Lecture Notes in Computer Science 11483

Commenced Publication in 1973
Founding and Former Series Editors:
Gerhard Goos, Juris Hartmanis, and Jan van Leeuwen

More information about this series at http://www.springer.com/series/7409

Paolo Giorgini · Barbara Weber (Eds.)

Advanced Information Systems Engineering

31st International Conference, CAiSE 2019
Rome, Italy, June 3–7, 2019
Proceedings

 Springer

Editors
Paolo Giorgini
University of Trento
Trento, Italy

Barbara Weber
University of St. Gallen
St. Gallen, Switzerland

ISSN 0302-9743 ISSN 1611-3349 (electronic)
Lecture Notes in Computer Science
ISBN 978-3-030-21289-6 ISBN 978-3-030-21290-2 (eBook)
https://doi.org/10.1007/978-3-030-21290-2

LNCS Sublibrary: SL3 – Information Systems and Applications, incl. Internet/Web, and HCI

This Springer imprint is published by the registered company Springer Nature Switzerland AG
The registered company address is: Gewerbestrasse 11, 6330 Cham, Switzerland

Preface

The 31th International Conference on Advanced Information Systems Engineering (CAiSE 2019) was held in Rome, Italy, during June 3–7, 2019.

The CAiSE conference continues its tradition as the premiere venue for innovative and rigorous research across the whole spectrum of Information Systems Engineering, while placing a special emphasis on the theme of "Responsible Information Systems." The theme acknowledges that trends like IoT, big data analytics, artificial intelligence, machine learning, as well as blockchain technology are expected to push digital transformation even further. While many of these technologies bear huge potential for information systems that are flexible enough for digital transformation and support high-velocity decision-making, they also pose new challenges for designing information systems that are responsible by considering privacy, security, and ethical concerns and providing trustworthiness.

The CAiSE program included three invited keynotes on important perspectives for Information Systems Engineering, by Prof. Annie Antón (Georgia Institute of Technology, USA), Dr. Ethan Hadar (Accenture Labs and Accenture Cyber Fusion Center in Tel Aviv, Israel), and Prof. Maurizio Lenzerini (Sapienza Università di Roma, Italy).

The accepted research papers (formal and/or technical, empirical, experience, exploratory) address facets related to the theme "Responsible Information Systems," as well as the core topics associated with IS Engineering: novel approaches; models, methods, and techniques; architectures and platforms; and domain-specific and multi-aspects IS.

We received 206 full paper submissions and we followed the selection process consolidated in the previous years: each paper was initially reviewed by at least two Program Committee (PC) members; papers with consistent negative evaluations were rejected; all papers with at least one positive evaluation were reviewed by a member of the Program Board (PB); all reviewers then engaged in an online discussion led by another PB member; finally, during the physical meeting of the PB meeting in Rome (February 21–22, 2019), the final decision was made about the acceptance or rejection of each paper. The overall evaluation process of the papers resulted in the selection of 41 high-quality papers, which amounts to an acceptance rate of 20%. The final program of CAiSE 2019 was complemented by CAiSE Forum, workshops, co-located working conferences, and a PhD consortium. For each of these events, separate proceedings were published.

We would like to thank the general chairs, Barbara Pernici and Massimo Mecella, and the whole organization team (Andrea Marrella, Francesco Leotta, Francesco Sapio, Lauren S. Ferro, Simone Agostinelli, Eleonora Bernasconi, Miguel Ceriani, Consulta Umbria – the organizing agency) for their support and incredible work. We thank also the forum chairs, Cinzia Cappiello and Marcela Ruiz, workshop chairs, Henderik A. Proper and Janis Stirna, tutorial chairs, Devis Bianchini and Marlon Dumas, doctoral consortium chairs, Manfred Reichert, Pierluigi Plebani, and Marcello La Rosa, publicity chairs, Artem Polyvyanyy, Estefania Serral Asensio, and Lin Liu, for their extraordinary and professional work. Finally, we would like to thank all PC and PB members, who played a fundamental role in the selection process.

CAiSE 2019 was organized with the support of Sapienza Università di Roma and Politecnico di Milano.

April 2019   Barbara Weber
                                                               Paolo Giorgini

Organization

General Chairs

Massimo Mecella   Sapienza Università di Roma, Italy
Barbara Pernici   Politecnico di Milano, Italy

Program Chairs

Paolo Giorgini   University of Trento, Italy
Barbara Weber   University of St. Gallen, Switzerland
     Technical University of Denmark, Denmark

Workshop Chairs

Henderik A. Proper   Luxembourg Institute for Science and Technology, Luxembourg
Janis Stirna   Stockholm University, Sweden

Forum Chairs

Cinzia Cappiello   Politecnico di Milano, Italy
Marcela Ruiz   Utrecht University, The Netherlands

Tutorial/Panel Chairs

Devis Bianchini   Università di Brescia, Italy
Marlon Dumas   University of Tartu, Estonia

Doctoral Consortium Chairs

Manfred Reichert   Ulm University, Germany
Pierluigi Plebani   Politecnico di Milano, Italy
Marcello La Rosa   University Melbourne, Australia

Organizing Local Chair

Andrea Marrella   Sapienza Università di Roma, Italy

Web and Social Media Chair

Francesco Leotta   Sapienza Università di Roma, Italy

Publicity Chairs

Artem Polyvyanyy	University of Melbourne, Australia
Estefania Serral A.	KU Leuven, Belgium
Lin Liu	Tsinghua University, China

Organizing Support Team

Francesco Sapio	Sapienza Università di Roma, Italy
Lauren S. Ferro	Sapienza Università di Roma, Italy
Simone Agostinelli	Sapienza Università di Roma, Italy
Consulta Umbria	(Organizing Agency)
Andrea Marrella	Sapienza Università di Roma, Italy
Francesco Leotta	Sapienza Università di Roma, Italy
Eleonora Bernasconi	Sapienza Università di Roma, Italy
Miguel Ceriani	Sapienza Università di Roma, Italy

Conference Steering Committee Chairs

Johann Eder	Alpen Adria Universitat Klagenfurt, Austria
John Krogstie	Norwegian University of Science and Technology, Norway
Eric Dubois	Luxembourg Institute of Science and Technology, Luxembourg

Conference Advisory Board

Janis Bubenko	KTH Stockholm, Sweden
Arne Solvberg	Norwegian University of Science and Technology, Norway
Colette Roland	Université Paris I Pantheon-Sorbonne, France
Oscar Pastor	Universidad Politécnica de Valencia, Spain
Barbara Pernici	Politecnico di Milano, Italy

Program Board Members

Eric Dubois	Luxembourg Institute of Science and Technology, Luxembourg
Schahram Dustdar	Vienna University of Technology, Austria
Johann Eder	Alpen-Adria-Universität Klagenfurt, Austria
Xavier Franch	Universitat Politècnica de Catalunya, Spain
Matthias Jarke	RWTH Aachen University, Germany
John Krogstie	Norwegian University of Science and Technology, Norway
Pericles Loucopoulos	The University of Manchester, UK
Heinrich C. Mayr	Alpen-Adria-Universität Klagenfurt, Austria

Program Committee

Additional Reviewers

Affia, Abasi-Amefon
Alahyari, Hiva
Aydemir, Fatma Başak
Back, Christoffer Olling
Bagozi, Ada
Batoulis, Kimon
Bazarhanova, Anar
Betzing, Jan Hendrik
Bock, Alexander
Breitmayer, Marius
Brunings, Mitchel
Böhm, Fabian
Camposano, José Carlos
Cantanhede da Silva, Gabriel
De Kinderen, Sybren
Del Río Ortega, Adela
Dietz, Marietheres
El-Khawaga, Ghada
Estrada Torres, Irene Bedilia
Farshidi, Siamak
Gallersdörfer, Ulrich
García, José María
Garda, Massimiliano
Ghidini, Chiara
Giraldo Velásquez, Fáber Danilo
Giraldo, Fáber D.
Groll, Sebastian
Guizzardi, Renata
Gulden, Jens
Halsbenning, Sebastian
Hartmann, Patrick
Hoffmeister, Benedikt
Holl, Patrick
Hoppenstedt, Burkhard
Ihde, Sven

Iqbal, Mubashar
Köpke, Julius
Ladleif, Jan
Lavbic, Dejan
Lefebvre, Armel
Leno, Volodymyr
Leotta, Francesco
Marquez Chamorro, Alfonso
Melchiori, Michele
Menges, Florian
Niemann, Marco
Nolte, Mario
Overbeek, Sietse
Parejo Maestre, José Antonio
Paukstadt, Ute
Pereira, Juanan
Pirelli, Blagovesta
Prakash, Deepika
Puchta, Alexander
Roth, Uwe
Ruiz, Marcela
Saltan, Andrei
Schmolke, Florian
Schobel, Johannes
Simonofski, Anthony
Stach, Michael
Steinau, Sebastian
Tinnes, Christof
Tom, Jake
Troya, Javier
van der Werf, Jan Martijn
Vielberth, Manfred
Weiss, Gregor
Zaman, Rashid
Zitnik, Slavko

Invited Keynote Talks

Keynote: The Post-digital Era – Technology Trends and Needed Research

Michal Biltz[1], Marc Carrel-Billiard[2], Paul R. Daugherty[1],
Ethan Hadar[3], and Edy R. Liongosari[1]

[1]Accenture, 1700 Sea Port Blvd, Redwood City, CA, San Francisco, USA
[2]Accenture, 400 avenue de Roumanille - Bt 1A, CS 80099,
Sophia Antipolis, France
[3]Accenture, Hamenofim Street 2, Herzliya Pituah, Israel
{michael.j.biltz,marc.carrel-billiard,
paul.r.daugherty,ethan.hadar,
edy.s.liongosari}@accenture.com

Abstract. The digital era is here. Digitization enables companies today to understand their customers with a new depth of granularity. There are more digital ecosystems and potential partners to help companies create holistic experiences. Companies are facing entirely new set of expectations from customers, employees and business partners, combining innovative services and hyper-personalization to change the way the market itself works. Now we are entering the post-digital era, where companies are asking what's next? Now, companies must first earn a level of trust that meets their customers, employees and business partners' goals, and they must use that trust responsibly. Such changes include addressing privacy, safety, ethics, and governance questions. This keynote presents Accenture Technology Vision 2019 which outlines five technology trends and challenges for research organizations and universities. The first trend outlines the new generation of technologies of Distributed Ledger, Artificial Intelligence, Extended Reality, and Quantum Computing, and applying these technologies in combination. The second through fifth trends describe what this post digital world will look like from the lens of consumers, employees, security and overall market dynamics.

The keynote contains insights from executive leaders of Accenture discussing the vision and trends definition including examples.

Keywords: Consumers · Personalization · Technology trends · Cyber security · New markets

Reference

1. Accenture Technical Vision 2019. https://www.accenture.com/t20190304T094157Z__w__/us-en/_acnmedia/PDF-94/Accenture-TechVision-2019-Tech-Trends-Report.pdf. Accessed 29 Mar 2019

Direct and Reverse Rewriting in Data Interoperability

Maurizio Lenzerini ⓘ

Dipartimento di Ingegneria Informatica, Automatica e Gestionale
"Antonio Ruberti", Sapienza Università di Roma, Rome, Italy
lenzerini@diag.uniroma1.it

Introduction

Data interoperability refers to the issue of accessing and processing data from multiple sources in order to create more holistic and contextual information for improving data analysis, for better decision-making, and for accountability purposes. In the era towards a data-driven society, the notion of data interoperability is of paramount importance. Looking at the research work in the last decades, several types of data interoperability scenarios emerged, including the following.

1. In Data Integration, we have a multitude of information sources, and we want to access them by means of a global schema, that somehow accommodates an integrated view of all data at the sources [12, 17].
2. In Data Exchange, we have a source database, and a target database, and we want to move the data from the source to the target according to some specified criteria [3, 15].
3. In P2P Data Coordination, we have a network of information nodes (peers), and we want to let them communicate to each other in order to exchange data or queries [5, 22].
4. In Ontology-Based Data Management (OBDM), we have a collection of data sources and an ontology representing a semantic model of the domain of interest, and we want to govern (i.e., query, update, monitoring, etc.) the data at the sources through the ontology, rather than by interacting directly with the sources [10, 18].

A fundamental component of all the above data interoperability frameworks is the mapping. Indeed, put in an abstract way, all the above scenarios are characterized by an architecture constituted by various autonomous nodes (called databases, data sources, peers, etc.) which hold information, and which are linked to other nodes by means of mappings. A mapping is a statement specifying that some relationship exists between pieces of information held by one node and pieces of information held by another node. Specifically, in Data Integration the mappings relate the data sources to the global schema, in Data Exchange they relate the source database to the target database, in P2P Coordination they relate the various peers in the network, and in OBDM they relate the various data sources to the ontology.

In the last years, many papers investigate the notion of mapping, from various points of view, and with different goals (see [16] and references therein). By looking at these papers, one could argue that one of the most important role of mapping is to allow reformulating queries expressed over a node into queries expressed over other mapped nodes.

Such reformulation task is crucial, for example, for answering queries expressed over the global schema in a data integration system. Indeed, to compute the answer, the system has to figure out which queries to ask to the data sources (where the real data are located), and this is done by a step that we call *direct rewriting*: rewrite the query over the global schema in terms of a query over the data sources. A similar task has been studied in the other data interoperability scenarios. In OBDM, for instance, given a user queries expressed over the ontology, the aim is to find a direct rewriting of the query, i.e., a query over the source schema, that, once executed over the data, provides the user query answers that are logically implied by the ontology and the mapping.

While the notion of direct rewriting has been the subject of many investigations in data interoperability in the last decades, in this paper we aim at discuss also a new notion of rewriting, that we call *inverse rewriting*. The importance of this new notion emerges when we consider the following task in the OBDM scenario: Given a query q over the sources, find the query over the ontology that characterizes q at best (independently from the current source database). Note that the problem is reversed with respect to the one where the traditional (direct) rewriting is used: here, we start with a source query, and we aim at deriving a corresponding query over the ontology. Thus, we are dealing with a sort of reverse engineering problem, which is novel in the investigation of data interoperability. We argue that this problem is relevant in a plethora of application scenarios. For the sake of brevity, we mention only three of them. *(1)* Following the ideas in [8], the notion of reverse rewriting can be used to provide the semantics of open data and open APIs published by organizations, which is a crucial aspect for unchaining all the potentials of open data. *(2)* Although the architecture of many modern Information Systems is based on data services, that are abstractions of computation done on data sources, it is often the case that the semantics of such computations is not well specified or documented. Can we automatically produce a semantic characterization of a data service, having an OBDA specification available? The idea is to exploit a new reasoning task over the OBDA specification, that works as follows: we express the data service in terms of a query over the sources, and we use the notion of reverse rewriting for deriving the query over the ontology that best describes the data service, given the ontology and the mapping. *(3)* It can be shown that the concept of reverse rewriting is also useful for a semantic-based approach to source profiling [1], in particular for describing the structure and the content of a data source in terms of the business vocabulary.

The goal of this paper is to provide a brief account of both direct and reverse rewritings in data interoperability, focusing in particular on OBDM. The plan of the paper is as follows: in Sect. 2 we describe the basic characteristics of the OBDM paradigm, in Sects. 3 and 4 we discuss the notions of direct and reverse rewriting, respectively, and in Sect. 5 we conclude the paper by illustrating some possible directions for the research on reverse rewriting.

Contents

Requirements and Modeling

Data Modeling and Analysis

Business Process Modeling and Engineering

Information System Security

Learning and Mining in Information Systems

CAiSE 2019 Tutorials

Invited Keynote Talk

Direct and Reverse Rewriting in Data Interoperability

Maurizio Lenzerini[✉][iD]

Dipartimento di Ingegneria Informatica, Automatica e Gestionale "Antonio Ruberti",
Sapienza Università di Roma, Rome, Italy
lenzerini@diag.uniroma1.it

1 Introduction

Data interoperability refers to the issue of accessing and processing data from multiple sources in order to create more holistic and contextual information for improving data analysis, for better decision-making, and for accountability purposes. In the era towards a data-driven society, the notion of data interoperability is of paramount importance. Looking at the research work in the last decades, several types of data interoperability scenarios emerged, including the following.

1. In Data Integration, we have a multitude of information sources, and we want to access them by means of a global schema, that somehow accommodates an integrated view of all data at the sources [12,17].
2. In Data Exchange, we have a source database, and a target database, and we want to move the data from the source to the target according to some specified criteria [3,15].
3. In P2P Data Coordination, we have a network of information nodes (peers), and we want to let them communicate to each other in order to exchange data or queries [5,22].
4. In Ontology-Based Data Management (OBDM), we have a collection of data sources and an ontology representing a semantic model of the domain of interest, and we want to govern (i.e., query, update, monitoring, etc.) the data at the sources through the ontology, rather than by interacting directly with the sources [10,18].

A fundamental component of all the above data interoperability frameworks is the mapping. Indeed, put in an abstract way, all the above scenarios are characterized by an architecture constituted by various autonomous nodes (called databases, data sources, peers, etc.) which hold information, and which are linked to other nodes by means of mappings. A mapping is a statement specifying that some relationship exists between pieces of information held by one node and pieces of information held by another node. Specifically, in Data Integration the mappings relate the data sources to the global schema, in Data Exchange they relate the source database to the target database, in P2P Coordination they

© Springer Nature Switzerland AG 2019
P. Giorgini and B. Weber (Eds.): CAiSE 2019, LNCS 11483, pp. 3–13, 2019.
https://doi.org/10.1007/978-3-030-21290-2_1

relate the various peers in the network, and in OBDM they relate the various data sources to the ontology.

In the last years, many papers investigate the notion of mapping, from various points of view, and with different goals (see [16] and references therein). By looking at these papers, one could argue that one of the most important role of mapping is to allow reformulating queries expressed over a node into queries expressed over other mapped nodes.

Such reformulation task is crucial, for example, for answering queries expressed over the global schema in a data integration system. Indeed, to compute the answer, the system has to figure out which queries to ask to the data sources (where the real data are located), and this is done by a step that we call *direct rewriting*: rewrite the query over the global schema in terms of a query over the data sources. A similar task has been studied in the other data interoperability scenarios. In OBDM, for instance, given a user queries expressed over the ontology, the aim is to find a direct rewriting of the query, i.e., a query over the source schema, that, once executed over the data, provides the user query answers that are logically implied by the ontology and the mapping.

While the notion of direct rewriting has been the subject of many investigations in data interoperability in the last decades, in this paper we aim at discuss also a new notion of rewriting, that we call *inverse rewriting*. The importance of this new notion emerges when we consider the following task in the OBDM scenario: Given a query q over the sources, find the query over the ontology that characterizes q at best (independently from the current source database). Note that the problem is reversed with respect to the one where the traditional (direct) rewriting is used: here, we start with a source query, and we aim at deriving a corresponding query over the ontology. Thus, we are dealing with a sort of reverse engineering problem, which is novel in the investigation of data interoperability. We argue that this problem is relevant in a plethora of application scenarios. For the sake of brevity, we mention only three of them. *(1)* Following the ideas in [8], the notion of reverse rewriting can be used to provide the semantics of open data and open APIs published by organizations, which is a crucial aspect for unchaining all the potentials of open data. *(2)* Although the architecture of many modern Information Systems is based on data services, that are abstractions of computation done on data sources, it is often the case that the semantics of such computations is not well specified or documented. Can we automatically produce a semantic characterization of a data service, having an OBDA specification available? The idea is to exploit a new reasoning task over the OBDA specification, that works as follows: we express the data service in terms of a query over the sources, and we use the notion of reverse rewriting for deriving the query over the ontology that best describes the data service, given the ontology and the mapping. *(3)* It can be shown that the concept of reverse rewriting is also useful for a semantic-based approach to source profiling [1], in particular for describing the structure and the content of a data source in terms of the business vocabulary.

The goal of this paper is to provide a brief account of both direct and reverse rewritings in data interoperability, focusing in particular on OBDM. The plan of the paper is as follows: in Sect. 2 we describe the basic characteristics of the OBDM paradigm, in Sects. 3 and 4 we discuss the notions of direct and reverse rewriting, respectively, and in Sect. 5 we conclude the paper by illustrating some possible directions for the research on reverse rewriting.

2   Framework for Ontology-Based Data Management

In this section we provide the definition of a general framework for OBDM. Our goal is to focus on the semantic and computational aspects related to the use of an ontology and of mappings to data sources in the OBDM paradigm. Thus, we do not address those issues, such as wrapping non-relational data, distributed query evaluation, or entity resolution, arising when the system includes *multiple*, *heterogeneous* data sources. Coherently, we assume in the following to deal with a single relational data source. In practice, such schema could derive from a data federation tool managing a set of heterogeneous data sources, all wrapped as a relational database. The framework is based on the notions of OBDM specification and OBDM system, that we now introduce.

An *OBDM specification* Σ is as a triple $\langle \mathcal{O}, \mathcal{S}, \mathcal{M} \rangle$, where $\mathcal{O}$ is an ontology, $\mathcal{S}$ is the source schema, and $\mathcal{M}$ is a mapping from $\mathcal{S}$ to $\mathcal{O}$. As we said before, we assume that $\mathcal{S}$ is a relational schema, but the framework can be easily adapted to the case where the data source has a different format. The various components of an OBDM specification can be described as follows:

- $\mathcal{O}$ represents the intensional knowledge about the domain of interest, expressed in a Description Logic (DL) TBox [4]. Essentially, a TBox is a set of logical axioms over a certain alphabet, where the symbols of such alphabet are the concepts and the relations that are relevant for describing the domain.
- $\mathcal{S}$ provides the structure of the repositories where the data are stored.
- $\mathcal{M}$ is a set of mapping assertions, each one relating a pattern in the data source with a pattern in the ontology. Essentially, a mapping assertions can be seen as a logical axiom expressing a relationship between a query over the source scheme, and a query over the ontology.

We obtain an OBDM system by pairing an OBDM specification with a concrete data source complying with the schema $\mathcal{S}$. Formally, an *OBDM system* is a pair (Σ, D) where Σ is an OBDM specification, and D is a database for the source schema $\mathcal{S}$, called source database for Σ. The semantics of (Σ, D) is given in terms of the logical interpretations that are models of Σ, i.e., that satisfy all axioms of $\mathcal{O}$, *and* satisfy $\mathcal{M}$ with respect to D. We denote by $Mod_D(\Sigma)$ the set of models of Σ.

In OBDM systems, like in all data interoperability scenarios, one of the main services of interest is *query answering*, i.e., computing the answers to user queries. In the case of OBDM, queries are posed over the ontology, and the data to be accessed for computing the answers are in the source database. Note that, while in the context of a traditional database, query answering can be seen as evaluating a logical formula in a single interpretation [2] (i.e., the database itself), an OBDM system is characterized by a set of interpretations (i.e., the set of its models). Therefore, it is not even obvious what does it mean for a tuple to be an answer to a query. The most popular approach is to sanction that a tuple is to be returned by the evaluation of the query if it is a *certain answer*, i.e., it satisfies the user query in all the interpretations in $Mod_D(\Sigma)$. Query answering in OBDM is thus a form of reasoning under incomplete information [13], and is much more challenging than classical query evaluation over a database instance.

From the computational perspective, query answering depends on *(1)* the language used for the ontology; *(2)* the language used to specify the queries in the mapping; *(3)* the language used for expressing user queries. In the following, we consider a particular instantiation of the OBDM framework, in which we choose each such language in such a way that query answering is guaranteed to be tractable w.r.t. the size of the data. We remark that the configuration we get is to some extent "maximal", i.e., as soon as we go beyond the expressiveness of the chosen languages, we lose this nice computational behaviour [7]. The instantiation we refer to is as follows:

– the ontology language is *DL-Lite*$_\mathcal{R}$;
– the mapping language is based on conjunctive queries, and follows the *global-and-local-as-view* (GLAV) approach [17],
– the user queries are unions of conjunctive queries.

Ontology Language. The DL *DL-Lite*$_\mathcal{R}$ is a member of the *DL-Lite* family of lightweight DLs [6], adopted as the basis of the OWL 2 QL profile of the W3C standard OWL (Ontology Web Language) [20]. As usual in DLs, *DL-Lite*$_\mathcal{R}$ allows for representing the domain of interest in terms of *concepts*, denoting sets of objects, and *roles*, denoting binary relations between objects. From the expressiveness point of view, *DL-Lite*$_\mathcal{R}$ is able to capture many features of Entity-Relationship diagrams and UML Class Diagrams, except for completeness of hierarchies. In particular, it allows for specifying ISA and disjointness between either concepts or roles, mandatory participations of concepts into roles, and the typing of roles. Formally, a *DL-Lite*$_\mathcal{R}$ TBox is a set of assertions obeying the following syntax:

$$B_1 \sqsubseteq B_2 \quad B_1 \sqsubseteq \neg B_2 \quad \text{(concept inclusions)}$$
$$R_1 \sqsubseteq R_2 \quad R_1 \sqsubseteq \neg R_2 \quad \text{(role inclusions)}$$

where B_1 and B_2 are basic concepts, i.e., expressions of the form A, $\exists P$, or $\exists P^-$, and R, R_1, and R_2 are a basic roles, i.e., expressions of the form P, or P^-. A and P denote an *atomic concept* and an *atomic role*, respectively, i.e., a unary and binary predicate from the ontology alphabet, respectively. P^- is the *inverse* of an atomic role P, i.e., the role obtained by switching the first and second components of P, and $\exists P$ (resp. $\exists P^-$), called existential unqualified restriction, denotes the projection of the role P on its first (resp. second) component. Finally

$\neg B_2$ (resp. $\neg R_2$) denotes the negation of a basic concept (resp. role). Assertions in the left-hand side (resp. right-hand side) of the first two rows are called positive (resp. negative) inclusions. *DL-Lite$_A$* poses some limitations on the way in which positive role inclusions and role functionalities interact. More precisely, in a *DL-Lite$_A$* TBox an atomic role that is either functional or inverse functional cannot be specialized, i.e., if (funct P) or (funct P^-) are in the TBox, no inclusion of the form $R \sqsubseteq P$ or $R \sqsubseteq P^-$ can occur in the TBox.

A *DL-Lite$_R$ interpretation* $I = (\Delta^I, \cdot^I)$ consists of a non-empty *interpretation domain* Δ^I and an *interpretation function* $\cdot^I$ that assigns to each atomic concept A a subset A^I of Δ^I, and to each atomic role P a binary relation P^I over Δ^I. In particular, for the constructs of *DL-Lite$_A$* we have:

$$A^I \subseteq \Delta^I \qquad\qquad (\exists R)^I = \{o \mid \exists o'. (o, o') \in R^I\}$$
$$P^I \subseteq \Delta^I \times \Delta^I \qquad\qquad (\neg B)^I = \Delta^I \setminus B^I$$
$$(P^-)^I = \{(o_2, o_1) \mid (o_1, o_2) \in P^I\} \qquad (\neg R)^I = (\Delta^I \times \Delta^I) \setminus R^I$$

Let C be either a basic concept B or its negation $\neg B$. An interpretation I satisfies a concept inclusion $B \sqsubseteq C$ if $B^I \subseteq C^I$. Similarly for role inclusions.

Mapping Language. As we said before, the mapping language in our tractable framework allows for GLAV mapping assertions, i.e., assertions of the following the form:

$$\forall \boldsymbol{x} \; (\phi_S(\boldsymbol{x}) \rightarrow \exists \boldsymbol{y} \; \psi_O(\boldsymbol{x}, \boldsymbol{y}))$$

where $\phi_S(\boldsymbol{x})$ is a conjunctive query over S, i.e., a conjunction of atomic formulas, with free variables $\boldsymbol{x}$, $\psi_O(\boldsymbol{x}, \boldsymbol{y}))$ is a conjunctive query over O with free variables $\boldsymbol{x}$, and $\rightarrow$ is the symbol for material implication in logic. Intuitively, the above assertion states that whenever a certain set of values satisfies the pattern corresponding to $\phi_S(\boldsymbol{x})$ in the source database, then there are values $\boldsymbol{y}$ such that the same set of values satisfies the pattern corresponding to $\psi_O(\boldsymbol{x}, \boldsymbol{y})$ in the ontology. Actually, in the mapping languages considered in ODBM (see [21]), the pattern corresponding to $\psi_O(\boldsymbol{x}, \boldsymbol{y})$ contains terms built using object constructors, so as to distinguish between the values in the source database and the constants satisfying the ontology predicates. However, for the sake of simplicity, we ignore this aspect here, and assume that the ontology constants are denoted by database values.

Formally speaking, given an OBDM system (Σ, D), and given an interpretation I for O, the mapping assertion $\forall \boldsymbol{x} \; (\phi_S(\boldsymbol{x}) \rightarrow \exists \boldsymbol{y} \; \psi_O(\boldsymbol{x}, \boldsymbol{y}))$ is satisfied by I if for all tuple t of the same arity of $\boldsymbol{x}$, $\phi_S(t)^I = \text{TRUE}$ implies $(\exists \boldsymbol{y} \; \psi_O(t, \boldsymbol{y}))^I = \text{TRUE}$. Note that, as usual in data interoperability, we are adopting the approach of assuming that mappings are *sound*, which intuitively means that the results returned by the source queries occurring in the mapping are a subset of the data that instantiate the corresponding ontology (or, target) query. This is coherent with the fact that we want to keep our domain knowledge (or, target schema) more general than the source data, so as to accommodate more data if needed. We also notice that our mapping language captures R2RML, the W3C recommendation for specifying mappings from relational database to

RDF datasets [9]. Indeed, an R2RML mapping assertion is simply an assertion having the above form, but where y is empty, and $\psi_\mathcal{O}$ is constituted by a single atom.

User Queries. User queries in our tractable framework are conjunctive queries (CQs) [2], or unions thereof. With $q(x)$, we denote a CQ with free variables x. A Boolean CQ is a CQ without free variables. Given an OBDA system (Σ, D) and a Boolean CQ $q_\mathcal{O}$ over Σ, i.e., over the ontology of Σ, we say that $q_\mathcal{O}$ is *entailed by* (Σ, D), denoted with $(\Sigma, D) \models q_\mathcal{O}$, if $q_\mathcal{O}$ evaluates to true in every $I \in Mod_D(\Sigma)$. We denote with $cert_{q_\mathcal{O},\Sigma}$ the query that, when evaluated over D, computes *certain answers* to $q_\mathcal{O}$ with respect to (Σ, D), i.e., the set of tuples t such that $(\Sigma, D) \models q_\mathcal{O}(t)$, where $q_\mathcal{O}(t)$ is the Boolean CQ obtained from $q_\mathcal{O}(x)$ by substituting x with t.

3 Direct Rewriting

In the tractable OBDA framework previously described, one can think of a simple chase procedure [2] for query answering, which first retrieves an initial set of concept and role instances (using appropriate "labeled nulls" for filling existential quantified variables) from the data source through the mapping, then, using the ontology axioms, "expands" such a set with all the logically entailed concept and role assertions, and finally evaluates the query on such an expanded set of assertions, seen as a database. Note that this is the approach pursued in the context of data exchange. Unfortunately, in *DL-Lite$_\mathcal{R}$* the materialization step of the above technique is not feasible in general, because the set of entailed instance assertions starting from even very simple OBDM specifications and small data sources may be infinite.

Fortunately, the notion of direct rewriting comes to the rescue. Indeed, most of the approaches to query answering in OBDM are based on query rewriting, in particular on what we call *direct rewriting*, or, equivalently, *perfect ontology-to-source rewriting*. Intuitively, such a rewriting w.r.t. an OBDM specification $\Sigma = \langle \mathcal{O}, \mathcal{M}, \mathcal{S} \rangle$ of a query $q_\mathcal{O}$ over $\mathcal{O}$ is a query over the source schema that, when evaluated over any source database D, returns the certain answers of q w.r.t. Σ and D. Thus, if we follow this approach, no materialization is needed, because answering query $q_\mathcal{O}$ is based on two steps: (1) we compute the rewriting $q_\mathcal{S}$ over $\mathcal{S}$ based on $q_\mathcal{O}$ and Σ, and then (2) we evaluate $q_\mathcal{S}$ over the source database D. The formal definition of perfect ontology-to-source rewriting suitable for this approach is as follows.

Definition 1. *Let $\Sigma = \langle \mathcal{O}, \mathcal{M}, \mathcal{S} \rangle$ be an OBDM specification, and let $q_\mathcal{O}$ be a query over $\mathcal{O}$. A query $q_\mathcal{S}$ over $\mathcal{S}$ is a perfect $\mathcal{O}$-to-$\mathcal{S}$ Σ-rewriting of $q_\mathcal{O}$ if for every source database D, we have $q_\mathcal{S}^D = cert_{q_\mathcal{O},\Sigma}^D$.*

One of the most studied problem in OBDM is how to compute the $\mathcal{O}$-to-$\mathcal{S}$ Σ-rewriting of a UCQ $q_\mathcal{O}$. Actually, the above described OBDM framework allows for modularizing the computation of the ontology-to-source rewriting. Indeed, the current techniques for OBDM consist of two phases: a phase of *direct rewriting w.r.t. the ontology of* Σ followed by a phase of *direct rewriting w.r.t. the mapping of* Σ. In the first phase, the initial query $q_\mathcal{O}$ is rewritten with respect to the ontology, producing a new query q_1, still over the ontology signature: intuitively, q_1 "encodes" the knowledge expressed by the ontology that is relevant for answering the query $q_\mathcal{O}$. In the second phase, the query q_1 is rewritten with respect to the mapping $\mathcal{M}$, thus obtaining a query $q_\mathcal{S}$ to be evaluated over the source data.

In our framework, the computation of the direct rewriting w.r.t. the mapping can be done by the techniques studied in data integration [12]. As for direct rewriting w.r.t. the ontology, many algorithms have been proposed in the last years, following the seminal work in [6,21].

Overall, the technique combining the two step shows that, in our tractable framework, query answering is *first-order rewritable*, i.e., for each union of CQ $q_\mathcal{O}$ over Σ, there always exists, and it is possible to compute, a first-order query q_r that is the $\mathcal{O}$-to-$\mathcal{S}$ Σ-rewriting of $q_\mathcal{O}$, i.e., such that, for each source database D, $t \in cert^D_{q_\mathcal{O},\Sigma}$, iff t is in the evaluation of q_r over D. In other words, in the tractable framework we can always compute a first-order query q_r over the source schema that is equivalent to $cert_{q_\mathcal{O},\Sigma}$.

Thus, $cert_{q_\mathcal{O},\Sigma}$ can be effectively expressed as an SQL query, and this implies that UCQ answering can be reduced to query evaluation over a relational database, for which we can rely on standard relational engines. The above property also implies that UCQ answering is in AC^0 in data complexity, which is the complexity of evaluating a first-order query over a relational database. Indeed, this is an immediate consequence of the fact that the complexity of the above phase of query rewriting is independent of the data source, and that the final rewritten query is an SQL expression. It can also be shown that conjunctive query answering in the OBDM setting is NP-complete w.r.t. combined complexity, i.e., the complexity of the problem with respect to the size of the whole input (data source, OBDM specification, and query). This is the same as the combined complexity of SQL query answering over the data source.

Finally, an important question is whether we can further extend the ontology specification language of OBDM without losing the above nice computational property of the direct rewriting. In [7] it is shown that adding any of the main concept constructors considered in Description Logics and missing in $DL\text{-}Lite_\mathcal{R}$ (e.g., negation, disjunction, qualified existential restriction, range restriction) causes a jump of the data complexity of conjunctive query answering in OBDM, which goes beyond the class AC^0, showing that the direct rewriting approach is unfeasible, if we aim at first-order rewriting.

As for the query language, we note that going beyond unions of CQs may become problematic for the direct rewriting approach, or even for solvability of the computation task. Aa an example, adding negation to CQs causes query answering to become undecidable [14].

4   Reverse Rewriting

In what follows, we implicitly refer to an OBDA specification $\Sigma = \langle \mathcal{O}, \mathcal{S}, \mathcal{M} \rangle$. As we said in the introduction, reverse rewritings are relevant when we consider the following problem: Given a query $q_\mathcal{S}$ over $\mathcal{S}$, we aim at finding the query over $\mathcal{O}$ that precisely characterizes $q_\mathcal{S}$ w.r.t. Σ. Since the evaluation of queries over $\mathcal{O}$ is based on certain answers, this means that we aim at finding a query over $\mathcal{O}$ whose certain answers w.r.t. Σ and D exactly capture the answers of $q_\mathcal{S}$ w.r.t. D for every $\mathcal{S}$-database D. So, we are naturally led to the notion of reverse rewriting, or, equivalently, perfect source-to-ontology rewriting. In the rest of this section, $q_\mathcal{S}$ refers to a query over $\mathcal{S}$, and $q_\mathcal{O}$ to a query over $\mathcal{O}$ of the same arity.

Definition 2. $q_\mathcal{O}$ is a perfect $\mathcal{S}$-to-$\mathcal{O}$ Σ-rewriting of $q_\mathcal{S}$ if for every $\mathcal{S}$-database D, $Mod_D(\Sigma) \neq \emptyset$ implies $q_\mathcal{S}^D = cert_{q_\mathcal{O}, \Sigma}^D$.

We observe that the above notion is similar, but not equivalent, to the notion of realization in [19]. Indeed, while the latter sanctions that $q_\mathcal{S}^D = cert_{q_\mathcal{O}, \Sigma}^D$ for *all* $\mathcal{S}$-databases, in our notion the condition is limited to the $\mathcal{S}$-databases that are consistent with Σ. As noted in [8,19] and illustrated in the next example, a perfect source-to-ontology rewriting of $q_\mathcal{S}$ may not exist.

Example 1. Let $\Sigma = \langle \mathcal{O}, \mathcal{S}, \mathcal{M} \rangle$ be as follows:

- $\mathcal{O} = \{$ Book $\sqsubseteq$ Product, $\exists$HasCategory $\sqsubseteq$ Product $\}$
- $\mathcal{S} = \{s_1, s_2, s_3\}$
- $\mathcal{M} = $
$$\{ \{(x) \mid s_1(x)\} \rightarrow \{(x) \mid \text{Product}(x)\},$$
$$\{(x) \mid s_2(x)\} \rightarrow \{(x) \mid \text{Product}(x)\},$$
$$\{(x) \mid s_2(x), s_3(x,y)\} \rightarrow \{(x) \mid \text{Book}(x)\},$$
$$\{(x) \mid s_2(x), s_4(x,y)\} \rightarrow \{(x) \mid \exists y\ \text{HasCategory}(x,y)\} \}$$

and consider the query $q_\mathcal{S}(x) = \{(x) \mid s_2(x)\}$. By inspecting the mappings, one can see that, since the certain answers of Product include the constants in both s_1, and s_2, such concept is too general for exactly characterizing s_2. Since both Book and $\exists$HasCategory are too specific, it follows that no perfect $\mathcal{S}$-to-$\mathcal{O}$ Σ-rewriting of $q_\mathcal{S}$ exists.

In order to cope with the situations illustrated in the example, we introduce the notions of sound and complete source-to-ontology rewritings, which, intuitively, provide sound and complete approximations of perfect rewritings, respectively.

Definition 3. $q_\mathcal{O}$ is a sound (respectively, complete) $\mathcal{S}$-to-$\mathcal{O}$ Σ-rewriting of $q_\mathcal{S}$ if for every $\mathcal{S}$-database D, $Mod_D(\Sigma) \neq \emptyset$ implies $cert_{q_\mathcal{O}, \Sigma}^D \subseteq q_\mathcal{S}^D$ (resp., $q_\mathcal{S}^D \subseteq cert_{q_\mathcal{O}, \Sigma}^D$).

Example 2. We refer to Example 1, and observe that $\{(x) \mid \text{Product}(x)\}$ is a complete $\mathcal{S}$-to-$\mathcal{O}$ Σ-rewriting of $q_\mathcal{S}$, whereas $\{(x) \mid \exists y\ \text{Book}(x) \wedge \text{HasCategory}(x,y)\}$ is a sound $\mathcal{S}$-to-$\mathcal{O}$ Σ-rewriting of $q_\mathcal{S}$.

Obviously, $q_{\mathcal{O}}$ is a perfect $\mathcal{S}$-to-$\mathcal{O}$ Σ-rewriting of $q_{\mathcal{S}}$ if and only if $q_{\mathcal{O}}$ is both a sound, and a complete $\mathcal{S}$-to-$\mathcal{O}$ Σ-rewriting of $q_{\mathcal{S}}$. There are also interesting relationships between the notions of $\mathcal{S}$-to-$\mathcal{O}$ Σ-rewritings introduced here and the notion of direct rewritings. In particular, the following two properties can be shown to hold:

1. $q_{\mathcal{O}}$ is a complete $\mathcal{S}$-to-$\mathcal{O}$ Σ-rewriting of $q_{\mathcal{S}}$ if and only if $q_{\mathcal{S}}$ is an $\mathcal{O}$-to-$\mathcal{S}$ Σ-rewriting of $q_{\mathcal{O}}$.
2. If $q_{\mathcal{S}}$ is a perfect $\mathcal{O}$-to-$\mathcal{S}$ Σ-rewriting of $q_{\mathcal{O}}$, then $q_{\mathcal{O}}$ is a perfect $\mathcal{S}$-to-$\mathcal{O}$ Σ-rewriting of $q_{\mathcal{S}}$.

It is easy to see that different sound or complete source-to-ontology rewritings of $q_{\mathcal{S}}$ may exist, and therefore it is reasonable to look for the "best" approximations of $q_{\mathcal{S}}$, at least relative to a certain class of queries. In what follows, if q_1 and q_2 are two queries over the same schema, we write $q_1 \sqsubseteq q_2$ to mean that for all database D, we have $q_1^D \subseteq q_2^D$.

Definition 4. $q_{\mathcal{O}} \in \mathcal{L}$ is an $\mathcal{L}$-maximally sound (respectively, $\mathcal{L}$-minimally complete) $\mathcal{S}$-to-$\mathcal{O}$ Σ-rewriting of $q_{\mathcal{S}}$ if no $q' \in \mathcal{L}$ exists such that (i) q' is a sound (resp., complete) $\mathcal{S}$-to-$\mathcal{O}$ Σ-rewriting of $q_{\mathcal{S}}$, (ii) $cert_{q_{\mathcal{O}},\Sigma} \sqsubseteq cert_{q',\Sigma}$ (resp., $cert_{q',\Sigma} \sqsubseteq cert_{q_{\mathcal{O}},\Sigma}$), and (iii) there exists an $\mathcal{S}$-database D s.t. $cert_{q_{\mathcal{O}},\Sigma}^D \subset cert_{q',\Sigma}^D$ (resp., $cert_{q',\Sigma}^D \subset cert_{q_{\mathcal{O}},\Sigma}^D$).

Example 3. We refer again to Example 1, and observe that while $\{(x) \mid$ Product$(x) \}$ is the minimally complete $\mathcal{S}$-to-$\mathcal{O}$ Σ-rewriting of $q_{\mathcal{S}}$ in the class of UCQs, both $\{(x) \mid$ Book$(x)\}$, and $\{(x) \mid \exists y$ HasCategory$(x,y)\}$ are maximally sound $\mathcal{S}$-to-$\mathcal{O}$ Σ-rewritings of $q_{\mathcal{S}}$ in the class of CQs, while $\{(x) \mid$ Book$(x) \vee \exists y$ HasCategory$(x,y)\}$ is so in the class of UCQs.

Analogously to the case of the direct rewriting, associated to the notion of $\mathcal{S}$-to-$\mathcal{O}$ Σ-rewriting, there is the following relevant computational problem: given $\Sigma = \langle \mathcal{O}, \mathcal{S}, \mathcal{M} \rangle$, and $q_{\mathcal{S}} \in \mathcal{L}_{\mathcal{S}}$ over $\mathcal{S}$ compute any $\mathcal{L}_{\mathcal{O}}$-maximally sound (resp., $\mathcal{L}_{\mathcal{O}}$-minimally complete, perfect) $\mathcal{S}$-to-$\mathcal{O}$ Σ-rewriting of $q_{\mathcal{S}}$, if it exists.

Two recent papers address this issue, namely [8,19]. Here, we concentrate on the computation of a $\mathcal{L}_{\mathcal{O}}$-minimally complete $\mathcal{S}$-to-$\mathcal{O}$ Σ-rewriting in our tractable framework, in particular in the case where both $\mathcal{L}_{\mathcal{O}}$ and $\mathcal{L}_{\mathcal{S}}$ denote the class of UCQs. This problem has been studied in [8], where it has been shown that (1) a UCQ-minimally complete $\mathcal{S}$-to-$\mathcal{O}$ Σ-rewriting of $q_{\mathcal{S}}$ always exists, (2) the UCQ-minimally complete $\mathcal{S}$-to-$\mathcal{O}$ Σ-rewritings of a query $q_{\mathcal{S}}$ are unique up to logical equivalence under Σ^1, (3) the problem can be solved in constant time in the size of $\mathcal{O}$, EXPTIME in the size of $\mathcal{M}$, and PTIME in the size of $q_{\mathcal{S}}$.

5 Conclusion

The investigation on reverse rewriting has started only very recently, and we believe that there are many interesting issues related to this notion that are

---

[1] The same holds for UCQ-maximally sound $\mathcal{S}$-to-$\mathcal{O}$ Σ-rewritings of $q_{\mathcal{S}}$.

worth exploring. For example, no algorithm for computing the UCQ-maximally sound S-to-$\mathcal{O}$ Σ-rewriting of a query q_S is known yet, even in the tractable framework. What is known is that there are cases where no sound reverse rewriting expressible as UCQ exists. Thus, it would be interesting to study the problem of checking for the existence of a UCQ-maximally sound source-to-ontology rewriting of a query, and computing it in case it exists. As a second example, it would be also interesting to explore the notion of reverse rewriting in OBDM settings that are more expressive than the tractable framework considered in this paper, for instance by considering as ontology languages other members of the *DL-Lite* family, or even other families of DLs, such as $\mathcal{EL}$. Also, although in this work we have analyzed the case where the reverse rewriting is expressed as a UCQ, one could wonder how the picture changes if we allow the reverse rewriting to be expressed in more powerful query languages. Finally, it would be interesting to explore possible usages of the notion of reverse rewriting in the context where the updates at the sources should be translated to updates at the level on the ontology [11].

Acknowledgement. The author would like to thank Gianluca Cima and Antonella Poggi for several discussions on the notion of reverse rewriting. This work has been partially supported by MIUR under the PRIN project "HOPE: High-quality Open data Publishing and Enrichment".

References

1. Abedjan, Z., Golab, L., Naumann, F.: Data profiling: a tutorial. In: Proceedings of the ACM SIGMOD International Conference on Management of Data, pp. 1747–1751 (2017)
2. Abiteboul, S., Hull, R., Vianu, V.: Foundations of Databases. Addison Wesley Publ. Co., Boston (1995)
3. Arenas, M., Barceló, P., Libkin, L., Murlak, F.: Foundations of Data Exchange. Cambridge University Press, Cambridge (2014)
4. Baader, F., Calvanese, D., McGuinness, D., Nardi, D., Patel-Schneider, P.F. (eds.): The Description Logic Handbook: Theory, Implementation and Applications, 2nd edn. Cambridge University Press, Cambridge (2007)
5. Calvanese, D., Damaggio, E., De Giacomo, G., Lenzerini, M., Rosati, R.: Semantic data integration in P2P systems. In: Proceedings of the International Workshop on Databases, Information Systems and Peer-to-Peer Computing (DBISP2P 2003) (2003)
6. Calvanese, D., De Giacomo, G., Lembo, D., Lenzerini, M., Rosati, R.: Tractable reasoning and efficient query answering in description logics: the DL-Lite family. J. Autom. Reason. **39**(3), 385–429 (2007)
7. Calvanese, D., De Giacomo, G., Lembo, D., Lenzerini, M., Rosati, R.: Data complexity of query answering in description logics. Artif. Intell. **195**, 335–360 (2013)
8. Cima, G.: Preliminary results on ontology-based open data publishing. In: Proceedings of the 30th International Workshop on Description Logic (DL), vol. 1879. CEUR Electronic Workshop Proceedings (2017). http://ceur-ws.org/

9. Das, S., Sundara, S., Cyganiak, R.: R2RML: RDB to RDF mapping language. W3C Recommendation, World Wide Web Consortium, September 2012. http://www.w3.org/TR/r2rml/

10. De Giacomo, G., Lembo, M., Lenzerini, A., Rosati, R.: Using ontologies for semantic data integration. In: Flesca, S., Greco, S., Masciari, E., Saccà, D. (eds.) A Comprehensive Guide Through the Italian Database Research Over the Last 25 Years. Studies in Big Data, vol. 31, pp. 187–202. Springer, Cham (2018). https://doi.org/10.1007/978-3-319-61893-7_11

11. De Giacomo, G., Lenzerini, M., Poggi, A., Rosati, R.: On the update of description logic ontologies at the instance level. In: Proceedings of the 21st National Conference on Artificial Intelligence (AAAI), pp. 1271–1276 (2006)

12. Doan, A., Halevy, A.Y., Ives, Z.G.: Principles of Data Integration. Morgan Kaufmann, Burlington (2012)

13. Greco, S., Molinaro, C., Spezzano, F.: Incomplete Data and Data Dependencies in Relational Databases. Synthesis Lectures on Data Management. Morgan & Claypool Publishers, Burlington (2012)

14. Gutiérrez-Basulto, V., Ibáñez-García, Y.A., Kontchakov, R., Kostylev, E.V.: Queries with negation and inequalities over lightweight ontologies. J. Web Semant. **35**, 184–202 (2015)

15. Kolaitis, P.G.: Schema mappings, data exchange, and metadata management. In: Proceedings of the 24th ACM SIGACT SIGMOD SIGART Symposium on Principles of Database Systems (PODS), pp. 61–75 (2005)

16. Kolaitis, P.G.: Reflections on schema mappings, data exchange, and metadata management. In: Proceedings of the 37th ACM SIGMOD-SIGACT-SIGAI Symposium on Principles of Database Systems, Houston, TX, USA, 10–15 June 2018, pp. 107–109 (2018)

17. Lenzerini, M.: Data integration: a theoretical perspective. In: Proceedings of the 21st ACM SIGACT SIGMOD SIGART Symposium on Principles of Database Systems (PODS), pp. 233–246 (2002)

18. Lenzerini, M.: Managing data through the lens of an ontology. AI Mag. **39**(2), 65–74 (2018)

19. Lutz, C., Marti, J., Sabellek, L.: Query expressibility and verification in ontology-based data access. In: Proceedings of the 16th International Conference on the Principles of Knowledge Representation and Reasoning (KR), pp. 389–398 (2018)

20. Motik, B., Fokoue, A., Horrocks, I., Wu, Z., Lutz, C., Grau, B.C.: OWL web ontology language profiles. W3C Recommendation, World Wide Web Consortium, October 2009. http://www.w3.org/TR/owl-profiles/

21. Poggi, A., Lembo, D., Calvanese, D., De Giacomo, G., Lenzerini, M., Rosati, R.: Linking data to ontologies. J. Data Semant. **X**, 133–173 (2008)

22. Roth, A., Skritek, S.: Peer data management. In: Data Exchange, Integration, and Streams. Dagstuhl Follow-Ups, vol. 5, pp. 185–215. Schloss Dagstuhl - Leibniz-Zentrum fuer Informatik (2013)

Information System Engineering

Efficient Engineering Data Exchange in Multi-disciplinary Systems Engineering

Stefan Biffl[1], Arndt Lüder[2], Felix Rinker[1,3], and Laura Waltersdorfer[1(✉)]

[1] Institute of Information Systems Engineering,
Technische Universität Wien, Vienna, Austria
{stefan.biffl,laura.waltersdorfer}@tuwien.ac.at
[2] Institute of Factory Automation,
Otto-von-Guericke University Magdeburg, Magdeburg, Germany
arndt.lueder@ovgu.de
[3] Christian Doppler Laboratory for Security and Quality Improvement
in the Production System Lifecycle (CDL-SQI), Technische Universität Wien,
Vienna, Austria
felix.rinker@tuwien.ac.at

Abstract. In the parallel engineering of industrial production systems, domain experts from several disciplines need to exchange data efficiently to prevent the divergence of local engineering models. However, the data synchronization is hard (a) as it may be unclear what data consumers need and (b) due to the heterogeneity of local engineering artifacts. In this paper, we introduce use cases and a process for efficient *Engineering Data Exchange (EDEx)* that guides the definition and semantic mapping of data elements for exchange and facilitates the frequent synchronization between domain experts. We identify main elements of an EDEx information system to automate the EDEx process. We evaluate the effectiveness and effort of the EDEx process and concepts in a feasibility case study with requirements and data from real-world use cases at a large production system engineering company. The domain experts found the EDEx process more effective and the EDEx operation more efficient than the traditional point-to-point process, and providing insight for advanced analyses.

Keywords: Production systems engineering · Data exchange · Data integration · Process design · Multi-aspect information system · Multidisciplinary engineering

1 Introduction

Engineering industrial, recently also cyber-physical, production systems, e.g., long-running and safety-critical systems for assembling automotive parts or for producing metal, is the business of multi-disciplinary *production system engineering* (PSE) companies [3,18]. In parallel engineering, the disciplines develop their engineering artifacts, such as plans, models, software code, or machine

© Springer Nature Switzerland AG 2019
P. Giorgini and B. Weber (Eds.): CAiSE 2019, LNCS 11483, pp. 17–31, 2019.
https://doi.org/10.1007/978-3-030-21290-2_2

configurations, independently, but have to consider dependencies between the engineering disciplines in order to build a common system. A key success factor is the capability to exchange selected data in the engineering artifacts with related domain experts efficiently and in a timely manner to reduce rework due to inconsistencies.

We illustrate the *engineering data exchange* (EDEx) process with a use case from simulation in PSE, as simulation is a major consumer of engineering data for assessing the safety and business risks of a production system before system construction. Goal of the simulation engineer is to design simulation systems that allow exploring dynamic properties of the designed production system, such as throughput or the physical feasibility of production steps. Therefore, the simulation engineer requires input data from several engineering data providers on key parameters of system parts, such as the rotation speed, torque, control signals, or power consumption of a motor, as foundation for calculating and analyzing the movement of work pieces and robots over time.

In the traditional EDEx process [1,5], domain experts communicate their engineering artifacts from point to point, typically in the form of spreadsheet tables, *pdf* or XML files. Unfortunately, in the traditional EDEx process, Lüder *et al.* [12] identified the following major challenges.

Ch1. Unclear Data Requirements of and Benefits for Stakeholders. For potential data providers, it is often not clearly defined which project participants require what kind of data at what point in time in the project. Even if general dependencies between stakeholders are known, the specific relations between engineering artifacts and their content within an engineering project can change during the project execution.

Ch2. Heterogeneous Engineering Data is Hard to Integrate for Sharing. Due to strongly practical and historical reasons, engineering tools are typically specific to one discipline and not designed for use with other disciplines. While the disciplines share some common concepts, such as the concept of a device or a signal, these concepts are not consistently modeled, making data integration for sharing error prone and hard to automate. Consequently, sharing engineering artifacts takes high effort for consuming domain experts and, thus, hinders comprehensive automated processing.

In this paper, we introduce a process for efficient data logistics to exchange engineering data in order to address these challenges and to automate data logistics for improving the value and for reducing the risks of EDEx. We investigate the following research questions (RQs) based on *Design Science* research methodology [19].

RQ1. What are main elements of an effective and efficient engineering data exchange (EDEx) process in Multi-Disciplinary Engineering? To address this research question, Sect. 2 summarizes related work on approaches for data exchange in multi-disciplinary *production systems engineering* (PSE). Section 3.1 discusses EDEx process requirements collected in workshops at a large PSE company. Section 3.2 proposes steps for an EDEx process that addresses these requirements. For designing the EDEx process, we adapt the *Multi-Model Dashboard* approach [5] from constraint evaluation to EDEx and replace the design requirement of an initial common concept model, which may not be available, with direct links between consumer and provider data elements.

RQ2. What are main information system mechanisms that enable engineering data exchange for Multi-Disciplinary Engineering? To address this research question, Sect. 3.3 derives requirements for effective and efficient *EDEx information system* (EDExIS) mechanisms. Section 4 reports on an evaluation of the effectiveness and effort of the proposed EDEx process with EDExIS mechanisms in a feasibility case study with requirements and data from real-world use cases with domain experts at a large PSE company. Section 5 discusses the findings and limitations. Section 6 concludes and proposes future research work. From the research, we expect the following contributions for the *information systems engineering* (ISE) community. The use cases and EDEx process give ISE researchers insight into the PSE domain, the foundation for Industry 4.0 applications. The EDEx process contributes capabilities for designing and investigating agile processes and information systems in PSE, a foundation for conducting engineering projects for *cyber-physical production systems* economically.

2   Related Work

This section summarizes related work on data exchange in production systems engineering, *information system* (IS) engineering, and software engineering.

2.1   Data Logistics in Production Systems Engineering

Due to the inherent dependencies between the local models in the *Production Systems Engineering* (PSE) process, e.g., the impact of electro-magnetic fields from electrical wiring on communication quality, domain knowledge is required both on the customer and the provider data models to interpret the data content [3]. Therefore, it is necessary to move from delivering engineering artifacts to *engineering data exchange* (EDEx).

Furthermore, the migration towards cyber-physical systems is a complex task due to challenges, such as heterogeneous tools and data formats as well as diverging views on artifacts and their versioning. Therefore, an extensive solution, covering technical, operational, and human dimensions, is required [7]. Optimizing the available engineering data is a possible quick impact that can be achieved by integrating EDEx [17] based on the machine understandable representation of knowledge.

Lüder *et al.* [12] introduced an architecture for engineering data logistics, based on *AutomationML* (IEC 62714) [18], an open, XML-based format for the exchange of engineering data. The proposed architecture allows exchanging data between discipline-specific data models with varying hierarchical key systems.

While this approach is useful in an *AutomationML* environment, it does not consider how to negotiate the EDEx between many data consumers and providers.

The *Multi-Model Dashboard* (MMD) [5] process guides the systematic definition, monitoring, and evaluation of PSE parameters and constraints. While we can build on the MMD strengths as foundation for the EDEx research in this paper, the MMD approach also requires significant adaptation for our context, since it does not consider the provision of data to consumers, and because well-defined common concepts in PSE are hard to implement in practice if several disciplines cooperate with each other, with no discipline clearly leading.

2.2 Data Exchange Contributions from Information Systems and Software Engineering

Methods from business process management provide useful approaches, such as *UML class diagrams* [6] or BPMN [13], for EDEx definition by characterizing the involved stakeholders, systems and, to some extent, data types and their relationships. However, these methods are generic and need to be adapted for new contexts, also in the case of heterogeneous engineering data integration [15]. In specialized domains, e.g., medicine or engineering, approaches need to be adapted to optimize data exchange according to domain-specific requirements [10,14].

Semantic Web technologies are recognized for facilitating data exchange across applications and organizations in the web and have proposed engineering data integration approaches following the *interchange standardization approach* [17]. However, the manifold types of dependencies in PSE data models are different from typical *Semantic Web* requirements [11] and the *Semantic Web* technology stack is, therefore, currently seldom used in engineering environments.

Software engineering design patterns [9] encapsulate best practices of software system design for commonly occurring problems, in our case data and tool integration. In the context of this work, we build on design patterns, such as *message passing* and *publish-subscribe*, to support the loose coupling of engineering work groups and tools.

3   Design of the Engineering Data Exchange Process and Information System

This section introduces requirements, use cases, and main elements for an *Engineering Data Exchange* (EDEx) process and derives mechanisms of an EDExIS.

3.1 Requirements for an Engineering Data Exchange Process

Following the *design science cycle* in [19], we set up an initial problem investigation with workshops [2], outlining the context and problem space of research, and deriving the following requirements addressing the challenges introduced in Sect. 1. A more detailed description can be found in [4].

Cap1. Engineering Data Representation. This capability concerns the representation of candidates for and specifics of typical engineering data structures, such as tree hierarchies of the functions of a production system, lists of objects, and objects and their attributes and relationships, both for data consumers and data providers.

Cap2. Semantic Link Knowledge Representation. This capability concerns the representation of candidates for and specifics for semantic links for data integration between selected consumer and provider data elements.

Cap3. Process Data Representation. This capability concerns the representation of meta-data on the EDEx process, e.g., who provided what data when, versions of data elements, data quality and validity (e.g., valid, invalid data).

Cap4. Consumer- and Benefit-Driven EDex Planning. This capability emphasizes on planning EDEx guided by business benefits coming from data consumer use cases to ensure the prioritization of EDEx with high benefits. This is an economic improvement to the traditional process, which focuses on the cost for set up and operation. This capability implies the requirement for providing an overview on stakeholders interested in requested or provided data as foundation for a data logistics marketplace.

3.2 Use Cases for Evaluation

From workshops at a large PSE company with 28 domain experts, who come from four different domains of expertise, and 6 researchers, we identified two illustrative EDEx consumer use cases (UCs) as foundation for the EDEx process design and evaluation. The engineering of a typical industrial *production system* (PS), such as automotive assembly, requires at least the collaboration of, and EDEx between, the *plant planner* (PP), who plans the layout of the PS, the *mechanical engineer* (ME), the *electrical engineer* (EE), and the *robot programmer* (RP).

UC Sim. Data Exchange for Production System Simulation. In a typical advanced engineering environment, a *simulation engineer* (SimE) designs and runs simulation models to check the engineering results and to optimize production system parameters, such as safety risks, production throughput, and energy consumption. The design of the simulation models depends on the input of several other domain experts. The PP, ME, EE, and RP may provide configuration parameters of motors and conveyors in a transport system and requirements of production processes, such as process duration (s), and production resource parameters, such as length (m), mass (kg), or power consumption (kW). The manual synchronization of these data typically requires additional effort, tends to be error prone, and induces avoidable project risks.

UC PM. Engineering Project Monitoring. The *project manager* (PM) wants to use the input from data providers to the SimE to assess project progress by analyzing the completeness and quality of the data with respect to the project phase and planned deliverables. Missing or inconsistent data may make sense in an early design phase, but may pose a major risk closer to a later design milestone and may require action by the PM. Unfortunately, the PM does not understand the various input engineering artifacts.

3.3 Engineering Data Exchange Process Design

To address the required capabilities in Sect. 3.1 and the use cases in Sect. 3.2, we introduce the main elements of an *engineering data exchange* (EDEx) process, design according to [19]. The EDEx process extends the *Multi-Model Dashboard* process [5] to multi-disciplinary engineering work groups in a PSE project. The EDEx process is independent of a concrete implementation technology.

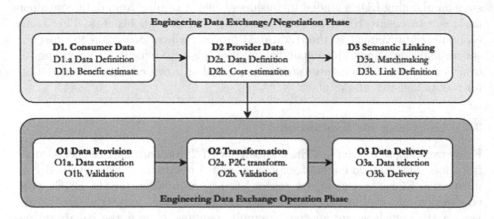

Fig. 1. Data Exchange process architecture with definition/negotiation and operation phases, based on [4].

Process Architecture. Figure 1 gives an overview on the EDEx definition and operation phases. The EDEx operation phase assumes an agreement between data consumers and data providers on the data model and concepts for EDEx.

EDEx Roles are the *data consumer*, the *data provider*, and the *EDEx curator*. The data consumer requests data according to her local consumer data model from providers to improve her business processes. The data provider has engineering artifacts that contain relevant data for a consumer. A domain expert may be both consumer and provider. The *EDEx curator* has background knowledge on the PSE business and relevant data models of all domain experts to mediate between consumers and data providers. The *EDEx curator* has the capability to link the local data models of consumers and providers with appropriate link definitions, such as mathematical formulae.

EDEx Definition Phase. The EDEx definition phase consists of three main steps to identify feasible and beneficial candidate instances for data exchange. At the end of this phase, the EDEx roles come to agreements on which data sets they plan to exchange as foundation for the technical design and implementation in a suitable EDEx environment. Figures 2 and 3 illustrate selected cases of the EDEx processes.

D1. Consumer Data Definition and Prioritization. Consumer candidates have to define their data requests. The *EDEx curator* validates with the consumer the definition of requested data and estimates the likely benefit of providing the data to focus on the most relevant EDEx instances first. This step results in a set of data model elements in the local consumer data view, with a semantic description understandable both to the *EDEx curator* and prospective providers based on the modelling concepts and vocabulary of the *EDEx curator* (see Fig. 3, tag D1). Note that this step is iterative to allow consumers adding data elements.

D2. Provider Data Definition and Cost Estimation. A provider can react to consumer data requests by agreeing to publish data that is semantically equivalent to the requested consumer data. Outcome of this activity is a set of data model elements in the local provider data view, with a semantic description understandable both to the *EDEx curator* and prospective providers based on the modelling concepts and vocabulary of the provider (see Fig. 3 for examples). The *EDEx curator* has to elicit the likely cost for data extraction and transformation into a format that is suitable for EDEx, such as *AutomationML*. The goal of this step is to give feedback to the provider whether the data is of sufficient quality and reasonable cost to continue setting up the EDEx (see Fig. 3, tag D2).

D3. Consumer-Provider Mediation and Semantic Link Definition. For each promising consumer data request, the *EDEx curator* tries to find a set of providers that would allow providing the requested data. In typical cases, the data elements may come from several providers in a variety of data formats (see Fig. 2). For each pair of requested and provided data items, the *EDEx curator* establishes a formal semantic link, i.e., a formula that specifies how to calculate the consumer data value from published provider data instances. More advanced semantic relationships [11] include string operations, mathematical calculations, and parameterized function calls to semantic transformation algorithms (see Fig. 4). Outcome of this step is a set of consumer data, semantically linked to a set of provider data as foundation for designing the EDEx operation, supported by an EDExIS.

EDEx Operation Phase. The EDEx definition phase provides the foundation for conducting the exchange of data instances (see Figs. 2 and 3).

O1. Data Provision and Validation. The provider extracts the data elements as agreed in the EDEx definition phase from their local engineering artifacts. Then

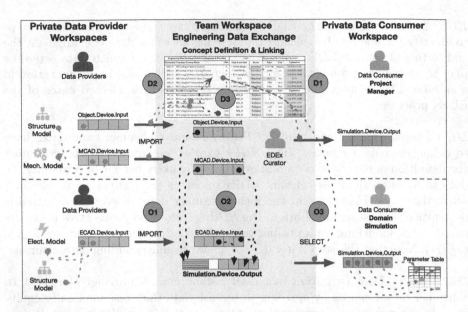

Fig. 2. Engineering data exchange definition/negotiation and operation for a customer data set, based on [4,5] (tags in green circles refer to EDEx process steps in Fig. 1). (Color figure online)

the provider transforms the extracted data into a data model and format that the *team workspace* can import (see Fig. 2, tag O1). The provider and the *EDEx curator* agree on a procedure to validate the data from extraction to input to *team workspace* to ensure that only correctly transformed data is imported. The *EDEx curator* imports valid data into the *team workspace.*

O2. Semantic Data Transformation and Validation. A transformation mechanism in the *team workspace* propagates the imported data along the semantic links to fill in or update consumer data sets (see Fig. 2, tag O2). The *EDEx curator* checks the correctness of the transformation of imported provider to consumer data.

O3. Data selection and Delivery. The consumer selects data instances by providing the *team workspace* with the type of and information to select the requested data instances, such as data identifiers or selection conditions, similar to a SQL query to a database. The *team workspace* delivers the result data to the consumer (see Fig. 2, tag O3).

3.4   Illustrating Use Cases

Figure 2 illustrates an overview on the roles, engineering artifacts, and exchanged data for the EDEx definition/negotiation and operation processes (see Fig. 1) for

Consumer	Consumer Concept Name	Prio	Link to provider	Status	Value	Unit	Updated at
SIM_01	ME.CuttingCell.Robot1.Location	A	= 10*ME.Weldin...	Subscribed	(113; 198)	(dm;dm)	2.2.2019; 17:49
SIM_01	RP.CuttingCell.Robot1.Cutting.Duration	A	= 1000*RP.We...	Subscribed	15,000	ms	10.4.2019; 16:20
SIM_01	RP.CuttingCell.Robot1.Handling.Duratio	A	= RP.CuttingC	scribed	6	s	.2019; 16:20
SIM_01	ME.CuttingCell.Robot1.Motor.Torque	C	N/A	ted	N/A	N	N/A
SIM_01	ME.CuttingCell.Conveyer.Speed	B	= 100*ME.Weld...	d	1500	cm/s	17.3.2019; 21:24
SIM_01	EE.CuttingCell.Conveyer.Drive1.Signal1	B	= PP.CuttingCell...	ed	False	Bool	13.3.2019; 06:49
Provider	Provider Concept Name	Cost	Used by consumer	Status	Value	Unit	Updated at
RP_02	RP.CuttingCell.Robot1.Cutting.Duration	Low	SIM_01	Published	15	s	10.4.2019; 16:20
RP_02	RP.CuttingCell.Robot1.Handling.Duration	Low	SIM_01	Published	6	s	.2019; 16:20
ME_03	ME.CuttingCell.Robot1.Location	High	SIM_01	Published	(11.3; 19.8)	(m;r	019; 17:49
ME_02	ME.CuttingCell.Conveyer.Size	Low	SIM_03	Published	1,325	mm	.2019; 21:24
ME_02	ME.CuttingCell.Conveyer.Speed	Low	SIM_01	Published	15	m/s	17.3.2019; 21:24
EE_04	EE.CuttingCell.Conveyer.Drive1.Signal1	High	SIM_01	Published	FALSE	Bool	14.8.2018; 07:43
EE_04	EE.CuttingCell.Conveyer.Drive1.Signal1	High	SIM_01	Published	FALSE	Bool	14.8.2018; 07:43

Fig. 3. EDEx definition/negotiation and operation overview table, based on MMD in [4,5] (tags in green circles refer to EDEx process steps in Fig. 1). (Color figure online)

one consumer data set, in this case device parameters collected for the SimE. The data providers and data consumers, such as the PP, ME, EE, and SimE, operate in *private workspaces*. The *team workspace* contains shared data views as foundation for preparing and operating the EDEx processes.

Parameter Exchange for Production System Simulation. In this use case, the SimE requires a set of parameters to configure the simulation for a device (see Fig. 2, lower right-hand part, red bar), such as a robot or conveyer. The SimE requests the set of parameters from providers, such as the PP, ME, EE, and RP, who may agree and publish their local engineering data corresponding to a consumer request (see Fig. 2, left-hand part). Then the *EDEx curator* links the set of parameters requested by the SimE with the set of parameters published by the PP, ME, EE, and RP (see Fig. 2, middle part) to enable the EDEx operation.

During the EDEx operation phase, the *team workspace* receives updates of provider data instances in engineering artifacts from the *private workspaces* of the PP, ME, EE, and RP (see Fig. 2, left-hand side for the ME and EE) and transforms this input data according to the semantic links into output data for delivery to the SimE (see Fig. 2, right-hand side, and example output data in Fig. 2, right-hand upper part). The SimE can be notified as soon as relevant data for a requested data set is available or changed.

Production System Engineering Project Monitoring. The PM can benefit from the EDEx for simple and advanced analyses. A simple analysis could be to subscribe to the same data sets as the SimE and analyze at specific points in the project for which data elements data is expected but missing.

Figure 3 shows a snapshot of the EDEx overview table during operation: data instances coming from the providers have been processed according to the linking formulae to fill in data instances for consumers (tags O1, O2, O3). For consumers, the EDEx overview (tag D1) shows the status of the data elements as requested, agreed for provision, or subscribed for delivery. The EDEx overview table (tag

D3) shows the status of linked data elements. For a requested data element, there may be several providers. Therefore, the EDEx overview table (see Fig. 3) indicates the cost of providing a data element and the engineering process phase. For example, $EE \ldots Signal1$ could be obtained from $PP \ldots Signal1$ at lower cost.

3.5   Engineering Data Exchange Information System Design

This section describes the main architectural components of mechanisms of an *EDex information system* (EDExIS) to address the requirements for capabilities of the EDex process described in Sect. 3.1 and the use cases described in Sect. 3.2. The design of these mechanisms is likely to vary depending on the application context.

EDEx Management and Overview. For managing the EDEx process, the EDExIS has to provide a mechanism providing the capabilities of the EDEx overview table illustrated in Fig. 3, including EDEx definition functions to request, agree on providing, publishing, and subscribing to data elements (see EDEx process steps D1 to D3), as well as setting relevant attributes of and searching the table for understanding the status of the EDEx definition in the project team.

EDEx Data Definition Languages. For EDEx definition, the EDExIS has to process the languages for the specification of consumer and provider data sets, and the language for semantic link definition specifying (a) the dependencies between consumer and provider data sets and (b) the transformation of imported provider data into consumer data.

Figure 4 illustrates examples of semantic link definitions between consumer and provider data models. In the simplest case, the output value is just an identical copy of an input instance value (see Fig. 4, formula DL1, assuming matching IDs for concepts welding cell, conveyor, etc.). Simple cases require scaling and/or shifting the input values, e.g., to adjust for different scales of units, such as m, cm, or mm, or s and ms (see Fig. 4, formula DL2). More advanced links may require more complex formulae including custom functions or combining the instance values from several data elements (see Fig. 4, formula DL3). A link formula can involve one or more providers and data elements as data sources and can encapsulate capabilities for string operations, advanced algorithms, and access to external knowledge, e.g., web services.

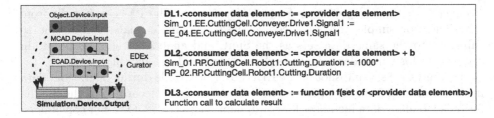

Fig. 4. Semantic link definition on consumer and provider data models, based on [4].

EDEx Operation Capabilities. For conducting the EDEx operation steps, the EDExIS has to be able (a) to import and validate provider data, (b) to store imported data versions including their metadata for processing, (c) to analyze the data and semantic links in order to correctly propagate the provider data to consumer data structures, and (d) to select and export consumer data.

4   Evaluation

This section reports on the evaluation of the *engineering data exchange* (EDEx) process and requirements (a) in an initial feasibility case study [16] with 19 domain experts at a large production systems engineering (PSE) company. The project coordinators for each domain were the same as in the initial workshop, a systems integrator for metallurgic production systems, and (b) in a cost/benefit comparison of the EDEx definition and operation processes to the traditional process of point-to-point exchange of engineering artifacts between domain experts, closing an iteration of the design cycle [19].

4.1   Feasibility Study

Goal of the feasibility study is to evaluate the basic concepts of the EDEx process with domain experts by following the steps of the EDEx process description (see Sect. 3.3 and Fig. 2). Based on the use cases introduced in Sect. 3.2, we designed prototypes of selected user interface elements, such as the overview table, specification, linking, and retrieval as mock-up artifacts. We collected data on the usability and usefulness of the EDEx process based on the *Technology Acceptance Model* uestionnaire [1,8].

Further, we developed technology prototypes of the IS capabilities to explore the feasibility of designing the EDExIS concepts with available technologies, including *AutomationML* for data specification (see [12]), an Excel dialect for the specification of dependency links, Java code for transformations, and BaseX as data storage. We conducted and discussed the EDEx steps in a workshop with domain experts representing the roles data provider (PP, ME, EE, RP in the use cases), data consumer (SimE, PM), and *EDEx curator*.

Overall, the domain experts found the EDEx process feasible, useful, and usable for basic cases that make up most of the data exchange use cases in their typical project context, assuming that the EDExIS provides effective tool support to automate the data transformation, storage, and selection tasks. The domain experts provided improvement suggestions for the user interfaces, and for describing the data transformation and linking formulae in their context. Further, the domain experts noted that more complex cases may take considerable effort to design and automate.

4.2   Cost/Benefit Considerations

To evaluate the costs and benefits of the EDEx process via a *team workspace* in comparison to the traditional manual process based EDEx, we elicited needs and estimates from domain experts, who are responsible for engineering and project management of large-scale metallurgic production system projects.

Table 1 presents an overview of the findings for of the EDEx process steps in the use case *Parameter exchange for production system simulation* by comparing the effectiveness, i.e., correctness of results for a task, and the effort of a stakeholder conducting a task. We applied a 5-point *Likert* scale (++, +, o, -, –), where "++" indicates very positive effects, and "–" very negative effects. Positive effects refer to high effectiveness of the investigated approaches and to low effort for implementation and application.

Table 1. Effectiveness and effort of *manual* and *EDEx* processes, based on [4].

EDEx Process steps	Effectiveness		Effort	
	Manual	EDEx	Manual	EDEx
D1. Consumer data definition & prioritization	o	+	+	o
D2. Provider data definition & cost estimation	–	+	+	-
D3. Consumer provider semantic link definition	–	++	N/A	-
O1. Data provision and validation	-	o	+	o
O2. Data transformation and validation	–	+	–	+
O3. Data selection and delivery	–	++	–	++

Regarding effectiveness, the EDEx process was found effective to very effective by the interviewed stakeholders, both providers and consumers, because they were able to exchange data elements in a traceable and validated way. In the traditional manual approach, the data consumers had to define, procure, transform, and validate the required data for each new delivery with significant effort and prone to errors. However, the application of the EDEx process requires additional effort, especially during the EDEx steps definition (D2) and linking (D3), in particular for providers and for the new role of the *EDEx curator*.

On the upside, the results of the linking step (D3) significantly improve the representation of shared knowledge in the engineering team, regarding an overview on the dependencies between the engineering roles on data element level. Domain experts and the PM can always get a current overview on the status of data deliveries and can identify missing engineering data and unfulfilled consumer requests.

5   Discussion

This section discusses results of the research questions introduced in Sect. 1.

RQ1. What are main elements of an effective and efficient engineering data exchange (EDEx) process in multi-disciplinary engineering? Section 3.3 introduced as main elements EDEx roles, process steps, and data structures. The new role of the *EDEx curator* mediates between data consumers and providers. In the feasibility study, a domain expert filling this role informally was identified. The EDEx data structures represent the necessary knowledge on engineering data, semantic links between consumer and provider data, and the status on the EDEx process as foundation for effective EDEx for the use cases and according to the required capabilities for EDEx in multi-disciplinary engineering. The EDEx process facilitates efficient EDEx (a) by considering the benefits of EDEx for consumers and the cost for providers to focus first on the data sets with the best cost-benefit balance and (b) by automating the EDEx operation with support by the EDExIS.

As potential drawbacks of the process, domain experts noted the need to convince data providers to take over the task and extra effort of extracting requested data from their engineering artifacts. For this task, specific tool support, adapted to the project context, will be required as well as appropriate compensation for the extra effort.

RQ2. What are main information system mechanisms that enable engineering data exchange for multi-disciplinary engineering? The EDExIS mechanisms for management and overview, data definition languages, and operation capabilities addressed the requirements for EDEx capabilities in Sect. 3.1 on a conceptual level. These mechanisms facilitate efficient *round-trip engineering*. The design of an operational EDExIS will have considerable impact on the efficiency of the EDEx process in the application context and needs further investigation.

Limitations. As all empirical studies the presented research has some limitations that require further investigation.

Feasibility Study. We evaluated the EDEx process with focus on specific use cases in cooperation with domain experts in a typical large company regarding the PSE of production systems that can be seen as representative for systems engineering enterprises with project business using a heterogeneous tool landscape. The evaluation results are based on observations from a limited sample of projects, stakeholder roles, and data models. To overcome these limitations, we plan a more detailed investigation in a wider variety of domains and application contexts.

The Expressiveness of Data Specification and Linking Languages, used in the evaluated prototype, can be considered as a limitation. The prototype is able to address an initial set of simple data types, while industrial scenarios showed more complex value ranges and aggregated ranges. While the evaluation worked well with data provided in tables, the evaluation of advanced data structures such as trees or graphs remains open.

6   Conclusion and Future Work

Digitalization in *production system engineering* (PSE) [18] aims at enabling flexible production towards the *Industry 4.0* vision and at shortening the engineering phase of production systems. This results in an increase of parallel PSE, where the involved disciplines have to exchange updates for synchronization due to dependency constraints between the engineering disciplines.

We introduced and investigated PSE use cases and the *engineering data exchange* (EDEx) process to provide domain experts in PSE with an approach to define and efficiently exchange agreed sets of data elements between heterogeneous local engineering models as foundation for agile and traceable PSE.

Ch1. Unclear Data Requirements of and Benefits for Stakeholders. The EDEx definition phase results in a network of stakeholders linked via data they exchange. This network can grow iteratively, going beyond a one-time process analysis. Therefore, the EDExIS facilitates frequent synchronization between work groups to reduce the risk of divergent local designs, rework, and delays.

Ch2. Heterogeneous Engineering Data is Hard to Integrate for Sharing. Semantic linking allowed the integration of heterogeneous data in the evaluated use cases. The semantic linking enables seamless traceability in the EDEx process that, for the first time, gives all stakeholders the opportunity to know and analyze which role provided or received which kind of engineering data. Further, the EDEx semantic linking improves the representation of shared knowledge in a machine-readable way, a prerequisite for introducing *Industry 4.0* applications.

Future Work. The EDEx meta-data will enable consumers and researchers to conduct advanced analyses, such as data validity and consistency, and symptoms for security risks. During the use of EDEx, the complexity of links may grow considerably with the number of data elements, consumers, and providers, which will require research on scalability of EDEx. However, centralizing knowledge in the EDExIS will require research on threats to the integrity of collected knowledge and of industrial espionage.

Acknowledgment. The financial support by the Christian Doppler Research Association, the Austrian Federal Ministry for Digital & Economic Affairs and the National Foundation for Research, Technology and Development is gratefully acknowledged.

References

1. Biffl, S., Eckhart, M., Lüder, A., Müller, T., Rinker, F., Winkler, D.: Data interface for coil car simulation (case study) part I. Technical report CDL-SQI-M2-TR02, TU Wien (2018)
2. Biffl, S., Eckhart, M., Lüder, A., Müller, T., Rinker, F., Winkler, D.: Data interface for coil car simulation (case study) part II - detailed data and process models. Technical report CDL-SQI-M2-TR03, TU Wien (2018)
3. Biffl, S., Gerhard, D., Lüder, A.: Introduction to the multi-disciplinary engineering for cyber-physical production systems. In: Biffl, S., Lüder, A., Gerhard, D. (eds.) Multi-Disciplinary Engineering for Cyber-Physical Production Systems, pp. 1–24. Springer, Cham (2017). https://doi.org/10.1007/978-3-319-56345-9_1

4. Biffl, S., Lüder, A., Rinker, F., Waltersdorfer, L., Winkler, D.: Introducing engineering data logistics for production systems engineering. Technical report CDL-SQI-2018-10, TU Wien (2018). http://qse.ifs.tuwien.ac.at/wp-content/uploads/CDL-SQI-2018-10.pdf
5. Biffl, S., Winkler, D., Mordinyi, R., Scheiber, S., Holl, G.: Efficient monitoring of multi-disciplinary engineering constraints with semantic data integration in the multi-model dashboard process. In: Proceedings of the 2014 IEEE Emerging Technology and Factory Automation (ETFA), pp. 1–10. IEEE (2014)
6. Brambilla, M., Cabot, J., Wimmer, M.: Model-driven software engineering in practice. Synth. Lect. Softw. Eng. **1**(1), 1–182 (2012)
7. Calà, A., et al.: Migration from traditional towards cyber-physical production systems. In: 2017 IEEE 15th International Conference on Industrial Informatics (INDIN), pp. 1147–1152. IEEE (2017)
8. Davis, F.D.: A technology acceptance model for empirically testing new end-user information systems: Theory and results. Ph.D. thesis, Massachusetts Institute of Technology (1985)
9. Hohpe, G., Woolf, B.: Enterprise Integration Patterns: Designing, Building, and Deploying Messaging Solutions. Addison-Wesley Professional, Boston (2004)
10. Jimenez-Ramirez, A., Barba, I., Reichert, M., Weber, B., Del Valle, C.: Clinical processes - the Killer application for constraint-based process interactions? In: Krogstie, J., Reijers, H.A. (eds.) CAiSE 2018. LNCS, vol. 10816, pp. 374–390. Springer, Cham (2018). https://doi.org/10.1007/978-3-319-91563-0_23
11. Kovalenko, O., Euzenat, J.: Semantic matching of engineering data structures. Semantic Web Technologies for Intelligent Engineering Applications, pp. 137–157. Springer, Cham (2016). https://doi.org/10.1007/978-3-319-41490-4_6
12. Lüder, A., Pauly, J.-L., Kirchheim, K., Rinker, F., Biffl, S.: Migration to AutomationML based tool chains - incrementally overcoming engineering network challenges. In: 5th AutomationML User Conference (2018)
13. Business Process Model. Notation (BPMN) Version 2.0. omg (2011)
14. Putze, S., Porzel, R., Savino, G.-L., Malaka, R.: A manageable model for experimental research data: an empirical study in the materials sciences. In: Krogstie, J., Reijers, H.A. (eds.) CAiSE 2018. LNCS, vol. 10816, pp. 424–439. Springer, Cham (2018). https://doi.org/10.1007/978-3-319-91563-0_26
15. Rosemann, M., vom Brocke, J.: The six core elements of business process management. In: vom Brocke, J., Rosemann, M. (eds.) Handbook on Business Process Management 1. IHIS, pp. 105–122. Springer, Heidelberg (2015). https://doi.org/10.1007/978-3-642-45100-3_5
16. Runeson, P., Höst, M.: Guidelines for conducting and reporting case study research in software engineering. Empirical Softw. Eng. **14**(2), 131 (2009)
17. Sabou, M., Ekaputra, F.J., Biffl, S.: Semantic web technologies for data integration in multi-disciplinary engineering. In: Biffl, S., Lüder, A., Gerhard, D. (eds.) Multi-disciplinary Engineering for Cyber-Physical Production Systems, pp. 301–329. Springer, Cham (2017). https://doi.org/10.1007/978-3-319-56345-9_12
18. Vogel-Heuser, B., Bauernhansl, T., Ten Hompel, M.: Handbuch industrie 4.0 bd. 4. Allgemeine Grundlagen, vol. 2 (2017)
19. Wieringa, R.J.: Design Science Methodology for Information Systems and Software Engineering. Springer, Heidelberg (2014). https://doi.org/10.1007/978-3-662-43839-8

Bing-CF-IDF+: A Semantics-Driven News Recommender System

Emma Brocken[1], Aron Hartveld[1], Emma de Koning[1], Thomas van Noort[1],
Frederik Hogenboom[1], Flavius Frasincar[1](✉)(iD), and Tarmo Robal[2](iD)

[1] Erasmus University Rotterdam,
Burgemeester Oudlaan 50, 3062 PA Rotterdam, The Netherlands
emmabrockenn@gmail.com, aronhartveld@gmail.com, emmadekoning@gmail.com,
thomasvnoort@gmail.com, {fhogenboom,frasincar}@ese.eur.nl
[2] Tallinn University of Technology,
Ehitajate tee 5, 19086 Tallinn, Estonia
tarmo.robal@ttu.ee

Abstract. With the ever growing amount of news on the Web, the need
for automatically finding the relevant content increases. Semantics-driven
news recommender systems suggest unread items to users by matching
user profiles, which are based on information found in previously read
articles, with emerging news. This paper proposes an extension to the
state-of-the-art semantics-driven CF-IDF+ news recommender system,
which uses identified news item concepts and their related concepts for
constructing user profiles and processing unread news messages. Due to
its domain specificity and reliance on knowledge bases, such a concept-
based recommender neglects many highly frequent named entities found
in news items, which contain relevant information about a news item's
content. Therefore, we extend the CF-IDF+ recommender by adding
information found in named entities, through the employment of a Bing-
based distance measure. Our Bing-CF-IDF+ recommender outperforms
the classic TF-IDF and the concept-based CF-IDF and CF-IDF+ recommenders in terms of the F_1-score and the Kappa statistic.

Keywords: News recommendation system ·
Content-based recommender · Semantic Web · Named entities ·
Bing-CF-IDF+

1 Introduction

The ever growing information stream on the Web is gradually overwhelming
the rapidly increasing population of Web users that try to access information
matching their needs. An automated and accurate approach for distinguishing
between relevant and non-relevant content is becoming of utmost importance
for fulfilling the basic needs of the people accessing the Web. Recommender
systems [1] have proven to be powerful tools for efficient processing of media
and news content. Such systems build up user profiles by gathering information

© Springer Nature Switzerland AG 2019
P. Giorgini and B. Weber (Eds.): CAiSE 2019, LNCS 11483, pp. 32–47, 2019.
https://doi.org/10.1007/978-3-030-21290-2_3

on recently viewed content, e.g., by exploiting domain models [18]. New content is analyzed in a similar fashion, so that similarities between user profiles and content can be computed, thus supporting a personalized Web experience [19,20] through efficient and intelligent procedures to deal with the information overload.

Traditionally, there are three kinds of recommender systems: content-based recommenders, collaborative filtering recommenders, and hybrid recommenders [5]. Content-based recommenders use the content of the unseen news items, media, etc., to match the interests of the user. Collaborative filtering recommenders find similar users and recommend new content of interest to the most similar users. Hybrid recommenders combine the former two methods. In this paper, a new content-based recommender is proposed that is aimed specifically towards news recommendation. Therefore, solely content-based recommender systems are discussed in the remainder of this paper.

Content-based news recommenders suggest unread news items based on similarities between the content of the news item and the user profile. The similarity can be computed in various ways, each measure utilizing different types of information. Some measures are based on terms (text strings) found in news items, while others are based on synsets or concepts. In this paper, we propose an extension to the previously proposed semantics-driven CF-IDF+ recommender [9] that has already proved to outperform the classic TF-IDF [21] and CF-IDF [12] recommenders. Where TF-IDF employs term-based similarities, CF-IDF adds the notion of concepts. CF-IDF+ additionally makes use of concepts that are related to concepts extracted from a news article or user profile, providing more accurate representations.

Another content-based recommendation method is based on named entities within a document. Named entities can be considered as real-world instantiations of objects, such as persons and locations. Typically, named entities are used for text analytics and information extraction purposes, e.g., by supporting more efficient search and question answering algorithms, text classification, and recommender systems [22]. The latter systems often have to deal with large amounts of (semi-)unstructured texts. By omitting the irrelevant words and only considering named entities, the dimensionality of similarity computations can be greatly reduced, thus allowing for less expensive, yet accurate recommendations. This is also in line with the usage of concepts and synsets employed in our news recommenders, and could be a beneficial addition to our systems.

Named entities appear often in news items, yet are mostly neglected because they are, for instance, not present in domain ontologies that underly concept-based recommenders. As a consequence, the CF-IDF+ method does not use all the information that is provided by named entities. A possible solution to this problem is the introduction of a methodology that takes into consideration page counts gathered by Web search engines such as Google or Bing for specific named entities. In earlier work, originally, we made use of Google named entities. However, we had to move to Bing as the usage of Google API was not for free anymore, while Bing API usage was still for free.

The recommender proposed in this paper extends the CF-IDF+ method by using information given in the named entities of news items. It combines the results of the CF-IDF+ method with similarities computed by the Bing search engine, which offered, at the time of conducting the research, a free API [3]. Our proposed recommender, Bing-CF-IDF+, consists of two individually weighted parts. The CF-IDF+ recommender computes the similarity based on concepts, whereas the Bing recommender computes the similarity based on named entities. Only the named entities that do not appear in the concepts are considered by the Bing-CF-IDF+ recommender. The main contribution of this work is the joint exploitation of concepts and their relationships from a domain ontology (CF-IDF+), on one side, and named entities and a search engine-based distance measure (Bing), on the other side, in a news recommender system.

The remainder of this paper is organized as follows. In Sect. 2, related work on previously proposed recommenders is discussed. Section 3 provides an introduction to our method and its implementation, and Sect. 4 evaluates the performance of Bing-CF-IDF+, compared against CF-IDF+, CF-IDF, and TF-IDF recommenders. Section 5 provides conclusions and some additional directions for future work.

2   Related Work

The research endeavours on profile-based (news) recommenders have been plentiful [14]. These recommenders compute similarity levels between news items and user profiles derived from previously read articles, and use these for recommending unseen items. In this section, we focus on recommenders employing terms, synsets, concepts, relations, and named entities.

2.1   Term-Based Recommendation

TF-IDF [21], one of the most commonly used methods for recommending news items, is based on news item terms. The method combines the Term Frequency (TF), which is the frequency of specific terms within a document, and the Inverse Document Frequency (IDF) [16], which is a measure of the fraction of documents that contain these terms. This method is often combined with the cosine similarity method to determine the similarity between users and news articles.

The term frequency of term $t \in T$ in document $d \in D$, $\mathrm{tf}(t, d)$, and its associated inverse document frequency $\mathrm{idf}(t, d)$ are computed as follows:

$$\mathrm{tf}(t, d) = \frac{n_{t,d}}{\sum\limits_{k} n_{k,d}}, \tag{1}$$

$$\mathrm{idf}(t, d) = \log \frac{|D|}{|d \in D : t \in d|}, \tag{2}$$

where term frequencies are calculated by dividing the frequency that term t occurs in news item d ($n_{t,d}$) by the total number of all terms in news item d.

The inverse document frequency is computed as a division of the total number of news items $|D|$ by the amount of news items in which term t can be found. Subsequently, TF-IDF is computed as a multiplication of TF and IDF:

$$\text{tf-idf}(t, d) = \text{tf}(t, d) \times \text{idf}(t, d). \tag{3}$$

This TF-IDF score is large for terms that occur frequently in a particular news item d, but not often in all other news items. Last, the similarity between unread news items and the user's interest is computed according to a cosine similarity function:

$$\text{sim}_{\text{TF-IDF}}(d_u, d_r) = \frac{d_r \cdot d_u}{||d_r|| \times ||d_u||}, \tag{4}$$

where d_r is the vector representation of the user's interest and d_u is the vector representation of an unread news item. The larger $\text{sim}_{\text{TF-IDF}}$ is, the more similar the unread news item and user's interest are. All unread news items that have a higher similarity value with a user profile than a certain cut-off value are recommended to the corresponding user.

2.2 Synset-Based Recommendation

A similar method to the TF-IDF method is the Synset Frequency - Inverse Document Frequency (SF-IDF) method [6]. This method uses synonym sets (synsets) associated to terms rather than terms alone. Synsets are provided by a semantic lexicon such as WordNet [10]. Due to ambiguity, a single term can have multiple synsets, thus requiring word sense disambiguation, e.g., by using the adapted Lesk algorithm proposed in [2] and implemented in [15]. The SF-IDF measure and its corresponding cosine similarity scores are computed using the same equations as introduced for TF-IDF, only by replacing term t by synset s, so that $\text{sf}(s, d) = n_{s,d} / \sum_k n_{k,d}$ and $\text{idf}(s, d) = \log |D| / |d \in D : s \in d|$, and hence

$$\text{sf-idf}(s, d) = \text{sf}(s, d) \times \text{idf}(s, d). \tag{5}$$

Then, the previously defined cosine similarity is used for computing $\text{sim}_{\text{SF-IDF}}$.

2.3 Concept-Based Recommendation

The Concept Frequency - Inverse Document Frequency (CF-IDF) method [12] calculates similarity measures using concepts from a domain ontology rather than terms or synsets. The concepts of an article are obtained using a Natural Language Processing (NLP) engine. For every document, the resulting concepts are then stored in a vector and these vectors can be used to calculate the CF-IDF measure. Similar to TF-IDF and SF-IDF, scores for concept c are computed as follows:

$$\text{cf-idf}(c, d) = \text{cf}(c, d) \times \text{idf}(c, d), \tag{6}$$

where frequencies and inverse document frequencies are defined as $\text{cf}(c, d) = n_{c,d} / \sum_k n_{k,d}$ and $\text{idf}(c, d) = \log |D| / |d \in D : c \in d|$, respectively. Cosine similarity computations remain unchanged for $\text{sim}_{\text{CF-IDF}}$.

2.4 Relation-Based Recommendation

Both SF-IDF and CF-IDF can be extended in such a way that also related synsets or concepts are taken into consideration. For this, the semantic lexicon and ontology can be used in order to derive related elements.

In SF-IDF+ [17], related synsets are considered to be synsets that are connected through a relation (27 unique semantic relationships, e.g., hyponymy, antonymy, synonymy, etc., exist in WordNet), and are added to the vector representation from SF-IDF. For each synset, scores are computed by multiplying the original SF-IDF score with a predefined weight. Weights always range between 0 and 1, as related synsets should never be more important that the synset itself. In Eq. 7, it is shown how the related synsets are added to the vector:

$$\text{sf-idf+}(s, d, r) = \text{sf}(s, d) \times \text{idf}(s, d) \times w_r, \tag{7}$$

where d is the news item, s and r are the original and related synsets, respectively, and w_r is the weight corresponding to the semantic relationship type the related synset has with s.

The same rules apply also for CF-IDF in its extended form (CF-IDF+ [9]). Related concepts are retrieved by taking into account related ontology concepts by three possible relationships, as a concept can have superclasses, subclasses, and domain-specific related concepts. Similarly, the CF-IDF+ value for a concept c and its related concept r in document d is computed as follows:

$$\text{cf-idf+}(c, d, r) = \text{cf}(c, d) \times \text{idf}(c, d) \times w_r, \tag{8}$$

where w_r represents the weight assigned to one of the three previously mentioned relationships present between c and r. If multiple weights are computed for the same concept (or synset), only the highest value is retained in the extended vector representation. The extended vector representation is used for computing the similarity between the user profile and the unread news items using the cosine similarity measure.

2.5 Named Entity-Based Recommendation

In recent endeavours, we additionally tried combining SF-IDF+ with named entities from Bing in Bing-SF-IDF+ [7], which showed promising results. Here, named entities that are not covered by the synsets from a semantic lexicon were still taken into account by consulting the Bing search engine and computing similarities based on page counts.

Computations are based on a weighted average of SF-IDF+ and Bing similarity scores, where the latter is computed using a co-occurrence similarity measure. Similarly, we would like to investigate the merits of the application of Bing named entities to (related) concepts.

Table 1. Average F_1-measures for the recommenders

Recommender	μ	
TF-IDF	0.449	[7]
SF-IDF	0.468	[6]
CF-IDF	0.485	[12]
SF-IDF+	0.548	[17]
CF-IDF+	0.571	[9]
Bing-SF-IDF+	0.579	[7]

2.6 Performance

The discussed methods have been thoroughly tested throughout the years. Some have served as a reference, and have been tested multiple times under different conditions. Overall, the performance of the methods (in terms of F_1) is as described in Table 1. In general, we can say that concept-based methods outperform synset-based methods and the baseline TF-IDF method. Moreover, relation-based recommenders show a performance improvement over their regular counterparts. Including named entities boosts recommendation quality even more.

3 Framework

We improve the existing methods by introducing a two-step procedure, in which we compute a Bing similarity score using point-wise mutual information similarities for Bing named entities, and a CF-IDF+ similarity score using cosine similarities based on concepts and related concepts. Bing-CF-IDF+ scores are computed as a weighted average between Bing and CF-IDF+ scores. Our approach makes use of a user profile, which can be constructed manually by a user by selecting either interesting concepts or interesting news items from which concepts and named entities can be extracted. Incoming news messages are processed similarly, while eliminating named entities that are already covered by the domain ontology.

3.1 Bing

Concept-based recommendation methods only make use of named entities that are included in the domain ontology. However, there could be many more named entities in a single article, that – if they would not be taken into consideration – could skew the entire similarity analysis. Therefore, the Bing similarity measure [7] takes all these named entities into account.

Let U and R be sets of named entities in an unread news item and the user profile:

$$U = \{u_1, u_2, \ldots, u_k\}, \tag{9}$$

$$R = \{r_1, r_2, \ldots, r_l\}, \tag{10}$$

where u_i is a named entity in unread item U, r_j a named entity in user profile R, and k and l are the number of named entities in the unread item and the user profile, respectively. Now let us define the set of possible named entity pairs from the unread news item and the user profile by taking their cartesian product:

$$V = U \times R = (\langle u_1, r_1 \rangle, \ldots, \langle u_k, r_l \rangle). \tag{11}$$

Subsequently, we compute the point-wise mutual information co-occurrence similarity measure as proposed by [4]. We search the named entities in a pair both separately and together in Bing to construct page counts. A page count is defined as the number of Web pages that are found by Bing. For every pair the similarity is computed as the difference between the actual and the expected joint probability. The similarity measure for a pair is defined as:

$$\mathrm{sim}_{\mathrm{PMI}}(u, r) = \log \frac{\frac{c(u,r)}{N}}{\frac{c(u)}{N} \times \frac{c(r)}{N}}, \tag{12}$$

where $c(u, r)$ is the Bing page count for pair (u, r), $c(u)$ and $c(r)$ the page counts for named entities u and r, and N the total number of Web pages that can be found by Bing. N is estimated to be around 15 billion. The Bing similarity measure $\mathrm{sim}_{\mathrm{Bing}}$ is then defined as:

$$\mathrm{sim}_{\mathrm{Bing}}(d_u, d_r) = \frac{\sum_{(u,r) \in V} \mathrm{sim}_{\mathrm{PMI}}(u, r)}{|V|}. \tag{13}$$

3.2   CF-IDF+

The CF-IDF+ method makes use of concepts and related concepts. A concept can be a class, which can have superclasses and subclasses. It can also be an instance and refer to other concepts using domain relationships. The relations between concepts contain valuable information about a news article and can therefore increase recommendation accuracy. Similar to the CF-IDF method, the CF-IDF+ method stores the concepts and related concepts of a news item into a vector. For every concept c, a new set of concepts is defined which contains all related concepts:

$$C(c) = \{c\} \bigcup_{r \in R(c)} r(c), \tag{14}$$

where c is a concept in the news item, $r(c)$ are concepts related to concept c by relation r, and $R(c)$ is the set of relationships of concept c.

The extended sets of concepts for all news items are now unified to one large set U:

$$U = \{C(u_1), C(u_2), \ldots, C(u_m)\}, \tag{15}$$

where $C(u_m)$ is the mth extended concept in the set of extended concepts of the news item. CF-IDF+ scores and their cosine similarities can be computed as introduced earlier using Eqs. 4 and 8. If these scores exceed a predetermined cut-off value, the news item is recommended to the user.

3.3 Bing-CF-IDF+

We can now calculate the Bing and the CF-IDF+ similarity measures between every unread news item and the user profile. Bing-CF-IDF+ is a weighed combination of the Bing and the CF-IDF+ similarity measures. For inter-comparability of the similarities, $\text{sim}_{\text{CF-IDF+}}$ and $\text{sim}_{\text{Bing}}(d_u, d_r)$ are normalized using a min-max scaling between 0 and 1:

$$\overline{\text{sim}}_{\text{CF-IDF+}}(d_u, d_r) = \frac{\text{sim}_{\text{CF-IDF+}}(d_u, d_r) - \min\limits_{u} \text{sim}_{\text{CF-IDF+}}(d_u, d_r)}{\max\limits_{u} \text{sim}_{\text{CF-IDF+}}(d_u, d_r) - \min\limits_{u} \text{sim}_{\text{CF-IDF+}}(d_u, d_r)}, \tag{16}$$

$$\overline{\text{sim}}_{\text{Bing}}(d_u, d_r) = \frac{\text{sim}_{\text{Bing}}(d_u, d_r) - \min\limits_{u} \text{sim}_{\text{Bing}}(d_u, d_r)}{\max\limits_{u} \text{sim}_{\text{Bing}}(d_u, d_r) - \min\limits_{u} \text{sim}_{\text{Bing}}(d_u, d_r)}, \tag{17}$$

where d_u and d_r are an unread news item and the user profile, respectively. The Bing-CF-IDF+ similarity measure $\text{sim}_{\text{Bing-CF-IDF+}}(d_u, d_r)$ is computed by taking a weighted average over both similarities:

$$\text{sim}_{\text{Bing-CF-IDF+}}(d_u, d_r) = \alpha \times \overline{\text{sim}}_{\text{Bing}} + (1 - \alpha) \times \overline{\text{sim}}_{\text{CF-IDF+}}, \tag{18}$$

where α is optimized using a grid search optimization on the training set. Again a news item is recommended when the similarity measures exceeds the predefined threshold value t. Please note that only named entities that are not found as denoting concepts are considered here.

3.4 Implementation

The Bing-CF-IDF+ recommender is implemented in the Hermes framework [11], which is a Java-based personalizing news service using Semantic Web technologies. Hermes ingests user queries and RSS feeds of news items, and supports multiple recommendation methods using an internal knowledge base for storing ontological concepts. Hermes provides recommendations based on user profiles that are constructed based on browsing behaviour. Hermes contains several plug-ins that extend the basic functionality. The Athena plug-in classifies and recommends news items using an internal OWL domain ontology [13]. Next to several concept-based recommender methods, Athena supports an additional profile builder, where a user is allowed to select relevant topics in a visual knowledge graph. The Ceryx plug-in [6] is an extension to Athena. Just like Athena, Ceryx works with a user profile. However, the algorithm to find related news items is slightly different. Besides classifying terms and concepts, Ceryx also determines the senses of words. Therefore, Ceryx is capable of handling recommender methods like SF-IDF+ and CF-IDF+. The Bing-CF-IDF+ recommender is also written for Ceryx.

4 Evaluation

In order to evaluate the performance of the newly proposed Bing-CF-IDF+ method, we compare it with its concept-based alternatives, i.e., CF-IDF and CF-IDF+, as well as the TF-IDF baseline. This section starts by elaborating on the experimental setup regarding data and performance measures. Next, the weights of the semantic relationships and their properties are discussed. Last, performance measures are compared.

4.1 Experimental Setup

In our experiments, we make use of an annotated data set of 100 news items from a Reuters news feed with news on technology companies. Domain experts related news messages to given subjects with an inter-annotator agreement of at least two thirds. The subjects (i.e., the user profiles) are listed in Table 2, accompanied by their inter-annotator agreements (IAA). The reported amounts of interesting (I+) and non-interesting (I−) news items are as determined by the experts.

Table 2. Amount of interesting (I+) and non-interesting (I−) news items, and the inter-annotator agreement (IAA)

Topic	I+	I−	IAA
Asia or its countries	21	79	99%
Financial markets	24	76	72%
Google or its rivals	26	74	97%
Web services	26	74	94%
Microsoft or its rivals	29	71	98%
National economies	33	67	90%
Technology	29	71	87%
United States	45	55	85%

The data set is randomly split into a training set and a test set, with respectively 60% and 40% of the data. First, a user profile is created by adding the interesting news items from the training set. The optimal weights are determined.

by using a validation set which is created by splitting the training set into two equally-sized sets, i.e., a validation set and a training set. We end up having three different sets: a validation set (30%), a training set (30%), and a test set (40%). The validation set and the test set are considered to consist of 'unread' news items. The validation set can now be used to determine the optimal weights, needed to calculate performance measures by using the test set later on.

Table 3. Mean and variance for the parameters of the Bing-CF-IDF+ recommender

	w_{super}	w_{sub}	w_{rel}	α
μ	0.426	0.384	0.523	0.170
σ^2	0.135	0.120	0.103	0.020

As discussed before, the CF-IDF+ recommender computes similarity measures for every unread news item. In case this similarity measure exceeds a certain cut-off value, the unread news item is recommended to the user. The results of the recommenders can be classified for news items as either true positive (TP), false positive (FP), true negative (TN), or false negative (FN). A selection of information retrieval metrics can be deduced from this confusion matrix: precision, recall (sensitivity), and specificity. Additionally, we can deduce the F_1-scores (i.e., the harmonic mean of precision and recall) and ROC-curve (i.e., the True Positive Rate or sensitivity plotted against the False Positive Rate or $1 -$ specificity) from these measures. Last, we compute the Kappa statistic [8] to verify whether the classification power is higher than a random guess. The parameters for semantic relationships are optimized individually through an incremental procedure, optimizing the global F_1-scores. Additionally, the α parameter that determines the weight of the Bing and CF-IDF+ parts is optimized similarly.

4.2 Optimizing Parameters

For each cut-off value, with an increment of 0.01, we optimize the weight parameters for superclass, subclass, and domain relationships, and the α that balances the two similarity measures. The results are displayed in Table 3, where the mean and variance of each of these parameters are computed.

On average, the Bing similarity measure has a lower weight than the CF-IDF+ measure, indicating that input from Bing has a lower impact on our recommender than the semantic relationships. This can be explained by the fact that concepts contain more informational value than named entities. Moreover, 44 out of 266 identified named entities appear in our employed ontology, indicating a loss of 20% of the available named entities. Nonetheless, α is greater than zero, and thus there is a use to employing named entities from Bing in the recommendation method. As for the semantic relationships, on average, concepts retrieved through domain relationships seem (w_{rel}) to be more important than sub- and superclasses (w_{sub} and w_{super}, respectively), and concepts retrieved through superclasses are more important than those deduced from subclass relations. This corresponds to the results of [9], and match our expectations, as superclasses give more general information about the topic of interest whereas subclasses risk to be too specific.

4.3 Experimental Results

Now that the optimal values of the parameters are determined for each cut-off value, we can compute the global precision, recall, and F_1-measures. Table 4 displays the mean F_1-scores for each recommender, underlining that Bing-CF-IDF+ outperforms the other recommenders. In fact, the more complex the recommender, the better the average performance. As shown in Table 5, all improvements are significant, except for CF-IDF over TF-IDF.

Table 4. Average F_1-measures for the recommenders

Recommender	μ
TF-IDF	0.449
CF-IDF	0.485
CF-IDF+	0.571
Bing-CF-IDF+	0.609

Table 5. Recommenders in columns outperforming recommenders in rows with respect to F_1 (p values where significance is $< 5e-02$)

Recommender	TF-IDF	CF-IDF	CF-IDF+	Bing-CF-IDF+
TF-IDF		7.046e−02	1.398e−07	5.836e−11
CF-IDF			6.525e−05	6.305e−08
CF-IDF+				3.361e−02
Bing-CF-IDF+				

Our observations are also supported by Fig. 1a. From the plot, it is evident that, throughout the range of cut-off values, Bing-CF-IDF+ outperforms the other recommenders consistently. TF-IDF is more performant for lower cut-off values (i.e., higher expected recall and lower expected precision) than CF-IDF and CF-IDF+. Due to the nature of CF-IDF variants, this is an expected outcome, because when using concepts rather than terms (or named entities for that matter), we enforce a much more restricted approach with a very limited amount of tokens (concepts) to match on.

This is also depicted in Figs. 1b and c. These figures also show that, while recall for Bing-CF-IDF+ and CF-IDF+ is very similar, the precision of Bing-CF-IDF+ clearly improves over CF-IDF+. Recall for CF-IDF (and TF-IDF) is much lower. Therefore, it seems that the addition of semantic relations improves recall, and the additional inclusion of Bing named entities improves precision, without making concessions to the recall of CF-IDF.

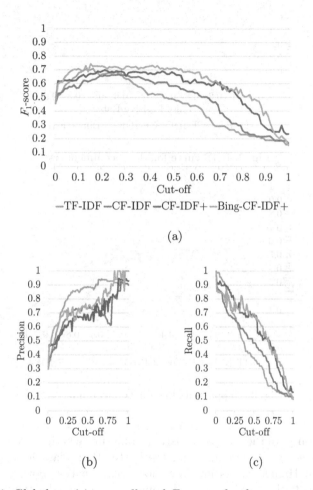

Fig. 1. Global precision, recall, and F_1 scores for the recommenders

Next we evaluate the Receiver Operating Characteristic (ROC) curves for the Bing-CF-IDF+, CF-IDF+, CF-IDF, and TF-IDF recommenders. The ROC curve in Fig. 2 shows that the Bing-CF-IDF+ and CF-IDF+ outperform CF-IDF and TF-IDF for low False Positive Rates. This indicates that recall (True Positive Rate) is higher for (Bing-)CF-IDF+ in more difficult situations against a handful of false positives, i.e., a higher precision. However, in the grand scale of things, the areas under the curve differ only slightly between the recommenders (value is approximately 0.85). This is in line with the higher precision and lower recall of Bing-CF-IDF+ when compared to TF-IDF.

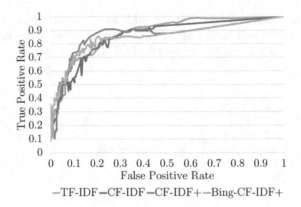

Fig. 2. ROC curve for the recommenders

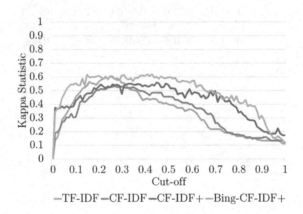

Fig. 3. Kappa statistics for the recommenders

Last, we compute the Kappa statistic to measure whether the proposed classifications made by the recommender are better than classification made by a
random guess. Higher values indicate more classification power, and are preferred. In Fig. 3, the results of the Kappa statistic can be found for varying
cut-off values. The plot shows that overall, the Kappa statistic of the Bing-
CF-IDF+ recommender is higher than the Kappa statistic of the other three
recommenders. Only for a cut-off value of 0.25, the statistics of the Bing-CF-
IDF+ and the TF-IDF are similar, and for cut-off value 0.70 the statistics of the
Bing-CF-IDF+ and the CF-IDF+ are alike. Because the Bing-CF-IDF+ recommender clearly has higher values for the Kappa statistic over all cut-off values,
we can state that overall, the Bing-CF-IDF+ has more classification power than
the CF-IDF+, CF-IDF, and TF-IDF recommenders.

5   Conclusion

In previous work, several new recommendation methods have been proposed. The traditional term-based TF-IDF was improved by methods like SF-IDF and CF-IDF, which take into account synsets from a semantic lexicon and concepts from a domain ontology, respectively. The CF-IDF+ similarity measure also matches news items based on related concepts like sub- and superclasses. However, named entities are not fully covered in recommendations whenever they are omitted in the domain ontology. Therefore, we have introduced the Bing-CF-IDF+ similarity measure, which is a two-step procedure that extends the CF-IDF+ similarity measure with Bing Web search similarity scores for named entities.

In order to evaluate the performance of the new Bing-CF-IDF+ recommender, we have optimized the weights for the semantic relationships between the concepts and for the Bing and CF-IDF+ recommenders themselves. These parameters are optimized using a grid search for both the semantic relationships and the concept-based and named entity-based recommenders, while maximizing the global F_1-measure per cut-off value, i.e., the minimum score for a news item to be recommended. We have tested the performance of Bing-CF-IDF+ against existing recommenders on 100 financial news items and 8 user profiles. In our evaluation, we have shown that the Bing-CF-IDF+ similarity measure outperforms TF-IDF, CF-IDF, and CF-IDF+ in terms of the F_1 measure and the Kappa statistic.

We envision various directions for future work. Parameter optimization has been performed using an incremental grid search. This could improved by applying more advanced optimization strategies, such as genetic algorithms. Moreover, we would like to investigate a larger collection of relationships. Now, we have considered the direct super- and subclasses, but hypothetically, non-direct super- and subclasses of concepts could be valuable as well. Last, a more thorough and powerful evaluation based on a larger set of news items would further underline the strong performance of Bing-CF-IDF+.

References

1. Adomavicius, G., Tuzhilin, A.: Toward the next generation of recommender systems: a survey of the state-of-the-art and possible extensions. IEEE Trans. Knowl. Data Eng. **17**(6), 734–749 (2005)
2. Banerjee, S., Pedersen, T.: An adapted lesk algorithm for word sense disambiguation using wordnet. In: Gelbukh, A. (ed.) CICLing 2002. LNCS, vol. 2276, pp. 136–145. Springer, Heidelberg (2002). https://doi.org/10.1007/3-540-45715-1_11
3. Bing: Bing API 2.0. Whitepaper (2018). http://www.bing.com/developers/s/APIBasics.html
4. Bouma, G.: Normalized (pointwise) mutual information in collocation extraction. In: Chiarcos, C., de Castilho, R.E., Stede, M. (eds.) Biennial GSCL Conference 2009 (GSCL 2009), pp. 31–40. Gunter Narr Verlag Tübingen (2009)
5. Burke, R.: Hybrid recommender systems: survey and experiments. User Model. User-Adapt. Interact. **12**(4), 331–370 (2002)

6. Capelle, M., Moerland, M., Frasincar, F., Hogenboom, F.: Semantics-based news recommendation. In: Akerkar, R., Bădică, C., Dan Burdescu, D. (eds.) 2nd International Conference on Web Intelligence, Mining and Semantics (WIMS 2012). ACM (2012)

7. Capelle, M., Moerland, M., Hogenboom, F., Frasincar, F., Vandic, D.: Bing-SF-IDF+: a hybrid semantics-driven news recommender. In: Wainwright, R.L., Corchado, J.M., Bechini, A., Hong, J. (eds.) 30th Symposium on Applied Computing (SAC 2015), Web Technologies Track, pp. 732–739. ACM (2015)

8. Cohen, J.: A coefficient of agreement for nominal scales. Educ. Psychol. Meas. **20**(1), 37–46 (1960)

9. de Koning, E., Hogenboom, F., Frasincar, F.: News recommendation with CF-IDF+. In: Krogstie, J., Reijers, H.A. (eds.) CAiSE 2018. LNCS, vol. 10816, pp. 170–184. Springer, Cham (2018). https://doi.org/10.1007/978-3-319-91563-0_11

10. Fellbaum, C.: WordNet: An Electronic Lexical Database. MIT Press, Cambridge (1998)

11. Frasincar, F., Borsje, J., Levering, L.: A semantic web-based approach for building personalized news services. Int. J. E-Bus. Res. **5**(3), 35–53 (2009)

12. Goossen, F., IJntema, W., Frasincar, F., Hogenboom, F., Kaymak, U.: News personalization using the CF-IDF semantic recommender. In: Akerkar, R. (ed.) International Conference on Web Intelligence, Mining and Semantics (WIMS 2011). ACM (2011)

13. IJntema, W., Goossen, F., Frasincar, F., Hogenboom, F.: Ontology-based news recommendation. In: Daniel, F., et al. (eds.) International Workshop on Business intelligencE and the WEB (BEWEB 2010) at 13th International Conference on Extending Database Technology and Thirteenth International Conference on Database Theory (EDBT/ICDT 2010). ACM (2010)

14. Jannach, D., Resnick, P., Tuzhilin, A., Zanker, M.: Recommender systems - beyond matrix completion. Commun. ACM **59**(11), 94–102 (2016)

15. Jensen, A.S., Boss, N.S.: Textual Similarity: comparing texts in order to discover how closely they discuss the same topics. Bachelor's thesis, Technical University of Denmark (2008)

16. Jones, K.S.: A statistical interpretation of term specificity and its application in retrieval. J. Doc. **28**(1), 11–21 (1972)

17. Moerland, M., Hogenboom, F., Capelle, M., Frasincar, F.: Semantics-based news recommendation with SF-IDF+. In: Camacho, D., Akerkar, R., Rodríguez-Moreno, M.D. (eds.) 3rd International Conference on Web Intelligence, Mining and Semantics (WIMS 2013). ACM (2013)

18. Robal, T., Haav, H.-M., Kalja, A.: Making web users' domain models explicit by applying ontologies. In: Hainaut, J.-L., et al. (eds.) ER 2007. LNCS, vol. 4802, pp. 170–179. Springer, Heidelberg (2007). https://doi.org/10.1007/978-3-540-76292-8_20

19. Robal, T., Kalja, A.: Conceptual web users' actions prediction for ontology-based browsing recommendations. In: Papadopoulos, G.A., Wojtkowski, W., Wojtkowski, W.G., Wrycza, S., Zupancic, J. (eds.) ISD 2008, pp. 121–129. Springer, Boston (2010). https://doi.org/10.1007/b137171_13

20. Robal, T., Kalja, A.: Applying user domain model to improve Web recommendations. In: Caplinskas, A., Dzemyda, G., Lupeikiene, A., Vasilecas, O. (eds.) Databases and Information Systems VII - Selected Papers from the Tenth International Baltic Conference (DB&IS 2012). Frontiers in Artificial Intelligence and Applications, vol. 249, pp. 118–131. IOS Press (2013)

21. Salton, G., Buckley, C.: Term-weighting approaches in automatic text retrieval. Inf. Process. Manag. **24**(5), 513–523 (1988)
22. Sekine, S., Ranchhod, E. (eds.): Named Entities: Recognition, Clasification and Use. John Benjamins Publishing Company, Amsterdam (2009)

Methodological Framework to Guide the Development of Continual Evolution Methods

Ornela Cela[✉], Mario Cortes-Cornax, Agnès Front,
and Dominique Rieu

University of Grenoble Alpes, CNRS, Inria, Grenoble INP, LIG,
38000 Grenoble, France
{ornela.cela,mario.cortes-cornax,agnes.front,
dominique.rieu}@univ-grenoble-alpes.fr

Abstract. Companies live in a fast-changing environment imposing to constantly evolve in order to stay competitive. Such an evolution is carried out through continuous improvement cycles or radical changes often based on innovation that concern their products, their processes, their internal organization, etc. We refer to this situation as continual evolution. There are two implications of such continual evolution from our viewpoint: (a) the instillation of the "no end point" philosophy in organizations and (b) the use of methods based (1) on continual evolution cycles (by opposition to project-based approaches that have delimited budget and dates) and, (2) on autonomous and collective implication of the organization's actors. This article presents a methodological framework, called As-Is/As-If framework to support method engineers in handling such continual evolution. The framework offers a process model and a product meta-model that are both reusable instruments, aiming to guide the construction of continual evolution methods. The process model and product meta-model can be seen as prototypical examples to be adapted in each situation at hand using heuristics proposed as part of the framework. The usefulness of the framework is illustrated through two methods adaptations.

Keywords: Method engineering · Continual evolution · Framework

1 Introduction

Today, companies live in a fast changing environment that demands them to constantly evolve in order to stay competitive [1]. This need implies to continually embrace improvement cycles or radical changes often based on innovation concerning their products, their processes, their internal organization, their collaboration with external partners, etc. Different methodologies have been proposed in order to guide these improvement cycles with a focus on process efficiency (Lean) [2], product quality (Six Sigma) [2], innovativeness of products by changing the organization's conception paradigm (Design thinking) [3] or the external knowledge use (open innovation) [4]. Despite their differences in focus, all the aforementioned methodologies consider the evolution cycle as a project, without taking into consideration that further improvement

© Springer Nature Switzerland AG 2019
P. Giorgini and B. Weber (Eds.): CAiSE 2019, LNCS 11483, pp. 48–63, 2019.
https://doi.org/10.1007/978-3-030-21290-2_4

or innovation cycles might follow. To emphasize this constantly changing situation, we introduce the concept of continual evolution, which refers to the idea that evolution imposes multiple cycles of change, as companies are constantly seeking for new opportunities to improve their competitiveness. This concept advocates that understanding the need for continual change must be instilled in the organization's culture [5]. This understanding will help in reducing the resistance toward the change and in facilitating its absorption by the organizational actors.

This holistic view of continual evolution, which we propose, has an impact on methods to be used for engineering the changes. Our view is that these methods must (1) be based on continual evolution cycles, (by opposition to project-based approaches that have delimited budget and dates) and (2) promote as much as possible the active and collective participation of actors of the organization, who will "take the method experts' place". For example, the process owner could replace the green belt consultant in Six Sigma and guide the process mapping. In this view, ludic and participative approaches are particularly adapted in order to lower the barrier of entry for the participants.

In this article, we propose a methodological framework, called As-Is/As-If framework to support method engineers in constructing or adapting methods matching the need of continual evolution. The framework has been constructed following a bottom-up approach that generalizes the concepts and phases proposed in continual evolution methods developed during research projects in which our team was involved from 2012 to 2018. It offers a process model and a product meta-model that are both reusable instruments to guide the method engineer in constructing or adapting methods for continual evolution. Both artefacts, can be seen as prototypical examples to be adapted for the situation at hand using heuristics that are proposed as part of the framework. The aforementioned adaptations produce a new method that we call the target method.

The paper is organized as follows: Sect. 2 provides an overview of our approach. Section 3 introduces the main concepts of the methodological framework and illustrates them with examples of two existing methods specifically dealing with continual evolution in two different domains. Section 4 presents the models of the framework (the product meta-model and process model). Section 5 introduces our position in comparison with related works. Finally, Sect. 6 concludes the article and introduces our future work perspectives.

2 Overview of the Approach

The As-Is/As-If framework offers a process model (expressed with the intentional MAP notation [6]) and a product meta-model (based on UML notation). MAP models are directed graphs with nodes representing intentions and labelled edges capturing strategies that model processes in a declarative manner. The MAP formalism allows the modeler to view a process at different levels of abstraction. Figure 1 introduces the top-level map representing the general view of the framework process model and the core meta-classes of the product meta-model. The detailed view of the models using different abstraction levels will be developed in Sect. 4.

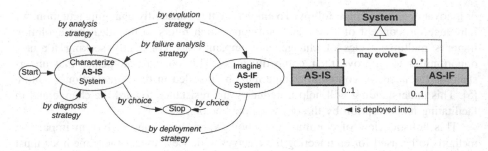

Fig. 1. General view of the process model and the product meta-model

As seen in Fig. 1, the **process model** has two mains intentions *Characterize As-Is System* and *Imagine As-If system,* which must be achieved in this order. It shall be noted that we use the term system to denote the product that will be produced by the method. The framework is not dedicated to a specific type of product. Thus the use of the term system that can denote an information system, an ecosystem or a business process model. Each evolution cycle firstly consists in analyzing the current system (*by analysis strategy*) and performing a diagnosis (*by diagnosis strategy*). Once the first intention is attained, the goal is to imagine (*by evolution strategy*) possible evolution scenarios based on the question "*And if?*". This strategy permits to determine **a set of possible *As-If* systems**, each of them corresponding to an evolution scenario. One of these multiple possibilities will be chosen and consolidated considering possible constraints (juridical, economic, social, technical, etc.). If no evolution scenario is chosen due to the impossibility to identify a satisfactory evolution (*by failure analysis strategy*), the analysis and the diagnosis strategies could be replayed. If an evolution scenario is chosen, it will be deployed becoming the new studied system (*by deployment strategy*). The decision to terminate the continual evolution cycle must be a collective choice of all actors. This possibility is represented through the *by choice* strategies. The framework **product meta-model** (right part of Fig. 1) shows a simplified version of the associations between the As-Is and the As-If systems. It represents the concepts used by the process model.

The two models illustrate the top-level patterns provided by the framework to reason about the cycle of evolution and to help in decisions making when adapting them to the new situation at hand. We will see in Sect. 4 how the refinement of the top-level will progressively guide the adaptation of the framework; (1) process model to produce the process model of the target method and (2) of the product meta-model to complete the definition of the target method.

The framework generalizes our empirical experience in building continual evolution methods: ADInnov [7], ISEACAP [8] and CEFOP [9] methods are developed within research projects in which our team was involved. This paper relies on CEFOP and ADInnov, used as target methods to illustrate the usage of the framework in adapting both methods. The following section introduces the concepts manipulated by both methods that are generalized in the framework.

3   ADInnov and CEFOP: Concepts and Examples

This section introduces the main concepts of the ADInnov and CEFOP methods and how they are generalized in order to obtain the concepts of the As-Is/As-If framework. This presentation mimics the bottom-up approach we used to construct the framework product meta-model and process model. To facilitate the reading, the following rule is used: the generalized concepts (meta-concepts) of the As-Is/As-If framework are in **Bold,** the terms concerning the methods are in ***bold italic***, and examples are in *italic* font. This section illustrates how the meta-concepts relate to either concept of ADInnov or of CEFOP. In addition, some examples of participative and ludic techniques used in these methods are provided as illustrations of concrete methodological fragments that a method engineer may reuse in the construction of a target method.

3.1   Concepts of ADInnov Generalized in the As-Is/As-If Framework

ADInnov is the method resulting from the InnoServ project[1], which aimed to analyze and diagnose ecosystems formed by fragile persons at home and to propose innovation services in such ecosystems. This project was financed by the French national research agency (ANR) from 2012 to 2016. Here, the system under study (**As-Is System**) is the *ecosystem* around a fragile person at home.

The **Analysis** shows that this *ecosystem* is composed of different **Components,** partially represented in Fig. 2. For instance, the *target* is the legal or physical person (*fragile person*) benefiting from the ecosystem services and over which *actors* operate under their own business (*nurse, physician, etc.*). ***Function*** corresponds to a skill or responsibility in the ecosystem involved in the realization of a concrete service in the *ecosystem* (*health professionals*). Several ***responsibility networks*** are defined in order to manage the ecosystem complexity; they are views determined by their proximity with the *target*. Three ***responsibility networks (RN)*** were identified in the InnoServ project: *Regulation* (laws and rules concerning home care of fragile people), *Coordination* (home care organization of fragile people) and *Execution* (direct interaction with fragile people at home). ***A point of view*** (*financial, medical, social, etc.*) relates to a crosscutting vision that determines a point of interest of a provided *service*. Indeed, *services* concern the provision of technical and intellectual capacity or of useful work for a *target*. A *service* is attached to a ***RN*** and is composed of one or several ***concrete services*** treating a ***point of view*** and performed by one or more ***functions*** (the *service Recognize the caregiver work* can be done from a legal *point of view recognizing the caregiver status* and from a financial *point of view establishing a salary for caregivers*). **Measures** such as the *quality of life of fragile people* or *the time to go back home after hospitalization* evaluate the *ecosystem*.

The **Diagnosis** of the ecosystem reveals several **Blocking Points**. In the context of the InnoServ project, the same term ***blocking point*** is used, which corresponds to a concrete issue in the context of a ***responsibility network*** or a ***point of view*** (in the *Execution RN*: *there is a problem of unavailability as well as lack of required actors*

---

[1] https://goo.gl/8HHZYQ.

for caregiving). A *point of view* is translated into one or more refined **Goals** (*have available actors in the fragile person's house*). **Constraints** are used to express the fact that some components can't evolve (*the fragile person is not supposed to evolve*).

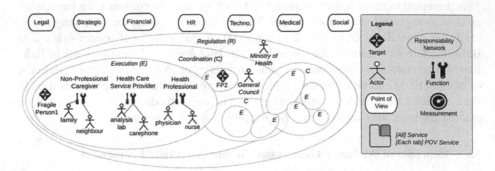

Fig. 2. Components of the As-Is ecosystem resulting from analysis in the ADInnov method

The **Innovation** phase aims to propose several **Changes** that make possible to reach the identified **Goals**. In ADInnov, **Changes** are named *innovation services* such as the proposition of new *services* (*a digital service of piloting*) or new *functions* (*orchestrator, coordinator*) [7]. The impact of these *innovation services* lead to **Evaluation** in order to identify their impact. The *innovation services* will introduce one or more *point of view service* (**Operational Changes**) corresponding to the implementation in the **As-Is system**. They can affect one or more **Components**: modifying them, deleting or adding new ones. For example, it is easy to imagine that the *innovation services* proposed above will have a great impact on the territory organization that will have to be at their turn, analyzed and diagnosed, hence considered as new *As-Is ecosystem*.

In order to come with the *ecosystem's components* (**Components**), detect the *blocking points* (**Blocking Points**) or propose *innovation services* (**Changes**) in the *ecosystem* (**System**), different strategies are used, which are considered here as reusable method fragments. Some of these method fragments such as serious games[2] to analyze the information flow between *functions*, post-its to study service dependency or CAUTIC workshops [10] to evaluate *innovation services* were proposed [7] and could be re-used in any other target method with similar needs.

3.2   Concepts of CEFOP Generalized in the As-Is/As-If Framework

The CEFOP method [9] is one of the results of ProMiNi[3], a research project in collaboration with NetInvaders, a French web development agency specialized in e-shop solutions and thin client software. The goal of this project was to apply a process

---

[2] http://www.lego.com/fr-fr/seriousplay/.

[3] https://en.net-invaders.com/.

mining approach to analyze the traces left in the company's information system in order to evolve its business processes to stay competitive in the fast changing environment. Here, the **As-Is System** is the *business process*.

The **Analysis** of the process (*the client's subscription process*) aims to elicit the **Components** (see Fig. 3): *inputs, outputs, tasks, actions, roles* and *tools*. The *inputs* (*Subscription request*) and *outputs* (*Successful subscription or Rejected subscription*) delimit the process under study. The *tasks* describe the activities performed in the process related to one *role* participating in the process (*client, etc.*). *Tasks* are composed of *actions* (*Create Account*), each of them describing an atomic activity supported by at most one *tool* (*mysql*). The performance of the process is evaluated by *indicators* (*the maximal number of days to subscribe*) that correspond to **Measure Elements** computed over the traces produced during the process execution. A set of indicators is defined relying on *goals* and *constraints*, elicited during the diagnosis.

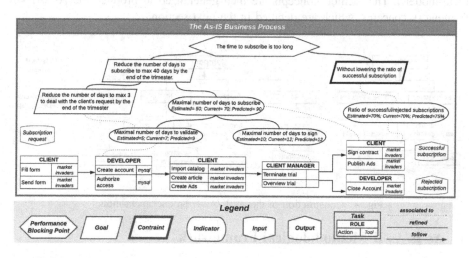

Fig. 3. Components of the As-Is business process elicited in the CEFOP method

The **Diagnosis** of a *business process* focusses on identifying the *performance blocking points* (*The time taken to subscribe is too long*). They describe performance elements currently missing or to be introduced in the evolution cycle. **Blocking Points** are translated into *goals* expressing the desired results to be achieved (*Reduce the number of days to subscribe to max 40 days by the end of the trimester*) and *constraints* that avoid changing specific values (*Without lowering the ratio of successful subscription*).

The **Evolution** phase starts by identifying possible **Changes** and translating them into **Operational Changes**. Each of them describes how the components of the **As-Is** are affected when generating the different **As-Ifs**. Indeed, several possible ways of evolving a process, implementing different changes, can be proposed (*As-If processes*). For example, a possible evolution (*As-If1*) for *the client's subscription* process could be generated by taking into consideration a *change* (*Hire an additional client manager*), implying two *operational changes* (*Increment the number of actors playing the client manager role* and *Recalculate the indicators*). In order to choose the most appropriate way to evolve the business process, the potential evolutions are subject to **Evaluation**. This implies to check if the *performance blocking points* are resolved, the *goals* are achieved without violating the *constraints,* and the steps to be deployed are defined.

When eliciting the above elements, CEFOP strongly requests the process partici- pants in order to reduce the need of external intervention. For that, the method inte- grates several ludic and participative methodological fragments [11].

3.3   Construction of the As-Is/As-If Product Meta-model

Figure 4 summarizes the As-Is/As-If product meta-model as resulting of the general- izations of specific concepts into generic ones that we illustrated in the previous sec- tions. Models of the specific projects (Innoserv and ProMiNi concepts) are instantiations of the ADInnov and CEFOP concepts (the meta-classes of the product meta-models). The method concepts are then generalized to produce the As-Is/As-If framework concepts, which are detailed in the next section.

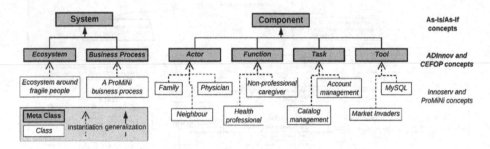

Fig. 4. Construction of the As-Is/As-If product meta-model

4   As-Is/As-If Methodological Framework

This section presents in detail the As-Is/As-If framework and illustrates its use to adapt the initial versions of the CEFOP and ADInnov methods. In this section we use a top- down approach to review the CEFOP and ADInnov methods using the framework. During this process, we discovered imperfections in these two methods. Thus, the use of the framework for these methods resulted in a second version of the product meta- model and process model for both methods as illustrated in the following subsections.

4.1   General View

According to the OMG modeling levels [13], a method is composed of a product meta- model (level M2) that defines the abstract syntax of the modeling language and a process model (level M1) whose execution produces product models that conform to the product meta-model. The As-Is/As-If framework (Fig. 5) proposes two models that can be reused and adapted to formalize continual evolution methods. The **process model** (left part) is formalized using intentional maps [6] and a **product meta-model** (right part) is formalized in a UML class diagram.

The process model defines the main strategies and intentions of any continual evolution process model and provide the starting point for eliciting the elements of the product meta-model. It is represented through a general map and three sub-maps that refine the Analysis, Diagnosis and Evolution sections of the top level map. Accordingly, the product meta-model is structured in 4 packages: the Core and three packages corresponding to Analysis, Diagnosis and Evolution.

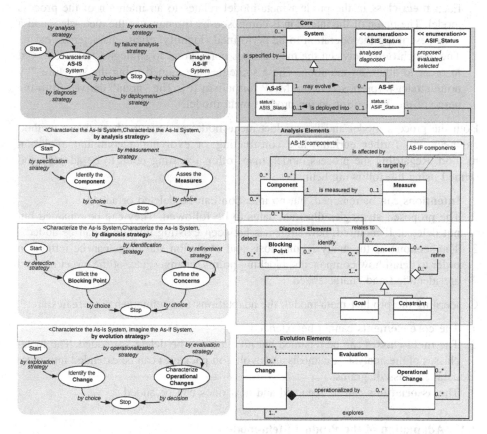

Fig. 5. The process model and the product meta-model proposed in the As-Is/As-If framework

The core package is composed of 3 mandatory meta-classes: the **System** meta-class and its two subclasses. An **As-Is System** can evolve into several possible evolution scenarios called **As-If Systems** (*may evolve* association). As mentioned before, only one **As-If System** will become the next **As-Is System** (*deployed into* association). The status attributes represent the **System State** with respect to its evolution process. An **As-Is System** can be **analyzed** (associated with elements of the Analysis Element package) or **diagnosed** (associated with the Diagnosis Element package). Also, the **As-If System** state can be **proposed** (associated to the Evolution Element package), **evaluated** (if an evaluation between the elements of Evolution and the Diagnosis exist) and **selected** (**As-If system** is deployed into an **As-Is System**).

It shall be noted that association naming provides the model-level traceability. For instance, the *indicator- maximal number of days to subscribe* of the **As-Is process** corresponds to the same *indicator* in the **As-If process** but it has different *values*, since the *activities* are affected by the *change*.

The product meta-model and the process model are closely related since the intentions of the process model define the elements of the product meta-model, so:

1. Each **meta-class** in the product meta-model relates to an intention of the process model. The name of the intention is composed by the name of the meta-class and a verb describing the operation to be performed (identify, elicit, characterize, etc.)
2. The **associations** between the meta-classes correspond to strategies to be followed in order to attain an intention. These strategies are named using the structure "by noun strategy" proposed in the MAP formalism [6]. The "noun" derives from the name of the association in the product meta-model.

Both the process model and the product meta-model provide the base that a method engineer will further enrich while constructing or evolving a continual evolution method. Regarding the process model, maps offer a starting point to be adapted and refined using the following heuristics:

1. **Intentions** can be renamed, but no intention can be deleted or added.
2. The proposed **strategies** illustrate paths to be followed. They can be renamed but not deleted. If required, new strategies between existing intentions can be added.
3. The **sections** of the analysis, diagnosis and evolution sub maps can be refined in order to detail how components, blocking points, changes, etc. of the target method are identified and characterized.

Concerning the product meta-model, the adaptations and refinements heuristics are:

1. The **core elements** cannot be extended.
2. The **meta-classes** can be renamed but no class can be deleted or added. The meta-classes of the analysis, diagnosis and evolution packages can be extended into more detailed class diagrams.
3. The **associations** can be renamed and new ones can be added.

4.2   Adaptation of the Product Meta-model

Undertaking continual evolution implies to adapt the product meta-model. This is guided by the use of the heuristics introduced in the above section. Figure 6 illustrates such an adaptation for two different target situations, namely the ones corresponding to the ADInnov and CEFOP methods (version 2). The Core package is not illustrated since it cannot be changed. The new associations identified when adapting the product meta-model are illustrated in thicker lines. Bold named meta-classes illustrate renaming or decomposition with regard to the framework. The languages corresponding to ADInnov and CEFOP are therefore defined by the abstract syntax given by the product meta-model in Fig. 6, and a concrete syntax introduced in the legends of the examples of Sects. 3.1 and 3.2, respectively.

The Analysis package essentially captures the **Components** of the system being studied and the **Measures** used to evaluate them. The **Component** meta-class is maintained but extended in the form of a class diagram containing all the components of the system. The refinement of this class permits the method engineer to adapt the method to a specific domain. The framework recommends that a model should never describe the entire system. Instead, it should be limited to the components targeted by the continual evolution. For instance, the CEFOP method does not take into account the synchronization of the control flows and therefore gateways are not considered as **Components**. During the continuous evolution process, new **Components** may appear, in particular in the case of disruptive evolution or innovation. In ADInnov, the concept of *responsibility network* (a new type of component) appeared in the first iteration cycle. **Components** are evaluated through **Measures**. For example, CEFOP uses *indicators* to measure the execution time of *activities*.

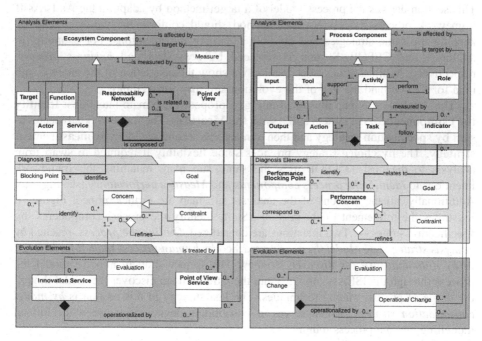

Fig. 6. Target methods adaptation corresponding to the abstract syntax of ADInnov and CEFOP

The Diagnosis package has two main meta-classes: **Blocking Point** and **Concern**. The former refers to a specific problem in the system that needs to be resolved and can be expressed as a simple sentence, a text or set of basic attributes. In a target method, the **Blocking Point** meta-class must be included in order to synthetize in a simple way the reason of an evolution. **Concern** is an abstract class that can be either a **Goal** or a **Constraint**. The target method must identify **Goals** to be reached and potential **Constraints** to be preserved in order to solve the corresponding **Blocking Point**. Concerning CEFOP, in order to resolve the *performance blocking points* (*the time* taken to subscribe is too long), the **goals** (*Reduce the number of days to subscribe [...] trimester*) must be achieved and the **constraints** (*without lowering the ratio of successful subscription*) preserved. CEFOP associate **goals** and **constraints** with the **process components** (*correspond to* association) to better conform to the studied domain.

The Evolution package proposes three meta-classes: **Change**, **Evaluation** and **Operational Change**. A **Change** is evaluated in relation to **Concerns**. Their implementation is detailed by **Operational Changes** that describe how **As-Is Components** are *affected* in order to generate the *targeted* **As-If Components**. For instance, in CEFOP a change was *operationalised by* two *operational changes* in order to describe how the possible evolution could be obtained.

4.3   Adaptation of the Process Model

This section derives the process model of a target method by adapting the As-Is/As-If framework process model. A target method should conform the top-level map by keeping the same strategies and possibly renaming the intentions. For example, in ADInnov and CEFOP, **System** is replaced by *ecosystem* and *business process,* respectively. As illustrations of adaptation we show the adaptation of the analysis sub map for CEFOP and the one of the evolution sub map for ADInnov.

The **Analysis** sub map illustrated in Fig. 5 proposed two main intentions: **Identify the Components** of the system and **Assess the Measures**. The framework advocates to start **by specification strategy** and then to reach the second intention **by measurement strategy**. The **by choice** strategy provides some flexibility if required to swap from analysis to diagnosis. CEFOP uses the same sub map, renaming the framework intentions to *Identify the process components* and *Measure performance* (see Fig. 7a). Additionally, all the sections of the analysis sub map are further refined. Figure 7b illustrates the refinement of the *section* <Start, Identify the process components, by specification strategy>. Two intentions are considered: *Outline the process*, reached *by analysis strategy* and *Model the process* reached *by human process modelling strategy* or *by automatic process discover strategy*. The former strategy aims to model the process through the ISEAsy tool [12] and the latter aims to discover the model though the usage of process mining techniques. The last strategy in this section is *by model consolidation strategy*, which serves to consolidate deviations between the human modelling and the process mining.

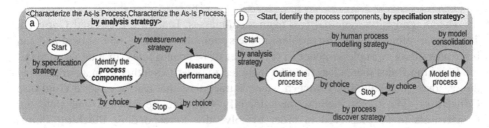

Fig. 7. The analysis map adapted by CEFOP and the refinement of the by specification section.

The adaptation of the **Evolution** strategy is illustrated for ADInnov. The main intentions to be achieved are the *Identify innovation services* and *Characterize innovations*. In the Evolution map (Fig. 8a), we just renamed the intentions to better fit the ADInnov domain and we added a new strategy *by enrichment strategy* that go back from the characterization to the identification. The second map in Fig. 8b refines the section <Characterize innovations, Characterize innovations, by evaluation strategy>. The intentions are *Consolidate the innovations* as well as *Illustrate the innovations* (by creating several videos illustrating the proposed innovations[4]). Strategies of this section are for instance, the use of serious games, the identification of service dependencies (using post-its) or an evaluation workshop using the CAUTIC method. More details about these re-usable method fragments can be found in [7].

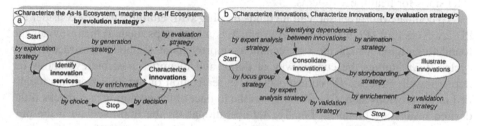

Fig. 8. The evolution map adapted by ADInnov and the refinement of the by evaluation section

5   Related Work

The As-Is/As-If framework belongs to the **Method Engineering** discipline, defined as the discipline to design, construct and adapt methods, techniques and tools for the development of information systems [14]. However, the framework is not limited to methods dealing with the development of information systems. It is wider in terms of target, since the type of studied system can be an ecosystem (ADInnov), a business processes (CEFOP), or any type of artefact. Vice-versa, the framework is not as generic as a typical method engineering solution would be as it focuses on the specific domain of continual evolution. Indeed, it proposes models (a process model and a product meta-model) dedicated to a specific method family [15], which is the family of continual evolution methods.

Different types of approaches are proposed in ME to deal with the construction of a new method by instantiation or adaptation of models [14–18]. The As-Is/As-If framework adopts the latter with specificity: the product meta-model and the process model of the target methods are at the same abstraction level as the framework models. These models have to be adapted in order to define the product meta-model (the abstract syntax of the language) and the process model of the target method. The product meta-model of the As-Is/As-If is therefore an instance of the MOF and does not benefit from the modeling power of UML. To solve this issue, OMG proposes the

---

[4] https://anrinnoserv.wordpress.com/.

UML profile mechanism to reduce the time and the cost of meta-model development [19]. The As-Is/As-If meta-classes would be UML stereotypes and the meta-classes of the target product meta-model are themselves stereotypes extending As-Is/As-If stereotypes (in UML, a stereotype can specialize another stereotype). The adaptation thus consists in using the profile mechanism to define the abstract syntax of the target product meta-model.

The product meta-model cannot be used without adaptation and thus does not provide a concrete syntax. When adapting the product meta-model, a concrete syntax (e.g., a graphical notation) associated with the most specialized level of stereotypes and corresponding to the concepts of the target method must be defined. In ADInnov, the profile approach is particularly interesting since it provides the possibility to define a Domain Specific Language dedicated to ecosystems and to introduce appropriate extensions for health ecosystems.

To compare our proposal with **methods dealing with changes** we first consider the PDCA cycle [20] (*Plan Do Check Act*) which is a four steps method that provides the foundations upon which most of continual improvement methods constructed their cycles. *Plan* studies the current way of doing and identifies possible evolutions for improving the process. *Do* corresponds to the realization of the improvements identified in the previous step. *Check* overviews the impact of the evolution and checks if the desired results are obtained. Finally, *Act* operationalizes the improvement if the previous check was positive. Our framework focuses on the coverage of the *Plan* phase through the As-Is/As-If cycle. To this intent, the *Plan* phase of the following methods has been analyzed. The deployment strategy implies going over the *Do, Check* and *Act* phases to obtain the new As-Is system.

The Lean cycle [21] is composed of 5 steps: *Value- Value stream mapping - Flow - Pull- Seek perfection*. The first two phases could be included in the PDCA *Plan*. They aim to detect the blocking points describing the problem as well as the client's needs and identifying the process and its wastage's causes. These steps are followed by the process improvement and monitoring and the trigger of further improvements if required. The DMAIC (*Define-Measure-Analyze-Improve-Control*) cycle [22], used by Six Sigma, correlates with the PDCA *Plan* in its three first phases: *Define* (aiming to identify the project scope and the resources composing the project), *Measure* (evaluating the current performance of the system) and *Analyze* (diagnosing performance problems and identifying their root causes).

Aligning the plan phase of the PDCA cycle with the previous methodologies is natural since their aim is continual improvement. This alignment is less evident when analyzing innovation methods. A comparison of the *Build-Measure-Learn* cycle of Lean Startup and the *Empathize-Define-Ideate-Prototype-Test* cycle of Design Thinking has been done [23]. The authors highlight that even through a different number of phases and names, their cycles aim to achieve similar goals. In particular, the *Learn* phase in Lean Startup has the same intention than the Design Thinking *Define* step. They both outline the context, elicit the clients and their requirements relating them to the *Plan* phase in the PDCA, as intended by our framework.

6   Conclusion and Perspectives

This paper proposes a methodological framework that guides the formalization of methods that support continual evolution. It provides a product meta-model and a process model to be adapted by method engineers to deal with a specific evolution domain. An important goal is that the target methods could be provided to organizations and be used in autonomy, minimizing the need of a method expert. The main force of the framework is the As-If dimension allowing constructing As-Ifs scenarios and evaluating their impact. The framework benefited from our experience in building continual evolution methods in different contexts and different research projects. Nevertheless, we are aware that the framework still needs to be tested in different contexts, evaluated, improved and enforced on several points.

First, a complete methodological guide is necessary to help the method engineers in adapting the product meta-model and the process model. The product meta-model will be completed with a dictionary to propose definitions, attributes and examples of each concept. Moreover, considering the strategies of the process model, guidance on the reuse of the aforementioned methodological fragments supported by participative, elicitation or creativity techniques, needs to be enhanced. We are currently working on solutions to guide the method engineer in choosing the best methodological fragment adapted to her/his specific context. One promising solution is the development of software tools supporting the library of methodological fragments deployed on MethodForChange[5], a platform aiming to collect and provide methods and tools related to innovation.

Second, in terms of evaluation and scaling up, more experiments are necessary. The framework has been used in adapting, generating new versions of three methods, which is insufficient, but new projects in our research team will allow us to test the As-Is/As-If framework. In the context of the IDEX CIRCULAR project[6] (2018–2021), a method to facilitate the transition towards circular economy in industrial supply chains will be proposed. In the AURA MOBIPA research project (2018–2021), a method will aim to improve the access of elderly people to mobility services. These two experiments will allow us to enrich the As-Is/As-If framework and support their construction. Indeed, the framework is easily extendable, adding new associations in the product meta-model and new strategies in the process model.

Acknowledgments. We sincerely thank Prof. C. Rolland for her valuable feedbacks.

References

1. Rashid, O.A., Ahmad, M.N.: Business process improvement methodologies: an overview. J. Inf. Syst. Res. Innov. **5**, 45–53 (2013)
2. Singh, J., Singh, H.: Continuous improvement philosophy – literature review and directions. Benchmarking Int. J. **22**(1), 75–119 (2015)

---

[5] https://methodforchange.com/.

[6] https://circular.univ-grenoble-alpes.fr/en/main-menu/circular/.

3. Brown, T., Wyatt, J.: Design thinking for social innovation. Dev. Outreach **12**(1), 29–43 (2010)
4. Chesbrough, H., Bogers, M.: Explicating open innovation: clarifying an emerging paradigm for understanding innovation. New Front. Open Innov. Oxford Univ. Press 3–28 (2014, forthcoming)
5. Georgiades, S.: Employee engagement and organizational change. In: Georgiades, S. (ed.) Employee Engagement in Media Management, pp. 19–37. Springer, Cham (2015). https://doi.org/10.1007/978-3-319-16217-1_2
6. Rolland, C.: Capturing system intentionality with maps. In: Krogstie, J., Opdahl, A.L., Brinkkemper, S. (eds.) Conceptual Modelling Information System Engineering, pp. 141–158. Springer, Heidelberg (2007). https://doi.org/10.1007/978-3-540-72677-7_9
7. Cortes-Cornax, M., Front, A., Rieu, D., Verdier, C., Forest, F.: ADInnov: an intentional method to instil innovation in socio-technical ecosystems. In: Nurcan, S., Soffer, P., Bajec, M., Eder, J. (eds.) CAiSE 2016. LNCS, vol. 9694, pp. 133–148. Springer, Cham (2016). https://doi.org/10.1007/978-3-319-39696-5_9
8. Movahedian, F., Front, A., Rieu, D., Farastier, A., et al.: A participative method for knowledge elicitation in collaborative innovation projects. In: International Conference on Research Challenges in Information Science (RCIS 2017), pp. 244–254. IEEE (2017)
9. Cela, O., Front, A., Rieu, D.: CEFOP: a method for the continual evolution of organisational processes. In: International Conference on Research Challenges in Information Science (RCIS 2017), pp. 33–43. IEEE (2017)
10. Forest, F., Mallein, P., Arhippainen, L.: Paradoxical user acceptance of ambient intelligent systems: : sociology of user experience approach. In: Proceedings of International Conference on Making Sense of Converging Media, pp. 211–218. ACM (2013)
11. Çela, O., Front, A., Rieu, D.: Model consolidation: a process modelling method combining process mining and business process modelling. In: Gulden, J., Reinhartz-Berger, I., Schmidt, R., Guerreiro, S., Guédria, W., Bera, P. (eds.) BPMDS/EMMSAD -2018. LNBIP, vol. 318, pp. 117–130. Springer, Cham (2018). https://doi.org/10.1007/978-3-319-91704-7_8
12. Front, A., Rieu, D., Santorum, M., Movahedian, F.: A participative end-user method for multi-perspective business process elicitation and improvement. Softw. Syst. Model. **16**(3), 691–714 (2017)
13. OMG: Meta Object Facility (MOF) Version 2.5 (2016). https://www.omg.org/spec/MOF
14. Brinkkemper, S.: Method engineering: engineering of information systems development methods and tools. Inf. Softw. Technol. ScienceDirect **38**(4), 275–280 (1996)
15. Deneckere, R., Kornyshova, E., Rolland, C.: Method family description and configuration. In: International Conference on Enterprise Information Systems (ICEIS 2011), pp. 384–387. SCITEPRESS (2011)
16. Ralyté, J., Rolland, C., Ben Ayed, M.: An approach for evolution driven method engineering. In: Information Modeling Methods and Methodologies, pp. 80–101. IGI Global, Hershey (2005)
17. Hug, C., Front, A., Rieu, D., Henderson-Sellers, B.: A method to build information systems engineering process metamodels. J. Syst. Softw. **82**(10), 1730–1742 (2009). Elsevier
18. Cervera, M., Albert, M., Torres, V., Pelechano, V.: A methodological framework and software infrastructure for the construction of software production methods. In: Münch, J., Yang, Y., Schäfer, W. (eds.) ICSP 2010. LNCS, vol. 6195, pp. 112–125. Springer, Heidelberg (2010). https://doi.org/10.1007/978-3-642-14347-2_11
19. Lakhal, F., Dubois, H., Rieu, D.: Pattern based methodology for UML profiles evolution management. In: IEEE - International Conference on Research Challenges in Information Science (RCIS 2013), pp. 1–12 (2013)

20. Deming, W.E.: Out of the Crisis. Cambridge, Massachusetts Institute of Technology (MIT), Center for Advanced Engineering Study, Cambridge (1986)
21. Womack, J., Jones, D.T.: Lean thinking: banish waste and create wealth for your corporation. J. Oper. Res. Soc. **48**(11), 1148 (1996)
22. Hambleton, L.: Define-measure-analyze- improve-control (DMAIC). In: Treasure Chest Six Sigma Growth Methods, Tools, Best Practices, pp. 13–27 (2007)
23. Mueller, R.M. Thoring, K.: Design thinking vs lean startup: a comparison of two user driven innovation strategies. In: Leading through Design, vol. 151, pp. 91–106 (2012)

Inter-organizational Integration in the AEC/FM Industry

Exploring the "Addressed" and "Unaddressed" Information Exchange Needs Between Stakeholders

José Carlos Camposano$^{(\boxtimes)}$ ⓘ and Kari Smolander ⓘ

LUT School of Engineering Science, LUT University, Lappeenranta, Finland
{jose.camposano,kari.smolander}@lut.fi

Abstract. This paper explores how the needs to exchange information across organizational boundaries in the Architecture, Engineering and Construction, and Facilities Management industry in Finland have been satisfied by means of stakeholder integration at the technical, business and socio-organizational levels. We interviewed practitioners about their motivations and goals for inter-organizational integration and observed different discourses. The information exchange needs in the context of individual building projects were often described as "addressed". These needs focused mainly on managing complex stakeholder relations or handling the variable conditions with other building projects. In the scope of the whole built environment lifecycle, the needs were rather portrayed as ongoing problems still "unaddressed". Existing information sources remained inadequate when the benefits of inter-organizational integration had not yet been clarified. The process workflow discontinuities demanded better understanding of the value of information beyond design as well as better coordination. The uncertainty of how much data to collect and for what purposes can be mitigated by defining "useful minimum" information exchange between stakeholders.

Keywords: Inter-organizational integration · Information exchange · Built environment · Building Lifecycle Management · Information systems · AEC/FM

1 Introduction

A prominent feature of the Architecture, Engineering and Construction, and Facilities Management industry (AEC/FM) is its complex network of interrelated stakeholders, who are becoming increasingly dependent on the exchange of information across organizational boundaries. This provides an interesting background context to study the systems integration and information management requirements to fulfill both shared and individual tasks. Unlike the manufacturing industry, the stakeholders of the AEC and FM sectors do not operate inside organizational structures with clear boundaries. They rather operate within project-based networks of partner organizations collaborating in a temporary arrangement [17], which do not always interact directly with each

© Springer Nature Switzerland AG 2019
P. Giorgini and B. Weber (Eds.): CAiSE 2019, LNCS 11483, pp. 64–79, 2019.
https://doi.org/10.1007/978-3-030-21290-2_5

other [26]. Besides the reliance on mutual data and information exchange to perform their activities effectively, the work of these various firms is generally framed within the same regulatory frameworks and customer demands. In this context, performance and competitiveness are not just within the control of a single organization but rather depend on the efficiency of whole network. Therefore, the technological strategies of these companies must often extend beyond their immediate boundaries, so the technologies they own can be managed effectively [11].

To address these issues, AEC/FM organizations may decide to implement information systems (IS) that integrate across organizational borders. Nam and Tatum [20] already observed more than two decades ago that the integration between design and production functions in AEC projects was linked to increased industry innovation. Since the early 2000s, industry stakeholders have increasingly adopted Building Information Modelling (BIM) solutions to improve their design and construction practices. BIM is generally understood as an overarching term for various object-oriented Computer-Aided Design (CAD) activities, which support the representation of building elements in terms of their 3D geometric and non-geometric (i.e. functional) attributes and relationships [12]. It has been credited for enhanced collaboration and productivity in AEC practices [4, 12].

The aim of this paper is to explore how the information needs of the Finnish AEC/FM industry stakeholders have been satisfied by integrating not only technical solutions such as BIM, but also by adapting at the business and socio-organizational levels. It has been previously argued that IT integration alone is insufficient to overcome the fragmentation of AEC operations and should be thus augmented by other means [20]. Bryde et al. [4] also claim that technical interoperability problems are more likely to be resolved over time by IT companies, but harder issues to solve are to make people agree on common IT platforms or to cooperate with each other. The present study approaches then the integration of IS from a holistic point of view, emphasizing not only the technical dimension of integration and interoperability, but also the business and socio-organizational aspects. From the perspective of AEC/FM practitioners, it can help to understand the implications of inter-organizational integration in the design, construction and operation of buildings. From the perspective of software engineers, it can also serve as a tool to design and develop more effective IT solutions that address the current problems faced by the industry.

During the course of this study, interviewees adopted different discourses when approaching the subject of integration across organizational boundaries. In the context of "building projects", informational needs were usually described as if they had been covered already by a combination of technologies, work processes or business models. At the same time, when the scope was broadened to the more abstract concept of "built environment lifecycle", participants rather provided descriptions of persistent ongoing problems, which they believe could be still mitigated through a more effective information exchange between stakeholders. Based on this discourse characterizing the needs for inter-organizational integration as surmounted or pending, this paper aims to answer the questions *"How have the stakeholders of the Finnish AEC/FM industry addressed their information exchange needs so far?"* and *"Which information exchange needs have yet to be addressed and why?"*.

The paper is structured as follows: Sect. 2 introduces the concepts of the built environment lifecycle and inter-organizational integration, which are essential for the study subject. Section 3 describes the research process, situating the reader within the case study context and providing a detailed account of the steps taken by the authors. Section 4 presents the most relevant findings grounded on the collected interview data without *a priori* hypotheses from academic literature. Section 5 discusses these findings in the context of previous studies. The paper ends by clarifying the research limitations, providing future research suggestions and recapping its main conclusions.

2 Background

2.1 The Built Environment Lifecycle

The AEC industry has been characterized as a loosely coupled system [8] or as a project-based productive network [11], utilizing separate firms with diverse technical capabilities in a temporary multidisciplinary arrangement to produce investment goods like buildings, roads or bridges according to unique specifications [17]. Construction projects can be considered within the scope of the broader field of studies known as the "built environment", a multidisciplinary concept comprising diverse aspects of urban design, land use and human activity within their physical environment [14].

The lifecycle of a building can be broadly articulated into two parts divided by the point in time when its construction has been completed. The first part refers to the planning, design and assembly activities in architecture, engineering and construction (AEC) projects, while the second part refers to the exploitation of the "completed" building which entails different facility management (FM) tasks. The teams that participate on either one of these parts rarely take part also in the other [26]. Throughout this paper, the first part will be referred to simply as "building project" or "construction project". On the other hand, the concept of "built environment lifecycle" will be used as a reference to all stages before, during (i.e. first part) and after (i.e. second part) the building project takes place.

Table 1. Identified stakeholders of the Finnish AEC/FM industry

Stakeholder	Group (Based on Gann and Salter [11])
State government agencies, local authorities	Regulatory and institutional framework
Designers (architects) and engineers (structural, HVAC, electrical, plumbing)	Project-based firms
Main contractors (construction companies)	Project-based firms
Sub-contractors (site workers, consultants)	Project-based firms
Professional associations	Technical support infrastructure
Universities and research institutes	Technical support infrastructure
Trade unions	Supply network
BIM or FM software providers	Supply network
Property owners, landlords	Projects
Facility managers, maintenance companies	Projects
Tenants	Projects

The analysis of relevant industry documentation and the primary data collected from interviews allowed the authors of this study to identify some key stakeholders of the AEC/FM industry in Finland, which are listed in Table 1. These have been mapped to each one of the groups described in the model of innovation and knowledge flows in construction industries by Gann and Salter [11].

2.2   Inter-organizational Integration

Previous scientific literature has approached integration issues in different ways according to the primary aim or focus of the study [2]. The disciplines studying systems of human endeavor, such as IS, management or software engineering, have widely discussed this topic under interchangeable terms such as "organizational integration" [2] or "enterprise integration" [5]. In this context, integration can be defined as "the extent to which distinct and interdependent organizational components constitute a unified whole" [2], where the term "component" refers to organizational units, departments or business partners, and includes in either case the business processes, people and technology involved [2, 21].

IS, management and software engineering scholars have also proposed different classifications of integration, which are often used to explain two intertwined but rather distinct aspects: *"what"* is to be integrated and *"at what scope"* is the integration occurring. In the case of *"what"*, Molina et al. [19], Vernadat [27] and Chen et al. [5] described three forms of integration: Physical systems, application and business/ knowledge, which aim to support the organizational needs for communication, cooperation and coordination/collaboration, respectively. As an example of *"at what scope"*, Barki and Pinssoneault [2] used the process chain of the organizations as an overarching concept to classify integration into internal (i.e. intra-organizational) and external (i.e. inter-organizational), with further subcategories each. This study adopts the classification by Kähkönen [16], who considers holistically both the *"what"* and *"at what scope"* by approaching integration from three perspectives that build on top of each other: Technical, business and socio-organizational. Throughout this paper, we refer to these categories interchangeably as levels or layers of integration. The present study approaches thus the concept of inter-organizational integration as the collaborative work of industry stakeholders using a combination of technical, business or socio-organizational methods. The following sections will describe some of the information exchange needs (or simply information needs) that can motivate such phenomena.

3   Research Process

This paper presents observations from a qualitative case study, taking the whole of the AEC/FM industry in Finland as unit of analysis. Case studies aim to provide in-depth understanding of a case or a set of cases. The unit of analysis is generally bound in time and place to a concrete entity within a real-life context, such as an individual or an organization, but at a more abstract level it can also refer to communities, relationships, programs, decisions, implementation projects or organizational changes [7, 29]. The findings of this study are grounded on data from semi-structured interviews conducted during the first half of 2018 with 24 stakeholders of AEC/FM industry in Finland, namely practitioners from private organizations in directive, managerial or project management roles, as well as public sector officers assigned to strategic projects. The participants represent altogether every stakeholder group from the model of innovation and knowledge flows in construction industries by Gann and Salter [11].

Semi-structured interviews combining specific and open-ended questions were selected as the primary data collection method, because they allowed to maintain consistency between interviews and keep focus on the relevant study topics, while providing also the opportunity to get unexpected insights into the participants' experiences [23]. Topics were covered without a predetermined order to allow for a more natural conversation [6]. Additionally, practitioners had the opportunity at the end of the interview to add anything else they considered important for the topic. To reduce potential biases in the questions and to confirm their relevance [9], the questionnaire[1] was pilot-tested with different researchers than the one who conducted the interviews.

Case studies employ purposive or theoretical sampling rather than random sampling, by selecting the cases which are most relevant to the study proposition [9, 10] and which are likely to replicate or extend the emergent theory. The network of participants in this study had been involved in key projects of the Finnish government to promote the digitalization of the local AEC/FM industry and were selected because they were likely to be more interested and informed about the topic of this study. The initial interviewees were the "gatekeepers" or main contacts in each organization. Each practitioner was asked to suggest names of other key people to interview later. This process was repeated until additional interviews did not provide any new relevant findings or contributions [22] or more specifically, when the concepts emerging from the data could not be developed further in terms of their properties or dimensional variation [6]. To decide whether this point of "saturation" had been reached, a discriminant sampling strategy [7] was applied, verifying if any codes and categories derived from early interviews held true to explain the answers provided by the subsequent participants as well. Table 2 shows a list of the study interviewees, along with the identifiers used in their quotes throughout this paper. Their names have been removed to preserve anonymity.

All interview sessions lasted between 45 and 90 min and were performed with a single participant, except for two interviews in which two participants were present in the room at the same time. The audio of the interviews was recorded for later transcription, coding and analysis using the Atlas.ti tool. Coding was done without *a priori* hypotheses in mind, so the categories could emerge directly from the data itself. This process was conducted first for each interview transcript and then across interviews, by comparing the similarities and differences in the participants' answers, adhering to the guidelines by Eisenhardt [10] of within-case data analysis followed by a cross-case search of patterns. Codes with a higher level of abstraction, or categories, were also derived from the constant comparison of the researcher's notes and memos.

---

[1] The interview guide can be accessed through this link: https://doi.org/10.5281/zenodo.2577038.

Besides the interviews, secondary data sources such as news articles and reports were employed to gain better understanding about the technical concepts and terminology of the AEC/FM disciplines, identify potential interviewees and place the answers of the study participants into the current context of the local industry.

Table 2. Study interview participants (*, ** = Interviewed simultaneously)

Interviewee ID	Organization	Role
n1	A: Construction contractor	Chief Information Officer
n2	A: Construction contractor	Development Manager
n3*	B: BIM software provider	Business Director
n4*	B: BIM software provider	Product Manager
n5**	C: BIM software provider	Product Development Director
n6**	C: BIM software provider	Customer Success Manager
n7	D: Property owners association	Project Manager
n8	E: Technology consultancy services	Senior Enterprise Architect
n9	F: Public-private partnership	Chief Digital Officer
n10	F: Public-private partnership	Project Assistant
n11	G: Trade union partnership	Development Manager
n12	H: Public sector, real estate	Senior Expert
n13	I: Public sector, State government	Senior Specialist
n14	J: FM software provider	Technology Director
n15	K: Universities and research institutes	BIM Professor, Architect
n16	L: Public sector, State government	R&D Specialist
n17	M: Public sector, local authorities	Special Planner
n18	N: Construction consultancy services	Partner and Senior Advisor
n19	O: Construction contractor	Chief Technology Officer
n20	O: Construction contractor	Development Manager
n21	P: Trade union	Managing Director
n22	Q: Engineering sub-contractor	Research Project Manager
n23	R: Public sector, State government	Senior Adviser
n24	S: Construction consultancy services	Project Manager

4   Findings

During the interviews, study participants had the opportunity to reflect upon and describe information exchange needs which demanded some form of inter-organizational integration at the technical, business or socio-organizational level. Rather than elaborating an exhaustive list of information requirements and integration methods for the AEC/FM industry stakeholders, this section focuses on the most relevant ones recognized by the interviewees. Based on the analysis, coding and categorization of their answers, the main findings have been summarized in Table 3.

The different narratives given by the study participants were carefully analyzed. When the questions and answers were constrained to the complexity within a single construction project or the variability between many of them, stakeholder information needs were often described as surmounted. At the same time, when the interview discussion was framed in the broader and more abstract concept of the built environment lifecycle (i.e. including phases before and after the building project) the integration needs – particularly those related to how the information is stored, managed or exchanged between stakeholders – were rather equated to ongoing issues yet to be solved. The different discourses can be observed in the following interview excerpts in the scope of building projects and the built environment lifecycle, respectively:

- n1: "In one of our big sites this is already functioning [...] when (our suppliers) deliver the slabs, the elements to the site [...] their logistics system (tells) our system when it is delivered and installed, and all that is visualized in this model. They integrate to our systems, so we know exactly where they are. And that is also good for them, because they know what is the status where we are in this particular project right now."
- n19: "We want to digitalize first the construction phase, so we can get the information flowing to the maintenance phase. It is like bridge building: Digitalize the site and automate the data collection [...] then the next step is to discuss with those who are maintaining the building. They have their own needs [...] it is very difficult to convert the data, even if it exists, but it is not available for their needs. So we have to somehow digitalize the construction phase first and then we will be ready to move on with the lifecycle."

These two discourses may not necessarily reflect the current maturity stage of inter-organizational integration within the individual organizations or the industry overall, but rather provide an indication that stakeholders are more or less certain on *"what"* has been integrated so far – or still needs to be integrated – when the dimension of *"at what scope"* changes. For this reason, the categories of "addressed" and "unaddressed" are presented between quotation marks ("") throughout this paper.

Table 3. Information needs and integration methods recognized by interviewees

Information exchange needs		Methods of inter-organizational integration
"Addressed" (Scope: Building projects)	Managing complexity within each project	Clarifying terms of stakeholder collaboration
		Improving coordination of distributed team members
		Exchanging detailed and standardized information
	Managing variability between different projects	Using separate software solutions from multiple providers
		Implementing interoperable software solutions
"Unaddressed" (Scope: Built environment lifecycle)	Improving adequacy of information sources	(No specific solutions described by interviewees)
	Reducing information gaps in the processes and workflows	
	Clarifying extent and purposes of data collection	

4.1 Recognized and "Addressed" Information Needs

Practitioners were prone to describe the information needs related to building projects as relatively covered by various technological or business methods of inter-organizational integration. Two categories were observed in this scope of discussion: The needs to manage the complex stakeholder relations within each single project and the needs to handle the variability between multiple projects.

Managing Complexity Within Each Project. When looking at each building project, the inter-organizational integration solutions described by interviewees were mainly focused on handling the large number of parts involved, one of the complexity factors influencing the managerial objectives in the industry [13].

- *Clarifying terms of stakeholder collaboration:* Interviewees often stated that "alliance model" contracts (i.e. various companies participating as consortium in a project) have become a common practice and an incentive for integrating with other stakeholders, as they could evidence the business value of their collaboration.
- *Improving coordination of distributed team members:* Interviewees also expressed that inter-organizational integration helped resolve clashes during the design and construction stages of the building project, occurring because of the split teamwork, or to track the changes occurring at the construction site. Practitioners have adopted different software tools for collaboration and communication on a per-project basis but gathering the decision-making representatives into the same physical space or "big room" was considered a more effective way to resolve any emerging conflicts.
- *Exchanging detailed and standardized information:* The increasing use of BIM tools has allowed the project-based firms to improve the technical quality of their designs, by specifying with greater level of detail the object information in domain-specific (e.g. structural, architectural, electrical, etc.) or combined models. BIM standardization and portability through.IFC format files was deemed by interviewees as a factor that facilitates the coordination between the parties involved in construction projects.

Managing Variability Between Different Projects. When interviewees looked across multiple building projects, information needs were rather aimed at working in different contexts, for instance due to the size and expertise of the companies involved. Discussions centered thus on how flexible the current software solutions were to allow such adaptation. Practitioners across all stakeholder groups and particularly main contractors expressed their lack of preference towards large applications developed by a single vendor, showing more interest on testing different kinds of software tools or adopting more interoperable solutions that could be easily combined. Rigid software products with many features were often labelled as too restrictive or belonging in the past, whereas the new kinds of software products that stakeholders aim for were frequently described using high-level terms such as "open", "integrated" or "platform".

The motivations of the interviewees from project-based firms (e.g. software users within AEC contractors) differed from those of the "supply network" stakeholders group (e.g. BIM software providers). The first ones indicated they were willing to test and use different software tools or applications depending on the project conditions, without committing to any particular software vendor. Some of the factors taken into account were the size of the other companies involved in the project, or the different levels of technical expertise of the sub-contracted staff.

- n1: "We optimize always those tools we are using, bringing in new ones and taking out old ones [...] It is actually up to the project to decide which tools and systems to use."
- n2: "Partnering [with the software providers] might be still a strong word. We are partnering in the sense that we are testing different companies' platforms."

The contractors' predisposition to switch easily between different software products has not gone unnoticed by the application vendors. From their perspective, it has become imperative to deliver more value for the users based on the existing technical resources they already provide. Interviewed software providers pointed out that such customer value may not come only from the features inherent to the offered products or services, but also from the flexibility given to the users to adapt, combine and maintain by themselves the applications from different vendors. Partnering was seen as a convenient alternative to avoid developing integrated software solutions from scratch, by combining instead the technical capabilities and expertise of different companies.

- n5: "We have not discussed [with our customers] if they are building their own software [...] if we can provide good solutions for our customers, even though they are using some different applications, then I think they will pay for our platform as well."
- n14: "We [different vendors] are giving three software [tools] that clients see as one [...] we are not dealing with gigantic systems which are closed, that's the dinosaur thinking."

4.2   Recognized but "Unaddressed" Information Needs

When interviewees discussed about information needs in the scope of the entire built environment lifecycle, they were less confident that their organizations were suitably integrated. The adequacy of the existing information sources, the process and workflow discontinuities, and the uncertainty of how much data to collect and for what purposes were three topics generally described as problems that still have to be solved.

Improving Adequacy of Information Sources. The prevalence of inadequate sources of building information was a concerning issue for most stakeholder groups, but appeared particularly pressing for the FM organizations, who must manage buildings that may have not been designed and constructed using modern software tools. These concerns referred to information from either analogue (i.e. paper-based) or digital sources. In the first case, interviewees mentioned that industry stakeholders still rely on paper-based designs, blueprints or models which are outdated or inconsistent. In terms of information already available in digital format, legacy IT systems, data silos and unnecessary replication were deemed as recurrent integration problems.

- n3: "There is one large construction company with a 300-point solution developed by themselves [...] they use it to solve a certain issue or task, but they recreate [every time] the whole information, which would be available if they looked at the bigger picture."
- n6: "When you import and export data from our database, it means that you will lack some information [...] we have customers who are exporting an XLS file [using] another software, so you get only like five columns of data."

Reducing Information Gaps in Processes and Workflows. Interviewees frequently commented about a critical breaking point in the flows of information between the AEC and FM phases of the built environment lifecycle. Their examples highlighted the improbability of the use/operation/maintenance stakeholders (e.g. FM staff, building inhabitants) to know in advance specific data to maintain the building, such as manufacturer name and model of the supplies they require. Interviewees in the FM segment claimed that most of the relevant information they needed was lost between AEC and FM, whereas unnecessary information is also transferred between the parties. Most practitioners attributed these information "continuity" problems to the temporary involvement of people rather than to the project scale. They suggested a leadership or coordination role was needed to oversee the information flows across the entire built environment lifecycle, as every stakeholder had just a limited view of the building data.

- n19: "Who can provide the 'as-built' model to the one [that] maintains the building? Basically what you get is the BIM model, which is 'as-designed' model, then you have lots of information in different documents where you describe what happened and that's it."
- n2: "You have different parties involved in different stages, but you don't have this *leadership role* [...] you don't have someone who looks at the whole lifecycle, which means there is a lot of data gaps and discontinuities."

Interviewees across different stakeholder groups believe BIM may become a solution to improve such process workflows, because the data contained in the models can be used for other purposes besides designing with high precision and improved quality. BIM was also seen as a method to reduce manual work and repetitive tasks, by automating the information exchange between stakeholders. Thus, study participants frequently interpreted the acronym BIM as "Building Information Management".

Uncertain Extent and Purposes of Data Collection. Research participants often expressed they already had the technical resources to collect and store vast amounts of information about the buildings. At the same time, interviewees also stated it was difficult to determine which data were valuable or could be shared between stakeholders, as in most cases the usage scenarios and benefits to the organization, its partners or customers were yet to be determined.

- n21: "We want this information to be given through the whole supply chain to the final customers [...] it is *too much* information that in different systems it's difficult to use."
- n24: "We have a project with the FM team about how they can use our data of design and construction [...] but FM doesn't need all that [...] there is *so much* information."

Interviewees gave multiple examples of use cases where it was not so important to collect *more* data but rather just *the right* pieces of data according to the user and purpose. This notion has been discussed among practitioners as the "useful minimum".

5   Discussion

A frequent aspect observed across all "addressed" information needs is how clearly the interviewees could articulate the resulting value of inter-organizational integration. From the perspective of the project-based firms, the flexibility to cope with variable conditions between multiple construction projects or dealing with many parties involved on each individual project are important motivations to integrate. Supply network stakeholders pursue rather better products and services built from existing technical resources. For interviewees of other stakeholder groups, the improved decision-making based on the lifecycle information can be considered an important incentive. Therefore, it can be argued that practitioners across all stakeholder groups aim at efficiency gains through inter-organizational integration.

Another element observed on both the "addressed" and "unaddressed" needs is the difficulty to make a clear distinction between levels of integration (i.e. technical, business and socio-organizational), because all of them are closely intertwined as Kähkönen [16] argues. Even the interoperability and compatibility between software products, which can be considered just a technical matter, is strongly associated to the business goals of both providers and end users. On one hand, contractors are willing to pay for interoperable solutions to minimize workload or automatize manual repetitive tasks. On the other hand, software vendors are keen on providing open APIs and develop partnerships with other companies to improve the value of their products in a way that could not be achieved otherwise. Thus, incorporating the features from potential competitors becomes a cost-effective alternative to avoid being replaced by them. In summary, the integration of software across organizational boundaries is perceived not so much as an incentive on its own right, but as the means to achieve higher-level business goals. This may also explain why the "addressed" information exchange needs have been often solved by establishing partnerships between AEC/FM stakeholders, ensuring that both the technical *and* business incentives are clear for the parties involved.

Table 4. "Unaddressed" information exchange needs and their possible reasons

"Unaddressed" information exchange needs	Possible reason(s)
Improving adequacy of information sources	Shared value of inter-organizational integration not clearly agreed upon
Reducing information gaps in processes and workflows	Value of utilizing BIM beyond design not fully understood
	Lack of leadership and coordination of inter-organizational integration
Clarifying extent and purposes of data collection	"Useful minimum" information exchange between stakeholders not yet identified

The remainder of this section will focus on the "unaddressed" information exchange needs summarized in Table 4, which appeared more often when interviewees had to reflect about integrating with other organizations of the whole built environment lifecycle (i.e. beyond construction projects). Understanding these issues and potential solutions can set the course of action for a better integration of the AEC/FM industry.

5.1 Improving Adequacy of Information Sources

Previous studies have noted that incomplete, obsolete or fragmented building information predominates in the industry, resulting in ineffective project management, time loss or cost increases in maintenance, retrofit or remediation processes [28]. According to Shen et al. [24, 25], incorporating legacy systems and achieving higher interoperability is an ongoing challenge of the construction industry. However, technical integration is not a standalone matter that can be analyzed in isolation from other layers of inter-organizational integration. The data silos mentioned by interviewees at technical level went hand in hand with key information gaps at the business level. Companies must invest time and money to develop interoperable solutions, an effort which may not translate into immediate economic benefits. Therefore, it may be necessary to study further how the shared value of inter-organizational integration projects, namely the benefits for every stakeholder, is agreed and communicated.

5.2 Reducing Information Gaps in Processes and Workflows

The "information breakpoint" between the construction and operation phases of the built environment lifecycle (i.e. between the AEC and FM of AEC/FM) has been already discussed in previous research [25, 26]. Information about the use of buildings can provide valuable feedback for project-based firms such as contractors. Future research should therefore focus on different use cases of building operation data collection and analysis aimed at providing more value back to the AEC stakeholders, for instance to improve their construction practices or help with the staff training.

Scholars have also acknowledged that applications primarily used to model and visualize building structures can serve other purposes besides design, for instance to facilitate shared understanding across the interdisciplinary groups participating in a building project [3]. The value of BIM beyond the scope of design activities has been covered in previous research [1, 12] and more recently, the interest has shifted toward the potential uses of BIM in FM processes such as maintenance and refurbishment [28], or to mitigate the sub-optimal management of information across the entire built environment lifecycle [4, 12, 28]. Researchers are currently studying how the principles of Product Lifecycle Management (PLM) from the manufacturing sector can be adopted by the AEC/FM industry, developing an emerging concept of "Building Lifecycle Management" (BLM) which emphasizes the need for a collaborative management of information throughout the entire building lifecycle, supported by existing and improved BIM solutions [18]. Further studies are needed to assess whether and to what extent these promised BIM benefits have been achieved with existing software solutions.

Another aspect observed in terms of reducing workflow gaps was the lack of a leading entity that can assume the coordination of inter-organizational information exchanges. Dubois and Gadde [8] have examined the different coupling patterns used in AEC projects to coordinate within supply chains, among firms and within firms. Future research could extend such approach to the whole built environment lifecycle.

5.3   Clarifying Extent and Purposes of Data Collection

The notion of "useful minimum" has been introduced in the scope of interoperability between software applications implementing IFC exchanges [15]. It emphasizes the need of passing only the most essential information to other stakeholders of the AEC/FM industry. These interdependencies should be understood and mapped at two levels: First among the actors collaborating *within* each phase of the built environment life-cycle and then *between* the actors taking over the building tasks in the consecutive phases (e.g. contractor handling out the HVAC/electrical product specifications to FM). These "useful minimum" pieces of information can be also seen as inter-organizational integration requirements and can help stakeholders understand how to keep the essential building data "flowing", particularly addressing the "unaddressed" integration needs outside the scope of building projects, as shown in Fig. 1.

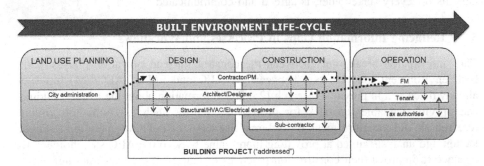

Fig. 1. "Useful minimum" information dependencies integrate stakeholders participating in the same stage (thin arrows) and in different stages (thick arrows) of the built environment lifecycle. Building projects denote boundaries between "addressed" and "unaddressed" integrations.

6 Limitations and Future Work

This paper has some limitations regarding data collection, coding and categorization, as these activities were mostly performed by a single researcher. The analysis could be thus enhanced with the inclusion of other researchers bringing different interpretations to the data. Another important limitation was the lack of Finnish-English translation of key industry reports and documents, requiring the occasional involvement of external assistant researchers. Our findings could be further complemented with additional data collection instruments such as surveys, in which the various needs for inter-organizational integration can be assessed or validated with different stakeholders.

This research does not analyze whether and to what extent the "useful minimum" can be attained with different types of IT solutions available during the building life-cycle. Therefore, future studies may benefit from including other research methods relying not only on the opinions of practitioners but also looking at the technical artefacts they refer to, i.e. their BIM tools and software platforms.

7 Conclusions

We explored how the information exchange needs in the Finnish AEC/FM industry have been covered by technical, business and socio-organizational integration methods. When the analysis was limited to building projects, practitioners often described their information needs as "addressed". In such cases, the value of inter-organizational integration was clear, as the involved parties aimed at managing the complex stakeholder relations or handling the variability between different projects. On the other hand, when the discussions about integration were framed in the scope of the whole built environment lifecycle, information needs were presented as "unaddressed" problems: Existing information sources may remain inadequate as long as the shared value of inter-organizational integration is not clearly agreed upon. Process and workflow discontinuities demand a better understanding of the value of BIM beyond design applications, as well as some leadership or coordination. The uncertainty of how much data to collect and for what purposes can be mitigated by establishing "useful minimum" information exchange between stakeholders. This study provides a basis for further IS engineering research focused on how to identify or manage such "useful minimum" dependencies that enable the inter-organizational integration in AEC/FM industry and other sectors.

Acknowledgements. The first author thanks the Department of Computer Science at Aalto University for the office facilities and technical resources to conduct this study.

References

1. Azhar, S.: Building information modeling (BIM): trends, benefits, risks, and challenges for the AEC industry. Leadersh. Manag. Eng. **11**(3), 241–252 (2011)
2. Barki, H., Pinsonneault, A.: A model of organizational integration, implementation effort, and performance. Organ. Sci. **16**(2), 165–179 (2005)
3. Bouchlaghem, D., et al.: Visualisation in architecture, engineering and construction (AEC). Autom. Constr. **14**(3), 287–295 (2005)
4. Bryde, D., et al.: The project benefits of building information modelling (BIM). Int. J. Proj. Manag. **31**(7), 971–980 (2013)
5. Chen, D., et al.: Architectures for enterprise integration and interoperability: past, present and future. Comput. Ind. **59**(7), 647–659 (2008)
6. Corbin, J.M., Strauss, A.L.: Basics of Qualitative Research: Techniques and Procedures for Developing Grounded Theory. SAGE, Los Angeles (2015)
7. Creswell, J.W., Poth, C.N.: Qualitative Inquiry & Research Design: Choosing Among Five Approaches. SAGE, Los Angeles (2018)
8. Dubois, A., Gadde, L.-E.: The construction industry as a loosely coupled system: implications for productivity and innovation. Constr. Manag. Econ. **20**(7), 621–631 (2002)
9. Easterbrook, S., et al.: Selecting empirical methods for software engineering research. In: Shull, F., et al. (eds.) Guide to Advanced Empirical Software Engineering, pp. 285–311. Springer, London, London (2008). https://doi.org/10.1007/978-1-84800-044-5_11
10. Eisenhardt, K.M.: Building theories from case study research. Acad. Manag. Rev. **14**(4), 532 (1989)
11. Gann, D.M., Salter, A.J.: Innovation in project-based, service-enhanced firms: the construction of complex products and systems. Res. Policy **29**(7–8), 955–972 (2000)
12. Ghaffarianhoseini, A., et al.: Building information modelling (BIM) uptake: clear benefits, understanding its implementation, risks and challenges. Renew. Sustain. Energy Rev. **75**, 1046–1053 (2017)
13. Gidado, K.I.: Project complexity: the focal point of construction production planning. Constr. Manag. Econ. **14**(3), 213–225 (1996)
14. Handy, S.L., et al.: How the built environment affects physical activity. Am. J. Prev. Med. **23**(2), 64–73 (2002)
15. Hietanen, J., Lehtinen, S.: The useful minimum. Tampere University of Technology (2006)
16. Kähkönen, T.: Understanding and managing enterprise systems integration. Lappeenranta University of Technology (2017)
17. Kamara, J.M., et al.: Knowledge management in the architecture, engineering and construction industry. Constr. Innov. **2**(1), 53–67 (2002)
18. Mangialardi, G., Di Biccari, C., Pascarelli, C., Lazoi, M., Corallo, A.: BIM and PLM associations in current literature. In: Ríos, J., Bernard, A., Bouras, A., Foufou, S. (eds.) PLM 2017. IAICT, vol. 517, pp. 345–357. Springer, Cham (2017). https://doi.org/10.1007/978-3-319-72905-3_31
19. Molina, A., Chen, D., Panetto, H., Vernadat, F., Whitman, L.: Enterprise integration and networking: issues, trends and vision. In: Bernus, P., Fox, M. (eds.) Knowledge Sharing in the Integrated Enterprise. ITIFIP, vol. 183, pp. 303–313. Springer, Boston, MA (2005). https://doi.org/10.1007/0-387-29766-9_25
20. Nam, C.H., Tatum, C.B.: Noncontractual methods of integration on construction projects. J. Constr. Eng. Manag. **118**(2), 385–398 (1992)

21. Oh, L.-B., et al.: Service-oriented architecture and organizational integration: an empirical study of IT-enabled sustained competitive advantage. In: ICIS 2007 Proceedings, vol. 18 (2007)
22. Runeson, P., Höst, M.: Guidelines for conducting and reporting case study research in software engineering. Empirical Softw. Eng. **14**(2), 131–164 (2009)
23. Seaman, C.B.: Qualitative methods in empirical studies of software engineering. IEEE Trans. Softw. Eng. **25**(4), 557–572 (1999)
24. Shen, W., et al.: A loosely coupled system integration approach for decision support in facility management and maintenance. Autom. Constr. **25**, 41–48 (2012)
25. Shen, W., et al.: Systems integration and collaboration in architecture, engineering, construction, and facilities management: a review. Adv. Eng. Inform. **24**(2), 196–207 (2010)
26. Vanlande, R., et al.: IFC and building lifecycle management. Autom. Constr. **18**(1), 70–78 (2008)
27. Vernadat, F.B.: 86. Enterprise Integration and Interoperability. In: Nof, S. (ed.) Springer Handbook of Automation, pp. 1529–1538. Springer, Heidelberg (2009). https://doi.org/10.1007/978-3-540-78831-7_86
28. Volk, R., et al.: Building information modeling (BIM) for existing buildings—literature review and future needs. Autom. Constr. **38**, 109–127 (2014)
29. Yin, R.K.: Case Study Research: Design and Methods. Sage Publications, Los Angeles (2009)

A Lightweight Framework for Multi-device Integration and Multi-sensor Fusion to Explore Driver Distraction

Gernot Lechner[1]([⊠]), Michael Fellmann[2], Andreas Festl[1],
Christian Kaiser[1], Tahir Emre Kalayci[1], Michael Spitzer[1],
and Alexander Stocker[1]

[1] Virtual Vehicle Research Center, Inffeldgasse 21a, 8010 Graz, Austria
{gernot.lechner,andreas.festl,christian.kaiser,
emre.kalayci,michael.spitzer,alexander.stocker}@v2c2.at
[2] University of Rostock, Albert-Einstein-Straße 22, 18059 Rostock, Germany
michael.fellmann@uni-rostock.de

Abstract. Driver distraction is a major challenge in road traffic and major cause of accidents. Vehicle industry dedicates increasing amounts of resources to better quantify the various activities of drivers resulting in distraction. Literature has shown that significant causes for driver distraction are tasks performed by drivers which are not related to driving, like using multimedia interfaces or glancing at co-drivers. One key aspect of the successful implementation of distraction prevention mechanisms is to know when the driver performs such auxiliary tasks. Therefore, capturing these tasks with appropriate measurement equipment is crucial. Especially novel quantification approaches combining data from different sensors and devices are necessary for comprehensively determining causes of driver distraction. However, as a literature review has revealed, there is currently a lack of lightweight frameworks for multi-device integration and multi-sensor fusion to enable cost-effective and minimally obtrusive driver monitoring with respect to scalability and extendibility. This paper presents such a lightweight framework which has been implemented in a demonstrator and applied in a small real-world study involving ten drivers performing simple distraction tasks. Preliminary results of our analysis have indicated a high accuracy of distraction detection for individual distraction tasks and thus the framework's usefulness. The gained knowledge can be used to develop improved mechanisms for detecting driver distraction through better quantification of distracting tasks.

Keywords: Driver distraction · Driver attention · Lightweight framework · Multi-device integration · Multi-sensor fusion

1 Introduction and Motivation

Driver distraction is a major challenge in road traffic, resulting in an enormous number of accidents and fatalities every year [1–3]. In a study based on the analysis of 997 crashes, Thomas et al. state that 11% of crashed drivers were distracted and 8% were

© Springer Nature Switzerland AG 2019
P. Giorgini and B. Weber (Eds.): CAiSE 2019, LNCS 11483, pp. 80–95, 2019.
https://doi.org/10.1007/978-3-030-21290-2_6

inattentive [4]. However, distraction does not only concern manual passenger vehicle driving but is also a key issue towards increasingly automated driving functions, Advanced Driver Assistance Systems (ADAS) and autonomous driving. When driving scenarios are not covered by an automation, the advanced driving functions fail, and a manual take-over is required [5, 6]. For this purpose, termed "to keep the *Human-in-the-loop*", drivers must be responsive and prepared all the time: drivers must end activities unrelated to driving and give enough attention to take manual control of the vehicle in an adequate manner.

Apart from the maturity level of the vehicle with respect to autonomous driving, one key point is correct measurement of driver distraction to assess driver's status. Further development of (partly) automated driving is highly dependent on qualitative and quantitative measurement of driver distraction to trigger appropriate measures to get drivers back into the loop. In addition, safety of drivers at the present time will be increased significantly through these measures by improving mechanisms to avoid distraction.

A major issue of measuring driver distraction is that in most existing approaches the sensors and devices are obtrusive, and already their application would distract the driver. For example, the methods of neuroimaging or eye tracking depend on bulky, distracting, and cost-intensive technical equipment and are therefore not applicable for daily use in real traffic but suitable only for experimental setups [7, 8]. Prototypical audiovisual systems for distraction measurement are in use but rarely in combination with other sensors [9]. However, available consumer-grade hardware such as smart-watches, wristbands, smartphones, or other types of wearables are already used by many drivers. Data captured by their sensors bears a huge potential to be used in driver distraction detection – a potential currently not fully exploited in research. A recent practice-oriented driver distraction study published by Zendrive.com – a startup dedicated to better inferring distraction by using smartphone sensors investigating 100 billion miles – found out that on an average day, over 60% of people use their phones at least once while being behind the wheel [10]. This determines the potential of using popular consumer electronics owned by drivers for distraction research. But how can data from multiple sensors in different devices be captured and made available for analysis in a convenient way? A literature review has indicated a lack of lightweight frameworks that integrate multiple sensors from multiple consumer devices in order to fuse data and enable a comprehensive analysis and detection of multiple distraction tasks.

Hence, the objective of the research presented in this paper is to answer the following research question: *What is a lightweight software framework for multi-device integration and multi-sensor fusion for comprehensive driver distraction detection?* Furthermore, this framework should serve as a baseline for potential interventions in the case of driver distraction and allow the measurement of interventions' success. Apart from being lightweight and cost-efficient, an important aspect of the proposed framework is easy extendibility, i.e. adding newly developed or improved sensors must be practical. This ensures the framework's adaption to various (distraction-related) data sources.

Concerning driver distraction and driver inattention, we follow the definitions provided by Regan et al. [11] who aim for better distinguishing driver distraction from other forms of inattention. They conclude that *Driver Inattention* means *insufficient or no attention to activities critical for safe driving* and *driver distraction* (they refer to *Driver Diverted Attention* as a synonym) as just one form of driver inattention.

2 Background

In the following sections, an overview of topics related to the presented research is provided. We discuss *driver inattention/distraction* followed by ways how to *quantify drivers and driving*, and finally we conclude with an *overview of frameworks*.

Driving a vehicle is a complex task, and *driver inattention and distraction* increase the risk of having a crash. Transport researchers have paid a lot of attention to explore both topics in review articles, simulation studies and field trials. Most of the highly cited articles are review papers: Sussman et al. [12] review research into driver attentional processes about safety implications of inattention, related psychological and physiological indices, and in-vehicle instrumentation for detection. Young and Regan [13] provide a literature review for driver distraction, which is a priority issue in road safety in many countries worldwide. They explicitly highlight the effect of in-vehicle devices (in particular mobile phones) on driving performance. Dong et al. [14] review technologies for driver inattention monitoring (distraction and fatigue) and discuss the application of hybrid measures to give more reliable solutions compared to single driver physical measures or single driving performance measures. Simulator studies and field trials are important for validating developed technical approaches. Horberry et al. [15] present the findings of a simulator study which examined the effects of driver distracted while having to perform in-vehicle distraction tasks. Klauer et al. [16] conducted a widely cited comprehensive study on the impact of driver inattention on near crash and crash risk, using data from the 100 Car naturalistic driving study. Their findings indicate higher risks when driving drowsy, or when engaging in complex tasks while driving. D'Orazio et al. [17] propose a visual approach based on image recognition for monitoring driver vigilance, detecting if a driver's eyes are open or closed while evaluating the temporal occurrence of eyes open to estimate the driver's attention level validated in experiments. Fletcher and Zelinsky [18] present a prototype system which can estimate a driver's observations and detect driver inattentiveness based on eye gaze – road event correlation validated in laboratory experiments and road trials.

Driving data resulting from *quantification of drivers and driving* is a valuable source for knowledge generation and can boost research in driver inattention and distraction. The quantification of human behavior termed *quantified self* [19] has sped-up the generation of data and is a very popular example for everyday life data analytics. Individuals engaged in self-tracking any kind of biological, physical, behavioral, or environmental information [20] have led to a multitude of data that can be used for different purposes including detecting health issues or developing personalized training plans. This pattern of self-tracking by using consumer devices can be easily transferred to vehicles, and in this sense, may be termed as *quantified vehicles* [21]. Sensors and electronic control units (ECUs) within modern vehicles create a plethora of vehicle operation data, but this data is hardly accessible for the reasons of safety and espionage. Although examples for real-time streaming of Controller Area Network (CAN) bus data are available (e.g. [22]), conversion of CAN data is restricted due to proprietary/manufacturer-specific standards (like SAE 1939 [23]). Yet, drivers and driving can be quantified either by using data accessed through the vehicles' on-board diagnostics (OBD) interface, or by utilizing the driver's wearables. While much of the data gained from the OBD interface is not suitable to detect driver distraction (e.g. ambient temperature), there are a few valuable measurements including vehicle speed or vehicle RPM (revolutions per minute) that can be explored. Additionally, smartphones provide a set of useful data for quantifying drivers and driving, for example through GPS, acceleration and gyroscope sensors. Analogously, many wearables like smartwatches have similar sensors and generated data may be used to quantify certain tasks of drivers.

Data collected by a driver's wearables using *Lightweight Frameworks for Multi-Device Integration and Multi-Sensor Fusion* can be used to enable driver distraction and inattention detection mechanisms which are independent from a car's built-in functionality. For instance, in the zendrive.com case which was introduced in Sect. 1, two sensors from the driver's smartphone have been used to quantify safety-critical smartphone usage during driving. But, for implementing such use cases, in-depth-knowledge about technical infrastructures for (multi-)sensor data acquisition, pre-processing, synchronization, and fusion is crucial. Much past research in multi-sensor integration has focused on hardware-based approaches for data acquisition (e.g., for physiological monitoring [24] or context awareness [25], to name two examples), which seems logical due to the former lack of devices with considerable computation power for dealing with software-based solutions. In search of such software solutions, a review of the scientific literature has shown that approaches for multi-device integration and multi-sensor fusion with a focus on wearables are not sufficiently reported. While some researchers (for example [26–29]) have already combined smartphone with smartwatch sensor data for recognizing human activities outside the driving domain, their papers lack the detailed description of applied technical frameworks for capturing and synchronizing measurement data. It is obvious that these papers are focused on the analytics part, which is obviously more interesting for data scientists, but lack on the technical part which should also be considered relevant. With respect to detecting unsafe driving, researchers [9, 30, 31] report on studies using sensor data from wearables. However, a description of their technical framework enabling the reported analysis is missing, too. Finally, de Arriba-Pérez et al. [32] present a research article elaborating on a technical framework, though embedded in an educational context.

3   A Technical Framework for Real-Time Fusion and Logging of Sensor Data

3.1   Requirements

In order to provide the basis for driver distraction detection, the framework must be able to record and integrate various data in a timely manner. Hence, requirements exist regarding which data should be recorded and how it should be stored and integrated. In the following, we describe fundamental requirements regarding these aspects.

- **Requirement 1**: The framework should be able to record data about the driver, vehicle state and the current GPS-position.

  Regarding the driver, physiological data is important such as movements of the driver's head (e.g. to detect if the driver is looking on the street or not), movements of arms/wrist (e.g. to detect if hands are placed on the steering-wheel) as well as the driver's heart rate (e.g. to detect situations of excessive stress). Regarding the vehicle state, data such as RPM or usage of the entertainment system is relevant (e.g. high RPM variation in combination with frequent gear reductions may indicate a more focused driving style, while excessive entertainment system usage may indicate the opposite). In order to detect the movement of the vehicle in the real world to obtain contextual information, GPS positioning data should also be recorded.

- **Requirement 2**: The framework should provide access to integrated data via a common query interface as well as the capability to store real-time time series data.

  Access to integrated data via a common interface is an important requirement to facilitate the analysis of diverse sensor data. The database should moreover be capable of processing large volumes of insert operations in almost real time (e.g. to store acceleration, gyroscope and GPS data). Regarding analysis, the database should provide support for time series data, i.e. querying large amounts of sensor values with a timestamp.

- **Requirement 3**: The framework should provide a mechanism for synchronizing data originating from various sensors from multiple devices.

  In order to synchronize sensor data such as GPS position, heart rate, head movement and RPM at a certain point in time, the timestamp of each sensor value could be used. As internal clocks of different sensors are not synchronized all sensors must agree on a common time. For this purpose, a GPS time stamp can be used since GPS sensors are available on many hardware devices such as smart glasses, smartwatches and inside vehicle data loggers used for experiments.

3.2 Generic Architecture

The generic architecture consists of an arbitrary number of *generic components (GC)* with various functions, thereby considering the requirements stated in the previous section. The GCs can acquire data from one or more sensors, but also – uni- or even bi-directionally – from other generic components through a receiver (GC reader). Such *data collection* is the primary and simplest function of a generic component. The *data transfer*-functionality makes the interchange of data between generic components possible and is built upon data collection, as collection of data is required before its transfer. For this purpose, a transmitter acting as a GC writer is integrated. *Data integration and processing* is an optional function separated from transfer and performed in a *data forwarder*. The data forwarder of the GC may thus act as an integrator, thereby processing data from one or more different data sources (individual sensors or generic components). In summary, as shown in Fig. 1, the GC is capable to perform following functions: (1) data collection, (2) data transfer, and (3) data integration and processing. In addition, the GC has a configuration layer providing basic configuration options which is accessible by users for specific configuration requirements.

These characteristics of the generic architecture allow to consider the framework as a general one which can be extended in various ways: as sensors quantify information from environment and bring them into a structured, machine-readable format, they can easily be connected to GCs. In particular, the structure of data in terms of measurement frequency and data types provided by different sensors is similar for many different sensors (as, e.g., accelerometers or gyroscopes), independent from specific brands or devices. However, the concrete implementation and respective performance of hardware determines both the number of performed tasks and sensors that can be added.

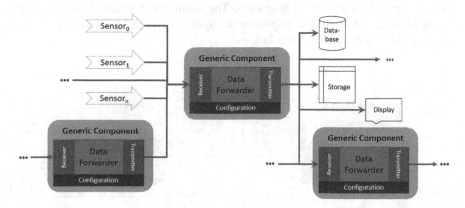

Fig. 1. Generic architecture for real-time fusion and logging of sensor data

3.3   Implementation

In order to explore driver distraction, an instance based on the generic architecture is implemented, satisfying the requirements stated previously (cf. Fig. 2). A smartwatch (top left) that delivers physiological data such as heart rate, but also movement-related data such as gyroscope and accelerometer data, is connected via Bluetooth to a smartphone (top right). Smart glasses (bottom right) are connected to a smartphone via WiFi in order to record head movements. The smartphone forwards data both from the smartwatch and the smart glasses to the central database (center) using a 4G LTE connection. Data about the vehicle state is collected by a vehicle data logger (bottom left) that also transfers data via a 4G LTE connection to the database. Results can be investigated in a user frontend on a web page. Regarding the concrete implementation of the system, four main components have been created. (1) An Android Wear App was developed that consists of one component running on the smartphone (Samsung Galaxy A5) interlinked with another component running on the smartwatch (Huawei Watch 2). This design is also referred to as "companion app". It provides the advantage that energy-intense tasks such as GPS data logging and writing data to the database over a network connection are delegated to the more powerful (in terms of battery and computing power) smartphone. One or more smartwatch-smartphone pairings can be used for data acquisition at the same time. (2) A smart glasses App for Microsoft HoloLens was developed for logging head movements. (3) A Vehicle Data Logger that accesses the ODB-II interface of the car provides real-time car data. (4) The time-series database InfluxDB was installed on a server to store all collected data and provide data for further analysis. A high-precision GPS-timestamp was added to all these data sources for synchronization. For more information on used hardware and sensors acting as data sources, we refer to Table 1.

The software architecture of the whole system follows the generic architecture. Figure 2 shows the system architecture. This architecture was implemented on several devices in several programming languages. The smart watch/smart phone implementation is in Java, the HoloLens implementation in C# and the Vehicle Data Logger implementation on the BeagleBone in C++.

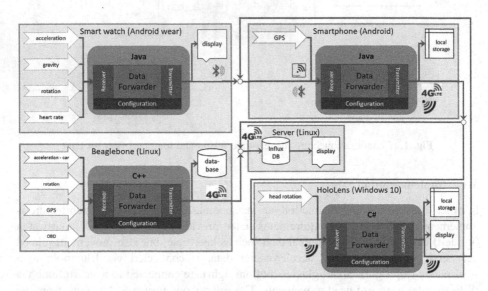

Fig. 2. System architecture

Figure 3 shows the interface specification of the C# implementation for the HoloLens. This principle was also applied to the other involved components written in C++ and Java. The *ISensorDataReceiver* is responsible for acquiring the current log point from the attached sensor. This could be done with a predefined sampling rate, but also asynchronous by triggering the *LogPointAvailable* event when a new sensor value is present. The *ISensorDataReceiver* reflects the receiver of the generic architecture.

Every measurement regardless of the sensor type is stored in a *LogPoint*. A log point consists of a timestamp, an array of captured values and names for the captured values.

The *IDataForwarder* interface reflects the data forwarder defined in the general architecture. It is responsible for connecting the *ISensorDataReceiver* (receiver) with any appropriate *IDataTransmitter* (transmitter). Additionally, start/stop of the data acquisition is controlled by the *IDataForwarder*. Various configuration settings such as URL endpoints, sampling rates, Sensor IDs, are also handled by the *IDataForwarder* interface. The *IDataTransmitter* interface reflects the transmitter of the general architecture. It is responsible for processing the acquired sensor value, e.g. store the value in a database, a local CSV file or to send the value over a WebSocket connection. All other devices and implementations follow the same generic architecture.

From a practical viewpoint, stability of connections between devices has to be tested intensively in order to avoid unwanted disconnections. In addition, battery runtime of devices must be considered when planning test setups, as continuous receiving and transmitting of data consumes much more power than standard operation. The easy-to-realize regular measurement of timestamps from GNSS-devices and related synchronization of multiple devices facilitates the joint usage of acquired data, as otherwise the devices in instances are prone to clock drift, what renders measurement data unusable.

Fig. 3. Interface definition in C# for HoloLens

3.4   Hardware and Equipment

The applied types of hardware and equipment were determined according to the requirements of the experimental setup. A thorough market and requirements analysis led to the application of the hardware and equipment listed in Table 1. In addition, details concerning the sensors of each device from which data was acquired are described. Please note that for all measurements along x-/y-/z-axis the reference system is provided by the sensor itself.

Table 1. Overview of applied hardware/equipment and acquired sensors.

Hardware & Equipment	Sensor description & acquired data from sensors
Huawei Watch 2 (2 units)	Off-the-shelf smartwatch based on Android Wear 2.0, offering a variety of sensors for data acquisition; one watch per wrist - Along x-/y-/z-axis: acceleration including/excluding gravity, measured acceleration (with/without bias compensation), force of gravity - Around x-/y-/z-axis: Euler angles, rate of rotation (with/without drift compensation), estimated drift - Scalar component of the rotation vector - Heart rate in beats per minute
Samsung Galaxy A5 (2 units)	Off-the-shelf smartphone serving running app for data acquisition (operating system: Android 7.0), one per smartwatch - Latitude/Longitude of smartphone's position & GPS timestamp
Microsoft HoloLens (1 unit)	Off-the-shelf mixed reality glasses (Operating system: Windows Mixed Reality) - Current absolute position of HoloLens-camera on x-/y-/z-axis - Component of quaternion (x/y/z/w): current rotation of camera - Angle between two sequenced quaternions - Component of Euler angle (x/y/z) representation of rotation
BeagleBone Vehicle Data Logger (1 unit)	Non-commercial OBD-II Vehicle Data Logger based on BeagleBoard-platform, including a sensor measurement cape, designed and manufactured at Virtual Vehicle Research Center. Although being a standalone data logger, data is synchronized with other acquired data by GPS timestamp - Acceleration x-/y-/z-axis including gravity [unit g] - Measured altitude above sea level - Rate of rotation around the x-/y-/z-axis - Latitude/Longitude of measured position & GPS timestamp - Various data according to OBD-II specification
GoPro cameras (2 units)	Mounted in the in-cabin room for videos about drivers. As only required for reasons of traceability during analysis phase, video data was not synchronized with remaining data in real-time - In-cabin video recording

4   Demonstration

The implemented lightweight framework was applied in a real-world study. The field study allows to develop improved systems for detecting driver distraction, as the results allow to better infer concrete distraction tasks. In addition, it makes the preliminary examination of the level of obtrusion possible.

4.1 Study Setup

The implemented framework was used for logging and fusing data from drivers and vehicles to gain insights into detection of distraction during driving. In an experimental series, ten drivers (5 female, 5 male) were asked to perform sequences of specific motions which simulate a variety of distraction tasks. The used vehicle was a Ford Mondeo with automatic transmission with a customized front video recorder capturing (non-synchronized) context of driving for reasons of traceability. Age of drivers ranged from 26 to 43 years, with a mean of 33.6 years (median: 34 years; standard deviation: 5.71). Depending on age, subjects were categorized as *digital natives* (age 18–30, 2:2), *middle age* (born in transition time to digital natives, age 31–40, 2:2), and *digital immigrants* (age 41+, 1:1). Six of the participants wore glasses, and 3 had prior experience with Smart Glasses. Test participants had to carefully read and sign an informed consent prior to the performance, where test purpose and procedure have been described without biasing the test participants for the tests. They could quit the study at any time, nevertheless, all participants finished all their tasks.

A comprehensive distraction detection requires the recording of a variety of different tasks. Thus, two different scenarios were tested: performing tasks in a stationary vehicle (static scenario) and while driving (dynamic scenario), with 10 repetitions for each. The sequence of motions in the static scenario consisted of (S1 – task not related to driving) turn a knob at the center console; (S2 – task related to driving) release and put on hand brake; (S3 – task not related to driving) look for at least 2 s into the eyes of the co-driver. In the dynamic case the tasks were (D1 – task related to driving) switch to Drive Mode, release the brake and accelerate to 5 km/h; (D2 – task not related to driving) turn a rotary knob at the center console; (D3 – task not related to driving) look for at least 2 s into the eyes of the co-driver; (D4 – task related to driving) stop the vehicle and switch to parking mode. The motions of the drivers were recorded and transmitted over the air to the database, applying the implemented framework. Drivers used smartwatches on both hands for acceleration and rotation of hand motions, and – despite the potential to be obtrusive – drivers wore smart glasses (HoloLens-device) in order to capture head motion data. A smartphone recorded the GPS position of the vehicle, and a data logger built on the BeagleBone Black-platform (beagleboard. org/black) recorded acceleration, rotation as well as data from the OBD interface of the vehicle (e.g. RPM and speed) to collect contextual information.

4.2 Evaluation of the Framework: Detection of Driver Distraction Tasks

In a preliminary, post-experimental step, data was analyzed and assessed with the objective to detect motion patterns related to driver distraction by applying advanced methods of data science. For this purpose, measurement data obtained from smartwatches, smartphones and smart glasses was used, while contextual information provided by the vehicle data logger was not required. Processing and manipulation of time series data was performed in *Jupyter Notebook* [33] with *Python* libraries *pandas* [34] and *numpy* [35], while *tsfresh* [36] for feature extraction and *scikit-learn* [37] for classification were used. Data quality (e.g. plausibility, completeness, …) was checked at first. Subsequently, the data was cleaned and manually split into labelled sequences by the help of the videos recorded by the GoPro cameras mounted in the car. Each sequence represented time series data of a specific distraction task. Sequences of the same type were bundled in sets of identical tasks. In order to have positive and negative examples in each bundle, we added time series sequences of comparable length that did not represent the distraction task to the bundle. These were chosen randomly from the available non-distraction data. Feature extraction from these extended bundles of time series data provided input values for machine learning algorithms. In the first step, importance of features was estimated using *ExtraTreesClassifiers*. Next, features were sorted by their estimated importance, and a limited number (2, 3, …, 33, 34) were provided to the machine learning algorithms. Algorithms applied on data covered *Support Vector Classification (SVC)* with linear/RBF kernels, *ExtraTreesClassifier*, *RandomForestClassifier*, *KNeighborsClassifier*, and *AdaBoostClassifier*, all imple-mented in *scikit-learn* and selected based on experience from similar approaches. Due to the limited amount of data we focused on a k-fold cross validation approach for each of the scenarios. Therefore, data was randomly partitioned into 10 subsamples of equal size. In each of the 10 training runs, 9 (different) subsamples acted as training data, while the model was tested and validated in terms of prediction accuracy using the remaining subsample.

Table 2 provides an overview of the results of these tests. In addition, the number of (positive and negative) input sequences, used sensor data, best performing algorithm and number of features used for obtaining the best prediction are given. The results show a satisfying accuracy in terms of distraction task classification. For all scenarios except (D4), the best average classification accuracy was greater or equal 90%, and for all except two, it was even greater than or equal to 95%. In general, classification was slightly worse in dynamic scenarios than in static ones, a fact that can be explained by less distinct data induced by vehicle movements. Apart from the finding that individual devices deliver sufficient information to detect simple movements, considering joint sensors like accelerometer and gyroscope does not necessarily lead to better results in such experiments with limited amount of data (see (S2), (D4)): although additional dimensions can increase the amount of available information, the available data becomes sparse due to the increased dimension of the feature space. In order to overcome this potential issue, more data must be provided. Please note that the implemented framework can detect single movements using sensor data from a single device but is also capable to detect different types of distraction by a combination of devices. In order to provide a comprehensive distraction detection, such a combination is required.

Table 2. Performance on classification of distraction tasks (A/G1: Accelerometer/Gyroscope smartwatch, G2: Gyroscope smart glasses).

Scenario	No. of sequences (pos. + neg.)	Sensor: source of data	Mean accuracy [%] (Std. Dev.)	Best algorithm	No. of features (best algorithm)
(S1)	29 + 29	A + G1	100% (0.000)	ExtraTreesClassifier	9
	29 + 29	A	98.0% (0.060)	SVC (linear)	21
	29 + 29	G1	100% (0.000)	ExtraTreesClassifier	3
(S2)	29 + 29	A + G1	97.5% (0.075)	SVC (linear)	4
	29 + 29	A	98.0% (0.060)	SVC (linear)	2
	29 + 29	G1	97.5% (0.075)	ExtraTreesClassifier	4
(S3)	62 + 62	G2	97.5% (0.038)	SVC (linear)	19
(D1)	60 + 60	A + G1	94.7% (0.043)	AdaBoostClassifier	33
	60 + 60	A	93.0% (0.077)	SVC (linear)	33
	60 + 60	G1	94.7% (0.043)	AdaBoostClassifier	33
(D2)	55 + 55	A + G1	95.4% (0.084)	RandomForestClassifier	2
	55 + 55	A	95.4% (0.084)	RandomForestClassifier	2
	55 + 55	G1	94.2% (0.077)	ExtraTreesClassifier	21
(D3)	62 + 62	G2	95.8% (0.042)	SVC (rbf)	28
(D4)	52 + 52	A + G1	88.8% (0.058)	ExtraTreesClassifier	7
	52 + 52	A	90.0% (0.045)	SVC (linear)	9
	52 + 52	G1	82.4% (0.074)	ExtraTreesClassifier	31

4.3 Participant Survey and Results

To evaluate comfort, usability and user experience of applied devices, all participants were asked to fill a questionnaire after the experiment to generate data for a qualitative evaluation of the experiment. In addition, drivers were also requested to provide answers on questions in a break between static and dynamic scenarios.

All participants had to answer some qualitative questions after both, the static and the dynamic scenarios. For example, regarding the wearing comfort of the smart glasses, on a scale from 1 (very uncomfortable) to 5 (very comfortable) all participants answered between 2 and 4 (standard deviation 0.6), on average with 3.2 after the static scenarios. Ratings had a greater variance and were more negative on overall in the dynamic scenario (2.8 on average), e.g. participant 7 rated the wearing comfort very uncomfortable, while participant 3 rated it as very comfortable.

All answers to the question if any technical or external issues occurred during the study were related to the smart glasses, but no other device was mentioned. Despite that, regarding the question if participants can imagine using the smart glasses regularly while driving using a 4-level Likert item (No = 1 to Yes = 4), results were rather towards Yes after the static scenario (mean: 3, std. dev.: 0.77), and surprisingly even more positive after the dynamic scenario (mean: 3.2, std. dev.: 0.75). Furthermore, participants were asked to answer the question "Describe the smart glasses experience. What do you think?" after static and dynamic scenarios. The answers showed a high variability in terms of weight, value of additional information, and interaction with the smart glasses. Selected positive statements after the static scenario include for example that "additional information using AR is good, as they are always in the visual field" (Participant 1), that the "weight is not annoying" (P2), that the "Experience is better than expected" (P3), or that it is "rather futuristic, but one could get used to it" (P5). In contrast, selected negative statements after the static scenario include for example an experienced "heavy weight" (P7), that the "Experience is worse than expected" (P8) and that it is "heavy, uncomfortable, difficult to interact" (P10). Participants 1, 2, 7 and 10 reported "heavy weight" after the dynamic scenario, too. However, positive statements after the static scenario include that "one gets used to it easily" (P2), that the "experience is better than expected" (P3), that the experience is "good in general. Visualization flickered often but did not disturb (in contrast to the expectation)" (P4), and that the map visualization is "nice, as you always know where you are" (P6).

5   Conclusion

In this work, we focused on exploring comprehensive detection of driver distraction based on a lightweight framework for multi-device integration and multi-sensor fusion. The research on similar frameworks in scientific literature revealed a lack of comparable approaches, what encouraged us to develop a generic architecture for connecting devices and respective sensors in order to achieve our research objective. The proposed generic architecture allows flexible configuration and linkage of generic components, thus being easily extendable by adding/removing generic components. In view of the very heterogeneous landscape, the generic architecture provided a standard frame of reference for all stakeholders involved in the development process. Thus, instantiating the generic architecture was straightforward. Beyond that, the architecture supported the communication with a remote software developer: a significant improvement in terms of software quality could be observed when comparing the first version without using the architecture with the second version based on the generic architecture. Although not being validated, the instance of the framework is expected to work also as baseline for potential interventions in the case of driver distraction: acquired data can directly serve as input for an analysis system with subsequent information of drivers. Of course, this gives rise to research on required real-time capabilities of such a system.

The evaluation of the study in terms of a proof-of-concept has indicated that the implemented framework is capable to acquire sufficient data with respect to quality and quantity from different sensors built into off-the-shelf consumer hardware to detect driver motions as a signal for driver distraction. Driver distraction mechanisms implemented in modern vehicles have a limited feasibility to fully capture all events to finally warn the driver and keep the driver in the loop, as they rely on data generated by the vehicles' own sensory and do not integrate data from external devices like wearables [38]. With a view to improvement of such systems, data from multiple wearables of a driver may enable a better detection of distraction-related events and thereby contribute to increasing driving safety. Obviously, combining both approaches can turn out to be an effective way. In view of this, fusing data of wearables with other (additional) sources' data would facilitate a more comprehensive distraction analysis.

Although the study size and subsequently the size of the collected data are a limitation of the presented research, the small amount of data generated and analyzed has delivered surprisingly accurate results concerning distraction task classification. Thus, a complete analysis, recognition and prediction of individual patterns is conceivable.

The developed framework has a wider application potential than being limited to the presented type of research. Besides the recognition of driver distraction through the classification of critical tasks, further applications based on data acquired by such a lightweight framework could cover, e.g. driving style detection and classification, storage of (driver-related) driving events in the case of accidents like black boxes in aviation, or the personalized adaption of features to habits.

Acknowledgements. Parts of this study were funded by the Austrian Research Promotion Agency (FFG) under project number 866781 (FFG FEMTech Project GENDrive). The authors would further like to acknowledge the financial support of the COMET K2 – Competence Centers for Excellent Technologies Programme of the Federal Ministry for Transport, Innovation and Technology (bmvit), the Federal Ministry for Digital, Business and Enterprise (bmdw), the Austrian Research Promotion Agency (FFG), the Province of Styria and the Styrian Business Promotion Agency (SFG).

References

1. NHTSA Risky Driving. https://www.nhtsa.gov/risky-driving/distracted-driving. Accessed 20 Nov 2018
2. Study on good practices for reducing road safety risks caused by road user distractions. https://ec.europa.eu/transport/road_safety/sites/roadsafety/files/pdf/behavior/distraction_study.pdf. Accessed 20 Nov
3. Research Note on Distracted Driving. https://crashstats.nhtsa.dot.gov/Api/Public/ViewPublication/812517. Accessed 20 Nov
4. Thomas, P., Morris, A., Talbot, R., Fagerlind, H.: Identifying the causes of road crashes in Europe. Ann. Adv. Automot. Med. **57**(13), 13–22 (2013)
5. Payre, W., Cestac, J., Dang, N.-T., Vienne, F., Delhomme, P.: Impact of training and in-vehicle task performance on manual control recovery in an automated car. Transp. Res. Part F: Traffic Psychol. Behav. **46**(A), 216–227 (2017)
6. Zeeb, K., Buchner, A., Schrauf, M.: What determines the take-over time? An integrated model approach of driver take-over after automated driving. Accid. Anal. Prev. **78**, 212–221 (2015)
7. Youtube Driver Distraction. https://www.youtube.com/watch?v=yVbPGmsG5sI. Accessed 20 Nov 2018
8. Youtube Understanding Driver Distraction. https://www.youtube.com/watch?v=XToWVxS_9lA. Accessed 20 Nov 2018
9. Detection of Driver Distraction. http://ppms.cit.cmu.edu/media/project_files/UTC_project_13_Multimodal_Detection_of_Driver_Distraction_-_final_report.pdf. Accessed 20 Nov 2018
10. Zendrive Distracted Driving. https://d1x6dm64pjo2h2.cloudfront.net/casestudies/Zendrive_Distracted_Driving_2018.pdf. Accessed 20 Nov 2018
11. Regan, M.A., Hallett, C., Gordon, C.P.: Driver distraction and driver inattention: definition, relationship and taxonomy. Accid. Anal. Prev. **43**(5), 1771–1781 (2011)

12. Sussman, E.D., Bishop, H., Madnick, B., Walters, R.: Driver inattention and highway safety. Transp. Res. Rec. **1047**, 40–48 (1985)
13. Young, K., Regan, M.: Driver distraction: a review of the literature. In: Faulks, I.J., Regan, M., Stevenson, M., Brown, J., Porter, A., Irwin, J.D. (eds.) Distracted driving, pp. 379–405. Australasian College of Road Safety, Sydney (2007)
14. Dong, Y., Hu, Z., Uchimura, K., Murayama, N.: Driver inattention monitoring system for intelligent vehicles: a review. IEEE Trans. Intell. Transp. Syst. **12**(2), 596–614 (2011)
15. Horberry, T., Anderson, J., Regan, M.A., Triggs, T.J., Brown, J.: Driver distraction: the effects of concurrent in-vehicle tasks, road environment complexity and age on driving performance. Accid. Anal. Prev. **38**(1), 185–191 (2006)
16. Klauer, S., Dingus, T., Neale, V., Sudweeks, J., Ramsey, D.: The Impact of Driver Inattention on Near-Crash/Crash Risk: An Analysis Using the 100-Car Naturalistic Driving Study Data. Virginia Tech Transportation Institute, Blacksburg (2006)
17. D'Orazio, T., Leo, M., Guaragnella, C., Distante, A.: A visual approach for driver inattention detection. Pattern Recogn. **40**(8), 2341–2355 (2007)
18. Fletcher, L., Zelinsky, A.: Driver inattention detection based on eye gaze—road event correlation. Int. J. Robot. Res. **28**(6), 774–801 (2009)
19. Swan, M.: Emerging patient-driven health care models: an examination of health social networks, consumer personalized medicine and quantified self-tracking. Int. J. Environ. Res. Public Health **6**(2), 492–525 (2009)
20. Swan, M.: The quantified self: fundamental disruption in big data science and biological discovery. Big data **1**(2), 85–99 (2013)
21. Stocker, A., Kaiser, C., Fellmann, M.: Quantified vehicles. Bus. Inf. Syst. Eng. **59**(2), 125–130 (2017)
22. CAN DBC File – Convert Data in Real Time. https://www.csselectronics.com/screen/page/dbc-database-can-bus-conversion-wireshark-j1939-example/language/en. Accessed 27 Nov 2018
23. SAE J1939 Standards Collection on the Web: Content. https://www.sae.org/standardsdev/groundvehicle/j1939a.htm. Accessed 27 Nov 2018
24. Pandian, P.S., Mohanavelu, K., Safeer, K.P., Kotresh, T.M., Shakunthala, D.T., Gopal, P., Padaki, V.C.: Smart Vest: wearable multi-parameter remote physiological monitoring system. Med. Eng. Phys. **30**(4), 466–477 (2008)
25. Gellersen, H.W., Schmidt, A., Beigl, M.: Multi-sensor context-awareness in mobile devices and smart artifacts. Mob. Netw. Appl. **7**(5), 341–351 (2002)
26. Ramos, F.B.A., Lorayne, A., Costa, A.A.M., de Sousa, R.R., et al.: Combining smartphone and smartwatch sensor data in activity recognition approaches: an experimental evaluation. In: Proceedings of the 28th International Conference on Software Engineering and Knowledge Engineering, SEKE 2016, Redwood City, pp. 267–272 (2016)
27. Shoaib, M., Bosch, S., Scholten, H., Havinga, P.J., Incel, O.D.: Towards detection of bad habits by fusing smartphone and smartwatch sensors. In: Proceedings of the 2015 IEEE International Conference on Pervasive Computing and Communication Workshops (PerCom Workshops), St. Louis, pp. 591–596 (2015)
28. Vilarinho, T., Farshchian, B., Bajer, D.G., Dahl, O.H., et al.: A combined smartphone and smartwatch fall detection system. In: Proceedings of the 2015 IEEE International Conference on Computer and Information Technology, Liverpool, pp. 1443–1448 (2015)
29. Casilari, E., Santoyo-Ramón, J.A., Cano-García, J.M.: Analysis of a smartphone-based architecture with multiple mobility sensors for fall detection. PLoS ONE **11**(12), e0168069 (2016)

30. Giang, W.C., Shanti, I., Chen, H.Y.W., Zhou, A., Donmez, B.: Smartwatches vs. smartphones: a preliminary report of driver behavior and perceived risk while responding to notifications. In: Proceedings of the 7th International Conference on Automotive User Interfaces and Interactive Vehicular Applications, Nottingham, pp. 154–161 (2015)

31. Liu, L., Karatas, C., Li, H., Tan, S., et al.: Toward detection of unsafe driving with wearables. In: Proceedings of the 2015 workshop on Wearable Systems and Applications, Florence, pp. 27–32 (2015)

32. De Arriba-Pérez, F., Caeiro-Rodríguez, M., Santos-Gago, J.M.: Collection and processing of data from wrist wearable devices in heterogeneous and multiple-user scenarios. Sensors **16** (9), 1538 (2016)

33. Kluyver, T., Ragan-Kelley, B., Pérez, F., Granger, B., et al.: Jupyter notebooks – a publishing format for reproducible computational workflows. In: Proceedings of the 20th International Conference on Electronic Publishing, pp. 87–90. IOS Press, Goettingen (2016)

34. McKinney, W.: Data structures for statistical computing in Python. In: Proceedings of the 9th Python in Science Conference, Austin, pp. 51–56 (2010)

35. Oliphant, T.E.: Guide to NumPy, 2nd edn. CreateSpace Independent Publishing Platform, USA (2015)

36. Christ, M., Braun, N., Neuffer, J., Kempa-Liehr, A.W.: Time series FeatuRe extraction on basis of scalable hypothesis tests. Neurocomputing **307**, 72–77 (2018)

37. Pedregosa, F., Varoquaux, G., Gramfort, A., Michel, V., et al.: Scikit-learn: machine learning in Python. J. Mach. Learn. Res. **12**, 2825–2830 (2011)

38. Kaiser, C., Stocker, A., Festl, A., Lechner, G., Fellmann, M.: A research agenda for vehicle information systems. ECIS (2018)

Exhaustive Simulation and Test Generation Using fUML Activity Diagrams

Junaid Iqbal[(✉)], Adnan Ashraf, Dragos Truscan, and Ivan Porres

Faculty of Science and Engineering,
Åbo Akademi University, Turku, Finland
{jiqbal,aashraf,dtruscan,iporres}@abo.fi

Abstract. The quality of the specifications used for test generation plays an important role in the quality of the generated tests. One approach to improve the quality of the UML specification is the use of executable models specified using the Foundational Subset for Executable UML Models (fUML) and the Action language for fUML (Alf). Due to their precise semantics, fUML and Alf models can be simulated or executed using an fUML execution engine. However, in order to execute the models exhaustively, one must provide input data required to reach and cover all essential elements not only in the graphical fUML models, but also in the textual Alf code associated with the graphical models. In this paper, we present an approach for exhaustive simulation and test generation from fUML activity diagrams containing Alf code. The proposed approach translates fUML activity diagrams and associated Alf code into equivalent Java code and then automatically generates: (1) input data needed to cover or execute all paths in the executable fUML and Alf models and (2) test cases and test oracle (expected output) for testing the actual implementation of the system under development. We also present a tool chain and demonstrate our proposed approach with the help of an example.

Keywords: fUML · Activity diagram · Alf · Simulation ·
Model-Based Testing · Test data generation · Eclipse · Papyrus · Moka

1 Introduction

The Unified Modeling Language (UML) is the de facto standard for modeling software systems. It allows to model the structure and the behavior of the software at a high level of abstraction. UML models can be used for Model-Driven Development (MDD) and Model-Based Testing (MBT). However, UML lacks precise semantics, which hinders the creation of high quality models. To address this problem, the Object Management Group (OMG) has published the Foundational Subset for Executable UML Models (fUML)[1] and Action Language for

---

[1] https://www.omg.org/spec/FUML.

© Springer Nature Switzerland AG 2019
P. Giorgini and B. Weber (Eds.): CAiSE 2019, LNCS 11483, pp. 96–110, 2019.
https://doi.org/10.1007/978-3-030-21290-2_7

fUML (Alf)[2] standards. fUML provides precise semantics and allows to create models that are not only executable, but also provide the basis to generate fully functional code.

fUML includes many basic modeling constructs of UML. To implement the precise behavior of the specified system, fUML Activity Diagram (AD) plays an import role. fUML ADs are similar to UML ADs, but they allow to combine and complement the graphical modeling elements with textual syntax specified using the Alf programming language, which is particularly useful for specifying detailed behaviors in complex activities.

There are several fUML implementations, including the open source fUML Reference Implementation[3] and the Moka[4] simulation engine for Papyrus[5], which is an open source Eclipse-based[6] UML editing tool. fUML ADs containing Alf code can be executed and tested in Moka. Model execution and testing allows to examine and improve the functional correctness and the overall quality of models. However, one must provide input data required to reach and execute all important elements in the graphical fUML and textual Alf models. Manual generation of input data might be suitable for small and simple models, but it is often not the case for real-life complex models. Similarly, test generation for executable models is a difficult and tedious task. The work presented in this paper addresses two research questions:

1. *How to automatically generate input data needed to simulate all execution paths in fUML ADs containing Alf code?*
2. *How to generate test cases with oracle from fUML ADs containing Alf code?*

To address these research questions, we present an approach for exhaustive simulation and test generation from fUML ADs containing Alf code. The proposed approach, called *MATERA2-Alf Tester* (M2-AT), translates fUML ADs and associated Alf code into equivalent Java code and then automatically generates: (1) input data needed to cover or execute all paths in the executable fUML and Alf models and (2) a test suite comprising test cases and test oracle (expected output) for testing the actual implementation of the system under development. The generated test cases in M2-AT satisfy 100% code coverage of the Java code. The generated input data is used for executing the original fUML and Alf models in the Moka simulation engine. The interactive execution in Moka allows to determine model coverage of the executable models. In addition, the generated Java code can be reused later on as a starting point for the actual implementation of the system. We also present our tool chain integrated with Papyrus and demonstrate our proposed approach with the help of an example.

The rest of the paper is organized as follows. Section 2 presents relevant background concepts including UML ADs and fUML. In Sect. 3, we present

---

[2] https://www.omg.org/spec/ALF.
[3] https://github.com/ModelDriven/fUML-Reference-Implementation.
[4] http://git.eclipse.org/c/papyrus/org.eclipse.papyrus-moka.git.
[5] http://www.eclipse.org/papyrus.
[6] http://www.eclipse.org.

our proposed M2-AT approach. Sections 4 and 5 present an example and an experimental evaluation, respectively. In Sect. 6, we review important related works. Finally, Sect. 7 presents our conclusions.

2   Preliminaries

The UML Activity Diagram (AD) is an important diagram for modeling the dynamic aspects of a system[7]. Following the Petri nets semantics, the UML ADs use Petri nets concepts such as places, tokens, and control flows [6, 20]. However, the UML AD specification is semi-formal.

UML ADs can depict activities (sequential and concurrent), the data objects consumed or produced by them, and the execution order of different actions. An action specifies a single step within an AD. Edges are used to control the execution flow of the nodes in an activity. A node does not begin its execution until it receives the control or input on each of its input flows. As a node completes its computation, the execution control transits to the nodes existing on its output flows. The execution of an AD is completed if it reaches a final node and/or returns a data object as a result of the internal computations. Passing parameters to an AD as data objects is possible and used for the exchange of information between two actions.

Executable modeling languages allow one to model the specification of the static and dynamic aspects, that is, the executable behavior of the system [4]. The main advantage of executable modeling languages is to specify a software system based on a limited subset of UML comprising class diagrams, state charts, and ADs. The class diagram outlines conceptual entities in the domain while the state chart for each class models the object life cycle. The AD is used to model the behavior of a state in the state chart by exhibiting the sequence of actions to be performed in a particular state [13]. An executable model executes dynamic actions such as creating class instances, establishing associations, and performing operations on attributes and call state events. Meanwhile, in executable UML, the aforementioned dynamic actions are executed via Alf action language which conforms to the UML Action Semantics.

The fUML standard defines the semantics of the class diagrams and ADs for a dedicated virtual machine (called fUML VM) that can interpret both class and activity diagrams [19]. fUML provides concepts similar to object-oriented programming languages, including implementation of operations either by graphical activities or via the Alf action language. Hence, fUML allows one to capture the detailed executable system behavior at the model level. Modeling system behavior in an executable form enables dynamic analysis to be carried out directly at the model level and paves ways for generating fully-functional code from models.

3   MATERA2-Alf Tester (M2-AT)

Figure 1 presents a high-level overview of our proposed *MATERA2-Alf Tester* (M2-AT) approach. The input to M2-AT consist of executable fUML ADs and

---

[7] https://www.omg.org/spec/UML/2.5/.

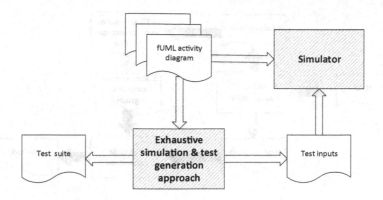

Fig. 1. A high-level overview of the proposed M2-AT approach

their associated Alf code. These executable models can be created in the model-ing phase of the software development process by refining software requirements and use cases, which define the desired system functionality. M2-AT produces: (1) input data needed for the exhaustive simulation of the fUML ADs and asso-ciated Alf code and (2) a test suite comprising test cases and test oracle for testing the actual implementation of the system under development. The gener-ated input data is transformed into an Alf script which allows to use these data in an automated manner.

Internally, the approach is composed of several steps. First, the fUML ADs and their associated Alf code are converted into Java code. Then, we obtain all the inputs of the Java program to achieve 100% coverage of the code. These inputs are used to simulate the AD. Since the Java code and the ADs are behav-iorally equivalent, the input will also satisfy 100% coverage of the AD. During the simulation, one can detect and fix problems in the specifications. In the next step, the Java code is used to generate input data and a test suite.

The proposed approach allows to left-shift testing activities in the software development process. In M2-AT, exhaustive simulation of fUML models helps in validating software specifications and improving their quality at an early stage. Moreover, test cases and test oracle are generated before the actual implemen-tation of the system is developed. In the following text, we present the two main phases of the approach namely, translation and input data and test suite generation phase.

3.1 Translation Phase

In order to translate fUML ADs and their associated Alf code into equivalent Java code, M2-AT performs the following steps: (1) separating structural and behavioral elements, (2) generating a dependency graph, (3) topologically sort-ing the dependency graph to solve node dependencies in the graph, and (4) generating Java code from the sorted dependency graph. Figure 2 presents the translation process.

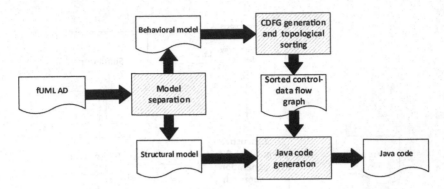

Fig. 2. Translation phase steps

Separating Structural and Behavioral Elements. In the first step, the structural and behavioral elements in the executable fUML and Alf models are separated. The structural elements include static features of the systems, while the behavioral elements have a dynamic nature and they represent different interactions among the structural elements. The structural elements can be directly translated into equivalent Java code. However, for behavioral elements a dependency graph is first constructed.

Dependency Graph. In order to identify data and control flow dependencies in the behavioral elements, M2-AT constructs a *Control-Data flow graph* (CDFG) [1]. A CDFG is a directed acyclic graph, in which a node can either be an operation node or a control node and an edge represents transfer of a value or control from one node to another.

Topological Sorting of Dependency Graph. To solve node dependencies in a CDFG and to decide a starting point for code generation, M2-AT applies topological sorting [11] on CDFGs. The topological sorting algorithm takes a directed acyclic graph G as input and produces a linear ordering of all nodes or vertices in G such that for each edge (v, w), vertex v precedes vertex w in the sorted graph.

Java Code Generation. After resolving node dependencies and the order of activity nodes in CDFGs, M2-AT translates structural model elements and sorted CDFGs into equivalent Java code. The structural elements such as packages, classes, interfaces, and associations are used to generator static structure of the Java code. An example of the structural mapping is shown in Fig. 3. The fUML class object in Fig. 3(a) is directly mapped to a Java class having fUML class properties as Java class attributes and fUML class operations as Java methods [10].

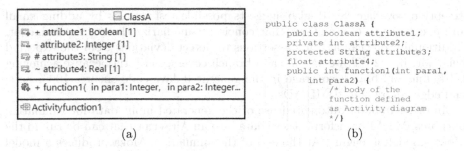

(a)   (b)

Fig. 3. Structural mapping between fUML class and Java code: (a) fUML Class with attributes and operations, and (b) Java code of fUML Class

Table 1. Java representation of fUML activity diagram nodes

fUML element	Java representation	fUML element	Java representation
ValueSpecificationAction → value	value = ValueSpecifcationAction.value;	AddStructuralFeatureValueAction (value, class) → class	class.attribute = value;
class → ReadStructuralFeatureAction → attribute	return = class.attribute;	CreateObjectAction → object	Object object = new Object();
para2, para → CallOperationAction → result, class	result = callOperationAction(*para1*, *para2*);	valueY, valueX → CallBehaviorAction → result	result = CallBehaviorAction(*valueX*, *valueY*);

The fUML ADs are translated into Java code using Java representation for UML activity as presented in the fUML standard. We support a subset of fUML diagram, which excludes asynchronous communication behaviors e.g, *Signal, Messages, and Reception*. Similarly, M2-AT currently does not support parallel execution of fUML nodes. Table 1 shows examples of some fUML AD model elements and their equivalent Java representation. To translate Alf code associated with fUML ADs, we devised a similar mapping that translates each element from Alf code to its equivalent code in Java.

3.2 Input Data and Test Suite Generation Phase

After translating the executable fUML and Alf models to their equivalent Java code, M2-AT uses the generated Java code to produce input data and test suite for exhaustive simulation and testing activities. Figure 4 presents the input data and test suite generation steps. The input data and test suite are generated by using EvoSuite [7]. EvoSuite generates and optimizes a test suite for different coverage criteria such as branch coverage, line coverage, method coverage, and exception coverage [8]. It also suggests possible test oracles by adding small and effective sets of assertions that concisely summarize the current behavior. Additionally, one can also use assertions to detect deviations from the expected behavior. In M2-AT, we use line and branch coverage criteria because achieving 100% line and branch coverage in the generated Java code ensures 100% node and edge coverage in fUML ADs.

In order to allow automated use of the generated input data for simulation purposes, M2-AT transforms these data into an Alf script that can be run in the Moka simulation engine. At the end of the simulation, Moka produces a model coverage report.

Fig. 4. Input data and test suite generation phase

3.3 M2-AT Tool Chain

Figure 5 presents the M2-AT tool chain comprising M2-AT components along with Papyrus[8] (an open source Eclipse-based UML editing tool), Moka[9] (a simulation engine for Papyrus), and EvoSuite [7] (a test generation tool for Java classes). Papyrus provides a graphical user interface for creating and editing UML and fUML models. In our proposed approach, Papyrus is used for creating fUML models including class diagrams and ADs containing Alf code. M2-AT translates these models into equivalent Java code.

EvoSuite is a search-based tool for automatic generation of test suites from Java classes. Given the name of a target class, EvoSuite produces a set of JUnit[10] test cases aimed at maximizing code coverage. M2-AT uses EvoSuite to generate input data and a test suite from Java code and then transforms the input data into an Alf script that can be run in the Moka simulation engine. Moka is an Eclipse plug-in for Papyrus [21]. It provides support for model execution or simulation, debugging, and logging facilities for fUML models. Moka also allows to measure model coverage and produces a model coverage report at the end of the simulation. When the Alf script is run in Moka, the fUML ADs along with their associated Alf code are executed and a coverage report is produced.

---

[8] http://www.eclipse.org/papyrus.
[9] http://git.eclipse.org/c/papyrus/org.eclipse.papyrus-moka.git.
[10] https://junit.org/.

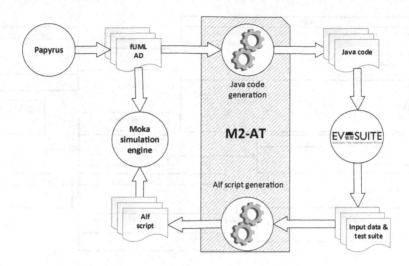

Fig. 5. M2-AT tool chain

3.4   Scalability of the Proposed Approach

The performance and scalability of the proposed approach is based on the time complexities of the M2-AT translation phase (Sect. 3.1) and the input data and test suite generation phase (Sect. 3.2). The M2-AT translation phase uses a linear-time topological sorting algorithm [11] that sorts a CDFG with $\mathcal{O}(|V| + |E|)$ complexity, where V and E represent CDFG vertices and edges, respectively. The overall time complexity of the M2-AT translation phase is also linear. Therefore, M2-AT provides highly scalable code generation. The scalability of the M2-AT input data and test suite generation phase is mainly based on the time complexity of EvoSuite, which uses several search-based test generation strategies to optimize test generation time and code coverage. The time complexity of the tool varies from one testing strategy to another and can not be generalized [17].

4   Example

In order to demonstrate the feasibility of our proposed approach, we use an automatic teller machine (ATM) system example originally presented in [15]. The structure of the ATM system is shown in Fig. 6. The ATM system can be used to perform withdrawal and deposit transactions in a bank account. The withdrawal operation is realized with the *withdraw* and *makeWithdrawal* methods in the *ATM* and *Account* classes, respectively. Similarly, the *ATM.deposit* and *Account.makeDeposit* methods implement the deposit operation. These operations can be modeled with fUML ADs and Alf code.

Figures 7 and 8 present the fUML ADs for the *ATM.withdraw* and *Account.makeWithdrawal* methods, respectively. To perform a withdrawal transaction, the user inserts an ATM card and enters the associated pin and the

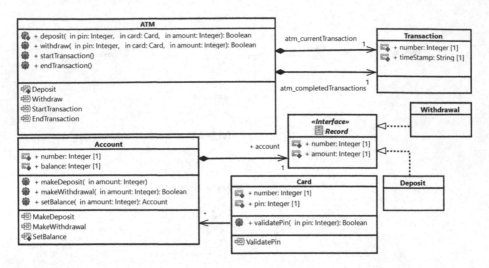

Fig. 6. Class diagram of the ATM system

amount of money to be withdrawn from the associated bank account. It invokes the *withdraw* method in the *ATM* class, which creates a new transaction and sets it as the current transaction (*startTransaction* method in *ATM* class). Next, it validates the entered pin (*validatePin* method in *Card* class). If *validatePin* returns true, the withdrawal transaction is successfully performed and the account balance is updated (*makeWithdrawal* method in *Account* class). Finally, the completed withdrawal transaction is recorded in the system (*endTransaction* method in *ATM* class).

Please note that the actions *startTransaction*, *validatePin*, *makeWithdrawal*, and *endTransaction* are call actions calling the declared operations. The explained functionality of these operations are implemented by dedicated activities. Additionally, the primitive behaviors such as addition and subtraction are encoded in Alf code. In the remainder of this paper, we use fUML ADs of the *ATM.withdraw* and *Account.makeWithdrawal* methods to demonstrate our proposed approach. ADs of all other operations in the ATM system are omitted due to space limitations.

5   Experimental Evaluation

As presented in Sect. 3.1, to translate fUML ADs and their associated Alf code into equivalent Java code, M2-AT first separates the structural and behavioral model elements and then generates a CDFG to identify and resolve data and control flow dependencies in the behavioral elements. Figure 9(a) presents the CDFG of the *ATM.withdraw* AD presented in Fig. 7. It shows that the *readAccount* method must be invoked before *makeWithdrawal*. Similarly, the *readAccount* requires a *Card* object to perform its execution. This data-dependency

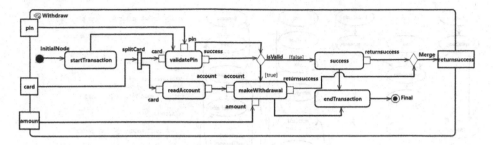

Fig. 7. fUML AD for *ATM.withdraw*

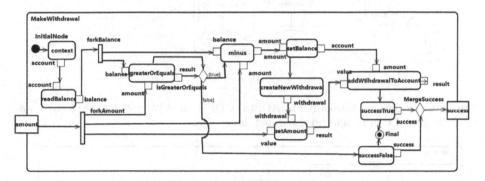

Fig. 8. fUML AD for *Account.makeWithdrawal*

path is independent of the main control-flow path in the AD, which consist of *InitialNode* → *startTransaction* → *validatePin* → *isValid* → *makeWithdrawal*. In such scenarios, manually deciding a starting point for code generation can be challenging and tedious. Figure 9(b) shows that by using topological sorting of the CDFGs, one can easily resolve all node dependencies in CDFGs and determine the starting point for code generation. Finally, Fig. 9(c) shows the Java code generated by traversing the topologically sorted CDFG in Fig. 9(b).

In the next step, M2-AT used the Java code in Fig. 9(c) to generate input data for model simulation and a test suite for testing the system under development. The initial test suite contained 8 test cases. However, 6 of them were not usable in the Moka simulation engine because they contained invalid *null* values. The invalid cases were also redundant for simulation purposes because they did not have any effect on the node and edge coverage of the *ATM.withdraw* AD. The remaining 2 valid test cases provided 100% node and edge coverage. We parsed the valid test cases to extract input data for model simulation and then transformed the extracted data into an Alf script. Listing 1 presents a fragment of the generated Alf script used for simulating the *ATM.withdraw* AD. Moreover, Fig. 10 shows the model coverage results, in which: (1) a solid line represents a covered edge, (2) a dashed line denotes an uncovered edge, and (3) a dotted line represents an unutilized object.

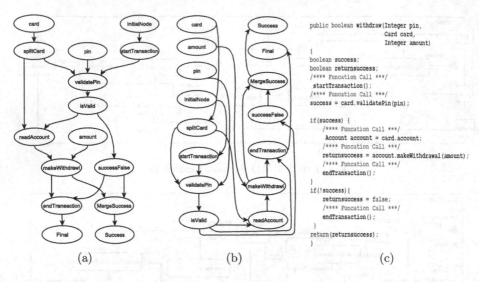

Fig. 9. Code generation from fUML AD: (a) CDFG for *ATM.withdraw* AD, (b) topologically sorted CDFG, and (c) generated Java code.

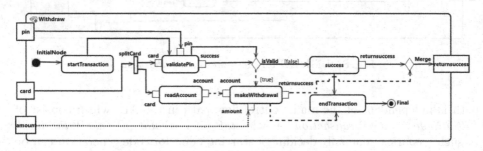

Fig. 10. Model coverage results

Listing 1. A fragment of the generated Alf script

```
namespace structure;
activity ActivityTester15() {
ATM aTM0 = new ATM();
Card card0 = new Card();
card0.pin = 234532;
card0.number=1;
Account account = new Account();
Boolean boolean0 = aTM0.withdraw(card0.number, card0, card0.number);
}
```

6   Related Work

In this section, we discuss the most important related works on verification of
ADs and test and code generation from ADs.

6.1 Verification of ADs

Model verification aims at verifying certain properties in the models under consideration. Model checkers like UPPAAL[11], NuSMV[12], and SPIN[13] verify several properties including deadlock-freeness, reachability, liveness, and safety. Using a model checker for fUML ADs requires that the original or extended ADs are first translated into a graph-based intermediate format and then the intermediate models are translated into the input language of the model checker. For example, for UPPAAL, the intermediate models are translated into UPPAAL Timed Automata (UTA). Daw and Cleaveland [6] translated extended UML ADs into flow graphs and then the flow graphs into the input language of several model checkers including UPPAAL, NuSMV, and SPIN.

Planas et al. [16] proposed a model verification tool called Alf-Verifier that checks the consistency of Alf operations with respect to integrity constraints specified in a class diagram using Object Constraint Language (OCL). For each inconsistency found in the Alf code, the tool returns corrective feedback comprising a set of actions and guards that should be added to the Alf operations to make their behavior consistent with the OCL constraints. Micskei et al. [14] presented a modeling and analysis approach for fUML and Alf. In their approach, the system behavior is first modeled as UML state machines, which are then translated to fUML ADs. In the next step, they manually enrich the fUML ADs with Alf code and then translate them to full Alf code. Finally, the Alf code is translated to UTA to perform model verification. In this approach, Alf is used as an intermediate modeling formalism.

6.2 Test Generation from ADs

Samuel and Mall [18] translated UML ADs to flow dependency graphs (FDGs) to generate dynamic slices for automated test case generation. In their approach, FDGs are created manually, but then an edge marking method is used to generate dynamic slices automatically from FDGs. To generate test data for a dynamic slice, a slice condition is formed by conjoining all conditional predicates on the slice and then function minimization is applied on the slice condition.

Mijatov et al. [15] presented a testing framework for fUML ADs, comprising a test specification language for defining assertions on fUML ADs and a test interpreter for evaluating the defined assertions to produce test verdicts. Tests are run by executing fUML ADs in an extended fUML VM, which allows to capture execution traces.

Arnaud et al. [2] proposed a timed symbolic execution [5] and conformance testing framework for executable models. Their approach checks correctness of fUML ADs with respect to high-level system scenarios modeled as UML

---

[11] http://www.uppaal.org/.
[12] http://nusmv.fbk.eu/.
[13] http://spinroot.com/.

MARTE[14] sequence diagrams. The test data is generated from sequence diagrams by using symbolic execution and constraint solving techniques. The fUML ADs are tested in the standardized fUML VM in Moka. Yu et al. [22] presented a model simulation approach for UML ADs. It uses model-based concolic execution [12], which combines concrete and symbolic execution.

6.3 Code Generation from ADs

Gessenharter and Rauscher [9] presented a code generation approach for UML class diagrams and UML ADs. For the structural part, their approach generates Java code from class diagrams comprising classes, attributes, and associations. For the behavioral part, additional code corresponding to UML activities and actions is added into the Java classes. Their code generator is designed for activities with at most one control node in an activity flow and does not provide support for more realistic, complex flows. Backhauß [3] proposed a code generation approach that translates UML ADs for realtime avionic systems into ANSI-C code. The approach works for control flow edges, but requires further investigations for data flow edges.

In comparison to the aforementioned model verification, test generation, and code generation approaches, the main focus of the proposed M2-AT approach is not on formal verification of ADs. M2-AT provides a light-weight approach that generates input data from fUML ADs containing Alf code and then uses the generated data to exhaustively simulate the original fUML models with the aim of improving their quality. The proposed approach also generates a test suite, which can be used for testing the actual implementation of the system under development. Moreover, it generates and uses topologically sorted CDFGs and Java code as intermediate formalisms. The generated Java code can also be reused for the actual implementation of the system.

7   Conclusion

The Foundational Subset for Executable UML Models (fUML) and the Action language for fUML (Alf) allow to create executable models, which can be simulated using an fUML execution engine. However, to execute such models exhaustively, one must provide input data required to reach and cover all essential elements not only in the graphical fUML models, but also in textual Alf code associated with the graphical models. In this paper, we presented an approach for exhaustive simulation and test generation from fUML ADs containing Alf code. The proposed approach, called *MATERA 2-Alf Tester* (M2-AT), translates fUML ADs and associated Alf code into equivalent Java code and then automatically generates: (1) input data needed to cover or execute all paths in the executable fUML and Alf models and (2) a test suite comprising test cases with oracle (expected output) for testing the actual implementation of the system

---

[14] https://www.omg.org/omgmarte/.

under development. The generated test cases in M2-AT satisfy 100% code coverage of the Java code. The generated input data is used for executing the original fUML and Alf models in the Moka simulation engine. The interactive execution in Moka allows to measure model coverage of the executable models. In addition, the generated Java code can be reused as a starting point for the actual implementation of the system. We also presented our tool chain and demonstrated our proposed approach with the help of an example. Our proposed tool chain integrates M2-AT code generation and Alf script generation components with the state-of-the-art model simulation and test generation tools allowing researchers and practitioners to generate test suites and input data for exhaustive model simulation at early stages of the software development life cycle.

Acknowledgments. This work has received funding from the Electronic Component Systems for European Leadership Joint Undertaking under grant agreement number 737494. This Joint Undertaking receives support from the European Unions Horizon 2020 research and innovation programme and Sweden, France, Spain, Italy, Finland, the Czech Republic.

References

1. Amellal, S., Kaminska, B.: Scheduling of a control data flow graph. In: 1993 IEEE International Symposium on Circuits and Systems, vol. 3, pp. 1666–1669 (1993)
2. Arnaud, M., Bannour, B., Cuccuru, A., Gaston, C., Gerard, S., Lapitre, A.: Timed symbolic testing framework for executable models using high-level scenarios. In: Boulanger, F., Krob, D., Morel, G., Roussel, J.C. (eds.) Complex Systems Design & Management, pp. 269–282. Springer, Cham (2015). https://doi.org/10.1007/978-3-319-11617-4_19
3. Backhauß, S.: Code generation for UML activity diagrams in real-time systems. Master's thesis, Institute for Software Systems, Hamburg University of Technology (2016)
4. Breton, E., Bézivin, J.: Towards an understanding of model executability. In: Proceedings of the International Conference on Formal Ontology in Information Systems - Volume 2001, FOIS 2001, pp. 70–80. ACM (2001)
5. Cadar, C., et al.: Symbolic execution for software testing in practice: preliminary assessment. In: Proceedings of the 33rd International Conference on Software Engineering, ICSE 2011, pp. 1066–1071. ACM (2011)
6. Daw, Z., Cleaveland, R.: Comparing model checkers for timed UML activity diagrams. Sci. Comput. Program. **111**, 277–299 (2015). Special Issue on Automated Verification of Critical Systems (AVoCS 2013)
7. Fraser, G., Arcuri, A.: EvoSuite: automatic test suite generation for object-oriented software. In: Proceedings of the 19th ACM SIGSOFT Symposium and the 13th European Conference on Foundations of Software Engineering, ESEC/FSE 2011, pp. 416–419. ACM (2011)
8. Gay, G.: Generating effective test suites by combining coverage criteria. In: Menzies, T., Petke, J. (eds.) SSBSE 2017. LNCS, vol. 10452, pp. 65–82. Springer, Cham (2017). https://doi.org/10.1007/978-3-319-66299-2_5

9. Gessenharter, D., Rauscher, M.: Code generation for UML 2 activity diagrams. In: France, R.B., Kuester, J.M., Bordbar, B., Paige, R.F. (eds.) ECMFA 2011. LNCS, vol. 6698, pp. 205–220. Springer, Heidelberg (2011). https://doi.org/10.1007/978-3-642-21470-7_15

10. Harrison, W., Barton, C., Raghavachari, M.: Mapping UML designs to Java. SIGPLAN Not. **35**(10), 178–187 (2000)

11. Kahn, A.B.: Topological sorting of large networks. Commun. ACM **5**(11), 558–562 (1962). https://doi.org/10.1145/368996.369025

12. Majumdar, R., Sen, K.: Hybrid concolic testing. In: Proceedings of the 29th International Conference on Software Engineering, pp. 416–426 (2007)

13. Mellor, S.J., Balcer, M.: Executable UML. A Foundation for Model-Driven Architecture. Addison-Wesley, Boston (2002)

14. Micskei, Z., Konnerth, R.A., Horváth, B., Semeráth, O., Vörös, A., Varró, D.: On open source tools for behavioral modeling and analysis with fUML and Alf. In: Bordelau, F., Dingel, J., Gerard, S., Voss, S. (eds.) 1st Workshop on Open Source Software for Model Driven Engineering (2014)

15. Mijatov, S., Mayerhofer, T., Langer, P., Kappel, G.: Testing functional requirements in UML activity diagrams. In: Blanchette, J.C., Kosmatov, N. (eds.) TAP 2015. LNCS, vol. 9154, pp. 173–190. Springer, Cham (2015). https://doi.org/10.1007/978-3-319-21215-9_11

16. Planas, E., Cabot, J., Gómez, C.: Lightweight and static verification of UML executable models. Comput. Lang. Syst. Struct. **46**, 66–90 (2016)

17. Rojas, J.M., Vivanti, M., Arcuri, A., Fraser, G.: A detailed investigation of the effectiveness of whole test suite generation. Empirical Softw. Eng. **22**(2), 852–893 (2017). https://doi.org/10.1007/s10664-015-9424-2

18. Samuel, P., Mall, R.: Slicing-based test case generation from UML activity diagrams. ACM SIGSOFT Softw. Eng. Notes **34**(6), 1–14 (2009)

19. Selic, B.: The less well known UML. In: Bernardo, M., Cortellessa, V., Pierantonio, A. (eds.) SFM 2012. LNCS, vol. 7320, pp. 1–20. Springer, Heidelberg (2012). https://doi.org/10.1007/978-3-642-30982-3_1

20. Störrle, H.: Semantics and verification of data flow in UML 2.0 activities. Electron. Notes Theor. Comput. Sci. **127**(4), 35–52 (2005)

21. Tatibouet, J., Cuccuru, A., Gérard, S., Terrier, F.: Principles for the realization of an open simulation framework based on fUML (WIP). In: Proceedings of the Symposium on Theory of Modeling & Simulation - DEVS Integrative M&S Symposium, DEVS 2013, pp. 4:1–4:6 (2013)

22. Yu, L., Tang, X., Wang, L., Li, X.: Simulating software behavior based on UML activity diagram. In: Proceedings of the 5th Asia-Pacific Symposium on Internetware, Internetware 2013, pp. 31:1–31:4. ACM (2013)

A Block-Free Distributed Ledger for P2P Energy Trading: Case with IOTA?

Joon Park[1], Ruzanna Chitchyan[1(✉)], Anastasia Angelopoulou[2], and Jordan Murkin[1]

[1] University of Bristol, Bristol BS8 1UB, UK
{jp17807,r.chitchyan,jordan.murkin}@bristol.ac.uk
[2] Columbus State University, Columbus, GA, USA
angelopoulou_anastasia@columbusstate.edu

Abstract. Across the world, the organisation and operation of the electricity markets is quickly changing, moving towards decentralised, distributed, renewables-based generation with real-time data exchange-based solutions. In order to support this change, blockchain-based distributed ledgers have been proposed for implementation of peer-to-peer energy trading platform. However, blockchain solutions suffer from scalability problems as well as from delays in transaction confirmation. This paper explores the feasibility of using IOTA's DAG-based block-free distributed ledger for implementation of energy trading platforms. Our agent-based simulation research demonstrates that an IOTA-like DAG-based solution could overcome the constraints that blockchains face in the energy market. However, to be usable for peer-to-peer energy trading, even DAG-based platforms need to consider specificities of energy trading markets (such as structured trading periods and assured confirmation of transactions for every completed period).

Keywords: Blockchain ·
Peer to peer energy trading platform ·
DAG-based distributed ledger · Block-free ledger · IOTA ·
Agent-based simulation

1 Introduction

In the current energy market, utility companies act as intermediaries between householders and the market, purchasing any excess generation that households produce. This is shown in Fig. 1a. In contrast to this, a **peer-to-peer (p2p) energy market** enables any two individuals to directly buy from and sell to each other, without the utility-intermediaries [1], as shown in Fig. 1b. Such households can be both prosumers (i.e., producing and consuming own electricity, as well as selling the excess to others), or only consumers (if they don't own any generation facilities). The key advantages here are in providing avenues for:

This work is supported by the UK EPSRC funding for Refactoring Energy Systems (EP/R007373/1) and Household Supplier Energy Market (EP/P031838/1) projects.

P. Giorgini and B. Weber (Eds.): CAiSE 2019, LNCS 11483, pp. 111–125, 2019.
https://doi.org/10.1007/978-3-030-21290-2_8

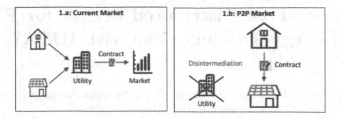

Fig. 1. Energy market disintermediation (from [2])

- Additional income streams to households with small-scale generation - via sale of their excess energy to other peers in the market[1]. Moreover, the price of the locally generated energy is likely to be more competitive than that of the grid supply, as the microgenerators would have lower generation costs, and no intermediation fees paid to utilities[2].
- Additional (non-monetary) value proposition of small-scale generation and energy storage - the microgenerators not only get return on their investment into generation equipment, but also support the energy needs of local communities, contributing to efforts on decarbonisation and energy security.
- Increased control over source/destination of supply - consumers are able to express their preferences on energy purchase: do they wish to buy solar or wind, from the local producer or from the cheapest supplier; do producers wish to donate their excess generation to the local school or sell it to the highest bidder? All these options become viable when peers directly buy and sell from/to each other.

Such an energy system, however, requires **a digital platform** which will remove intermediation from the utilities (so that control is fully retained by the market participants), advertise the sale and purchase orders between the trading parties, undertake matching of these orders, based on the users' preferences, ensure security of the transactions, transparency of the trades, and accountability of the transaction participants.

Recently a number of researchers have advocated use of the blockchain ledgers to create such a p2p energy trading platform. This is due to the functionality that the blockchains enable. They:

- provide full support for **distributed, decentralised data storage and processing**. Thus, there is no need to use and pay for any centralised data storage organisations and facilities.

---

[1] Currently in the UK the excess generation must be sold back to the utility provider at a set rate (the so called "feed in tariff" set by the UK government). However, for many types of household generation this scheme will cease as of March 31 2019.
[2] Please note: each locality remains interconnected with the grid, the energy costs will still include grid connection and maintenance charges. This is because the households wish to be insured against the intermittency of the renewables-based generation, and the grid provides such insurance and balancing services.

- **remove the need for trusting a third party intermediary**, as the blockchain ledgers rely on agreement of the majority of the participants on the state of the chain, not on any external party;
- maintain tampering-resistant and **accountable records** of transactions.

Yet, the unpermissioned blockchains [25] (i.e., ledgers where all participants have unrestricted right to participate in transaction validation and data access - which is critical for an open and trusted p2p trading environment) also suffer from a number of **drawbacks**, such as:

- Scalability limitations when handling a large number of transactions, due to block size constraints and increasingly high transaction processing fees,
- Latency of transaction confirmation (particularly for low-fee transactions) due to low incentives to the miners to include such transactions into blocks.

In this paper, employing the IOTA ledger as a sample, we explore the feasibility of using the Directed Acyclic Graph-based block-free ledgers (abbreviated to DAG-BF) for p2p energy trading. Unlike blockchains, DAG-BF ledgers do not structure transaction records into blocks, and do not rely on specialist miners to process the transactions. Thus, we expect that the above mentioned blockchain limitations would be addressed. Moreover, the DAG-FB ledgers maintain transparent and decentralised transaction records, which fit with the needs of the p2p energy trading domain.

This paper proceeds by outlining the current state of the research and developments of blockchain solutions in the energy sector (Sect. 2). An introduction to the key characteristics of the DAG-BF ledgers is also presented (Sect. 2). Section 3 of the paper presents the p2p energy trading model and outlines the study design. Employing agent-based simulation, this study then sets out to investigate the feasibility of using DAG-BF ledgers for p2p energy trading. The findings of this study suggest that such ledgers could indeed be used for p2p-based energy trading (Sect. 4). A discussion on how the peculiarities of the energy market would align with the present findings is also presented (Sect. 4).

2 Distributed Ledgers in the Energy Sector: A Background Overview

A distributed ledger is a database architecture which facilitates peer-to-peer transactions in a distributed and decentralised way without the need for an intermediary or a centralised authority [25]. The following subsections provide a brief overview of blockchains and DAG-FB distributed ledgers in the energy sector.

2.1 Blockchains in the Energy Sector

Blockchain is a distributed ledger which records transactions, agreements, contracts, and sales [6,25]. Here, a set of transactions is collected into a *block*.

Each block of transactions is then validated by specialised peers on the network, called *miners*. Miners are rewarded for the validation effort with *transaction fees*. The validated transactions are recorded into the *ledger* (or chain).

The idea of using blockchains in the energy sector is becoming increasingly popular, as shown by the growing number of pilots and research projects [7]. It is often considered to be a game-changer for the energy industry [3,25], as it has the potential to enable transition to low-carbon sustainable energy systems [4]; foster innovation in development of IoT platforms [5], digital applications for P2P energy trading and smart grids [7,8].

Various electricity and gas distributors in different countries (such as Vector in New Zealand, Vattenfall in Sweden, EDF Energy and Verv in the UK to name a few) are already testing blockchain platforms for local p2p energy markets [7].

The research community has also explored the use of blockchain ledgers in P2P energy trading. Mengelkamp at el. [9] simulated a local energy market of 100 residential households where consumers and prosumers can trade energy within their community on a private blockchain platform. Murkin et al. [10] proposed a p2p electricity trading platform under a blockchain scheme to automatically buy and sell electricity in each household as microgeneration increases. Pop at el. [11] used a blockchain mechanism to manage the demand response in smart grids. Oh et al. [12] implemented an energy-trading system using MultiChain and demonstrated that transactions worked correctly over blockchain. The use of blockchains for sharing of renewable electricity through smart contracts was studied in NRGX-Change [13] and the Crypto-Trading projects [14].

However, the structure of blockchain-based solutions has recently been criticised due to the difference between mining and other nodes, as well as block size restrictions [9,12]. The miners (i.e., block validator nodes) are motivated by transaction processing fees for including a transaction into the block-to-be-validated. Consequently, the transactions willing to pay higher fees are given priority for inclusion into the blocks, pushing the fees to increase as the number of waiting transactions increases. Transactions with low allocated processing fees may remain in the queue of unconfirmed transactions for a long time, as the block sizes are limited and higher-fee transactions are always chosen first.

2.2 DAG-based Block Free Distributed Ledgers

In a block-free ledger the individual transactions are directly introduced into the ledger (without aggregation into blocks). The newly introduced transactions also cross-verify other transactions, thus carrying out the task which was done by the dedicated miners in the blockchain. Thus, the block-free distributed ledger removes the distinction between miner and participant nodes. Here all nodes of the network must participate in the transaction approval.

In many current block-free ledgers (BF) [15–17] the cross-validating transactions are structured into a Directed Acyclic Graph (DAG). Such a DAG consists of vertices and edges, where each vertex represents a transaction and each directed edge a reference. The referencing edges validate and approve the transactions to which they point. The DAG serves as a truly distributed ledger, which reaches consensus by accumulating information about the state of the network.

It must be noted that a DAG structure can also be used within blockchains, for instance, Ethereum [18] employs a DAG where *blocks of transactions* comprise the vertices. The problems of block size, transaction validation latency, and use of dedicated miners, however, remain. Thus, we focus on DAG-based block-free (DAG-BF) alternative in our study.

Several DAG-BF cryptocurrencies have recently gained recognition, such as RaiBlocks [15], Byteball [16] and IOTA [17]. These differ from each other in the details of implementation and consensus protocols. For instance, IOTA requires that each transaction is referenced by two other transactions for verification, while, for Byteball, references to a number of trusted nodes are necessary. IOTA achieves consensus via the cumulative proof-of-work of confirmed transactions, while, in RaiBlocks, consensus is achieved via balance-weighted vote on conflicting transactions. Yet, they all have a common set of characteristics which are relevant for implementing a distributed ledger-based platform for a p2p energy trading market:

1. transactions are processed *individually*, without block formation, which overcomes the processing latency due to block size constraint;
2. processing is carried out *asynchronously*, "upon arrival" of each new transaction, tackling the delay of block formation;
3. each network participant is also a validator, *without distinction between mining and other nodes*;
4. newly arriving transactions are added as leaf nodes into a DAG, and are to be *confirmed by accumulating references* within the DAG.

In this work IOTA is used as a sample DAG-BF ledger to investigate the feasibility of using such ledgers in p2p energy trading. While the details of the simulation are, by necessity, aligned with the IOTA specifics (e.g., referencing 2 parent nodes, cumulative weight calculation method), the results that relate to the above DAG-BF ledger characteristics could be considered of wider relevance.

2.3 IOTA

IOTA is a DAG-BF distributed ledger; its DAG is called the Tangle [19]. When a new transaction enters the Tangle, it selects two existing transactions to approve, and an edge is created between the new transaction and each of its selected predecessors. The new transaction then approves the two selected transactions (by solving a cryptography puzzle that links it to its approved transactions) and waits for another transaction to approve it (e.g., see Fig. 2).

An unconfirmed transaction in a DAG is called a "tip" (e.g., the transactions A, B, X, C, E in Fig. 2, as these have less than 2 incoming transactions confirming them). The average time that a transaction remains unconfirmed in the Tangle (i.e., *transaction confirmation latency*) and the *number of unconfirmed transactions* (i.e. tips) at any given time are key parameters when considering the use of Tangle as a candidate for a p2p energy trading platform.

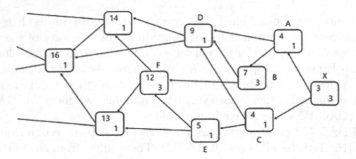

Fig. 2. View of IOTA Tangle (from [19]. Boxes represent transactions, number at the bottom of a box is own weight, number at the top is the cumulative weight.)

Both the *transaction confirmation latency* and the *number of unconfirmed tips at any given time* are heavily dependent on how new transactions select the tips to validate, i.e., on their tip-selection algorithm [19]. Additionally the *number of unconfirmed tips* is also dependent on the rate of arrival of new transactions into the Tangle. Examples of tip selection algorithms are:

- *Uniform random selection*, whereby each new transaction randomly selects two tips to confirm, (without having to traverse the graph);
- *Unweighted random walk*, whereby starting from the genesis node, the walker chooses which transaction to move to with equal probability; and
- *Weighted random walk* where each transaction is assigned a weight (e.g., 1 for D in Fig. 2) and a cumulative weight [19] (e.g., 9 for D in Fig. 2). The weight defines how much work has been invested into each transaction by the issuing node. Cumulative weight is the sum of the weights of the given transaction and all other transactions that directly or indirectly reference the given one. For instance, cumulative weight for D in Fig. 2 is 9, and it comprises the weight of D (1), weights of B(3), A (1), X (3) which indirectly references D through A, and C (1). Under the weighted random walk selection algorithm, a validating node selects a tip based on the tip's weight.

The complexity of the weights is introduced into the tip selection algorithms so as to penalise the so-called lazy (and/or malicious) nodes [19]. Lazy nodes send new transactions and attach them to already approved transactions, instead of approving new ones. Such behaviour saves computation time for the lazy nodes, but results in a larger number of unconfirmed transactions. Neither uniform random selection nor unweighted random walk algorithms can discriminate against the lazy nodes. The weighted random walk, on the other hand, can use the cumulative weights as an indicator for selection of 'honest' transactions. IOTA does this through use of the α parameter that can be set between 0 and 1, biasing the graph traversing towards the selection of higher-weighted transactions [19]. Thus (as shown in [19]) if y approves x then the transition probability P_{xy} is:

$$P_{xy} = \exp\left(-\alpha(H_x - H_y)\right) / \sum_{z:z \to x} \exp\left(-\alpha(H_x - H_z)\right) \tag{1}$$

where H_x and H_y are the cumulative weights of nodes x and y respectively. If z approves x, then $z \to x$ and $\alpha > 0$ needs to be chosen. When α is set to 0 the algorithm reverts to unweighted random walk, as then there is no bias towards choosing the path through transactions with a higher cumulative weight. As α approaches 1, the walker will always choose only the path through the transaction with the highest cumulative weight, continuously increasing the weight of transactions in that path (by adding new indirect references).

3   Modelling a Block-Free P2P Energy Trading Platform

In this exploratory study we wish to investigate whether p2p energy trading would be feasible on a DAG-BF ledger with respect to transaction confirmation latency and large volume of transactions to be processed. As noted before, we opt to use IOTA as the sample DAG-BF ledger, as it is one of the most widely publicised such ledgers. Yet IOTA's current implementation is also strongly criticised [26–28]. For instance, presently IOTA relies on a centralised coordinator[3] node, which renders it a centrally controlled network [28] (though there are claims that the coordinator will be removed imminently [29]). It could also suffer from replay vulnerability [27].

In order to abstract from the specifics of the current implementation, while retaining the key characteristics of IOTA's DAG-FB ledger, we turn to an agent-based simulation (instead of on-chain implementation), assuming that the coordinator-free version of the ledger is in place. Agent-based (AB) modelling is particularly suitable for the present research as it allows us to focus on the defining properties of DAG-BF.

Thus, we set the characteristics and behavioural rules for each individual undertaking the transactions (i.e., agent) in the simulation, then observe the collective impact of these behaviours and interactions among agents [21,22] and their impact on the ledger. To build an AB model, we must detail its constituent parts, i.e.:

- **Agents**, who are defined as heterogeneous entities with different characteristics and individual behaviours. They are situated in an environment and perform actions.
- **Interactions** between agents change the agents' state;
- **Environment** is the space in which agents are located (e.g., longitude and latitude), and the rules under which they operate (e.g., the excess energy that has been generated is to be sold).

3.1   Study Design

To develop a P2P energy trading platform, we must first consider the characteristics of the energy market (i.e., the environment within which the actors operate), including trade organisation, and the properties of traders.

---

[3] Note: in case of the energy sector such a coordinator may be acceptable, if run by the energy regulator providing governance to the system.

Market Structure: Trade Periods. On the current energy market, energy is bought and sold per 30 min. intervals. This structure is dictated by the nature of the market itself, as the amounts of electricity generation and consumption (and so its prices) vary due to:

- *external environmental conditions* (especially for renewables-based generation) as, for instance, PV panels generate more in the summer than in the winter and consumers use more electricity in cold weather, as well as
- *time of day*, e.g., PV panels have highest output around midday; while most individuals wake up and have breakfast between 6.30 AM and 9 AM on weekdays, (causing increased demand in the morning), yet
- the electricity *grid must be balanced for every time period*, which requires for the peak-time energy use (when grid is under stress to meet the high consumption requirements) to be more expensive than off-peak.

Thus, we too keep to the period-based trading, where the trading is carried out every t period (where t can be 30 min, or less). During each current period the sellers and buyers publish their desired sell/buy request for the next period. At the end of the current period the buy and sell requests are matched and recorded as transactions into the ledger. A new period then begins. For simplicity we do not consider cases where advertised sell/buy requests are not satisfied and further settlement is required, as this does not affect the ledger's scalability or latency, but depends on the trading and settlement algorithm used [23]. Similarly, though the matching algorithm allows for partial trading, where one individual buys/sells to many in a given trading period, to fill his/her order, these are simply extra transactions to the ledger, and are not further discussed. The key result of such trade structuring decision is that all the sell/buy requests are processed together, and *their results are released for committing into the ledger at the same time.*

Households and Interactions. We model individual households as *automated software buyer or seller agents* that express their trading preferences, and can generate (as producers) or use (as consumers) energy. The households periodically (e.g., every 30 min) advertise the amount of generation (sell requests) and use (buy requests) they provide/require. A p2p trading algorithm then calculates a stable match for each of the buyer-seller pair of agents, while taking into account their individual preferences (e.g., as much as possible, buy only solar energy, or sell to local buyers). The national grid acts as the default seller/buyer where the p2p market under/over produces. Once the stable match is found (i.e., there is no buyer/seller pair that would prefer to be matched to a different partner), transactions are sent to the distributed ledger by the buyers. The attributes of the agents are illustrated in Table 1.

A seller agent's properties are the amount of electricity to sell, the location, the generation type, the distance preference (how far the buyer can be located), and the minimum price at which the seller is willing to sell. A buyer agent's

Table 1. Agent structure.

Properties	Definition
Agent ID	Unique agent identifier
Agent location	Agent location in terms of latitude and longitude
Amount of electricity	Amount of electricity to buy or sell for every trading period
Generation type	Generation type (i.e., solar PV, wind, anaerobic digestion, hydro, and micro CHP)
Distance preference	Distance preference for the trade
Price preference	Minimum price (willing to sell) for seller agent or maximum price (willing to buy) for buyer agent

properties are the amount of electricity to buy, his/her location, distance preferences, the maximum price at which the buyer is willing to buy, and the preferred generation-type to purchase (as a priority list, ranked from 1 to 5).

The agents' attributes are used to express agent preferences and to influence with which other agents a given agent will trade. Thus, the distance preferences of each seller/buyer are used to determine which potential trading partners are located within his/her preferred distance. If a party is located outside the distance preference, then the matching score to this party will be lowered. The seller's minimum price at which (s)he is willing to sell is the minimum sales price per 1 kWh of electricity, and the buyer's maximum price at which (s)he is willing to buy should be greater than the seller's minimum sales price in order for these two agents to enter into a transaction.

The p2p electricity trading process starts with sellers and buyers publishing their desired sell/buy requests. Then, the trading algorithm[4] scores each buyer-seller combination, and ranks the matches based on their scores. The highest scoring pairs are matched. The buyer then creates a transaction, which is recorded into the ledger. The transaction is initiated by the buyer, as it is fully dependent on his/her willingness to pay. Each transaction contains the transaction ID, the buyer's ID, the seller's ID, the amount of electricity exchanged, the unit price, and the timestamp. This information about each transaction is saved in a file and is used to check the shape of the transaction graph using the GraphViz [24] visualisation tool. The AB model was developed with the AnyLogic [20] simulation tool[5].

---

[4] The details of the matching algorithm are not the focus of this study. The base algorithm is given in [23], though this study uses an extended version.

[5] This model can be accessed via: https://cloud.anylogic.com/model/966f6846-62e0-460e-bf69-2a1b00317128?mode=SETTINGS from the Anylogic Cloud.

Model Setup. Before the model can be executed, it needs to be set up. The accounts are randomly generated for the simulation. We assume that buyers and seller of the p2p electricity market area are located in an arbitrary area in the UK, with latitude randomly chosen between 50.956870 and 52.438562, and longitude between -2.386779 and 0.292914. Sellers' generation types are uniformly distributed, and sellers generate from 5 to 10 kWh every trading period. Five types of generation are used: solar, wind, hydro, anaerobic digestion, and micro CHP. Distance preference is set for all accounts between 5–10 km. For buyers, the maximum price to buy is set randomly between 14 p and 16 p per kWh, and the demand is set randomly between 1 kWh and 6 kWh. Buyers' generation-type preferences are set randomly. During model testing, a percentage of these accounts were assigned to be sellers. Simulations were run for 16 replications for each model, where the percentage of sellers in the market ranged from 5% to 20% in 5% increments, and the number of participants ranged from 500 to 3000 in increments of 500.

4   Findings and Discussion

After setting the number of sellers and buyers that participate in the electricity trading market, as well as their location, sales volume, and demand quantity, we can observe the changes in the metrics and monitor the transactions that occur among them. The metrics of this feasibility study are the transaction confirmation latency and the number of unconfirmed tips per trading period.

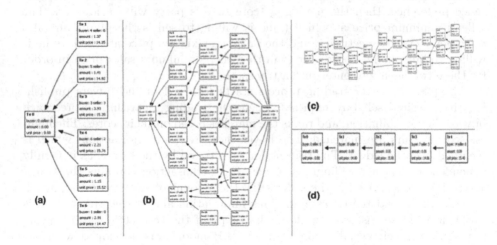

Fig. 3. Shapes of Tangle under various transaction release rates (the last nodes in parts b and c are termination nodes, see Sect. 4.1).

4.1 Impact of Market Structure

Trade Periods: As previously discussed, the nature of the energy market requires that trades are structured into fixed time intervals[6]. As the trades are agreed at the end of the trading period, the buyers' agents will simultaneously[7] send the transactions into the ledger. Simultaneous arrival of large groups of transactions into the ledger could result in several transactions simultaneously selecting and confirming the same tip with some other tips remaining unconfirmed for a longer time [19]. For instance, as shown in Fig. 3a, all transactions released in the first group confirm solely the genesis node, while they themselves remain unconfirmed until transactions from the next group are released.

Figure 3 illustrates the shape of the block-free distributed ledger under various (uniformly distributed) delay ranges in sending transactions (Fig. 3(b) delay of 0.1 s to 0.3 s, (c) from 0.7 s to 0.9 s, (d) from 1.3 s to 1.5 s.)[8]. As the agents' delay in setting out transactions increases, the shape of the Tangle of the block-free distributed ledger converges to the shape of a chain.

Termination Nodes: The interval-based market structure in energy trading (e.g., per 30 min) implies that transactions which were not confirmed at the end of one trading period cannot be settled until the next trading period releases transactions. Yet, energy generation and consumption cannot be postponed until the next period during which transactions would be confirmed. To address this concern, we suggest the need for a termination node that would confirm all unconfirmed transactions at the end of each trading period. The work for creation of a termination node could be allocated to all network participants, with one or two participants randomly selected for such node generation at the end of each trading period. Two nodes will ensure that each unconfirmed transaction has two validators (as required per Iota's protocol). The termination nodes can then serve as the starting nodes for the DAG of the next set of trade transactions, as illustrated in Fig. 4. This structure both ensures the transactions are confirmed for each trading period and the DAG nodes are clearly allocated to each trading period. IOTA's current solution whereby all nodes maintain statistics on new transactions received from the neighbours [19] could still be sufficient in excluding transactions from "too lazy" nodes, and prevent a behaviour where nodes expect that the termination node "will confirm all transaction anyhow".

---

[6] While this study considers buy/sell requests published at period (t) for period (t+1), further periods (e.g., t+10, as different markets) can also be studied with this model.

[7] Specific implementations of the trading algorithms could vary the transaction release rate. For instance, when the ranked order algorithm is applied in trade matching, the matching is carried out in several cycles, and trades are agreed and released into the ledger in groups [23]. In this case, the following discussion relates to a single group release.

[8] As we focus on the shape of the ledger not transaction content, figure readability is not strictly necessary. Yet, if need be, the figures can be accessed via: https://jmp.sh/WNkIbZp.

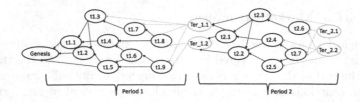

Fig. 4. Connecting two Directed Acyclic Graphs

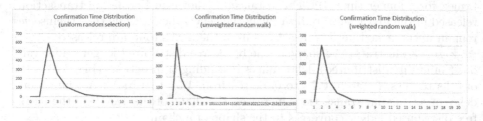

Fig. 5. Confirmation time distribution using (a) uniform random selection (b) unweighted random walk (c) weighted random walk.

4.2 Impact of Tip Selection Algorithm

As previously discussed, the transaction confirmation time and the number of unconfirmed tips present in the ledger at any given time are dependant on the tip selection algorithm [19].

To analyse the impact of the tip selection algorithms, the market in the AB model was simulated for 2,500 buyers and 375 sellers, with an average of 1,000 transactions generated and recorded into the block-free distributed ledger during the trading period. The delay of releasing the transactions into the ledger is uniformly distributed between 0.3 to 0.9 s.

Transaction Confirmation Time: The transaction confirmation time is defined as the difference between the time when a transaction is connected to the block-free distributed ledger and the time of its first transmission into the network.

The transaction confirmation times aggregated from the above discussed simulation are depicted in Fig. 5 when (a) uniform random selection, (b) unweighted random walk, and (c) weighted random walk are used.

While all 3 tip selection algorithms confirm between 500 and 600 transactions within 2 s, the average confirmation time varies from 2.26 for uniform random walk to 2.63 for unweighted and 7.91 s for weighted random walk. The length of the last case is due to delays in confirming some outlier transactions.

Unconfirmed Transactions (Tips): The number of unconfirmed transactions recorded from the above noted simulation are depicted in Fig. 6 with: (a) uniform random selection, (b) unweighted random walk, and (c) weighted random walk.

Fig. 6. Number of unconfirmed tips under (a) uniform random selection, (b) unweighted random walk, and (c) weighted random walk.

We observe that both uniform random selection and unweighted random walk maintain stable ranges of unconfirmed tips (2 to 14 for random selection and 2 to 16 for unweighted random walk). However, under the weighted random walk, the number of unconfirmed tips could become divergent. Here the range stability depends on the alpha value (which was discussed in Sect. 2.2 Eq. (1).

To analyse this, we recorded the number of unconfirmed transactions per unit time for the following α values: 0.02, 0.05, 0.1, 0.2 and 0.5 (see Fig. 6c). We noticed that as the value of alpha increases, the number of unconfirmed transactions shows an upwards trend, rather than being stably maintained. Thus, as alpha approaches 1, predominantly the transactions with larger cumulative weight are selected for confirmation, while other tips remain unconfirmed (see Fig. 6c). On the other hand, when alpha approaches zero, the number of unconfirmed tips becomes stabilised.

Thus, though the weighted random walk tip selection algorithm can penalise lazy and malicious behaviour by isolating lazy nodes, our experiment suggests that it could also lead to increased transaction confirmation delay. As discussed in Sect. 2.3, as α increases, the algorithm will converge to a single traversal path. Thus, any transactions that had chosen to confirm any tips outside of this "main path" will forever remain unconfirmed. Consequently, should α be wrongly chosen, the ledger will be destabilised.

5   Conclusions

Using the IOTA as an example, this paper explores the feasibility of utilising (IOTA-like) DAG-based block-free distributed ledgers for implementation of peer-to-peer energy trading platforms. This effort is motivated by the promise of the DAG-BF ledgers to remove the need for specialist miners/validators and their respective fees, threat of over-centralisation due to dominance of large mining pools, and the risk of long transaction confirmation delays for some (low value) transactions.

Our agent-based simulation experiments for a p2p energy market suggest that the functioning of this simulated market can indeed be successfully supported by a IOTA and similar DAG-FB ledgers. However, we also noted the need to carefully design the shape of the block-free ledger:

1. The peculiarity of the p2p energy market structure (i.e., the need to trade over discrete time periods, where all trade transactions agreed for one period could

potentially be released simultaneously) necessitates a uniformly randomised process of releasing transactions into the ledger for each trading period.

2. As energy generation and consumption have to be continuously balanced in the grid, all trades for a given period should be confirmed and completed before the start of the next period. We have suggested to use a dedicated kind of nodes, (so called termination nodes) that guarantee confirmation of all 'honest' transactions at the end of each trading period. They help to both finalise sales for each period and to clearly structure records per each trading period. We also note that the termination nodes provide an ideal location for the so-called ledger maintenance tasks (such as pruning and confirmation) [19]. This, however, also leaves an open question as to if and how exactly should the termination nodes avoid confirmation of transactions from lazy nodes. For instance, one could explore the impact of choosing the lazy nodes as the main workers in the generation of the termination nodes, thus forcing them into active participation.

3. There is no single "best" tip selection algorithm, as some of the most frequently used solutions (i.e., uniform random walk and unweighted random walk) do not safeguard against potential lazy and malicious behaviour of some nodes at the expense of the others. The choice of the weighted random walk, on the other hand, could lead to an increased average transaction confirmation delay (due to some outlier tips and/or inappropriately set α).

Finally, we must also note that, though this simulation study suggests that IOTA (and similar DAG-FB ledgers) appear(s) to be feasible for implementation of p2p energy trading platforms, this conclusion cannot be fully verified without an actual implementation of such a platform. Such an implementation is our immediate future work.

References

1. Zhang, C., Wu, J., Long, C., Cheng, M.: Review of existing peer-to-peer energy trading projects. Energy Procedia **105**, 2563–2568 (2017)
2. Murkin, J., Chitchyan, R., Ferguson, D.: Towards peer-to-peer electricity trading in the UK (2018). https://reedexpo.app.box.com/s/plwhcfaqp6pnhxc8mcjznh7jtkevg9h1/file/292636529562. Presented at All Energy
3. Burger, C., Kuhlmann, A., Richard, P., Weinmann, J.: Blockchain in the energy transition a survey among decision makers in the German energy industry (2016)
4. Mattila, J., et al.: Industrial blockchain platforms: an exercise in use case development in the energy industry (2016). https://www.etla.fi/julkaisut/industrial-blockchain-platforms-an-exercise-in-use-case-development-in-the-energy-industry/
5. Stojkoska, B.L.R., Trivodaliev, K.V.: A review of Internet of Things for smart home: challenges and solutions. J. Clean Prod. **140**, 1454–64 (2017)
6. Christidis, K., Devetsikiotis, M.: Blockchains and smart contracts for the IoTs. IEEE Access **4**, 2292–2303 (2016)
7. Chitchyan, R., Murkin, J.: Review of blockchain technology and its expectations: case of the energy sector. arXiv preprint arXiv:1803.03567 (2018)

8. Andoni, M., et al.: Blockchain technology in the energy sector: a systematic review of challenges and opportunities. Renew. Sustain. Energy Rev. **100**, 143–174 (2019)

9. Mengelkamp, E., et al.: A blockchain-based smart grid: towards sustainable local energy markets. Comput. Sci.-Res. Dev. **33**, 207–214 (2018)

10. Murkin, J., Chitchyan, R., Byrne, A.: Enabling peer-to peer electricity trading. In: 4th International Conference on ICT for Sustainability, pp. 234–235 (2016)

11. Pop, C., et al.: Blockchain based decentralized management of demand response programs in smart energy grids. Sensors **18**(1), 162 (2018)

12. Oh, S.-C., et al.: Implementation of blockchain-based energy trading system. Asia Pac. J. Innov. Entrepreneurship **11**(3), 322–334 (2017)

13. Mihaylov, M., et al.: NRG-X-change-a novel mechanism for trading of renewable energy in smart grids. In: Smartgreens, pp. 101–106 (2014)

14. Mannaro, K., Pinna, A., Marchesi, M.: Crypto-trading: blockchain-oriented energy market. In: AEIT International Annual Conference, pp. 1–5. IEEE (2017)

15. LeMahieu, C.: RaiBlocks: a feeless distributed cryptocurrency network (2017). https://raiblocks.net/media/RaiBlocks_Whitepaper_English.pdf

16. Churyumov, A.: Byteball: a decentralized system for storage and transfer of value (2015). https://byteball.org/Byteball.pdf

17. IOTA: A cryptocurrency for the Internet of Things. www.iota.org

18. Buterin, V.: Ethereum white paper. GitHub repository, pp. 22–23 (2013)

19. Popov, S.: The tangle (2017). https://iota.org/IOTA_Whitepaper.pdf

20. XJ Technologies Company Ltd. http://www.anylogic.com/

21. Macal, C.M., North, M.J.: Tutorial on agent-based modelling and simulation. J. Simul. **4**(3), 151–162 (2010)

22. Macal, C.M., North, M.J.: Agent-based modeling and simulation: ABMS examples. In: Proceedings of 40th Conference on Winter Simulation, pp. 101–112 (2008)

23. Murkin, J., Chitchyan, R., Ferguson, D.: Goal-based automation of peer-to-peer electricity trading. In: Otjacques, B., Hitzelberger, P., Naumann, S., Wohlgemuth, V. (eds.) From Science to Society. PI, pp. 139–151. Springer, Cham (2018). https://doi.org/10.1007/978-3-319-65687-8_13

24. Graphviz: Graphviz-Graph Visualization Software. https://www.graphviz.org

25. UK Government Office for Science, Distributed Ledger Technology: Beyond Block Chain (2016). https://www.gov.uk/government/news/distributed-ledger-technology-beyond-block-chain

26. Ito, J.: Our response to "a cryptocurrency without a blockchain has been built to outperform bitcoin". https://www.media.mit.edu/posts/iota-response/. Accessed 15 Mar 2018

27. Siim, J.: DAG-Based Distributed Ledgers (2018)

28. Wall, E.: IOTA is centralized. https://medium.com/@ercwl/iota-is-centralized-6289246e7b4d. Accessed 15 Mar 2018

29. IOTA Foundation: Coordinator. https://blog.iota.org/coordinator-part-1-the-path-to-coordicide-ee4148a8db08. Accessed 15 Mar 2018

Profile Reconciliation Through Dynamic Activities Across Social Networks

Suela Isaj[1,2(✉)], Nacéra Bennacer Seghouani[1], and Gianluca Quercini[1]

[1] Laboratoire de Recherche en Informatique LRI, 91190 Gif-sur-Yvette, France
{nacera.bennacer,gianluca.quercini}@lri.fr
[2] Aalborg University, 9220 Aalborg, Denmark
suela@cs.aau.dk

Abstract. Since today's online social media serve diverse purposes such as social and professional networking, photo and blog sharing, it is not uncommon for people to have multiple profiles across different social networks. Finding or reconciling these profiles would allow the creation of a holistic view of different facets of a person's life that can be used by recommender systems, human resource management, marketing activities and also raise awareness about the potential threats to one person's privacy. In this paper, we propose a new approach for reconciling profiles based on their temporal activity (i.e., timestamped posts) shared across similar-scope social networks. The timestamped posts are compared by considering different dynamic attributes originating from what the user shares (geographical data, text, tags, and photos) and static attributes (username and real name). Our evaluation on Flickr and Twitter social networks datasets shows that the temporal activity is a good predictor of two profiles referring or not to the same user.

Keywords: Social networks · Reconciliation · Entity resolution

1 Introduction

Social media popularity keeps growing. According to Pew Research Center, 69% of U.S adults use social media as of the end of 2016, as opposed to 5% at the beginning of 2005 (http://www.pewinternet.org/fact-sheet/social-media/). Social networks are information systems since their information can be further processed and analyzed in order to make decisions such as choosing an influential user, propagating information, analyzing trends, etc. Since today's online social media platforms serve diverse purposes, from social (e.g., Facebook, Twitter) and professional networking (e.g, Linkedin) to photo sharing (e.g., Flickr) and blogging (e.g., Livejournal), it comes as no surprise that 56% of U.S. adults use many of them at the same time [7]. As a result, the personal data of a social media users are scattered across different platforms, each holding a *profile* of the user that reflects a particular facet (e.g., social, professional) of her life.

P. Giorgini and B. Weber (Eds.): CAiSE 2019, LNCS 11483, pp. 126–141, 2019.
https://doi.org/10.1007/978-3-030-21290-2_9

The different profiles need to be linked in order to obtain a global profile of a user, which is key to certain applications, such as recommender systems, advertisement companies, investigations, police surveillance, and cross-network dynamics analysis [25]. The benefit of using a reconciliation algorithm is of having holistic and more prosperous information about a user, which can be input to information systems that make decisions based on social network profiles. The focus of this work is on the automatic identification of the profiles of a user across social networks, a process known as *user identity linkage* or *profile reconciliation*. The reconciliation is based on the hypothesis that two different profiles of the same user have some overlapping information, be it the values of some *attributes* (e.g., username, name, current location) or the content of the posts, essentially text and photos published in the profiles. An individual is likely to use a similar alias (full name or even a nickname) across social networks. Moreover, at a given place and time, he might share similar content across social networks. These occurrences alone sometimes are a solid ground to unveil the identity of an individual. In this paper, we propose a novel temporal approach that compares the activities (i.e., posts) that occur in two profiles; the approach organizes the activity in time intervals and compares activity across social networks that happens close in time. In contrast to the previous research, we are able to prove that an individual is highly likely to express similar behavior across similar-scope social networks and these traces are sufficient to reveal the link between the profiles.

Here are our main contributions. (i) We propose an approach that considers the activity across social networks (i.e., the user's posts) and reconciles profiles Since the approach only considers the activity, it can also be applied when the data is anonymized. Additionally, the approach can also use profile attributes (e.g., the username) whenever they are available. (ii) We propose a parallel implementation of the approach to improve its efficiency. Additionally, we significantly reduce the pairwise comparisons of the posts by indexing the time intervals and using a heuristic that decides whether two posts originate from the same user based on the geographical information attached to the posts. (iii) We evaluate our approach on real datasets obtained from Twitter and Flickr, with and without using the pruning heuristic, using only activity attributes and using both activity and profile attributes. The results show a higher precision when only the activity attributes are used and a higher recall when adding the profile attributes. The paper is organized as follows. A review of the scientific literature is presented in Sect. 2; we formally define the problem and introduce the terminology used throughout the paper in Sect. 3. We describe thoroughly our approach, the features that we use, and the parallel implementation in Sect. 4. The evaluation and the comparison with state-of-art approaches are described in Sect. 5, followed by conclusions in Sect. 6.

2   Related Work

The approaches that have been proposed to reconcile profiles across social networks are based on supervised, semi-supervised and unsupervised methods and use different types of features, such as the profile attributes [4,16,18,22,23, 27], the topology of the networks [12,14,17,19], the content generated by the users [5,15,24] or a combination of these [1,2,6,10,11,20,28,29].

Attributes-Based Approaches. Their rationale is that two profiles are likely to refer to the same user if the values of some (or all) of their attributes (e.g., nickname, name, birth date) are equal or similar. Most of the approaches that fall into this category calculate a syntactic similarity between the values of the attributes [4,16], especially the nickname [22,23,27]; others measured the similarity between profile photos [16] or used face recognition techniques [18]. The main limitation of all these approaches is that they cannot reconcile profiles when the values of the attributes are missing or dissimilar. Our approach overcomes this limitation by also exploiting the activity of the users.

Topology-Based Approaches. People tend to connect to the same subgroup of individuals when they have profiles in different social networks [6]. Topology-based approaches reconcile profiles by calculating the connections that they share across social networks [12,19] or by using embedding methods to learn latent network features [14,17]. These approaches have the merit to reconcile profiles that are completely anonymous. However, the reconciliation fails when the network topology cannot be fully extracted, which is the case of many social networks, such as Facebook and LinkedIn.

Content-Based Approaches. Some approaches compute the similarity of two profiles by comparing the spatial signatures [5] and the spatio-temporal trajectories [24] aggregated from the user's posts. Two profiles that refer to the same user are likely to show near-simultaneous activity and have similar spatial *histograms*. Although our approach is close in spirit, it is different in three key aspects: (i) it compares pairwise posts close in time by computing their similarity, thus not limiting only to counting the number of near-simultaneous posts; (ii) it uses the location of the posts, in combination with time, to determine whether two posts are authored by the same user, instead of condensing all locations in a histogram—profiles with similar location histograms might still not refer to the same person; (iii) it uses the profile attributes whenever available, instead of ignoring them, that provide important clues as to the reconciliation process.

Hybrid Approaches. They use profile attributes in combination with the network topology [1,2,6,20,28,29], and/or user-generated content [10,11]. Only the approach proposed by Kong et al. uses the location and the temporal distributions of the posts of two profiles [11]; unlike our approach, location and temporal features are used independently and not to compare posts pairwise.

3   Preliminaries and Problem Definition

A social media *profile* typically consists of *static attributes* (e.g., name and username), that are never or rarely changed, and *posts*, which form the *activity* of the user. Each post is characterized by attributes such as the content (either text, or photo, or both), the *tags*, and the geographic location; we call them *dynamic attributes* because they are associated with the activity of the user, which, by definition, is constantly evolving in time.

Let $\mathcal{A}$ and $\mathcal{D}$ be the set of static and dynamic attributes respectively. A user profile $p < \{a_i\}, \{e_t\} >$ consists of a set $\{a_i\}$ of values of static attributes defined in $\mathcal{A}$ and a set $\{e_t\}$ of posts that occurred at different times t. Each post $e_t < \{d_i\} >$ is defined by the set of values d_i of dynamic attributes defined in $\mathcal{D}$. The problem of reconciling the profiles referring to the same individual across different social networks is formalized as follows. The **input** is a set $\mathcal{P} = \bigcup_{i=1,...,N} \mathcal{P}^i$ of user profiles across N social networks, with $\mathcal{P}^i$ being the set of user profiles belonging to the i-th social network. The **output** is a set of triples $\{< p^i, p^j, \rho >\}$, where p^i and p^j are two profiles from the i-th and j-th social network respectively and ρ is a boolean value indicating whether the profiles p^i and p^j are owned by the same individual (i.e., they are *reconciled*) or not.

The rationale of the approach that we propose in this paper is that *two profiles are likely to be owned by the same individual if they contain similar posts shared in a short time frame*. For instance, the fact that the individual A shares a photo of the Eiffel Tower on her profile p^i at 22:12:14 on 2017-01-09 and the same photo is found on the profile p^j only four minutes later is a strong indication that p^i and p^j are both owned by A. The similarity of the static attributes (e.g., the username) associated to p^i and p^j can also be used as a supporting evidence for the reconciliation of p^i and p^j.

4   Profile Reconciliation

The comparison of the values of static attributes (if present) sometimes suffices to reconcile profiles. Gross and Acquisti showed that 89% of the names in Facebook appear to be real [8]. Thus, in this work, we assume reliable profile attributes. However, a profile cannot be readily identified only by the static attributes. Given two profiles p^i and p^j that belong to two different social network platforms i and j, our approach computes the similarity (a value between 0 and 1) of the dynamic attributes of all the pairs of posts $(e_t, e_{t'})$ in p^i and p^j respectively that occur in the same time interval. The similarity (value between 0 and 1) of the static attributes, when available, is computed (Sect. 4.1). In order to compare the posts, we propose an algorithm called *Bubble Matching* or BM (Sect. 4.2). that compares pairwise the posts that happened in a time interval Δt and computes the similarity of their attributes. The algorithm takes in a set of posts $\{e_t\}$ and returns a set $R = \{< e_t^i, e_{t'}^j, S >\}$ of compared posts and a vector S containing the similarity scores of their attributes.

To avoid useless comparisons, we propose a pruning technique that discards posts that are unlikely to represent the same activity because their spatial distance is too large with respect to Δt. Suppose that two posts e_t^1 and $e_{t'}^2$ contain a photo of the Eiffel Tower, but one has been uploaded from China and the other from France. Although the two posts have a similar content, they are unlikely to be posted by the same user, because that same user would have needed to travel from China to France in 20 min. The output of BM is the input of a logistic regression (Sect. 4) that defines the contribution of each of the attributes in determining whether two profiles are owned by the same person or not.

4.1 Similarities of Attributes

Dynamic Attributes. Geographic data, photo, text and tags.

Geographic data, or *geo-data*, is metadata encapsulated in a post that indicates the position in space of the individual when s/he shares the post. The position might be a precise point, identified by its latitude and longitude, or an area, expressed in the form of a polygon (as it is the case in most of the Twitter posts). The similarity between two locations is given by their distance. Instead of computing this distance "as the crow flies", which would result in an underestimation, we use Google Maps API (https://developers.google.com/maps/), where the distance is expressed as the time needed to travel from one location to the other. As there might be more than one option to travel (e.g., walking, biking, riding a bus) between the two locations, we select the fastest on the grounds that a person would most probably choose it.

The **Photo** is a media resource that could be extracted either as an input stream (stream of bytes), or a buffered image (object for images, storing its characteristics, color model etc). Comparison between input streams is extremely fast but sensitive to image editing or altering. Since social networks photos have different resolutions and they might be altered with the use of filters, this technique would not be appropriate. For this reason, we use the *feature matching algorithm* [13], that has been shown to be robust to photo edits and computationally efficient [9]; the algorithm extracts a vector of features (e.g., color, texture, shape) from the two photos and computes the cosine similarity of the two vectors. We use the implementation provided by the Open CV libraries (http://opencv.org/).

Text is almost always present in the content of posts. To compute the similarity of two texts, we first tokenize them into their constituent words, we remove the stop words and we stem the remaining with Porter's algorithm. Next, we represent the texts as two vectors of tf-idf weights associated to their words. Given a word w, a *text* and the set $C_{\Delta t}$ of textual posts shared in the time interval Δt, we have that tf-idf$(w, text, C_{\Delta t}) = tf(w, text) * idf(w, C_{\Delta t})$; $tf(w, post)$ is the frequency of w in *text*; $idf(w, C_{\Delta t})$ is the inverse frequency of w in $C_{\Delta t}$ computed as: $idf(w, C_{\Delta t}) = log \frac{|C_{\Delta t}|}{\{txt \in C_{\Delta t} : w \in txt\}}$. The frequency of words in $C_{\Delta t}$ is affected by viral posts that are shared in Δt (e.g., "Earthquake happening right now"). Thus, the tf-idf weights degrade the importance of words that occur in viral posts. Finally, the similarity between two textual posts $text_1$ and $text_2$ is computed as the cosine similarity between the two corresponding vectors.

Tags (or, *hashtags*) are keywords or terms that are often added to the posts by the users as an indicator of the topics covered by the post. As tags are a textual resource, we process them in the same way as the content of the post. Note that we treat tags separately from the text to measure their contribution to profile reconciliation.

Static Attributes. We consider two: username and real name.

Username. To compare two usernames, we use the Lenvenshtein distance whose effectiveness was shown in [2,4,20,23]. The distance $d(s_1, s_2)$ between two strings s_1 and s_2 (e.g., "johnsmith" and "johnsmeet") is expressed as the minimum number of edits (insertion, deletion or replacement of characters) that are necessary to convert s_1 to s_2 (e.g., 2 in our example). The similarity of s_1 and s_2 is expressed by $1 - d_{s_1,s_2}/max(len(s_1), len(s_2))$, where len is the function that returns the length of a string. Therefore, the similarity of "johnsmith" and "johnsmeeth" is $1 - \frac{2}{10} = 1 - 0.2 = 0.8$.

Realname. For the comparison of two real names r_1 and r_2 we use the Jaccard similarity. A real name may contain one or several words, depending on the number of first and family names of an individual (e.g., "John Smith", "Louis Ramon Blanco"), put in whatever order decided by the individual himself (e.g., "Smith John"). For the comparison, we split r_1 and r_2 into its constituent sets of words $W(r_1)$ and $W(r_2)$ and compute the Jaccard similarity of these two sets given by $|W(r_1) \cap W(r_2)|/|W(r_1) \cup W(r_2)|$. This way, two usernames that are identical, modulo the order of their words (e.g., "John Smith" and "Smith John"), would receive the highest similarity 1.

The attribute similarity methods described above are used in the *Bubble Matching* algorithm when comparing posts that happen in the same time interval, detailed in the following section.

4.2 The Algorithm Bubble Matching

The algorithm *Bubble Matching* BM is grounded on the hypothesis that an individual has similar activities across social networks within a short time interval and might express similar feelings through text, tags and photos. We define a *bubble* as the set of posts in two profiles that happened within a fixed time frame Δt. These posts are pairwise compared in order to determine the similarity score of their attributes.

Given two profiles p^i and p^j, the **input** of BM consists in two parameters, $\{e_t\}$ and Δt. The first is the set of posts from p^i and p^j that occurred in a given timeline, and the second is the length of the time interval. The **output** is the set of pairs of compared posts $R = \{< e_t^i, e_{t'}^j, S >\}$. e_t^i and $e_{t'}^j$ are resp. the posts of profiles p^i and p^j that occurred respectively in t and t' such that $|t' - t| \leq \Delta t$. S is the vector of the similarity scores of the attributes of the two posts. In order to understand the rationale of BM, the Fig. 1 illustrates the case of the set of five posts $e_1, \ldots, e_5$ that happened at time $t_1, \ldots, t_5$ respectively. Starting with the first post, we use the timestamp t_1 of e_1 as the starting point. BM finds that the posts that happened in the interval $[t_1, t_1 + \Delta t]$, indicated by the curved arrow, are e_1, e_2 and e_3 and therefore compares e_1 to e_2, e_1 to e_3 and e_2 to e_3. Continuing on the timeline, BM considers the timestamp t_2 of the post e_2. For the interval $[t_2, t_2 + \Delta t]$, BM compares e_2 to e_3, e_2 to e_4 and e_3 to e_4.

Our solution is similar in spirit to a time window that slides in the timeline of activities, where the start time is explicitly defined by the timestamp of posts in order to avoid passing in an empty timeline. Even though the idea of sliding time windows exists in several applications, it has not been applied in this context. Moreover, we can relate to the blocking techniques presented in [21] given that we arrange posts together in a time-defined block. However, the pre-processing of the blocks such as merging would violate the time restriction (Δt) by creating blocks that cover a larger timespan and discarding large blocks would cause missing potential matches. A temporal matching algorithm used in DBLP dataset is proposed in [3]. Even though the temporal aspect is used, the authors focus on the probability that an attribute value reappears over time. The records are processed in an increasing order depending on the time and their evolution is monitored. In our case, the change of the values of attributes are not tracked in time but we rather treat the sharing of content as a discrete post in time. The timestamp is used to compare the posts that are shared close in time, not to model the evolution of the behavior. Thus, time series approaches are not applicable in our case. As Fig. 1 clearly shows, the posts that occur in two overlapping bubbles (zones A and B, for instance) are compared twice. In order to avoid redundant comparisons, we index the previous bubble (Fig. 2), so that the comparisons of the posts in the interval $[t_2, t_{index}]$ are not repeated; instead, BM compares all the posts in $[t_{index}, t_2]$ and the posts in $[t_2, t_{index}]$ against the posts in $[t_{index}, t_2]$.

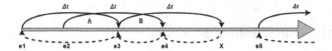

Fig. 1. Example of bubbles with redundancy

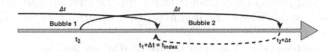

Fig. 2. Example of bubbles without redundancy

Algorithm 1 describes the comparison of the posts within the bubbles. For each timestamp t in the timeline T, the algorithm compares (Lines 8–9) all the posts in $E_{out} = [t, t+\Delta t]$ (outer loop) against all the posts in $E_{in} =\,]t_{index}, t+\Delta t]$ (inner loop), where t_{index} is the index of the previous bubble; if the current and the previous bubbles do not overlap ($t_{index} < t$), t_{index} is updated to t (Lines 3–4). The similarity δ_d between dynamic attribute values is computed for each $< e_t, e_{t'} >$ (Lines 10–12). Additionally, BM computes the similarity δ_a between the static attributes of the profiles of e_t and $e_{t'}$; the similarity values are saved to a list L so they are computed only once (Lines 13–18). The compared posts $< e_t, e_{t'} >$ and their set of attribute similarities S is added to R (Lines 19). The update of t_{index} is done after the bubble comparison is finished (Line 20).

Algorithm 1. The algorithm Bubble Matching

Input: Set of ordered posts $E = \{e_{t_1}, e_{t_2}, ...\}$,
  $T = \{t_1, t_2, ...\}$; Δt
Output: Set of compared posts pairs R
1: $R \leftarrow \emptyset$; $t_{index} \leftarrow t_1$; $L \leftarrow \emptyset$
2: **for each** t in T **do**
3:   **if** $t_{index} < t$ **then**
4:     $t_{index} \leftarrow t$
5:   **end if**
6:   $E_{out} \leftarrow$ set of posts in $[t, t + \Delta t]$
7:   $E_{in} \leftarrow$ set of posts in $]t_{index}, t + \Delta t]$
8:   **for each** $e_t \in E_{out}$ **do**
9:     **for each** $e_{t\prime} \in E_{in} \land e_{t\prime} \neq e_t$ **do**
10:      **for** $d \in \mathcal{D}$ **do**
11:        $S \leftarrow S \cup \delta_d(e_t, e_{t\prime})$
12:      **end for**
13:      **if** $< profile(e_t), profile(e_{t\prime}) > \not\subseteq L$ **then**
14:        **for** $a \in \mathcal{A}$ **do**
15:          $S \leftarrow S \cup \delta_a(profile(e_t), profile(e_{t\prime}))$
16:        **end for**
17:        Add $< profile(e_t), profile(e_{t\prime}) >$ to L;
18:      **end if**
19:      Add $< e_t, e_{t\prime}, S >$ to R
20:    **end for**
21: **end for**
22: $t_{index} \leftarrow t + \Delta t$
23: **end for return** R

Theorem 1. *Given a set of posts that happened in time interval Δt, Algorithm 1 does not compute redundant comparisons.*

Proof. Let us assume that two posts e_t and $e_{t'}$ are compared in both $bubble_i$ ($[t_i, t_i + \Delta t]$) and $bubble_{i+1}$ ($[t_{i+1}, t_{i+1} + \Delta t]$). If $< e_t, e_{t'} >$ is compared in $bubble_i$, then $t < t_i + \Delta t$ and $t' < t_i + \Delta t$. If $< e_t, e_{t'} >$ is compared again in $bubble_{i+1}$, then e_t and/or $e_{t'}$ happened in the inner loop $]t_i + \Delta t, t_{i+1} + \Delta t]$. Thus, we would have the contradictory conclusion that $t > t_i + \Delta t$ and $t' > t_i + \Delta t$. The contradiction proves the theorem.

Theorem 2. *Given a set of posts that happened in a given timeline, Algorithm 1 does not miss any comparison for a fixed time interval Δt.*

Proof. Consider a pair $< e_t, e_{t'} >$ such that $t - t' \leq \Delta t$. There exists at least one bubble $bubble_i$ that contains e_t and $e_{t'}$. Two cases can occur. The case $t_{i-1} + \Delta t < t_i$ is simple because $bubble_i$ and $bubble_{i-1}$ do not overlap; all the posts in $bubble_i$, including $< e_t, e_{t'} >$, are compared. The case $t_{i-1} + \Delta t \geq t_i$ causes the overlap of $bubble_i$ and $bubble_{i-1}$. Four scenarios could appear. **(i)** $t \in]t_{i-1} + \Delta t, t_i + \Delta t]$ and $t\prime \in]t_{i-1} + \Delta t, t_i + \Delta t]$. Obviously both posts fall in $bubble_i$ since $]t_{i-1} + \Delta t, t_i + \Delta t] \subset [t_i, t_i + \Delta t]$. **(ii)** $t \in [t_i, t_{i-1} + \Delta t]$ and $t' \in]t_i, t_{i-1} + \Delta t]$. The comparison will not happen in $bubble_i$, because t' is outside the inner loop of $bubble_i$. If $t_{i-2} + \Delta t \leq t_i$ (which means that $bubble_{i-2}$ does not overlap with $bubble_i$), then $bubble_{i-1}$ has $[t_{i-1}, t_{i-1} + \Delta t]$ as the outer loop, where $[t_i, t_{i-1} + \Delta t]$ is included, and $]t_{i-2} + \Delta t, t_{i-1} + \Delta t]$ as the inner interval, which also includes $]t_i, t_{i-1} + \Delta t]$. Therefore in this case the two posts are compared. If $t_{i-2} + \Delta t > t_i$ (which means that $bubble_{i-2}$ does overlap with $bubble_i$), we can propagate the same reasoning to the previous bubble. **(iii)** $t \in [t_i, t_{i-1} + \Delta t]$ and $t' \in]t_{i-1} + \Delta t, t_i + \Delta t]$. The comparison falls perfectly in $bubble_i$, because t is in the outer loop and t' is in the inner loop. **(iv)** $t \in [t_{i-1} + \Delta t, t_i + \Delta t]$ and $t\prime \in]t_i, t_{i-1} + \Delta t]$. The comparison falls perfectly in $bubble_i$, because t is in the inner loop and t' is in the outer loop. Considering all possible scenarios, there is no case where Algorithm 1 fails to compare e_t against $e_{t'}$.

Geo Pruning Procedure. The number of comparisons could be very high and also depends on the value of Δt. In order to reduce this number, we exploit the geographic data attribute values. Our rationale is that it is impossible for an individual to share a post from Paris and New York City within four minutes; as a result, we only keep pairs of posts such that the distance between the locations of the posts that can be covered within the time interval of the posts themselves. More precisely, any pair of posts $< e_t, e_{t'} >$, such that $|t - t'| \leq \Delta t$, is *geo-pruned* if the duration of the travel from the location of e_t to the location of $e_{t'}$ is greater than Δt. Using this procedure, the Algorithm 1 could prune drastically all the pairs of posts belonging to these profiles. In fact, if e_t and $e_{t'}$ (that come from the profile p^i and p^j, respectively) are found to be too far to be posted by the same individual, p^i and p^j are likely to be owned by two different individuals and, therefore, all the post pairs coming from these two profiles are removed too. **Complexity.** If we were to compare all the posts against any other, the cost of the algorithm would be $O(M^2)$, where M is the total number of posts. The algorithm BM only compares posts that co-occur in the same bubble; therefore, its computational cost is $O(m \cdot k^2)$, where $m \ll M$ is the number of bubbles and k is the average number of posts in a bubble. The geo-pruning procedure reduces even more the number of comparisons k (Sect. 5).

4.3   Reconciling Profiles

The output of BM is the set of pairs of posts $< e_t^i, e_{t'}^j >$ that happened within the predefined Δt and the set of their similarity scores S. In order to decide if p^i and p^j belong to the same individual, we learn in a training set through logistic regression the combination of the similarity scores of each attribute in uncovering the identity of profiles p^i and p^j. The **input** is the set $R = \{< e_t^i, e_{t'}^j, S\} >$ of compared posts pairs accompanied by the set $S = \{\delta_k\}$ of similarity scores of k attributes. The **output** is the set $\{< p^i, p^j, \rho >\}$ of reconciled ($\rho = true$) or unreconciled ($\rho = false$) profiles pairs. S is the set of similarity scores δ_k of the compared posts e_t^i and $e_{t'}^j$ from profiles p^i and p^j respectively. We decide on a Boolean value $\rho(e_t^i, e_{t'}^j)$, which predicts the class of the posts e_t^i and $e_{t'}^j$ by learning with logistic regression on the input R. Each δ_k in R acts as a predictor (where k is the number of attributes), the logistic regression learns $\rho(e_t^i, e_{t'}^j)$. A *true* value of $\rho(e_t^i, e_{t'}^j)$ means that e_t^i and $e_{t'}^j$ indicate a strong similarity that can imply a link between profiles p^i and p^j. However, there might be pairs of events from the same profiles that show a strong link but even others with a weak link. Nevertheless, the profiles p^i and p^j are not expected to have *consistently* similar posts, therefore even a single pair of posts can detect a *true* class of the profiles. Reconciling profiles is the set of triples $\{< p^i, p^j, \rho >\}$ where ρ is *true* if p^i and p^j are reconciled and ρ is *false* if otherwise. The value of ρ is true if $\exists \rho(e_t^i, e_{t'}^j) = true$; in other words, *Two profiles will be reconciled only if there exists at least one true class of their post pairs.*

5   Evaluation

Dataset. We obtained data from two popular social networks, Flickr and Twitter, by using the APIs that they provide. As opposed to other approaches

[1,2,4,23], which extract a subgraph by visiting the social networks starting from a set of manually selected seed users (thus, obtaining a local sample), we retrieved user profiles by extracting the recent activity on the two social networks. We selected the profiles from Flickr and Twitter that provide an explicit link to each other ("Website" attribute). We chose a dataset with declared cross-links for two reasons: (1) the evaluation is not ambiguous since the ground truth is available. A non-labeled dataset would require human evaluation which is erroneous (accuracy of 0.6 in [26]). (2) the users disclose their links openly; thus we respect the privacy of those who do not want to disclose. However, we acknowledge the risks associated with the bias of the already disclosed links. Nevertheless, even though the users share the cross-link publicly, this does not guarantee the similarity of the profiles. For each pair of cross-linked profiles, we retain the 400 latest posts, i.e., 200 tweets in Twitter and 200 photos in Flickr. In the end, we gather a sample of the two networks that is not local to some seed users and consists of 2,716 profiles and 481,575 posts, equally distributed over the two networks (cf. Table 1). For each profile, we extracted two static textual attributes (username and real name) and each post may consist of photo, text, tags and geotags.

Table 1. Statistics on the dataset.

	# Profiles	# Posts	Username	Real name	Photo	Text	Tags	Geo
Flickr	1,358	223,023	100%	75%	100%	100%	47%	12%
Twitter	1,358	258,552	100%	100%	17%	100%	17%	6%

Parallel Implementation. Since two posts that belong to two different bubbles do not need to be compared, we can easily parallelize the comparisons. More specifically, we deploy a master/slave model that consists of a machine (referred to as the *master*) that assigns tasks to five machines (referred to as the *slaves*) while balancing the workload. The details of the machines are as follows: (i) Master - Intel(R) Core(TM) i3-2330M CPU @2.20 GHz with 4.0 GB RAM; (ii) Slaves - Intel(R) Xeon(R) CPU E5-2609 @ 2.50 GHz with 62 GB RAM.

Each slaves takes an interval I, which he splits into bubbles of predefined Δt to process. A naive solution would be dividing the timeline into equal-sized time intervals I. However, whether we set $\Delta t = 60$ (Fig. 4a)—a low value—or $\Delta t = 3600$ (Fig. 4b)—a high value—recent time intervals have more and larger bubbles than earlier years, especially for larger values of Δt. As a result, the slaves that are assigned time intervals from early years will have considerably less workload than the slaves that are assigned recent time intervals. Based on these observations, we divide the timeline in such a way that the early time intervals I are longer than the recent ones and, consequently, the number of bubbles is more balanced across the intervals. Note that Δt does not change. Figure 3 illustrates how the parallel execution works. First, the set of pairs $< t, n_t >$ (t is a timestamp and n_t is the bubble size) is extracted from the dataset (1) and processed by the master (2). The master creates the intervals and adds them to a queue Q (3). The master takes the interval I_1 from Q and assigns it to S_3, the first slave in the queue S_{free} (4). The process continues until Q contains intervals. Whenever a slave finishes processing an interval, it is put into the queue S_{free} (6). As shown in Fig. 5[1], the parallel implementation is three times faster compared to a sequential implementation. The execution time for the whole dataset is presented in Fig. 6. The values vary depending on Δt. With the increase in bubble size, the execution time rises. For example, for $\Delta t = 60$ the runtime is 15 min whereas for $\Delta t = 3600$ the runtime reaches 5,4 days.

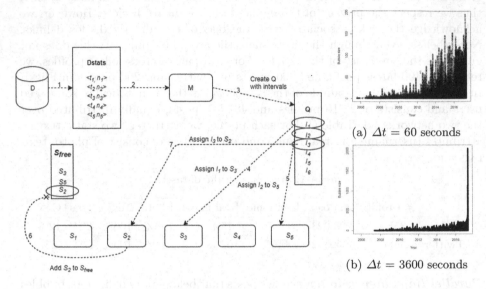

(a) $\Delta t = 60$ seconds

(b) $\Delta t = 3600$ seconds

Fig. 3. Parallel bubble matching execution

Fig. 4. Workload

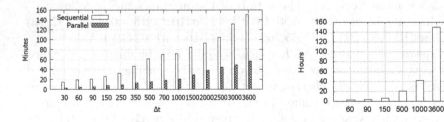

Fig. 5. Parallel versus sequential

Fig. 6. Execution time

Evaluation metrics. Given two posts from two different social networks, either they are generated by the same user, in which case they are referred to as a *positive* instance, or they don't (*negative* instance). We define the *true positives*

---

[1] The graph is obtained by running the algorithm on a sample of the dataset (7%) consisting of posts of March 2017 only. The sequential version is very time-consuming to be run on the whole dataset.

TP (resp., the *false positives* FP) as the set of all post pairs that our algorithm determined as positive instances and they are (resp., not) so; similarly, we define the *true negatives* TN and *false negatives* FN. For the evaluation, we use *precision* ($P = |TP|/(|TP| + |FP|)$)—that measures how many of the instances determined as positives by the algorithm are actually so—and *recall* ($R = |TP|/(|TP| + |FN|)$)—that measures how many of the instances that are actually positive are determined as such by the algorithm. Moreover, we report the values of the area under ROC curve (AUC) as the metric of the overall accuracy of the algorithm.

Evaluation results. When only considering dynamic attributes (Fig. 7a), our algorithm has a precision of 0.8 for $\Delta t \leq 3$ minutes and above 0.6 for higher values of Δt; this is remarkable, considering that ignoring the static attributes is tantamount to having anonymized profiles. The recall is high for small values of Δt, which means that the algorithm can reconcile profiles that display near-simultaneous activity; as Δt increases, the bubbles contain posts that are not close in time and therefore the algorithm does not "dare" to make any conclusion, resulting in a lower recall. When the algorithm also considers the static attributes (Fig. 7b), both precision and recall increases, which comes as no surprise, as the algorithm can exploit more information. In the dataset that we use, the coverage of static attributes is very high (all Twitter profiles disclose the real name), which explains why the improvement obtained is significant. However, not always are static attributes so easily available in social networks.

Evaluation of Geo-pruning. Fig. 8a shows the total number of post pairs (thick line) that are pruned and those that are actually negative (dashed line), that is posts made by two different users. As expected, the number of post pairs pruned decreases with Δ_t; for small values of Δ_t (e.g., few seconds to few minutes), the distance between the locations of two posts is unlikely to be covered, even if the two locations are proximate. In other words, with small values of Δ_t, the heuristic prunes all the posts for which the location is not exactly (almost) the same. As a result, as the geocodes attached to two posts is almost never 100% accurate, the heuristic is likely to mistakenly prune posts that are originated by the same user. The gap between the two graphs in Fig. 8a represents these mistakes and is clearly wider for small values of Δ_t, as discussed. Interestingly, this gap tightens while increasing the value of Δ_t (fewer mistakes are committed) and it becomes constant for $\Delta t \geq 1440$ (24 min). Similarly, we recorded the pruned pairs of users for each of the models while changing Δt. We pruned around 3602 pairs for the model with 0 s, out of which 32 pairs were wrongly pruned. While increasing Δt, we are less conservative regarding pruning and we diminish the gap between the total pruned pairs of users and the actual negatives (Fig. 8b). After $\Delta t = 3060$ s (51 min), this gap stays constant at 4 pairs wrongly pruned. This could happen when users share a late post, putting a geo location of an old post in one of the social networks, while in the other they share the actual location of the moment.

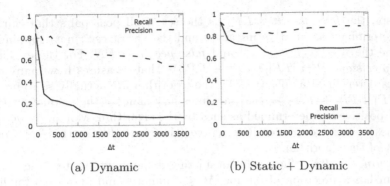

(a) Dynamic   (b) Static + Dynamic

Fig. 7. Precision and recall for different values of Δt

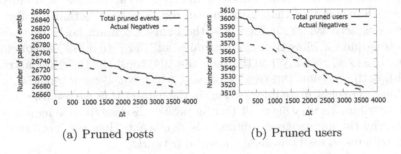

(a) Pruned posts   (b) Pruned users

Fig. 8. Evaluation of geo-pruning

Comparison. We intend to compare the impact of only using the static attributes against the use of dynamic attributes. For this purpose, we selected from the literature the approaches only using static attributes that reported the best values of precision/recall. Pachenko et al. [20] fix the threshold $\alpha = 0.6$ and $\beta = 0.8$ for the first name and last name respectively using Levenshtein and then calculate the similarities of their friends to rank candidates and choose the highest ranked. In our dataset, we do not have information about the network of friends. However, we implemented the pair-wise comparisons for the first name and last name. Quercini et al. [23] propose 1-rule (rule based on one attribute) based on a threshold of 0.9 for the username similarity derived from Levenshtein distance and the 2-rule (based on two attributes) thresholds of 0.9 for both username similarity with Levenshtein and real name similarity with Jaccard. Another attribute-based approach that uses the username, profile photo and location is presented by Edwards at el. [4]. The authors use logistic regression for training the model. We apply the same idea but using only our static attributes. The results are presented in Table 2. Although the use of static attributes allows the identification of the profiles with very high precision, the recall is generally extremely low. This confirms our statement that *the use of static attributes is quite effective (if the values are available and are correctly disclosed) but for a better overall model, the analysis of the activities is needed.* Thus, a higher recall is achieved by our method.

Table 2. Evaluation of attribute-based approaches

Approach	Recall	Precision	AUC
Edwards et al.	0.407	0.970	0.788
Gianluca et al. - 1 rule	0.425	1.000	0.635
Gianluca et al. - 2 rule	0.423	0.995	0.711
Pachenko et al.	0.222	0.990	0.611
Bubble matching 20 min	0.631	0.822	0.815
Bubble matching 1 h	0.698	0.886	0.849

6 Conclusions and Future Work

In this paper, we described an approach that identifies with high precision individuals only from their posts; as a result, profiles can be reconciled when static attributes are missing or incomplete. This raises interesting privacy concerns. Static attributes, when they are available, contribute to a significant improvement in precision and recall. However, for those individuals who fake their profile attributes in order to avoid profile linkage, there is still a high risk of getting exposed through time-related activity. Our model using only dynamic attributes reports high values of precision for detecting profiles that share similar content even with an hour delay. There are several directions that could be considered in the future work. Our parallel implementation proved to be quite efficient, compared to the sequential. We intent to address the scalability of the approach in the future work. We used feature extraction algorithm for photo comparison since we are comparing the photos of the posts, which are not necessarily pictures of people. However, face recognition methods could be combined with the feature extraction algorithm and produce a combined similarity measure for photo comparison. We used Google Maps API to get the distance between two locations but other tools can be applied.

References

1. Bartunov, S., Korshunov, A., Park, S.T., Ryu, W., Lee, H.: Joint link-attribute user identity resolution in online social networks. In: SNA-KDD. ACM (2012)
2. Buccafurri, F., Lax, G., Nocera, A., Ursino, D.: Discovering missing me edges across social networks. Inf. Sci. **319**, 18–37 (2015)
3. Chiang, Y.H., Doan, A., Naughton, J.F.: Modeling entity evolution for temporal record matching. In: SIGMOD, pp. 1175–1186. ACM (2014)
4. Edwards, M., Wattam, S., Rayson, P., Rashid, A.: Sampling labelled profile data for identity resolution. In: IEEE Big Data, pp. 540–547. IEEE (2016)
5. Goga, O., Lei, H., Parthasarathi, S.H.K., Friedland, G., Sommer, R., Teixeira, R.: Exploiting innocuous activity for correlating users across sites. In: WWW, pp. 447–458. ACM (2013)
6. Golbeck, J., Rothstein, M.: Linking social networks on the web with FOAF: a semantic web case study. AAAI **8**, 1138–1143 (2008)

7. Greenwood, S., Perrin, A., Duggan, M.: Social media update 2016. Pew Research Center, November 2016
8. Gross, R., Acquisti, A.: Information revelation and privacy in online social networks. In: WPES Workshop, pp. 71–80. ACM (2005)
9. Hassaballah, M., Abdelmgeid, A.A., Alshazly, H.A.: Image features detection, description and matching. In: Awad, A.I., Hassaballah, M. (eds.) Image Feature Detectors and Descriptors. SCI, vol. 630, pp. 11–45. Springer, Cham (2016). https://doi.org/10.1007/978-3-319-28854-3_2
10. Iofciu, T., Fankhauser, P., Abel, F., Bischoff, K.: Identifying users across social tagging systems. In: ICWSM (2011)
11. Kong, X., Zhang, J., Yu, P.S.: Inferring anchor links across multiple heterogeneous social networks. In: CIKM, pp. 179–188. ACM (2013)
12. Korula, N., Lattanzi, S.: An efficient reconciliation algorithm for social networks. Proc. VLDB Endow. **7**(5), 377–388 (2014)
13. Laganière, R.: OpenCV Computer Vision Application Programming Cookbook, 2nd edn. Packt Publishing Ltd., Birmingham (2014)
14. Liu, L., Cheung, W.K., Li, X., Liao, L.: Aligning users across social networks using network embedding. In: IJCAI, pp. 1774–1780 (2016)
15. Liu, S., Wang, S., Zhu, F., Zhang, J., Krishnan, R.: HYDRA: large-scale social identity linkage via heterogeneous behavior modeling. In: SIGMOD, pp. 51–62. ACM (2014)
16. Malhotra, A., Totti, L., Meira, W., Kumaraguru, P., Almeida, V.: Studying user footprints in different online social networks. In: ASONAM. ACM (2012)
17. Man, T., Shen, H., Liu, S., Jin, X., Cheng, X.: Predict anchor links across social networks via an embedding approach. In: IJCAI, pp. 1823–1829 (2016)
18. Minder, P., Bernstein, A.: Social network aggregation using face-recognition. In: ISWC 2011 Workshop: Social Data on the Web. Citeseer (2011)
19. Narayanan, A., Shmatikov, V.: De-anonymizing social networks. In: 30th IEEE Symposium on Security and Privacy, pp. 173–187. IEEE (2009)
20. Panchenko, A., Babaev, D., Obiedkov, S.: Large-scale parallel matching of social network profiles. In: Khachay, M.Y., Konstantinova, N., Panchenko, A., Ignatov, D.I., Labunets, V.G. (eds.) AIST 2015. CCIS, vol. 542, pp. 275–285. Springer, Cham (2015). https://doi.org/10.1007/978-3-319-26123-2_27
21. Papadakis, G., Ioannou, E., Niederée, C., Palpanas, T., Nejdl, W.: Beyond 100 million entities: large-scale blocking-based resolution for heterogeneous data. In: WSDM, pp. 53–62. ACM (2012)
22. Perito, D., Castelluccia, C., Kaafar, M.A., Manils, P.: How unique and traceable are usernames? In: Fischer-Hübner, S., Hopper, N. (eds.) PETS 2011. LNCS, vol. 6794, pp. 1–17. Springer, Heidelberg (2011). https://doi.org/10.1007/978-3-642-22263-4_1
23. Quercini, G., Bennacer, N., Ghufran, M., Nana Jipmo, C.: LIAISON: reconciLIAtion of Individuals profiles across SOcial Networks. In: Guillet, F., Pinaud, B., Venturini, G. (eds.) Advances in Knowledge Discovery and Management. SCI, vol. 665, pp. 229–253. Springer, Cham (2017). https://doi.org/10.1007/978-3-319-45763-5_12
24. Riederer, C., Kim, Y., Chaintreau, A., Korula, N., Lattanzi, S.: Linking users across domains with location data: theory and validation. In: WWW, pp. 707–719 (2016)
25. Shu, K., Wang, S., Tang, J., Zafarani, R., Liu, H.: User identity linkage across online social networks: a review. SIGKDD Explor. Newslett. **18**(2), 5–17 (2017)

26. Vosoughi, S., Zhou, H., Roy, D.: Digital stylometry: linking profiles across social networks. SocInfo 2015. LNCS, vol. 9471, pp. 164–177. Springer, Cham (2015). https://doi.org/10.1007/978-3-319-27433-1_12
27. Zafarani, R., Liu, H.: Connecting users across social media sites: a behavioral-modeling approach. In: KDD, pp. 41–49. ACM (2013)
28. Zhang, Y., Tang, J., Yang, Z., Pei, J., Yu, P.S.: COSNET: connecting heterogeneous social networks with local and global consistency. In: KDD, pp. 1485–1494. ACM (2015)
29. Zhou, X., Liang, X., Zhang, H., Ma, Y.: Cross-platform identification of anonymous identical users in multiple social media networks. TKDE **28**(2), 411–424 (2016)

Requirements and Modeling

Towards an Ontology-Based Approach for Eliciting Possible Solutions to Non-Functional Requirements

Rodrigo Veleda and Luiz Marcio Cysneiros[(✉)]

School of Information Technology, York University, Toronto, Canada
{rveleda, cysneiro}@yorku.ca

Abstract. Requirements Engineering plays a crucial role in the software development process. Many works have pointed out that Non-Functional Requirements (NFRs) are critical to the quality of software systems. NFRs, also known as quality requirements, can be difficult to elicit due to their subjective diversity nature. In this paper, we introduce the QR Framework which uses an ontology-based approach to support the collection of knowledge on possible solutions to implement NFRs, semi-automatically connecting related NFRs. Preliminary search mechanisms are provided in a tool to facilitate the identification of possible solutions to an NFR and their related consequences to other solutions and/or other NFRs. To evaluate whether our approach aids eliciting NFRs, we conducted a controlled experiment performing a software development scenario. Our results suggest that reusing NFR knowledge can drive software engineers to obtain a closer to complete set of possible solutions to address quality concerns.

Keywords: Non-Functional Requirements · Knowledge reuse · Ontology · Quality requirements

1 Introduction

Non-Functional Requirements (NFR), also known as quality requirements, frequently express constraints to be imposed on functional requirements as well as general quality properties that will apply to software. Examples of NFRs are Privacy, Usability, Reliability, Security, and Trust.

Despite many new works going from elicitation to verification and validation [1], there is still no convergence towards an amalgamated approach to deal with NFRs. NFRs are frequently fuzzy in nature, hard to identify, and it is even harder to elicit how to satisfice[1] them. Choosing solutions to cope with one particular NFR frequently introduce synergies and, most likely, conflicts with other NFRs. Identifying and modelling these interdependencies is the most challenging task for effectively eliciting NFRs.

---

[1] We use the term satisfice in the same way as it is used in the NFR Framework [2] denoting that an NFR is expected to be satisfied within acceptable limits.

© Springer Nature Switzerland AG 2019
P. Giorgini and B. Weber (Eds.): CAiSE 2019, LNCS 11483, pp. 145–161, 2019.
https://doi.org/10.1007/978-3-030-21290-2_10

One way of representing knowledge on *satisficing* NFRs is to build catalogues using *Softgoal Interdependency Graphs* (SIG) [2, 3], where softgoals represent NFRs and their refinements can be further refined using an And/Or decomposition approach until it reaches possible operationalizations to satisfice the softgoals.

In a previous work [4], we detail an empirical study that suggests the use of NFR catalogues helps identifying a larger and more appropriate set of NFRs that should be used in a project as well as a broader set of possible solutions to operationalize these NFRs.

Other works such as [5, 6] also conducted empirical experiments pointing out to catalogues helping to elicit NFRs in different situations. However, these works recognize that the use of catalogues faces some challenges, among them, the scalability problem. Catalogues can grow quite fast and become difficult to visualize. Another problem relies on the ability to discover conflicts among solutions to different NFRs. Typically, NFR catalogues contain very few if any conflicts clearly typified. More importantly, when dealing with catalogs for several NFRs at the same time, which is a common situation, even when these conflicts are mentioned in one catalogue, realizing the connection among these catalogs for such interdependencies is a visual task quite prone to mistakes and omissions.

To mitigate these problems, we started to investigate a framework that can semi-automate the acquisition of knowledge linking possible interdependencies (positive and negative ones) portrait in several different catalogues while at the same time providing an environment that can facilitate searches to guide requirements engineer (RE) to identify possible NFRs and operationalizations that could be needed in a project. The retrieved set of NFRs and possible operationalizations would help the RE to model *all possible solutions* to only then evaluate which solution will fit best the interests of this specific project. We understand that NFRs solutions will vary from one project to another and hence, the best approach is to provide as many possible solutions as possible to guide a better cost vs. benefit analysis for each project. As such, our approach does not suggest one solution. Instead, it suggests a *whole set of solutions* to be studied as possible solutions to guide the cost vs. benefit analysis.

We have investigated the use of ontologies and semantic web techniques to represent SIGs in a machine-readable format [7]. It aims to facilitate the reuse of the knowledge captured in SIGs. Veleda [8] introduced the requirements for the Quality Requirements (QR) Framework and its supporting tool, which aims at eliciting knowledge on how to develop software that will deliver appropriated solutions for needed NFRs.

The objective of this paper is to present the initial results of implementing the first step of the QR Framework, which focus on providing an environment that can semi-automate the acquisition of knowledge and at the same time provide mechanisms to efficiently search for the knowledge embedded in this knowledge base. We have implemented these mechanisms on the QR tool and carried out an empirical study to evaluate how well the current approach helps to identify a more comprehensive set of possible NFRs and its operationalizations and correlations. Correlations model the impact, either positive or negative, of one NFR solution into other NFR solution [2], and it is one of the most challenging goals of eliciting and negotiating NFRs satisficing. Initial results suggest that participants using the QR tool were able to identify a much broader set of possible operationalizations, but perhaps more importantly, they were also able to identify a significantly higher number of possible conflicts.

The paper is structured as follow: Sect. 2 tackles some of the related work while Sect. 3 describes the QR Framework and details the QR tool which is central to support the QR Framework. Section 4 depicts the experiment used to validate our hypotheses followed by a discussion of the results. Section 5 concludes this work.

2   Related Work

SIGs were introduced by the NFR Framework [2] and have been used to describe quality attributes. Many works have used SIGs to represent knowledge related to NFRs such as [2, 9, 10]. Empirical works have suggested that the use of catalogues have a positive impact on the quality of the developed software [4, 6]. However, catalogues do not scale efficiently [5, 6] hence, the larger the amount of knowledge we gather the more difficult it is to reuse it.

On a different path, Sancho et al. [11] suggested to use an ontological database and exemplified its use with the Software Performance Engineering Body of Knowledge. Their proposal consists of two ontologies both written in OWL [12]: the NFR ontology and the SIG ontology. The NFR Ontology describes the NFRs concept and relationships among them. The SIG Ontology depicts SIG constructs and their relationships. We have identified two shortcomings of this ontology. First, the SIG ontology does not define any class to describe the correlation interdependency between softgoals. Second, it does not enforce the use of the proper kind of softgoals as parent and offspring of each refinement. A few other semantic-based approaches have been proposed in the NFR context. ElicitO [13] is an ontology-based tool that supports NFRs elicitation; it provides a knowledge base about NFR requirements and associated metrics. Hu [14] proposed an ontology model as a baseline for modeling NFRs.

However, these works do not facilitate the required reasoning for a RE to analyze the tradeoffs involving different NFRs. Neither have they tackled the important aspect of creating methods to retrieve knowledge using searches with varying levels of granularity and filters to help visualize the retrieved knowledge. The QR Framework aims at mitigating some of these gaps. The following sections will illustrate how the QR Framework proposes to tackle these issues. More specifically we will focus on the first part of the framework targeting the elicitation and reasoning of NFRs solutions for a given project.

3   The Core of the QR Framework

In this work, we present an initial approach to providing the QR Framework with basic capabilities that will form the core of the framework, i.e., instruments to facilitate the elicitation of NFRs. In order to facilitate NFR elicitation, we departure from the idea that using Catalogues indeed help eliciting NFRs but do present a challenge in dealing with the acquisition of knowledge to create these catalogues and moreover, how to store and represent its knowledge in such a way that retrieving all pertinent information can be done efficiently [4–6].

The QR Framework was introduced in [8] and allows storage and retrieval of as many as possible options for satisficing NFRs, together with the consequences of choosing one option over another and its effects in other NFRs. The QR Framework is centered on the use of ontologies and semantic web techniques to facilitate reuse. The use of techniques such as RDF schemas [15] and SPARQL [16] aims at exploring the possibility of having rules that can help to identify interdependencies among operationalizations that could easily go unnoticed otherwise. It may also facilitate the ability to explore different levels of granularity in queries to retrieve knowledge [8].

Ontologies are frequently associated with description logic and represented with languages like OWL [12] which provides a vocabulary to describe classes, their properties, relations among them and cardinalities. The NDR Ontology [7] maps the NFR Framework [2] allowing us to describe well-formed SIGs in a machine-readable format allowing software engineers to explore the knowledge embedded in SIGs together with any rationale associated with possible design decisions.

However, we need to provide an environment that can hide all the details of handling ontologies concepts and querying it. A prototype of the QR tool is presented in this paper to provide such environment handling domain-independent catalogues of NFRs together with the interdependencies among these catalogues. As a future work, it will be extended to allow these catalogues to be instantiated into domain-specific alternatives. It is important to note that the QR Framework does not intend to propose one single solution (operationalization) to satisfice one or more NFRs. It aims at recovering **as many as possible alternatives** so developers can choose the one that fits better to their project. For example, the use of contextual metadata may hurt privacy expectations in the healthcare domain but may play an essential role in self-driving cars where the expectation of privacy would be much lower and less important.

3.1   The QR Framework Architecture

The QR Framework is first mentioned in [8]. In this present work, we introduce the first version of the QR tool that includes the acquisition of data from several SIGs and demonstrate the many possibilities from retrieving possible operationalizations together with their eventual correlations with other NFRs. We designed the tool to be deployed in a cloud environment. In other words, our approach implements a RESTful API, promoting a Web Service behavior. We believe that this design choice supports our application's extensibility. Furthermore, the framework will be more capable of integrating with multiple third-party modeling applications. Additionally, by following Web Service standards, the tool may provide NFR knowledge on demand as a resource for smart applications and self-adaptive systems. Perhaps more importantly, in the future, the knowledge base will be able to be used by anyone, researchers or practitioners, interested in reusing knowledge on NFR satisficing. It may even be possible to open the knowledge base to be updated in a controlled manner by other researchers.

3.2   The QR Tool

The QR tool contains two repositories: Knowledge and Ontology. The knowledge repository stores the NFR information extracted from SIG catalogues, maintaining the knowledge evolution associated with a particular ontology model. On the other hand, the ontology repository holds different ontology models. Consequently, within this approach, we envision to provide support to multiple ontologies that are also capable of representing NFRs and design rationale knowledge, other than limit the tool operation solely to the NDR ontology. The meta-ontology used here is described in [7]. To fulfill its functioning and achieve needed requirements, the QR tool incorporates multiple technologies. We mainly adopted alternatives that have an open-source implementation and active community support. Further details can be found in [8].

NFR Knowledge Acquisition. The QR tool acquires NFR information through a three-fold process: (i) Knowledge Extraction (ii) Knowledge Conversion and (iii) Ontology Update.

To better emphasize and describe each knowledge acquisition steps, we propose the following scenario: a SIG catalogue containing information about Transparency being imported into our platform.

Once the SIG catalogue is uploaded into the platform, the QR tool performs a series of actions to interpret and extract NFR information provided within the model. Firstly, it parses each XML element and transforms them into memory-based candidates for new NDR ontology individuals.

Subsequently, the platform verifies if each recently created candidate already exists in the knowledge repository. If a candidate is already persisted as an individual of NFR knowledge, the tool disregards it and utilizes the already existent instance from the knowledge repository. This candidate verification occurs iteratively throughout the knowledge extraction step.

After verifying the status of each candidate, the tool converts the information extracted from the original representation to OWL format, complying with the model proposed by the NDR ontology [7]. In other words, at this point, the platform converts the verified new candidates into fresh ontology individuals and references linked to the already existent ones within the NDR ontology during the knowledge conversion step. For each new reference for already existent information, the tool relies on inference techniques provided using ontologies to identify and suggest possible interdependencies among the ontology individuals. Therefore, the knowledge extraction and conversion steps adequately express how the QR tool practices knowledge evolution through the reutilization of NFR information already existent in the knowledge repository. The reason for applying such knowledge evolution originates from the constraints of the NFR Framework [2]. Since the NDR ontology follows the NFR Framework definitions, our approach enforces its restrictions during the knowledge acquisition phase.

Within the Semantic Web, Inferences are meant to discover new relationships among diverse resources [17]. Therefore, the tool leverages this Semantic Web-native feature during the knowledge extraction process to identify interdependencies between several SIG catalogues automatically. As a result, when new NFR information is imported into the knowledge repository, the QR tool would assume that when a decomposition or operationalization is described in more than one catalogue, a potential correlation between the primary NFRs described in each catalogue should be defined.

Identifying these interdependencies is one of the most significant challenges REs face when evaluating how one solution for one specific NFR might affect other NFRs. For example, in a catalog for Privacy that is already stored in the knowledge base, some of the softgoals in Privacy have operationalizations that are also used in the Transparency catalog. For example, while *Anonymity* may help to operationalize Privacy, it would hurt *Completeness, Clarity, and Operability* regarding Transparency. By the same token, while operationalizations such as *Data Collection, Cloud and Exposure to Personal Information* could help to operationalize Transparency, it would hurt Privacy. In that way, when the RE is searching for solutions to implement Privacy concerns he/she will be pointed out to look at Transparency issues and vice versa.

It is true that linking NFRs during the importation process still relies on the matching of terms used to naming softgoals and operationalizations. We have started to investigate how to overcome this problem using synonymies and dictionaries among other techniques, but this is future work. However, even as it stands right now, we were able to merge catalogs developed by at least four different people (two associate professors and two master students from different universities that have worked independently for generating these catalogs) and yet finding many matches linking the SIGs, which suggests the mechanism is useful even with the current limitation. A near-match process to suggest possible missed correlation is being developed to start tackling this issue.

Finally, after handling the knowledge extraction and conversion, the QR tool updates the target ontology with the new information. This step occurs directly at the SPARQL server and is defined in an OWL level.

Searching and Visualizing NFR Knowledge. The QR tool provides two main possibilities for searching specific NFR Knowledge across the repository: (i) Selection of one specific NFR and (ii) Input of a custom search term.

Suppose our knowledge base has acquired the knowledge for the NFRs of Security, Privacy, Usability, Traceability, and Transparency. One could select one specific NFR by using the dropdown menu option "Choose an NFR" as it can be seen in Fig. 2. After selecting one of them, the tool will then display the SIG that represents the chosen NFR together with a list of correlated catalogues. Based on the constraints of the NFR Framework, the tool uses two distinct colors to reason about the nature of an association between two elements. Therefore, it applies the Green color when an association has a positive nature and employs the Red color when an association has a negative nature. For instance, a decomposition that may help *to satisfice* a given softgoal is highlighted in green color. On the other hand, a correlation that may hurt *satisficing* a particular softgoal is represented using red color.

As a consequence of demonstrating the occurrences of a queried element, the QR Tool may infer existent correlations when a parent NFR is utilized as a query term. After searching for Usability, the tool graphically outputs the complete existent knowledge associated with Usability showing subgoals such as *Conduct Usability*

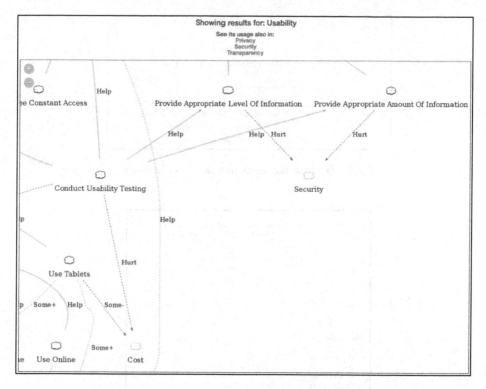

Fig. 1. QR tool: partial SIG for usability and some correlations

Testing, *Provide Appropriate Level of Information* and *Provide Appropriate amount of Information*. Figure 1 illustrates the resulting partial SIG after using the "zoom in" capability provided by the + and − buttons in the upper left part of the Figure (Print Screen). Correlations with other SIGs can be seen on the upper part of the screen where one ca0n read "See its usage also in Privacy, Security, and Transparency".

The partial SIG illustrated in Fig. 1 shows for example that Conduct Usability Testing helps to satisfice the subgoals *Provide Appropriate Level of Information* and *Provide Appropriate amount of Information* but hurts Performance concerns as well as *Cost*. On the other Hand, while *Provide Appropriate Level of Information* and *Provide Appropriate amount of Information* helps to satisfice Usability it also presents a possible conflict with the Security SIG. Performance does not appear together with the other three NFRs on the list of correlations ("See its usage also in") because at this point it is not a SIG in our knowledge base yet.

To explore different levels of granularity regarding how solutions are developed and modeled, the tool provides the capability to use a custom search term. Typing one or more words in a search box will trigger the tool to look for any element that contains the term provided. The QR tool performs a non-restrictive search for custom terms. Therefore, it will produce a list with all the occurrences of this term in different SIGs.

Figure 2 illustrates this mentioned scenario. Let us suppose one wants to investigate where disclosure of data may be an issue. Filling up the search box with the term

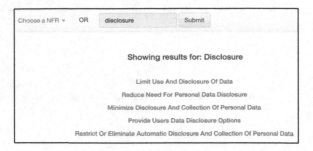

Fig. 2. QR tool: non-restrictive search – disclosure

```
PREFIX rdfs: <http://www.w3.org/2000/01/rdf-schema#>
PREFIX ndr: <http://www.yorku.ca/itec/ontologies/2014/9/NDR.owl#>
PREFIX rdf: <http://www.w3.org/1999/02/22-rdf-syntax-ns#>

#1
SELECT ?type ?label
WHERE {
    ?type rdf:type ndr:NFRsoftgoal;
    rdfs:label ?label
    FILTER regex(?label, searchTerm, 'i')
}

#2
SELECT ?interlinkId ?label ?tail ?headtype ?tailtype
WHERE {
    ?interlinkId rdf:type ndr:NFRDecomposition.
    ?interlinkId ndr:nfrDecHead targetElement.
    ?interlinkId ndr:contributionKind ?label.
    ?interlinkId ndr:nfrDecTail ?tail.
    ?tail rdf:type ?tailtype.
    targetElement rdf:type ?headtype
}
```

Fig. 3. QR tool: non-restrictive search – SPARQL queries

"disclosure" will trigger the tool to produce a series of SPARQL queries. These queries are then executed on the SPARQL server side in a recursive manner. Hence, the system can retrieve every interdependency associated with each element related to the search. Figure 3 depicts an example of two SPARQL queries: the former is produced and applied by the tool during the search term process, and the latter is employed just before the tool begins with the drawing process. As a result, the system outputs a partial graphic visualization starting from the chosen search possibility, in this case, five possible operationalizations as demonstrated in Fig. 2. If necessary, the user can still select among the subgoals/operationalizations associated with the term "disclosure" one of the five possible operationalizations to be further explored. Figure 4 illustrates the partial graphic output originated from clicking on the *Reduce Need For Personal Data Disclosure*.

The search capability provided by the QR tool works on different levels of granularity. In other words, a RE can search for any NFR related capabilities (subgoals or operationalizations), ranging from early refinements to a particular refinement level. This characteristic provides a versatile mechanism for scenarios where the granular level of a needed NFR related solution is unknown.

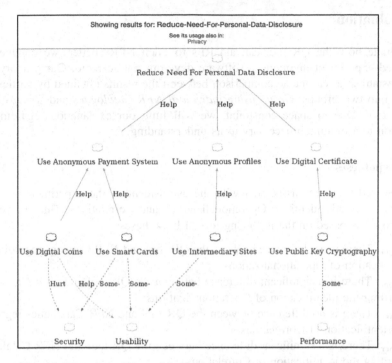

Fig. 4. QR tool: partial graphic output resulted from search – disclosure

Any correlations are displayed using a type of hyperlink between solution patterns where the RE can navigate through those patterns. Put that together with the non-restricted search capability as well as the search for specific NFRs and REs have a powerful and flexible search mechanism at hand. It helps the scalability problem allowing one to search for one specific NFR and yet be directed to look where a specific solution will hurt or help another solution either for this NFR or another.

By the same token, the search by substring where the tool searches the complete knowledge base for all the occurrences of this substring helps to find information in a vast SIG as well as looking at many different SIGs at once. We believe that such kind of tool facilitates the reuse of solutions patterns previous elicited helping REs to evaluate many different possible alternatives to comply with stakeholder's demands.

We understand that each project will face different challenges, eventually addressing different types of users and therefore stakeholders, in general, may need different solutions for different domains and even for different companies in the same domain. That is the main reason why our SIGs do not evaluate which alternative would be better to use nor do we weigh different solutions against each other. We aim at providing a *general approach that can be used in various projects* regardless of the type of development process being used or the domain in which it is being used.

4 Evaluation

To evaluate how the QR tool can aid REs to elicit NFRs better, we conducted a controlled experiment involving a software development scenario. Our primary goal was to establish a reasonable comparison between the results obtained by participants divided into two groups: *Group using individual NFR Catalogues* and *Groups using the QR tool*. Due to space constraint, we will limit our explanation regarding the evaluation to a minimum necessary to its understanding.

4.1 Hypotheses

The observed measures associated with the assessment of the experiment were the number of correctly identified Operationalizations and Correlations. Thus, our experimentation was based on the following formal hypotheses:

- H_{0oper}: There is no difference between the QR tool and NFR Catalogs regarding the identification of Operationalizations
- H_{1oper}: There is a significant difference between the QR tool and NFR Catalogues regarding the identification of Operationalizations
- H_{0corr}: There is no difference between the QR tool and NFR Catalogues regarding the identification of Correlations
- H_{1corr}: There is a significant difference between the QR tool and NFR Catalogues regarding the identification of Correlations

4.2 Methodology

To properly test our formal hypotheses, we designed an empirical evaluation with participants randomly assigned to a control group (Group using individual NFR Catalogues) and to an experimental group (Group using QR tool). Participants within the control group could only rely on pure printed NFR Catalogues as a knowledge-assistance method for eliciting and modeling NFRs. Pure NFR Catalogues were represented in a SIG format and defined as static images. On the other hand, members of the experimental group used the QR tool as a knowledge-assistance technique for eliciting and modeling NFRs. Moreover, both knowledge-assistance techniques covered the same amount of domain-free NFR Knowledge. Both had the same NFRs and the same set of operationalizations. The key differences were related to how each group could access and explore a needed NFR Knowledge. Additionally, both groups had to elicit and model NFRs following an identical software development context.

The participants targeted for this study were 4th-year undergraduate students attending a Requirements Management course from the Information Technology program at York University, Toronto - Canada. Their participation was on a voluntary basis, and each participant attended twelve non-consecutive hours of training provided in a workshop manner before performing the experiment. The training workshop mainly consisted of lessons on how to model appropriate SIGs representing solutions to expected NFRs for a particular software scenario.

The expected outcome from each participant was a set of SIGs catalogues representing a complete as possible set of NFRs and operationalizations that could be used in the proposed software development scenario. The main idea was to compare each developed SIG catalogue to an authoritative control, which was produced based on the literature on SIG catalogues and represented the expected NFRs for the proposed scenario. For comparing results, we mainly focused the number of correctly identified Operationalizations and Correlations for a particular NFR. We followed the notion that the higher the number of correctly identified Operationalizations, the higher the chance of satisficing an NFR. The same assumption applies to Correlations since it expresses possible synergies and conflicts among NFRs. We repeated this evaluation for every SIG developed by every participant. Additionally, by following the idea that different projects may lead to distinct solutions for the same NFR, our goal was to evaluate whether the QR tool could help a RE to recognize a more comprehensive set of possible alternatives for satisficing a particular NFR together with the possible implications for each possibility.

The set of SIGs developed for the authoritative controls followed the same idea and contained all possible Operationalizations and Correlations for each possible necessary NFR applicable to the problem. It was first developed by the first author and later validated by the second author.

To measure the similarity between a participant's SIG catalogue and the authoritative set of SIG models, we counted the number of correctly identified Operationalizations and Correlations in the participant's response model. An Operationalization or Correlation had to be explicitly expressed in the authoritative set of SIG catalogues to be considered accurate. Our comparison strategy also took into the account the taxonomy variations regarding the name of elements used for both Correlations and Operationalizations. We manually verified these taxonomy variations due to the subjective nature of NFRs. For instance, we manually validated that an operationalization involving "*Use Desktop*" in the authoritative model was correctly expressed in a participant's SIG catalogue as "*Use Computer*". Thus, similar terms can be applied to emphasize the same solution for satisficing an NFR. However, most of the time we were able to find exact matches quietly likely due to the use of the catalogues in both formats.

Additionally, students were randomly assigned to each of the two groups and our comparison was conducted in a blind evaluation manner. Hence, the comparison between the participant's responses and the authoritative control was performed in a random approach, disregarding the group information about the target participant.

4.3 Proposed Scenario

To bring this study as close to reality as possible, we proposed a hypothetical software development scenario involving a system for an *autonomous taxi service* company. The idea originated from the current discussions regarding autonomous systems in our present society and intended to trigger the participant's interest, demanding a significant number of NFRs to be elicited. At the same time, it intended to use a non-trivial problem in which we would find a large number of NFRs and possible

Operationalizations and Correlations. Finally, it also intended to minimize the influence of *participants using their own expertise* instead of the guidance of the catalogues.

Participants were asked to model a set of SIGs representing the expected NFRs and their Operationalizations and Correlations. We provided full documentation regarding the demanded system to each participant, including a Requirements Table characterizing every needed Functional Requirement. We also provided documentation based on Use Case diagrams, Class diagrams, and Sequence diagrams.

The identification of NFRs by the participants was part of the experiment. In other words, our documentation did not provide information about NFRs. Each participant had to elicit as many NFRs as he/she thought was necessary, relying on their own interpretation. Our authoritative control highlighted **Privacy, Security, Traceability, Transparency, Usability,** and **Performance NFRs** since those were the catalogues students were given to work with. The whole set of expected NFRs within the authoritative control featured a total number of 52 Operationalizations and 28 Correlations. Figure 5 demonstrates an example of the authoritative SIG depicting solutions for Security. It is noteworthy to mention that the goal of the SIGs composing the authoritative control was to represent the largest set of alternatives that could be used under the target domain.

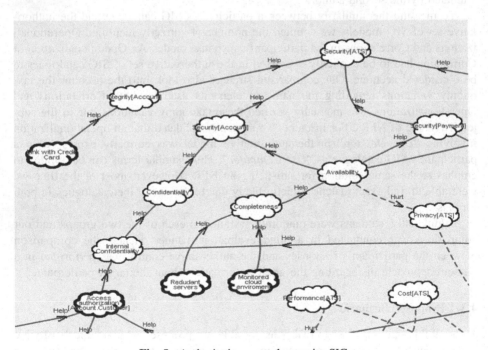

Fig. 5. Authoritative control: security SIG

4.4   Analysis

As a result of our evaluation, we were able to collect a sample composed of 18 participants. Half of the participants used the QR tool as a knowledge-assistance technique, while the other half performed the experiment using pure NFR Catalogues as a knowledge-assistance method. The data collected from each participant's response was essentially the percentage of Operationalizations and Correlations correctly identified. For example, if a particular participant found 8 correct Operationalizations out of the total of 52, we considered 15.38% as the quantified data for our analysis. The same logic was applied to the total of Correlations correctly identified.

Correspondingly, both groups define a population positively skewed. The central tendency measure indicates that the average of results from the Group with QR tool (*Median = 36.54%*) is significantly higher than the one from the Group with NFR Catalogues (*Median = 13.46%*). Additionally, the Group with QR tool demonstrated a higher variability among the obtained results in comparison to the Group with NFR Catalogues. Moreover, the distribution of results from the Group with NFR Catalogues concentrates towards the minimum possible value. This observation suggests that most of the participants in Group with NFR Catalogues identified a low percentage of operationalizations in comparison to Group with QR tool.

When analyzing both groups regarding the percentage of correctly identified correlations, both groups presented a positively skewed dataset. Also, the central tendency measure shows that the average for the Group with QR tool (*Median = 25%*) is significantly greater than the average presented by the Group with NFR Catalogue (*Median = 3.57%*), which seems to have the same value as the first quartile value within the dataset. Furthermore, the Group with QR tool demonstrated a higher variability among the obtained results. Additionally, in this comparison, both groups demonstrated a distribution more concentrated towards the minimum value from each dataset. However, it is noticeable that participants within the Group with QR tool could still elicit a high percentage of correlations since their minimum presented value (*17.86%*) can be considered as a medium-high percentage value in comparison to the results obtained from the Group with NFR Catalogues.

To test our formal hypotheses, we also conducted an inferential statistical analysis. We carried out a Mann-Whitney U test for both Hypotheses. The results indicate that for the first hypothesis (H_{1oper}), the null hypothesis (H_{0oper}) should be rejected (*2-tailed sigma of 0.015*). Consequently, we can confirm our first hypothesis: There is a significant difference between the QR tool and NFR Catalogues regarding the identification of operationalizations. For the second hypothesis (H_{1corr}), the results also indicate that the null hypothesis (H_{0corr}) should be rejected (*2-tailed sigma of 0.002*). Consequently, we assume the confirmation of our second hypothesis: There is a significant difference between the QR tool and NFR Catalogues regarding the identification of correlations. Also, in both comparisons, the Group with QR tool presented a significantly higher mean rank value than Group with NFR Catalogues.

4.5   Threats to Validity

From the perspective of Internal Validity, Maturation was not considered a threat to our study since each participant had to perform the tasks for the experiment only once. As for Instrumentation, we controlled this threat by providing identical conditions for every subject regarding tools and execution time. Also, we designed the experiment in a similar manner to an optional academic course assignment. Biased subject selection prevailed partially uncontrolled in our study since each target subject consisted of an undergraduate student attending a Requirements Management course. However, among this population, we randomly choose who was going to participate in each group from the available participants. To mitigate Experimental mortality, we provided the entire essential material through a web-portal, and we let each subject perform the experiment in their timely manner until a specific due date.

Regarding External Validity, there is the issue of interactions between selection biases and the independent variable: This threat remained uncontrolled due to our target population in this study. We acknowledge that using only students may raise doubts on whether results could be extrapolated to experienced REs. However, studies such as the one from Salman et al. [18] show that, as well as in other studies, when applying new technology students results do not statistically differ from professional results. Recently, editors of the Empirical Software Engineering engaged in discussion with other authors and the authors in Salman et al. discussed the validity of using students [19]. Several arguments are made both in favor of using students and the preference for using professionals. However, it is acknowledged the use of professionals can be prohibitive, and in many situations, the use of students can lead to equivalent results.

Our results suggest that the QR tool may facilitate the reuse of NFR Knowledge and therefore contribute to elicit a more comprehensive set of possible NFRs. Given the statistical outcome, we believe that the features provided by the QR tool offered convenience and helped participants to navigate through the available NFR Knowledge in a more efficient way. Among these features we emphasize: (i) The capability to navigate from one NFR to another, (ii) The ability to query one particular NFR and retrieve it operationalizations together with possible correlations, (iii) The non-restrictive search capability that covers different granularity levels regarding NFR operationalizations and interdependencies and (iv) The provided inference mechanism for identifying occurrences of a particular element across the knowledge repository, leading to correlations.

We also consider that these features assisted the participants in identifying more possible synergies and conflicts regarding an element involved in satisficing an NFR. For instance, a participant wondering whether Transparency correlates with another NFR could easily use the tool to search for "Transparency" and quickly see its occurrence across the Knowledge Repository. At this point, a participant would also be able to verify every correlation associated with Transparency according to the NFR Knowledge in the repository.

Regarding the sample size of the experiment, we understand that a larger dataset would produce more accurate results regarding both groups. We aim to reproduce this study in the future with a bigger population. However, we believe that the number of participants is enough to support our conclusions.

We also understand that as pointed out by Gramatica [6] the use of catalogues may differ for expert users when compared to novice users and in our experiment, we only used novice participants. Nevertheless, we believe that both would gain from using our framework.

Additionally, it is important to mention the current limitations of our approach. At this moment, we consider the tool's Knowledge Acquisition feature as a semi-automated process. Currently, the platform assumes that every SIG provided as a knowledge input contains substantial NFR information. Therefore, the QR tool still relies on a manual knowledge validation as pre-step for the knowledge acquisition phase. We aim to address this challenge by applying the use of a custom and automated ontology reasoner during the importation of NFR Knowledge into the repository in the future to facilitate this semi-automated process.

As mentioned before, the use of catalogues brings the question of the expressions used to name both NFRs and operationalizations. We are currently researching mechanisms such as the use of lexicons, thesaurus ad non-restrictive searches to mitigate this problem. Nevertheless, we believe that despite the current limitation the use of our approach already presents relevant results.

Although we have initially tackled some issues exploring the ability to use different levels of granularity to search the knowledge base, we understand that we still must improve it.

Lastly, the current version of the QR tool is designed to handle domain-free NFR Knowledge only. However, the NDR Ontology already envisions domain-specific knowledge, and we believe that the current implementation of the NDR needs minimal improvement to support domain-specific NFR Knowledge. Nevertheless, extensive tests and validations are still required to be performed. Therefore, we believe that the next version of the QR tool will include the support of domain-specific NFR Knowledge.

In an overall manner, we consider that our approach can be highlighted as an alternative for dealing and facilitating the reuse of NFR Knowledge during the early phases of the software development lifecycle. We believe that our work arises as an important contribution to the relatively few alternatives for promoting the reuse of NFR Knowledge. On a longer perspective, we will investigate how to facilitate the integration of possible solutions into models depicting the whole solution for the problem.

5 Conclusions

This paper introduces a Framework to promote the elicitation and modelling of NFRs. At this point, we present the initial approach to this framework focusing on the elicitation part. We introduce the QR tool as a support mechanism based on a previously defined ontology [7] to support the acquisition of knowledge to satisfice NFRs while allowing queries to be made on this knowledge base. The tool supports a semi-automated process of knowledge acquisition linking related SIGs. It also provides a retrieval approach that allows the requirements engineering to query the existent knowledge base using different levels of granularity as well as different approaches to search and visualize results.

We carried out a controlled experiment to evaluate how the use of the tool would help to find solutions to address needed NFRs. The experiment suggests that not only we could identify more NFRs, but perhaps more importantly, we could identify a significantly higher number of possible conflicts and synergies among possible solutions.

Future work will involve replicating this experiment with other groups to further evaluate the use of the tool and to identify possible angles to amplify the ability to provide different levels of granularities for searching solutions. We also aim at investigating mechanisms to tackle the problem of expressing one NFR or operationalization using different names/expressions. On a longer perspective, we will investigate how to facilitate the integration of possible solutions into models depicting the whole solution for the problem.

Acknowledgment. This research was partially supported by NSERC. We would also like to thank the valuable comments received from the reviewers for improving the paper.

References

1. Hasan, M.M., Loucopoulos, P., Nikolaidou, M.: Classification and qualitative analysis of non-functional requirements approaches. In: Bider, I., et al. (eds.) BPMDS/EMMSAD - 2014. LNBIP, vol. 175, pp. 348–362. Springer, Heidelberg (2014). https://doi.org/10.1007/978-3-662-43745-2_24
2. Chung, L., Nixon, B.A., Yu, E., Mylopoulos, J.: Non-Functional requirements in software engineering. International Series in Software Engineering, vol. 5. Springer, Boston (2000). https://doi.org/10.1007/978-1-4615-5269-7
3. Webster, I., Ivanova, V., Cysneiros, L.M.: Reusable knowledge for achieving privacy: health information technologies perspective. In: Proceedings of Requirements Engineering, Porto, Portugal, vol. 112, pp. 752–972 (2005). ISBN 0790
4. Cysneiros, L.M.: Evaluating the effectiveness of using catalogues to elicit non-functional requirements. In: WER, pp. 107–115 (2007)
5. Cardoso, E., Almeida, J.P., Guizzardi, R.S., Guizzardi, G.: A method for eliciting goals for business process models based on non-functional requirements catalogues. In: Frameworks for Developing Efficient Information Systems: Models, Theory, and Practice: Models, Theory, and Practice, pp. 226–242 (2013)
6. de Gramatica, M., Labunets, K., Massacci, F., Paci, F., Tedeschi, A.: The role of catalogues of threats and security controls in security risk assessment: an empirical study with ATM professionals. In: Fricker, S.A., Schneider, K. (eds.) REFSQ 2015. LNCS, vol. 9013, pp. 98–114. Springer, Cham (2015). https://doi.org/10.1007/978-3-319-16101-3_7
7. Lopez, C., Cysneiros, L.M., Astudillo, H.: NDR ontology: sharing and reusing NFR and design rationale knowledge. In: 2008 1st International Workshop on Managing Requirements Knowledge, MARK 2008 (2008)
8. Veleda, R., Cysneiros, L.M.: Towards a tool to help exploring existing non-functional requirements solution patterns. In: 2017 IEEE 25th International Requirements Engineering Conference Workshops (REW), pp. 232–239. IEEE (2017)
9. Cleland-Huang, J., Settimi, R., Benkhadra, O., Berezhanskaya, E., Christina, S.: Goal-centric traceability for managing non-functional requirements. In: Proceedings of the 27th International Conference on Software Engineering, New York, NY, USA, pp. 362–371. ACM (2005)

10. Supakkul, S., Hill, T., Chung, L., Tun, T.T., do Prado Leite, J.C.S.: An NFR pattern approach to dealing with NFRs. In: 2010 18th IEEE International Requirements Engineering Conference, pp. 179–188. IEEE (2010)

11. Sancho, P.P., Juiz, C., Puigjaner, R., Chung, L., Subramanian, N.: An approach to ontology-aided performance engineering through NFR framework. In: Proceedings of the 6th International Workshop on Software and Performance, New York, NY, USA, pp. 125–128. ACM (2007)

12. Van Harmelen, F., McGuinness, D.: OWL web ontology language overview. W3C Recommendation (2004)

13. Al Balushi, T.H., Sampaio, P.R.F., Dabhi, D., Loucopoulos, P.: ElicitO: a quality ontology-guided NFR elicitation tool. In: Sawyer, P., Paech, B., Heymans, P. (eds.) REFSQ 2007. LNCS, vol. 4542, pp. 306–319. Springer, Heidelberg (2007). https://doi.org/10.1007/978-3-540-73031-6_23

14. Hu, H., Ma, Q., Zhang, T., Tan, Y., Xiang, H., Fu, C., Feng, Y.: Semantic modelling and automated reasoning of non-functional requirement conflicts in the context of softgoal interdependencies. IET Softw. **9**, 145–156 (2015)

15. Brickley, D., Guha, R.V: RDF Vocabulary Description Language 1.0: RDF Schema (2002). https://www.w3.org/TR/2002/WD-rdf-schema-20021112/

16. The W3C SPARQL Working Group: SPARQL Query Language for RDF. http://www.w3.org/TR/rdf-sparql-query/

17. Berners-Lee, T., Hendler, J., Lassila, O., et al.: The semantic web. Sci. Am. **284**, 28–37 (2001)

18. Salman, I., Misirli, A.T., Juristo, N.: Are students representatives of professionals in software engineering experiments? In: 2015 IEEE/ACM 37th IEEE International Conference on Software Engineering, pp. 666–676. IEEE (2015)

19. Feldt, R., et al.: Four commentaries on the use of students and professionals in empirical software engineering experiments. Empir. Softw. Eng. **23**, 3801–3820 (2018)

Using a Modelling Language to Describe the Quality of Life Goals of People Living with Dementia

James Lockerbie and Neil Maiden[(⊠)]

Centre for Creativity in Professional Practice, Cass Business School,
106 Bunhill Row, London EC1Y 8TZ, UK
{James.Lockerbie.1,n.a.m.maiden}@city.ac.uk

Abstract. Although now well established, our information systems engineering theories and methods are applied only rarely in disciplines beyond systems development. This paper reports the application of the $i*$ goal modelling language to describe the types of and relationships between quality of life goals of people living with dementia. Published social care frameworks to manage and improve the lives of people with dementia were reviewed to synthesize, for the first time, a comprehensive conceptual model of the types of goals of people living with dementia. Although the quality of life goal model was developed in order to construct automated reasoning capabilities in a new digital toolset that people with dementia can use for life planning, the multi-stage modelling exercise provided valuable insights into quality of life and dementia care practices of both researchers and experienced practitioners in the field.

Keywords: Dementia · Quality of life · Interactive toolset · Goal modeling

1 Introduction

Information systems engineering theories and methods are well established in their disciplines. Outcomes from basic and applied research results that are reported in conferences such as CAiSE have transformed into maturing information systems engineering practices. Examples of these practices include business modelling formalisms [1], product variability and configuration management mechanisms [4], and goal modelling techniques [31]. In turn, these maturing practices have created new research opportunities in information systems engineering and other disciplines.

Unsurprisingly, however, most reported information systems engineering practices have been undertaken by people working to model and analyze more traditional types of information systems in domains such as person-centric healthcare [5] and air traffic management systems [15]. By contrast, there has been relatively little cross-discipline use made of the research and practices in domains as diverse as creative leadership, sports training and the care of older people. Alas, this current limited use represents missed opportunities.

One missed opportunity, which is the focus of this paper, is to support the care for people living with chronic diseases such as dementia. Dementia has emerged over the

© Springer Nature Switzerland AG 2019
P. Giorgini and B. Weber (Eds.): CAiSE 2019, LNCS 11483, pp. 162–176, 2019.
https://doi.org/10.1007/978-3-030-21290-2_11

last decade as a major societal challenge due to the increased ageing of populations, especially in more advanced economies. As well as becoming a new social care challenge and a source of individual human distress, it has major economic impacts – the economic cost of dementia worldwide has been estimated to be US$818 billion annually, rising to US$2 trillion by 2029 [20].

In this paper we report the use of an advanced goal modelling method from information systems engineering to understand, model and synthesise existing social care frameworks of quality of life of people living with dementia. The paper presents a new goal model of quality of life to be used for the development and implementation of automated reasoning capabilities to be embedded in *EnableSelfCare*, a new toolset for quality of life planning by people living with dementia.

The rest of this paper is in 5 sections. Section 2 summarises dementia and its impacts, and reports on examples of social care and digital research and practices that have been developed to improve the lives of people living with dementia. Sections 3 and 4 outline the new *EnableSelfCare* toolset under development and the rationale for using the *i** goal modelling language to model quality of life as part of the toolset. Section 5 reports the development of the new quality of life goal model, and demonstrates the model's characteristics with indicative examples. The paper ends with an exposé of insights gained from the application of the goal modelling language to a social care problem, and draws first conclusions for uses in other non-engineering domains.

2 Dementia Care Practices and Technologies

Dementia is a decline in mental ability that affects memory, thinking, concentration and perception. It occurs because of the death of brain cells or damage in parts of the brain that deal with thought processes. The number of people with it worldwide has been estimated at 47.8 million, a figure expected to double in 20 years. Alzheimer's disease is a common cause of dementia that accounts for up to 70% of all cases.

The presence of dementia impacts substantially on the person's defined quality of life, often from before diagnosis to end of life. A defined quality of life [22] derives from the World Health Organization's definition of *health*, and concerns not only the absence of disease or infirmity but also the presence of physical, mental and social wellbeing [30]. Quality of life has increasingly been used as an outcome of medical research. However, whilst there is a considerable literature relating to it (e.g. [28]), a single and accepted model of quality of life is still missing [25]. Furthermore, many people with dementia also have co-morbidities – other illnesses such as Parkinson's disease, diabetes and anaemia – that add to barriers to a defined quality of life.

Over the last 20 years, different activities of daily life with the potential to overcome barriers and maintain aspects of quality of life have been reported widely. Better-known examples of these activities include the person listening to their favourite music and reminiscing about past experiences [29]. In response, professional services such as the UK's Alzheimer's Society have started to provide online information about the more common types of these activities. However, most of these common activities improve some but not all aspects of the quality of the lives of people with dementia.

Moreover, the associations between the common types of meaningful activities and the quality of life benefits that are claimed for them are still poorly understood, and there is no single source that defines these associations.

2.1   Digital Technologies to Support People Living with Dementia

Most of the computer science research related to dementia has focused on technologies to support the early and effective diagnosis of the condition using, for example brain images [26] and magnetic resonance spectroscopy data [17]. To design such technologies, researchers such as [23] have reported the elicitation of new causal models of dementia diagnosis with domain experts.

More relevant to our work, some interactive digital technologies have been demonstrated to support people living with dementia to improve aspects of their quality of life after diagnosis. For example, Cowans et al. [7] reported early work that utilized interactive multimedia to stimulate long-term memory to prompt communication as part of reminiscence therapy for people with dementia. Cahill et al. [3] argued that assistive technologies can make a significant difference to the lives of people with dementia and to their care workers if delivered at home in a thoughtful and sensitive and ethical way. Wallace et al. [27] described the use of computing devices designed as furniture pieces by older residents to provide notions of home, intimacy and possessions with which to develop a sense of personhood. Thiry et al. [24] reported work in which older people made personal digital timelines using technologies designed to support the building of memory. Lazar et al. [14] reported the design and exploration of *Moments*, a prototype system that allowed individuals living with dementia to share their artwork with others in the network by manipulating their physical environment. And immersive interactions with virtual environments of familiar places and activities have been shown to improve some aspects of the physical and emotional wellbeing of people with dementia [10].

As these examples demonstrate, most of the research to develop new technologies to support people living with dementia relies on action research focusing on early digital prototypes in use by people living with dementia. One consequence is that few of the reported research prototypes have been evolved into production-level systems. By contrast, no applications of information systems engineering to the problems of people living with dementia have been reported, and little digital support for wider quality of life planning and improvement is available.

More generally, the types of artificial intelligence technique that have been applied successfully to support healthcare include case-based reasoning to plan radiotherapy treatments, Bayesian Belief Networks to diagnose liver disorders and artificial neural networks to predict Parkinson's tremor onset. Although effective, most were developed to manage individual medical conditions, rather than support people living with complex degenerative conditions and co-morbidities such as dementia. Now, the emerging need to support people to achieve quality of life with complex degenerative conditions such as dementia creates new opportunities for artificial intelligence in social care and healthcare – opportunities that, on the whole, have yet to be taken.

2.2 Social Care Approaches to Supporting People Living with Dementia

Social care research has led to different quality of life frameworks to help people with dementia understand and communicate their life preferences and needs. Most of these still focus on selected aspects of the person's preferences and needs, such as framing a person's quality of life choices [13], describing personal outcomes [2] or documenting preferred meaningful activities [18]. None support all of a person's quality of life preferences and needs.

Furthermore, these frameworks were developed for carers to use manually, so there are no reported attempts to make the guidance from these frameworks automatic and accessible to carers with all but the most simple of digital tools. Indeed, guidance is normally reported using informal language. For example, practical guidance for care professionals for describing personal outcomes [19] is presented as narrative and tables such as in Table 1. The guidance is informal, the presented concepts are not defined, and no structure between these concepts is reported (e.g. between *health* and *mobility*, or between *being listened to* and *being respected*), which results in ambiguities, inconsistencies and overlaps between concepts (e.g. between *I see people* and *I belong to a community*).

Table 1. Lists of outcomes important to people living in care homes, as described in a practical guide for personal outcomes in [19]

Quality of life	Process	Change
• I feel safe and secure	• I am treated as an individual	• My skills are improved
• I see people	• I am valued and respected	• My confidence and morale are improved
• I have things to do	• I am listened to	• My mobility is improved
• I live in a nice place	• I have a say in decisions about my care and support	• My health has improved or my symptoms are reduced
• I live life as I want and where I want	• I am supported to live well and plan for a good end of life	

Although an experienced carer can interpret the ambiguities and inconsistencies in the guidance for the needs of each individual, the informality impedes the development of all but the most basic digital support based on these frameworks.

Furthermore such frameworks, in their current forms, are not usable to support the use of emerging technologies that increase automation in dementia care using, for example, the Internet of Things, big data analytics and machine learning. Indeed, these frameworks were designed to be used with volumes of data that are orders of magnitude smaller than can be collected using digital sensors, and process this data less frequently than is possible with real-time data collection.

To conclude, our review of social care frameworks revealed an opportunity to apply information systems engineering theories and methods to model and synthesise concepts related to the quality of life of people with dementia. One planned outcome of this modelling work would be to inform the development of a new digital toolset for use by people with dementia to plan to improve the qualities of their lives. The next section introduces one such toolset, and the pivotal role of a new quality of life goal model in that toolset.

3   The *EnableSelfCare* Toolset

The use of documented plans for the lives of people with dementia – plans that describe the life requirements and the meaningful activities to undertake to contribute to these requirements to maintain and acquire – is becoming commonplace. Increasingly, these plans are documented using digital tools. However, although domestic sensors are also now available and used to monitor people with dementia [12], these sensors are not integrated meaningfully with their digital plans that describe the requirements and associated activities to be monitored. This gap can result in interventions that might be inconsistent with the person's requirements.

Therefore, the future *EnableSelfCare* toolset will allow a person with dementia living in their own home to plan, monitor and self-manage his or her life and wellbeing. The person will interact with the toolset using a simple interface to describe and change requirements and meaningful activities that s/he desires to maintain, achieve and undertake. These requirements will be used to configure a simple set of low-cost sensors to collect data about, for example, movement and applied pressure associated with the activities. Data fusion algorithms will generate descriptions of the person's activities from data collected from these sensors – descriptions that will provide the input data to a computational version of a new quality of life goal model. The model will use these descriptions to infer whether desired requirements associated with these activities are achieved. The toolset architecture is depicted in Fig. 1. Its intelligence will derive from the completeness and accuracy of the model.

Therefore, development of this goal model became a major research task.

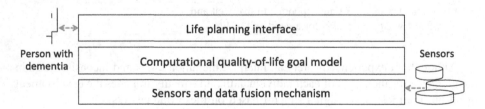

Fig. 1. Simplified architecture of the *EnableSelfCare* toolset

4   Using the *i** Goal Modelling Language

To enable precise representation of and analyses about the goal types derived from the existing social care frameworks, the model was developed using the *i** goal modeling language [31] from information systems engineering. The *i** language enables the modeling of intentions of different actors in a social system, and has been applied to analyze goals and associations in complex systems in, for example, healthcare monitoring systems [16]. With *i**, an actor seeks to achieve or attain an end element, which in *i** can be a soft goal or a goal. An actor also has the means to achieve or attain the end element. In *i** a means can be a goal, soft goal, a task, or a resource. The actor seeks to attain a goal (a desirable state) and undertake a task (so that a goal might be attained). With soft goal contributes-to links, the achievement of one soft goal can contribute positively or negatively to achieving another soft goal. Where the end element of the links is a soft goal, the relationship can be attributed with values that specify the modality and type of the contribution (*Some +*, *Some–, Help, Hurt, Make, Break, Unknown*), as reported in [31].

Some of the *i** model semantics mapped well to content that was extracted from the different quality of life framework elements, indicating that it could be an effective language with which to describe the intentions of people living with dementia. *i** soft goals were effective for describing types of state that the person desired to achieve, such as qualities of life and personal outcomes. Examples of these soft goal types included *social life maintained* and *cognitive function maintained*. *i** tasks were effective for describing the meaningful activity types that the person sought to undertake, for example *to stroll in garden* and *to make own lunch*. And *i** contributes-to links could be applied to describe how the completion of types of meaningful activity contributed to achieving different types of soft goals, and how soft goal type achievement contributed to the achievement of other soft goal types.

5 Developing the New Quality of Life Goal Model

To develop a first version of the new quality of life model, we conducted a review of academic literature on quality of life. At stages, to direct the review, we consulted about the review findings with leading academics and practitioners in dementia care. Based on these consultations we sometimes reviewed other literatures. And during these reviews, we developed informal versions of the model by extracting goal types from the frameworks and documented these types using semi-structured graphical notations. When it was assessed to be sufficiently complete, the informal model was described formally using the *i** goal modeling language.

The model was developed to be a general model that would describe the types of goal that would hold for most people living with dementia. As a consequence it described types of goal such as *engaged with neighborhood* rather than instance-level goals such as *engaged with my village's neighborhood watch*. The rest of this section reports each of the model development stages.

The literature review revealed a wide-range of treatments of quality of life in disciplines such as health and nutrition, so we restricted the literature review to quality of life of people living with dementia. Lawton [13] reported that whilst quality of life emerged as a concept at the forefront of gerontology research, much of this research neglected the quality of lives of people with Alzheimer's disease. His subsequent research of quality of life for people living with dementia provided a baseline for many care practice approaches, and was subsequently referenced by other quality of life dementia frameworks such as the *Bath Assessment of Subjective Quality of Life in Dementia (BASQID)* and *dementia quality of life instrument (DQoL)*. Moreover,

Lawton's model is cited as the most pervasive influence on conceptualizing quality of life in dementia [21]. Therefore, the first version of the model and the types of goal that it described was based on Lawton's framework [13].

Although Lawton's framework identified important elements with which to structure the model, it did not define personal goal types of importance to people living with dementia. Person-centred care is now a dominant form of caring for older people with dementia. It is a form of care that seeks an individualized approach that recognizes the uniqueness of the world from the perspective of the person with dementia [4]. After consultations with care academics and practitioners, we conducted a review of the personal outcomes literature (e.g. [2]) associated with person-centred care practices. Personal outcome goals are, by definition, specific to individuals [6], so the review revealed numerous examples of personal goals rather than a comprehensive list of goal types. Therefore, the extracted examples of personal goals were clustered to enable us to generate a smaller set of goal types that represented most of the collected personal goal examples uncovered in the literature. Then, to associate the personal goal types with types of meaningful activities that people can undertake to improve quality of life, we reviewed taxonomies of activities for people with dementia [8]. These taxonomies were used to generate types of goals that a person achieves by completing a single or few instances of types of meaningful activities. The resulting goal types were then associated with a larger set of meaningful activity types that people living with dementia in their own homes might undertake in order to improve the qualities of their lives in different ways.

The basic structure of the goal model is depicted in Fig. 2. This model describes a small number of types of soft goal associated with qualities of life that all people living with dementia would seek to achieve. These types of soft goal were then associated with a larger number of types of soft goal that were extracted from goal examples from the personal outcome frameworks. New associations between these soft goal types were then discovered and added to the model. The types of soft goals extracted from the meaningful activities were also then added, and associated via further modelling with both the personal outcomes soft goal types and the larger number of meaningful activity types associated with achieving quality of life.

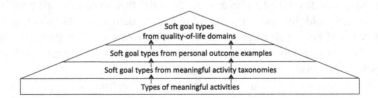

Fig. 2. The basic structure of the quality of life goal model derived from social care frameworks

At different points in the process, experienced professional domiciliary carers validated the emerging versions of the quality of life goal model. A total of 7 workshops took place to validate the completeness and the accuracy of the goal types and contributes-to links. The input model to each workshop was updated with changes after the first 3 workshops. To encourage hands-on changes by the carers, the model's digital representation was transformed into a physical one of cards, pins and string, as depicted in Fig. 3. Most model transformations were additions of new content such as new types of meaningful activity and changes to contributes-to links between soft goal types. Outcomes from these workshops led to many implemented model changes.

 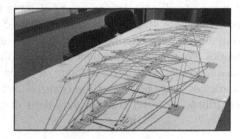

Fig. 3. Examples of physical versions of the quality of life goal model used in the workshops

Each part of the new quality of life goal model is described in turn.

5.1 The Modeled Overall Quality of Life Goal Types

Lawton's definition of quality of life with Alzheimer's disease [13] specified 6 quality of life domains: the *ability to perform activities of daily living, engaging in the meaningful use of time, competent cognitive functioning, physical health, socially appropriate behavior,* and a *favorable balance between positive and negative emotion* [13]. As Lawton's framework has had a far-reaching influence on conceptualizations of quality of life of people with dementia, 5 of these 6 domains were used to define 5 soft goal types that each person would seek to achieve. The 6th quality of life domain identified by Lawton – *engaged in the meaningful use of time* – was not converted into a soft goal type because it was the premise of all the meaningful activities, and therefore represented by all of the modelled meaningful activity soft goal types. The remaining 5 quality of life soft goal types that structure the quality of life goal model are summarized graphically in Fig. 4.

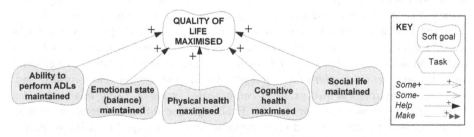

Fig. 4. The soft goal types used to structure the quality of life goal model, and key of used i* graphical modelling elements

5.2   The Modeled Personal Outcomes Goal Types

The different types of soft goal generated from examples of personal outcomes in the frameworks (e.g. [2, 6]) were described in the new quality of life goal model. After analyses of multiple personal goal examples and validation exercises with the professional carers, a total of 40 personal outcome soft goal types were added to the model. Figure 5 depicts 9 of these 40 soft goal types and contributes-to links to 2 of the 5 types of soft goal derived from Lawton's framework [13]. Most of the associations between these 40 soft goal types and the 5 different soft goal types from Lawton's framework were inferred from examples reported in the personal outcomes frameworks. For example, the model describes that the increased achievement of *communication skills maintained, learning maintained, active mind brain function maintained, perceived state of memory maximized* and *ability to concentrate maximized* each contributes positively to achieving the soft goal *cognitive health maximized.*

Fig. 5. Different types of soft goal generated from the personal outcomes literature associated to quality of life soft goal types

Unsurprisingly, the review revealed a lack of explicit associations between quality of life goals reported in the different sources, so the validation workshops were used to discover and validate missing contribute-to links between soft goal types.

5.3   The Modeled Goal Types Associated with Meaningful Activities

Meaningful activities include physical, social and leisure activities such as *gardening, reading* and *singing*. There are many factors that make activities meaningful to an individual that can relate to that person's values, beliefs, past roles, interests and routines [9]. Han et al. [8] synthesized qualitative studies of meaningful activities of people with dementia (e.g. [9]), categorized these meaningful activities and identified themes related to *connectedness* with which to categorize them. The 3 themes described how a person with dementia might seek to connect: (1) to oneself (for example *through maintenance of personal routines, engaging in activities to benefit health* and *having personal time and rest*); (2) to others (for example *having social contact, doing activities with others* and *maintaining meaningful relationships*) and: (3) to one's environment (for example *being settled at home, being involved in the community* and *getting out into nature*). Enabling these different senses of purpose through meaningful activities had been shown to improve the quality of life of people living with dementia (e.g. [18]).

Therefore, we drew on the reported categories of meaningful activities and their descriptions to extract equivalent possible types of soft goal of people living with dementia associated with the 3 themes. Two additional types – *engaged in creative activity achieved* and *engaged in personal finances achieved* – were added to these soft goal types from other sources. After the workshops with professional carers, the model was composed of 17 different types of soft goal that described outcomes associated directly with the completion of common meaningful activities. Examples of these extracted soft goal types are depicted graphically in Fig. 6.

CONNECTED TO ENVIRONMENT			CONNECTED TO SELF				CONNECTED TO OTHERS			
Engaged with own home environment	Engaged in neighbourhood activities	Engaged with nature achieved	Engaged for continuity achieved	Engaged in relaxation achieved	Engaged in physical activity achieved	+ 7 more	Engaged in helping others achieved	Engaged in the company of others	Engaged in relationship based activity	Engaged in support activity for condition

Fig. 6. Examples of goal types achieved directly by the successful completion of types of meaningful activities, structured by the connectedness model reported in [10]

5.4 The Modelled Contribute-to Links Between Quality of Life Soft Goal Types

The literature review and validation workshops revealed that most modelled contributes-to links were *Help* rather than *Make* links. The achievement of most meaningful activity or quality of life soft goal types contributed positively to achieving other quality of life soft goal types, but on its own, each contribution was insufficient to achieve the quality of life soft goal type. Only a small number of contributes-to links were *Make* links, for which achievement of a meaningful activity or quality of life soft goal type was sufficient to achieve a quality of life soft goal type. In cases where the *Some* + contributes-to links were modelled, we took consensus across the workshops to remove each link or change it to a *Help* contribution.

Example contributes-to links of both types are shown in Fig. 7, which depicts *Make* contributions arising from achieving the soft goal type *engaged in intellectual brain activity achieved*. The model describes that engaging in *intellectual brain activities* is sufficient, on its own, to *maximise cognitive health*. By contrast, maximizing cognitive health is not, on its own, sufficient to maximize *quality of life*.

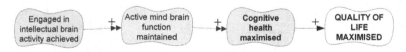

Fig. 7. Flattened representation a goal contribution thread through the new quality of life model showing the contribution of having engaged in intellectual brain activity

5.5 Modelled Tradeoffs Between Quality of Life Soft Goal Types

The validation workshops also uncovered trade-offs between types of soft goal that were true in most care contexts. Trade-offs were needed because the *EnableSelfCare* toolset is required to support someone with dementia to evaluate the impact of their activities on quality of life over a given time period. Understanding trade-offs would inform their decision making about qualities to achieve and activities to plan. Whilst professional carers reported that there was scope to achieve most quality of life soft goal types without tradeoffs, some tradeoffs did hold for most cases of people living with dementia. One tradeoff, which is depicted in Fig. 8, was between the soft goals *sense of freedom achieved* and *sense of safety achieved*. Other soft goal trade-offs that were modelled were between *activity* and *relaxation, support/nurture* and *independence*, and family *involvement* and *respite*.

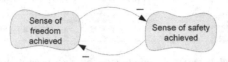

Fig. 8. A two-way trade-off expressed using contributes-to links between types of soft goals

5.6   Modelled Meaningful Activity Types Contributing to Quality of Life

The types of meaningful activities that were modelled were extracted from examples in the literature (e.g. [8]) and classified into domains to link to modelled soft goal types. Classes such as *physical, spiritual, intellectual* and *social* were refined by sub-classes e.g. *tennis* as a subclass of *sport*, as shown in Fig. 9. Other sub-classes of meaningful activities were then elicited from the validation exercises. Once the classification was stable, additional data from an additional published source – the *Compendium of Physical Activities* [32] – was analyzed in order to generate additional meaningful activity types and task attributes such as such as how much physical energy needs to be expended on typical activity types, to enable comparisons when making decisions.

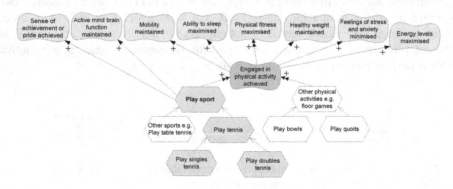

Fig. 9. Mapping classified meaningful activities to the quality of life soft goal types

5.7   The Resulting Quality of Life Goal Model

The resulting descriptive version of the quality of life goal model was composed of 63 different soft goal types and a larger number of contributes-to links between these soft goal types, see Fig. 10. The model also described another 744 different task types representing types of meaningful activities that contribute to the modelled quality of life soft goal types, but these are not shown in Figure.

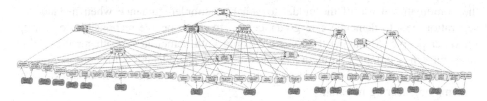

Fig. 10. The final version of the quality of life goal model, showing types of soft goal sought by people living at home with dementia, accessible at [33]

This descriptive model of quality of life goal was subsequently transformed into a computational version in the *EnableSelfCare* toolset. This new version receives as inputs data about the degree of completion of meaningful activities of different types, then computes and propagates values representing the degree of achievement to quality of life goal types, to provide feedback on qualities of life being achieved and alternative activities to achieve better the quality of life goal types not being achieved. We look forward to reporting on this computational model in future publications.

6   Insights and Lessons

As well as produce the new model of quality of life goals for people living with dementia, the application of the goal modelling provided a series of unexpected insights by the researchers and professional care practitioners about the social care literature.

The conceptual analysis confirmed that no single existing social framework (e.g. [2, 6, 8] provided complete guidance to describe all of the quality of life goals that were described in the model. Instead, the model was a synthesis of overlapping goals identified in and extracted from different frameworks. Indeed, our conceptual analysis using the goal modelling language [31] was essential to undertake a cost-effective synthesis of quality of life goals from different frameworks, based on the identification of overlapping goals and associations between goals. Moreover, the validation workshops with the professional carers revealed that our codification of the informal using the *i** goal modelling language based on available literature had been relatively accurate, and that the model omissions reflected the gaps between the partial frameworks. This outcome revealed that reviewing and interpreting a complex and inconsistent literature in order to produce a complex goal model in a new discipline can be an effective means of undertaking research.

One possible reason for the partial guidance offered by the reviewed social care frameworks (e.g. [2, 6]) was the need for simple forms of guidance that carers appeared to require. Most carers were not educated to degree level and had little time to read or learn guidance to undertake care work. Indeed, many were not professional, and had received limited training. Therefore, most published guidance appeared not to incorporate or report underlying complex concepts, even though those concepts were important for understanding and delivering dementia care. By contrast, our reported use of the goal modelling language separated the description of complex phenomena from the computational use of the model to generate simpler guidance when needed – a separation new to dementia care guidance and to many people responsible for caring for older people. Managing the lives of people with dementia and other chronic diseases remains a complex problem lacking solutions. To understand this complexity, the authors used a new method to describe this complexity – a method from information systems engineering research.

Furthermore, model validation in the workshops often externalized care knowledge that was semi-tacit. This new externalization of care knowledge, in turn, encouraged the care professionals to reflect on their care practices. For example, the professionals in the workshops reported that the model supported them to contextualize their care expertise. One said: "*To us, we just do what we do. You know, we don't class it as a job. So looking at that now [the model] you don't realize what you do looking at it on paper. You think oh gosh, do I do that, do I do that? Ooh, you know isn't it. We don't realize a lot of it.*". Whilst the care professionals had knowledge of quality of life frameworks and experience with different types of meaningful activity in their work, they had not seen a framework that connected both. As a consequence two commented: "*It's like a flow isn't it*" and "*I found it surprising that something down there can come to up there actually*". Although the use of conceptual modelling visualizations is now familiar in business analysis, engineering and even healthcare, the use in dementia care appeared to be new, especially to externalize and model concepts associated with quality of life. The modelling experience revealed the benefits of applying information systems engineering methods in new domains.

Finally, use of the $i*$ goal modelling language was a critical enabler for the authors to design and implement a new computational model of quality of life goals as part of the *EnableSelfCare* toolset. We are beginning to evaluate the completeness and accuracy of this computational model.

7   Conclusions

This paper reports the use of the $i*$ goal modelling language from information systems engineering to understand, model and synthesise existing frameworks of quality of life of people living with dementia. It presents a new goal model of quality of life for the development and implementation of automated reasoning capabilities.

The authors believe that this research can inspire and guide other researchers to explore new avenues and opportunities for the use of information systems engineering methods. For example, the goal modelling languages can be applied to model and analyse the quality of life goals of people living with other chronic conditions such as

Parkinson's and different forms of cancer. And understanding and support the qualities of the lives of citizens have become increasingly important to governments, such as the *Good Society Framework* [11] applied by a previous UK government. Again, conceptual modelling can be applied to support such work. As engineers, we have responsibilities to deploy our knowledge and skills for the wider good.

Acknowledgements. This work is supported by the EPSRC-funded SCAMPI project Grant EP/P010024/1.

References

1. Bhattacharya, K., Gerede, C., Hull, R., Liu, R., Su, J.: Towards formal analysis of artifact-centric business process models. In: Alonso, G., Dadam, P., Rosemann, M. (eds.) Business Process Management, LNCS, vol. 4714, pp. 288–304. Springer, Heidelberg (2007). https://doi.org/10.1007/978-3-319-45348-4
2. Bowers, H., Bailey, G., Sanderson, H., Easterbrook, L., Macadam, A.: Person Centred Thinking with Older People: Practicalities and Possibilities. HSA Press, Stockport (2007)
3. Cahill, S., Macijauskiene, J., Nygard, A., Kaulkner, J., Hagen, I.: Technology in dementia care. Technol. Disabil. **19**(2/3), 53–54 (2007)
4. Chen, L., Babar, M.A.: A systematic review of evaluation of variability management approaches in software product lines. Inf. Softw. Technol. **53**(4), 344–362 (2011)
5. Chiasera, A., Creazzi, E., Brandi, M., Baldessarini, I., Vispi, C.: Continuous improvement, business intelligence and user experience for health care quality. In: Krogstie, J., Reijers, Hajo A. (eds.) CAiSE 2018. LNCS, vol. 10816, pp. 505–519. Springer, Cham (2018). https://doi.org/10.1007/978-3-319-91563-0_31
6. Cook, A., Miller, E.: Talking Points Personal Outcomes Approach: Practical Guide. JIT, Edinburgh (2012)
7. Cowans, G., Campbell, J., Alm, N., Dye, R., Astell, A., Ellis, M.: Designing a multimedia conversation aid for reminiscence therapy in dementia care environments. In: Proceedings CHI 2004 Extended Abstracts, pp. 825–836. ACM Press (2004)
8. Han, A., Radel, J., McDowd, J., Sabata, D.: Perspectives of people with dementia about meaningful activities: a synthesis. Am. J. Alzheimer's Dis. Other Dementias **31**(2), 115–123 (2016)
9. Harmer, B., Orrell, M.: What is meaningful activity for people with dementia living in care homes? a comparison of the views of older people with dementia, staff and family carers. Aging Ment. Health **12**(5), 548–558 (2018)
10. Hodge, J., Balaam, M., Hastings, S., Morrissey, K.: Exploring the design of tailored virtual reality experiences for people with dementia. In: Proceedings CHI2018 Conference, Paper No. 514. ACM Press (2018)
11. Jordan, P.: The Good Society Framework. http://www.patrickwjordan.com/15/business-psychology-models. Accessed on 23 Nov 2018
12. Karakostas, A., ILazarou, I., Meditskos, G., Stavropoulos, T., Kompatsiaris, I., Tsolaki, M.: Sensor-based in-home monitoring of people with dementia using remote web technologies. In: Proceedings of International Conference on Interactive Mobile Communication Technologies and Learning (IMCL), Thessaloniki, 2015, pp. 353–357 (2005)
13. Lawton, M.: Quality of life in Alzheimer Disease. Alzheimer Dis. Assoc. Disord. **8**(3), 138–150 (1994)

14. Lazar, A., Edasis, C., Hazelrig, A.: Supporting people with dementia in digital social sharing. In: Proceedings CHI2017 Conference, pp. 2149–2162. ACM Press (2017)
15. Lockerbie, J., Bush, D., Maiden, N.A.M., Blom, H., Everdij, M.: Using i* modelling as a bridge between air traffic management operational concepts and agent-based simulation analysis. In: Proceedings 18th IEEE International Requirements Engineering Conference, pp. 351–356. IEEE Computer Society Press (2010)
16. Lockerbie, J., Maiden, N.A.M., Engmann, J., Randall, D., Jones, S., Bush, D.: Exploring the impact of software requirements on system-wide goals: a method using satisfaction arguments and i* goal modelling. Requirements Eng. J. **17**(3), 227–254 (2012)
17. Munteanu, C., et al.: Classification of mild cognitive impairment and Alzheimer's Disease with machine-learning techniques using H magnetic resonance spectroscopy data. Expert Syst. Appl. **42**(15–16), 6205–6214 (2015)
18. Palacios-Ceña, D., Gómez-Calero, C., Cachón-Pérez, J.M., Velarde-García, J.F., Martínez-Piedrola, R., Pérez-De-Heredia, M.: Is the experience of meaningful activities understood in nursing homes? a qualitative study. Geriat. Nurs. **37**(2), 110–115 (2015)
19. Nolan, M., Brown, J., Davies, S., Nolan, J., Keady, J.: The senses framework: improving care for older people through a relationship-centred approach. Getting Research into Practice (GRiP) Report No 2. Sheffield Hallam University (2006)
20. Prince, M., Wimo, A., Guerchet, M., Ali, G., Wu, Y., Prina, M.: World Alzheimer Report 2015, The Global Impact of Dementia: An Analysis of Prevalence, Incidence, Cost and Trends. Alzheimer's Disease International, London (2015)
21. Ready, R., Ott, B.: Quality of Life measures for dementia. Health Qual. Life Outcomes **1**, 11 (2003)
22. Riepe, M., et al.: Quality of life as an outcome in Alzheimer's Disease and other dementias - obstacles and goals. BMC Neurol. **9**, 47 (2009)
23. Sutcliffe, A., et al.: Known and unknown requirements in healthcare. Requirements Eng. J., pp. 1–20 (2018). https://doi.org/10.1007/s00766-018-0301-6
24. Thiry, E., Lindley, S., Banks, R., Regan, T.: Authoring personal histories: exploring the timeline as a framework for meaning making. In: Proceedings CHI 2013 Conference, pp. 1619–1628. ACM Press (2013)
25. Vaarama, M.: Care-related quality of life in old age. Eur. J. Ageing **6**(2), 113–125 (2009)
26. Veeramuthu, A., Meenakshi, S., Manjusha, P.: A New approach for Alzheimer's Disease diagnosis by using association rule over PET images. Int J. Comput. Appl. (0975 – 8887) **91** (9), 9–14 (2014)
27. Wallace, J., Thieme, A., Wood, G., Schofield, G., Oliver, P.: Enabling self, intimacy and a sense of home in dementia: an enquiry into design in a hospital setting. In: Proceedings CHI 2012 Conference, pp. 2629–2638. ACM Press (2012)
28. Wilhelmsen, K., Andersson, C., Waern, M., Allebeck, P.: Elderly people's perspectives on quality of life. Ageing Soc. **25**(4), 585–600 (2005)
29. Woods, B., Spector, A., Jones, C., Orrell, M., Davies, S.: Reminiscence therapy for dementia. Cochrane Database Syst. Rev. **18**(2), CD001120 (2005)
30. World Health Organization, Constitution of WHO: Principles. http://www.who.int/about/mission/en/. Accessed 23 Aug 2018
31. Yu, E., Giorgini, P., Maiden, N., Mylopoulos, M.: Social Modeling for Requirements Engineering. MIT Press, Cambridge (2010)
32. Ainsworth, B., et al.: 2011 Compendium of physical activities: a second update of codes and MET values. Med. Sci. Sports Exerc. **43**(8), 1575–1581 (2011)
33. SCAMPI website (2019). http://scampi.city.ac.uk/files/QoL_Model_Winter_2018_CAiSE.pdf

Multi-platform Chatbot Modeling and Deployment with the Jarvis Framework

Gwendal Daniel[1]($\boxtimes$), Jordi Cabot[1,2], Laurent Deruelle[3], and Mustapha Derras[4]

[1] Internet Interdisciplinary Institute (IN3),
Universitat Oberta de Catalunya (UOC), Barcelona, Spain
gdaniel@uoc.edu
[2] ICREA, Barcelona, Spain
jordi.cabot@icrea.cat
[3] Berger-Levrault, Pérols, France
laurent.deruelle@berger-levrault.com
[4] Berger-Levrault, Labège, France
mustapha.derras@berger-levrault.com

Abstract. Chatbot applications are increasingly adopted in various domains such as e-commerce or customer services as a direct communication channel between companies and end-users. Multiple frameworks have been developed to ease their definition and deployment. They typically rely on existing cloud infrastructures and artificial intelligence techniques to efficiently process user inputs and extract conversation information. While these frameworks are efficient to design simple chatbot applications, they still require advanced technical knowledge to define complex conversations and interactions. In addition, the deployment of a chatbot application usually requires a deep understanding of the targeted platforms, increasing the development and maintenance costs. In this paper we introduce the Jarvis framework, that tackles these issues by providing a Domain Specific Language (DSL) to define chatbots in a platform-independent way, and a runtime engine that automatically deploys the chatbot application and manages the defined conversation logic. Jarvis is open source and fully available online.

Keywords: MDE · DSL · Chatbot design · Chatbot deployment

1 Introduction

Instant messaging platforms have been widely adopted as one of the main technology to communicate and exchange information [9,22]. Nowadays, most of them provide built-in support for integrating *chatbot applications*, which are automated conversational agents capable of interacting with users of the platform [18]. Chatbots have proven useful in various contexts to automate tasks and improve the user experience, such as automated customer services [32],

© Springer Nature Switzerland AG 2019
P. Giorgini and B. Weber (Eds.): CAiSE 2019, LNCS 11483, pp. 177–193, 2019.
https://doi.org/10.1007/978-3-030-21290-2_12

education [16], and e-commerce [30]. Moreover, existing reports highlight the large-scale usage of chatbots in social media [29], and emphasize that chatbot design will become a key ability in IT hires in the near future [12].

This widespread interest and demand for chatbot applications has emphasized the need to be able to quickly build complex chatbot applications supporting natural language processing [13], custom knowledge base definition [27], as well as complex action responses including external service composition. However, the definition of chatbots remains a challenging task that requires expertise in a variety of technical domains, ranging from natural language processing to a deep understanding of the API of the targeted instant messaging platforms and third-party services to be integrated.

So far, chatbot development platforms have mainly addressed the first challenge, typically by relying on external *intent recognition providers*, that are natural language processing frameworks providing user-friendly interfaces to define conversation assets. As a trade-off, chatbot applications are tightly coupled to their *intent recognition providers*, hampering their maintainability, reusability and evolution.

This work aims to tackle both issues by raising the level of abstraction at what chatbots are defined, and can be summarized by the following design research question [31]

Can we improve the development of chatbot applications by abstracting out the platforms complexity and deployment configurations in order to allow designers to focus on the logic of the designed chatbot?

In this paper we introduce Jarvis, a novel model-based chatbot development framework that aims to address this question using Model Driven Engineering (MDE) techniques. Jarvis embeds a dedicated chatbot-specific modeling language to specify user intentions, computable actions and callable services, combining them in rich conversation flows. The resulting chatbot definition is independent of the intent recognition provider and messaging platforms, and can be deployed through the Jarvis runtime component on a number of them while hiding the technical details and automatically managing the conversation. Jarvis is employed in a joint project with the Berger-Levrault company.

The rest of the paper is structured as follows: Sect. 2 introduces preliminary concepts used through the article. Section 3 shows an overview of the Jarvis framework, while Sects. 4 and 5 detail its internal components. Section 6 presents the tool support, and Sect. 7 compare our approach with existing chatbot design techniques. Finally, Sect. 8 summarizes the key points of the paper, draws conclusions, and present our future work.

2   Background

This section defines the key concepts of a chatbot application that are reused through this article.

Chatbot design [19] typically relies on parsing techniques, pattern matching strategies and Natural Language Processing (NLP) to represent the chatbot knowledge. The latter is the dominant technique thanks to the popularization of libraries and cloud-based services such as DialogFlow [8] or IBM Watson Assistant [11], which rely on Machine Learning (ML) techniques to understand the user input and provide user-friendly interfaces to design the conversational flow.

However, Pereira and Díaz have recently reported that chatbot applications can not be reduced to raw language processing capabilities, and additional dimensions such as complex system engineering, service integration, and testing have to be taken into account when designing such applications [24]. Indeed, the conversational component of the application is usually the front-end of a larger system that involves data storage and service execution as part of the chatbot reaction to the user intent. Thus, we define a chatbot as an application embedding a *recognition engine* to extract *intentions* from user inputs, and an *execution component* performing complex event processing represented as a set of *actions*.

Intentions are named entities that can be matched by the recognition engine. They are defined through a set of *training sentences*, that are input examples used by the recognition engine's ML/NLP framework to derive a number of potential ways the user could use to express the intention[1]. Matched intentions usually carry *contextual information* computed by additional extraction rules (e.g. a typed attribute such as a city name, a date, etc) available to the underlying application. In our approach, *Actions* are used to represent simple responses such as sending a message back to the user, as well as advanced features required by complex chatbots like database querying or external service calling. Finally, we define a *conversation path* as a particular sequence of received user *intentions* and associated *actions* (including non-messaging actions) that can be executed by the chatbot application.

3   Jarvis Framework

Our approach applies Model Driven Engineering (MDE) principles to the chatbot building domain. As such, chatbot models become the primary artifacts that drive all software (chatbot) engineering activities [4]. Existing reports have emphasized the benefits of MDE in terms of productivity and maintainability compared to traditional development processes [10], making it a suitable candidate to address chatbot development and deployment. In the following we first introduce a running example and then we present an overview of our MDE-based chatbot approach and its main components.

3.1   Running Example

Our case study is a simple example of a multi-platform chatbot aiming to assist newcomers in the definition of issues on the Github platform, a reported concern in the open source community [15]. Instead of directly interacting with

---

[1] In this article we focus on ML/NLP-based chatbots, but the approach could be extended to alternative recognition techniques.

the GitHub repository, users of our software could use the chatbot to report a new issue they found. The chatbot helps them to specify the repository to open the issue in and the relevant class/es affected by the issue, and opens the issue on their behalf. The chatbot is deployed as a Slack app (i.e. the conversation between the user and the chatbot takes place on the Slack messaging platform) and, beyond creating the issue itself, the chatbot sends an alert message to the repository's development team channel hosted on the Discord platform.

Although this chatbot is obviously a simplification of what a chatbot for GitHub could look like, we believe it is representative enough of the current chatbot landscape, where chatbots usually need to interact with various input/output platforms to provide rich user experiences.

In the following we show how this chatbot is defined with the help of the Jarvis modeling language, and we detail how the runtime component manages its concrete deployment and execution.

3.2   Framework Overview

Figure 1 shows the overview of the Jarvis Framework. A designer specifies the chatbot under construction using the **Jarvis Modeling Language**, that defines three core packages:

– **Intent Package** to describe the user *intentions* using training sentences, contextual information extraction, and matching conditions (e.g. the intention to open an issue or the intention to select a repository, in our running example)
– **Platform Package** to specify the possible *actions* available in the potential target platforms, including those existing only on specific environments (e.g. posting a message on a Slack channel, opening an issue on Github, etc).

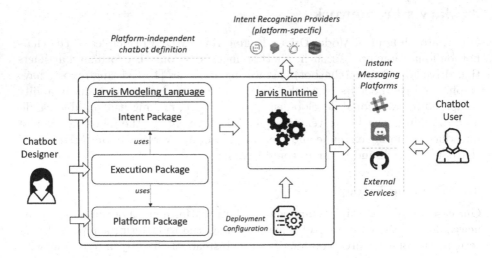

Fig. 1. Jarvis framework overview

– **Execution Package** to bind user *intentions* to *actions* as part of the chatbot behaviour definition (e.g. sending a welcome message to the user when he intents to open a new issue).

These models are complemented with a *Deployment Configuration* file, that specifies the *Intent Recognition Provider* platform to use (e.g Google's DialogFlow [8] or IBM Watson Assistant [11]), platform specific configuration (e.g. Slack and Discord credentials), as well as custom execution properties.

These assets constitute the input of the **Jarvis Runtime** component that starts by deploying the created chatbot. This implies registering the user *intents* to the selected *Intent Recognition Provider*, connecting to the *Instant Messaging Platforms*, and starting the *External Services* specified in the *execution* model. Then, when a user input is received, the runtime forwards it to the *Intent Recognition Provider*, gets back the recognized intent and performs the required action based on the chatbot *execution* model.

This infrastructure provides three main benefits:

– The *Jarvis Modeling Language* packages decouple the different dimensions of a chatbot definition, facilitating the reuse of each dimension across several chatbots (e.g. the Slack platform definition can be reused in all chatbots interacting with Slack).
– Each sublanguage is totally independent of the concrete deployment and intent recognition platforms, easing the maintenance and evolution of the chatbot.
– The *Jarvis Runtime* architecture can be easily extended to support new platform connections and computable actions. This aspect, coupled with the high modularity of the language, fosters new contributions and extensions of the framework that are further discussed in Sect. 5.

In the following we detail the **Jarvis Modeling Language** (Sect. 4) and **Jarvis Runtime** components (Sect. 5), and we show how they are used to define and deploy our example chatbot over multiple platforms.

4   Jarvis Modeling Language

In the following we introduce the Jarvis Modeling Language, a chatbot Domain Specific Language (DSL) that provides primitives to design the user intentions, execution logic, and deployment platform of the chatbot under construction.

The DSL is defined through two main components [17]: (i) an abstract syntax (metamodel) defining the language concepts and their relationships (generalizing the primitives provided by the major intent recognition platforms [1,8,11]), and (ii) a concrete syntax in the form of a textual notation to write chatbot descriptions conforming to the abstract syntax[2]. In the following we use the former to describe the DSL packages, and the latter to show instance examples based on our running case study. A modeling IDE for the language is also introduced in our tool support.

---

[2] A graphical notation sharing the same metamodel is left as further work.

4.1   Intent Package

Figure 2 presents the metamodel of the *Intent Package*, that defines a top-level *IntentLibrary* class containing a collection of *IntentDefinitions*. An *IntentDefinition* is a *named* entity representing an user intention. It contains a set of *Training Sentences*, which are input examples used to detect the user intention underlying a textual message. *Training Sentences* are split into *TrainingSentenceParts* representing input text fragments—typically words—to match.

Each *IntentDefinition* defines a set of *outContexts*, that are named containers used to persist information along the conversation and customize intent recognition. A *Context* embeds a set of *ContextParameters* which define a mapping from *TrainingSentenceParts* to specific *EntityTypes*, specifying which parts of the *TrainingSentences* contain information to extract and store. A *Context* also defines a *lifespan* representing the number of user inputs that can be processed before deleting it from the conversation, allowing to specify information to retain and discard, and customize the conversation based on user inputs.

IntentDefinitions can also reference *inContexts* that are used to specify matching conditions. An *IntentDefinition* can only be matched if its referenced *inContexts* have been previously set, i.e. if another *IntentDefinition* defining them as its *outContexts* has been matched, and if these *Contexts* are active with respect to their *lifespans*. Finally, the *follow* association defines *IntentDefinition* matching precedence, and can be coupled with *inContext* conditions to finely describe complex conversation paths.

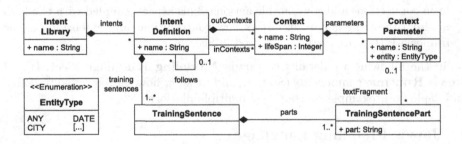

Fig. 2. Intent package metamodel

Listing 1 shows an example instance of the *Intent Package* from the running example introduced in Sect. 3.1. The model defines the *IntentLibrary* Example, that contains three *IntentDefinitions*: OpenNewIssue, SpecifyRepository, and SpecifyClass.

OpenNewIssue is a simple *IntentDefinition* that does not *follow* any other intent nor require *inContext* value, and thus will be the first intent matched in the conversation. It contains three training sentences specifying alternative inputs used to initiate the conversation. The SpecifyRepository intent follows the OpenNewIssue one, and defines one *outContext* RepositoryContext, with a *lifespan* of 5^3, and a single parameter **name**. Note that this example shows the two syntax variants used to define parameters, the first one (line 13) is an inline definition, while the second one (line 14–21) is an explicit definition that matches the user input replacing the **MyRepo** fragment. While inline definitions are simpler to specify, explicit definitions allow to express advanced matching rules, such as parameters spanning over multiple *TrainingSentenceParts* or multi-context parameters.

Finally, the **SpecifyClass** *IntentDefinition* defines a single training sentence, and the *inContext* rule specifying that the **RepositoryContext** must be active in order to match it. This implies that the **SpecifyRepository** *IntentDefinition* must have been matched in the last 5 interactions, according to the context's *lifespan*.

Listing 1. Example Intents for the Github Case Study

```
1   library Example
2
3   OpenNewIssue {
4     inputs {
5       "I want to create an issue", "Open an issue", "New issue"
6     }
7   }
8   SpecifyRepository follows OpenNewIssue {
9     inputs {
10      "In repository (RepositoryContext:name=@any)",
11      "The issue is located in repo MyRepo",
12      "MyRepo"
13    }
14    outContext "RepositoryContext" (lifespan=5) {
15      param name <- "MyRepo" (@any)
16    }
17  }
18  SpecifyClass {
19    inputs {
20      "In class (ClassContext:name=@any)"
21    }
22    inContext "RepositoryContext"
23  }
```

4.2   Platform Package

The *Platform Package* (Fig. 3) defines the capabilities of a given implementation platform (e.g. Slack, Discord, and Github) through a set of *ActionDefinitions* and *InputProviderDefinitions*.

A *Platform* is defined by a *name*, and provides a *path* attribute that is used by the **Jarvis Runtime** component (see Sect. 5) to bind the model to its concrete implementation. A *Platform* holds a set of *ActionDefinitions*, which are signatures of its supported operations. *ActionDefinitions* are identified by a *name* and define a set of *required Parameters*. A *Platform* can be *abstract*, meaning that it does not provide an implementation for its *ActionDefinitions* but it represents, instead, a family of similar platforms. This feature allows to define chatbots in a more generic way.

---

[3] DialogFlow uses a default lifespan value of 5 that allows 5 unrecognized user inputs before forgetting the conversation contexts.

As an example, the `Chat` *Platform* in Listing 2 is an *abstract* platform that defines three *ActionDefinitions*: `PostMessage`, `PostFile`, and `Reply`. The first two *ActionDefinitions* require two parameters (the message/file and the channel to post it), and the third one defines a single parameter with the content of the reply. The `Github` *Platform* (Listing 3) defines a single *ActionDefinition* `OpenIssue` with the parameters `repository`, `title`, and `content`.

A *Platform* can *extend* another one, and inherit its *ActionDefinitions*. This mechanism is used to define specific implementations of *abstract Platforms*. As an example, the concrete `Slack` and `Discord` *Platforms extend* the `Chat` one and implement its *ActionDefinitions* for the Slack and Discord messaging applications, respectively.

Finally, *InputProviderDefinitions* are named entities representing message processing capabilities that can be used as inputs for the chatbot under design. Messaging *Platforms* typically define a *default provider*, that can be complemented with additional *providers* with specific capabilities (e.g. listen to a specific channel or user). Note that *default providers* are implicitly set in the *Platform* language.

Listing 2. Chat Platform Example

```
1    Abstract Platform Chat
2        path "jarvis.ChatPlatform"
3        actions
4            PostMessage(message, channel)
5            PostFile(file, channel)
6            Reply(message)
7
8    Platform Slack    extends Chat
9        path "jarvis.SlackPlatform"
10   Platform Discord extends Chat
11       path "jarvis.DiscordPlatform"
```

Listing 3. Github Platform Example

```
1    Platform Github
2
3    path "jarvis.Github"
4
5    actions
6        OpenIssue(repository, title,
7            content)
```

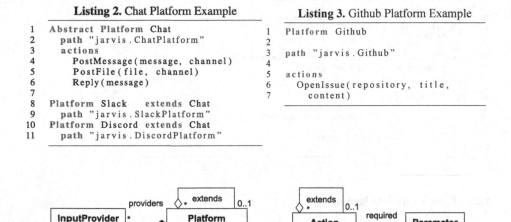

Fig. 3. Platform package metamodel

4.3   Execution Package

The *Execution Package* (Fig. 4) is an event-based language that represents the chatbot execution logic.

An *ExecutionModel* imports *Platforms* and *IntentLibraries*, and specifies the *IntentProviderDefinitions* used to receive user inputs. The *ExecutionRule* class

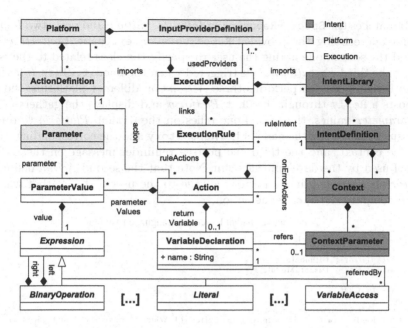

Fig. 4. Execution package metamodel

is the cornerstone of the language, which defines the mapping between received *IntentDefinitions* and *Actions* to compute.

The *Action* class represents the reification of a *Platform ActionDefinition* with concrete *ParameterValues* bound to its *Parameter* definitions. The *value* of a *ParameterValue* is represented as an *Expression* instance. Jarvis *Execution* language currently supports *Literals*, *Unary* and *Binary Operations*, as well as *VariableAccesses* that are read-only operations used to access *ContextParameters*.

An *Action* can also define an optional *returnVariable* that represents the result of its computation, and can be accessed from other *Actions* through *VariableAccess Expressions*, allowing to propagate information between computed actions. Finally, an *Action* can also contain *onErrorActions*, which are specific *Actions* that are executed when the base one errored.

Listing 4 shows the *Execution* model from our running example. It *imports* the **Example** *IntentLibrary*, the generic **Chat** *Platform*, as well as the concrete **Github** and **Discord** *Platforms*. Note that Jarvis *Execution* language allows to *import* both concrete and *abstract Platforms*, the concrete implementations of the latter can be specified to the **Jarvis Runtime** component (see next section).

The defined *ExecutionModel* specifies a single *InputProviderDefinition* that will receive user inputs from the **Chat** *Platform*. Resulting *IntentDefinitions* are handled by three *ExecutionRules* following the conversation path. The first one (lines 8–9) is triggered when the **OpenNewIssue** *IntentDefinition* is matched, and posts a simple **Reply** message starting the conversation. The second one (lines

11–13) matches the `SpecifyRepository` *IntentDefinition*, and posts two *Replies*: the first one echoing the provided `RepositoryContext.name` *ContextParameter*, and the second one asking the user to specify the class related to the issue. Finally, the third *ExecutionRule* is triggered when the `SpecifyClass` *IntentDefinition* is matched, and performs three *Actions* on different platforms: the first one posts a `Reply` through the `Chat` *Platform* and displays the gathered *ContextParameter* values, the second one relies on the `Github` *Platform* to open a new issue by accessing the `name` of the `Repository` and the corresponding `Class` from the context, and the third one posts a reminder message on the Discord channel used by the development team. Note that the second *Action* defines an *onError* clause that prints an error message to the user if the chatbot was not able to compute the `openIssue` action.

Listing 4. Chatbot Execution Language Example

```
1   import library Example
2   import platform Chat
3   import platform GithubModule
4   import platform DiscordModule
5
6   listen to Chat
7
8   on intent OpenNewIssue do
9       Chat.Reply("Sure, I'll help you to write it! Which repository would you like to
            report an issue for?")
10
11  on intent SpecifyRepository do
12      Chat.Reply("Alright, I have noted that your issue is related to repository {
            $RepositoryContext.name}")
13      Chat.Reply("Which class is affected by the issue?")
14
15  on intent SpecifyClass do
16      Chat.Reply("Ok! I am opening an issue in repository {$RepositoryContext.name}
            for the class {$ClassContext.name}, thanks!"
17      GithubModule.openIssue({$RepositoryContext.name}, {$ClassContext.name}, "There
            is an issue in class {$ClassContext.name}")
18          on error do Chat.Reply("I can't open the issue on the repository, please
                try again later")
19      DiscordModule.PostMessage("A new issue has been opened on repository {
            $RepositoryContext.name}", "dev−channel")
```

5 Jarvis Runtime

The **Jarvis Runtime** component is an event-based execution engine that deploys and manages the execution of the chatbot. Its inputs are the chatbot model (written with the **Jarvis Modeling Language**) and a *configuration* file holding deployment information and platform credentials. In the following we detail the structure of this *configuration* file, then we present the architecture of the **Jarvis Runtime** component. Finally, we introduce a dynamic view of the framework showing how input messages are handled by its internal components.

5.1 Jarvis Deployment Configuration

The Jarvis *deployment configuration* file provides runtime-level information to setup and bind the platforms with whom the chatbot needs to interact either to get user input or to call as part of an action response. Listing 5 shows a possible configuration for the example used through this article. The first part (lines 1–4) specifies `DialogFlow` as the concrete *IntentRecognitionProvider* service used to match received messages against *IntentDefinitions*, and provides the necessary credentials. The second part of the configuration (lines 5–6) binds the concrete `Slack` platform (using its *path* attribute) to the abstract `Chat` used in the *Execution* model (Listing 4). This runtime-level binding hides platform-specific details from the *Execution* model, that can be reused and deployed over multiple platforms. The last part of the configuration (lines 7–10) specifies platform credentials.

Listing 5. Chatbot Deployment Configuration Example

```
1   // Intent Recognition Provider Configuration
2   jarvis.intent.recognition     = DialogFlow
3   jarvis.dialogflow.project     = <DialogFlow Project ID>
4   jarvis.dialogflow.credentials = <DialogFlow Credentials>
5   // Abstract Platform Binding
6   jarvis.platform.chat          = jarvis.SlackPlatform
7   // Concrete Platform Configuration
8   jarvis.slack.credentials      = <Slack Credentials>
9   jarvis.discord.credentials    = <Discord Credentials>
10  jarvis.github.credentials     = <Github Credentials>
```

5.2   Architecture

Figure 5 shows an overview of the **Jarvis Runtime** internal structure, including illustrative instances from the running example (light-grey). The *JarvisCore* class is the cornerstone of the framework, which is *initialized* with the *Configuration* and *ExecutionModel* previously defined. This initial step starts the *InputProvider* receiving user messages, and setups the concrete *IntentRecognitionProvider* (in our case `DialogFlow`) employed to extract *RecognizedIntents*, which represent concrete instances of the specified *IntentDefinitions*.

The input *ExecutionModel* is then processed and its content stored in a set of *Registries* managing *IntentDefinitions*, *Actions*, and *Platforms*. The *PlatformRegistry* contains *PlatformInstances*, which correspond to concrete *Platform* implementations (e.g. the `Slack` platform from the running example) initialized with the *Configuration* file. *PlatformInstances build ActionInstances*, that contain the execution code associated to the *ActionDefinitions* defined in the *Intent* language, and are initialized with *Actions* from the *Execution* model. These *ActionInstances* are finally sent to the *ActionRunner* that manages their execution.

The *JarvisCore* also manages a set of *Sessions*, used to store *Context* information and *ActionInstance* return variables. Each *Session* defines an unique identifier associated to a user, allowing to separate *Context* information from one user input to another.

Figure 6 shows how these elements collaborate together by illustrating the sequence of operations that are executed when the framework receives a user message. To simplify the presentation, this sequence diagram assumes that all

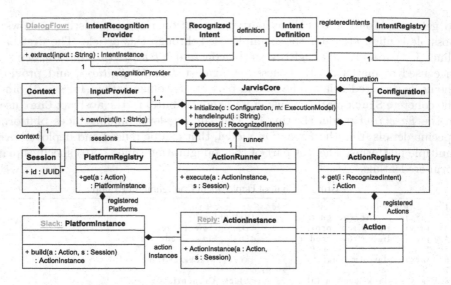

Fig. 5. Jarvis runtime engine architecture overview

the internal structures have been *initialized* and that the different registries have been populated from the provided *ExecutionModel*.

User inputs are received by the framework through the *InputProvider*'s *newInput* method (1), that defines a single parameter *i* containing the raw text sent by the user. This input is forwarded to the *JarvisCore* instance (2), that calls its *IntentRecognitionProvider*'s *extract* method (3). The input is then matched against the specified *IntentDefinitions*, and the resulting *RecognizedIntent* (4) is returned to the *JarvisCore* (5).

The *JarvisCore* instance then performs a lookup in its *ActionRegistry* (6) and retrieves the list of *Actions* associated to the *RecognizedIntent* (7). The *JarvisCore* then iterates through the returned *Actions*, and retrieves from its *PlatformRegistry* (8) their associated *PlatformInstance* (9). The user's *Session* is then retrieved from the *JarvisCore*'s *sessions* list (10). Note that this process relies on both the user input and the *Action* to compute, and ensures that a client *Session* remains consistent across action executions. Finally, the *Jarvis-Core* component calls the *build* method of the *PlatformInstance* (11), that constructs a new *ActionInstance* from the provided *Session* and *Action* signature (12) and returns it to the core component (13). Finally, the *JarvisCore* component relies on the *execute* method of its *ActionRunner* to compute the created *ActionInstance* (14) and stores its result (15), in the user's *Session* (16).

Note that due to the lake of space the presented diagram does not include the fallback logic that is triggered when the computation of a *ActionInstance* returns an error. Additional information on fallback and *on error* clauses can be found in the project repository.

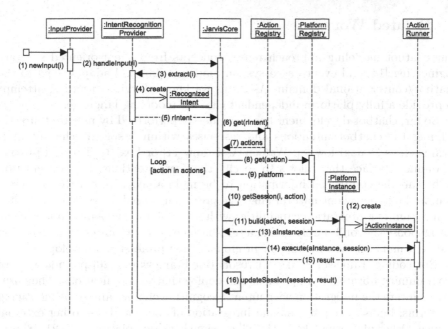

Fig. 6. Runtime engine sequence diagram

6   Tool Support

The Jarvis framework is open source and released under the Eclipse Public License v2[4]. The source code of the project and the Eclipse update site are available on Github[5], which also includes a wiki providing installation instructions as well as developer resources to extend the framework.

The concrete syntax of the Jarvis modeling language is implemented with Xtext [2], an EBNF-based language used to specify grammars and generate the associated toolkit containing a meta-model of the language, a parser, and textual editors. The provided editors support auto-completion, syntactic and semantic validation, and can be installed from the Jarvis Eclipse update site.

The **Jarvis Runtime** engine is a Java library that implements all the execution logic presented in this paper. In addition, Jarvis provides a full implementation of the *IntentRecognitionProvider* interface for Google's DialogFlow engine [8], as well as the concrete *PlatformInstance* implementations for the Slack, Discord, and Github platforms used in the running example. The runtime component can be downloaded and deployed on a server as a standalone application, or integrated in an existing application using a dedicated Maven dependency.

---

[4] https://www.eclipse.org/legal/epl-2.0/.
[5] https://github.com/SOM-Research/jarvis.

7   Related Work

Our chatbot modeling approach reuses concepts from agent-oriented software engineering [14] and event-based system modeling [26] and adapts them to the chatbot/conversational domain. As far as we know, Jarvis is the first attempt to provide a fully platform-independent chatbot modeling language.

So far, chatbot development has been mostly performed by means of directly defining the chatbot intentions and responses within a specific chatbot platform such as DialogFlow [8], Watson Assistant [11] or Lex [1]. They all provide an online interface that allows to specify the user intentions, the conversation path, and the contextual information to be maintained through the conversation, and offer excellent natural language processing capabilities. However, they all have limited integration capabilities with other platforms. Any complex chatbot response (beyond purely giving a text-based answer) requires manual coding and API management, making them unfit for non-professional developers.

Bot coding frameworks like Microsoft Bot Frameworks [20] provide a set of programming libraries to implement and deploy chatbot applications. They usually facilitate the integration with intent recognition engines and some messaging platforms, but still require manual integration of those and any other external service. Other platforms like Botkit [3] or some low-code platforms [5,21,28] predefine a number of integrations with major messaging platform. While this helps if we are aiming at building simple conversational chatbots they still need to be tightened to one of the above platforms (for powerful language skills, e.g. for intent recognition) and require, as before, manual coding of advanced chatbot action. Finally, a few low-code platforms such as FlowXO [7] also provide support for triggering actions within the conversation. However, they are typically defined as a closed environment that cannot be easily extended by the designer with new actions and/or intent recognition platforms.

Conversely, Jarvis proposes an MDE approach that combines the benefit of platform-independent chatbot definition, including non-trivial chatbot actions and side effects, together with an easy deployment on any major chatbot platform for optimal natural language processing. Moreover, the extensibility of our modular design facilitates the integration of any external API and services as input/output source of the chatbot. These integrations can be shared and reused in future projects. On the other hand, Jarvis' generic chatbot design may hide useful platform-specific features that are not supported by all the vendors (e.g. DialogFlow's small talk). This could be addressed by adding a step in the design process that would refine Jarvis' platform independent model into a platform-specific model where designers could enrich the bot with specific features of the platform.

8   Conclusion

In this paper we introduced Jarvis, a multi-platform chatbot modeling framework. Jarvis decouples the chatbot modeling part from the platform-specific aspects, increasing the reusability of the conversational flows and facilitating the deployment of chatbot-enabled applications over a variety of chatbot service providers. The runtime component can be easily extended to support additional platform-specific actions and events.

Jarvis is the core component of an industrial case study in collaboration with Berger-Levrault that aims to generate chatbots for citizen portals (chatbots' mission is to help citizens navigate the portal to autonomously complete a number of city-related obligations). As part of this project we plan to perform a detailed evaluation of the expressiveness of the chatbot modeling language and the overall usability and productivity of the framework relying on evaluation techniques such as [23,25].

We also plan to enrich the Jarvis framework with advanced conversation capabilities such as intent recognition confidence level and conditional branching that are not supported for the moment. We are also exploring the support of generic events such as webhooks and push notifications. This would allow the modeling of reactive bots that can actively listen and respond to non-conversational events as well (e.g. a bot that wakes up as soon as a new issue is created on Github and immediately engages with the user to help clarifying the issue description). We are also studying how to extend our approach to support chatbot deployment over smart assistants such as Amazon Alexa. Another future work is the extension of the presented DSLs to support variation points at the metamodel level allowing to generate families of chatbots, e.g. using product line techniques [6].

Acknowledgement. This work has been partially funded by the Electronic Component Systems for European Leadership Joint Undertaking under grant management No. 737494 (MegaMRt2 project) and the Spanish government (TIN2016-75944-R project).

References

1. Amazon: Amazon Lex Website (2018). https://aws.amazon.com/lex/
2. Bettini, L.: Implementing Domain-Specific Languages with Xtext and Xtend. Packt Publishing Ltd., Birmingham (2013)
3. Botkit: Botkit Website (2018). https://botkit.ai
4. Brambilla, M., Cabot, J., Wimmer, M.: Model-driven software engineering in practice. Synth. Lect. Softw. Eng. **1**(1), 1–182 (2012)
5. Chatfuel: Chatfuel Website (2018). https://chatfuel.com/
6. Clements, P., Northrop, L.: Software Product Lines: Practices and Patterns, vol. 3. Addison-Wesley, Reading (2002)
7. FlowXO: FlowXO Website (2019). https://flowxo.com/
8. Google: DialogFlow Website (2018). https://dialogflow.com/
9. Grinter, R.E., Palen, L.: Instant messaging in teen life. In: Proceedings of the 5th CSCW Conference, pp. 21–30. ACM (2002)
10. Hutchinson, J., Whittle, J., Rouncefield, M.: Model-driven engineering practices in industry: social, organizational and managerial factors that lead to success or failure. SCP **89**, 144–161 (2014)

11. IBM: Watson Assistant Website (2018). https://www.ibm.com/watson/ai-assistant/
12. Gartner Inc.: The Road to Enterprise AI. RAGE Frameworks (2017)
13. Jackson, P., Moulinier, I.: Natural Language Processing for Online Applications: Text Retrieval, Extraction and Categorization, vol. 5. John Benjamins Publishing, Amsterdam (2007)
14. Jennings, N.R., Wooldridge, M.: Agent-oriented software engineering. In: Handbook of Agent Technology, vol. 18 (2001)
15. Kavaler, D., Sirovica, S., Hellendoorn, V., Aranovich, R., Filkov, V.: Perceived language complexity in GitHub issue discussions and their effect on issue resolution. In: Proceedings of the 32nd ASE Conference, pp. 72–83. IEEE (2017)
16. Kerlyl, A., Hall, P., Bull, S.: Bringing Chatbots into Education: Towards Natural Language Negotiation of Open Learner Models. In: Ellis, R., Allen, T., Tuson, A. (eds.) Applications and Innovations in Intelligent Systems XIV, pp. 179–192. Springer, London (2007). https://doi.org/10.1007/978-1-84628-666-7_14
17. Kleppe, A.: Software Language Engineering: Creating Domain-Specific Languages Using Metamodels. Pearson Education, London (2008)
18. Klopfenstein, L.C., Delpriori, S., Malatini, S., Bogliolo, A.: The rise of bots: a survey of conversational interfaces, patterns, and paradigms. In: Proceedings of the 12th DIS Conference, pp. 555–565. ACM (2017)
19. Masche, J., Le, N.-T.: A review of technologies for conversational systems. In: Le, N.-T., Van Do, T., Nguyen, N.T., Thi, H.A.L. (eds.) ICCSAMA 2017. AISC, vol. 629, pp. 212–225. Springer, Cham (2018). https://doi.org/10.1007/978-3-319-61911-8_19
20. Mayo, J.: Programming the Microsoft Bot Framework: A Multiplatform Approach to Building Chatbots. Microsoft Press, Redmond (2017)
21. Mendix: Mendix Website (2018). https://www.mendix.com/
22. Nardi, B.A., Whittaker, S., Bradner, E.: Interaction and outeraction: instant messaging in action. In: Proceedings of the 3rd CSCW Conference, pp. 79–88. ACM (2000)
23. Pereira, J., Díaz, Ó.: A quality analysis of Facebook Messenger's most popular chatbots. In: Proceedings of the 33rd SAC Symposium, pp. 2144–2150. ACM (2018)
24. Pereira, J., Díaz, Ó.: Chatbot dimensions that matter: lessons from the trenches. In: Mikkonen, T., Klamma, R., Hernández, J. (eds.) ICWE 2018. LNCS, vol. 10845, pp. 129–135. Springer, Cham (2018). https://doi.org/10.1007/978-3-319-91662-0_9
25. Radziwill, N.M., Benton, M.C.: Evaluating quality of chatbots and intelligent conversational agents. arXiv preprint arXiv:1704.04579 (2017)
26. Rozsnyai, S., Schiefer, J., Schatten, A.: Concepts and models for typing events for event-based systems. In: Proceedings of the 1st DEBS Conference, pp. 62–70. ACM (2007)
27. Shawar, A., Atwell, E., Roberts, A.: FAQchat as in information retrieval system. In: Proceedings of the 2nd LTC Conference, pp. 274–278. Wydawnictwo Poznanskie, Poznan (2005)
28. Smartloop: Smartloop Website (2018). https://smartloop.ai/
29. Subrahmanian, V.S., et al.: The DARPA Twitter bot challenge. arXiv preprint arXiv:1601.05140 (2016)
30. Thomas, N.T.: An E-business chatbot using AIML and LSA. In: Proceedings of the 5th ICACCI Conference, pp. 2740–2742. IEEE (2016)

31. Wieringa, R.J.: Design Science Methodology for Information Systems and Software Engineering. Springer, Heidelberg (2014). https://doi.org/10.1007/978-3-662-43839-8
32. Xu, A., Liu, Z., Guo, Y., Sinha, V., Akkiraju, R.: A new chatbot for customer service on social media. In: Proceedings of the 35th CHI Conference, pp. 3506–3510. ACM (2017)

Information Systems Modeling: Language, Verification, and Tool Support

Artem Polyvyanyy[1]([⊠]), Jan Martijn E. M. van der Werf[2], Sietse Overbeek[2], and Rick Brouwers[2]

[1] The University of Melbourne, Parkville, VIC 3010, Australia
`artem.polyvyanyy@unimelb.edu.au`
[2] Utrecht University, Princetonplein 5, 3584 CC Utrecht, The Netherlands
`{j.m.e.m.vanderwerf,s.j.overbeek}@uu.nl,`
`r.a.c.m.brouwers@students.uu.nl`

Abstract. Information and processes are both important aspects of information systems. Nevertheless, most existing languages for modeling information systems focus either on one or the other. Languages that focus on information modeling often neglect the fact that information is manipulated by processes, while languages that focus on processes abstract from the structure of the information. In this paper, we present an approach for modeling and verification of information systems that combines information models and process models using an automated theorem prover. In our approach, set theory and first-order logic are used to express the structure and constraints of information, while Petri nets of a special kind, called Petri nets with identifiers, are used to capture the dynamic aspects of the systems. The proposed approach exhibits a unique balance between expressiveness and formal foundation, as it allows capturing a wide range of information systems, including infinite state systems, while allowing for automated verification, as it ensures the decidability of the reachability problem. The approach was implemented in a publicly available modeling and simulation tool and used in teaching of Information Systems students.

Keywords: IS modeling · Verification of IS models · Tools for IS modeling

1 Introduction

An *information system* is an organized collection of concepts and constraints for storing, manipulating, and disseminating information. Finding the right balance between concepts and constraints for specifying static and dynamic aspects is essential when designing an information system. However, existing modeling languages often focus on one of the two aspects, leaving the other to play the second fiddle. Many information modeling notations introduce concepts to capture and verify domain constraints, but neglect that information is populated through processes. Similarly, process modeling languages often contain dedicated constructs

© Springer Nature Switzerland AG 2019
P. Giorgini and B. Weber (Eds.): CAiSE 2019, LNCS 11483, pp. 194–212, 2019.
https://doi.org/10.1007/978-3-030-21290-2_13

to represent information/data, e.g., documents and messages, and data/information flows, but are of limited help when specifying beyond trivial information constraints imposed by the domain.

This work is motivated by the need, as witnessed by research in the last decade [6,10,18,27], for theoretical and practical languages, methods, and tools to effectively integrate processes driven and information managed by information systems, as well as on our experiences in teaching information systems [33]. We propose a language for conceptual modeling of information systems that fulfills these requirements:

R1. Can be used to model concepts and constraints that govern the aspects related to the information that a system can manage, i.e., data, and the semantics of the data, that the processes of the system can manipulate;

R2. Can be used to model concepts and constraints that govern the aspects related to the dynamic behavior that a system can exercise, i.e., processes that manipulate the information managed by the system;

R3. Can be used to specify an aspect of an information system using information and/or process concepts and constraints;

R4. Has a formal foundation that allows automated verification.

The language we propose, called Information Systems Modeling Language (ISML), builds upon established formalisms for modeling process- and information-related concepts and constraints. Other criteria for assessing the quality of conceptual modeling languages, such as clarity, semantic stability, semantic relevance, and abstraction mechanisms (cf. [15]), are not considered in this work. These are addressed in isolation by the languages that constitute our formalism. Studies of manifestations of these criteria for the proposed overarching language are left for future work.

Requirements R1–R4 are standard for IS modeling languages [6,10,18,27]. We use *mathematical modeling* and *formal proof* methods to develop a formalism that instantiates them in a *unique* way, as listed below (this claim is justified in Sect. 2):

I1. The create, read, update, and delete (CRUD) operations over information facts are supported, along with the expressiveness of the *first-order logic over finite sets with equality* for specifying information constraints;

I2. The process constraints of an information system, captured using *Petri nets with identifiers*, can induce a finite or countably infinite number of reachable states;

I3. An aspect of an information system can be captured using either process only, information only, or a combination of process and information concepts and constraints;

I4. The reachability problem, which given a model of an information system, its initial state, and some other state of the system consists of deciding if the information system can evolve from the initial into the given state, is computable.

These instantiations allow capturing a wide range of systems in a flexible way while ensuring a solid formal foundation. Instantiation I1 ensures standard support for CRUD operations over information facts and the ability to specify arbitrary constraints over them. Instantiation I2 ensures that the dynamic behavior of a captured system can be analyzed based on a wide range of semantics, including the interleaving/noninterleaving and linear/branching time semantics [29]. Consequently, the support of noninterleaving semantics necessitates the support for infinite collections of reachable states, as it often breaks the by-construction-guarantee of a bound on a number of reachable states. Instantiation I3 addresses the standard mechanism for balancing information and process concepts and constraints in models of information systems. We argue that instantiation I4 sets a solid formal foundation. For example, for the well-established formalism of Petri nets for describing distributed systems, many interesting verification problems were demonstrated to be recursively equivalent to the reachability problem [12]; these are the problems of liveness, deadlock-freedom, and several variants of the reachability problem, e.g., submarking reachability, zero reachability, and single-place zero reachability. The in this work presented reachability result is yet to be capitalized on in future studies to extend the repertoire of decidable verification problems for ISML models.

The next section discusses related work. Section 3 presents our modeling language. Section 4 is devoted to the decidability of the reachability problem. Then, Sect. 5 discusses a proof-of-concept implementation of a tool that supports modeling and simulation of information systems captured using the proposed language and reports on a preliminary evaluation of the approach with a cohort of Information Systems students. The paper closes with conclusions and an outlook at future work.

2   Related Work

To identify existing techniques for modeling information systems, we looked into survey papers on the topic of integrated data and process modeling. The survey papers, in turn, were identified by first using Scopus to find papers with titles that contain strings "data-centric process", "data-aware process", "process-centric data", or "process-aware data", and have the subject area of Computer Science (18 papers), then taking only survey papers (2 papers), and finally including other survey papers that cite any of the papers related to data and process modeling among the initially identified 18 papers. This procedure resulted in four identified survey papers, concretely [6,10,18,27]. In what follows, we discuss those techniques included in the identified surveys that were assessed to deliver the best balance of expressiveness and verifiability. We classify the techniques based on their origin in one of the requirements R1 or R2 from Sect. 1. The discussions of languages for capturing exclusively process or exclusively information concepts and constraints are omitted, because of the space limitations. Hence, for instance, Entity Relationship diagrams or Object Role Model diagrams, as well as Petri nets, reset nets, or transfer nets, are not discussed.

Data-Aware Process Models. The core formalism for describing data-aware processes is arguably colored Petri nets (CPNs). CPNs extend classical Petri nets by equipping each token with a data value, or color, which can be of an arbitrarily complex type [19]. For CPNs, reachability is undecidable unless the finiteness of the color domain is imposed. In [1], CPNs were used for modeling process-aware information systems. This instantiation of CPNs allows token manipulations to be captured as arbitrary programs, which benefits expressiveness but hinders analysis, as reachability stays undecidable.

In a Petri net with data, every token carries a data value and executions of transitions depend on and augment values associated with tokens. If data values are tested only for equality, like in the case of ν-PNs, the reachability problem is undecidable [28]. However, coverability, termination, and some boundedness problems are decidable for ν-PNs. The coverability, termination, and boundedness are decidable if in addition to the equality testing data values are drawn from a totally ordered domain [21]. However, the reachability problem remains undecidable even under this additional constraint [20].

In [9], the authors propose another model, called RAW-SYS, that combines Petri nets with relational databases. A RAW-SYS may induce an infinite state transition system, which complicates the analysis. In fact, the authors indeed conclude that, unless one limits the number of objects that can co-exist in a reachable state, the reachability problem is undecidable. Note that we do not impose this requirement on our models.

In [8], the authors integrate Petri nets, first-order logic, and specifications of how nets update data populations. Although closely related, this approach is limited to workflows represented as classical Petri nets only. The authors do not report any results on the decidability of verification problems for the proposed integrated modeling approach.

In [24], the authors take inspiration from [9] and propose a three-layered model of DB-nets. In a DB-net, the persistence layer maintains data values in a relational database, the control layer uses a variant of colored Petri nets to describe processes, and the data logic layer provides methods to extract and augment data values. The authors demonstrate that for a special class of bounded DB-nets that use string and real data types and may (despite the name) induce infinite collections of reachable states, the problem of reachability of a nonempty place is decidable.

Process-Aware Data Models. A business artifact describes information about a business entity that evolves over time according to a well-defined life-cycle [26]. In [14], the authors study systems of artifacts that exhibit collective behaviors captured as Kripke structures and demonstrate that certain CTL properties are decidable for these systems when values of attributes and variables (scalars) that encode information managed by the system range over bounded or unbounded (but ordered) domains. Note that a Kripke structure cannot be used to encode the noninterleaving semantics of a system and can only be used to describe a finite number of reachable states. In [5], the authors study the problems of verifying whether an execution of a system can complete, the existence of an execution that leads to a dead-end, and redundancy of an attribute in a given system. These problems are shown to be decidable only under various restrictions, such as abstracting from actual attribute values or imposing restrictions on information manipulations, e.g., a value of an attribute is allowed to be modified at most once. The behavior of the overall system is captured as a set of declarative constraints that describe a collection of allowed executions and interpreted using the interleaving semantics. Differently from the approaches in [5,14], our formalism does not impose restrictions over domains or structure of values used to encode information facts.

In [25], the authors propose to use state transition systems to capture life cycles of data objects. The life cycles of such data objects are then linked according to the relationships between the objects. Consequently, such an integrated system is capable of describing only a finite number of states. A similar approach is followed in artifact-centric modeling [13]. Each artifact has a life cycle, represented by a state machine that manipulates a data model via OCL. Verification may not always terminate, and, as shown in [7], verification is only possible in limited cases.

In [11], the authors present some decidability results on verification of a rich artifact model that surpasses the previous work from IBM on artifact systems at expressiveness. However, the results are obtained under eight restrictions, which limit the management of data and recursive computation. The authors demonstrate that lifting any of the eight restrictions leads to undecidability of the verification. In [4], the authors formalize artifact systems as multi-agent systems and study the decidability of the problem of verifying some temporal logic properties. The authors state the undecidability of the problem for the general class of systems and derive at the decidability result for the subclass of systems whose behavior does not depend on the data values in reachable states.

A relational transducer [3,30] based on Gurevich's Abstract State Machine (ASM) is a relational database along with an ASM that governs management of the database. The problems of verifying temporal properties, log equivalence, and finite log validation are undecidable for transducers [30]. Some decidability results were obtained by a priori limiting the number of possible relations in each transducer state, limiting the number of database changes, and restricting the behavior of the transducers [3,30]. Active XML (AXML) is an extension of XML with embedded service calls [2]. Some decidability results for AXML models for verifying data and process related properties were shown to be decidable under several restrictions, e.g., by ensuring a static bound on the total number of function calls in an execution of the system.

In [16], the authors address verification of data-centric dynamic systems (DCDSs). In a DCDS data is maintained in a relational database, while the process is captured as a set of condition-action rules that govern updates in the database. A DCDS can induce infinite collections of reachable states. As shown in [16], verification, in terms of some temporal logic properties, is undecidable in general and becomes decidable under constraints over data values in the reachable states.

Summary. None of the existing formalisms for describing process and information aspects of information systems is capable of describing an infinite amount of states while imposing no bounds on the values of governed information facts and enjoying the decidability of the reachability problem. Hence the work at hand to address the gap. In addition, our formalism supports CRUD operations over information facts and can be interpreted using interleaving/noninterleaving and linear/branching time semantics.

3   Information Systems Modeling Language

The language we propose has three constituents: an information model to describe the domain, a Petri net with identifiers to describe dynamic processes, and a specification defining how the processes manipulate information. In the remainder, we use the following running example to demonstrate the proposed language.[1]

Running Example. The educational institute "Private Teaching Institute" (PTI) offers different education tracks, such as Information Sciences and Computer Science. Each track at PTI has a small team, called the track management team, and a small student administration for all tracks together. For each track, different courses can be followed. Every person is entitled to register for a track. Once registered, and accepted by the track management, a person becomes a student of that track. A student accepted for a track must create a study plan, consisting of the courses she wants to follow. This plan has to be approved by the track management. Students enroll for courses. A student of a track is allowed to follow up to two courses concurrently. A lecturer decides whether a student fails or passes the course. In case a student fails, she is allowed to retake the course, until she passes it. Once the student passed all courses approved upon in the study plan, the student can request a diploma for that track. The track management verifies the certificates and the plan, after which they award the diploma.

3.1   Information Models

Many languages are available that satisfy the goal of requirement R1 to govern information and its manipulations, such as ERDs, UML class diagrams, and ORM diagrams. Each notation comes with its constructs and ways to express constraints. Yet, all these notations are similar in that they are founded in set theory and first-order logic. In ISML, we do not advocate the use of specific

---

[1] Related materials can be found at: http://informationsystem.org/ismsuite/.

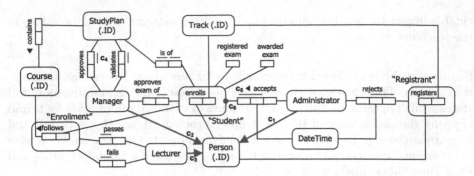

Fig. 1. An information model of the running example in ORM notation.

notations, but rather focus on the underlying principles. An *information model* consists of a set of possible entity types and relations, which are characterized by finite sequences of entity types, together with a set of conditions, specified in first-order logic on finite sets with equality.

Let $\mathcal{I}$ and Λ be a universe of *identifiers* and a universe of *labels*, respectively.

Definition 3.1 (Information model)
An *information model* is a 4-tuple (E, R, ρ, Ψ), where:

- $E \subseteq \mathcal{P}(\mathcal{I})$ is a finite set of *entity types*;
- $R \subseteq \Lambda$ is a finite set of *relation types*;
- $\rho : R \to E^*$ is a *relation definition function* that maps every relation type onto a finite sequence of entity types for which it holds that for every $e \in E$ there exists $r \in R$, called the *entity relation* of e, such that $\rho(r) = \langle e \rangle$; and
- Ψ is a collection of *constraints* defined as a formal theory of the first-order logic statements over a collection of predicates that for every $r \in R$ contains a predicate with the domain $\prod_{i=1}^{|\rho(r)|} \rho(r)(i)$.

An information model of our running example in ORM notation is shown in Fig. 1. Boxes with rounded corners denote entity types, while rectangles stand for relation types, or facts using the ORM terminology. The diagram allows for traceability between the visual notation and the formalism. Note that in classical ORM, the running example would normally be captured using value types and objectified fact types, refer to [15].

Each entity and relation type of an information model is identified by a label and a corresponding sequence of entity types. For example, entity type **Person** is characterized by entity relation *Person* and the sequence of entity types $\rho(Person) = \langle \texttt{Person} \rangle$. To indicate that a person can enroll into a track, one can define relation *enrolls* such that $\rho(enrolls) = \langle \texttt{Person}, \texttt{Track} \rangle$. Figure 2 gives the relation definition function of the running example (without the entity relations).

An information model can be instantiated with entities and relations, called *facts*, which define its *population*. Every population is typed, i.e., every relation obeys its definition given by the relation definition function.

$\rho(\textit{registers}) = \langle\texttt{Person, Track}\rangle$
$\rho(\textit{rejects}) = \langle\texttt{Administrator, DateTime, Person, Track}\rangle$
$\rho(\textit{accepts}) = \langle\texttt{Administrator, DateTime, Person, Track}\rangle$
$\rho(\textit{enrolls}) = \langle\texttt{Person, Track}\rangle$
$\rho(\textit{isOf}) = \langle\texttt{StudyPlan, Person, Track}\rangle$
$\rho(\textit{contains}) = \langle\texttt{StudyPlan, Course}\rangle$
$\rho(\textit{approves}) = \langle\texttt{Manager, StudyPlan}\rangle$

$\rho(\textit{follows}) = \langle\texttt{Person, Track, Course}\rangle$
$\rho(\textit{fails}) = \langle\texttt{Person, Track, Course, Lecturer}\rangle$
$\rho(\textit{passes}) = \langle\texttt{Person, Track, Course, Lecturer}\rangle$
$\rho(\textit{registeredExam}) = \langle\texttt{Person, Track}\rangle$
$\rho(\textit{validates}) = \langle\texttt{Manager, StudyPlan}\rangle$
$\rho(\textit{approvesExamOf}) = \langle\texttt{Manager, Person, Track}\rangle$
$\rho(\textit{awardedExam}) = \langle\texttt{Person, Track}\rangle$

Fig. 2. Relation definition function for our running example, also visualized in Fig. 1.

Definition 3.2 (Population, Fact)

A *population* of an information model (E, R, ρ, Ψ) is a function $\pi : R \to \mathcal{P}(\bigcup_{n\in\mathbb{N}} \mathcal{I}^n)$ such that every element in the population is correctly typed, i.e., for every $r \in R$ it holds that $\pi(r) \in \mathcal{P}(\prod_{i=1}^{|\rho(r)|} \rho(r)(i)).$[2] An element in $\pi(r)$ is called a *fact*.

Domain constraints are captured as first-order logic statements that define the formal theory of the information model. Based on the structure, one can distinguish various classes of constraints. In the context of the running example, we discuss several classes of constraints. In the remainder, let (E, R, ρ, Ψ) be an information model.

Subtyping. Each entity of one type $(X \in E)$ belongs to another type $(Y \in E)$ iff $\forall_{x\in\mathcal{I}} : [x \in X \Rightarrow x \in Y]$. In Fig. 1, arrows c_1, c_2, and c_3 capture subtype constraints.

Uniqueness. A combination of elements in a tuple is unique within a population. In Fig. 1, c_5 specifies that the last three elements of a tuple in *accepts* are unique: $\forall_{x,y,z,u,v\in\mathcal{I}} : [((x, z, u, v) \in \textit{accepts} \land (y, z, u, v) \in \textit{accepts}) \Rightarrow x = y]$.

Mandatory. An element or fact must take part in another fact. For example, constraint c_6, denoted by a small filled circle in Fig. 1, specifies that *enrolls* must appear in *accepts*: $\forall_{x,y\in\mathcal{I}} : [\exists_{u,v\in\mathcal{I}} : [(x, y) \in \textit{enrolls} \Rightarrow (u, v, x, y) \in \textit{accepts}]]$.

Domain-specific. Constraints that do not fall into predefined categories, like those listed above, for which typically no corresponding graphical notations exist. For example, administrators are not allowed to cheat: $\forall_{x,y,z\in\mathcal{I}} : [(x, y, x, z) \notin \textit{accepts}]$, i.e., an administrator cannot accept herself for a track.

A population may invalidate the constraints. Thus, we say that a population π is *valid* if it satisfies all the constraints of the information model, denoted by $\pi \models \Psi$; otherwise the population is *invalid*. By $\Pi(D)$ and $\Lambda(D)$ we denote the set of all possible populations of information model D and the set of all possible valid populations of D, respectively.

The population of an information system changes frequently. Entities and facts can be added, deleted, or updated. We define two operations for manipulating populations: inserting entities into a relation and removing entities from

---

[2] $\mathbb{N}$ denotes the set of all natural numbers, i.e., $\mathbb{N} = \{1, 2, 3, \ldots\}$, set $\mathbb{N}^0 = \mathbb{N} \cup \{0\}$.

a relation. Note that an update can be interpreted as a delete followed by an insert.

Definition 3.3 (Transaction)

Let $D = (E, R, \rho, \Psi)$ be an information model. Let $r \in R$ be a relation, let $v \in \prod_{i=1}^{|\rho(r)|} \rho(r)(i)$ be a fact, and let $\pi \in \Pi(D)$ be a population. An *operation* o is a tuple $o \in \mathcal{O}(D)$ with $\mathcal{O}(D) = \left(R \times \{\oplus, \ominus\} \times \bigcup_{n \in \mathbb{N}} \mathcal{I}^n\right)$.

- Operation $o = (r, \oplus, v)$ *inserts* fact v into r in π, i.e., it results in population $\pi' \in \Pi(D)$, denoted by $(D : \pi \xrightarrow{r \oplus v} \pi')$, iff $\pi' = (\pi \setminus \{(r, \pi(r))\}) \cup \{(r, \pi(r) \cup \{v\})\}$.
- Operation $o = (r, \ominus, v)$ *deletes* fact v from r in π, i.e., it results in population $\pi' \in \Pi(D)$, denoted by $(D : \pi \xrightarrow{r \ominus v} \pi')$, iff $\pi' = (\pi \setminus \{(r, \pi(r))\}) \cup \{(r, \pi(r) \setminus \{v\})\}$.

A *transaction* $s \in (\mathcal{O}(D))^*$ is a finite sequence of operations, such that every subsequent operation is performed in a population resulting from the previous operation. A transaction is *valid* if the starting and resulting populations are valid.

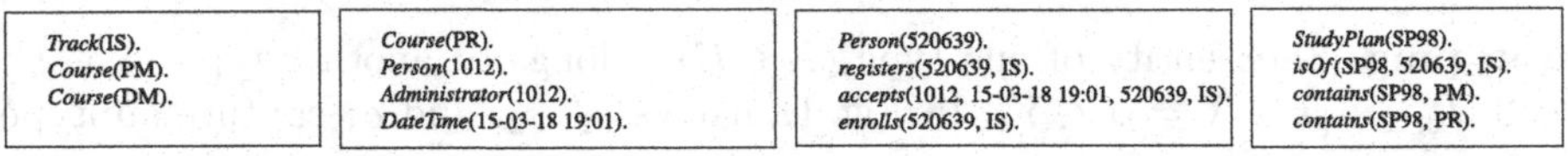

Track(IS). *Course*(PM). *Course*(DM).	*Course*(PR). *Person*(1012). *Administrator*(1012). *DateTime*(15-03-18 19:01).	*Person*(520639). *registers*(520639, IS). *accepts*(1012, 15-03-18 19:01, 520639, IS). *enrolls*(520639, IS).	*StudyPlan*(SP98). *isOf*(SP98, 520639, IS). *contains*(SP98, PM). *contains*(SP98, PR).

Fig. 3. A valid population for the running example.

When the context is clear, i.e., the scope of the information model and its current population are known, we write insert(r, v) and delete(r, v) instead of $(D : \pi \xrightarrow{r \oplus v} \pi')$ and $(D : \pi \xrightarrow{r \ominus v} \pi')$, respectively. A valid population of the information model of Fig. 2 is depicted in Fig. 3. Suppose student 520639 is working on her study plan. Updating the course Programming (PR) into Data Modeling (DM) can be expressed as follows:

$$\langle \text{delete}(contains, (\text{SP98}, \text{PR})), \text{insert}(contains, (\text{SP98}, \text{DM})) \rangle.$$

As the initial population is valid, and the result of executing the transaction will not violate any constraint, the above transaction is valid.

3.2   Process Models

Many different approaches for modeling processes exist that satisfy requirement R2. Each comes with its own notation and applications. For requirement R4 and its instantiation I4, a formal grounding of process modeling is required. Similar to [1], we utilize Petri nets to model processes. Notice that many languages can be translated into Petri nets, thus allowing tools to rely on a grounding formalism, while the modeler is using their own preferred modeling language. The Petri net in Fig. 4 reflects the process model of the running example.

Many analysis techniques for processes ignore data, i.e., tokens in places resembling the state of the process are considered to be indistinguishable. However, this results in an over-approximation of the possible firings, as shown with the following example: Starting with two tokens in place i, resembling two students, the model can eventually mark place *max concurrent courses* with four tokens, refer to Fig. 4; note that places with tokens encode all the corresponding entity instances currently kept in the population of the information model. Now, each student can start following one course by firing *register course*. As two tokens remain in place *max concurrent courses*, transition *register exam* remains enabled. However, if considering the students in isolation, this transition would not have been enabled.

The literature describes several approaches to address requirement R4, refer to Sect. 2. In ν-PN, tokens carry identifiers, while markings map places to bags of identifiers, indicating how many tokens in each place carry the same identifier.

In this paper, we extend the idea of tokens carrying identifiers to vectors of identifiers, to obtain Petri nets with identifiers (PNIDs). Vectors of identifiers have the advantage that a single token can represent multiple entities at the same time. In this way, a token may resemble a (composed) fact from a population of an information model.

In a PNID, each arc is labeled with a vector of variables. Similar to ν-PN, a valuation instantiates the variables to identifiers. The size of the vector on the arc is implied by the *cardinality* of the place it is connected to. Tokens carrying vectors of size 0 represent classical – black – tokens. If for a transition some variable only appears on outgoing arcs, it is called a *creator variable*. Let Σ denote a universe of variables.

Definition 3.4 (Petri net with identifiers)
A *Petri net with identifiers* (PNID) is a 5-tuple (P, T, F, α, β), where:

- (P, T, F) is a Petri net, with a set of places P, a set of transitions T, such that $P \cap T = \emptyset$, and a flow function $F : ((P \times T) \cup (T \times P)) \to \mathbb{N}^0$; if for $n, m \in P \cup T$, $F(n, m) > 0$, an arc is drawn from n to m;
- $\alpha : P \to \mathbb{N}^0$ defines the *cardinality* of a place, i.e., the length of the vector carried on the tokens residing at that place; its *color* is defined by $C(p) = \mathcal{I}^{\alpha(p)}$;
- β defines the *variable vector* for each arc, i.e., $\beta \in \prod_{f \in F} V_f$, where $V_{(p,t)} = V_{(t,p)} = \Sigma^{\alpha(p)}$ for $p \in P, t \in T$.

A marking of a PNID defines for each place the amount of tokens per vector identifier.

Definition 3.5 (Marking)
Given a PNID $N = (P, T, F, \alpha, \beta)$, its set of all possible markings is defined as $\mathcal{M}(N) = \prod_{p \in P} C(p) \to \mathbb{N}^0$. For $m \in \mathcal{M}(N)$, pair (N, m) is a *marked PNID*.

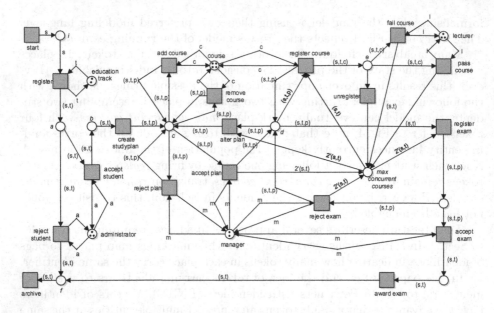

Fig. 4. PNID that describes processes students follow at PTI.

A transition is enabled if a *valuation* of variables to identifiers exists, such that each input place contains sufficient tokens with vectors of identifiers induced by the instantiated variable vector of the corresponding arc. The same valuation is used to determine which vectors of identifiers are produced in the output places. Note that a transition can only create new identifiers through variables that do not occur on its input arcs.

Definition 3.6 (Transition firing in a PNID)
Let (N, m) be a marked PNID with $N = (P, T, F, \alpha, \beta)$. Let *valuation* $\nu : \Sigma \to \mathcal{I}$ be an injective function that maps each variable to an identifier. A transition $t \in T$ is enabled in (N, m) if $[\nu(\beta((p, t)))^{F(p,t)}] \leq m(p)$ for all places $p \in P$. Its firing, denoted by $(N : m \xrightarrow{(t,\nu)} m')$, results in a marking m' with $m'(p) + [\nu(\beta((p, t)))^{F(p,t)}] = m(p) + [\nu(\beta((t, p)))^{F(t,p)}]$, for all places $p \in P$. ⌙

Details on the semantics of PNIDs are in [34]. Consider again the net in Fig. 4. This net is a PNID. Transition *start* creates a token with a single identifier, representing a person entering PTI. Place *education track* contains all the tracks PTI offers. Firing transition *register*, models that some person s chooses a track t and registers for that track. The result is a token with a vector containing two identifiers: one for the person and one for the track. A token in place d resembles a student with an accepted plan. Similarly, place e represents students following a course, and carries three identifiers: the student (person and track), and the course.

| insert(*Person*, (*s*))
insert(*registers*, (*s, t*)) | insert(*Person*, (520639))
insert(*registers*, (520639, IS)) |

Fig. 5. Abstract transaction for transition *register*, and its instantiation with valuation $\{s \mapsto 520639, t \mapsto \text{IS}\}$.

3.3 Information Systems Modeling Language

A transition firing can resemble some fact manipulation in the information model. Its firing requires a valuation that determines which identities can be used. For example, transition *register* resembles adding a fact to the population: insert(*register*, (p, t)), for some person p and track t. The intent of requirement R2 is to make this relation explicit. In our proposed formalism, each transition is specified with an *abstract transaction* that describes how the transition manipulates the population of the information model. Similar to transition firings in PNID, valuations are used to compute the transaction by instantiating the abstract transaction. For example, transition *accept student* from Fig. 4 can have the abstract transaction depicted in Fig. 5, that inserts two facts into a population: one to add the student as a person, and one to relate the person to the track.

Definition 3.7 (Abstract transaction)
Let $D = (E, R, \rho, \Psi)$ be a data model. An *abstract transaction* is a sequence of *abstract operations* $o \in \left(R \times \{\oplus, \ominus\} \times \bigcup_{n \in \mathbb{N}} (\Sigma \cup \mathcal{I})^n\right)^*$, using variables from Σ and identifiers $\mathcal{I}$. An abstract transaction o is instantiated using a *valuation* $\nu : \Sigma \to \mathcal{I}$, denoted by $\nu(o)$, which results in a transaction by replacing all variables by their valuation. The set of all abstract transactions for data model D is denoted by $\mathcal{T}(D)$.

Starting with a valid population, a transaction should not invalidate the population. Hence, we only allow transitions to fire if both the transition is enabled and its corresponding transaction is valid in the current population. This forms the basis of an ISM, whereas ISML consists of three languages for specifying information models, PNIDs, and specifications which define abstract transactions of the transitions of PNIDs.

Definition 3.8 (Information System Model, Semantics)
An *Information System Model* (ISM) is a tuple $IS = (D, N, S)$, where $D = (E, R, \rho, \Psi)$ is an information model, $N = (P, T, F, \alpha, \beta)$ is a PNID, and $S : T \to \mathcal{T}(D)$ is a specification. A *state* of an information system is a pair (π, m), with population $\pi \in \Lambda(D)$ and marking $m \in \mathcal{M}(N)$. Given markings $m, m' \in \mathcal{M}(N)$ and valid populations $\pi, \pi' \in \Lambda(D)$, transition $t \in T$ with valuation ν is enabled in (π, m) iff $(D : \pi \xrightarrow{\nu(S(t))} \pi')$ and $(N : m \xrightarrow{(t,\nu)} m')$. Its firing results in the new state (π', m'), and is denoted by $(IS : (\pi, m) \xrightarrow{(t,\nu)} (\pi', m'))$. A state (π_n, m_n) is said to be *reachable* from (π_0, m_0) if intermediate states (π_i, m_i) and transitions t_i with valuations ν_i exist such that $(IS : (\pi_i, m_i) \xrightarrow{(t_i, \nu_i)} (\pi_{i+1}, m_{i+1}))$ for all $0 \le i < n$.

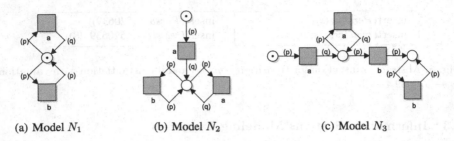

(a) Model N_1 (b) Model N_2 (c) Model N_3

Fig. 6. Three process models of ISMs that capture the same behavior (subject to the information model); ISMs that rely on models N_1 and N_3 are information- and process-driven, respectively.

A Spectrum of Information System Models. Domain constraints can be expressed in the information model or in the process model, or in both. As an example, consider the models in Fig. 6. Suppose we have information model D with relation types defined by $\rho(P) = \langle \mathsf{P} \rangle$ and $\rho(Q) = \langle \mathsf{P}, \mathsf{P} \rangle$. Let the information model be constrained by $\forall_{x,y \in \mathcal{I}} : [(x,y) \in Q \implies ((x) \in P \wedge (y) \in P)]$. Let the specification map all the transitions in Fig. 6 labeled a to the transaction $\langle \mathrm{delete}(P,(p)), \mathrm{insert}(P,(q)) \rangle$, and all the transitions labeled b to the transaction $\langle \mathrm{insert}(Q,(p,p)) \rangle$. The three process models result in the following ISMs: $IS_1 = (D, N_1, S)$, $IS_2 = (D, N_2, S)$, and $IS_3 = (D, N_3, S)$. Suppose, we start from the empty population. In all three ISMs, transition b is only enabled after a transition with label a has fired at least once; it requires a fact $(x) \in P$, which initially does not hold. Similarly, suppose we have a population with fact $(x) \in P$. Firing a transition with label b results in the population with facts $(x) \in P$ and $(x,x) \in Q$. Removing fact $(x) \in P$ is not allowed anymore, as this will violate the constraint. Hence, transition a is never enabled once transition b fired. Consequently, given the initial empty population, all three ISMs model exactly the same behavior.

The above example shows that different ISMs can describe exactly the same behavior. Model N_1 does not impose any order on the process. Hence, always if a transaction in N_1 is valid, the corresponding transition is enabled. We call this behavior *information-driven*. On the other hand, in model N_3 it becomes directly apparent that there is a constraint on the order of firing transitions a and b: always if the transition is enabled in the net, the corresponding transaction is valid. We say such transitions are *process-driven*. Model N_2 is a combination of the two: the top transition a and transition b are both process- and information-driven, whereas the other transition a is only information-driven. These examples show the existence of a spectrum of ISMs:

Definition 3.9 (Information- and process-driven ISMs)
Let $IS = (D, N, S)$ be an ISM with $N = (P, T, F, \alpha, \beta)$. Transition $t \in T$ is called:

- *information-driven* if $(D : \pi \xrightarrow{\nu(S(t))} \pi')$ implies $(IS : (\pi, m) \xrightarrow{(t,\nu)} (\pi', m'))$,

- *process-driven* if $(N : m \xrightarrow{(t,\nu)} m')$ implies $(IS : (\pi, m) \xrightarrow{(t,\nu)} (\pi', m'))$,

for any two markings $m, m' \in \mathcal{M}(N)$, valuation ν, and populations $\pi, \pi' \in \Lambda(D)$. If all transitions in the PNID are information-driven (process-driven), the ISM is called *information-driven* (*process-driven*).   ⌋

Most transitions are neither information- nor process-driven. Instead, for each transition, the modeler balances between information and process. As an example, consider transition *register exam* from Fig. 4. Suppose PTI prescribes that registering for an exam is only allowed if all courses the student listed in the study plan are passed. In the current model, if the student has its study plan accepted, but did not yet follow a single course, transition *register exam* is enabled. Although the above constraint could be modeled in the process model, it adds unnecessary complexity, whereas the constraint is relatively simple to be expressed in first-order logic (see Fig. 7). Therefore it can be added to the information model, rather than to encode it in the process model.

Being aware of how constraints manifest in the different models and their consequences is essential when designing information systems. This is the main idea behind requirement R3 and our instantiation of this requirement with ISMs, i.e., that designers of information systems are aware of which constraints are imposed and how they interplay within the system, as these are a possible cause of mistakes, as experienced by many students [33]. ISML allows modelers to decide how to specify constraints, and to verify the consequences of that decision.

4   Automated Verification

Automated verification assists designers in checking whether their system satisfies expected properties. An important class of properties are reachability related [12]: Given some current state of an IS, it should always be possible to reach some other state of the system. For example, a student that starts studying a track, should always be able to finish the track. This results in the following definition of the reachability problem:

Definition 4.1 (Reachability problem)
Given an initial state (π_0, m_0) of an ISM (D, N, S), the reachability problem consists in deciding whether a state (π, m) is reachable from (π_0, m_0).   ⌋

Combining information and process models is almost a guarantee to violate requirement R4 [6]. In general, the reachability problem is undecidable for Petri nets with identifiers, as there is no structure on the countably infinite set of identifiers; this observation is similar to the one for ν-PNs [21,28]. In ISMs, identifiers represent elements in the information model. Under the assumption that no information model becomes infinite, which is a reasonable assumption [6], there is a bound on the number of elements the identifiers represent. Further assuming that each identifier is generated consecutively, provides an ordering on the identifiers. These two assumptions form the basis of the class of *counter-valued PNIDs* [17]. In this class, identifiers are mapped on the natural numbers, and an implicit *counter place* is used to generate the next, fresh, identifier for every fresh element in the information model. As the last generated identifier for a given net is always known, the net can be translated into a classical Petri net [34], for which the reachability problem is decidable [12].

Based on the same assumptions, one can conclude that the set of populations for an information model induced from a finite set of elements is finite. In addition, the set of transactions possible on these populations is finite. Consequently, the process of moving between populations can be represented by a deterministic finite automaton. Hence, given an upper bound k on the identifiers, the semantics of the information system model becomes the synchronous product of a classical Petri net, the one constructed from the corresponding counter-valued PNID, and a deterministic finite automaton, the one obtained from the information model, for which reachability is again decidable [23]. All these observations lead to the main reachability result for ISMs.

Theorem 4.2 (Decidability of the reachability problem)
Given an ISM (D, N, S), where N is a counter-valued PNID, it is decidable whether some state (π, m) is reachable from the initial state (π_0, m_0) of the ISM.

Proof (sketch). Let $\bar{N}$ be the classical Petri net derived from the k-bounded net N, where $k \in \mathbb{N}^0$ is the last generated identifier in N, cf. [34]. Let Q be the automaton induced by the up-to-k-bounded populations of D. Then Q is finite and deterministic. As each transition in $\bar{N}$ maps to a transaction in Q via specification S, one can construct the synchronous product of $\bar{N}$ and Q that describes the semantics of the ISM. Hence, the reachability of the k-bounded ISM translates to the reachability of the synchronous product, which is decidable [23]. $\square$

Based on the result in [22], we conclude that the proposed decision procedure requires at least $2^{c \times (2^{k^{u \times v}} + p \times k^w)}$ space for some constant $c > 0$, where k, as in the above proof sketch, is the identifier in the counter place of N, u is the number of relations in D, v is the length of the shortest relation in D, w is the minimal sum of all incoming and outgoing arcs of some place of N, and p is the number of places in N. Details on obtaining this result and for the rigorous proof of Theorem 4.2 can be found in [34].

5   Tool Support and Initial Evaluation

To show the applicability of ISML, we have implemented our approach in a prototype called ISM Suite.[3] In this prototype, we build upon CPN tools [35] for simulating the PNID, and an own implementation of a theorem prover on finite sets. Constraints of the information model are specified in TPTP syntax [32]; an example constraint is shown in Fig. 7. The specification uses a special format to

---

[3] The source code is available from https://github.com/information-systems/ismsuite.

```
tff(register_for_exam), conjecture,
  ! [p: Person, t: Track]:
    ( registeredExam(p,t) =>
    ? [s: StudyPlan]: ( isOf(s,p,t)
      & ! [c: Course]: ( contains(s,c) =>
        ? [l: Lecturer] :
          passes(p,t,c,l) ) )
  ) ).
```

```
process Student {
  ...
  transition register(p: Person,
                      t: Track) {
    register p;
    insert (p) into Person;
    insert (p,t) into registers;
  } ... }
```

Fig. 7. Constraint in TPTP-format.   **Fig. 8.** Excerpt of the specification.

define transactions of transitions. An excerpt of the specification of the running example is in Fig. 8. The specification language has three constructs that can be used to define transactions: *register*, to register an element in the population, and *insert* and *remove* to add and remove facts, respectively. If an unregistered element is used in a fact, the resulting population is invalid.

All enabled transitions that result in valid populations are listed in the user interface, from which the user can select a transition to fire. For each transition that yields an invalid population, the violated constraints can be requested, to support the designer in better understanding the reasons of the violation.

In [33], we reported on an initial evaluation of the modeling component of ISM Suite with a cohort of Information Systems students in a real teaching and learning environment; the students used our tool to solve an information system modeling task. The initial results are promising, as evidenced by the collected qualitative comments from the students, refer to [33]. This and subsequent collected feedback will be used to inform evolution of our tool.

6 Conclusions and Future Work

The paper at hand proposes an approach for modeling an information system as an integration of an information model and a process model via a specification on how processes manipulate information. The proposal constitutes a unique instantiation of standard requirements for capturing concepts and constraints of an information system. Using the proposed formalism, one can express an infinite state system that supports CRUD operations over arbitrary finite populations of information facts governed by the constraints expressed in first-order logic with equality. At the same time, the proposed formalism enjoys the decidability of the reachability problem, which sets a solid foundation for verification of formal properties of the described systems.

Future work will strengthen the results reported in this paper to allow the adoption of the language by practitioners. The concrete next steps include studies of other verification problems and data flow anomalies [31], studies of the interplay between information and process concepts and constraints, improvement of the tool support, development of methodologies for designing information systems using our formalism, and empirical studies aimed at improving the usability of the approach. Finally, the high lower bound on the space requirement reported at the end of Sect. 4 justifies that one can use ISML to capture a wide range of systems. It is interesting to study how often do the extremely complex cases manifest in the problems encountered in the real world.

Acknowledgment. Artem Polyvyanyy was partly supported by the Australian Research Council Discovery Project DP180102839.

References

1. van der Aalst, W.M.P., Stahl, C.: Modeling Business Processes—A Petri Net-Oriented Approach. Cooperative Information Systems Series. MIT Press, Cambridge (2011)
2. Abiteboul, S., Segoufin, L., Vianu, V.: Modeling and verifying active XML artifacts. IEEE Data Eng. Bull. **32**(3), 10–15 (2009)
3. Abiteboul, S., Vianu, V., Fordham, B.S., Yesha, Y.: Relational transducers for electronic commerce. J. Comput. Syst. Sci. **61**(2), 236–269 (2000)
4. Belardinelli, F., Lomuscio, A., Patrizi, F.: Verification of agent-based artifact systems. J. Artif. Intell. Res. **51**, 333–376 (2014)
5. Bhattacharya, K., Gerede, C., Hull, R., Liu, R., Su, J.: Towards formal analysis of artifact-centric business process models. In: Alonso, G., Dadam, P., Rosemann, M. (eds.) BPM 2007. LNCS, vol. 4714, pp. 288–304. Springer, Heidelberg (2007). https://doi.org/10.1007/978-3-540-75183-0_21
6. Calvanese, D., De Giacomo, G., Montali, M.: Foundations of data-aware process analysis: a database theory perspective. In: PODS, pp. 1–12. ACM (2013)
7. Calvanese, D., Montali, M., Estañol, M., Teniente, E.: Verifiable UML artifact-centric business process models. In: CIKM. ACM Press (2014)
8. De Giacomo, G., Oriol, X., Estañol, M., Teniente, E.: Linking data and BPMN processes to achieve executable models. In: Dubois, E., Pohl, K. (eds.) CAiSE 2017. LNCS, vol. 10253, pp. 612–628. Springer, Cham (2017). https://doi.org/10.1007/978-3-319-59536-8_38
9. De Masellis, R., Di Francescomarino, C., Ghidini, C., Montali, M., Tessaris, S.: Add data into business process verification: bridging the gap between theory and practice. In: AAAI, pp. 1091–1099. AAAI Press (2017)
10. Deutsch, A., Hull, R., Li, Y., Vianu, V.: Automatic verification of database-centric systems. SIGLOG News **5**(2), 37–56 (2018)
11. Deutsch, A., Li, Y., Vianu, V.: Verification of hierarchical artifact systems. In: PODS, pp. 179–194. ACM Press (2016)
12. Esparza, J., Nielsen, M.: Decidability issues for Petri nets–a survey. EATCS Bulletin, vol. 52 (1994)
13. Estañol, M., Sancho, M.-R., Teniente, E.: Verification and validation of UML artifact-centric business process models. In: Zdravkovic, J., Kirikova, M., Johannesson, P. (eds.) CAiSE 2015. LNCS, vol. 9097, pp. 434–449. Springer, Cham (2015). https://doi.org/10.1007/978-3-319-19069-3_27
14. Gerede, C.E., Su, J.: Specification and verification of artifact behaviors in business process models. In: Krämer, B.J., Lin, K.-J., Narasimhan, P. (eds.) ICSOC 2007. LNCS, vol. 4749, pp. 181–192. Springer, Heidelberg (2007). https://doi.org/10.1007/978-3-540-74974-5_15

15. Halpin, T.A., Bloesch, A.C.: Data modeling in UML and ORM: a comparison. J. Database Manag. **10**(4), 4–13 (1999)
16. Hariri, B., Calvanese, D., De Giacomo, G., Deutsch, A., Montali, M.: Verification of relational data-centric dynamic systems with external services. In: PODS. ACM Press (2013)
17. van Hee, K.M., Sidorova, N., Voorhoeve, M., van der Werf, J.M.E.M.: Generation of database transactions with Petri nets. Fundam. Inform. **93**(1–3), 171–184 (2009)
18. Hull, R., Su, J., Vaculín, R.: Data management perspectives on business process management: tutorial overview. In: SIGMOD, pp. 943–948. ACM (2013)
19. Jensen, K.: Coloured Petri Nets-Basic Concepts, Analysis Methods and Practical Use. Monographs in Theoretical Computer Science. An EATCS Series, vol. 1. Springer, Heidelberg (1996). https://doi.org/10.1007/978-3-662-03241-1
20. Lasota, S.: Decidability border for Petri nets with data: WQO dichotomy conjecture. In: Kordon, F., Moldt, D. (eds.) PETRI NETS 2016. LNCS, vol. 9698, pp. 20–36. Springer, Cham (2016). https://doi.org/10.1007/978-3-319-39086-4_3
21. Lazic, R., Newcomb, T.C., Ouaknine, J., Roscoe, A.W., Worrell, J.: Nets with tokens which carry data. Fundam. Inform. **88**(3), 251–274 (2008)
22. Lipton, R.J.: The reachability problem requires exponential space. Research report, Department of Computer Science, Yale University (1976)
23. Mayr, E.W.: Persistence of vector replacement systems is decidable. Acta Inf. **15**(3), 309–318 (1981)
24. Montali, M., Rivkin, A.: DB-Nets: on the marriage of colored Petri nets and relational databases. In: Koutny, M., Kleijn, J., Penczek, W. (eds.) Transactions on Petri Nets and Other Models of Concurrency XII. LNCS, vol. 10470, pp. 91–118. Springer, Heidelberg (2017). https://doi.org/10.1007/978-3-662-55862-1_5
25. Müller, D., Reichert, M., Herbst, J.: Data-driven modeling and coordination of large process structures. In: Meersman, R., Tari, Z. (eds.) OTM 2007. LNCS, vol. 4803, pp. 131–149. Springer, Heidelberg (2007). https://doi.org/10.1007/978-3-540-76848-7_10
26. Nigam, A., Caswell, N.S.: Business artifacts: an approach to operational specification. IBM Syst. J. **42**(3), 428–445 (2003)
27. Reijers, H.A., et al.: Evaluating data-centric process approaches: does the human factor factor in? SoSyM **16**(3), 649–662 (2017)
28. Rosa-Velardo, F., de Frutos-Escrig, D.: Decidability and complexity of Petri nets with unordered data. Theor. Comput. Sci. **412**, 4439–4451 (2011)
29. Sassone, V., Nielsen, M., Winskel, G.: Models for concurrency: towards a classification. Theor. Comput. Sci. **170**(1–2), 297–348 (1996)
30. Spielmann, M.: Verification of relational transducers for electronic commerce. J. Comput. Syst. Sci. **66**(1), 40–65 (2003)
31. Sun, S.X., Zhao, J.L., Nunamaker Jr., J.F., Sheng, O.R.L.: Formulating the dataflow perspective for business process management. Inf. Syst. Res. **17**(4), 374–391 (2006)
32. Sutcliffe, G., Schulz, S., Claessen, K., Van Gelder, A.: Using the TPTP language for writing derivations and finite interpretations. In: Furbach, U., Shankar, N. (eds.) IJCAR 2006. LNCS (LNAI), vol. 4130, pp. 67–81. Springer, Heidelberg (2006). https://doi.org/10.1007/11814771_7
33. van der Werf, J.M.E.M., Polyvyanyy, A.: An assignment on information system modeling. In: Daniel, F., Sheng, Q.Z., Motahari, H. (eds.) BPM 2018. LNBIP, vol. 342, pp. 553–566. Springer, Cham (2019). https://doi.org/10.1007/978-3-030-11641-5_44

34. van der Werf, J.M.E.M., Polyvyanyy, A.: On the decidability of reachability problems for models of information systems. Technical report UU-CS-2018-005, Utrecht University (2018)
35. Westergaard, M., Kristensen, L.M.: The Access/CPN framework: a tool for interacting with the CPN-tools simulator. In: Franceschinis, G., Wolf, K. (eds.) PETRI NETS 2009. LNCS, vol. 5606, pp. 313–322. Springer, Heidelberg (2009). https://doi.org/10.1007/978-3-642-02424-5_19

Expert2Vec: Experts Representation in Community Question Answering for Question Routing

Sara Mumtaz[✉], Carlos Rodriguez, and Boualem Benatallah

School of Computer Science and Engineering, UNSW Sydney, Sydney, NSW 2052, Australia
{s.mumtaz,carlos.rodriguez,boualem}@unsw.edu.au

Abstract. Communities of Question Answering (CQAs) are rapidly growing communities for exchanging information in the form of questions and answers. They rely on the contributions of users (i.e., members of the community) who have appropriate domain knowledge and can provide helpful answers. In order to deliver the most appropriate and valuable answers, identification of such users (experts) is critically important. However, a common problem faced in CQAs is that of poor expertise matching, i.e., routing of questions to inappropriate users. In this paper, we focus on Stack Overflow (a programming CQA) and address this problem by proposing an embedding based approach that integrates users' textual content obtained from the community (e.g., answers) and community feedback in a unified framework. Our embedding-based approach is used to find the best relevant users for a given question by computing the similarity between questions and our user expertise representation. Then, our framework exploits feedback from the community to rank the relevant users according to their expertise. We experimentally evaluate the performance of the proposed approach using Stack Overflow's dataset, compare it with state-of-the-art models and demonstrate that it can produce better results than the alternative models.

Keywords: Experts finding · Question and answering communities · Embeddings models · Stack overflow · Expert representation

1 Introduction

Following the boom of web 2.0 technologies, there has been a dramatic increase in the number and variety of knowledge sharing communities. One such community is the Community Question Answering (CQA), which imparts knowledge in the form of questions and answers. Some of these communities are open to general discussions (e.g., Yahoo Answers[1]), whereas others (e.g., Stack Overflow

---

[1] https://answers.yahoo.com/.

© Springer Nature Switzerland AG 2019
P. Giorgini and B. Weber (Eds.): CAiSE 2019, LNCS 11483, pp. 213–229, 2019.
https://doi.org/10.1007/978-3-030-21290-2_14

$(SO)^2$) are specialized communities focusing on technical knowledge (SO, in particular, focuses on programming knowledge). The goal of these communities is to provide accurate and timely answers to questions posted by users of the platform supporting the communities. Achieving this goal entails the recommendation of the question to the right user (answerer) for which knowledge and expertise in the question's topic is essential. The process that identifies such user is called Expert Identification [22] and involves finding a skillful and knowledgeable user that can answer a given question. Unlike general CQAs, specialized communities not only require more technical skills but also demand various levels of expertise on specific topics in order to provide answers with long lasting relevance for the community [1].

Despite the success, CQAs face a number of problems and challenges that are still far from being solved. Among them, poor expertise matching [21] is one of the most significant problems. Poor expertise matching implies that a new question may not be matched with the appropriate user who possesses the expertise to correctly answer the question. This may result in answers either being given incorrectly, scammed or not given at all [19]. To address this problem, a wide range of models have been developed, among them the well known probabilistic language models [3], which estimate users expertise from their relevant documents based on co-occurrences. Here, the answers provided by users are considered to be the reflection of their expertise [16]. Although, these approaches have achieved reasonable performance, they are prone to term mismatch problems [11] between search queries and documents (or questions and experts, in the context of CQAs). Topic models, such as Latent Dirichlet Allocation (LDA) and its variants [4], have been introduced thereafter to overcome this problem by capturing the latent semantic relationship between users and their queries (see, e.g., [21]). These approaches, however, do not perform well when dealing with short-text documents (which is typically the case for posts in CQAs) where only limited word co-occurrence instances can be found [20].

In order to address these limitations, in this paper, we focus on the specialized community of SO and propose a framework for better representation of user expertise that leverages on word embedding techniques [17]. This framework not only makes use of textual content as evidences of user expertise within the community, but it also leverages the community feedback and interactions of users with one another to better match user expertise for routing questions. In a nutshell, the contributions of this paper are as follows:

- We propose an effective framework for representation of user expertise via word embedding techniques applied on the content of their contributions. We furthermore leverage on community feedback in order to rank users based on their contributions and performance within the community.
- We build our own word embedding model from SO's corpus to better capture domain-specific semantics within this community.
- We evaluate the performance of our proposed solution through experiments on SO's dataset and by comparing it with state-of-the-art models.

---

[2] https://stackoverflow.com/.

The rest of the paper proceeds as follows. The problem statement and the characteristics of SO platform is introduced in Sect. 2. Section 3 explains the framework for our proposed approach. The experiments and evaluations are presented in Sect. 4. Related work is given in Sect. 5, and, finally, Sect. 6 concludes the paper with ideas for future work.

2   Preliminaries

This section formally presents the problem statement and provides background information to better understand the different Q&A elements and mechanisms in SO's platform.

2.1   Problem Statement

Given a question Q, our goal is to find a set of experts $\mathcal{U}$ that best match to the required skills and domain knowledge to answer Q.

Definition 1. *Experts in CQA [16]. Given a new question Q on topic X, a user can be considered as an expert to answer Q if he/she has already answered a set of similar questions $Y = \{y_1, y_2, ..., y_z\}$ in the past. In addition, his/her expertise can also be inferred from his/her behavior and interactions within the community.*

More specifically, if we are given a new question Q and n number of users $U = \{u_1, u_2, ..., u_n\}$ having a set of m answer posts $P = \{p_1, p_2, ..., p_m\}$, our goal is to find a set of k users $\mathcal{U} = \{u_1, u_2, ..., u_k\}$ capable of answering Q. To be aligned with the definition of experts in CQA, we consider the users' answers as an indicator of their expertise on the question's topic and estimate their performance through community feedback.

As we will explain in the following section, our work leverages on users' textual content (i.e., answers) to match questions and experts. Therefore, a key *challenge* we face is the representation of user expertise for matching the newly posted question and users (experts) using a content-based method [16]. Given that SO is a focused programming community, unlike general CQAs (such as Yahoo Answers), it requires sufficient technical expertise for a user to answer a question. Keeping this in view, the second challenge entails quantifying the level of expertise of users.

2.2   Stack Overflow

SO is an interactive knowledge sharing platform in the area of computer programming and software development. It managed to get the attention of a large audience with nearly 8 million users and 41 million posts (25 million answers and 16 million questions)[3]. Users in SO interact by asking and answering questions

---

[3] https://insights.stackoverflow.com/survey/2018/.

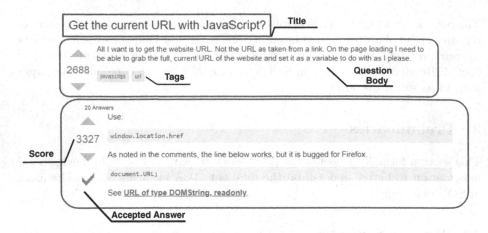

Fig. 1. An example of stack overflow Q&A post.

as well as editing and commenting on posts in order to curate content. Similarly, they acknowledge the most helpful answers by up/down voting and expressing their opinion on the quality of posts. SO also incorporates a reputation system that reflects the users' activities and their engagement toward contributions that encourage users' participation.

As an example, Fig. 1 illustrates the different elements of a Q&A post in SO. The asker posts a question that consists of three parts: (i) title, (ii) body and (iii) tags. The title of a question is a short description of the essence of the question, whereas the body explains the question in more details. A tag (which can be considered a metadata) provides a glimpse into the topic of the question. The example question in Fig. 1 has two tags, *JavaScript* and *URL*, which indicates that the question is related to JavaScript and URLs. Users provide different answers according to their knowledge and expertise (20 answers for our example question). Moreover, the asker can accept one answer among all answers, which is typically referred to as the best answer. Furthermore, other users can also up/down vote questions and answers. Such feedback mechanisms are built upon the important concepts of trust and reputation [1], which allow SO to associate reputation scores and badges to users[4].

3   Representing Users' Expertise and Recommending Users to Questions

This section presents our proposal for representing user expertise and recommending users to questions. Given the nature of the contributions in SO (which is made mainly of textual content), the key intuition behind our proposal is that we can leverage on such contributions to derive a suitable representation for user

---

[4] https://stackoverflow.com/help/whats-reputation.

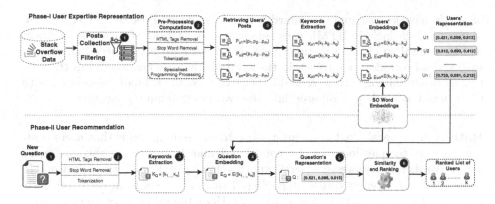

Fig. 2. Overall framework for our proposed solution.

expertise. As we will discuss next, we leverage on state-of-the-art techniques to embed such expertise into a vector space that can be later used to match users with questions. The framework for our proposed solution is outlined in Fig. 2 and consists of two main phases: (i) *user expertise representation*, and (ii) *user recommendation*. We discuss the details of each of these phases next.

3.1 User Expertise Representation

A key requirement for a good matching of user expertise and a new question consists in having a good representation of the expertise of users participating in a CQA. In this phase, users' answers and their expertise are represented by using embedding models [14], which form the basis for capturing the semantic relationship between a new question and users' expertise. Word embeddings stem from the distributional hypothesis [17], which states that words occurring in similar contexts tend to have similar meanings. This is a powerful property that have been leveraged in the literature to develop robust semantic similarity techniques in various domains [8]. In the following, we describe step-by-step how our framework (see Fig. 2) leverages on this property for user expertise representation in CQAs.

Posts Collection and Filtering. The first step in our framework involves the collection of Q&A posts from SO. The collected posts are filtered based on two requirements: (i) already resolved posts (i.e., question with answers), and (ii) having accepted (best) answer marked by the question poster. The purpose of this early filtering is to filter out low quality posts and reduce noise in the dataset.

Pre-Processing Computations. Pre-processing is an essential step that transforms raw text into a format suitable for further processing. In Step 2 of our framework, we apply standard Natural Language Processing (NLP) techniques[5], which include HTML tags removal, tokenization, stop words/frequent words removal and lemmatization. Apart from standard text processing, we also take special consideration to retain the symbols that are meaningful in the context of programming such as & and $. For example, the symbols associated with C++ and C# are key to differentiate the two programming languages.

Retrieving Users' Posts. In our approach, our assumption is that users posting answers to questions can be considered knowledgeable on the question's topic. We therefore represent users' expertise in CQAs through their answers. In order to do so, after pre-processing, Step 3 retrieves posts from each user (see, e.g., $P = \{p_1, p_2, ..., p_m\}$ in Step 3 of Fig. 2). Here, the selection of users/answers are also based on satisfying specific criteria, i.e., (i) users with at least one best (accepted) answer, and (ii) answers with score (upvotes - downvotes) of 5 or more (users with high expertise get high score/votes for their answers [7]). This step filters out users with low quality posts.

Keywords Extraction. Step 4 involves taking answer posts from users and decomposing them into a set of keywords $\{k_1, k_2, ..., k_q\}$ with the help of a part-of-speech tagger[6]. It is important to note that, unlike other CQAs, users' answers from programming CQAs usually contain massive code snippets. Filtering out such codes snippets during the pre-processing stage results in a very sparse set of keywords for each post. In order to deal with this problem, we combine the keywords from a post with tags (associated to the post) and their description for better representation (tags in SO come with their own description). This enriched set of keywords is then used to represent users in an embedding space as explained next.

User Embeddings. Following keywords extraction, Step 5 in our framework consists in representing users via these keywords with proper semantic embeddings/vector representation, which will be used in the next phase to capture the semantic similarity between a question being asked and users' expertise. The vector representation can be computed in various ways. One popular technique is the vector space model [2], which considers users' answers as a bag of words and uses occurrences count of words as features. A typical problem with this model is that it classifies semantically similar words such as *car* and *automobile* differently [26]. To avoid this problem, we employ embedding-based models that utilise the (contextual) co-occurrences of words to represent them in a lower dimensional vector space and capture their contextual and semantic relationship.

More specifically, to compute the vector representation $\overrightarrow{U}$ for each user expertise, we first learn a vector representation of words from SO's corpus using Word2Vec Skip-gram model [17]. The Skip-gram model uses a neural network

---

[5] https://www.nltk.org/.

[6] https://nlp.stanford.edu/software/tagger.shtml.

architecture to learn distributed word embeddings. This enables the prediction of the surroundings of words in associated context(s) from a corpus. We trained this model on SO's full dataset (more details is given in experimental section) to obtain domain-specific word embeddings v_w for each word w in SO's corpora. Using this word embedding model, denoted by $\mathcal{WE}$, we then generate each user expertise embedding $\overrightarrow{U}$. To do so, we make use of *vectors averaging* and *weighted vectors averaging* as discussed next.

Vectors Averaging (VecAvg). A simple yet powerful way for text representation through embeddings consists in aggregating its individual word embeddings through sum or averaging [8]. In this work, using $\mathcal{WE}$, we compute the average of the word vectors of each keyword $k_i \in K_{ui}$ in the user's answer post to obtain the semantic representation of users' expertise. That is, for each user u_j, we compute:

$$\overrightarrow{P_m} = \frac{1}{q} \sum_{i=1}^{q} e(k_i) \tag{1}$$

where $\overrightarrow{P_m}$ is the vector representation of user u_j's answer post, q is the number of keywords obtained from the post and $e(k_i)$ is a function that obtains the embedding of keyword $k_i \in K_{uj}$ from $\mathcal{WE}$ (notice that, for simplicity, the right hand side of Eq. (1) is represented as function $E(k_1, k_2, .., k_q)$ in Step 5 of Fig. 2). Similarly, the vector representation $\overrightarrow{U_j}$ for users can be obtained by averaging the vectors of all their answer posts.

Weighted Vector Averaging. The vector averaging method above considers all keyword in an answer post as equally important, which leads to vector representations of users' expertise that ignore the role that certain keywords play within an answer. To address this limitation, we use the weighted vector averaging method. Here, weights are assigned to each keyword to reflect their importance in an answer post. In this work, these weights are determined by the IDF (Inverse Document Frequency) weighting scheme [6]. The IDF is computed as the inverse of the number of user posts that contain a specific keyword, i.e.,

$$IDF_k = log\frac{m}{PC_k} \tag{2}$$

where IDF_k is the IDF of keyword k, m is the total number of answer posts of a user u_j and PC_k represents the number of answer posts containing keyword k. Thus, the weighed vector averaging not only leverages on the distributional semantics of word embedding techniques but also takes into consideration the information about the distribution of keywords appearing in different user posts. The actual computation of a users' expertise representation ($\overrightarrow{U}$) using this method can be obtained by weighting the embedding of each keyword k in Eq. (1) by the corresponding IDF_k obtained through Eq. (2).

3.2 User Recommendation

This phase of our framework aims to route a newly posted question to users that are expert on the topic of the question. We achieve this in two steps: (i) *similarity computation*, and (ii) *user ranking via statistical features*.

Upon receiving a new question Q, phase-II performs similar pre-processing and keyword extraction steps as given in phase-I. Then, it leverages $\mathcal{WE}$ to generate a vector $\vec{Q}$ for the given question using the vector averaging method, which is used for similarity computations as detailed next.

Similarity Computations. After learning the vector representation of users' expertise $\vec{U}$ and question $\vec{Q}$, we compute the similarity score $sim(Q,U)$ via cosine similarity [26], which is defined as follows:

$$sim(Q,U) = \frac{\vec{Q}.\vec{U}}{|\vec{Q}||\vec{U}|} \tag{3}$$

The closer the value of the cosine similarity to 1, the greater the relevancy of the new question with the users' expertise. This similarity computation is done for each user u_j, which results in a ranked list of users U_s, such that $U_s \subset U$ and:

$$U_s = sim(Q,U) \tag{4}$$

Here, the rank in U_s is determined by the results of the cosine similarity. Next, we show how we employ statistical features to further improve this ranking.

Users Ranking via Statistical Features. In addition to domain knowledge, the expertise of users can also be inferred from their activities and behaviour in CQAs. These activities comprise different signals based on user performance, reputation and impact in the community. Table 1 presents a list of statistical features from SO that can be used as expertise indicators. We consider all these signals and features in our work as given in [12]. The key intuition behind this choice is that expertise can be defined collectively by a set of indicators on the platform that capture the characteristics of users indicating their expertise on a given topic. We elaborate more on these features next.

Activity Features. These are features related to users' activities on the platform. Prior research [10] has shown that this set of features is useful in finding experts. For example, the best answers measure is an indication of a user being an expert in that domain area. Another example includes the z-score $z(q,a) = \frac{a-q}{\sqrt{a-q}}$ measure introduced in [23], where q and a are the number of users' questions and answers, respectively. This score combines users' asking and replying patterns with the intuition that asking a lot of questions often indicates the lack of expertise on some topics and vice versa.

Community Features. This set of features shows how much the community trusts an answerer. Feedback from the community indicates the quality of users' contributions [7]. Intuitively, users with high reputation get more votes for their posts as compared to others. Similarly, badges are given to users to reward them for their contributions once they reach a certain threshold.

Table 1. Set of features comprising different signals from platform.

Features Set	Features
Activity(A)	Number of questions, number of answers and number of accepted answers, z-score computation
Community(C)	Number of badges/awards, number of page views, number of favourites, total reputation and average answers score
Time-Aware(T)	Time interval (days between joining and n-th best answers) and average answers time

Time-Aware Features. We also include this feature to observe user activities over a period of time. One sample feature in this category includes the days between a user a joining the community and his/her n-th best answer.

We leverage on the statistical features introduced previously and apply different linear combinations of these features. More formally, the aim is to rank a user with respect to his/her level of expertise and knowledge through his/her performance in the community. To do so, an expertise score $exp(Q, U_s)$ of each user in U_s for a question Q is computed as follows:

$$exp(Q, U_s) = \alpha(A) + \beta(C) + \gamma(T) \tag{5}$$

where α, β and γ are weights that range from 0 to 1. These weights distribute the importance of activity, community and time-aware features in determining the expertise of users.

We briefly describe the usage of these features in our work next. The level of user expertise is derived from Eq. (5) by aggregating the features given in Table 1. A is an aggregation of user *activity features*. More concretely, $A(Q, U_s) = x + y$ where x computes the acceptance ratio of a users' answers, i.e., $x = \frac{B(A_Q)}{A_Q}$. Here, $B(A_Q)$ represents the number of a user's *best* answers and A_Q is the total number of his/her answers. Similarly, y quantifies the z score ($\frac{a-q}{\sqrt{a-q}}$) introduced previously. Intuitively, a high z score indicates a high knowledge of the user of the topic related to Q. Likewise, *community features* represent the influence of a user in the community and it is expressed as $C(Q, U_s) = p + q + r + s$. Where p represents the number of badges a user received, q combines the number of favourites with number of page views of a user's posts, r computes user reputation relative to the overall reputation in the community, and s is the average answer score of a user. The *time-aware feature* (T) is another factor that indicates user expertise over a period of time, with the intuition that expert users take less time in answering questions. Here, $T(U_s) = t_{ba} + t_{avg}$, where t_{ba} is the number of days between user joining the community and the n-th best answers, and t_{avg} is the average answer time of a user. The less time the user takes in answering questions, the greater the expertise of the user.

Recommendation Score. The last step in our framework is to recommend an appropriate set of users to answer a question Q. Hence, a recommendation score is calculated based on the user relevance and expertise to Q. More precisely, we integrate the Eqs. (4) and (5) to get the final ranking of users as:

$$R(Q, U_s) = \psi(U_s) + (1 - \psi)exp(Q, U_s) \qquad (6)$$

The first term in Eq. (6) deals with the contribution of a user relevance to a question Q whereas the second term is the contribution of user expertise in relation to Q. Here, ψ is a weight in the range $[0, 1]$ showing the importance of the terms in Eq. (6) in recommending expert users for answering Q. In the end, this step returns $top-k$ expert users in decreasing order of their recommendation score, i.e., $\mathcal{U} = \{u_1, u_2, ..., u_k\}$. Here, the user with the highest score (i.e., best ranked) is the best user to answer the given question.

4   Experiments

This section evaluates the performance of our proposed approach through a set of experiments with the aim of answering the following research questions:

RQ1: How effective is our proposed approach for experts representation via embedding models in question-to-expert matching?
RQ2: What is the impact of the statistical features employed in our approach in improving question-to-expert matching?

4.1   Experimental Setup

We run our experiments using real data from SO. In the following, we provide the details of our experiments, which includes data preparation, parameters setting along with models and metrics used for comparison purposes.

Data Preparation. We first start with the details regarding data preparation. We describe next the dataset, ground truth and test data used for experimentation purposes.

Dataset. The subset of data is obtained from SO's dataset[7] covering the period from August 2008 to August 2018, which consists of posts tagged by Java and its co-occurred tags (*Java Script, HTML, etc.*). Java tag has the highest ratio of Q&A posts in our dataset, and thus covers a large amount of data with 3,345,038 posts. As stated earlier in Sect. 3, the selection of users and posts are based on certain requirements: Firstly, we prune questions with no answers, which results in 2,904,208 posts. Secondly, we extract only the stabilised posts. Stabilised posts refer to resolved questions which have an accepted (best) answer. Similarly, users are also selected based on two criteria: (i) the user has at least

---

[7] https://archive.org/details/stackexchange.

one best answer, and (ii) his/her reputation score in the community must be more than the average reputation in the community. Furthermore, only answer posts with a score of 5 or more are selected. In the end, our dataset consists of 778,418 posts and 54,851 users.

Ground Truth. As for the ground truth for our approach, we make use of heuristics instead of manual labeling, as the latter does not scale well with the sheer amount of data. Following the experimental settings given in [10] for ground truth, we also define users expertise based on their accepted (best answers). A user is considered as an expert if: (i) he/she has at least ten or more accepted (best) answers, and (ii) his/her answers' acceptance ratio as well as their reputation score must be higher than the average user ratio on the platform. Thus, following these heuristics, the ground truth is made of users that have shown expertise on the topics corresponding to the answered questions.

Test Data. We prepare two different test datasets to carry out our experiments. The first one consists in a collection of Java unanswered questions (so the training and test data do not overlap), while the second one comprises randomly collected questions related to Java with actual best answerers.

Parameters Setting. To obtain domain specific embeddings, we trained our own embedding model instead of making use of already available pre-trained model over general dataset such as Wikipedia[8]. For instance, the domain specific word "cmd" (typically, short for "command") might not be available in the general trained model. Similarly, a word such as "Python" has different contextual meaning in software engineering vs. other domains. The parameters required to train this model are set as follows: The vector dimension to 200 and a sliding window for word co-occurrences to 5. In addition, a minimum word count set to 20 means that a word must occur at least 20 times in the training set. This setting of parameters gave best performance in term of matching accuracy.

Environment and Implementation. This work is implemented in Python 3 and experiments are conducted on a Linux machine with Intel Xeon 2.80 GHz CPU and 16 GB memory.

Performance Comparison. In order to demonstrate the effectiveness and matching accuracy of our approach, we compare it with the following models.

Language Model (LM) [3]. It is a classical language model for expert finding, which considers documents associated with users as their expertise. We use Jelinek Mercer (JM) smoothing with parameter $\lambda = 0.25$ for experiment purposes.

Latent Dirichlet Allocation (LDA) [4]. LDA is an unsupervised generative probability model that represents documents into a latent semantic space and then

---

[8] https://github.com/3Top/word2vec-api.

extracts topics. We use LDA to extract the topic vectors of users' answers and then compute the cosine similarity to match with the given question. The number of topics is set to 100 for this purpose.

Latent Semantic Indexing (LSI) [9]. LSI is essentially a bag of words and is used to identify the similarity between queries and user expertise.

Document Representation (Doc2vec) [14]. Doc2vec is an extension of word2vec [17]. It is based on the distributed bag of words' representations to extend the learning from word to word sequences. In this paper, we use the distributed bag of words idea to learn vectors directly by predicting all words in the answers. To be aligned with word level representation, we use the same hypermeters as of word2vec model with a sample size of $1e - 5$.

Word Movers Distance (WMD) [13]. WMD is the minimal cumulative distance between words of two documents. It retrieves word vectors from pre-trained word embedding model and considers each text document as a normalised bag of words. The weight of each word is considered as the number of times the word occurs in the document. The high occurrences show the importance of each word in that document. This approach does not require any hypermeters.

Evaluation Metrics. We evaluate the performance of our proposed solution based on one of the most used information retrieval measures for expert finding [3] and question routing in CQA [24], i.e., $P@N$ (precision at N). It measures the percentage of relevant users/experts found at the top N retrieved results. More specifically, it is the ratio of the number of relevant users $@N$ to the total number of users until N. For example, if our system returns 10 users for a given Q, where the relevant users are ranked at 1, 5, 6 and 9. Then P@5 is $\frac{2}{5}$ in this case. We also use Mean Averaged Precision (MAP), which is the average precision of all precisions for all test questions. Besides this, a user can also be ranked via the metric Success@N ($S@N$) introduced in [15] for finding the best answerers. If a system returns the actual best answerer for a given question, then prediction is successful. Otherwise, it is not. For a test question, if the best answerer is among the top N experts returned by the system, then the value of the $S@N$ is the reciprocal rank (RR), i.e., $1/N$. From here, we can also calculate the Mean Averaged Reciprocal (MRR) across multiple questions as follows:

$$MRR = \frac{1}{|M|} \sum_{i=1}^{|M|} \frac{1}{Rank_i} \tag{7}$$

where $|M|$ is the number of questions and $Rank_i$ is the position of the best answerer in the ranked list returned by the system for the i-th question.

4.2 Results and Discussions

RQ1: Effectiveness of Embedding Models. The first set of experiments investigates how well users' expertise matched a given question using embedding models. The performance of different models in terms of precision@N and MAP is summarised and reported in Table 2. It is interesting to note that the simple word level representation, i.e., *VecAvg*, achieved better performance over others in terms of recommending relevant experts. LSI and LDA have also achieved reasonable performance. Despite this, the embedding models outperformed both of them. Overall, results suggest that simple word level representation works better in representing user expertise and routing questions.

Table 2. Performance comparison of different methods.

Method	P@1	P@5	P@10	MAP
LM	0.36	0.34	0.36	0.43
LSI	0.40	0.36	0.30	0.53
LDA	0.50	0.36	0.34	0.45
Doc2Vec	0.60	0.41	0.38	0.56
WMD	0.50	0.44	0.35	0.56
VecAvg	0.60	0.48	0.42	0.62
Weighted VecAvg	0.60	0.45	0.44	0.63

RQ2: Effect of Statistical Features. The second research question explores the importance of statistical features in ranking a user. For this purpose, we evaluate the performance of our approach through MRR for best answerers prediction and list the results in Table 3. The $MRR(R)$ measure in Table 3 ranks users based on the relevance between their answers and questions (see Eq. (4)). Whereas $MRR(S)$ make use of statistical features and combines the user relevance with expertise to rank them accordingly (Eq. (6)). The larger the value for these metrics, the better the performance of the corresponding technique. It can be observed from the results that there is a small improvement in the ranking using the expertise indicators. These results show that the usage of expertise indicators improves user ranking, and thus, the prediction of best answerers for a given question.

Table 3. Best answerer prediction.

Method	MRR(R)	MRR(S)
LM	0.041	0.045
WMD	0.154	0.155
VecAvg	0.161	0.163

Discussions. The results reported in Tables 2 and 3 show that expertise representation via embeddings indeed produce better results w.r.t. the more traditional techniques of LM, LSI, LDA and WMD. When considering P@1, the embedding models outperform their counterparts by approximately 20% (WMD) to 67% (LM). When comparing performances w.r.t. the usage (or not) of statistical features, we can see modest improvements across the representative models in Table 3, ranging from 1.2% (VecAvg) to 9.8% (LM). Overall, these results are promising and encouraging, and opens up new opportunities for further research into this direction.

The experiment reported in this work comes with its own *limitations*. Firstly, we used only a subset of SO's dataset (focused only on Java-related posts), which limits our ability to generalize our conclusions to the whole platform (and for all topics in SO). Secondly, given the lack of a labeled dataset for expertise in SO, we relied on heuristics to determine the expertise of users. While this is a best-effort attempt to cope with such issue, the heuristics we used have proven useful also in previous work [10]. Finally, we trained our word embedding model (with Word2Vec) only on SO's dataset. More robust embeddings could be obtained by considering additional corpus from other sources such as Github[9] and programming-related wikis and forums.

5 Related Work

The concept of expert finding has been well-studied in information retrieval and knowledge management [22]. More recently, an increased attention has been given to the analysis of CQAs. As a result, many algorithms and models have been employed that can be categorised into three types: Graph based, content based and deep learning based approaches.

Graph Based Approaches. These approaches are based on graph analysis. They are built upon underlying interactions among users in the community [18] to understand their activities. An early work in this direction was introduced [23] for the online help seek community to find people who can provide helpful answers. For this purpose, they applied network algorithms such as PageRank [6] to estimate relative expertise of users from their interactions. Similarly, [5] proposed a model called InDegree that considers the number of best answers provided by users as an expertise indicator. The higher the degree of a user, the more likely he/she is an expert. These approaches, however, are based only on user interactions in the community rather than their textual contents as an evidence of their expertise. Thus, graph based approaches are helpful in finding the influential users in the community but not the topical expertise.

Content Based Approaches. Content based approaches usually consider expert finding as an Information Retrieval problem. For example, seminal works like [3] on probabilistic language modeling technique consider documents associated with users as the reflection of their expertise. In the context of CQAs, questions being asked can be considered as queries, while answers provided by users are considered the reflection of their expertise [16]. Here, the need for an exact overlap between query and document terms leads to a vocabulary gap

---

[9] https://github.com.

problem. Topic modeling [4] based approaches, such as [21], address this problem by incorporating semantic similarity to discover the latent topics in contents of question and identifies the interests of users. Compared to language models, topic modeling achieves better performance in terms of retrieving expert users.

Despite the improved performance shown by content based approaches, it is usually difficult to decide which features are to be used for a specific dataset. Moreover, these methods require more efforts and time due to the excessive dependence on handcrafted features. Therefore, more recently, increased attention has been given to deep learning techniques.

Deep Learning Based Approaches. Deep learning approaches have been widely used primarily for their effectiveness and promising results with little human involvement in feature selection and engineering. Work in the context of expert finding was introduced by [25], which leverages the textual contents and social interactions among users for better similarity matching. Their method utilises DeepWalk for social relations and Recurrent Neural Networks (RNNs) for modelling users' relative quality rank to questions. Similar to this work, [24] proposed a framework, which models questions, answers and users as a heterogeneous network and trains a deep neural network on random walks to enhance matching. A very recent work [26] makes use of the Convolutional Neural Network (CNN) for expert identification in CQAs. Their approach combines question and user representations for finding questions that are similar to a given question. The user representations in their framework is build up using DeepWalk and word embeddings are used to represent questions. [19] proposes an approach that not only addresses the problem of matching degree between users' expertise with the query but also the likelihood of an expert to answer the query after inviting him/her to do so.

There is also a large body of work addressing the same problem in other professional communities such as LinkedIn[10]. For example, [12] focuses on determining the topical expertise based on the skills dataset available within the company. Similarly, expert finding is also studied in bibliographical information networks [26] to mitigate the vocabulary gap problem by introducing locally trained embedding with network ranking algorithm. Unlike the approaches above, in our work, we combine content- and embedding-based techniques along with statistical features stemming from both user activities and feedback provided by the community (crowd).

6 Conclusion

In this work, we apply the state-of-the-art embedding models for representation of users' expertise to address the problem of poor expertise matching in CQAs. The key of our approach is the use of user content as well as community feedback in formulating their expertise. Firstly, we introduce the embedding models that

---

[10] https://www.linkedin.com.

map the newly posted question and users' contents into low dimensional semantic space and then relevance between them is computed via cosine similarity. Secondly, we take the advantage of the community feedback from the platform and incorporate it as an expertise indicator that helps rank the relevant users according to their level of expertise. We performed extensive experiments on Stack Overflow's dataset and compared the results with previous models. The experimental results show that our proposed framework outperforms the previous models and baseline approaches in terms of routing questions to experts.

In future work, we would like to extend the proposed approach for expert representation to heterogeneous data sources combining, e.g., Stack Overflow, Github and other programming communities.

Acknowledgement. The work of the second and third authors is supported by Data to Decisions CRC (D2D-CRC).

References

1. Anderson, A., Huttenlocher, D., Kleinberg, J., Leskovec, J.: Discovering value from community activity on focused question answering sites: a case study of stack overflow. In: Proceedings of KDD 2012, pp. 850–858 (2012)
2. Baeza-Yates, R., Ribeiro, B.: Modern Information Retrieval (2011)
3. Balog, K., Bogers, T., Azzopardi, L., de Rijke, M., van den Bosch, A.: Broad expertise retrieval in sparse data environments. In: Proceedings of SIGIR 2007, pp. 551–558 (2007)
4. Blei, D.M., Ng, A.Y., Jordan, M.I.: Latent dirichlet allocation. J. Mach. Learn. Res. **3**, 993–1022 (2003)
5. Bouguessa, M., Dumoulin, B., Wang, S.: Identifying authoritative actors in question-answering forums: the case of Yahoo! answers. In: Proceedings of SIGKDD 2008, pp. 866–874 (2008)
6. Christopher, D.M., Prabhakar, R., Hinrich, S.: Introduction to Information Retrieval. Cambridge University Press, Cambridge (2008). An Introduction to Information Retrieval **151**(177), 5
7. Dalip, D.H., Gonçalves, M.A., Cristo, M., Calado, P.: Exploiting user feedback to learn to rank answers in q&a forums: a case study with stack overflow. In: Proceedings of SIGIR 2013, pp. 543–552 (2013)
8. De Boom, C., Van Canneyt, S., Demeester, T., Dhoedt, B.: Representation learning for very short texts using weighted word embedding aggregation. Pattern Recogn. Lett. **80**, 150–156 (2016)
9. Deerwester, S., Dumais, S.T., Furnas, G.W., Landauer, T.K., Harshman, R.: Indexing by latent semantic analysis. J. Am. Soc. Inf. Sci. **41**(6), 391–407 (1990)
10. van Dijk, D., Tsagkias, M., de Rijke, M.: Early detection of topical expertise in community question answering. In: Proceedings of SIGIR 2015, pp. 995–998 (2015)
11. Gui, H., Zhu, Q., Liu, L., Zhang, A., Han, J.: Expert finding in heterogeneous bibliographic networks with locally-trained embeddings. CoRR abs/1803.03370 (2018)
12. Ha-Thuc, V., Venkataraman, G., Rodriguez, M., Sinha, S., Sundaram, S., Guo, L.: Personalized expertise search at LinkedIn. In: 2015 IEEE International Conference on Big Data (Big Data), pp. 1238–1247. IEEE (2015)

13. Kusner, M., Sun, Y., Kolkin, N., Weinberger, K.: From word embeddings to document distances. In: ICML 2015, pp. 957–966 (2015)
14. Le, Q., Mikolov, T.: Distributed representations of sentences and documents. In: ICML 2014, pp. 1188–1196 (2014)
15. Liu, M., Liu, Y., Yang, Q.: Predicting best answerers for new questions in community question answering. In: International Conference on Web-Age Information Management, pp. 127–138 (2010)
16. Liu, X., Croft, W.B., Koll, M.: Finding experts in community-based question-answering services. In: CIKM 2005, pp. 315–316 (2005)
17. Mikolov, T., Sutskever, I., Chen, K., Corrado, G.S., Dean, J.: Distributed representations of words and phrases and their compositionality. In: Advances in Neural Information Processing Systems, pp. 3111–3119 (2013)
18. Mumtaz, S., Wang, X.: Identifying Top-K influential nodes in networks. In: CIKM 2017, pp. 2219–2222 (2017)
19. Qian, Y., Tang, J., Wu, K.: Weakly learning to match experts in online community. In: IJCAI 2018, pp. 3841–3847 (2018)
20. Quan, X., Kit, C., Ge, Y., Pan, S.J.: Short and sparse text topic modeling via self-aggregation. In: IJCAI 2015 (2015)
21. Yang, L., et al.: CQARank: Jointly model topics and expertise in community question answering. In: Proceedings of CIKM 2013, pp. 99–108 (2013)
22. Yimam-Seid, D., Kobsa, A.: Expert-finding systems for organizations: Problem and domain analysis and the DEMOIR approach. J. Organ. Comput. Electron. Commer. 13(1), 1–24 (2003)
23. Zhang, J., Ackerman, M.S., Adamic, L.: Expertise networks in online communities: structure and algorithms. In: WWW 2007, pp. 221–230 (2007)
24. Zhao, Z., Lu, H., Zheng, V.W., Cai, D., He, X., Zhuang, Y.: Community-based question answering via asymmetric multi-faceted ranking network learning. In: AAAI 2017, pp. 3532–3539 (2017)
25. Zhao, Z., Yang, Q., Cai, D., He, X., Zhuang, Y.: Expert finding for community-based question answering via ranking metric network learning. In: IJCAI 2016, pp. 3000–3006 (2016)
26. Zheng, C., Zhai, S., Zhang, Z.: A deep learning approach for expert identification in question answering communities. CoRR abs/1711.05350 (2017)

A Pattern Language for Value Modeling in ArchiMate

Tiago Prince Sales[1,2(✉)], Ben Roelens[3], Geert Poels[4], Giancarlo Guizzardi[5],
Nicola Guarino[2], and John Mylopoulos[1]

[1] University of Trento, Trento, Italy
{tiago.princesales,john.mylopoulos}@unitn.it
[2] ISTC-CNR Laboratory for Applied Ontology, Trento, Italy
nicola.guarino@cnr.it
[3] Open University, Heerlen, The Netherlands
ben.roelens@ou.nl
[4] Ghent University, Ghent, Belgium
geert.poels@ugent.be
[5] Free University of Bozen-Bolzano, Bolzano, Italy
giancarlo.guizzardi@unibz.it

Abstract. In recent years, there has been a growing interest in modeling value in the context of Enterprise Architecture, which has been driven by a need to align the vision and strategic goals of an enterprise with its business architecture. Nevertheless, the current literature shows that the concept of value is conceptually complex and still causes a lot of confusion. For example, we can find in the literature the concept of value being taken as equivalent to notions as disparate as goals, events, objects and capabilities. As a result, there is still a lack of proper support for modeling all aspects of value as well as its relations to these aforementioned notions. To address this issue, we propose in this paper a pattern language for value modeling in ArchiMate, which is based on the Common Ontology of Value and Risk, a well-founded reference ontology developed following the principles of the Unified Foundation Ontology. This enables us to delineate a clear ontological foundation, which addresses the ambiguous use of the value concept. The design of the Value Pattern Language will be guided by the Design Science Research Methodology. More specifically, a first iteration of the build-and-evaluate loop is presented, which includes the development of the pattern language and its demonstration by means of a case study of a low-cost airline.

Keywords: Value modeling · Enterprise architecture · ArchiMate

1 Introduction

In the last decades, several value modeling languages have been introduced, such as e^3value [9] and VDML [19]. However, it is only recently that there is an interest in modeling value in the context of Enterprise Architecture (EA)

© Springer Nature Switzerland AG 2019
P. Giorgini and B. Weber (Eds.): CAiSE 2019, LNCS 11483, pp. 230–245, 2019.
https://doi.org/10.1007/978-3-030-21290-2_15

[24]. This integration is important as the concept of value enables to bridge the gap that exists between the goals that an organization wants to achieve and the processes that are needed to achieve these goals [3]. In other words, the notion of value enables the alignment of the Architecture Vision with the Business Architecture of an organization [24], which is needed for a company to deliver a positive end-to-end experience to their customers [15].

Despite this growing interest, it is largely recognized that value is a polisemic *term* [4,27] that might refer to several conceptually complex phenomena for which there has not been shared agreement. This issue is evinced in the current proposals to model value in ArchiMate [25]. For instance, value has been described as a goal (e.g. "Being insured" [1], "Anonymity" [8], "Security" [17]), as an object that has value (e.g. "Warehouse Space" [23]), as an event (e.g. "Payment" [1]), and as a capability (e.g. "Computer Skills" [23]).

To address this ambiguity, a value modeling approach for ArchiMate should be based on a proper ontological theory, which provides adequate real-world and formal semantics for such a language's vocabulary [10]. In particular, we make use of the concepts and relations defined in the Common Ontology of ValuE and Risk (COVER) [21] (Sect. 2.2), a novel well-founded reference ontology that explains value and risk as two ends of the same spectrum. COVER is grounded on several theories from marketing, service science, strategy and risk management. It is specified in OntoUML [10] and thus, compliant with the meta-ontological commitments of the Unified Foundational Ontology (UFO) [10].

Based on COVER, we propose a Value Pattern Language (VPL) for ArchiMate that consists of a set of interrelated modeling patterns. ArchiMate was chosen as it is a widely used modeling standard in the EA field, which is also aligned to the TOGAF standard [26]. The advantage of a pattern language [5] is that it offers a context in which related patterns can be combined, thus, reducing the space of design choices and design constraints [7].

We designed VPL according to a first cycle of Design Science Research [13]. As a first step in the design, a set of requirements is identified for the language (Sect. 3.1). These requirements ensure that the contribution of this paper is clear and verifiable, and they are needed for a formal evaluation of the language [13]. Afterwards the individual modeling patterns that compose VPL are presented (Sect. 3.3), as well as method for combining them (Sect. 3.4). We demonstrate how the VPL can be used using the case example of a low-cost airline (Sect. 4). The actual evaluation of the VPL is outside the scope of this paper, but it will be addressed by future research.

2 Research Baseline

2.1 ArchiMate

ArchiMate is a modeling standard to describe the architecture of enterprises [25]. The language is organized in six layers, namely Strategy, Business, Application, Technology, Physical, and Implementation & Migration [25]. For this paper, only elements of the Strategy and Business layers are particularly relevant. Each element is classified in the language according to its nature, referred to as "aspect" in ArchiMate: a Behavior Element represents *a unit of activity performed by one or more active structure elements*, an Active Structure Element represents *an entity that is capable of performing behavior*, a Passive Structure Element represents *a structural element that cannot perform behavior*, a Motivation Element is one that *provides the context of or reason behind the architecture of an enterprise*, and a Composite Element is simply one that aggregates other elements. Table 1 lists the most relevant ArchiMate elements and relations for the VPL. The underlying logic for the relevance of each concept in this paper can be found in Sect. 3.2. We refer the reader to the ArchiMate specification for a detailed definition of the concepts [25], while their concrete syntax can be inferred from the patterns in Sect. 3.3.

Table 1. Overview of the relevant ArchiMate concepts for the VPL.

Type	Elements
	Concepts
Motivation	Stakeholder, Driver, Assessment, Goal, Value
Structure	Resource
Behavior	Capability, Business Process, Business Interaction, Business Event
Composite	Grouping
	Relations
Structure	Composition, Realization
Dependency	Influence
Dynamic	Triggering
Other	Association

2.2   COVER: Common Ontology of ValuE and Risk

The Common Ontology of ValuE and Risk (COVER) [21] formalizes a particular sense in which the term value is used, namely that of *use value*. Briefly put, use value is the quality that summarizes a utility assessment of an object or experience from the perspective of a given subject. This is the meaning of value in sentences such as "A waterproof jacket is valuable when in a rainy city" and "A messenger app that no one uses is of no value to anyone". The notion of use value should not be confused with those of exchange and ethical value, which are also frequently used in daily life. The former refers to the worth of something in the context of an exchange and is usually measured in monetary terms (e.g. a startup valued at € 1.000.000). The latter refers to a high-level constraint that guides the behavior of individuals, as in "one of Google's core values is that Democracy on the web works".

COVER makes the following ontological commitments on the nature of value:

- **Value emerges from impacts on goal.** Value emerges from events that affect the degree of satisfaction of one or more goals of an agent. For example, sunscreen is valuable to a tourist in a hot summer day at the beach, as it allows to achieve the goal of protection from ultraviolet radiation–and thus premature aging.
- **Value is neither "good" or "bad".** Even though people intuitively assume a positive connotation for the term value, use value emerges from events that impact goals either positively or negatively. For instance, consider an event in which Vittoria drops and breaks her new phone. Assuming she had the goal of keeping it intact so she could text her friends, the break event has hurt her goal, and thus has a negative value for her.
- **Value is relative.** The same object or experience may be valuable to a person and of no value to another. For instance, a cigarette has value for a smoker and virtually no value for a non-smoker.
- **Value is experiential.** Even though value can be ascribed to objects, it is ultimately grounded on experiences. For instance, in order to explain the value of a smartphone, one must refer to the experiences enabled by it. These could include sending a text message, watching a video, or paying a bill via a banking app. Then, by valuating each experience and aggregating them according to a given function, one can "compute" the smartphone's value.
- **Value is contextual.** The value of an object can vary depending on the context in which it is used. Consider a winter jacket, for instance. If worn in a cold evening in the Italian Dolomites, it creates value by protecting one from the cold. Conversely, if worn on a warm day, it is of little use.

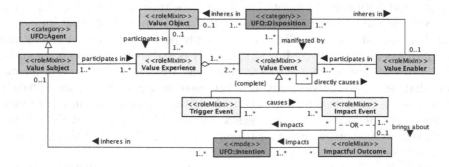

Fig. 1. A fragment of COVER depicting value experiences, their parts and participants. (Color figure online)

The aforementioned ontological commitments are captured in the COVER diagrams presented in Figs. 1 and 2[1]. The former is centered around the

---

[1] We adopt the following color coding in the OntoUML diagrams presented in this paper: events are represented in yellow, objects in pink, qualities and modes in blue, relators in green, and situations in orange.

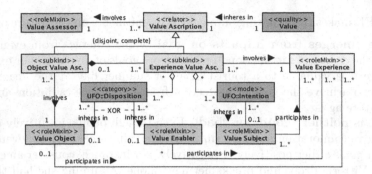

Fig. 2. A COVER fragment formalizing relationships of value ascription. (Color figure online)

experiences that create value. It depicts the VALUE SUBJECT class as the role played by an AGENT from whose perspective a value ascription is made. If the target of such an ascription is an object, it is said to play the role of a VALUE OBJECT. Conversely, if the target is an event, it is said to play the role of a VALUE EXPERIENCE. Naturally, a VALUE EXPERIENCE involves VALUE SUBJECTS and VALUE OBJECTS as participants. Additionally, it can also involve other objects, which are labelled VALUE ENABLERS. These allow the ontology to represent participants which contribute to or are necessary for an experience, but are not the focal targets of a given valuation. Examples include a browser application, which someone needs to navigate on the internet using a computer, or a road, on which someone drives a car. COVER breaks down VALUE EXPERIENCES into "smaller" events, dubbed VALUE EVENTS. These are classified into IMPACT and TRIGGER EVENTS. The former are those that directly impact a goal or bring about a situation (named IMPACTFUL OUTCOME) that impacts a goal. On contrast, TRIGGER EVENTS are simply parts of an experience that are identified as causing IMPACT EVENTS, directly or indirectly. To formalize goals, COVER reuses the concept of INTENTION from UFO [11], as a type of mental state that describes a class of state-of-affairs that an agent, the VALUE SUBJECT in our case, is committed to bring about. Note that, since agents in UFO's view includes both physical and social agents, we are able to represent value being ascribed from the perspective of a customer and an employee, but also from that of a business unit or even a whole enterprise.

The diagram in Fig. 2 is centered around the VALUE ASCRIPTION relationship, which represents an assessment made by an AGENT, the VALUE ASSESSOR, that "attaches" a quality VALUE to a given VALUE OBJECT or EXPERIENCE from the perspective of a VALUE SUBJECT. As COVER commits to grounding value on experiences, it distinguishes between OBJECT- and EXPERIENCE VALUE ASCRIPTION relationships, with the former being composed by the latter.

2.3 On Patterns and Pattern Languages

A *modeling pattern* describes a situation-independent well-proven solution to a recurring modeling problem. Its use favors the reuse of encoded experiences and good practices. As discussed in depth in [7], a particular modeling pattern of interest is an Ontology Design Pattern (ODP). As demonstrated in [7], ODPs can be systematically extracted from so-called core ontologies, i.e., ontologies that capture phenomena that are recurrent in a number of domains.

As pointed out by Alexander et al. [2], each pattern can exist only to the extent that it is supported by other patterns. According to Schmidt et al. [22], in Software Engineering (SE), the trend is defining pattern languages, rather than stand-alone patterns. The term "pattern language" in SE refers to a network of interrelated patterns that defines a process for systematically solving coarse-grained software development problems [22]. In [7], the authors make a case demonstrating the viability and benefits of this approach for conceptual model engineering. As shown there, from a core ontology, one can systematically extract a set of ODPs as well as their ties (comprising relations of aggregation, precedence, dependence, mutual exclusion, etc.). Languages that prescribe how ODPs extracted from the same core ontology can be used together are termed Ontology Pattern Languages (OPLs). The method proposed in [7] has been successfully employed to construct OPLs for the modeling of Enterprises, Services, Software Processes, among others. Following this method, in next section, we propose a Pattern Language for Value Modeling.

3   A Pattern Language for Value Modeling

3.1 Language Requirements

In the context of modeling language design, it is useful to identify two types of requirements. The first, named an *analysis requirement*, refers to what the models produced with the language should help users to achieve, either by means of automated or manual analysis. The second, named an *ontological requirement*, refers to the concepts and relations the language should have in order to accurately represent its domain of interest and thus support its intended uses. Let us consider a case for ArchiMate to exemplify these notions. By allowing the representation of how the various elements of an architecture are related, such as services being realized by business processes, which in turn are supported by applications (an ontological requirement), ArchiMate allows users to perform an impact-of-change analysis (an analysis requirement) [16].

For the VPL, we established the following *analysis requirements*:

R1. *Design-time value analysis:* An enterprise should be able to understand how it creates value for a given stakeholder, as well as identify opportunities to improve its offerings so that it can maximize value creation.

R2. *Run-time value analysis:* An enterprise should be able to identify which indicators it needs to monitor value creation for a given stakeholder, so that it can detect deviations from planned experiences, as well as identify opportunities for innovation.

R3. *Competitive analysis:* By modeling the value experiences an enterprise offers to its customers and those of its competitors, an enterprise should be able to identify its competitive advantages.

Given that we are leveraging COVER for the design of the VPL, its ontological requirements are fairly straightforward, i.e., they consist of an isomorphic representation of all concepts and relations defined in the ontology (as argued in [10]). In addition to the aforementioned requirements, we assumed the following *constraints* for the VPL:

R4. It should rely exclusively on constructs available in ArchiMate 3.0.1 [25]. This is to avoid adding to the complexity of the language.
R5. It should map value-related concepts into ArchiMate constructs maintaining, as much as possible, their original meaning as described in the standard. Stereotypes should only be used if strictly necessary to refine the meaning of particular constructs.

3.2 Mapping

Table 2 shows the mapping of COVER concepts into ArchiMate elements.

Table 2. Representation of value-related concepts in ArchiMate.

Concept	Representation in archimate
Value Subject	Stakeholder
Value Object	Structure Element connected to a «ValueExperience»
Value Enabler	Structure Element connected to a Value Event
Value Experience	«ValueExperience» Grouping
Value Event	Business Process, Business Interaction, Business Event
Disposition	Capability
Quality	«Quality» Driver
Intention	«QualityGoal» Goal, «FunctionalGoal» Goal
Value	Value
Value Assessor	Stakeholder connected to a «Valuation»
Object Value Asc.	«Valuation» Assessment connected to a Value Object
Experience Value Asc.	«Valuation» Assessment connected to a «ValueExperience»
Likelihood	«Likelihood» Assessment connected to a triggering association between Value Events or to a «ValueExperience»

3.3 Value Modelling Patterns

Value Object. This pattern allows modelers to express which object will be the focus of a valuation, as well as which kind of experiences enabled by the object are being considered to deduce its value. Its generic structure is depicted on the left side of Fig. 3. It consists of a STRUCTURE ELEMENT–the Value Object–connected to a «ValueExperience» GROUPING that realizes a «FunctionalGoal» GOAL and for which there is a «Likelihood» ASSESSMENT. The likelihood element allows modelers to represent how frequent an experience involving the value object will occur. This assessment serves as a "weight" to the overall use value of an object.

We suggest that modelers represent one experience per type of goal that someone can accomplish with a given value object. For instance, if the value object under analysis is a car, the experiences could include driving it to work, to travel, or to buy groceries. If relevant, modelers can also represent multiple experiences that fulfill the same goal, but that take place in different contexts, such as travelling by car through highways or through dirt roads in the country-side.

Value Experience. This pattern refines the former w.r.t detailing value experiences. As depicted on the right side of Fig. 3, it consists of «ValueExperience» Grouping connected to a STAKEHOLDER acting as the value subject, and its decomposition into value events, which can be represented using BUSINESS PROCESSES, BUSINESS EVENTS and/or BUSINESS INTERACTIONS.

This pattern is neutral with regard to the level of detail at which an experience is modelled. For instance, let us consider the experience of a football fan watching a match at a stadium. It could simply include the events of going to the stadium, watching the match, and then going home. Alternatively, it could be further detailed to account for the ticket purchase, the movement within the stadium to find one's designated seat, and the consumption of food and drinks. Still, note that the more an experience is detailed, the more accurate the description is of how value is created, and thereby, more insights can be obtained.

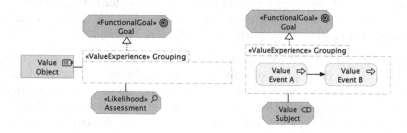

Fig. 3. Generic structures of the value object and value experience patterns.

Value Subject. In order to account for what creates value for a given stakeholder, we introduce the Value Subject Pattern, as depicted in Fig. 4. It allows one to represent every relevant GOAL of a STAKEHOLDER, as well as to specify their importance by means of a numeric REWARD attribute (represented in the figure between brackets for clarity). Adding "weights" to goals is a modeling strategy that has shown to be very useful for analyzing models, such as the optimization algorithms proposed in [18]. Moreover, to represent the various goals of a value subject in a more compact manner, we propose to represent them within a «Motivation» GROUPING associated to their owner. This modeling strategy is directly inspired by those proposed in goal modeling languages, such as i* [28].

Fig. 4. Generic structure of the value subject pattern.

Note that we differentiate between functional and quality goals, following the semantics proposed in [12]. Simply put, functional goals refer to what change in the state-of-affairs an agent wants to bring about, while a quality goal refers to how this change should occur. For instance, traveling to a destination is a functional goal, while doing so in less then two hours is a quality goal. One should note that this distinction is not equivalent to that of hard and soft goals. This second classification refers to how clearly a goal is defined, and thus, is orthogonal to the former. Our previous example of traveling under two hours is considered a hard goal, whilst traveling quickly is a soft goal.

We are aware that providing concrete values for rewards given by goals is challenging. Such numbers may feel artificially chosen and contradictions may quickly arise. Nonetheless, it is fundamental to be able to articulate the motivations driving different stakeholders. To explain why, let us consider customers of low-cost and regular airlines. All of them want to reach their destination, have a comfortable trip, and minimize their financial efforts. However, customers of low-cost airlines prefer to minimize their financial efforts over having a comfortable trip, i.e. they ascribe a higher reward to the former goal than to the latter. To help modelers define these rewards, we suggest the use of prioritization techniques, such as the Analytic Hierarchy Process (AHP) [20].

Value Event. Given that we described the motivation driving a value subject, we go back to the description of value experiences. In order to account for how parts of an experience affect goals, and thus, increase or reduce its value, we propose the Value Event Pattern. Its three variants are presented in Fig. 5.

The first variant, depicted in Fig. 5a, has a very simple structure, consisting of a value event associated to a «FunctionalGoal» GOAL by means of a REALIZA-TION relation. One could use this variant to represent that the event of watching a movie realizes the goal of being entertained.

The second variant, depicted in Fig. 5b, has a more complex structure. It consists of a value event, a «QualityGoal» GOAL, a «Quality» DRIVER and a quality ASSESSMENT. The value event INFLUENCES the GOAL (either positively or negatively) because the magnitude of one of its qualities is directly related to the satisfaction of the goal. For instance, consider the event of waiting in line at the post office. Since most people want to minimize the time they waste doing chores, its satisfaction is directly related to the duration of the waiting event.

In the third variant, depicted in Fig. 5c, the quality related to the satisfaction of a goal does not inhere in the event, but in one of its participants. Let us consider again the post office case. One's value perception of such an experience is also influenced by qualities like the politeness of the post office attendants, the number of seats available in the waiting room, and the number of complaints being made by other customers.

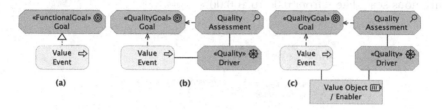

Fig. 5. The three variants of the value event pattern.

Disposition. This pattern further characterizes value events, in the sense of accounting for what allows them to happen (ontologically, events are always manifestations of dispositions). As shown on the left side of Fig. 6, it consists on modelling the dispositions (i.e., CAPABILITIES in ArchiMate) whose manifestations are the value events, as well as the value objects or enablers, in which these dispositions inhere. This pattern allows one to represent that a banking app has capabilities to enable customers to check their balance and make payments. It also allows the representation of dispositions that are manifested as unwanted value events, such as a car that has a disposition to overheat.

Causality. This pattern connects value events that composed a value experience to allow its characterization as an ordered sequence of steps. Its general structure, depicted on the right side of Fig. 6, consists of two value events connected by a TRIGGERING relation, for which a «Likelihood» ASSESSMENT is made. This means that a value event has a probability to cause (or be followed by) another value event. To exemplify this pattern, let us consider the experience of using an on-demand video streaming service. A modeler could use this pattern to represent that after choosing a movie on the platform library, a viewer actually watches it, or that while watching, there is a chance that the viewer dislikes it and then proceeds to search for an alternative content to watch.

Fig. 6. Generic structures of the disposition and the causality patterns.

Experience Valuation. This pattern allows modelers to describe value judgments made towards experiences. As shown in Fig. 7, it consists of a «Valuation» ASSESSMENT made by a STAKEHOLDER that a «ValueExperience» GROUPING creates VALUE for another STAKEHOLDER. Note that the actual VALUE element here is not described in textual terms, but rather as an entry in a scale chosen by the modeler. Just as we are used to see in risk management methodologies, value can be described in a discrete scale like $<Low, Medium, High>$ or in a continuous scale like <from 0.00 to 100.00>.

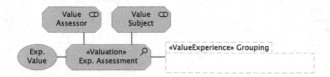

Fig. 7. Generic structure of the experience valuation pattern.

Object Valuation. The last VPL pattern is very similar to the previous one, as it also represents a value judgment. The difference is that the judgment is made towards a value object, as seen in Fig. 8. As we previously discussed, the value ascribed to objects is computed from the experiences they afford. Thus, a «Valuation» ASSESSMENT associated to a value object is composed by «Valuation» ASSESSMENTS associated to «ValueExperience» GROUPINGS that are associated to the focal value object. We also represent a derived INFLUENCE association between the VALUE attached to each ASSESSMENT, so that we can clearly see the process of value aggregation.

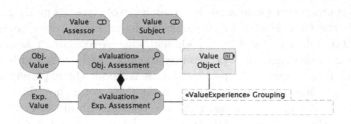

Fig. 8. Generic structure of the object valuation pattern.

3.4   Combining the Patterns

To use VPL, a modeler may start with the application of: (i) the Value Object pattern, if the valuation focus is an object (e.g. a product offered by the enterprise or a resource owned by it); (ii) the Value Experience pattern, if the valuation focus is an experience (e.g. a service provided by the enterprise); or (iii) the Value Subject pattern, if the focus is the value perceived by a stakeholder in multiple contexts (e.g. as a partner and as a provider).

When starting with a Value Object pattern, a user may iteratively apply it to account for the relevant ways in which an object can create value, as well as in which contexts it may do so. Each application should be followed by that of the Value Experience. Then, for every experience, the user should iteratively apply the three patterns that detail the inner structure of a value experience: the Value Event, Disposition, and Causality patterns. For each detailed experience, the modeler should apply the Experience Valuation pattern in order to represent its value for the chosen value subject. If one is valuating an object, the Object Valuation pattern should be used to group the experience valuations, and thus derive the aggregate value of the object.

The detailed diagrams presenting the complete process of combining the patterns can be found at https://github.com/ontouml/vpl.

4 Case Study

We now present a realistic case study in which we use the VPL to describe how a low-cost airline creates value for its customers. In particular, we model the experience of flying with such a company following a customer journey mapping approach [15], a marketing framework that proposes to map, evaluate and redesign customers' experiences when engaging with companies. Given the limited space available, we only present relevant fragments of the resulting model. The complete case study is available at https://github.com/ontouml/vpl.

Since our case focuses on an experience, rather than a product, we start with the application of the Value Experience pattern, as shown in Fig. 9. As the value subject, we use a persona that exemplifies the prototypical customer of a low-cost airline, here named PRICE SENSITIVE LEISURE TRAVELER. Naturally, the main functional goal of air travelling is to TRAVEL TO A DESTINATION, and thus, we represent it as the goal the experience realizes. We also decompose the experience into 4 main steps: BOOKING, PRE-FLIGHT, FLIGHT and POST-FLIGHT.

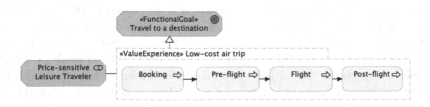

Fig. 9. Usage of the value experience pattern.

In order to describe how our subject perceives value, we apply the Value Subject pattern, as depicted in Fig. 10. In addition to the travelling goal, we

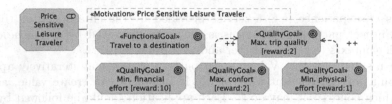

Fig. 10. Application of the value subject pattern.

assume that the subject wants to minimize her efforts, both monetary and non-monetary. The former refers to how much she pays to book a flight, choose a seat, and dispatch her luggage, whilst the latter refers to any physical, emotional, cognitive or time effort [6] she has to endure throughout her experience. To each goal, we ascribe a reward between 1 and 10, which reflects their importance to the subject. This prioritization evinces that the subject rather prefers to minimize her financial effort than to enjoy a high quality trip.

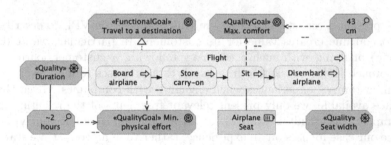

Fig. 11. Application of all three variants of the value event pattern.

We now further detail the travelling experience by applying the Value Event pattern three times, as depicted in Fig. 11. We first use the pattern to represent that the FLIGHT process realizes the traveling goal. Then, we apply it to express that the DURATION of the flight is inversely related to the satisfaction of the goal of minimizing physical effort. Lastly, we apply it to represent that, the WIDTH of the AIRPLANE SEAT negatively impacts the subject's comfort goal.

Using the Causality pattern, we represent alternative paths the air traveling experience can take. In Fig. 12, we present a refinement of the PRE-FLIGHT step that captures a choice the subject can make after checking in on the flight. She can either download her boarding pass on a smartphone or print it at a totem the airline provides at the airport. Moreover, we use the Disposition pattern to model that the DOWNLOAD BOARDING PASS process depends on the SMARTPHONE, a value enabler, having a CONNECTIVITY disposition to access the internet.

Lastly, we demonstrate the application of the Experience Valuation pattern in Fig. 13. With it, we express that a CUSTOMER EXPERIENCE ANALYST, an

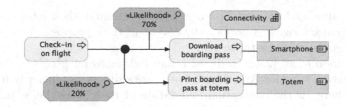

Fig. 12. Usage of the causality and of the disposition pattern.

employee of the low-cost airline, judges that our subject, the Price Sensitve Leisure Traveler ascribes a High value to the low-cost traveling experience.

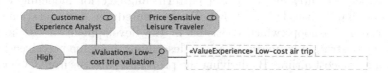

Fig. 13. Application of the experience valuation pattern.

5   Related Work

Iacob et al. [14] proposed to extend ArchiMate 2.0 so that it could model strategy- and value-related constructs. As we did, the authors also argue for a relative perspective on value, although it is not clear if they mean taking the perspective of the value subject or the assessor. They also explicitly relate value and risk, although they do not elaborate on the relation itself. Nonetheless, compared to this paper, an interesting aspect of their proposal is to model value from a quantitative perspective, one that is often neglected in the literature.

A second extension was proposed by Aldea et al. [1]. In their work, the authors are clearly concerned with properly grasping the nature of value, as they recognize the difference between use and exchange value. They account for the relative notion of use value by representing it as being perceived by a stakeholder, as well as the relation between value and goals. Nonetheless, the lack of clearly defined ontological foundations hinders the clarity of their proposal, as the authors seem to contradict themselves by using the value element in the sense of a goal ("Being insured") and in the sense of a value creating event ("Payment").

More recently, Feltus and colleagues introduced a value co-creation extension for ArchiMate [8]. They grounded their proposal on the Value Co-creation Ontology, a reference ontology designed from a Service-dominant Logic perspective that formalizes the concept of use value. Despite their more narrow focus on co-creation, the authors also assume a relative view on value, by representing that it benefits some stakeholder. They do distinguish between value, the events that create value, and the participating objects, although their interrelations are not clearly characterized. A noteworthy caveat to their proposal, however, is the omission of goals to characterize value.

Lastly, Singh et al. [23] introduced a method based on e^3value [9] to design a Value Creation view for ArchiMate. Their work differs significantly from what we propose here, as the conceptual foundation of their work, i.e. e^3value, aims at modeling the exchange of value objects between economic agents. Their work focuses on *what* has value, as evinced by their use of "Warehouse Space" as a value element, whereas we focus on *what*, *why* and *how* things have value.

6   Final Remarks

In this paper, we introduced VPL, a pattern language for modeling value in ArchiMate that is based on COVER. We presented the first iteration of the build-and-evaluate loop, which consisted in the development of the language and its demonstration by means of a case describing the value perceived by customers of a low-cost airline. By deriving the proposed patterns from COVER, we provided clear real-world semantics for its constituting elements, thus reducing the ambiguity and conceptual complexity found in previous approaches. In particular, we can represent: (i) *what* we can ascribe value to–objects and events; (ii) *why* these have value–because of their impact on goals; (iii) *how* value emerges–by means of value experiences that are composed of value events; and (iv) *who* participates in a value ascription–value subjects and assessors.

As future work, we plan to evaluate VPL by means of case studies in which we will assess: (i) its suitability to model the value domain, (ii) the usability and completeness of the patterns, (iii) the adequacy of the pattern application process, and (iv) the scalability of the language. Moreover, we want to further explore the business insights one may get from using VPL.

References

1. Aldea, A., Iacob, M.E., van Hillegersberg, J., Quartel, D., Franken, H.: Modelling value with ArchiMate. In: Persson, A., Stirna, J. (eds.) CAiSE 2015. LNBIP, vol. 215, pp. 375–388. Springer, Cham (2015). https://doi.org/10.1007/978-3-319-19243-7_35
2. Alexander, C., et al.: A Pattern Language: Towns, Buildings, Construction. Oxford University Press, Oxford (1977)
3. Andersson, B., Johannesson, P., Zdravkovic, J.: Aligning goals and services through goal and business modelling. Inf. Syst. e-Bus. Manag. **7**(2), 143–169 (2009)
4. Boztepe, S.: User value: competing theories and models. Int. J. Des. **1**(2), 55–63 (2007)
5. Buschmann, F., Henney, K., Schimdt, D.: Pattern-Oriented Software Architecture: on Patterns and Pattern Languages, vol. 5. Wiley, Hoboken (2007)
6. Clark, M., Bryan, A.: Customer effort: help or hype? Henley Business school (2013)
7. Falbo, R.A., et al.: Ontology pattern languages. In: Ontology Engineering with Ontology Design Patterns: Foundations and Applications. IOS Press (2016)

8. Feltus, C., Proper, E.H., Haki, K.: Towards a language to support value cocreation: an extension to the ArchiMate modeling framework. In: Federated Conference on Computer Science and Information Systems, vol. 15, pp. 751–760. IEEE (2018)
9. Gordijn, J., Akkermans, J.: Value-based requirements engineering: exploring innovative e-commerce ideas. Requirements Eng. **8**(2), 114–134 (2003)
10. Guizzardi, G.: Ontological Foundations for Structural Conceptual Models. Telematics Instituut, Enschede (2005)
11. Guizzardi, G., Falbo, R., Guizzardi, R.S.S.: Grounding software domain ontologies in the Unified Foundational Ontology (UFO). In: 11th Ibero-American Conference on Software Engineering (CIbSE), pp. 127–140 (2008)
12. Guizzardi, R.S., et al.: An ontological interpretation of non-functional requirements. In: International Conference on Formal Ontology in Information Systems, pp. 344–357 (2014)
13. Hevner, A.R., March, S.T., Park, J., Ram, S.: Design science in information systems research. MIS Q. **28**(1), 6 (2008)
14. Iacob, M.E., Quartel, D., Jonkers, H.: Capturing business strategy and value in enterprise architecture to support portfolio valuation. In: 16th International Enterprise Distributed Object Computing Conference, pp. 11–20. IEEE (2012)
15. Kalbach, J.: Mapping Experiences: A Complete Guide to Creating Value through Journeys, Blueprints, and Diagrams. O'Reilly Media Inc., Sebastopol (2016)
16. Lankhorst, M.: Enterprise Architecture at Work: Modelling, Communication and Analysis. TEES. Springer, Heidelberg (2013). https://doi.org/10.1007/978-3-642-29651-2
17. Meertens, L., et al.: Mapping the business model canvas to ArchiMate. In: ACM Symposium on Applied Computing, pp. 1694–1701. ACM (2012)
18. Nguyen, C.M., Sebastiani, R., Giorgini, P., Mylopoulos, J.: Multi-objective reasoning with constrained goal models. Requirements Eng. **23**(2), 189–225 (2018)
19. Object Management Group (OMG): Value delivery metamodel v1.0 (2015)
20. Roelens, B., Steenacker, W., Poels, G.: Realizing strategic fit within the business architecture: the design of a process-goal alignment modeling and analysis technique. Softw. Syst. Model. **18**, 1–32 (2017)
21. Sales, T.P., Baião, F., Guizzardi, G., Almeida, J.P.A., Guarino, N., Mylopoulos, J.: The common ontology of value and risk. In: Trujillo, J.C., et al. (eds.) ER 2018. LNCS, vol. 11157, pp. 121–135. Springer, Cham (2018). https://doi.org/10.1007/978-3-030-00847-5_11
22. Schmidt, D.C., Stal, M., Rohnert, H., Buschmann, F.: Pattern-Oriented Software Architecture: Patterns for Concurrent and Networked Objects. Wiley, Hoboken (2000)
23. Singh, P.M., et al.: Modeling value creation with enterprise architecture. Int. Conf. Enterp. Inf. Syst. (ICEIS) **3**, 343–351 (2014)
24. Svee, E.-O., Zdravkovic, J.: Extending enterprise architectures to capture consumer values: the case of TOGAF. In: Persson, A., Stirna, J. (eds.) CAiSE 2015. LNBIP, vol. 215, pp. 221–232. Springer, Cham (2015). https://doi.org/10.1007/978-3-319-19243-7_22
25. The Open Group: ArchiMate v3.0.1 Specification. Standard C179 (2017)
26. The Open Group: TOGAF v9.2 (2018)
27. Vargo, S.L., Maglio, P.P., Akaka, M.A.: On value and value co-creation: a service systems and service logic perspective. Eur. Manag. J. **26**(3), 145–152 (2008)
28. Yu, E., Giorgini, P., Maiden, N., Mylopoulos, J.: Social Modeling for Requirements Engineering. MIT Press, Cambridge (2011)

Paving Ontological Foundation for Social Engineering Analysis

Tong Li$^{(\boxtimes)}$ and Yeming Ni

Beijing University of Technology, Beijing, China
litong@bjut.edu.cn, niyemingyou@gmail.com

Abstract. System security analysis has been focusing on technology-based attacks, while paying less attention on social perspectives. As a result, social engineering are becoming more and more serious threats to socio-technical systems, in which human plays important roles. However, due to the interdisciplinary nature of social engineering, there is a lack of consensus on its definition, hindering the further development of this research field. In this paper, we propose a comprehensive and fundamental ontology of social engineering, with the purpose of prompting the fast development of this field. In particular, we first review and compare existing social engineering taxonomies in order to summarize the core concepts and boundaries of social engineering, as well as identify corresponding research challenges. We then define a comprehensive social engineering ontology, which is embedded with extensive knowledge from psychology and sociology, providing a full picture of social engineering. The ontology is built on top of existing security ontologies in order to align social engineering analysis with typical security analysis as much as possible. By formalizing such ontology using Description Logic, we provide unambiguous definitions for core concepts of social engineering, serving as a fundamental terminology to facilitate research within this field. Finally, our ontology is evaluated based on a collection of existing social engineering attacks, the results of which indicate good expressiveness of our ontology.

Keywords: Social engineering · Ontology · Psychology · Attacks

1 Introduction

With the rapid growth of system scales, modern information systems include more heterogeneous components other than software. In particular, human has played an increasingly important role in the entire system, who can be seen as a system component and interacts with other system components (e.g., human, software, hardware) [9]. As such, security analysis should cover not only software security, but also concerns the security of human in order to ensure holistic security of systems. However, traditional security analysis has been focusing on technology-based attacks, while paying less attention on the social perspective [6]. As a result, social engineering has become more and more serious threats

© Springer Nature Switzerland AG 2019
P. Giorgini and B. Weber (Eds.): CAiSE 2019, LNCS 11483, pp. 246–260, 2019.
https://doi.org/10.1007/978-3-030-21290-2_16

to socio-technical systems. A famous social engineer Kevin Mitnick has clearly pointed out that nowadays human has become the most vulnerable part of systems [11].

Due to the interdisciplinary nature of social engineering, there is a lack of consensus on its definition, hindering the further development of this research field. Researchers from different research fields are likely to use their own terminology to describe social engineering. Even researchers in the same research field may have totally different definitions. A notable example is about inclusion or exclusion of *shoulder surfing*, which is traditionally treated as a social engineering attack [3], but some other researchers explicitly vote for excluding it from social engineering attacks [14]. The main reason for this phenomenon is because there lacks of a well-defined ontology for social engineering. Especially, all social engineering researchers only present social engineering in a descriptive way by using natural languages, which is by no means precise and unambiguous. As a result, without having a consensus on the definition of social engineering, even social engineering researchers are confusing about concepts of social engineering, not mention industrial practitioners.

In this paper, we aim to provide a rigorous and comprehensive ontology of social engineering in order to form a fundamental terminology for research of social engineering. Specifically, we first review existing social engineering ontologies in detail, investigating aspects they focus on and comparing their conceptual coverage. Based on such a review, we propose a comprehensive ontology of social engineering, which offers a unified set of concepts of social engineering and covers various perspectives in order to be easily comprehended by researchers from different communities. The proposal is founded on top of typical security requirements ontologies, and is embedded with extensive knowledge from psychology and sociology, providing a complete picture of social engineering. We have formalized the proposed ontology by using Description Logic (DL) in order to provide unambiguous semantics and enable class inferences, serving as a theoretic foundation for carrying out follow-up research in this field. Finally, we evaluate the coverage and correctness of our approach by using it to analyze real social engineering attacks reported in literature.

In the remainder of this paper, we first report the findings of our literature survey in Sect. 2. Based on the results of the survey, we then present our main contribution, a comprehensive social engineering ontology in Sect. 3. After that we evaluate the expressiveness of our ontology in Sect. 4, and eventually conclude the paper in Sect. 5.

2   Review of Existing Approaches

A number of studies have been carried out to investigate the taxonomy and ontology of social engineering, each of which emphasizes different perspectives. In this section, we present an in-depth survey of existing taxonomies and ontology of social engineering with the purpose of comprehensively understanding various conceptual elements in social engineering. Base on such a survey, we then report our findings about a number of challenges with existing studies. In particular, we focus on investigating social engineering attacks and their categories. Moreover, other social engineering-specific concepts (e.g., human vulnerability) are also surveyed and presented.

2.1 Social Engineering Attacks

Many researchers have investigated social engineering by focusing on social engineering attacks, and have proposed several taxonomies of social engineering attacks [2–4, 8, 13, 14]. Note that social engineering attacks are described as attack vector [8], attack technique [2], or attack method [5]. Table 1 shows the comparison of various studies regarding social engineering attacks. We have tried to cluster similar attacks in a row to better present the similarity and difference among various studies (i.e., C1-C5). It is worth noting that the last row C5 presents attacks that are different from each other and cannot be related to any of the previous attacks.

Table 1. Comparison of social engineering attacks defined in different studies

No.	Gulati [2]	Nyamsuren [13]	Krombholz [8]	Peltier [14]	Ivaturi [4]	Harley [3]
C1	Spying and Eavesdropping; Dumpster Diving	Shoulder Surfing; Digital Dumpster Diving	Shoulder Surfing; Dumpster Diving	Dumpster Diving and Shoulder Surfing		Dumpster Diving; Leftover
C2	Technical Expert; Support Stuff			Impersonation and Important User; In Person	Impersonation	Masquerading
C3	Voice of Authority; Direct Approach		Reverse Social Engineering	Third-Party Authorization	Reverse Social Engineering; Tailgating; Pretexting	Direct Psychological Manipulation
C4	Trojan Horse; Pop-Up Windows	Phishing		Pop-Up Windows; Mail Attachments; Web Sites	Phishing; SMSishing; Cross Site Request Forgery; Malware; Vishing	Spam
C5		Signal Hijacking; Network Monitoring; Theft on Mobile Device; Denial of Service	Baiting; Waterholing; Advanced Persistent Threat			Hoax Virus Alerts and Other Chain Letters; Password Stealing

Having a closer look at these studies, Harley first presents a taxonomy of social engineering attacks [3], in which he enumerated seven social engineering attacks, including *masquerading, password stealing, spam* etc. Such attacks are summarized at a rather coarse-grained level, describing the common procedure for carrying out the attacks. Krombholz et al. also describe attacks in a coarse manner, such as *shoulder surfing*, *baiting*, and *waterholing* [8]. Ivaturi and Janczewski identify social engineering attacks by focusing on particular approaches used by attackers, such as *pretexting*, *cross site request forgery*, and *malware* [4]. Also, they distinguish attacks that are carried out via different media. For example, *phishing*, *smsishing*, and *vishing* characterize three attacks that are carried out via email, short message, and voice. Peltier summarizes a list of social engineering attacks from real attack scenarios [14]. Similar to Ivaturi's taxonomy, he looks into the media via which attacks are carried out, e.g., *popup windows* and *mail attachments*. Gulati enumerates social engineering attacks at a fine-grained level [2]. In particular, he distinguishes impersonation attacks based on the person to be impersonated, such as *technical expert* and *supporting stuff*. Nyamsuren and Choi discuss social engineering attacks in the context of ubiquitous environment [13]. Thus, they present some attacks specific to the ubiquitous environment in addition to typical ones, e.g., *signal hijacking*.

Challenges. Although such studies all tried to enumerate a full list of social engineering attacks, each of them came out with a particular taxonomy that is inconsistent and even conflicting with others. In particular, we have observed the following challenges that should be addressed.

- No Clear Definition. As clearly shown in Table 1, different studies have proposed quite different social engineering attacks (as shown in row C5), and none of them are complete. The most important issue is that there is no clear definition for social engineering attacks. Thus, the scope of social engineering attacks varies from studies to studies. A notable example is *Dumpster Diving*. Although most studies treat it as a social engineering attack, Ivaturi and Janczewski argue that such an attack does not involve social interactions with the victim and thus explicitly exclude it from their taxonomy [4]. Such a clarification is reasonable, but we cannot determine which proposal is correct without a clear definition.
- Inconsistent Granularity. Different researchers characterize social engineering attacks at different granularity levels. For instance, Peltier emphasizes particular scenarios of carrying out psychological manipulation, such as *third-party authorization* and *creating a sense of urgency*. While other researchers [3] view such attacks at a higher abstraction level as *direct psychological manipulation*.
- Incomplete Enumeration. In addition to common social engineering attacks, each study has proposed unique attacks from their own perspective. For example, Nyamsuren and Choi extend *dumpster diving* to propose *digital dumpster diving*; Ivaturi and Janczewski propose *smsishing*, which is similar to *phishing* but is carried out via mobile phone message. However, such new attacks have not been summarized and proposed in a systematic way, and thus none of existing studies can come out with a complete enumeration of social engineering attacks. Not to mention some of the newly proposed attacks should not be classified as a new type of attack. For example, *password stealing*

describes a possible damage caused by *impersonation* [3], which should not be positioned as a particular type of social engineering attack.

- Different Terminologies. Different researchers are likely to name social engineering attacks based on their own terminology. For example, *masquerading* [3] and *impersonation* [4] describe the same type of attacks, in which attackers use fake identities. Also, *digital dumpster diving* and *leftover* are describing the same thing according to their explanation [3,13].

2.2   Categories of Social Engineering Attacks

Researchers have proposed various categories to manage and navigate social engineering attacks, among which the mostly accepted proposal is to classify attacks as *human-based attacks and technology-based attacks* [1,2,5,14]. Specifically, as long as a social engineering attack involves using any computer-related technology, it is deemed as a technology-based attack; otherwise, it is a human-based attack.

In addition to the above simple categories, Krombholz et al. have defined a more comprehensive taxonomy for classifying social engineering attacks [8]. In particular, they view a social engineering attack as a scenario that attackers perform physical actions, apply socio-psychological or computer technique over a variety of different channels. As such, they propose to classify social engineering attacks in terms of *Operator*, *Channel*, and *Type*. Mouton et al. emphasize the communication between attackers and victims, and propose to classify social engineering attacks into direct attacks and indirect attacks [12]. Furthermore, they classify direct attacks into two ways of communicating: bidirectional communication or unidirectional communication.

Challenges. We argue the binary classification, i.e., human-based attacks and technology-based attacks, is too general to be useful. Especially, a social engineering attack, in many cases, actually belongs to multiple categories depending on its different attributes. For example, *voice of authority* can be reasonably classified as *psychological manipulation*; however, if an attacker opts to perform actions via email with attachments, then such an attack can be classified as *email attachment*. As such, we believe a well-defined categorization of social engineering attacks is essential for people to understand the ever-increasing set of social engineering attacks. To this end, we need to identify meaningful dimensions for characterizing social engineering attacks as many as possible, which is a challenging task. As reviewed above, Krombholz et al. and Mouton et al. have tentatively explored such dimensions, serving as good starting points.

2.3   Vulnerability

In contrast to typical information security attacks which exploit software vulnerability to carry out malicious actions, social engineering attacks exploit human as targets. Several researchers have explicitly point this out, and present a list of human traits and behaviors that are vulnerable to be exploited by social engineers. Harley present seven personality traits, namely *gullibility, curiosity, courtesy, greed, diffidence, thoughtlessness*, and *apathy* [3]. Similarly, Gulati also mentions seven vulnerable behaviors [2], parts of which are different from Harley's proposal, including *trust, fear of unknown*. Finally, Peltier summarizes four vulnerable factors, including *diffusion of responsibility, chance of ingratiation, trust relationship*, and *guilt* [14].

Challenges. The challenges regarding the human vulnerability research are twofold.

- Enumeration of Human Vulnerability. As an interdisciplinary research field, the research of human vulnerability requires knowledge from psychology and sociology, which is difficult for information security researchers. This explains why our reviewed studies all come out with different sets of human vulnerabilities. It is also one of the most important reasons that hinders the development of this research field.
- Linkages between Human Vulnerability and Social Engineering Attacks. Security analysts need not only identify human vulnerabilities, but also well understand how attackers exploit known human vulnerabilities. Thus, a follow-up challenge is linking the human vulnerabilities to corresponding social engineering attacks.

3   A Comprehensive Ontology of Social Engineering

In this section, we present a comprehensive social engineering ontology, dealing with the research challenges we identified in Sect. 2. A well-defined ontology should preserve a number of characteristics, e.g., completeness, consistency, disjointness [15]. In addition, based on our survey analysis, we argue the ontology of social engineering should meet the following requirements.

1. Inconsistent understanding about social engineering is the primary challenge that hinders the development of this research topic. Consequently, the ontology should have an unambiguous definition towards social engineering attacks, which can be used to precisely distinguish social engineering attacks from other attacks.
2. Social engineering attacks are a particular type of security attack, which has been used together with technical attacks (e.g., SQL injection) to cause more serious damage [11]. As argued by Li et al. [10], social engineering analysis should be part of a holistic system security analysis, in which human is deemed as a particular type of system component. Thus, it is important to align core concepts of social engineering with existing security concepts as much as possible. Moreover, such alignment can greatly help information security analysts to comprehend social engineering.

3. As an interdisciplinary research field, social engineering attacks are evolving along with the advances of related research fields, e.g., information security, sociology and psychology. For one thing, design of the ontology should appropriately take into account knowledge from those related research fields. For another, the ontology should be extensible to incorporate emerging social engineering attacks.
4. Researchers from different research communities are likely to take their particular perspectives to classify social engineering attacks at different abstraction levels. As a result, the ontology should support a hierarchical classification schema, helping people to better understand social engineering.

   Taking into account such requirements, in the remaining parts of this section, we first present and explain core concepts and relations of social engineering in detail. Then we formalize such a concepts and relations using Description Logic (DL) in order to assign formal and unambiguous semantics to the proposed ontology.

3.1   Core Concepts of Social Engineering

Security ontology has been investigated for decades, resulting in many different variants [17]. Among all such proposals, there are four essential concepts have been universally identified, i.e., *Asset*, *Attacker*, *Attack*, and *Vulnerability*. In particular, an asset is anything that is valuable to system stakeholders; an attacker is a proactive agent who carries out attack actions to harm assets; a vulnerability is any weakness exists in system assets that can be exploited by corresponding attack actions.

To align social engineering analysis with typical security analysis, we identify core concepts and relations of social engineering based on the aforementioned security concepts. Based on our in-depth survey over existing social engineering research, we come out with the conclusion that all the security concepts can be specialized into subconcepts in the context of social engineering. Furthermore, two additional concepts are also introduced to more comprehensively characterize social engineering attacks. The core concepts of social engineering and their connections with security concepts are presented in Fig. 1.

Specifically, *Human* is a subclass of *Asset*, acting as the target of social engineering attacks. We argue that **targeting human is a distinguishing feature of social engineering attack**. *Vulnerability* of an asset is then specialized as *Human Vulnerability*. Different from software vulnerability, which is typically a defect, human vulnerability is not always a negative characteristic. For example, desiring to be helpful is a good for people in most contexts, but such a characteristic can increase the likelihood of being manipulated by social engineering attackers. Defining human vulnerability requires additional psychology and sociology knowledge, which is detailed and explained in the next subsection. In contrast, *Attacker* and *Attack* are more intuitive to be specialized into *Social Engineer* and *Social Engineering Attack*, respectively. During the survey of social engineering studies, we realized that human as an attack target can

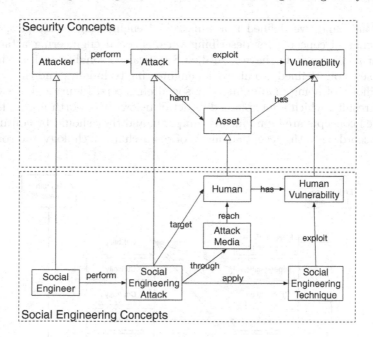

Fig. 1. Connect social engineering concepts with security concepts

be reached by a social engineer through various ways, e.g., email, telephone, each of which presents a particular attack scenario. As such we define *Attack Media* as an important dimension for characterizing social engineering attacks and consider seven particular types of media, including *Email, Instant Message, Telephone, Website, Malware, Face to Face*, and *Physical*. Finally, another distinguish feature of social engineering attacks is to apply particular *Social Engineering Techniques* in order to manipulate human. In particular, each social engineering attack can apply one or multiple social engineering techniques, while each technique exploits one or multiple human vulnerabilities. Detailed explanation of this concept involves psychological knowledge and thus is presented in the next subsection.

3.2 Incorporate Social and Psychological Knowledge

As an interdisciplinary topic, the investigation of social engineering ontology inevitably requires social and psychological knowledge, especially when dealing with social attack techniques and human vulnerabilities. To this end, we survey and summarize relevant knowledge from existing social engineering studies [2, 3, 11, 14]. Moreover, we refer to psychological publications that discuss psychopathy and manipulative people [7, 16] in order to better understand how people is psychologically manipulated. Eventually, we here elaborate and define detailed *Social Engineering Technique* and *Human Vulnerability*, as well as their *exploit* relationships, based on the core social engineering concepts we identified before.

On the one hand, we defined 9 atomic social engineering techniques, serving as fundamental concepts for describing various social engineering attacks. On the other hand, we so far have identified 8 typical personality traits, which are vulnerable to our defined atomic social engineering techniques and thus increase the likelihood of being manipulated by social engineers. Figure 2 shows our full research results, which are explained in detail below. It is worth noting that the elaborated concepts are by no means complete, and they should be continuously revised according to the recent advances of research in psychology and sociology.

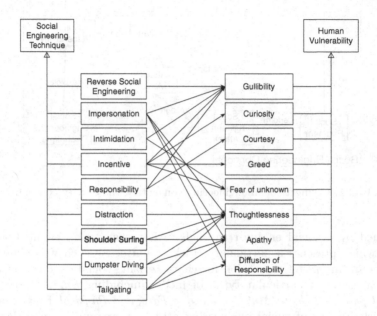

Fig. 2. Detailed social engineering techniques and human vulnerabilities

Social Engineering Technique. We divide social engineering techniques into two categories, *direct approach* and *indirect approach*. The former category contains techniques that are directly applied to human, i.e., the social engineer directly interacts with the victim. Specifically, all direct approaches aim to first turn victims into certain situations/states, in which the victims will likely follow what the social engineer asks them to do.

- *Reverse social engineering* is a means to establish trust between a social engineer and a victim, i.e., turn the victim into a trusting situation. Typically, the social engineer creates a situation in which the victim requires help and then present themselves as problem solvers to gain trust from the victim. After that the social engineer can easily manipulate the victim to disclose confidential information or to perform certain actions.
- *Impersonation* is one of the most valued techniques that a social engineer impersonates himself with a particular identity that affects the state of the

victim. In particular, the social engineer can achieve various malicious goals by impersonating different identities, depending on the roles of the identities. For example, impersonating as a supporting staff can get access to restricted areas, while impersonating as an authoritative person can ask the victim for confidential information.

- *Intimidation* is a manipulation strategy with the purpose of turning victims into scared states in which they have to follow requests of the social engineer. It is worth noting that this technique can be carried out together with the impersonation technique, which can significantly increase its success rate.
- *Incentive* is a manipulation strategy to make victim motivated to do something. For example, bribery is one of the most simple and effective behaviors to implement this strategy. Similar to the intimidation technique, incentive can also be applied together with impersonation. One common scenario is that a social engineer pretends to be a lottery company and send an email to victims saying they hit the jackpot and have to do certain things to get their rewards.
- *Responsibility* manipulates victims to feel that they should do something in order to comply with certain laws, regulations, or social rules. For example, a social engineer may lie to the victim that his manager asks him to do something. More effectively, the social engineer can directly impersonate an authoritative person, i.e., combining with the impersonation technique.
- *Distraction* is a direct approach to attract victims' attention in order to carry out malicious actions without being detected. This strategy is commonly applied when more than one social engineer attack together.

The *indirect approach* category concerns techniques that do not involve direct interactions with the victim. Some researchers argue such techniques are outside the boundary of social engineering as victims have not been manipulated via interactions [14]. In this paper, we include these techniques as social engineering techniques as they do exploit human vulnerabilities, which we argue is the essential criterion of being a social engineering attack. More formal definition will be presented in the next subsection.

- *Shoulder Surfing* is a simple but effective approach where a social engineer monitors the physical activity of victims in close proximity.
- *Dumpster Diving* is to sift through the trash of individuals or companies with the aim of finding discarded items that include sensitive information.
- *Tailgating* is a means to entry into a restricted area by following an authorized person. Note that although this technique might not require any interactions with any people, the behavior of the social engineer implies that he is an authorized person as well. As such some researchers classify this techniques as a subclass of impersonation [4].

Human Vulnerability. In the context of social engineering, personality traits that can increase the success rate of social engineering techniques are defined as human vulnerabilities. As shown in Fig. 2, among the identified 8 vulnerabilities, some of them are vulnerable to many social engineering techniques (e.g., gulli-bility), while others are only related to one particular technique (e.g., curiosity). We here explain each of them in detail.

- *Gullibility* is the most exploited vulnerability. All social engineering tech-niques that involve deception take advantage of the gullibility of victims. As most people by nature are prone to believe what other people say instead of questioning, people have to be specially trained in order to avoid such attacks.
- *Curiosity* is a trait which encourages people to disclose unknown things. When a social engineer sends mysterious messages to victims, such a trait will drive the victims to follow instructions to reveal the mysterious mask of the mes-sage.
- *Courtesy* describes the fact that many people are by default desiring to be helpful. As a result, when they feel that they are responsible to do something, they tend to offer more than they should, violating the need-to-know policy.
- *Greed* leads a victim to be vulnerable to incentive techniques (e.g., bribery).
- *Fear of unknown* is vulnerable to both intimidation and incentive techniques. On the one hand, people's fear can be significantly increased due to the unknown threats; On the other hand, people also are afraid of not know-ing potential monetary rewards.
- *Thoughtlessness* is common in reality, as we cannot expect all people being thoughtful all the time. When people are thoughtless, they are more vulner-able to distraction, shoulder surfing, dumpster diving and tailgating tech-niques.
- *Apathy* is a trait that makes people ignore things that they think are not worthwhile to do, making shoulder surfing, dumpster diving and tailgating much easier to success. In many cases, such situation can be attributed to a management problem, which makes people's morale low.
- *Diffusion of Responsibility* describes that people are reluctant to do something even if he is responsible (e.g., asking a stranger to show his ID when he tries to enter confidential places), as they think other responsible people will do that. Taking advantages of this vulnerability, social engineers can easily apply perform impersonation and tailgating techniques.

3.3   Formal Definition of the Social Engineering Ontology

Based on the previously discussed concepts and relations of social engineering, we here provide a formal definition of our proposed social engineering ontology using Description Logic (DL), which is shown in Table 2. As defined at Axiom_1, we formally define a social engineering attack is an attack which applies one or multiple social engineering attack techniques, targets one particular person who has at least one human vulnerability, and is performed by a social engi-neer through a particular type of attack media. In particular, we here empha-size that **the most distinguishing characteristic of a social engineering attack is exploiting human vulnerabilities.** This explains why our ontology includes *shoulder surfing* as a social engineering attack, because it exploits people's *thoughtlessness* and *apathy*. Moreover, Axiom_2–4 formally define human vulnerabilities, social engineering techniques and attack media, respectively.

Table 2. Formal social engineering ontology

Core concepts:
$Axiom\_1$: $SocialEngineeringAttack \equiv Attack$
$\sqcap = 1\ performed\_by.SocialEngineer \sqcap = 1\ through.AttackMedia$
$\sqcap = 1\ target.(Human \sqcap \exists has.HumanVulnerability)$
$\sqcap \geq 1apply.SocialEngineeringTechnique$
$Axiom\_2$: $HumanVulnerability \equiv Gullibility \sqcup Curiosity \sqcup Courtesy \sqcup Greed \sqcup$ $FearOfUnknown \sqcup Thoughtlessness \sqcup Apathy \sqcup DefussionOfResponsibility$
$Axiom\_3$: $SocialEngineeringTechnique \equiv ReverseSocialEngineering \sqcup$ $Impersonation \sqcup Intimidation \sqcup Incentive \sqcup Responsibility \sqcup Distraction \sqcup$ $ShoulderSurfing \sqcup DumpsterDiving \sqcup Tailgating$
$Axiom\_4$: $AttackMedia \equiv Email \sqcup InstantMessage \sqcup Telephone \sqcup Website \sqcup$ $Malware \sqcup FaceToFace \sqcup Physical$

Our proposed ontology comprehensively includes important dimensions for characterizing social engineering attacks, i.e., attack media, human vulnerability, and social engineering technique. Thus, we propose to base various classification schemata of social engineering attacks on our ontology, offering a shared terminology to related researchers. Taking a notable example, many studies roughly classify social engineering attacks a human-based attacks and technology-based attacks [1,5,14]. However, none of these studies precisely defines such a classification schema, and in fact their classification results are inconsistent with each other. Our ontology can be used to formally and unambiguously define such classification schema, and contribute to the communication and development of this research field. Axiom_5–7 in Table 3 show such formal definitions. Specifically, we define a social engineering attack as non-technology attack if it is carried out through either face to face or physical means, while all other social engineering attacks are then defined as technology-based attacks. Axiom_8–10 illustrate another example, in which we formally classify social engineering attacks as either an indirect attack or a direct attack. The former category includes social engineering attacks that apply shoulder surfing, dumpster diving, or tailgating techniques, and all other attacks are classified as direct social engineering attacks.

We have implemented our formal ontology in Protégé[1], which is shown Fig. 3. With the implementation support, we are able to leverage inference engines to automatically classify social engineering attacks according to particular classification schemata (such as those defined in Table 3), which is essential for

---

[1] https://protege.stanford.edu/.

Table 3. Social engineering attack classifications

Attack classification:
$Axiom\_5 : SocialEngineeringAttack \equiv NonTechnologySocialEngineeringAttack$ $\sqcup TechnologyBasedSocialEngineeringAttack$
$Axiom\_6 : NonTechnologySocialEngineeringAttack \equiv SocialEngineeringAttack$ $\sqcap \exists trhough.(FaceToFace \sqcup Physical)$
$Axiom\_7 : TechnologyBasedSocialEngineeringAttack \equiv SocialEngineeringAttack$ $\sqcap \neg NonTechnologySocialEngineeringAttack$
$Axiom\_8 : SocialEngineeringAttack \equiv DirectSocialEngineeringAttack \sqcup$ $IndirectSocialEngineeringAttack$
$Axiom\_9 : IndirectSocialEngineeringAttack \equiv SocialEngineeringAttack \sqcap$ $\exists apply.(ShoulderSurfing \sqcup DumpsterDiving \sqcup Tailgating)$
$Axiom\_10 : DirectSocialEngineeringAttack \equiv SocialEngineeringAttack \sqcap$ $\neg IndirectSocialEngineeringAttack$

people to understand the ever-increasing set of social engineering attacks. Regrading our research objective, we plan to offer our ontology to social engineering researchers and contribute to this research community. The ontology file can be found online[2].

4 Evaluation

In this section, we evaluate the expressiveness of our ontology by using it to characterize and classify all social engineering attacks we have collected during our literature review [2–4,8,13,14], i.e., attacks we have shown in Table 1. The attack classification is done strictly based on its original descriptions, even some of the descriptions might not be complete. In such a way, we try to make the evaluation clear and repeatable. The results of our evaluations lead us to the following observations and conclusions:

– Our ontology has good expressiveness and is able to characterize all social engineering attacks we have collected in terms of attack technique, human vulnerability, and attack media.
– As shown clearly in the table, the three dimensions are very helpful for classifying and comprehending social engineering attacks. More importantly, the results clearly present us which attacks are actually describing the same things and should be merged to avoid misunderstanding. For instance, *Impersonation* and *Masquerading* are the same type of attacks.
– Interpreting various social engineering attacks based on our ontology can help with identifying useful categories of social engineering attacks. For instance,

---

[2] https://www.dropbox.com/s/cff40r0e1e6qvj5/SEA.owl?dl=0.

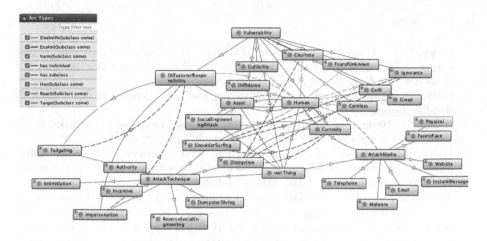

Fig. 3. Implement the ontology in Protege

Phishing, *Vishing*, and *SMSishing* leverage the same social engineering techniques and exploit the same vulnerabilities, but through different attack media. In such a case, it is reasonable to consider a parent class of these three attacks.

5 Conclusions and Future Work

In this paper, we present our work towards an unambiguous and comprehensive ontology of social engineering. Our major research objective is to prompt the development of this research field, which is becoming more and more important. In particular, we have reviewed existing social engineering ontologies in detail and discovered current research challenges, motivated by which we propose a unified set of concepts of social engineering to covers various perspectives. To deal with the interdisciplinary nature of social engineering, we have systematically review and incorporate related psychology and sociology knowledge, and formalize the ontology using Description Logic (DL) . Finally, we evaluate the coverage and correctness of our approach by using it to analyze real social engineering attacks reported in literature. In the future, we are first planning to have researchers other than the authors to apply our ontology in order to evaluate its usability. Also, we aim to analyze industrial cases in a real word setting to validate the effectiveness of our ontology.

Acknowledgements. This work is supported by National Key R&D Program of China (No. 2018YFB0804703, 2017YFC0803307), the National Natural Science of Foundation of China (No. 91546111, 91646201), International Research Cooperation Seed Fund of Beijing University of Technology (No. 2018B2), and Basic Research Funding of Beijing University of Technology (No. 040000546318516).

References

1. Foozy, F.M., Ahmad, R., Abdollah, M., Yusof, R., Mas'ud, M.: Generic taxonomy of social engineering attack. In: Malaysian Technical Universities International Conference on Engineering & Technology, pp. 1–7 (2011)
2. Gulati, R.: The threat of social engineering and your defense against it. SANS Reading Room (2003)
3. Harley, D.: Re-floating the titanic: dealing with social engineering attacks. European Institute for Computer Antivirus Research, pp. 4–29 (1998)
4. Ivaturi, K., Janczewski, L.: A taxonomy for social engineering attacks. In: International Conference on Information Resources Management, pp. 1–12. Centre for Information Technology, Organizations, and People (2011)
5. Janczewski, L.J., Fu, L.: Social engineering-based attacks: model and New Zealand perspective. In: Proceedings of the 2010 International Multiconference on Computer Science and Information Technology (IMCSIT), pp. 847–853. IEEE (2010)
6. Jürjens, J.: UMLsec: extending uml for secure systems development. In: Jézéquel, J.-M., Hussmann, H., Cook, S. (eds.) UML 2002. LNCS, vol. 2460, pp. 412–425. Springer, Heidelberg (2002). https://doi.org/10.1007/3-540-45800-X_32
7. Kantor, M.: The psychopathy of everyday life (2006)
8. Krombholz, K., Hobel, H., Huber, M., Weippl, E.: Advanced social engineering attacks. J. Inf. Secur. Appl. **22**, 113–122 (2015)
9. Li, T., Horkoff, J.: Dealing with security requirements for socio-technical systems: a holistic approach. In: Jarke, M., et al. (eds.) CAiSE 2014. LNCS, vol. 8484, pp. 285–300. Springer, Cham (2014). https://doi.org/10.1007/978-3-319-07881-6_20
10. Li, T., Horkoff, J., Mylopoulos, J.: Holistic security requirements analysis for socio-technical systems. Softw. Syst. Model. **17**(4), 1253–1285 (2018)
11. Mitnick, K.D., Simon, W.L.: The Art of Deception: Controlling the Human Element of Security. Wiley, Hoboken (2011)
12. Mouton, F., Leenen, L., Malan, M.M., Venter, H.S.: Towards an ontological model defining the social engineering domain. In: Kimppa, K., Whitehouse, D., Kuusela, T., Phahlamohlaka, J. (eds.) HCC 2014. IAICT, vol. 431, pp. 266–279. Springer, Heidelberg (2014). https://doi.org/10.1007/978-3-662-44208-1_22
13. Nyamsuren, E., Choi, H.-J.: Preventing social engineering in ubiquitous environment. In: Future Generation Communication and Networking (FGCN 2007), vol. 2, pp. 573–577. IEEE (2007)
14. Peltier, T.R.: Social engineering: concepts and solutions. Inf. Secur. J. **15**(5), 13 (2006)
15. Roussey, C., Pinet, F., Kang, M.A., Corcho, O.: An introduction to ontologies and ontology engineering. In: Falquet, G., Métral, C., Teller, J., Tweed, C. (eds.) Ontologies in Urban Development Projects, vol. 1, pp. 9–38. Springer, London (2011). https://doi.org/10.1007/978-0-85729-724-2_2
16. Simon, G.K., Foley, K.: In Sheep's Clothing: Understanding and Dealing with Manipulative People. Tantor Media, Incorporated, Old Saybrook (2011)
17. Souag, A., Salinesi, C., Comyn-Wattiau, I.: Ontologies for security requirements: a literature survey and classification. In: Bajec, M., Eder, J. (eds.) CAiSE 2012. LNBIP, vol. 112, pp. 61–69. Springer, Heidelberg (2012). https://doi.org/10.1007/978-3-642-31069-0_5

Improving Traceability Links Recovery in Process Models Through an Ontological Expansion of Requirements

Raúl Lapeña[1]([⊠]), Francisca Pérez[1], Carlos Cetina[1], and Óscar Pastor[2]

[1] SVIT Research Group, Universidad San Jorge, Zaragoza, Spain
{rlapena,fperez,ccetina}@usj.es
[2] Centro de Investigación en Métodos de Producción de Software,
Universitat Politècnica de València, Valencia, Spain
opastor@pros.upv.es

Abstract. Often, when requirements are written, parts of the domain knowledge are assumed by the domain experts and not formalized in writing, but nevertheless used to build software artifacts. This issue, known as tacit knowledge, affects the performance of Traceability Links Recovery. Through this work we propose LORE, a novel approach that uses Natural Language Processing techniques along with an Ontological Requirements Expansion process to minimize the impact of tacit knowledge on TLR over process models. We evaluated our approach through a real-world industrial case study, comparing its outcomes against those of a baseline. Results show that our approach retrieves improved results for all the measured performance indicators. We studied why this is the case, and identified some issues that affect LORE, leaving room for improvement opportunities. We make an open-source implementation of LORE publicly available in order to facilitate its adoption in future studies.

Keywords: Traceability Links Recovery · Business Process Models · Requirements Engineering

1 Introduction

Traceability Links Recovery (TLR) has been a subject of investigation for many years within the software engineering community [11,21]. Traceability can be critical to the success of a project [25], leads to increased maintainability and reliability of software systems [10], and decreases the expected defect rate in developed software [16]. However, TLR techniques rely greatly on the language of the studied documents. Often, when requirements are written, parts of the domain knowledge are not embodied in them, or embodied in ambiguous ways. This phenomena is known as tacit knowledge. The tacit knowledge is assumed by all the domain experts, and never formalized in writing. This behavior has been

© Springer Nature Switzerland AG 2019
P. Giorgini and B. Weber (Eds.): CAiSE 2019, LNCS 11483, pp. 261–275, 2019.
https://doi.org/10.1007/978-3-030-21290-2_17

reported by previous works [3,22]. As a result, both the text of the requirements and the tacit knowledge are used to build software artifacts, which in turn contain elements that are related to the text of the requirement, and elements that are related to the tacit knowledge. However, since part of the knowledge is not reflected in the text of the requirement, recovering the most relevant software artifact for a requirement through TLR becomes a complex task.

Through this work, we propose LORE, a novel approach that minimizes the impact that tacit knowledge has on TLR. To that extent, Natural Language Processing (NLP) techniques are used to process the requirements, and then an ontology is used to expand the processed requirements with concepts from the domain. Finally, TLR techniques are applied to analyze the requirements and software artifacts in search for software artifact fragments that match the requirements. We have evaluated our approach by carrying out LORE between the requirements and process models that comprise a real-world industrial case study, involving the control software of the trains manufactured by our industrial partner. Results show that our approach guides TLR to enhanced results for all the measured performance indicators, providing a mean precision value of 79.2%, a mean recall value of 50.2%, a combined F-measure of 66.5%, and an MCC value of 0.62. In contrast, the baseline used for comparison presents worse results in these same measurements. Through our work, we have also identified a series of issues related to the ontology and the requirements that prevent our approach from achieving better solutions. These issues could be tackled in the future to further improve the TLR process between requirements and process models.

Through the following pages, Sect. 2 presents the background for our work. Sections 3 and 4 provide details on our approach, and on the leveraged Traceability Links Recovery technique. Section 5 describes the evaluation of our approach. Section 6 introduces the obtained results. Section 7 discusses the outcomes of our work. Section 8 presents the threats to the validity of our work. Section 9 reviews works related to this one. Finally, Sect. 10 concludes the paper.

2   Background

In industrial scenarios, companies tend to have a myriad of products with large and complex models behind, created and maintained over long periods of time by different software engineers, who often lack knowledge over the entirety of the product details. Through this section, we provide an overview of the models in our case study, and of the problem that our approach intends to mitigate.

2.1   Case Study Models

Figure 1 depicts one example of a model, taken from a real-world train, specified through a process model. The model has the expressiveness required to describe the interaction between the main pieces of equipment installed in a train unit, and the non-functional aspects related to regulation. Specifically, the example of the figure presents the station stop process, where a human sets the stop mode and the system opens the platform passenger doors. The elements of Fig. 1 highlighted in gray conform an example model fragment.

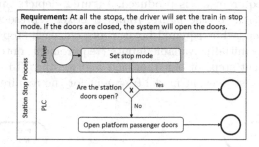

Fig. 1. Example of requirement, model and model fragment

2.2 Tacit Knowledge in Requirements

However, the requirement in Fig. 1 is lacking important information, known by the engineers and kept as tacit knowledge. A literal interpretation of the second sentence of the requirement implies that at all stations, all the doors of the train will open. However, the sentence embodies tacit knowledge that is not written but that is obvious to the domain engineers: (1) the train has doors on both sides, but only the doors on the side of the platform will open; and (2) not all the doors will open, the door of the control cabin will remain closed for the safety of the driver and the train. Thus, only the platform passenger doors will open.

3   Our Approach

3.1   Approach Overview

Through the presented approach, we tackle the tacit knowledge issue presented in the prior section, by expanding requirements through a domain ontology. The approach runs in a two-step process:

1. First, we use Natural Language Processing (NLP) techniques to process the requirement and the ontology. The NLP techniques unify the language of the software artifacts, which facilitates the expansion process.
2. Secondly, we propose an Ontological Requirement Expansion (ORE) process that uses the processed requirement and ontology in order to expand the requirement with related domain knowledge, diminishing the amount of tacit knowledge in the requirement.

The expanded requirement is used along with the NLP-treated process models from our case study as an input for Latent Semantic Indexing (LSI) [12], a widely accepted TLR process [26]. Through LSI, a model fragment, candidate solution for the requirement, is produced. Figure 2 depicts an overview of the steps of the approach. In the figure, rounded boxes represent the inputs and outputs of each step, while squared boxes represent each step. The highlighted boxes represent the initially available inputs (requirement, ontology, and model) used for the different steps of our approach and for the TLR process, and the final output (the most relevant model fragment for the requirement).

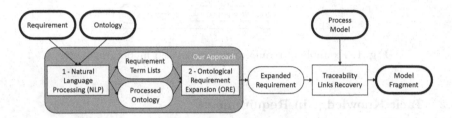

Fig. 2. Approach overview

3.2 Natural Language Processing (NLP)

This section describes the NLP techniques taken in account for our approach. Figure 3 is used to illustrate the whole compendium of techniques, detailed through the following paragraphs.

Splitting: As seen in Sect. 2, the tacit knowledge lies within the sentences of the requirements. Thus, in order to better isolate the tacit knowledge issue, we split the text of the requirements into the sentences that compose it. These smaller parts of text will help expand the requirement more accurately further on in our approach. Figure 3 depicts the two sentences that result from splitting the running example requirement.

Syntactical Analysis: Syntactical Analysis (SA) techniques analyze the specific roles of each one of them in the sentence and determine their grammatical function. These techniques (referred to as Parts-Of-Speech Tagging, or POS Tagging) allow engineers to implement filters for words that fulfill specific grammatical roles in a requirement, usually opting only for nouns [5]. In Fig. 3, it is possible to appreciate the SA process, with the POS Tagged Tokens associated to each sentence of the requirement as outcome.

Root Reduction: The technique known as Lemmatizing reduces words to their semantic roots or lemmas. Thanks to lemmas, the language of the NL requirements is unified, avoiding verb tenses, noun plurals, and other word forms that interfere negatively with the TLR process. The unification of the language semantics is an evolution over pure syntactical role filtering, allowing for a more advanced filtering of words in NL requirements. In Fig. 3, it is possible to appreciate the RR process, with the Root-Reduced Tokens as outcome of the semantic analysis of the POS Tags derived from the NL requirement (keeping only nouns). This process is also applied to the ontology, treating all the concepts as nouns, since domain terms always name important characteristics of the trains.

Human NLP: The inclusion of domain knowledge through experts and software engineers in the TLR process is regarded as beneficial. Human NLP is often carried out through Domain Terms Extraction or Stopwords Removal. In our approach, domain terms are checked for after splitting the requirement into sentences. We analyze each sentence in search for the domain terms provided by the software engineers, and add the found domain terms to the final processed sentence. On the other hand, stopwords are filtered out of the Root Reduced sentences. Figure 3 depicts the Human NLP process, where a software engineer provides both lists of terms, which are consequently introduced into the final query, or filtered out of it.

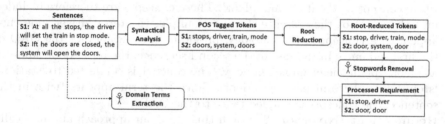

Fig. 3. Natural language processing techniques

3.3 Ontological Requirement Expansion (ORE)

The process that we propose in order to ontologically expand a requirement is detailed through the paragraphs of this section. The process runs in two steps: (1) calculation of the Ontological Affinity Documents associated to the requirement, and (2) expansion of the requirement.

1. **Ontological Affinity:** Ontological Affinity Documents (OADs) are documents that contain a set of ontological concepts related to a certain input. The first step of the Ontological Requirement Expansion process is to calculate the OADs associated to the requirement. We designed an algorithm that utilizes a processed domain ontology and a processed requirement to generate the OADs. The algorithm first selects one of the processed sentences generated through NLP. Then, the algorithm takes one term in the sentence, searching for it in the ontology. If the term matches a concept that is present in the ontology, all the concepts directly connected to the concept are added to an OAD. The algorithm iterates over all the terms in the sentence, generating the OAD associated to the sentence. The process is repeated for every

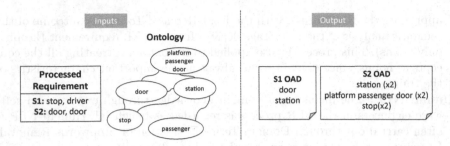

Fig. 4. Ontological affinity documents calculation

sentence in the processed requirement, generating one OAD per sentence. This process is illustrated through our running example in Fig. 4. In the figure, for space reasons, only a small part of the domain ontology is represented. In the case of the first sentence, the term 'stop' appears both in the sentence and as an ontology concept. The concepts that are directly related to the 'stop' concept are 'station' and 'door'. These concepts are therefore included into the OAD of the sentence. In our example, the term 'driver' does not appear as a concept in the ontology, providing no concepts for the OAD of the first sentence. In the case of the second sentence, the term 'door' appears as a concept in the example ontology. The concept is connected to 'station', 'stop', and 'platform passenger door'. Since the term appears twice in the sentence, the concepts are added twice to the OAD.

2. **Requirement Expansion:** Through this step, our approach automatically reformulates the processed requirement to expand it with terms of the OADs using a technique that is based on Rocchio's method [18], which is perhaps the most commonly used method for query reformulation [20]. Rocchio's method orders the terms in the OADs based on the sum of the importance of each term of the documents using the following equation:

$$Rocchio = \sum_{d \in R} TF(c,d) \cdot IDF(t,R) \tag{1}$$

Where R is the set of OADs, d is a document in R, and c is a concept in d. The first component of the measure is the Term Frequency (TF), which is the number of times the concept appears in a document; it is an indicator of the importance of the concept in the document compared to the rest of the concepts in that document. The second component is the Inverse Document Frequency (IDF), which is the inverse of the number of documents that contain that concept; it indicates the specificity of that concept for a document that contains it. The IDF measurement is calculated as:

$$IDF(t,R) = \log \frac{|R|}{|\{d \in R : c \in d\}|} \tag{2}$$

Where $|R|$ is the number of documents and $|\{d \in R : c \in d\}|$ is the number of documents where the concept is present.

To illustrate this calculation, consider the processed requirement from our running example. After calculating the OADs presented in Fig. 4, Rocchio's method is applied to the concepts of the documents in order to retrieve the importance of said concepts. Take in account the concept 'platform passenger door'. In the first document, the concept does not appear ($TF = 0$), immediately leading to a $TF \cdot IDF$ value of $TF \cdot IDF = 0$. The concept appears twice in the second document ($TF = 2$) and appears in one of two documents ($IDF = \log \frac{2}{1} \approx 0.3$), which leads to a $TF \cdot IDF$ value of $TF \cdot IDF \approx 0.6$. The sum of both $TF \cdot IDF$ values leads to a total $Rocchio$ value of $Rocchio \approx 0.6$. Using Rocchio's method, the concepts of the OADs associated to the sentences of the requirement are ordered from highest to lowest sum of importance into a single document of concepts. Once ordered, we take in consideration only the first 10 suggestions and discard the rest, as is recommended in the literature [6]. The list of the 10 first suggested concepts conforms the OAD associated to the requirement.

Since the objective of our approach is to mitigate the tacit knowledge of the requirement, our aim is to find new domain knowledge to include in the requirement, and therefore we refine the requirement OAD by discarding those concepts in the OAD that already appear in any sentence of the requirement. In our running example, this process would produce a requirement OAD consisting of the terms 'station' and 'platform passenger door', since both 'door' and 'stop' are already present in the sentences of the requirement. The terms of the processed sentences and the concepts on the refined OAD are then concatenated into a single list of terms. This final list of terms is the ultimate goal that our approach seeks to obtain: an expanded requirement, enriched with ontological domain knowledge. The expanded requirement is the final output of the Ontological Requirement Expansion process, and is used as query for the Traceability Links Recovery process.

4   Traceability Links Recovery

LORE can be applied to any TLR technique that uses a requirement as input. Through this work, we utilize Latent Semantic Indexing (LSI), the TLR technique that obtains the best results when performing TLR between requirements and software artifacts [26]. Latent Semantic Indexing (LSI) [12] constructs vector representations of a query and a corpus of text documents by encoding them as a *term-by-document co-occurrence matrix*. In our approach, *terms* are each of the words that compose the expanded requirement and NL representation of the input model (extracted through the technique presented in [15]), *documents* are the model elements in the input model, and the *query* is the expanded requirement. Each cell in the matrix contains the frequency with which the *term* of its row appears in the *document* denoted by its column. Once the matrix is built, it is normalized and decomposed into a set of vectors using a matrix factorization technique called Singular Value Decomposition (SVD) [12].

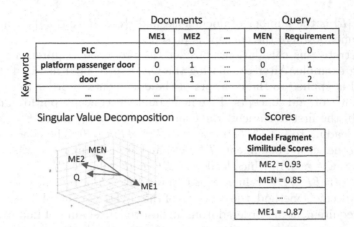

Fig. 5. Traceability link recovery through latent semantic indexing example

The similarity degree between the query and each document is calculated through the cosine between the vectors that represent them. Figure 5 shows an example matrix, built from our running example, the result of applying the SVD technique to the matrix, and the resulting scores associated to each document. In our approach, we use the top ranked model elements to build a model fragment that serves as a candidate for realizing the requirement. Of all the model elements, only those that have a similarity measure greater than x must be taken into account. A widely used heuristic is $x = 0.7$. This value corresponds to a 45° angle between the corresponding vectors. Even though the selection of the threshold is an issue under study, the chosen heuristic has yielded good results in other similar works [14,17].

5   Evaluation

This section presents the evaluation of our approach, including the experimental setup, a description of the case study where we applied the evaluation, and the implementation details of our approach.

5.1   Experimental Setup

The goal of this experiment is to perform TLR between requirements and models through LORE, comparing its results against the baseline. The baseline against which we compare our work is the technique that obtains the best results when recovering Traceability between requirements and models according to the literature, TLR through LSI. The baseline utilizes the processed requirement, without performing the ontological expansion in use in LORE. Figure 6 shows an overview of the process followed to evaluate our approach (LORE) and the baseline (TLR). The top part of the figure shows the inputs, as provided by our industrial partner. The requirements and models are used to build the test cases

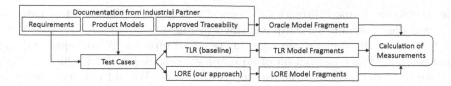

Fig. 6. Experimental setup

(one requirement and one model each) and the approved Traceability is used to build the oracles against which the results of the approaches are compared.

For each test case, both LORE and TLR generate one model fragment each. The model fragments generated for each test case are compared against their respective oracles (ground truth), and a confusion matrix is calculated for each of the two approaches. A confusion matrix is a table used to describe the performance of a classification model on a set of test data for which the true values are known. In our case, the presence or absence of each model element is considered as a classification. The confusion matrix arranges the results of the classifications into four categories: (1) True Positive (predicted true, true in the real scenario), (2) False Positive (predicted true, false in the real scenario), (3) True Negative (predicted false, false in the real scenario), and (4) False Negative (predicted false, true in the real scenario). From the confusion matrix, it is possible to extract some measurements that evaluate the performance of the approach. We report four performance measurements for both LORE and TLR: Recall, Precision, F-measure, and MCC (Matthews Correlation Coefficient). Recall measures the number of elements of the solution that are correctly retrieved by the proposed solution, precision measures the number of elements from the solution that are correct according to the ground truth, and the F-measure corresponds to the harmonic mean of precision and recall. The MCC is a correlation coefficient between the observed and predicted binary classifications [14, 19].

Recall values can range between 0% (no single model element from the oracle is present in the retrieved model fragment) to 100% (all the model elements from the oracle are present in the retrieved model fragment). Precision values can range between 0% (no model elements from the retrieved model fragment appear in the oracle) to 100% (all the model elements from the retrieved model fragment appear in the oracle). MCC values can range between -1 (no correlation between the prediction and the oracle) to 1 (perfect prediction). Moreover, an MCC value of 0 corresponds to a random prediction.

5.2 Case Study

The case study where we applied our approach was provided by our industrial partner, CAF (http://www.caf.es/en), a worldwide provider of railway solutions. Our evaluation includes 140 test cases, with each test case comprising one requirement, one model, and the approved Traceability between the requirement and the model. The requirements have about 25 words on average, and the models are formed through 650 elements on average. For each test case, we followed the experimental setup described in Fig. 6.

Regarding the domain ontology in use, it comprises 27 concepts and 176 relationships. The construction of an ontology is a major effort which requires the study of the domain structure and terminology. We did not try to address the creation of a new ontology in this paper but instead, our industrial partner provided us with the ontology they use for training new employees. The ontology is an important artifact and that its quality, size, and completeness may have an impact on the results. In a future work, we intend to analyze the extent of this impact on the results of LORE.

5.3   Implementation Details

For the development of the Natural Language Processing operations used in both our approach and the baseline, we have used the OpenNLP Toolkit [2]. To implement the LSI and SVD techniques, the Efficient Java Matrix Library (EJML) was used [1]. For the evaluation, we used a Lenovo E330 laptop, with a processor Intel(R) Core(TM) i5-3210M@2.5 GHz with 16 GB RAM and Windows 10 (64-bit). A prototype of LORE can be found at bitbucket.org/svitusj/lore.

6   Results

Table 1 outlines the results of the TLR baseline and our LORE approach. Each row shows the Precision, Recall, F-measure, and MCC values obtained through each of the two approaches. The LORE approach achieves the best results for all the performance indicators, providing a mean precision value of 79.2%, a mean recall value of 50.2%, a combined F-measure of 66.5%, and an MCC value of 0.62. In contrast, the TLR baseline presents worse results in all the measurements, attaining a mean precision value of 59.3%, a mean recall value of 45.5%, a combined F-measure of 52.4%, and an MCC value of 0.31. We also included the values of the measurements for the top 20 and the bottom 20 results for TLR and LORE, to better highlight how the results obtained by LORE improve those obtained by the TLR baseline.

Table 1. Mean values and standard deviations for precision, recall and F-measure

	Precision	Recall	F-measure	MCC
TLR	59.3% ± 29.6%	45.5% ± 34.2%	52.4% ± 31.9%	0.31 ± 0.13
LORE	79.2% ± 33.6%	50.2% ± 30.6%	66.5% ± 38.6%	0.62 ± 0.32
Top 20 - TLR	81.3% ± 7.3%	55.4% ± 3.2%	68.3% ± 5.2%	0.41 ± 0.03
Top 20 - LORE	93.4% ± 8.4%	69.8% ± 4.6%	81.6% ± 6.5%	0.86 ± 0.04
Bottom 20 - TLR	48.3% ± 6.9%	19.8% ± 4.2%	34.1% ± 5.5%	0.22 ± 0.04
Bottom 20 - LORE	66.2% ± 5.7%	41.2% ± 5.1%	53.7% ± 5.4%	0.38 ± 0.08

7 Discussion

The results presented in the previous section suggest that by embedding domain knowledge into requirements the TLR process retrieves enhanced results. Taking a closer look at the test cases, we found out that there are many terms in the models that do not appear in the requirements. Through the ontological expansion of the requirements, they are enriched with otherwise missing terms, retrieving more and better links. However, we also noticed a series of facts that prevent LORE from achieving better results than it does. We should tackle these issues in the future to further improve our line of work:

1. Our analysis of the results raised awareness about the importance of the quality and completeness of the ontology in LORE. If a particular concept does not have quality connections, the quality of the expansion process is diminished, also affecting the quality of the final outcome. Equally, if a concept is missing from the ontology, the concept itself and its would-be related concepts cannot be introduced in the expanded requirement. This issue leaves parts of the domain knowledge out from the requirement, causing a decrease in recall. In order to tackle this issue, we plan to automatically identify words and patterns of words that occur repeatedly in the requirements and models, and suggest their inclusion in the ontology as concepts, entrusting the creation of their relationships to the software engineers.

2. In the ontology, we identified some terms that have a large number of connections to other terms. Matching one of those terms through LORE leads to the inclusion of several unwanted ontological concepts into the expanded requirement. This concatenation of events reflects into LSI noise, strongly affecting in a negative manner the precision of the results, since elements that are not part of the oracle can be added to the proposed solution due to this issue. To tackle this issue, we plan to automatically identify the overly connected ontological concepts and suggest their inclusion in the stopwords list to the software engineers, so they can be kept out of the LORE analysis.

3. Another possible consideration towards the obtained results is the parameter tuning of our approach. Many Information Retrieval approaches have parameters that can be tuned in order to improve the results (such as the LSI similitude threshold), and our approach is no exception. So far, we have considered only the directly related ontological concepts when performing the expansion (one jump or ontological affinity level 1). In the future, we plan to study how using different levels of affinity may impact the results. We believe this could help us further explore the ontology and the relationships between the concepts, although at a risk of including noise into LSI. Analyzing the tuning of this parameter and its implications and impact on the outcomes of the LORE approach remains as future work.

4. Regarding recall, we have inspected the results and have determined that the low recall levels are not dependent solely on the techniques under use, but are also affected by the quality of the received queries, which in several occasions, are poorly formulated. Focusing only on these particular cases, recall values

obtained by TLR range at 20%, while recall values obtained by LORE range
at 40%. However, for better quality queries, TLR recall results range at 55%,
while those of LORE range at 70%. The point is, considering ontological
knowledge in the process helps improve traceability results. That is, in the
face of poor quality inputs, the results improve, but if we feed LORE with
better queries, the results improve as well. Studying the quality of the inputs
and how to ensure it remains as an interesting research topic for a future
work in which we might as well design another experiment to research how
LORE improves the results of TLR for top-quality queries. In any case, as a
naive experiment and in order to ensure the usefulness of the obtained results,
we have discussed them with one of the software engineers working for our
industrial partner, who has confirmed that the model fragments obtained by
LORE serve as a better starting point for requirement-model tracing than
those obtained by plain TLR.

5. Finally, in many cases, different terms are used to reference the same concept
   in the requirements, models, and ontology alike. In industrial environments,
   the engineers in charge of writing requirements may not be assigned with the
   building of the models or the ontology in any ways, being those tasks left for
   different engineers. Moreover, the artifacts can be manipulated by different
   engineers. This issue is known as vocabulary mismatch. Even though LORE
   uses NLP to homogenize the language between requirements and models, the
   vocabulary mismatch continues to be a disregarded issue in our work. The
   lack of awareness caused by the vocabulary mismatch makes it impossible
   to locate the elements from the model that are relevant to the requirement,
   which in turn negatively impacts both precision and recall. To mitigate this
   issue, we plan on adding a third human-made list, comprising in-house terms
   and their possible synonyms, allowing us to further map ontology concepts
   and requirements.

8   Threats to Validity

In this section, we use the classification of threats to validity of [27] to acknowledge the limitations of our approach.

1. **Construct Validity:** This aspect of validity reflects the extent to which the
   operational measures that are studied represent what the researchers have in
   mind. To minimize this risk, our evaluation studies four measures that are
   widely accepted in the software engineering research community: precision,
   recall, F-measure, and MCC.
2. **Internal Validity:** This aspect of validity is of concern when causal relations are examined. There is a risk that the factor being investigated may be
   affected by other neglected factors. The number of requirements and models
   presented in this work may look small, but they implement a wide scope of
   different railway equipment.
3. **External Validity:** This aspect of validity is concerned with to what extent
   it is possible to generalize the findings, and to what extent the findings are

of relevance for other cases. Both requirements and process models are frequently leveraged to specify all kinds of different software. LSI is a widely accepted and utilized technique which has proven to obtain good results in multiple domains. The NLP techniques studied through this work are also commonly used in the whole of the SE community. Therefore, our experiment does not rely on the particular conditions of our domain. In addition, the real-world models used in our research are a good representative of the railway, automotive, aviation, and general industrial manufacturing domains. Nevertheless, the experiment and its results should be replicated in other domains before assuring their generalization.

4. **Reliability:** This aspect is concerned with to what extent the data and the analysis are dependent on the specific researchers. To reduce this threat, all the software artifacts were provided by our industrial partner.

9 Related Work

Some works focus on the impact and application of Linguistics to TLR at several levels of abstraction. Works like [23,24] or [7] use Linguistic approaches to tackle specific TLR problems and tasks. In [9], the authors use Linguistic techniques to identify equivalence between requirements, also defining and using a series of principles for evaluating their performance when identifying equivalent requirements. The authors of [9] conclude that, in their field, the performance of Linguistic techniques is determined by the properties of the given dataset over which they are performed. They measure the properties as a factor to adjust the Linguistic techniques accordingly, and then apply their principles to an industrial case study. The work presented in [4] uses Linguistic techniques to study how changes in requirements impact other requirements in the same specification. Through the pages of their work, the authors analyze TLR between requirements, and use Linguistic techniques to determine how changes in requirements must propagate.

Our work differs from [23,24] and [7] since our approach is not based on Linguistic techniques as a means of TLR, but we rather use an ontological expansion process to enrich requirements before performing TLR, using NLP techniques only as a preprocess in our work. Moreover, we do not study how Linguistic techniques must be tweaked for specific problems as [9] does. In addition, differing from [4], we do not tackle changes in requirements nor TLR between requirements, but instead focus our work on TLR between requirements and models.

Other works target the application of LSI to TLR tasks. De Lucia et al. [13] present a Traceability Links Recovery method and tool based on LSI in the context of an artifact management system, which includes models. [8] takes in consideration the possible configurations of LSI when using the technique for TLR between requirements artifacts, namely requirements and test cases. In their work, the authors state that the configurations of LSI depend on the datasets used, and they look forward to automatically determining an appropriate configuration for LSI for any given dataset. Through our work, we do not focus on the usage of LSI or its tuning, but rather expand requirements with ontological domain knowledge before carrying out TLR between said requirements and the models.

10   Conclusions

Through this work, we propose a novel approach (LORE), based on an Ontological Requirement Expansion process, that can be used to minimize the impact that tacit knowledge has on TLR. We evaluated our approach by carrying out LORE between the requirements and process models that comprise a real-world industrial case study. Results show that our approach guides TLR to the best results for all the measured performance indicators, providing a mean precision value of 79.2%, a mean recall value of 50.2%, a combined F-measure of 66.5%, and an MCC value of 0.62. In contrast, the baseline used for comparison presents worse results in these same measurements. In addition, we identified a series of issues that prevent our approach from achieving better solutions, and that should be tackled in the future in order to further improve the TLR process between requirements and process models. To facilitate the adoption of LORE, we made a reference implementation freely available for the Eclipse environment.

Acknowledgements. This work has been partially supported by the Ministry of Economy and Competitiveness and ERDF funds under the project *Model-Driven Variability Extraction for Software Product Lines Adoption* (TIN2015-64397-R). We also thank the ITEA3 15010 REVaMP2 Project.

References

1. Abeles, P.: Efficient Java Matrix Library (2017). http://ejml.org/. Accessed 9 Nov 2017
2. Apache: OpenNLP Toolkit for the Processing of Natural Language Text (2017). https://opennlp.apache.org/. Accessed 12 Nov 2017
3. Arora, C., Sabetzadeh, M., Briand, L., Zimmer, F.: Extracting domain models from natural-language requirements: approach and industrial evaluation. In: Proceedings of the ACM/IEEE 19th International Conference on Model Driven Engineering Languages and Systems, pp. 250–260. ACM (2016)
4. Arora, C., Sabetzadeh, M., Goknil, A., Briand, L.C., Zimmer, F.: Change impact analysis for natural language requirements: an NLP approach. In: IEEE 23rd International Requirements Engineering Conference (2015)
5. Capobianco, G., De Lucia, A., Oliveto, R., Panichella, A., Panichella, S.: On the role of the nouns in IR-based traceability recovery. In: IEEE 17th International Conference on Program Comprehension, ICPC 2009, pp. 148–157. IEEE (2009)
6. Carpineto, C., Romano, G.: A survey of automatic query expansion in information retrieval. ACM Comput. Surv. **44**, 1:1–1:50 (2012)
7. Duan, C., Cleland-Huang, J.: Clustering support for automated tracing. In: Proceedings of the 22nd IEEE/ACM International Conference on Automated Software Engineering (2007)

8. Eder, S., Femmer, H., Hauptmann, B., Junker, M.: Configuring latent semantic indexing for requirements tracing. In: Proceedings of the 2nd International Workshop on Requirements Engineering and Testing (2015)
9. Falessi, D., Cantone, G., Canfora, G.: Empirical principles and an industrial case study in retrieving equivalent requirements via natural language processing techniques. Trans. Softw. Eng. **39**(1), 18–44 (2013)
10. Ghazarian, A.: A research agenda for software reliability. IEEE Reliability Society 2009 Annual Technology Report (2010)
11. Gotel, O.C., Finkelstein, C.: An analysis of the requirements traceability problem. In: Proceedings of the First International Conference on Requirements Engineering, pp. 94–101. IEEE (1994)
12. Landauer, T.K., Foltz, P.W., Laham, D.: An introduction to latent semantic analysis. Discourse Process. **25**(2–3), 259–284 (1998)
13. de Lucia, A., et al.: Enhancing an artefact management system with traceability recovery features. In: Proceedings of the 20th IEEE International Conference on Software Maintenance, pp. 306–315. IEEE (2004)
14. Marcus, A., Sergeyev, A., Rajlich, V., Maletic, J.: An information retrieval approach to concept location in source code. In: Proceedings of the 11th Working Conference on Reverse Engineering, pp. 214–223 (2004). https://doi.org/10.1109/WCRE.2004.10
15. Meziane, F., Athanasakis, N., Ananiadou, S.: Generating natural language specifications from UML class diagrams. Requirements Eng. **13**(1), 1–18 (2008)
16. Rempel, P., Mäder, P.: Preventing defects: the impact of requirements traceability completeness on software quality. IEEE Trans. Softw. Eng. **43**(8), 777–797 (2017)
17. Salman, H.E., Seriai, A., Dony, C.: Feature location in a collection of product variants: combining information retrieval and hierarchical clustering. In: The 26th International Conference on Software Engineering and Knowledge Engineering, pp. 426–430 (2014)
18. Salton, G.: The SMART Retrieval System - Experiments in Automatic Document Processing. Prentice-Hall Inc., Upper Saddle River (1971)
19. Salton, G., McGill, M.J.: Introduction to Modern Information Retrieval. McGraw-Hill Inc., New York (1986)
20. Sisman, B., Kak, A.C.: Assisting code search with automatic query reformulation for bug localization. In: Proceedings of the 10th Working Conference on Mining Software Repositories, pp. 309–318 (2013)
21. Spanoudakis, G., Zisman, A.: Software traceability: a roadmap. Handb. Softw. Eng. Knowl. Eng. **3**, 395–428 (2005)
22. Stone, A., Sawyer, P.: Using pre-requirements tracing to investigate requirements based on tacit knowledge. In: ICSOFT (1), pp. 139–144 (2006)
23. Sultanov, H., Hayes, J.H.: Application of swarm techniques to requirements engineering: requirements tracing. In: 18th IEEE International Requirements Engineering Conference (2010)
24. Sundaram, S.K., Hayes, J.H., Dekhtyar, A., Holbrook, E.A.: Assessing traceability of software engineering artifacts. Requirements Eng. **15**(3), 313–335 (2010)
25. Watkins, R., Neal, M.: Why and how of requirements tracing. IEEE Softw. **11**(4), 104–106 (1994)
26. Winkler, S., Pilgrim, J.: A survey of traceability in requirements engineering and model-driven development. Softw. Syst. Model. (SoSyM) **9**(4), 529–565 (2010)
27. Wohlin, C., Runeson, P., Höst, M., Ohlsson, M.C., Regnell, B., Wesslén, A.: Experimentation in Software Engineering. Springer, Heidelberg (2012). https://doi.org/10.1007/978-3-642-29044-2

Requirements Engineering for Cyber Physical Production Systems

Pericles Loucopoulos[1] , Evangelia Kavakli[2(✉)] ,
and Natalia Chechina[3]

[1] Institute of Digital Innovation and Research, Dublin 9, Ireland
periloucopoulos@me.com
[2] University of the Aegean, Mytilene, Greece
kavakli@aegean.gr
[3] Department of Computing and Informatics,
Bournemouth University, Poole, UK
nchechina@bournemouth.ac.uk

Abstract. Traditional manufacturing and production systems are in the throes of a digital transformation. By blending the real and virtual production worlds, it is now possible to connect all parts of the production process: devices, products, processes, systems and people, in an informational ecosystem. This paper examines the underpinning issues that characterise the challenges for transforming traditional manufacturing to a Cyber Physical Production System. Such a transformation constitutes a major endeavour for requirements engineers who need to identify, specify and analyse the effects that a multitude of assets need to be transformed towards a network of collaborating devices, information sources, and human actors. The paper reports on the e-CORE approach which is a systematic, analytical and traceable approach to Requirements Engineering and demonstrates its utility using an industrial-size application. It also considers the effect of Cyber Physical Production Systems on future approaches to requirements in dealing with the dynamic nature of such systems.

Keywords: Requirements Engineering · Industry 4.0 ·
Factories of the Future (FoF) · Cyber Physical Production Systems (CPPS) ·
Capability-Oriented modelling

1 Introduction

A term that has come to represent the blending of the physical with the digital towards a new industrial era is that of Industry 4.0 [1]. More specifically to production systems, terms that have come to dominate the debate are those of Factory of the Future (FoF) and Cyber Physical Production Systems (CPPS) [2]. The purpose of CPPS is to transform current Physical Production Systems (PPS) towards those that, underpinned by ICT-related capabilities, could achieve a greater degree of connectivity of production entities and processes.

The aforementioned transformation could have a profound impact on operational, tactical and strategic aspects of a manufacturing company. *Operations* would be directly impacted on a daily basis through the augmentation of traditional physical production machines with devices capable of providing valuable information on the functioning of these machines. *Tactical* decisions could result in more efficient, streamlined production lines through the provision of data analyses for optimized planning, improved scheduling, and reactive as well as predictive event handling. *Strategically*, the 'smart factory' could be transformed into a profitable innovation centre through its ability to be quickly 'reprogrammed' to provide faster time-to-market responses to global consumer demand, effectively addressing mass-customization needs and bringing life to innovative new products.

The *challenge* to designers of systems aimed at facilitating this type of organisational transformation is that ".... the boundaries between the real world and the virtual world become increasingly blurred" [3] with the resulting hybrid systems being regarded as ".... online networks of social machines that are organised in a similar way to social networks" [1]. In such a setting, all *assets* of the manufacturing enterprise, whether human, physical or digital, need to be considered synergistically if the transformation is to be successful.

The *motivation* for the work presented in this paper is threefold. First, to present a methodological approach that addresses the aforementioned challenge, especially how an asset-centric view is utilised for a robust, analytical and traceable way for requirements for CPPS. This is done by introducing the e-CORE (early Capability Oriented Requirements Engineering) framework in terms of its conceptual foundations and its way of working. Second, to demonstrate the utility of this approach in the context of a real manufacturing situation. This is done through a detailed walkthrough of the way the approach was applied to two major transformational needs of a major automobile manufacturer, henceforth referred to as FCA, and which was done in the context of the Horizon 2020 project DISRUPT. Third, to present a reflective discussion on the way that e-CORE could facilitate the definition of self-awareness requirements for dealing with the interplay between system and its environment.

The paper is organised as follows. Section 2 sets the context of Physical Production Systems (PPS) in a general sense, in terms of the key concepts involved in a manufacturing production topology, and which will be influenced when incorporating a cyber-centric production chain. The e-CORE approach, is introduced in Sect. 3, together with the support arguments for the reason to deploy a capability-orientated method to transforming PPS to CPPS. Section 4 demonstrates the complete e-CORE lifecycle in the FCA case noting that due to space limitation the conceptual models presented in this paper represent a small but nevertheless fully representative part of the actual results from this industrial case. Finally, Sect. 5 concludes this paper with a short commentary on the value of the approach to CPPS applications and defines research initiatives for extending the approach towards dealing also with emergent system behaviours.

2   Challenges in the Transformation Towards CPPS

The term "Smart Factory" or "Factory of the Future" is used to define a flexible factory that can be dynamically transformed to respond to various events emanating from disruptions in the supply chain or in the production line. To this end, *production topologies* need to achieve dynamic re-configurability and scaling, to facilitate decision support by accommodating value chain collaboration and to enable decentralised (self-) adjustment of production, while also incorporating resource optimisation.

Production topologies define the context within which a transformation in manufacturing is to take place. Production topologies, according to the Instrument Society of America [4, 5], the taxonomic analysis of manufacturing systems [6–8], and ontologies for manufacturing and logistics [9], can be considered in terms of concepts that fall into two broad categories: *external* (e.g. SUPPLIER, TRANSPORTER and ORDER) and *internal* (e.g. MATERIAL, PERSONNEL, PRODUCTIONLINE, WORKCELL, and EQUIPMENT).

The challenges to be considered by requirements engineers are of a technical, organisational and social nature such as: "what are the assets, human, physical, cyber, whose unique combination can provide strategic advantage to the enterprise?"; "what is the gap between existing and desired capabilities?"; "what is the requirements process such that one can reason about the choices available and the choices made in transforming existing assets to cyber-oriented ones?". These challenges are addressed by the e-CORE approach which is a systematic way of proceeding from high-level early requirements to late requirements.

3   The e-CORE Approach

3.1   Background and Related Work

The requirements of new complex, emergent systems, such as smart factories, intelligent transportation, and smart cities, has brought new challenges to the RE discipline [10, 11]. These complex, heterogeneous systems of systems, consist of digital structures (e.g., software, data) that interact with physical constructs (e.g., sensors, devices) and with social elements (e.g., persons, organisations). The interplay between the different worlds of physical, digital and social has thus become more intricate, complex, dynamic, and generative. The challenges presented by production systems' transformation towards cyber-physicality requires a new metaphor [12]. We posit that the notion of *capability* represents a most suitable metaphor that provides the means of considering the intertwining of concerns in these different worlds in a way such that it is possible to connect strategic objectives and high-level organizational requirements to technological artefacts in a unified manner.

The general consensus is that an enterprise capability represents a conceptual service that a group of processes and people, supported by the relevant application, information and underlying technology, performs [13, 14]. There has been a number of attempts at incorporating the notion of 'capability' in frameworks, most notably those of the Open Management Group [15], the Department of Defence Architecture Framework (DOFAF) [16] and the NATO Architecture Framework (NAF) [17] as well as considering capability as a way of developing organisational strategies [18, 19]. In the context of information systems engineering, capability has been examined from a software development and management perspective, most notably in the Capability as a Service (CaaS) project [20].

In a capability-oriented paradigm we are interested in identifying possession of *valuable, rare, inimitable* and *non-substitutable* resources of enterprise as a source of sustainable advantage [21], whether these are existing capabilities or new ones that need to be introduced. Using capabilities as the starting point one can begin investigating and analysing what lies behind these fundamental enterprise assets, what goals govern them, what actors are involved and how they collaborate to synergistically meet requirements for enterprise transformation.

3.2   The e-CORE Conceptual Framework

The *conceptual modelling* framework underpinning e-CORE has been developed and applied in recent work [22–25]. It employs a set of complimentary and intertwined modelling paradigms based on enterprise *capabilities, goals, actors,* and *information objects.*

In CPPS applications, a key consideration is to focus on physical assets and in the way that these are transformed into on-line networks of collaborating social machines in a similar way to social networks [1]. In this context the e-CORE approach is particularly suitable since it focuses attention on assets and their collaboration for achieving a certain enterprise goal. This notion is shown in the meta-model of Fig. 1.

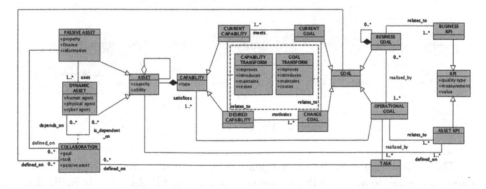

Fig. 1. The e-CORE top level meta-model

Referring to the meta-model in Fig. 1, one can see that a CAPABILITY is a generalisation of ASSETS (capacities and abilities) where ASSETS are distinguished between PASSIVE (resources) and DYNAMIC (agents). DYNAMIC ASSETS represent the social dimension, focusing on the COLLABORATION between these agents, which is defined as dependencies between them. These dependencies may involve the exchange of PASSIVE ASSETS (resources), or on execution of some TASK or the achievement of a GOAL.

In a RE setting we are interested in both CURRENT CAPABILITIES and DESIRED CAPABILITIES in order to model the necessary transformations from the former to the latter. There is a symmetry between CURRENT CAPABILITIES and DESIRED CAPABILITIES in the sense that each set is related to enterprise goals, the former to CURRENT GOALS and the latter to CHANGE GOALS. In e-CORE, requirements are modelled and analysed in terms of the juxtaposition of CHANGE GOALS against CURRENT GOALS and their corresponding capabilities.

3.3   The Way-of-Working

The e-CORE process and detailed activities are summarized in the three phases, as shown in Fig. 2.

Information elicitation refers to the collection of information related to the user case using a number of instruments (online forms, structures elicitation forms, collaborative workshops, onsite visits). It results in user narratives of the existing enterprise situation, as well as the user needs and aspirations with respect to the foreseen functionality and quality of the new system under development. The use of natural language in these user narratives has the advantage of ease of transferability but is prone to ambiguity and inconsistencies.

Defining those concepts that are relevant to the CPPS in a clear and consistent manner is done through e-CORE concept identification, which results in the list of concepts that describe the application domain. However, it does not define their structure, nor the interrelationships that exist between these concepts which in turn hinders any potential analysis.

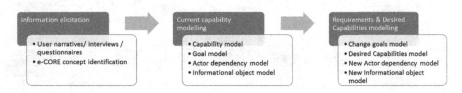

Fig. 2. The e-CORE process

This is ameliorated by the second phase which is that of *current capability modelling,* according to the e-CORE meta-model, as discussed in Sect. 3.2. In particular, 4 different types of modelling are considered each focusing on specific conceptual perspectives:

- The capability model focuses on the capacities and abilities necessary for a particular application.

- The goal model focuses on enterprise's objectives for retaining, acquiring or developing the necessary capabilities for the application.
- The actor – dependency model focuses on the socio-technical components of the enterprise that relate to specific capabilities for the application.
- The informational model focuses on the logical structure of the informational resources that are part of the enterprise's capabilities and act as the medium of communication between enterprise actors when they are trying to meet specific enterprise goals.

This model-driven approach encourages modellers to focus on those elements that are deemed to be key drivers in the dynamic change of enterprises and their systems, whilst ensuring that consistency is achieved across all four, through appropriate relationships between model concepts as defined in the e-CORE meta-model.

The third phase, *requirements and desired capabilities modelling*, focuses on the business requirements for change and the way these are mapped onto new capabilities and in the way these capabilities are operationalised in terms of actor dependencies. Change goals provide a way of identifying and reasoning about the user requirements and as such they express a desired state the user wishes to achieve. Reasoning about change goals is based on the premise that the desired changes are derived through the comparison of the 'desired' vision against the 'present' reality (the current goal model). This process aims to re-interpret each change requirement in relation to the existing goals, involving the key business stakeholders, most of whom would have been involved in the definition of current goals. The result of this activity is the construction of a revised goal model (the Change Goals Model) detailing stakeholders' requirements for change. In the standard goal decomposition manner, the change goal model shows operational goals for the new improved situation. These operational goals, according to the e-CORE meta-model (Fig. 1), motivate new capabilities in terms of the new assets which may be further elaborated in the desired actor dependency model. In detailing the actor dependency model, it is then possible to proceed with the detailed functional and non-functional requirements of the desired system and its components.

4 Application of the e-CORE Framework on the FCA Case

FCA being one of the largest automotive manufacturers in the world has automated its production planning and scheduling according to the capabilities of the current software configuration. However, FCA still faces problems when there is a disruption in either its external topology, e.g. the *supply chain* (delays, errors in the supply of components) or in its internal topology, e.g. the *production process* (machine breakdown, unscheduled maintenance, software problems). The e-CORE approach has been used in collaboration between requirements engineers and a variety of FCA stakeholders (production planners, production engineers, and logistics teams). Sections 4.1, 4.2 and 4.3 provide details of all 3 e-CORE process phases applied on the FCA case.

4.1   Information Elicitation

Initially FCA requirements are expressed in natural language by the users, as shown in Fig. 3.

The narrative reveals a number of FCA business capabilities that can be informally mapped onto e-CORE, detailed in terms of the assets (in the form of human, physical and software actors) that the company possesses and the ability, (in the form of means or skills), inherent in these assets. For example, `Production Scheduling` deploys the `Production Planner` (referred to as Valentina in the narrative) in collaboration with the software applications of `OSS`, `MES` and `MRP` , having the knowledge, expertise and software ability for `Scheduling` and `Rescheduling` .

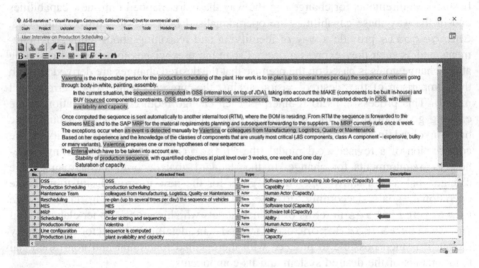

Fig. 3. e-CORE concept identification from user narrative

4.2   Current Capability Modelling

Starting from the concepts that were identified in Sect. 4.1, we can construct the FCA current capability model shown in Fig. 4, which defines 5 main capabilities denoted as `CAP1:Inbound Logistics` , `CAP2: Material Management` , `CAP3: Production Planning` , `CAP4: Production Scheduling` and `CAP5: Production` .

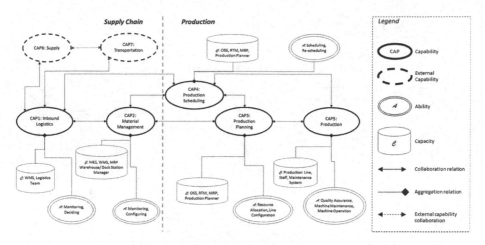

Fig. 4. The FCA current capability model

The model of Fig. 4 provides the scoping for the FCA application. `CAP1`   and `CAP2` relate to the first problem area of supply of materials whilst `CAP3`, `CAP4` and `CAP5` relate to the second namely that of the production process.

In addition to these internal capabilities, there are two external capabilities that are owned by enterprises with which FCA collaborate but whose capabilities are not owned, controlled or subject to any influence by FCA. These are capabilities `CAP6: Supply` and `CAP7: Transportation` . They are included in the capability model in order to externalize these relationships, which may be very significant if in the transformed situation there may be opportunities for a closer collaboration of FCA with external entities for example suppliers and logistics companies, by making use of Internet of Things (IoT) functionalities.

The capability model acts as an *anchor point* for the rest of the e-CORE models, which for reasons of brevity are not presented here individually, but segments of these are shown in Fig. 5 which also provides a visual representation of how these models, driven by the capability model are formally interrelated. These interrelationships objectively provide answers to the following questions: *"why does the enterprise need these capabilities?"* (answered by the *goal model*), *"what socio-technical actors are involved and how do they co-operate in order to meet these enterprise goals?"* (answered by the *actor dependency model*), and *"what kind of information is used in this co-operation?"* (answered by the *informational object model*).

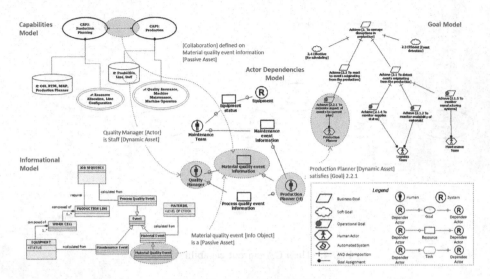

Fig. 5. Cross model relationships

As shown in Fig. 5, the dynamic asset of 'Staff' of capability 'CAP5' motivates the analysis in the actor-dependency model of this asset, which resulted in the actors 'Quality Manager' and 'Maintenance Team'.

The collaboration between capabilities 'CAP3' and 'CAP5', gave rise to the 'Material quality event information' exchange of resource between 'Quality Manager' and 'Production Planner'. This resource is then identified as an informational resource, which was modelled in the informational model as 'Material Quality Event'.

Finally, the existence of 'Production Planner' in the actor-dependency model is due to the enterprise goal of 'G2.2.1 . To estimate impact of to current plan' which is met by 'CAP3' through the asset 'Production Planner' which is found in both the goal assignment of 'G2.2.1' and in the capacity of 'CAP3'.

4.3   Requirements Modelling

The 4 different types of modelling shown in Fig. 5 represent the dimension of abstraction being applied. Orthogonal to this is the dimension of requirements lifecycle, which is a set of phases for progressing from an existing situation to a new desired situation, driven by the FCA's needs and wishes as well as perceived opportunities with respect to the CPPS technologies. The potential transformation is modelled in terms of change goals.

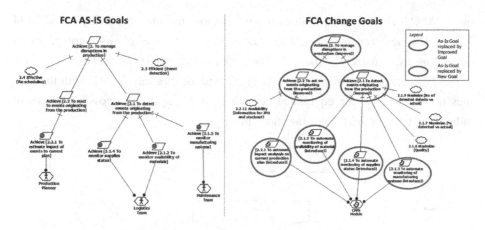

Fig. 6. Transformation from current to change FCA Goals

The change goals model is constructed in a top down stepwise manner, by generating the change goals either as *improvements* of the current goals or by *introducing* new goals. This process iterates on three main activities: (i) Determining the impact of perceived 'automation' on current business goals; (ii) Modifying the current goal hierarchy to reflect these changes; and (iii) Re-assigning operational goals to existing or foreseen actors (the CPPS modules). The result of this process is illustrated in Fig. 6, which depicts a segment of the change goal hierarchy corresponding to goal `G2. To manage    disruptions in production (improve)` ·

As shown in this model the initial requirement to improve management of disruptions in production, is gradually operationalised through the introduction of a number of new goals, which are ultimately assigned to CPPS modules. These modules will represent a new set of assets and therefore capabilities. These new capabilities will give FCA a competitive advantage, as well as dealing with current difficulties in solving problems mentioned in Sect. 4.1 with their current set of capabilities.

Some of these system goals replace existing current goals, previously assigned to specific human actors. For example, change goal `G2.1.5. To automate monitoring of manufacturing    systems (introduce)`   assigned to `CPPS Module` , replaces the   current   goal   `G2.1.5. To monitor manufacturing systems` currently assigned to the `Maintenance Team` . Thus, it becomes obvious that the improvement sought by FCA will affect the dependencies between current actors and associated capabilities.

Therefore, the defined change goals express the CPPS requirements from a user perspective and motivate the desired transformation of FCA capabilities. For example, the FCA change goals (see Fig. 6) `G2.1.5. To automate monitoring of manufacturing systems`   and `G2.2.1 . To automate impact analysis on    current production plan` , motivate the introduction of a new capability `CAP8: Smart Event Monitoring`   and the transformation of an existing capability, that of `CAP4: Production Scheduling` , to that of 'CAP4' . This new situation is shown in the capability model of Fig. 7. The new capability 'CAP8: Smart Event Monitoring' comprises of three assets, namely the 'Cyber Physical System (CPS)' , the 'Complex Event Processing (CEP)' and the 'Dashboard' , with the abilities to 'monitor' the equipment condition, to 'diagnose' possible causes of failure and to 'inform' the shop floor manager.

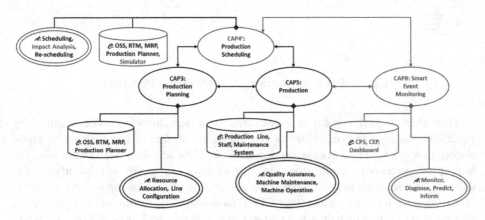

Fig. 7. Desired FCA capabilities for the production case

Similarly, the transformed capability 'CAP4' is augmented with the ability of 'impact analysis' that is the prediction of the effect of detected events on the production. This ability is effected through a new asset, that of the 'Simulator' . Note that these new assets, are elaborations of the CPPS modules mentioned above (see the Change Goal model in Fig. 6).

As shown in the model of Fig. 7, the new set of capabilities also gives rise to new collaborations between capabilities and involved actors. The identification of these relationships is significant because it enables us to define the way that actors coordinate between themselves in order to make capabilities realisable, further detailed in a new actor model, as shown in Fig. 8. For example, the collaboration between the new capability 'CAP8' and the existing capability 'CAP5' gives rise to the 'Monitor Shopfloor' task dependency between the 'Shopfloor Manager' (a human actor) and the 'Dashboard' (a CPPS module) in the new actor dependency model.

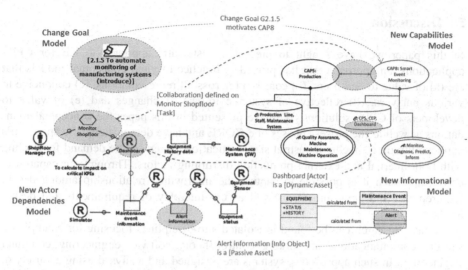

Fig. 8. Cross model relationships between change goals, desired capabilities and actors

Thus, starting from change requirements, new capabilities are modelled and these in turn give rise to details in a new actor model, which essentially defines operational requirements. This is even more explicit in the information model, also shown in Fig. 8, whereby the resource dependencies are elaborated. For example, the actor dependency on 'Alert information', which is a passive asset, leads to a revised information model that now incorporates the information object 'Alert'.

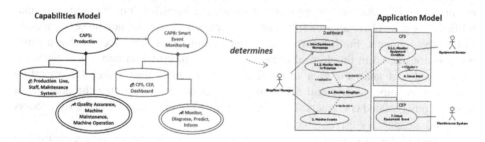

Fig. 9. Desired capabilities determine system models for late requirements

In summary, the process shown schematically in Fig. 8, provides a robust, analytical and traceable way of proceeding from high level strategic change goals to detailed operational requirements and the desired capabilities. Continuing with the capability driven paradigm, the identified desired capabilities determine the system components, in UML notation, as shown in Fig. 9.

5   Discussion

In this paper we have sought to present a systematic approach to RE for CPPS applications, an approach that has proved in practice to yield conceptual models that are (a) of value to end users, (b) consistent across all representations, (c) conducive to various analyses, (d) reflective of systemic impact of changes and (e) of value to developers of CPPS solutions. We have presented in this paper the conceptual foundations as well as the process phases of e-CORE and have demonstrated the approach's applicability on a specific industrial size application driven by the demand for dealing with both internal and external production disrupting factors. Through our capability-driven approach it is possible to capture the intertwined relationship among design requirements and environment, as well as the interplay of requirements and design artefacts [10].

Related research can be found in isolated sub-disciplines focusing for example on sensors, communications, networking, control theory, software engineering, computer engineering. In such approaches, systems are designed and analysed using a variety of modelling formalisms and tools whereby each representation highlights certain features and disregards others to make analysis tractable. These attempts may suffice to support a component-based approach to development but fails short on the intertwining of the multitude of agents whose interconnection is the very essence of cyber physicality. The importance of cooperating agents, has received attention in research work addressing intelligent systems [26]. However, this collaboration is considered at a physical level and these approaches are mostly concerned with disruption at the operational layer [27, 28]. Our approach complements the aforementioned works, by considering the influences of external factors on internal system networking and collaboration.

It is reported that work in cyber-physical systems pays less attention to early requirements [29, 30]. In our approach, through the identification of enterprise capabilities, it is possible to address fully early requirements, and to relate these seamlessly to late requirements. Furthermore, a key contribution of our approach is that a capability is considered in ontological terms and as such information about it is captured, represented and analysed in a methodical manner rather than either (a) regarding capability as some generic and nebulous construct or (b) considering the analysis in terms of other related constructs. This has the important implication that the RE process is indeed a capability-driven process.

Further to the early requirements issues discussed in this paper, we recognise that there are a number of significant CPPS challenges that still need to be addressed. These are linked to the specific nature of CPPSs which are neither static, nor isolated entities. CPPSs being composed of elements which may frequently constantly change impact their interconnectivity and their environment around them. Due to the scale of emerging CPPSs being Systems of Systems and the variety of events being generated, requirements cannot be expected to arrive in synchronised batches any longer, but rather as a consistent flow.

Part of CPPSs dynamicity is their mobility– their position and location are not fixed anymore, now they move in space and independently collaborate with other physical and cyber agents. Ocado and Amazon warehouses are great examples of the types of industrial operations we may expect in coming years. Therefore, requirements engineering for CPPS should take mobility into account [31, 32].

CPPS dynamicity and mobility raise challenges with respect to quality properties of the live systems which need to be considered at requirements stage, properties that are often referred to as non-functional requirements (NFR) such as completeness, availability, reliability, consistency, relevance, and security [33]. We need to consider these NFRs as a way of monitoring and providing feedback on one hand from the system to the environment and on the other hand from the environment to the system.

Following the recommendations in [10], we recognise the following three cases of requirements challenges.

First, the *design* challenge related to the emergent behaviour and dynamics of the system and its environment. This implies that further to the fixed goals of the system which is the traditional way of specifying requirements we need to consider whether the system will continue to meet any emergent goals during the system's lifetime.

Second, the *modelling* challenge related to the anticipation and representation of the emergent behaviours of the system. In this sense we need to develop approaches for representing, communicating and analysing dynamic systems and their emergent requirements in ways that guarantee that these meet functional and non-functional requirements.

Third, the *predictability* challenge related to the impact that the system and its behaviour will have on its environment. In other words, we need to pay particular attention to the continuous dynamic composition of the system and its environment and how to predict the impact of the system on the environment, and vice versa.

The common thread in all these issues is that we need to define *self-awareness requirements* about the run-time success or failure or even the level and quality of service of other requirements. We posit that addressing such self-awareness requirements, is dealt by considering transformational capabilities that will lead to feedback functionality of the established system configuration.

To address these challenges we need models that should be capable of describing and reasoning about how the system monitors itself and its environment, how the system adapts itself and how the system coordinates monitoring and adaptation [34]. To this end, we envision extensions to the e-CORE approach by incorporating the notion of adaptation capabilities in its meta-model and its way-of-working. Such capabilities refer to run-time mechanisms that bring about changes to system capabilities defined at design time. Adaptation capabilities are triggered when the monitoring of NFRs (e.g. system availability, response time, etc.) detects signs of failures and to aid the system to reconfigure (predefined) system capabilities in order to restore the achievement of system goals. Adaptation capabilities may be considered as predictive or reactive, depending on the emergent properties that trigger the necessity for adaptation. In extending e-CORE we envision considering similar works in the area of requirements for self-awareness [35].

Acknowledgment. The notion of 'capability' in the context of digital enterprises was first investigated by the authors in the EU-FP7 funded project CaaS (# 611351). The e-CORE approach was developed as part of the Open Models Initiative and series of NEMO Summer Schools. It was extended and applied in the Qatar National Research Fund project i-Doha (# NPRP 7-662-2-247). Aspects of the FCA use case described in this paper were part of the work carried out by the authors for the EU H2020-FOF-11-2016 project DISRUPT (# 723541). The authors wish to express their gratitude to all their colleagues with whom they collaborated in the aforementioned projects.

References

1. Deloitte, Industry 4.0: Challenges and solutions for the digital transformation and use of exponential technologies (2016)
2. IEC: Factory of the Future - A White Paper, IEC (2016)
3. ITRE, Industry 4.0: Study of the ITRE Committee. Directorate General for Internal Policies, European Parliament (2016)
4. Instrument Society of America, Enterprise - Control System Integration Part 1: Models and Terminology (1999)
5. Instrument Society of America, Enterprise - Control System Integration Part 3: Activity Models of Manufacturing Operations Management (2004)
6. Garetti, M., Fumagalli, L.: P-PSO ontology for manufacturing systems. In: 14th IFAC Symposium on Information Control Problems in Manufacturing, Bucharest, Romania (2012)
7. Lemaignan, S., et al.: MASON: a proposal for an ontology of manufacturing domain. In: IEEE Workshop on Distributed Intelligent Systems: Collective Intelligence and Its Applications (DIS'06) (2010)
8. Lin, H.K., Harding, J.A.: A manufacturing system engineering ontology model on the semantic web for inter-enterprise collaboration. Comput. Ind. **58**, 428–437 (2007)
9. Fumagalli, L., Pala, S., Garetti, M., Negri, E.: Ontology-based modeling of manufacturing and logistics systems for a new MES architecture. In: Grabot, B., Vallespir, B., Gomes, S., Bouras, A., Kiritsis, D. (eds.) APMS 2014. IAICT, vol. 438, pp. 192–200. Springer, Heidelberg (2014). https://doi.org/10.1007/978-3-662-44739-0_24
10. Jarke, M., et al.: The brave new world of design requirements. Inf. Syst. **36**(7), 992–1008 (2011)
11. Loucopoulos, P.: Requirements engineering for emergent application software. In: Cordeiro, J., Maciaszek, Leszek A., Filipe, J. (eds.) ICEIS 2012. LNBIP, vol. 141, pp. 18–28. Springer, Heidelberg (2013). https://doi.org/10.1007/978-3-642-40654-6_2
12. Cao, J., et al.: Capability as requirement metaphor. In: 2011 IEEE 10th International Conference on Trust, Security and Privacy in Computing and Communications (2011)
13. Danesh, M.H., Yu, E.: Modeling enterprise capabilities with i*: reasoning on alternatives. In: Iliadis, L., Papazoglou, M., Pohl, K. (eds.) CAiSE 2014. LNBIP, vol. 178, pp. 112–123. Springer, Cham (2014). https://doi.org/10.1007/978-3-319-07869-4_10
14. Rosen, M.: Business Processes Start with Capabilities. BP Trends (2010). http://www.bptrends.com/publicationfiles/12-07-10-COL-BPM%20&%20SOA–BusProcesses%20begin%20with%20Capabilities%201003%20v01–Rosen.pdf
15. OMG: Value Delivery Metamodel, v. 1.0 (2013). http://www.omg.org/spec/VDML/1.0/
16. DoD: Systems engineering guide for systems of systems, Washington DC (2008)
17. MoD: NATO architecture framework v4.0 documentation (2013). http://nafdocs.org/modem

18. Teece, D.J.: Dynamic Capabilities and Strategic Management. Oxford University Press, New York (2009)
19. Helfat, C.E., Peteraf, M.A.: The dynamic resource-based view: capability lifecycles. Strat. Manag. J. **24**, 997–1010 (2003)
20. Sandkuhl, K., Stirna, J. (eds.): Capability Management in Digital Enterprises. Springer, Heidelberg (2018). https://doi.org/10.1007/978-3-319-90424-5
21. Barney, J.: Firm resources and sustained competitive advantage. J. Manag. **17**, 99–120 (1991)
22. Loucopoulos, P., Kavakli, E.: Capability oriented enterprise knowledge modeling: the CODEK approach. Domain-Specific Conceptual Modeling, pp. 197–215. Springer, Cham (2016). https://doi.org/10.1007/978-3-319-39417-6_9
23. Loucopoulos, P., Kavakli, E.: Capability modeling with application on large-scale sports events. In: AMCIS 2016, San Diego, USA (2016)
24. Loucopoulos, P.: Capability modeling as a strategic analysis tool - keynote extended abstract. In: IEEE Conference on Requirements Engineering: RePa Workshop. IEEE Computer Society, Beijing (2016)
25. Dimitrakopoulos, G., et al.: A capability-oriented modelling and simulation approach for autonomous vehicle management. Simul. Model. Pract. Theory **91**, 28–47 (2018)
26. Reza, H., et al.: Toward requirements engineering of cyber-physical systems: modeling cubesat. In: 2016 IEEE Aerospace Conference (2016)
27. Bertolino, A., et al.: A tour of secure software engineering solutions for connected vehicles. Softw. Qual. J. **26**, 1223–1256 (2017)
28. Singh, I., Lee, S.W.: Self-adaptive requirements for intelligent transportation system: a case study. In: 2017 International Conference on Information and Communication Technology Convergence (ICTC) (2017)
29. Braun, P., et al.: Guiding requirements engineering for software-intensive embedded systems in the automotive industry. Comput. Sci.-Res. Dev. **29**(1), 21–43 (2014)
30. Chowdhury, N.M., Mackenzie, L., Perkins, C.: Requirement analysis for building practical accident warning systems based on Vehicular Ad-Hoc Networks. In: 2014 11th Annual Conference on Wireless On-demand Network Systems and Services (WONS) (2014)
31. Nelson, R.: Robots pick groceries, make sushi, assist amputees. EE-Eval. Eng. **57**(2), 28–29 (2018)
32. Bogue, R.: Growth in e-commerce boosts innovation in the warehouse robot market. Ind. Robot.: Int. J. **43**(6), 583–587 (2016)
33. Breivold, H.P., Sandström, K.: Internet of things for industrial automation–challenges and technical solutions. In: 2015 IEEE International Conference on Data Science and Data Intensive Systems, pp. 532–539. IEEE (2015)
34. Weyns, D., Malek, S., Andersson, J.: FORMS: unifying reference model for formal specification of distributed self-adaptive systems. ACM Trans. Auton. Adapt. Syst. (TAAS) **2012**(7), 1–61 (2012)
35. Souza, Vítor E.Silva, Lapouchnian, Alexei, Mylopoulos, John: Requirements-driven qualitative adaptation. In: Meersman, Robert, et al. (eds.) OTM 2012. LNCS, vol. 7565, pp. 342–361. Springer, Heidelberg (2012). https://doi.org/10.1007/978-3-642-33606-5_21

Data Modeling and Analysis

A Fourth Normal Form
for Uncertain Data

Ziheng Wei and Sebastian Link[(✉)]

Department of Computer Science, The University of Auckland,
Auckland, New Zealand
{z.wei,s.link}@auckland.ac.nz

Abstract. Relational database design addresses applications for data
that is certain. Modern applications require the handling of uncertain
data. Indeed, one dimension of big data is veracity. Ideally, the design of
databases helps users quantify their trust in the data. For that purpose,
we need to establish a design framework that handles responsibly any
knowledge of an organization about the uncertainty in their data. Naturally, such knowledge helps us find database designs that process data
more efficiently. In this paper, we apply possibility theory to introduce
the class of possibilistic multivalued dependencies that are a significant
source of data redundancy. Redundant data may occur with different
degrees, derived from the different degrees of uncertainty in the data.
We propose a family of fourth normal forms for uncertain data. We justify our proposal showing that its members characterize schemata that
are free from any redundant data occurrences in any of their instances at
the targeted level of uncertainty in the data. We show how to automatically transform any schema into one that satisfies our proposal, without
loss of any information. Our results are founded on axiomatic and algorithmic solutions to the implication problem of possibilistic functional
and multivalued dependencies which we also establish.

Keywords: Database design · Functional dependency ·
Multivalued dependency · Normal form · Redundancy · Uncertainty

1 Introduction

Big data has given us big promises. However, their realization comes with big
responsibilities. One dimension of big data is veracity, or the uncertainty in data.
According to an IBM study, one in three managers distrust the data that they
use to make decisions[1]. Our community needs to establish design frameworks
that produce responsible systems, that is, systems which establish trust in the
data that they manage. A first step is to provide a capability for data stewards
to quantify the degrees of uncertainty in data that they deem appropriate. It is
natural to think that such information helps tailor database designs according

---

[1] http://www-01.ibm.com/software/data/bigdata/.

© Springer Nature Switzerland AG 2019
P. Giorgini and B. Weber (Eds.): CAiSE 2019, LNCS 11483, pp. 295–311, 2019.
https://doi.org/10.1007/978-3-030-21290-2_19

to application requirements on the certainty in data. With such a framework data would meet the requirements of applications by design. This would provide a solid foundation for trust in data and data-driven decision making.

In [11,12] the authors presented a design framework of relational databases for uncertain data. Based on possibility theory [2], records are assigned a discrete degree of possibility (p-degree) with which they occur in a relation. Intuitively, the p-degree quantifies the level of confidence an organization is prepared to assign to a record. The assignment of p-degrees can be based on many factors, specific to applications and irrelevant for developing the framework. In addition, an integrity constraint is assigned a degree of certainty (c-degree) that quantifies to which records it applies. Intuitively, the higher the c-degree of a constraint the lower the minimum p-degree of records to which the constraint applies. For example, a constraint with the highest c-degree applies to all records, and one with the lowest c-degree only applies to records with the highest p-degree. The design framework of [12] was developed for possibilistic functional dependencies (pFDs) [11]. Generalizations of Boyce-Codd and Third Normal Forms were established that characterized schemata that eliminated, minimized across all dependency-preserving decompositions respectively, from every instance, every redundant data value occurrence from every record whose p-degree meets a given target. Consequently, the normalization effort is tailored to the application requirements for the minimum p-degrees required from data.

Our main goal is to establish a design framework for the combined class of pFDs and possibilistic multivalued dependencies (pMVDs). That is, tailor relational schema design up to Fagin's Fourth Normal Form (4NF) [3] to uncertain data. One key motivation follows the relational framework since MVDs cause data redundancy that is not covered by FDs. However, modern applications provide stronger motivation as they need to integrate data from various sources, in which companies have varying degrees of trust. In fact, the integration process often relies on joins which are a frequent source of data redundancy that is caused by MVDs. In fact, a relation exhibits an MVD if and only if the relation is the lossless join over two of its projections [3]. As modern information systems have the responsibility to process uncertain data efficiently, we require a design framework for uncertain data that can eliminate sources of data redundancy as required by applications. Our main goal poses new challenges. Indeed, the framework in [11,12] is founded on the *downward closure property* of FDs, which says that an FD that is satisfied by a relation is also satisfied by every subset of records in the relation. Unfortunately, MVDs are not closed downwards and it is unclear whether the achievements of [12] for pFDs can be extended to pMVDs.

Contributions. (1) We introduce the class of pMVDs, generalizing both MVDs and pFDs, as a rich source of redundancy in uncertain data. (2) We establish axiomatic and algorithmic characterizations for the implication problem of pFDs and pMVDs. (3) For pFDs and pMVDs we characterize schemata that do not permit any instances with any redundant data value occurrence of a targeted minimum p-degree. This is achieved by a fourth normal form proposal on conditions of pMVDs that apply to data in which redundancy of the targeted p-degree can occur. (4) We show how to transform any schema into one that meets the fourth normal form condition, without loss of information. Our contributions subsume Fagin's 4NF as the special case with one p-degree.

Organization. Section 2 introduces our running example. We discuss related work in Sect. 3. Preliminaries are provided in Sect. 4. A design theory is established in Sect. 5. Our normal form proposal and semantic justification is developed in Sect. 6. Section 7 explains how our normal form can always be achieved. Section 8 concludes and comments briefly on future work. Proofs can be found in a technical report [16].

2 Running Application Scenario

We introduce a running example chosen small enough to illustrate our concepts and findings throughout the paper. The application scenario integrates data about the supply of products that record which *p)roducts* are supplied by which *s)upplier* from which *l)ocation* on which *d)ate*. The data originates from different sources. Data about products, suppliers, and date originate from source 1, while data about suppliers and their location originate from source 2 and source 3. The integrated relation is the result of joining source 1 with the union of sources 2 and 3. Importantly, there is more confidence in records that occur in both source 2 and 3 than in records that occur in either source 2 or source 3. As a means to distinguish between these levels of confidence, records that occur in both source 2 and 3 are assigned the confidence label *high*, while the remaining ones have label *medium*.

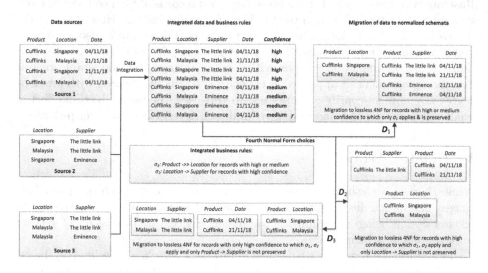

Fig. 1. 4NF normalization strategies for data with different confidence levels

A specific instance of this application scenario is depicted in Fig. 1, in which relation r originates from the given instances of the three sources. We can observe that the sub-relation r_1 of r, that consists of the four records with confidence label *high*, exhibits the FD σ_2 : *location* $\rightarrow$ *supplier* while r does not satisfy σ_2. Indeed, the location of supplier *Eminence* is not certain. Recall that an FD $X \rightarrow Y$ with attribute subsets X, Y is satisfied by a relation whenever two records with matching values on all the attributes in X have also matching values on all the attributes in Y. On the other hand, the entire relation r does exhibit the MVD σ_1 : *product* $\twoheadrightarrow$ *location*. Indeed, an MVD $X \twoheadrightarrow Y$ with attribute subsets $X, Y \subseteq R$ is satisfied by a relation whenever for every two records with matching values on all the attributes in X there is a record that has matching values with the first record on all the attributes in $X \cup Y$ and matching values with the second record on all the attributes in $X \cup (R - Y)$. In other words, r satisfies $X \twoheadrightarrow Y$ if and only if r is the join of its projections $r(XY)$ and $r(X(R - Y))$.

Following Vincent's notion of data redundancy [15], σ_2 causes all occurrences of supplier *The little link* to be redundant: every change in value for one of these occurrences causes a violation of σ_2. These redundant values only occur in records of *high* confidence, since σ_2 only applies to those records. However, every value occurrence in columns *location*, *supplier*, and *date* is also redundant. These redundancies are caused by the MVD σ_1 which applies to all records. This illustrates that MVDs are a major source of data redundancy that cannot be captured by FDs, but also that the uncertainty in data causes different degrees of data redundancy. The latter point is further highlighted in Fig. 1. In applications with records of high or medium confidence, we only need the MVD σ_2 for normalization, because the FD σ_1 does not apply. The 4NF decomposition $\mathbf{D}_1$ illustrates this case in Fig. 1. In applications with records of high confidence only, we require both the FD σ_1 and the MVD σ_2 for normalization. Here, $\mathbf{D}_2$ and $\mathbf{D}_3$ are lossless decompositions into 4NF, respectively. The scenario also illustrates that redundancy in records with higher p-degrees require a higher normalization effort than redundancy in records with lower p-degrees, for the simple reason that more dependencies apply to fewer records. Arguably, records with lower p-degree are more susceptible to updates. In this case, the normalization effort is smaller as fewer dependencies cause redundancy in records with lower p-degrees.

3   Related Work

While there is a plethora of interest in uncertain data, research on query languages and probabilistic approaches dominate. Instead, we are interested in schema design using a possibilistic approach. Hence, our discussion of related work centers on schema design.

The article is a natural continuation of our work on schema design [12], based on pFDs introduced in [11]. As illustrated before, pFDs cannot capture many instances of redundancy in uncertain data for which pMVDs are responsible. This is particularly relevant in modern applications where data is joined from various sources of information. Our article is the first to introduce pMVDs, and therefore also the first with a 4NF proposal targeted at uncertain data. As we capture the combined class of pFDs and pMVDs, our results subsume previous findings on schema design based on pFDs alone [12].

Our framework subsumes Fagin's well-known MVDs and 4NF from relational databases as the special case with only one p-degree [3]. This includes results on the implication problem for the combined class of FDs and MVDs [4,8], as well as the semantic justification of 4NF by the absence of data redundancy caused by MVDs [15].

Few other papers address schema design for uncertain data [1,14]. In [14] an "FD theory for data models whose basic construct for uncertainty is *alternatives*" is developed. That work is thus fundamentally different from the current approach. In particular, p-relations cannot always be expressed by the uncertain relations of [14]. For example, the simple two-tuple p-relation $\{(t_1, \alpha_1), (t_2, \alpha_2)\}$ with the possible worlds $w_1 = \{t_1\} \subseteq \{t_1, t_2\} = w_2$ cannot be expressed: The world w_1 says there is at most one record in which t_1 is an alternative, while the world w_2 says that there must be at least two records, namely one record in which t_1 is an alternative and one record in which t_2 is an alternative. Indeed, t_1 and t_2 cannot be alternatives of the same record since possible worlds in [14] result from choosing one alternative from each record. The article [1] models fuzziness in an Entity-Relationship model, so addresses schema design by a conceptual approach and not by a logical approach as we do. [1] derives the uncertainty of their fuzzy FDs from fuzzy similarity relations between attribute values, as proposed in [13]. That means that classical normalization is applied to data value redundancy with weaker notions of value equality, but always to the same set of records and the same set of FDs. Instead, the certainty of pFDs in our approach is derived from the largest possible world of records to which they apply. That means classical normalization is still applied to data value redundancy based on value equality, but optimized in terms of the number of FDs that apply to a possible world. Both approaches are therefore incomparable, even if only FDs are considered.

4 Possibilistic Relations

We summarize our model of uncertain data, introduced in [11] and further used in [12].

A relation schema, usually denoted by R, is a finite non-empty set of *attributes*. Each attribute $A \in R$ has a *domain* $dom(A)$ of values. A *tuple* t over R is an element of the Cartesian product $\prod_{A \in R} dom(A)$ of the attributes' domains. For $X \subseteq R$ we denote by $t(X)$ the *projection* of t on X. A *relation* over R is a finite set r of tuples over R. As a running example we use the relation schema SUPPLY with attributes *Product, Location, Supplier,* and *Date,* as introduced before.

We define possibilistic relations as relations where each tuple is associated with some confidence. The confidence of a tuple expresses up to which degree of possibility a tuple occurs in a relation. Formally, we model the confidence as a *scale of possibility*, that is, a finite, strictly linear order $\mathcal{S} = (S, <)$ with

$k + 1$ elements where k is some positive integer, which we denote by $\alpha_1 > \cdots > \alpha_k > \alpha_{k+1}$, and whose elements $\alpha_i \in S$ we call *possibility degrees* (p-degrees). The top p-degree α_1 is reserved for tuples that are 'fully possible' to occur in a relation, while the bottom p-degree α_{k+1} is reserved for tuples that are 'not possible at all', that is 'impossible', to occur in a relation currently. The use of the bottom p-degree α_{k+1} in our model is the counterpart of the classical closed world assumption. Humans like to use simple scales in everyday life, for instance to communicate, compare, or rank. Simple usually means to classify items qualitatively, rather than quantitatively by putting a precise value on it. Note that classical relations use a scale with two elements, that is, where $k = 1$.

In our running example, source one says which products are supplied on which days from which location, while sources two and three say which suppliers are found at these locations. While both sources confirm "The little link" as supplier at "Singapore" and "Malaysia", only source two mentions supplier "Eminence" at "Singapore" and only source three mentions supplier "Eminence" at "Malaysia". Accordingly, (The little link, Singapore) and (The little link, Malaysia) have p-degree α_1, while (Eminence, Singapore) and (Eminence, Malaysia) only have p-degree α_2. This is a natural technique to assign p-degrees to records based on the number k of sources in which they appear: they obtain the highest p-degree α_1 when they appear in all sources, the second highest p-degree α_2 when they appear in all but one source, and so on until records that appear in only one source obtain the lowest p-degree α_k and the bottom p-degree α_{k+1} is reserved for records that do not appear in any source.

Formally, a *possibilistic relation schema* (p-schema) (R, S) consists of a relation schema R and a possibility scale S. A *possibilistic relation* (p-relation) over (R, S) consists of a relation r over R, together with a function $Poss_r$ that maps each tuple $t \in r$ to a p-degree $Poss_r(t)$ in the possibility scale S. Sometimes, we simply refer to a p-relation $(r, Poss_r)$ by r, assuming that $Poss_r$ has been fixed. For example, Table 1

Table 1. Possibilistic relation $(r, Poss_r)$

Product	Location	Supplier	Date	$Poss_r$
Cufflinks	Singapore	The little link	04/11/2018	α_1
Cufflinks	Malaysia	The little link	21/11/2018	α_1
Cufflinks	Singapore	The little link	21/11/2018	α_1
Cufflinks	Malaysia	The little link	04/11/2018	α_1
Cufflinks	Singapore	Eminence	04/11/2018	α_2
Cufflinks	Malaysia	Eminence	21/11/2018	α_2
Cufflinks	Singapore	Eminence	21/11/2018	α_2
Cufflinks	Malaysia	Eminence	04/11/2018	α_2

shows our p-relation $(r, Poss_r)$ over (SUPPLY, $S = \{\alpha_1, \alpha_2, \alpha_3\}$).

P-relations enjoy a well-founded semantics in terms of possible worlds. In fact, a p-relation gives rise to a possibility distribution over possible worlds of relations. For $i = 1, \ldots, k$ let r_i denote the relation that consists of all tuples in r that have a p-degree of at least α_i, that is, $r_i = \{t \in r \mid Poss_r(t) \geq \alpha_i\}$. The linear order of the p-degrees results in a linear order of possible worlds of relations. Indeed, we have $r_1 \subseteq r_2 \subseteq \cdots \subseteq r_k$. The possibility distribution π_r for this linear chain of possible worlds is defined by $\pi_r(r_i) = \alpha_i$. Note that r_{k+1} is not considered to be a possible world, since its possibility $\pi(r_{k+1}) = \alpha_{k+1}$

means 'not possible at all'. Vice versa, the possibility $Poss_r(t)$ of a tuple $t \in r$ is the possibility of the smallest possible world in which t occurs, that is, the maximum possibility $\max\{\alpha_i \mid t \in r_i\}$ of a world to which t belongs. If $t \notin r_k$, then $Poss_r(t) = \alpha_{k+1}$. The top p-degree α_1 takes on a distinguished role: every tuple that is 'fully possible' occurs in every possible world - and is thus - 'fully certain'. This confirms our intuition that p-relations subsume relations (of fully certain tuples) as a special case.

4.1 Functional and Multivalued Dependencies

Recall that an FD $X \rightarrow Y$ is satisfied by a relation r whenever every pair of tuples in r that have matching values on all the attributes in X have also matching values on all the attributes in Y [3]. For example, the FD $Location \rightarrow Supplier$ is not satisfied by r_2 but by r_1. An MVD $X \twoheadrightarrow Y$ is satisfied by a relation r over relation schema R whenever for every pair of tuples in r that have matching values on all the attributes in X there is some tuple in r that has matching values on all the attributes in XY with the first tuple and matching values on all the attributes in $X(R - Y)$ with the second tuple [3]. For example, the MVD $Product \twoheadrightarrow Location$ is satisfies by relations r_1 and r_2.

For a given FD or MVD σ, the marginal certainty with which a σ holds in a p-relation corresponds to the p-degree of the smallest possible world in which σ is violated. Therefore, dually to a scale $\mathcal{S}$ of p-degrees for tuples we use a scale $\mathcal{S}^T$ of certainty degrees (c-degrees) for FDs and MVDs. We commonly use subscripted versions of the Greek letter β to denote c-degrees associated with FDs and MVDs. Formally, the duality between p-degrees in $\mathcal{S}$ and the c-degrees in $\mathcal{S}^T$ can be defined by the mapping $\alpha_i \mapsto \beta_{k+2-i}$, for $i = 1, \ldots, k + 1$. Assuming that the world r_{k+1} cannot satisfy any FD or MVD, the marginal certainty $C_{(r,Poss_r)}(\sigma)$ with which the FD or MVD σ holds on the p-relation $(r, Poss_r)$ is the c-degree β_{k+2-i} that corresponds to the smallest world r_i in which σ is violated, that is,

$$C_{(r,Poss_r)}(\sigma) = \min\{\beta_{k+2-i} \mid \not\models_{r_i} \sigma\}.$$

In particular, if r_k satisfies σ, then $C_{(r,Poss_r)}(\sigma) = \beta_1$. We can now define the syntax and semantics of pFDs and pMVDs.

Definition 1. *A possibilistic FD (pFD) over a p-schema $(R, \mathcal{S})$ is an expression $(X \rightarrow Y, \beta)$ where $X, Y \subseteq R$ and $\beta \in \mathcal{S}^T$. A possibilistic MVD (pMVD) over a p-schema $(R, \mathcal{S})$ is an expression $(X \twoheadrightarrow Y, \beta)$ where $X, Y \subseteq R$ and $\beta \in \mathcal{S}^T$. A p-relation $(r, Poss_r)$ over $(R, \mathcal{S})$ satisfies the pFD or pMVD (σ, β) if and only if $C_{(r,Poss_r)}(\sigma) \geq \beta$.*

The following comment illustrates a difference between FDs and MVDs that is important for Definition 1 of their possibilistic variants. FDs are downwards-closed: whenever a relation r satisfies an FD, then every sub-relation $s \subseteq r$ also satisfies the FD. This is not the case for MVDs: For example, the relation r_1 satisfies the MVD $Product \twoheadrightarrow Supplier$, while every sub-relation with either 2 or

3 records violates this MVD. The downward-closure property of FDs provides a very natural definition of its possibilistic counterpart: If the FD is satisfied by some world, then it is satisfied by every smaller world as well. This means that every FD that holds with c-degree β also holds with every smaller c-degree β'. However, even though MVDs are not downward-closed, they still permit the same natural definition for their possibilistic counterpart: whenever there are two tuples $t, t' \in r$ with p-degrees α_i and α_j, respectively, then an MVD that is satisfied by $r_{\max\{i,j\}}$ also generates a tuple $t'' \in r_{\max\{i,j\}}$, that is, t'' has minimum p-degree $\min\{\alpha_i, \alpha_j\}$. In particular, if $t, t' \in r_i$, then $t'' \in r_i$, too. In other words, if an MVD is satisfied by some world, then it is also satisfied by every smaller world. This means that every MVD that holds with c-degree β also holds with every smaller c-degree β'. For example, the world r_2 satisfies the MVD $Product \twoheadrightarrow Supplier$, and also the world r_1. In summary, our definition of the marginal certainty applies to both FDs and MVDs, but is motivated by different properties: namely by the downward-closure property of FDs and the tuple-generating property of MVDs.

5   Possibilistic Design Theory

Relational normalization for 4NF [3] is founded on the theory of functional and multivalued dependencies, in particular the axiomatic and algorithmic solutions to their implication problem [3,4]. Consequently, we now establish a design theory for pFDs and pMVDs as a foundation for a possibilistic 4NF normal form, its semantic justification, and normalization of p-schemata. First, we establish a strong link between the implication problem of pFDs and pMVDs and the implication problem of FDs and MVDs, which is a consequence of the downward closure property of FDs and the tuple-generating property of MVDs. Based on this link, we then establish axiomatic and algorithmic solutions to the implication problem of pFDs and pMVDs. Our design theory for pFDs and pMVDs subsumes the design theory for classical FDs and MVDs as the special case where $k = 1$, and also subsumes the design theory for pFDs as the special case with no pMVDs.

5.1 β-Cuts

We establish a precise correspondence between instances of the implication problem for pFDs and pMVDs and instances of the implication problem for relational FDs and MVDs. Let $\Sigma \cup \{\varphi\}$ denote a set of pFDs and pMVDs over a p-schema $(R, \mathcal{S})$. We say that Σ *implies* φ, denoted by $\Sigma \models \varphi$, if every p-relation $(r, Poss_r)$ over $(R, \mathcal{S})$ that satisfies every pFD and pMVD in Σ also satisfies φ.

Example 1. Let Σ consist of the pMVD $(Product \twoheadrightarrow Location, \beta_1)$ but also the pFD $(Location \rightarrow Supplier, \beta_2)$ over $(\text{SUPPLY}, \{\alpha_1, \alpha_2, \alpha_3\})$. Further, let φ denote the pFD $(Product \rightarrow Supplier, \beta_1)$. Then Σ does not imply φ as the following p-relation witnesses.

Product	Location	Supplier	Date	P-degree
Cufflinks	Singapore	The little link	04/11/2018	α_1
Cufflinks	Singapore	Eminence	04/11/2018	α_2

For a set Σ of pFDs and pMVDs on some p-schema $(R, \mathcal{S})$ and c-degree $\beta \in \mathcal{S}^T$ where $\beta > \beta_{k+1}$, let

$$\Sigma_\beta = \{X \to Y \mid (X \to Y, \beta') \in \Sigma \text{ and } \beta' \geq \beta\}$$

be the β-*cut* of Σ. The major strength of our framework is engraved in the following result. It says that a pFD or pMVD (σ, β) with c-degree β is implied by a set Σ of pFDs and pMVDs if and only if the FD or MVD σ is implied by the β-cut Σ_β of Σ.

Theorem 1. *Let $\Sigma \cup \{(\sigma, \beta)\}$ be a set of pFDs and pMVDs over a p-schema $(R, \mathcal{S})$ where $\beta > \beta_{k+1}$. Then $\Sigma \models (\sigma, \beta)$ if and only if $\Sigma_\beta \models \sigma$.*

The following example illustrates Theorem 1.

Example 2. Let Σ and φ be as in Example 1, in particular Σ does not imply φ. Theorem 1 reduces the implication problem of pFDs and pMVDs to that of FDs and MVDs, namely Σ_{β_1} does not imply *Product* $\to$ *Supplier*. Indeed, the possible world r_2 of the p-relation from Example 1

Product	Location	Supplier	Date
Cufflinks	Singapore	The little link	04/11/2018
Cufflinks	Singapore	Eminence	04/11/2018

satisfies the MVD *Product* $\twoheadrightarrow$ *Location* that forms Σ_{β_1}, and violates the FD *Product* $\to$ *Supplier*.

5.2   Axiomatic Characterization

The *semantic closure* $\Sigma^* = \{\varphi \mid \Sigma \models \varphi\}$ contains all pFDs and pMVDs implied by Σ. We compute Σ^* by applying *inference rules* of the form $\frac{\text{premise}}{\text{conclusion}}$ condition, where rules without premise are *axioms*. For a set $\mathfrak{R}$ of inference rules let $\Sigma \vdash_{\mathfrak{R}} \varphi$ denote that there is an *inference* of φ from Σ by $\mathfrak{R}$. That is, there is some sequence $\sigma_1, \ldots, \sigma_n$ such that $\sigma_n = \varphi$ and every σ_i is in Σ or the result of applying a rule in $\mathfrak{R}$ to some premises in $\{\sigma_1, \ldots, \sigma_{i-1}\}$. Let $\Sigma^+_{\mathfrak{R}} = \{\varphi \mid \Sigma \vdash_{\mathfrak{R}} \varphi\}$ denote the *syntactic closure* of Σ under inferences by $\mathfrak{R}$. $\mathfrak{R}$ is *sound* (*complete*) if for every p-schema $(R, \mathcal{S})$ and for every set Σ we have $\Sigma^+_{\mathfrak{R}} \subseteq \Sigma^*$ ($\Sigma^* \subseteq \Sigma^+_{\mathfrak{R}}$). The (finite) set $\mathfrak{R}$ is a (finite) *axiomatization* if $\mathfrak{R}$ is both sound and complete.

Table 2. Axiomatization $\mathfrak{P}$ of pFDs and pMVDs

$$\frac{}{(XY \to X, \beta)}$$
(FD reflexivity, $\mathcal{R}$)

$$\frac{(X \to Y, \beta)}{(X \to XY, \beta)}$$
(FD extension, $\mathcal{E}$)

$$\frac{(X \to Y, \beta) \quad (Y \to Z, \beta)}{(X \to Z, \beta)}$$
(FD transitivity, $\mathcal{T}$)

$$\frac{}{(\emptyset \twoheadrightarrow R, \beta)}$$
(MVD complement, $\mathcal{C}$)

$$\frac{(X \twoheadrightarrow Y, \beta) \quad (X \twoheadrightarrow Z, \beta)}{(X \to YZ, \beta)}$$
(MVD union, $\mathcal{U}$)

$$\frac{(X \twoheadrightarrow Y, \beta) \quad (Y \twoheadrightarrow Z, \beta)}{(X \twoheadrightarrow Z - Y, \beta)}$$
(MVD pseudo-transitivity, $\mathcal{P}_M$)

$$\frac{}{(\sigma, \beta_{k+1})}$$
(bottom rule, $\mathcal{B}$)

$$\frac{(X \to Y, \beta)}{(X \twoheadrightarrow Y, \beta)}$$
(FD-MVD implication, $\mathcal{I}$)

$$\frac{(X \twoheadrightarrow Y, \beta) \quad (Y \to Z, \beta)}{(X \to Z - Y, \beta)}$$
(FD-MVD pseudo-transitivity, $\mathcal{P}_{FM}$)

$$\frac{(\sigma, \beta)}{(\sigma, \beta')} \beta \geq \beta'$$
(weakening, $\mathcal{W}$)

Table 2 shows the axiomatization $\mathfrak{P}$ of pFDs and pMVDs. For a rule in $\mathcal{R} \in \mathfrak{P} - \{\mathcal{B}, \mathcal{W}\}$ let $\mathcal{R}'$ denote the rule that is obtained from $\mathcal{R}$ by omitting the c-degree β and the parenthesis, and let $\mathfrak{P}' = \{\mathcal{R}' \mid \mathcal{R} \in \mathfrak{P} - \{\mathcal{B}, \mathcal{W}\}\}$. It is known that $\mathfrak{P}'$ forms an axiomatization for FDs and MVDs [5]. In fact, $\mathfrak{P}$ subsumes the axiomatization for FDs and MVDs as the special case where the scale $\mathcal{S}^T$ consists of just two c-degrees. In the rules all attribute sets X, Y, Z are subsets of the given relation schema R, the c-degrees β and β' belong to the given certainty scale $\mathcal{S}^T$, and β_{k+1} denotes the bottom c-degree. For a completeness proof of $\mathfrak{P}$ we could use the classical strategy to write down a two-tuple p-relation that violates a given pFD or pMVD (σ, β) that cannot be inferred from a given pFD and pMVD set Σ using $\mathfrak{P}$. Instead, we establish the completeness of $\mathfrak{P}$ directly by showing that a given pFD or pMVD (σ, β) that is implied by Σ can be also be inferred from Σ using the rules in $\mathfrak{P}$. This direct proof shows how the bottom axiom $\mathcal{B}$ and weakening rule $\mathcal{W}$ can be applied to reduce the inference of (σ, β) from Σ to an inference of σ from Σ_β. However, the completeness of $\mathfrak{P}'$ guarantees immediately that σ can be inferred from Σ_β, due to Theorem 1 and the assumption that (σ, β) is implied by Σ.

Theorem 2. $\mathfrak{P}$ *forms a finite axiomatization for the implication of pFDs and pMVDs.*

Example 3. Let $\Sigma = \{(Product \twoheadrightarrow Location, \beta_1), (Location \to Supplier, \beta_2)\}$ and $\varphi = (Product \to Supplier, \beta_2)$ over SUPPLY, and $\varphi' = (Product \to Supplier, \beta_1)$. We show an inference of φ from Σ by $\mathfrak{P}$.

$$\frac{\dfrac{(Product \twoheadrightarrow Location, \beta_1)}{\mathcal{W}: (Product \twoheadrightarrow Location, \beta_2)} \quad (Location \to Supplier, \beta_2)}{\mathcal{P}_{FM}: \qquad\qquad (Product \to Supplier, \beta_2)}$$

Of course, φ' cannot be inferred from Σ by $\mathfrak{P}$, as Example 1 shows.

5.3   Algorithmic Characterization

In practice it is often unnecessary to compute the closure Σ^* from a given set Σ. Instead, rather frequently occurs the problem of deciding whether a given Σ implies a given φ.

PROBLEM: IMPLICATION	
INPUT:	Relation schema R,
	Scale $\mathcal{S}$ with $k+1$ possibility degrees,
	Set $\Sigma \cup \{\varphi\}$ of pFDs and pMVDs over $(R, \mathcal{S})$
OUTPUT:	Yes, if $\Sigma \models \varphi$, and No, otherwise

One may compute Σ^* and check if $\varphi \in \Sigma^*$, but this is inefficient and does not make effective use of the additional input φ. For pFDs and pMVDs, we can exploit Theorem 1 to derive an almost linear time algorithm that decides the implication problem. Given a pFD and pMVD set $\Sigma \cup \{(\sigma, \beta)\}$ we return *true* if $\beta = \beta_{k+1}$ (since this is the trivial case where β_{k+1} is the bottom c-degree), otherwise it is sufficient to check if $\Sigma_\beta \models \sigma$. The latter test can be done in almost linear time [4].

Theorem 3. *The implication problem $\Sigma \models \varphi$ of pFDs and pMVDs can be decided in time $\mathcal{O}(\|\Sigma\| \cdot \log \|\Sigma\|)$.*

We illustrate the algorithm on our running example.

Example 4. Let $\Sigma = \{(Product \twoheadrightarrow Location, \beta_1), (Location \rightarrow Supplier, \beta_2)\}$ and $\varphi = (Product \rightarrow Supplier, \beta_2)$ over SUPPLY, and $\varphi' = (Product \rightarrow Supplier, \beta_1)$. Indeed, *Product $\rightarrow$ Supplier* is not implied by Σ_{β_1} while *Product $\rightarrow$ Supplier* is implied by Σ_{β_2}. That is, Σ implies φ but Σ does not imply φ'.

6   Possibilistic Fourth Normal Form Design

In p-relations different tuples may have different p-degrees, and different pFDs and pMVDs may apply to them. Hence, data value redundancy is caused by pFDs or pMVDs with different c-degrees and occurs in tuples of different p-degrees. Indeed, the smaller the p-degree for which data value redundancy is to be eliminated, the smaller the number of pFDs and pMVDs that can cause this redundancy. Consequently, the smaller the normalization effort will be, too. We will now exploit this observation to tailor relational schema design for applications with different requirements for the uncertainty of their data. For this purpose, we will introduce notions of data value redundancy that target the p-degree of tuples in which they occur. This results in a family of semantic normal forms by which data value redundancy of varying p-degrees are eliminated. We characterize each of the semantic normal forms by a corresponding syntactic normal form, and establish strong correspondences with Fagin's 4NF in relational databases [3, 15].

6.1   Redundancy-Free Normal Form

Motivated by our running example we propose different degrees of data value redundancy that are tailored towards the different p-degrees of tuples in a p-relation. For this, we exploit the classical proposal by Vincent [15]. Let R denote a relation schema, A an attribute of R, t a tuple over R, and Σ a set of constraints over R. A *replacement* of $t(A)$ is a tuple $\bar{t}$ over R such that: (i) for all $\bar{A} \in R-\{A\}$ we have $\bar{t}(\bar{A}) = t(\bar{A})$, and (ii) $\bar{t}(A) \neq t(A)$. For a relation r over R that satisfies Σ and $t \in r$, the data value occurrence $t(A)$ in r is *redundant* for Σ if and only if for every replacement $\bar{t}$ of $t(A)$, $\bar{r} := (r - \{t\}) \cup \{\bar{t}\}$ violates some constraint in Σ. A relation schema R is in *Redundancy-Free normal form* (RFNF) for a set Σ of constraints if and only if there are no relation r over R that satisfies Σ, tuple $t \in r$, and attribute $A \in R$ such that the data value occurrence $t(A)$ is redundant for Σ [15].

Definition 2. *Let $(R, \mathcal{S})$ denote a p-schema, Σ a set of pFDs and pMVDs over $(R, \mathcal{S})$, $A \in R$ an attribute, $(r, Poss_r)$ a p-relation over $(R, \mathcal{S})$ that satisfies Σ, and t a tuple in r_i. The data value occurrence $t(A)$ is α_i-redundant if and only if $t(A)$ is redundant for $\Sigma_{\alpha_i} = \{X \to Y \mid (X \to Y, \beta) \in \Sigma \text{ and } \beta \geq \beta_{k+1-i}\}$.*

This definition meets the intuition of data value redundancy in our running example. For instance, each occurrence of *The little link* is α_1-redundant, and each occurrences of *Eminence* is α_2-redundant. Importantly, α_i-redundant data value occurrences can only be caused by pFDs or pMVDs (σ, β) that apply to the world of the occurrence, that is, where $\beta \geq \beta_{k+1-i}$. Hence, α_1-redundancy can be caused by pFDs or pMVDs with any c-degree $\beta_1, \dots, \beta_k$, while α_k-redundancy can only be caused by pFDs or pMVDs with c-degree β_1. This motivates the following definition.

Definition 3. *A p-schema $(R, \mathcal{S})$ is in α_i-Redundancy-Free Normal Form (α_i-RFNF) for a set Σ of pFDs and pMVDs over $(R, \mathcal{S})$ if and only if there do not exist a p-relation $(r, Poss_r)$ over $(R, \mathcal{S})$ that satisfies Σ, an attribute $A \in R$, and a tuple $t \in r_i$ such that $t(A)$ is α_i-redundant.*

For example, (SUPPLY, $\mathcal{S}$) is neither in α_1-RFNF nor in α_2-RFNF for Σ. The negative results follow directly from the redundant occurrences in Fig. 1. Indeed, α_i-RFNF characterizes p-schemata that permit only p-relations whose possible world r_i is free from data redundancy caused by the classical FDs and MVDs that apply to it.

Theorem 4. *$(R, \mathcal{S})$ is in α_i-RFNF for Σ if and only if R is in RFNF for Σ_{α_i}.*

6.2   Possibilistic Fourth Normal Form

Our goal is now to characterize α-RFNF, which is a semantic normal form, purely syntactically. Therefore, we propose qualitative variants of the classical 4NF condition [3]. Recall that a relation schema R is in Fourth normal form

(4NF) for a set Σ of FDs and MVDs over R if and only if for all $X \twoheadrightarrow Y \in \Sigma_{\mathfrak{P}'}^+$ where $Y \not\subseteq X$ and $Y \neq R$, we have $X \to R \in \Sigma_{\mathfrak{P}'}^+$. Here, $\Sigma_{\mathfrak{P}'}^+$ denotes the syntactic closure of Σ with respect to the axiomatization $\mathfrak{P}'$ of FDs and MVDs [5]. While α-RFNF is defined semantically using the p-degree α of a possible world, qualitative variants of 4NF are defined syntactically using the c-degrees of the given pFDs and pMVDs.

Definition 4. *A p-schema $(R, \mathcal{S})$ is in β-4NF for a set Σ of pFDs and pMVDs over $(R, \mathcal{S})$ if and only if for every pMVD $(X \twoheadrightarrow Y, \beta) \in \Sigma_{\mathfrak{P}}^+$ where $Y \not\subseteq X$ and $Y \neq R$, we have $(X \to R, \beta) \in \Sigma_{\mathfrak{P}}^+$.*

Recall that sets Σ and Θ are *covers* of one another if $\Sigma^* = \Theta^*$ holds. The property of being in β-4NF for Σ is independent of the representation of Σ. That is, for every cover Σ' of Σ, $(R, \mathcal{S})$ is in β-4NF for Σ if and only if $(R, \mathcal{S})$ is in β-4NF for Σ'. The β-4NF condition for a pFD and pMVD set Σ can be characterized by the 4NF condition for the FD and MVD set Σ_β.

Theorem 5. *$(R, \mathcal{S})$ is in β-4NF for Σ if and only if R is in 4NF for Σ_β.*

We can now characterize the semantic α_i-RFNF by the syntactic β_{k+1-i}-4NF.

Theorem 6. *For all $i = 1, \ldots, k$, $(R, \mathcal{S})$ with $|\mathcal{S}| = k + 1$ is in α_i-RFNF with respect to Σ if and only if $(R, \mathcal{S})$ is in β_{k+1-i}-4NF with respect to Σ.*

Figure 2 shows the correspondences between the syntactic and semantic normal forms, and their relationships to classical normal forms.

Due to the cover-insensitivity of the β-4NF condition, one may wonder about the efficiency of checking whether a given p-schema $(R, \mathcal{S})$ is in β-4NF with respect to a set Σ. Indeed, as in the classical case it suffices to check some pFDs and pMVDs in Σ instead of checking all pMVDs in $\Sigma_{\mathfrak{P}}^+$.

$$
\begin{array}{cc}
\Sigma_{\beta_2}\text{-}BCNF & \Sigma_{\beta_1}\text{-}BCNF \\
\updownarrow & \updownarrow \\
\beta_2\text{-}BCNF & \beta_1\text{-}BCNF \\
\updownarrow & \updownarrow \\
\alpha_1\text{-}RFNF & \alpha_2\text{-}RFNF \\
\updownarrow & \updownarrow \\
\Sigma_{\alpha_1}\text{-}RFNF & \Sigma_{\alpha_2}\text{-}RFNF
\end{array}
$$

Fig. 2. Normal forms

Theorem 7. *A p-schema $(R, \mathcal{S})$ is in β-4NF for a set Σ of pFDs and pMVDs over $(R, \mathcal{S})$ if and only if for every pFD $(X \to Y, \beta') \in \Sigma$ where $\beta' \geq \beta$ and $Y \not\subseteq X$ and for every pMVD $(X \twoheadrightarrow Y, \beta') \in \Sigma$ where $\beta' \geq \beta$ and $Y \not\subseteq X$ and $Y \neq R$, we have $(X \to R, \beta) \in \Sigma_{\mathfrak{P}}^+$.*

Example 5. Let $(\text{SUPPLY}, \mathcal{S})$ and Σ. Using Theorem 7 we can observe that the schema is neither in β_1- nor β_2-4NF for Σ. By Theorem 6 we conclude that the schema is neither in α_2- nor α_1-RFNF for Σ. By Theorem 5 it follows that SUPPLY is neither in 4NF for Σ_{β_1}, nor Σ_{β_2}. Finally, by Theorem 4, it follows that SUPPLY is neither in RFNF for Σ_{α_2} or Σ_{α_1}.

7 Qualitative Normalization

We now establish algorithmic means to design relational
database schemata for applications with uncertain data.
For that purpose, we normal-
ize a given p-schema $(R, \mathcal{S})$ for
the given set Σ of pFDs and
pMVDs. Our strategy is to fix
some c-degree $\beta \in \mathcal{S}^T$ that
determines which possible world
we normalize for which FDs and
MVDs. For each choice of a c-

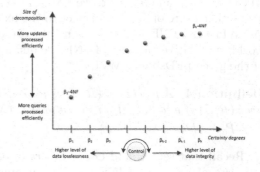

Fig. 3. C-degrees to control design tradeoffs

degree, we pursue 4NF normalizations to obtain lossless decompositions free
from any data value redundancy but potentially not dependency-preserving (that
is, some FDs or MVDs may require validation on the join of some relations).
Applying our strategy to different c-degrees provides organizations with a variety of normalized database schemata, each targeted at different levels of data
integrity, data losslessness, and the efficiency of different updates and queries.
In this sense, our c-degrees are parameters that allow stakeholders to control
trade-offs between data integrity and data losslessness, as well as between query
efficiency and update efficiency, as illustrated in Fig. 3.

7.1 4NF Decomposition

We recall basic terminology from relational databases. A *decomposition* of relation schema R is a set $\mathcal{D} = \{R_1, \ldots, R_n\}$ of relation schemata such that
$R_1 \cup \cdots \cup R_n = R$. For $R_j \subseteq R$ and an FD and MVD set Σ over R,
$\Sigma[R_j] = \{X \rightarrow Y \mid X \rightarrow Y \in \Sigma_{\mathfrak{A}}^+ \text{ and } X, Y \subseteq R_j\}$ denotes the *projection*
of Σ onto R_j. A decomposition $\mathcal{D}$ of a relation schema R with FD and MVD
set Σ is *lossless* if and only if every relation r over R that satisfies Σ is the
join of its projections on the elements of $\mathcal{D}$, that is, $r = \bowtie_{R_j \in \mathcal{D}} r[R_j]$. Here,
$r[R_j] = \{t(R_j) \mid t \in r\}$. A *4NF* decomposition of a relation schema R with FD
and MVD set Σ is a decomposition $\mathcal{D}$ of R where every $R_j \in \mathcal{D}$ is in 4NF for
$\Sigma[R_j]$. Theorem 5 motivates the following definition of a 4NF decomposition
that is lossless for a given p-degree.

Definition 5. *Given a p-schema* $(R, \{\alpha_1, \ldots, \alpha_{k+1}\})$, *an* α_{k+1-i}-*lossless 4NF
decomposition for the pFD and pMVD set* Σ *is a lossless 4NF decomposition of
R for Σ_{β_i}.*

Instrumental to Definition 5 is the following decomposition theorem, which
follows directly from Theorem 1. It covers the classical decomposition theorem
[3] as the special case of having just one possible world.

Theorem 8. *Let $(X \to Y, \beta_i)$ be a pFD and $(X \twoheadrightarrow Y, \beta_i)$ be a pMVD with $1 \leq i < k + 1$ that satisfies the p-relation $(r, Poss_r)$ over the p-schema $(R, \mathcal{S})$. Then $r_{k+1-i} = r_{k+1-i}[XY] \bowtie r_{k+1-i}[X(R - Y)]$, that is, the possible world r_{k+1-i} of r is the lossless join of its projections on XY and $X(R - Y)$.*

Therefore, an α_{k+1-i}-lossless 4NF decomposition for a pFD and pMVD set Σ can simply be obtained by performing a classical lossless 4NF decomposition for the β_i-cut Σ_{β_i} of Σ. This suggests a simple lossless 4NF decomposition strategy.

PROBLEM: Qualitative 4NF Decomposition	
INPUT:	Possibilistic Relation Schema $(R, \mathcal{S})$
	Set Σ of pFDs and pMVDs over $(R, \mathcal{S})$
	Certainty degree $\beta_i \in \mathcal{S}^T - \{\beta_{k+1}\}$
OUTPUT:	α_{k+1-i}-lossless 4NF decomposition of $(R, \mathcal{S})$ with respect to Σ
METHOD:	Perform a lossless 4NF decomposition of R with respect to Σ_{β_i}

We illustrate the decomposition on our running example.

Example 6. Let $(\text{SUPPLY}, \mathcal{S})$ and Σ be as in Example 1. As $(\text{SUPPLY}, \mathcal{S})$ is not in β_1-4NF for Σ, we perform an α_2-lossless 4NF decomposition for Σ_{β_1}. The result consists of $R_1 = \{Product, Location\}$ and $R_2 = \{Product, Supplier, Date\}$. Note that the MVD in Σ_{β_1} is satisfied by the join of any relation over R_1 with any relation over R_2. That means our 4NF decomposition is β_1-dependency-preserving.

The last example is rather special, since one cannot expect to preserve all FDs and MVDs in the 4NF decomposition process. Recall that a decomposition $\mathcal{D}$ of relation schema R with FD and MVD set Σ is *dependency-preserving* if and only if the join $\bowtie_r$ relation over $_{D \in \mathcal{D}}$ r of every relation r over every $D \in \mathcal{D}$ satisfies Σ. Note here that we consider only relations r over D of the join that satisfy all the FDs and MVDs in the projection of Σ onto D.
This is illustrated with another example.

Example 7. Let $(\text{SUPPLY}, \mathcal{S})$ and Σ be as in Example 1. As $(\text{SUPPLY}, \mathcal{S})$ is not in β_2-4NF for Σ, we perform an α_1-lossless 4NF decomposition for Σ_{β_2}. The result is $R_1 = \{Product, Location\}$ and $R_2 = \{Product, Supplier\}$ with projected FD/MVD set

$$\Sigma_{\beta_2}[R_2] = \{Product \to Supplier\}$$

and $R_3 = \{Product, Date\}$. Note that the FD *Location $\to$ Supplier* is not preserved by this decomposition. Since the pFDs and pMVDs in Σ apply only to world r_1 from Fig. 1, this decomposition may be applied to r_1 to obtain the instance $\mathcal{D}_2$ shown in Fig. 1.

Definition 6. *A β-dependency-preserving decomposition of a p-schema $(R, \mathcal{S})$ for the pFD and pMVD set Σ is a dependency-preserving decomposition of R for Σ_β.*

The α_2-lossless 4NF decomposition from Example 6 is β_1-dependency-preserving, but the α_1-lossless 4NF decomposition from Example 7 is not β_2-dependency-preserving. In practice, lost dependencies can only be validated by joining relations after inserts or modification. For example, to validate the FD *Location* $\rightarrow$ *Supplier* after an update, one would have to join R_1 and R_2 from Example 7. This can be prohibitively expensive. While 3NF synthesis algorithms exist that can transform any relational database schema into one that is dependency-preserving, such normal form is unknown for MVDs.

8   Conclusion and Future Work

We have extended Fagin's 4NF from certain to uncertain data. Our results show how traditional database design can make the most of information about the uncertainty in data. Future work includes extensions to partial [9] data over fixed and undetermined schemata [10], and to referential integrity [6,7].

References

1. Chaudhry, N.A., Moyne, J.R., Rundensteiner, E.A.: An extended database design methodology for uncertain data management. Inf. Sci. **121**(1–2), 83–112 (1999)
2. Dubois, D., Prade, H.: Possibility theory. In: Meyers, R.A. (ed.) Computational Complexity: Theory, Techniques, and Applications, pp. 2240–2252. Springer, New York (2012). https://doi.org/10.1007/978-1-4614-1800-9_139
3. Fagin, R.: Multivalued dependencies and a new normal form for relational databases. ACM Trans. Database Syst. **2**(3), 262–278 (1977)
4. Galil, Z.: An almost linear-time algorithm for computing a dependency basis in a relational database. J. ACM **29**(1), 96–102 (1982)
5. Hartmann, S., Link, S.: On a problem of Fagin concerning multivalued dependencies in relational databases. Theor. Comput. Sci. **353**(1–3), 53–62 (2006)
6. Köhler, H., Link, S.: Inclusion dependencies and their interaction with functional dependencies in SQL. J. Comput. Syst. Sci. **85**, 104–131 (2017)
7. Levene, M., Vincent, M.W.: Justification for inclusion dependency normal form. IEEE Trans. Knowl. Data Eng. **12**(2), 281–291 (2000)
8. Link, S.: Charting the completeness frontier of inference systems for multivalued dependencies. Acta Inf. **45**(7–8), 565–591 (2008)
9. Link, S.: On the implication of multivalued dependencies in partial database relations. Int. J. Found. Comput. Sci. **19**(3), 691–715 (2008)
10. Link, S.: Characterisations of multivalued dependency implication over undetermined universes. J. Comput. Syst. Sci. **78**(4), 1026–1044 (2012)
11. Link, S., Prade, H.: Possibilistic functional dependencies and their relationship to possibility theory. IEEE Trans. Fuzzy Syst. **24**(3), 757–763 (2016)
12. Link, S., Prade, H.: Relational database schema design for uncertain data. In: Mukhopadhyay, S., et al. (eds.) Proceedings of the 25th ACM International Conference on Information and Knowledge Management, CIKM 2016, Indianapolis, IN, USA, 24–28 October 2016, pp. 1211–1220. ACM (2016)
13. Raju, K., Majumdar, A.K.: Fuzzy functional dependencies and lossless join decomposition of fuzzy relational database systems. ACM Trans. Database Syst. **13**(2), 129–166 (1988)

14. Sarma, A.D., Ullman, J.D., Widom, J.: Schema design for uncertain databases. In: Arenas, M., Bertossi, L.E. (eds.) Proceedings of the 3rd Alberto Mendelzon International Workshop on Foundations of Data Management, Arequipa, Peru, 12–15 May 2009, CEUR Workshop Proceedings, vol. 450 (2009)
15. Vincent, M.W.: Semantic foundations of 4NF in relational database design. Acta Inf. **36**(3), 173–213 (1999)
16. Wei, Z., Link, S.: A fourth normal form for possibilistic data. Technical report 533, The University of Auckland, CDMTCS (2019)

Revealing the Conceptual Schemas of RDF Datasets

Subhi Issa[✉], Pierre-Henri Paris, Fayçal Hamdi, and Samira Si-Said Cherfi

CEDRIC - Conservatoire National des Arts et Métiers,
292 Rue Saint Martin, Paris, France
{subhi.issa,faycal.hamdi,samira.cherfi}@cnam.fr,
pierre-henri.paris@upmc.fr

Abstract. RDF-based datasets, thanks to their semantic richness, variety and fine granularity, are increasingly used by both researchers and business communities. However, these datasets suffer a lack of completeness as the content evolves continuously and data contributors are loosely constrained by the vocabularies and schemes related to the data sources. Conceptual schemas have long been recognized as a key mechanism for understanding and dealing with complex real-world systems. In the context of the Web of Data and user-generated content, the conceptual schema is implicit. In fact, each data contributor has an implicit personal model that is not known by the other contributors. Consequently, revealing a meaningful conceptual schema is a challenging task that should take into account the data and the intended usage. In this paper, we propose a completeness-based approach for revealing conceptual schemas of RDF data. We combine quality evaluation and data mining approaches to find a conceptual schema for a dataset, this model meets user expectations regarding data completeness constraints. To achieve that, we propose LOD-CM; a web-based completeness demonstrator for linked datasets.

Keywords: Conceptual modeling · Completeness · Model quality ·
Conceptual schema mining · Schema mining

1 Introduction

Data became a strategic asset in the information-driven world. One of the challenges for companies and researchers is to improve the display and understandability of the data they manage and use.

However, exploiting and using open linked data, even if it is more and more accessible, is not an easy task. Data is often incomplete and lacks metadata. This means that the quality of published data is not as good as we could expect leading to a low added value and a low reliability of the derived conclusions. In [10], the authors believe that existing approaches which describe datasets focus on their statistical aspects rather than on capturing conceptual information.

© Springer Nature Switzerland AG 2019
P. Giorgini and B. Weber (Eds.): CAiSE 2019, LNCS 11483, pp. 312–327, 2019.
https://doi.org/10.1007/978-3-030-21290-2_20

A conceptual schema is an abstraction of a reality that can serve as a vehicle for understanding, communicating, reasoning and adding knowledge about this reality.

In traditional information system development, conceptual modeling is driven by intended usage and needs. In the Web of Data, as in all user-generated content, data is rather use-agnostic [15]. Consequently, data is represented from many individual viewpoints and the overall semantics, although necessary to reasoning of data, is missing. We believe that a conceptual schema that creates an abstract representation upon data would help to overcome the disparity of visions and will reveal the underlying semantics [17]. Let us consider, for instance, that we have a collaboratively built dataset. In this case, the traditional top down vision of a predefined schema is no more applicable. Both data and underlying schema evolve continuously, as data are described by several communities with different views and needs. In this situation, a conceptual schema, defined as an abstract and consensual representation about the reality that is derived from requirements, could not be applied. The challenge is then to find a way to create a suitable conceptual schema having instances as a starting point.

In this paper, we are interested in conceptual modeling of RDF Data (Resource Description Framework) [13]. Our objective is to define an approach for deriving conceptual schemas from existing data. The proposed solution should cope with the essential characteristics of a conceptual schema that are the ability to make an abstraction of relevant aspects from the universe of discourse and the one of meeting user's requirements [19]. The approach we propose in this paper takes into account the two facets; namely the universe of discourse represented by the data sources, and the user's needs represented by the user's decisions during the conceptual schema construction. As the model should express the meaningful state of the considered dataset, we rely on a mining approach leading to taking into consideration the data model from a more frequent combination of properties. The relevancy of properties is handled by integrating a completeness measurement solution that drives the identification of relevant properties [6,9]. To meet user's requirements, we propose to construct the conceptual schema on a *scratch card* manner where the user decides about the parts of the conceptual schema to reveal according to her needs and constraints. The main contributions are:

1. We use a mining approach to infer a model from data, as we consider that no predefined schema exists. The underlying assumption is that the more frequent a schema is, the more representative for the dataset it is.
2. We introduce a novel approach, called *LOD-CM*, for Conceptual Model mining based on quality measures, and, in this paper, on completeness measures as a way to drive the conceptual schema mining process.

The remainder of this paper is organized as follows: Sect. 2 summarizes a related literature on the subject while Sect. 3 details the mining-based approach for RDF data conceptual modeling. This section explains the tight link with the completeness quality criterion. Section 4 presents two use cases of LOD-CM. Finally, Section 5 draws conclusions and future research directions.

2   Related Work

RDF data is described as sets of statements called *triples*. A triple $< s, p, o >$ is a fact where a subject s has a property p, and the property value is the object o. As an example, $< England, capital, London >$ means that London is the capital city of England. Understanding and reasoning about this data requires at least knowledge about its abstract model. Consequently, schema discovery has attracted several researchers originating from several communities. The research directions address objectives such as efficient storage, efficient querying, navigation through data or semantic representation, etc.

Completeness of Linked Data is one of the most important data quality dimension [1]. This dimension is defined as the degree to which all required information is present in a particular dataset [23]. We have to know that a reference schema (or a gold standard) should be available to compare against a given dataset.

In the database community, the question was how to store this kind of data. Levandoski et al. [14] proposed a solution that derives a classical relational scheme from an RDF data source in order to accelerate the processing of queries. In the FlexTable method [22], authors proposed to replace RDF triples by RDF tuples resulting from the unification of a set of triples having the same subject. All these approaches do not target a human readable schema and are more concerned with providing suitable structure for a computer processing of data.

The Semantic Web community is more aware of data semantics through the usage of *ontologies* and *vocabularies*. Several semi-automatic or automatic proposals, mainly based on classification, clustering, and association analysis techniques are proposed. In [21] a statistical approach based on association rules mining allows generating ontologies from RDF data. Other works, such as those presented in [2,12,18], are closer to modeling. Authors propose to derive a data structure using a clustering algorithm. After a manual labeling of clusters representing groups of frequent properties, a schema is derived. These approaches, however, do not consider user's needs and preferences and the derived schema is the result of automatic preprocessing, apart from the labeling task.

In traditional conceptual modeling, models are generally derived from user's requirements. However, with the increasing use of external data sources in information systems, there is a need to apply a bottom-up modeling from instances. This is motivated by the expressiveness and the analysis facilities that conceptual models could provide for such data. Similarly to our bottom-up approach, [16] proposed a conceptual modeling grammar based on the assumption that instances play a major role while human beings try to represent the reality. In [15] authors presented a set of principles for conceptual modeling within structured user-generated content. The authors highlighted the problem of quality in such produced content. They focused on the importance of capturing relevant properties from instances. However, the proposal does not provide an explicit solution for deriving such models. Concerning unstructured data, we can cite [3] where authors addressed the problem of deriving conceptual models based on regular-expression pattern recognition.

Recognizing that conceptual modeling is a powerful tool for data understanding, our proposal addresses the problem of deriving a conceptual schema from RDF data. By exploring instances, our approach integrates a completeness measurement as a quality criterion to ensure the relevancy of the derived schema as data from RDF data sources is the result of a free individual publication effort. The result would be a conceptual schema enriched with completeness values.

3   Conceptual Schemas Derivation

To illustrate our proposed approach, let us consider a user willing to obtain a list of artists with their names and birth places from an RDF data source; To do so, she can write the following SPARQL query[1]:

```
SELECT * WHERE {
    ?actor rdf:type dbo:Actor .
    ?actor foaf:name ?name .
    ?actor dbo:birthPlace ?birthPlace .}
```

Writing such a query is much more difficult in a Linked Open Data (LOD) source context than in a relational database one. In a relational context, the database schema is predefined and the user writing the query is aware of it. In a LOD context, in addition to the fact that the schema does not exist, there is another problem related to data completeness. Actually, the expressed query returns only the list of actors having values for all the properties listed in the query. In our example, only actors having values for both *foaf:name* and *dbo:birthPlace* are included in the result. Knowing that at most 74% of actors have a value for *dbo:birthPlace*, the user should probably appreciate getting this information to add for example OPTIONAL to the second pattern of the query and obtain more results. Besides, she would be aware of the fact that the result is complete to a certain degree (i.e. *dbo:birthPlace* is present in only 74% of actors).

To tackle these two problems, we propose an approach that aims to help "revealing" a conceptual schema from a LOD RDF source. This conceptual schema is driven by the user for both its content and completeness quality values. In the context of the Web of Data, most of the datasets published in the Web are described by models called, in the linked data jargon, vocabularies (or ontologies). However, these models are not used in a prescriptive manner. Consequently, a person who publishes data is not constrained by the underlying ontology leading to sparse descriptions of concepts. For example, the category *Actor* from DBpedia has around 532 properties that are not equally relevant.

From these observations, it is clear that checking data (instances) is necessary to infer a relevant model that can be used to guarantee, for example, an expected completeness value. The approach that we propose deals with this issue through an iterative process which infers a conceptual schema complying the expected completeness. Figure 1 gives an overview of this process.

---

[1] Performed on: http://dbpedia.org/sparql.

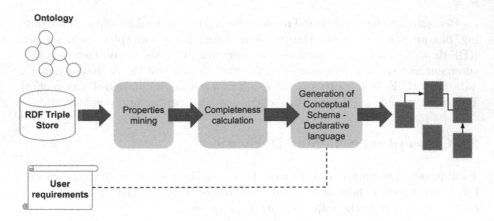

Fig. 1. The *LOD-CM* workflow

The process of inferring a conceptual schema goes through four steps: First, a subset of data that corresponds to the user's scope is extracted from the triple store (cf. Sect. 3.1). This subset is then transformed into transactions and a mining algorithm is applied. In our approach, for efficiency reasons, we chose the well-known FP-growth algorithm [7,8] (any other itemset mining algorithm could obviously be used). From the generated frequent itemsets, only a subset of these frequent itemsets, called "Maximal" [4,5,11], is captured. This choice is motivated by the fact that, on the one hand, we are interested in the *expression* of the frequent pattern and, on the other hand, the number of frequent patterns could be exponential when the transaction vector is very large (cf. Sect. 3.2). $\mathcal{MFP}$ is the set containing all maximal frequent patterns. Each pattern in $\mathcal{MFP}$ is then used to calculate the completeness of each transaction (regarding the presence or absence of the pattern) and, hence, the completeness of the whole dataset regarding this pattern. The final completeness value will be the average of all completeness value calculated for each $\mathcal{MFP}$ pattern (cf. Sect. 3.3). Finally, based on the completeness value and $\mathcal{MFP}$ that guarantees this value, a conceptual schema is generated. The classes, the attributes, and the relations of the model will be tagged with the completeness value (cf. Sect. 3.4). All these steps are integrated in an iterative process in such a way that the user could choose some parts in the generated model to refine. The data corresponding to the parts to refine is then extracted from the triple store, and the same steps are carried out to generate a new model.

In the following subsections, we give a detailed description of each step of the workflow.

3.1 Scope and Completeness Specification

In this step, a subset of data is extracted from the triple store. This subset could correspond to a category or a set of categories such as *Actor*, *Film* or

Organization. This defines what we call the user's scope that corresponds to the categories that the user plans to use in a query, to the information she wants to explore or any kind of usage based on data consumption.

The user is also asked to indicate the degree of the desired completeness. Indeed, properties for a given category are not equally valuated. For example, for the category *Artist*, the property *foaf:name* has a value for 99% of the instances whereas the *dbo:birthPlace* property has a value for at most 74% of the instances. Our approach gives the possibility to express a constraint on the completeness values desired for mined properties and associations. Once the categories are identified, the data is converted into transaction vectors and a mining algorithm is applied to obtain a set of frequent itemsets.

Table 1 illustrates some instances of the *Film* category in the form of triples, taken from DBpedia. Each Category is described by a set of properties (predicates) and an instance of this category could have a value for all the properties or only for a subset of these properties. This subset is called transaction. Table 2 represents the set of transactions constructed from the triples of Table 1.

More formally, let us define a dataset $\mathcal{D}$ to be the triple (C, I_C, P), where C is the set of categories (e.g., *Film*, *Artist*), I_C is the set of instances for categories in C (e.g., *The_Godfather* is an instance of the *Film* category), and $P = \{p_1, p_2, ..., p_n\}$ is the set of properties (e.g *director(Film, Person)*).

Let $\mathcal{T} = \{t_1, t_2, ..., t_m\}$ be a set of transactions with $\forall k, 1 \leq k \leq m : t_k \subseteq P$ be a vector of transactions over P, and $E(t_k)$ be the set of items in transaction t_k. Each transaction is a set of properties used in the description of the instances of the subset $\mathcal{I}' = \{i_1, i_2, ..., i_m\}$ with $\mathcal{I}' \subseteq I_C$ (e.g., properties used to describe the *The_Godfather* instance are: *director* and *musicComposer*). We consider $\mathcal{CP}$ the completeness of $\mathcal{I}'$ against properties used in the description of each of its instances.

3.2   Properties Mining

In the RDF model, all statements having the same subject represent the same category that will be modeled in our approach by a class. The related properties could consequently constitute, either the attributes (properties) of the classes or relationships to other classes, when the property value (the object in the triple $< s, p, o >$) refers to another category. In this step, the objective is to find the properties patterns that are the most shared by the subset of instances extracted from the triple store related to the same category. This set will be then used to calculate a completeness value regarding these patterns.

Let $\mathcal{D}(C, I_C, P)$ be a dataset (stored in the triple store) and $\mathcal{I}'$ be a subset of data (instances) extracted from $\mathcal{D}$ with $\mathcal{I}' \subseteq I_C$. We first initialize $\mathcal{T} = \emptyset$, $\mathcal{MFP} = \emptyset$. For each $i \in \mathcal{I}'$ we generate a transaction t. Indeed, each instance i is related to values (either resources or literals) through a set of properties. Therefore, a transaction t_k of an instance i_k is a set of properties such that $t_k \subseteq P$. Transactions generated for all the instances of $\mathcal{I}'$ are then added to the $\mathcal{T}$ set.

Example 1. Referring Table 1, let $\mathcal{I}'$ be a subset of instances such that: $\mathcal{I}' = \{The\_Godfather, Goodfellas, True\_Lies\}$. The set of transaction $\mathcal{T}$ would be:

$$\mathcal{T} = \{\{director, musicComposer\}, \{director, editing\},$$
$$\{director, editing, musicComposer\}\}$$

The objective is then to compute the set of frequent patterns $\mathcal{FP}$ from the transaction vector $\mathcal{T}$.

Table 1. A sample of triples from DBpedia

Subject	Predicate	Object
The_Godfather	director	Francis_Ford_Coppola
The_Godfather	musicComposer	Nino_Rota
Goodfellas	director	Martin_Scorsese
Goodfellas	editing	Thelma_Schoonmaker
True_Lies	director	James_Cameron
True_Lies	editing	Conrad_Buff_IV
True_Lies	musicComposer	Brad_Fiedel

Table 2. Transactions created from triples

Instance	Transaction
The_Godfather	director, musicComposer
Goodfellas	director, editing
True_Lies	director, editing, musicComposer

Definition 1. *(Pattern) Let $\mathcal{T}$ be a set of transactions. A pattern $\hat{P}$ is a sequence of properties shared by one or several transactions t in $\mathcal{T}$. It is sometimes called an* itemset.

For any pattern $\hat{P}$, let $E(\hat{P})$ be the corresponding set of items (constitutes, in our case, of properties), and $T(\hat{P}) = \{t \in \mathcal{T} \mid E(\hat{P}) \subseteq E(t)\}$ be the corresponding set of transactions. $E(\hat{P})$ designates the *expression* of $\hat{P}$, and $|T(\hat{P})|$ the *support* of $\hat{P}$. A pattern $\hat{P}$ is frequent if $\frac{1}{|\mathcal{T}|}|T(\hat{P})| \geq \xi$, where ξ is a user-specified threshold.

Example 2. Referring Table 2, let $\hat{P} = \{director, musicComposer\}$ and $\xi = 60\%$. $\hat{P}$ is frequent as its relative support (66.7%) is greater than ξ.

To find all the frequent patterns $\mathcal{FP}$, we used, as we mentioned above, the FP-growth itemsets mining algorithm. However, according to the size of the transactions vector, the FP-growth algorithm could generate a very large $\mathcal{FP}$ set. As our objective is to see how a transaction (a description of an instance) is *complete* against a set of properties, we focus on the pattern *expression* (in terms of items it contains) instead of its *support*.

For completeness calculation, we need to select a pattern to serve as a reference schema. This pattern should present a right balance between frequency and expressiveness, therefore we use the concept, called "Maximal" frequent patterns, to find this subset. Thus, to reduce $\mathcal{FP}$, we generate a subset containing only "Maximal" patterns.

Definition 2. *(*$\mathcal{MFP}$*) Let $\hat{P}$ be a frequent pattern. $\hat{P}$ is maximal if none of its proper superset is frequent. We define the set of Maximal Frequent Patterns $\mathcal{MFP}$ as:*

$$\mathcal{MFP} = \{\hat{P} \in \mathcal{FP} \mid \forall \hat{P}' \supsetneq \hat{P} : \frac{|T(\hat{P}')|}{|T|} < \xi\}$$

Example 3. Referring Table 2, let $\xi = 60\%$ and the set of frequent patterns $\mathcal{FP} = \{\{director\}, \{musicComposer\}, \{editing\}, \{director, music\text{-}Composer\}, \{director, editing\}\}$. The $\mathcal{MFP}$ set would be:

$$\mathcal{MFP} = \{\{director, musicComposer\}, \{director, editing\}\}$$

3.3 Completeness Calculation

In this step, we carry out for each transaction a comparison between its corresponding properties and each pattern of the $\mathcal{MFP}$ set (regarding the presence or the absence of the pattern). An average is, therefore, calculated to obtain the completeness of each transaction $t \in \mathcal{T}$. Finally, the completeness of the whole $t \in \mathcal{T}$ will be the average of all the completeness values calculated for each transaction.

Definition 3. *(Completeness) Let $\mathcal{I}'$ be a subset of instances, $\mathcal{T}$ the set of transactions constructed from $\mathcal{I}'$, and $\mathcal{MFP}$ a set of maximal frequent pattern. The completeness of $\mathcal{I}'$ corresponds to the completeness of its transaction vector $\mathcal{T}$ obtained by calculating the average of the completeness of $\mathcal{T}$ regarding each pattern in $\mathcal{MFP}$. Therefore, we define the completeness $\mathcal{CP}$ of a subset of instances $\mathcal{I}'$ as follows:*

$$\mathcal{CP}(\mathcal{I}') = \frac{1}{|\mathcal{T}|} \sum_{k=1}^{|\mathcal{T}|} \sum_{j=1}^{|\mathcal{MFP}|} \frac{\delta(E(t_k), \hat{P}_j)}{|\mathcal{MFP}|} \tag{1}$$

such that: $\hat{P}_j \in \mathcal{MFP}$, and

$$\delta(E(t_k), \hat{P}_j) = \begin{cases} 1 \text{ if } \hat{P}_j \subset E(t_k) \\ 0 \text{ otherwise} \end{cases}$$

The Algorithm 1 shows the pseudo-codes for calculating $CP(\mathcal{I}')$.

Example 4. Let $\xi = 60\%$. The completeness of the subset of instances in Table 1 regarding $\mathcal{MFP} = \{\{director, musicComposer\}, \{director, editing\}\}$ would be:

$$CP(\mathcal{I}') = (2 * (1/2) + (2/2))/3 = 0.67$$

This value corresponds to the completeness average value for the whole dataset regarding the inferred patterns in $\mathcal{MFP}$.

Algorithm 1. Completeness calculation

Input: $\mathcal{D}, \mathcal{I}', \xi$
Output: $CP(\mathcal{I}')$
    for each $i \in \mathcal{I}'$ **do**
        $t_i = |p_1 \, p_2 \dots p_n|$
        $\mathcal{T} = \mathcal{T} + t_i$
    ▷ *Properties mining*
    $\mathcal{MFP} = Maximal(FP\text{-}growth(\mathcal{T}, \xi))$
    ▷ *Using equation 1*
    return $CP(\mathcal{I}') = CalculateCompleteness(\mathcal{I}', \mathcal{T}, \mathcal{MFP})$

3.4 Generation of Enriched Conceptual Schemas

In this step, the goal is to generate a conceptual schema enriched with the completeness values calculated in the previous step. The $\mathcal{MFP}$ patterns used to get the completeness values are transformed into a class diagram. Figure 2 illustrates the user's interface of our LOD-CM web service. Using the graphical interface[2], the user can choose her own constraints. The web service permits the

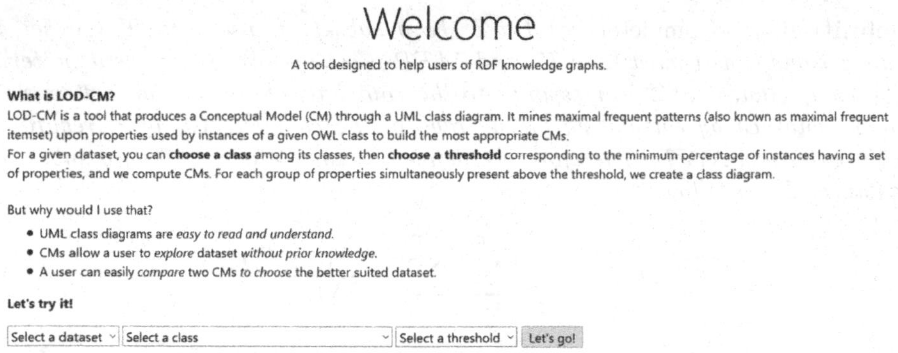

Welcome

A tool designed to help users of RDF knowledge graphs.

What is LOD-CM?

LOD-CM is a tool that produces a Conceptual Model (CM) through a UML class diagram. It mines maximal frequent patterns (also known as maximal frequent itemset) upon properties used by instances of a given OWL class to build the most appropriate CMs.

For a given dataset, you can **choose a class** among its classes, then **choose a threshold** corresponding to the minimum percentage of instances having a set of properties, and we compute CMs. For each group of properties simultaneously present above the threshold, we create a class diagram.

But why would I use that?

- UML class diagrams are *easy to read and understand.*
- CMs allow a user to *explore* dataset *without prior knowledge.*
- A user can easily *compare* two CMs *to choose* the better suited dataset.

Let's try it!

| Select a dataset ˅ | Select a class | ˅ | Select a threshold ˅ | Let's go! |

Fig. 2. LOD-CM main interface

---

[2] http://cedric.cnam.fr/lod-cm.

user to enter the class name in the text box and the user may select the threshold completeness she wants to apply. Currently, our demo supports DBpedia.

After the user selects the class name and desired completeness and clicks Submit button, the algorithm runs to find the attributes, relationships and the missed domains/ranges based on user's constraints.

The structure of the model is constructed regarding the definitions of the patterns properties in the ontology describing the dataset. Figure 3 represents a class diagram derived by our approach, from a set of films extracted from DBpedia.

A First Iteration: In this example, the expectation of the user is a model that guarantees at least 50% of completeness. To generate the model, the first step consists of obtaining the set of properties $p \in \bigcup_{j=1}^{n} E(\hat{P_j})$, and $\hat{P_j} \in \mathcal{MFP}$ that composes the union of all the $\mathcal{MFP}$, mined from the extracted subset, with a minimum support $\xi = 50\%$. For this example, the set of properties are: {*director, label, name, runtime, starring, type*}, {*director, label, name, starring, type, writer*} and {*label, name, runtime, type, writer*}. OWL distinguishes between two main categories of properties: (i) datatype properties, where the value is a data literal, and (ii) object properties, where the value is an individual (i.e., an other instance with its own type). Each property is considered as an attribute (e.g. name) of the class or a relationship (e.g. director) with another class, depending on the nature of the value. Therefore, according to the nature of the value of each property, it is considered as an attribute of the class or a relationship with another class. Two types of links will be used during generating of conceptual schemas: inheritance and association links. Inheritance link describes the relation between the class and the superclass, and association link describes the relation between two classes and point to the property. A dotted link was added to illustrate that a class has been inferred to complete the relationship. For this reason, based on the approach that has been proposed in [20], we infer missed domains (and/or ranges) of properties. In our example, the names of the classes and the inheritance links between the classes are derived from categories names and organization described in the ontology of the data source DBpedia. We do not derive new names nor new organization of the classes as the conceptual schema should conform to the data used. Indeed, even if the derived conceptual schema is not satisfactory from conceptual modeling principles, it should faithfully reflect the reality of data while taking into account user preferences. Finally, the diagram is enriched by the completeness values calculated in the previous step. These values are associated to each component of the model.

A Second Iteration: A new iteration is triggered when the user chooses to get more details about a part of the model (e.g. the *Artist* class). In this case, a new query is executed on the triple store to extract data corresponding to this part. The previous three steps are then executed in order to generate a new model integrating the new desired details. Figure 4 shows an example that details a

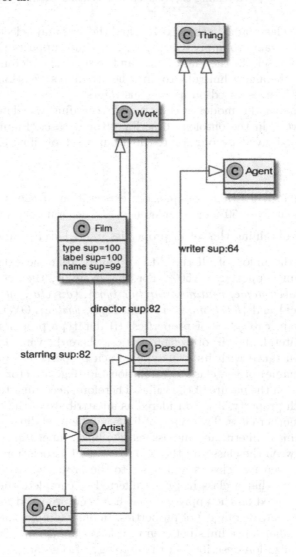

Fig. 3. The *Film* conceptual schema as a class diagram

part of the model from Fig. 3. In this example, a set of classes, relationships and attributes are added to the *Artist* class with corresponding completeness values. This way of revealing the conceptual schema is similar to a magnifying glass that allows the user navigating around a targeted concept, here the *Film* category.

The output of our algorithm is a file written in a declarative language. The file includes the chosen category, the attributes, and the relationships tagged by completeness values. We use PlantUML[3] to transfer this generated file into a picture to illustrate it to the user.

---

[3] http://plantuml.com/.

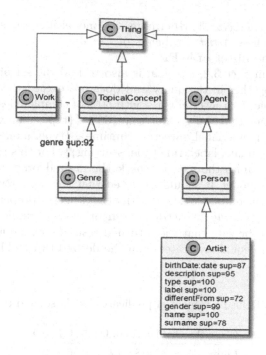

Fig. 4. The *Artist* diagram class

4 Use Cases

The objective of the Linked Open Data cloud is to enable large-scale data integration, so that we can have a contextually relevant Web and find quick answers to a much wider range of questions. LOD-CM is a web-based completeness demonstrator for linked datasets. It is used to display data related to the chosen class of a dataset. In this section, we provide a brief summary of two use cases related to schema discovery based on user's needs. The displayed model could help the user to understand the schema and discover the related properties. LOD-CM only supports DBpedia at the moment.

1. **Class diagram to facilitate data browsing**
   LOD-CM aims basically to visualize the discovered schema based on user's requirements. Suppose a user wants to find the directors and budgets of a list of films. Actually, 82% of films have a director in DBpedia dataset. In addition, only 15% of films have budget value for the same dataset. Only the list of films that have the properties (director and budget) will be displayed (i.e., at most 15% of the films). The outcome model could help the user to present the properties that are related to the chosen class and that are greater than a specified threshold. Besides, it illustrates the relation between the concerned classes such as the classes *Person* and *Film* that are linked

by the property *director*. Furthermore, the model illustrates the inheritance relationship such as *Artist* is subclass of *Person*.

2. **Discovering a subset of MFP**

   As mentioned in Sect. 3.2, our goal is also to find the set of properties that can be used together in the query and does not exceed the selected threshold. For example, for the *Film* class with 60% of completeness, there are four sets of properties that are greater than 60% {{type, name, label, director, writer}, {type, name, label, director, runtime}, {type, name, label, director, starring},{type, name, label, runetime, starring}}. For this reason, our LOD-CM interface enables the user to check the desired properties that appear in the returned model. It should be noted that the property which does not achieve the completeness threshold with other selected properties will be inactivated, such as *starring* and *writer* in our previous example. This case could help the user to be sure that the returned results for its query with this set of properties are equal or greater than the desired threshold.

Table 3. DBpedia number of predicates by classes and thresholds

Class/threshold	0.1	0.3	0.5	0.7	0.9
Film	18	12	7	6	3
Settlement	18	14	8	5	4
Organisation	18	4	4	3	3
Scientist	19	16	12	9	5

Finally, Table 3 shows the number of properties we get (at the end of our pipeline) for several classes according to several thresholds. The lower the threshold is, the more properties there are, obviously. Thus, lower thresholds produce more complex conceptual schemas but with more noise. Hence, this tool can help the user to find the right balance between those two.

5 Conclusion

We have presented an approach for revealing conceptual schemas from RDF data sources. The approach is an iterative process that computes a plausible model from the data values. We have shown how to automatically extract schema and represent it as a model from a data source using a user-specified threshold. The inferred model takes into account the data and the user quality expectations. The result is a conceptual schema enriched by both completeness values as a relevancy indicator on the elements of the models, and existence constraints that inform about how often these elements co-exist or co-appear in the real data.

The elements composing the model (classes, relationships and properties) are obtained by applying a mining algorithm with an underlying assumption stating that the more frequent a schema is, the more relevant it is. The user can decide on the desired completeness, the parts of the data for which the model will be inferred and the possibility to focus on a different category through an iterative process. Currently, our demo supports only the DBpedia dataset.

We have provided several use cases to demonstrate the usefulness of such a tool. We believe that it can help in the discovery of a new dataset and its internal structure, therefore, it can help in the adoption of LD datasets.

Our analysis revealed some interesting characteristics allowing the characterization of the sources and the behavior of the community that maintains each of the data sources. The results show the rich opportunities of analysis offered by our approach and underlying outputs.

In the future, we plan to investigate the role of conceptual modeling in an integration context where the universe of discourse is not only one data source but an integrated system upon several Linked Open Data. We plan to make more datasets available and allow the user to easily compare two conceptual schemas side by side (from two datasets). We believe that the ability to compare two conceptual schemas of two datasets side by side can help to choose the one that is best suited for its use.

References

1. Batini, C., Scannapieco, M.: Erratum to: data and information quality: dimensions, principles and techniques. In: Batini, C., Scannapieco, M. (eds.) Data and Information Quality. DSA, pp. E1–E1. Springer, Cham (2016). https://doi.org/10.1007/978-3-319-24106-7_15
2. Christodoulou, K., Paton, N.W., Fernandes, A.A.A.: Structure inference for linked data sources using clustering. In: Hameurlain, A., Küng, J., Wagner, R., Bianchini, D., De Antonellis, V., De Virgilio, R. (eds.) Transactions on Large-Scale Data- and Knowledge-Centered Systems XIX. LNCS, vol. 8990, pp. 1–25. Springer, Heidelberg (2015). https://doi.org/10.1007/978-3-662-46562-2_1
3. Embley, D.W., Liddle, S.W.: Big data—conceptual modeling to the rescue. In: Ng, W., Storey, V.C., Trujillo, J.C. (eds.) ER 2013. LNCS, vol. 8217, pp. 1–8. Springer, Heidelberg (2013). https://doi.org/10.1007/978-3-642-41924-9_1
4. Gouda, K., Zaki, M.J.: Efficiently mining maximal frequent itemsets. In: Proceedings of the 2001 IEEE International Conference on Data Mining, ICDM 2001, pp. 163–170. IEEE Computer Society, Washington, DC (2001)
5. Grahne, G., Zhu, J.: Efficiently using prefix-trees in mining frequent itemsets. In: Goethals, B., Zaki, M.J. (eds.) FIMI 2003, Frequent Itemset Mining Implementations, Proceedings of the ICDM 2003 Workshop on Frequent Itemset Mining Implementations, 19 December 2003, Melbourne, Florida, USA, CEUR Workshop Proceedings, vol. 90. CEUR-WS.org (2003)
6. Hamdi, F., Cherfi, S.S.S.: An approach for measuring rdf data completeness. BDA 2015 Gestion de Données-Principes, Technologies et Applications 29 septembre au 2 octobre 2015 Ile de Porquerolles p. 32 (2015)

7. Han, J., Pei, J., Yin, Y.: Mining frequent patterns without candidate generation. In: Chen, W., Naughton, J.F., Bernstein, P.A. (eds.) Proceedings of the 2000 ACM SIGMOD International Conference on Management of Data, 16–18 May 2000, Dallas, Texas, USA, pp. 1–12. ACM (2000)
8. Han, J., Pei, J., Yin, Y., Mao, R.: Mining frequent patterns without candidate generation: a frequent-pattern tree approach. Data Min. Knowl. Discov. 8(1), 53–87 (2004)
9. Issa, S., Paris, P.-H., Hamdi, F.: Assessing the completeness evolution of DBpedia: a case study. In: de Cesare, S., Frank, U. (eds.) ER 2017. LNCS, vol. 10651, pp. 238–247. Springer, Cham (2017). https://doi.org/10.1007/978-3-319-70625-2_22
10. Jain, P., Hitzler, P., Yeh, P.Z., Verma, K., Sheth, A.P.: Linked data is merely more data. In: Linked Data Meets Artificial Intelligence, Papers from the 2010 AAAI Spring Symposium, Technical Report SS-10-07, Stanford, California, USA, 22–24 March 2010 (2010). http://www.aaai.org/ocs/index.php/SSS/SSS10/paper/view/1130
11. Bayardo Jr., R.J: Efficiently mining long patterns from databases. In: Haas, L.M., Tiwary, A. (eds.) SIGMOD 1998, Proceedings ACM SIGMOD International Conference on Management of Data, 2–4 June 1998, Seattle, Washington, USA, pp. 85–93. ACM Press (1998)
12. Kellou-Menouer, K., Kedad, Z.: Schema discovery in RDF data sources. In: Johannesson, P., Lee, M.L., Liddle, S.W., Opdahl, A.L., López, Ó.P. (eds.) ER 2015. LNCS, vol. 9381, pp. 481–495. Springer, Cham (2015). https://doi.org/10.1007/978-3-319-25264-3_36
13. Klyne, G., Carroll, J.J.: Resource description framework (RDF): Concepts and abstract syntax (2006)
14. Levandoski, J.J., Mokbel, M.F.: RDF data-centric storage. In: IEEE International Conference on Web Services, ICWS 2009, pp. 911–918. IEEE (2009)
15. Lukyanenko, R., Parsons, J.: Principles for modeling user-generated content. In: Johannesson, P., Lee, M.L., Liddle, S.W., Opdahl, A.L., López, Ó.P. (eds.) ER 2015. LNCS, vol. 9381, pp. 432–440. Springer, Cham (2015). https://doi.org/10.1007/978-3-319-25264-3_32
16. Lukyanenko, R., Parsons, J., Samuel, B.M.: Representing instances: the case for reengineering conceptual modelling grammars. Eur. J. Inf. Syst. 28(1), 68–90 (2019)
17. Olivé, A.: Conceptual Modeling of Information Systems. Springer, Heidelberg (2007). https://doi.org/10.1007/978-3-540-39390-0
18. Pham, M., Passing, L., Erling, O., Boncz, P.A.: Deriving an emergent relational schema from RDF data. In: Gangemi, A., Leonardi, S., Panconesi, A. (eds.) Proceedings of the 24th International Conference on World Wide Web, WWW 2015, Florence, Italy, 18–22 May 2015, pp. 864–874. ACM (2015). http://doi.acm.org/10.1145/2736277.2741121
19. Rolland, C., Prakash, N.: From conceptual modelling to requirements engineering. Ann. Softw. Eng. 10(1–4), 151–176 (2000)
20. Töpper, G., Knuth, M., Sack, H.: Dbpedia ontology enrichment for inconsistency detection. In: Proceedings of the 8th International Conference on Semantic Systems, pp. 33–40. ACM (2012)
21. Völker, J., Niepert, M.: Statistical schema induction. In: Antoniou, G., et al. (eds.) ESWC 2011. LNCS, vol. 6643, pp. 124–138. Springer, Heidelberg (2011). https://doi.org/10.1007/978-3-642-21034-1_9

22. Wang, Y., Du, X., Lu, J., Wang, X.: FlexTable: using a dynamic relation model to store RDF data. In: Kitagawa, H., Ishikawa, Y., Li, Q., Watanabe, C. (eds.) DAS-FAA 2010. LNCS, vol. 5981, pp. 580–594. Springer, Heidelberg (2010). https://doi.org/10.1007/978-3-642-12026-8_44
23. Zaveri, A., et al.: Quality assessment methodologies for linked open data. Semant. Web J. (2013, submitted)

Modeling and In-Database Management of Relational, Data-Aware Processes

Diego Calvanese[1], Marco Montali[1], Fabio Patrizi[2], and Andrey Rivkin[1(✉)]

[1] Free University of Bozen-Bolzano, Bolzano, Italy
{calvanese,montali,rivkin}@inf.unibz.it
[2] Sapienza Università di Roma, Roma, Italy
patrizi@dis.uniroma1.it

Abstract. It is known that the engineering of information systems usually requires a huge effort in integrating master data and business processes. Existing approaches, both from academia and the industry, typically come with ad-hoc abstractions to represent and interact with the data component. This has two disadvantages: *(i)* an existing database (DB) cannot be effortlessly enriched with dynamics; *(ii)* such approaches generally do not allow for integrated modelling, verification, and enactment. We attack these two challenges by proposing a declarative approach, fully grounded in SQL, that supports the agile modelling of relational data-aware processes directly on top of relational DBs. We show how this approach can be automatically translated into a concrete procedural SQL dialect, executable directly inside any relational DB engine. The translation exploits an in-database representation of process states that, in turn, is used to handle, at once, process enactment with or without logging of the executed instances, as well as process verification. The approach has been implemented in a working prototype.

Keywords: Data-aware processes · Process engines · Relational databases

1 Introduction

During the last two decades, increasing attention has been given to the challenging problem of resolving the dichotomy between business process and master data management [3,10,18]. Devising integrated models and corresponding enactment platforms for processes and data is now acknowledged as a key milestone, which cannot be reduced to implementation-level solutions at the level of enterprise IT infrastructures [8].

This triggered a flourishing line of research on concrete languages for data-aware processes, and on the development of tools to model and enact such processes. The main unifying theme for such approaches is a shift from standard activity-centric business process meta-models, to a paradigm that focuses

© Springer Nature Switzerland AG 2019
P. Giorgini and B. Weber (Eds.): CAiSE 2019, LNCS 11483, pp. 328–345, 2019.
https://doi.org/10.1007/978-3-030-21290-2_21

first on the elicitation of business entities (and data), and then on their behavioral aspects. Notable approaches in this line are artifact-centric [10], object-centric [12] and data-centric models [19]. In parallel to these new modeling paradigms, also BPMS based on standard, activity-centric approaches a là BPMN, have increased the tool support of data-related aspects. Many modern BPM platforms provide (typically proprietary) data models, ad-hoc user interfaces to indicate how process tasks induce data updates, and query languages to express decisions based on data. While this approach has the main advantage of hiding the complexity of the underlying relational database (DB) from the modeler, it comes with two critical shortcomings. First, it makes it difficult to conceptually understand the overall process in terms of general, tool-agnostic principles, and to redeploy the same process in a different BPMS. This is witnessed by a number of ongoing proposals that explicitly bring forward complex mappings for model-to-model transformation (see, e.g., [11,23]). Second, this approach cannot be readily applied in the recurrent case where the process needs to be integrated with existing DB tables. In fact, updating an underlying DB through a more abstract data model is challenging and relates to the long-standing, well-known *view update problem* in the database literature [9].

We approach these issues by addressing three main research questions in a setting in which *the database can be directly accessed and updated by running processes*:

RQ1 Is it possible to ground data-centric approaches based on condition-action rules in the SQL standard, also accounting for the interaction with external systems?

RQ2 Is it possible to develop a corresponding enactment engine running directly on top of legacy DBMSs, and providing logging functionalities?

RQ3 Is it possible to implement the foundational techniques for the (abstract) state-space construction of data-centric approaches based on condition-action rules?

To answer **RQ1**, we propose a declarative language, called dapSL, that introduces minimal changes to the SQL standard, allowing one to: *(i)* encapsulate process tasks into SQL-based, parameterized actions that update the DB, possibly injecting values obtained from external inputs (e.g., ERP systems, user forms, web services, external applications), and *(ii)* define rules determining which actions are executable and with which parameter bindings, based on the answers obtained by querying the DB. Notably, the last feature is intrinsic to many artifact- and data-centric approaches [1,2,6,13] since the data manipulation in them is handled via rules. In practice, dapSL can be used either in a bottom-up manner, as a scripting language that enriches DBs with processes, or in a top-down manner, as a way to complement standard, control flow-oriented process modelling languages with an unambiguous, runnable specification of conditions and tasks. From the formal point of view, dapSL represents the concrete counterpart of one of the most sophisticated formal models for data-aware processes [1], which comes with a series of (theoretical) results on the conditions

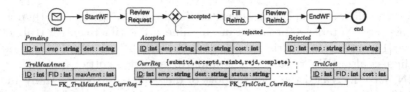

Fig. 1. The travel management process and a corresponding data model

under which verification can be carried out. In fact, a wide range of foundational results tackling the formalization of data-ware processes, and the identification of boundaries for their verifiability has been obtained [3], but the resulting approaches never resulted in actual modeling and enactment tools. In this sense, dapSL constitutes the first attempt to bridge the gap between such formal approaches and concrete modeling and execution.

To address **RQ2**, we propose a framework, called DAPHNE, where data-aware processes are directly specified on top of standard relational DBs. To support such specifications, an automatic translation of dapSL into a concrete procedural SQL dialect is presented, in turn providing direct in-database process execution support. The framework has been implemented within the DAPHNE engine, whose back-end consists of a relational storage with corresponding stored procedures to manage the action-induced updates, and whose JAVA front-end provides APIs and functionalities to inspect the current state of the process and its underlying data, as well as to interact with different concrete systems for acquiring external data.

Thanks to a sophisticated encoding of the dapSL process state and related data into SQL, DAPHNE seamlessly accounts for three key usage modalities: enactment with and without logging of historical data, and state space construction for formal analysis. The third modality is fully addressed within the scope of **RQ3**. Relying on DAPHNE, we propose a solution that constructs the state space invoking the same mechanism used for enactment. This ensures that the analysis is carried out on the exact same model that is enacted, differently from usual approaches in formal verification, where an abstract version of a concrete model is constructed in ad-hoc way for verification purposes.

DAPHNE is available at https://bit.ly/2KIbMvN.

2   Data-Aware Process Specification Language

We approach **RQ1** by introducing a declarative, SQL-based *data-aware process specification language* (dapSL) to describe processes operating over relational data. dapSL can be seen as a SQL-based front-end language for specifying *data-centric dynamic systems* (DCDSs) [1]. A dapSL specification consists of two main components: *(i)* a *data layer*, representing the structural aspects of the domain, and storing corresponding extensional data; *(ii)* a *control layer*, which queries and evolves the data of the data layer.

Example 1. As a running example, we consider a travel reimbursement process inspired by [7], whose control flow is depicted in Fig. 1. The process starts (StartWF) by checking pending employee travel requests in the DB. Then, after selecting a request, the system examines it (ReviewRequest), and decides whether to approve it or not. If approved, the process continues by calculating the maximum refundable amount, and the employee can go on her business trip. On arrival, she is asked to compile and submit a form with all the business trip expenses (FillReimb). The system analyzes the submitted form (ReviewReimb) and, if the estimated maximum has not been exceeded, approves the refunding. Otherwise the reimbursement is rejected.   ◁

Data Layer. The *data layer* is a standard relational DB, consisting of an intensional (schema) part, and an extensional (instance) part. The intensional part is a *DB schema*, that is, a pair $\langle \mathcal{R}, \mathcal{E} \rangle$, where $\mathcal{R}$ is a finite set of *relation schemas*, and $\mathcal{E}$ is a finite set of *integrity constraints* over $\mathcal{R}$. To capture a DB schema, dapSL employs the standard SQL data definition language (DDL). For presentation reasons, in the remainder of the papers we refer to the components of a DB schema in an abstract way, following standard definitions. dapSL tackles three fundamental types of integrity constraints: a *primary key* for a relation R is denoted PK(R); a *foreign key* from attributes B of relation S to attributes A of R is denoted $S[\mathsf{B}] \rightarrow R[\mathsf{A}]$; a *domain constraint* enumerates the values assigned to a relation attribute. Note that such constraints are expressed in dapSL by using the standard SQL DDL. The extensional part of the data layer is a *DB instance* (DB for short). dapSL delegates the representation of this part to the relational storage of choice. We always assume that a DB is consistent, that is, satisfies all constraints in $\mathcal{E}$. While the intensional part is fixed in a dapSL model, the extensional part starts from an initial DB that is then iteratively updated through the control layer, as dictated below.

Example 2. The dapSL DB schema for the process informally described in Example 1 is shown in Fig. 1. We recall of the relation schemas: *(i)* requests under process are stored in the relation *CurrReq*, whose components are the request UID, which is the primary key, the employee requesting a reimbursement, the trip destination, and the status of the request, which ranges over a set of predefined values (captured with a domain constraint); *(ii)* maximum allowed trip budgets are stored in *TrvlMaxAmnt*, whose components are the id (the primary key), the request reference number (a foreign key), and the maximum amount assigned for the trip; *(iii)* *TrvlCost* stores the total amount spent, with the same attributes as in *TrvlMaxAmnt*.   ◁

Control Layer. The *control layer* defines how the data layer can be evolved through the execution of actions (concretely accounting for the different process tasks). Technically, the control layer is a triple $\langle \mathcal{F}, \mathcal{A}, \rho \rangle$, where $\mathcal{F}$ is a finite set of *external services*, $\mathcal{A}$ is a finite set of *atomic tasks* (or actions), and ρ is a *process specification*.

Each service is defined as a function signature that indicates how externally generated data can be brought into the process, abstractly accounting for a variety of concrete data injection mechanisms, e.g., user forms, web services, external ERP systems, internal generation of primary keys etc. Each service comes with a signature indicating the *service name*, its *formal input parameters* and their *types*, as well as the *output type*.

Actions are the basic building blocks of the control layer, and represent transactional operations over the data layer. Each action comes with a distinguished name and a set of formal parameters, and consists of a set of *parameterized SQL statements* that inspect and update the current state of the dapSL model (i.e., the current DB), using standard insert-delete SQL operations. operations are parameterized so as to allow referring with the statements to the action parameters, as well as to the results obtained by invoking a service call. Both kind of parameters are substituted with actual values when the action is concretely executed. Hence, whenever a SQL statement allows for using a constant value, dapSL allows for using either a constant, an action parameter, or a placeholder representing the invocation of a service call. To distinguish service invocations from action parameters, dapSL prefixes the service call name with @.

Formally, a dapSL *action* is an expression $\alpha(p_1, \ldots, p_n) : \{e_1; \ldots; e_m\}$, where: *(i)* $\alpha(p_1, \ldots, p_n)$ is the action *signature*, constituted by *action name* α and the set $\{p_1, \ldots, p_n\}$ of *action formal parameters*; *(ii)* $\{e_1, \ldots, e_m\}$ is a set of parameterized effect specifications, which are SQL insertions and deletions performed on the current DB. We assume that no two actions in $\mathcal{A}$ share the same name, and then use the action name to refer to its corresponding specification.

A *parameterized SQL insertion* has the form **INSERT INTO** $R(\mathsf{A}_1, \ldots, \mathsf{A}_k)$ **VALUES** $(t_1, \ldots, t_k)$, where $R \in \mathcal{R}$, and each t_j is either a value, an action formal parameter or a service call invocation (which syntactically corresponds to a scalar function call in SQL). Given a service call @F with parameters p, an invocation for F is of the form @F$(x_1, \ldots, x_p)$, where each x_j is either a value or an action formal parameter. **VALUES** can be substituted by a complex SQL inner selection query, which in turn supports *bulk insertions* into R by using all answers obtained by evaluating the inner query.

A *parameterized SQL deletion* has the form **DELETE FROM** R **WHERE** ⟨*condition*⟩, where $R \in \mathcal{R}$, and the **WHERE** clause may internally refer to the action formal parameters. This specification captures the simultaneous deletion of all tuples returned by the evaluation of *condition* on the current DB. Following classical conceptual modeling approaches to domain changes [17], we allow for overlapping deletions and insertions in such a way that first all deletions, and then all insertions are applied. This allows to unambiguously capture update effects (by deleting certain tuples, and inserting back variants of those tuples). Introducing explicit SQL update statements would create ambiguities on how to prioritize updates w.r.t. potentially overlapping deletions and insertions.

The executability of an action, including how its formal parameters may be bound to corresponding values, is dictated by the process specification ρ – a set of condition-action (CA) rules, again grounded in SQL, and used to declaratively capture the control-flow of the ᴅᴀᴘSL model. For each action α in $\mathcal{A}$ with k parameters, ρ contains a single CA rule determining the executability of α. The CA rule is an expression of the form:

$$\textbf{SELECT } A_1, \ldots, A_s \textbf{ FROM } R_1, \ldots, R_m \textbf{ WHERE } \langle condition \rangle \textbf{ ENABLES } \alpha(A_{n_1}, \ldots, A_{n_k}),$$

where each A_i is an attribute, each $R_i \in \mathcal{R}$, $\alpha \in \mathcal{A}$, and $\{A_{n_1}, \ldots, A_{n_k}\} \subseteq \{A_1, \ldots, A_s\}$. Here, the SQL **SELECT** query represents the rule condition, and the results of the query provide alternative actual parameters that instantiate the formal parameters of α. This grounding mechanism is applied on a per-answer basis, that is, to execute α one has to choose how to instantiate the formal parameters of α with one of the query answers returned by the **SELECT** query. Multiple answers consequently provide alternative instantiation choices. Notice that requiring each action to have only one CA rule is w.l.o.g, as multiple CA rules for the same action can be compacted into a unique rule whose condition is the **UNION** of the condition queries in the original rules.

Example 3. We focus on three tasks of the process in Example 1, showing their encoding in ᴅᴀᴘSL. StartWF creates a new travel reimbursement request by picking a pending requests from the current DB. We represent this in ᴅᴀᴘSL as an action with three formal parameters, denoting a pending request id, its responsible employee, and her intended destination:

SELECT id, emp, dest **FROM** *Pending* **ENABLES** StartWF(id, emp, dest);
StartWF(id, emp, dest) : {**DELETE FROM** *Pending* **WHERE** *Pending*.id = id;
  INSERT INTO *CurrReq*(id, emp, dest, status) **VALUES**(@genpk(), emp, dest, submitd)}

Here, a new request is generated by removing from *Pending* the entry that matches the given id, then inserting a new tuple into *CurrReq* with the emp and dest values of the deleted tuple, and the status set to 'submitd'. To get a unique id for such a tuple, we invoke the nullary service call @genpk, returning a fresh primary key value. ReviewRequest examines an employee trip request and, if accepted, assigns its maximum reimbursable amount. The action can be executed only if a request in *CurrReq* actually exists:

SELECT id, emp, dest **FROM** *CurrReq* **WHERE** *CurrReq*.status = 'submitd'
  ENABLES RvwRequest(id, emp, dest);
RvwRequest(id, emp, dest) : {**DELETE FROM** *CurrReq* **WHERE** *CurrReq*.id = id;
          INSERT INTO *CurrReq*(id, emp, dest, status)
          VALUES(id, emp, dest, @status(emp, dest));
          INSERT INTO *TrvlMaxAmnt*(tid, tfid, tmaxAmnt)
          VALUES(@genpk(), id, @maxAmnt(emp, dest))}

The request status of *CurrReq* is updated by calling service @status, that takes as input an employee name and a trip destination, and returns a new status value. Also, a new tuple containing the maximum reimbursable amount is added to *TrvlMaxAmnt*. To get the maximum refundable amount for *TrvlMaxAmnt*, we employ service @maxAmnt with the same arguments as @status.

Task FillReimb updates the current request by adding a compiled form with all the trip expenses. This can be done only when the request has been accepted:

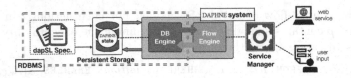

Fig. 2. Conceptual architecture of DAPHNE

SELECT id, emp, dest **FROM** *CurrReq* **WHERE** *CurrReq*.status = 'acceptd'
    ENABLES FillReimb(id, emp, dest);
FillReimb(id, emp, dest): { **INSERT INTO** *TrvlCost*(id, fid, cost)
                    VALUES (@genpk(), id, @cost(emp, dest)) }

Again, @genpk and @cost are used to obtain values externally upon insertion.

◁

Execution Semantics. The semantics mimics that of DCDSs [1]. Let $\mathcal{I}$ be the current DB for the data layer of the ⅾⲁⲡSL model of interest. An action α is *enabled* in $\mathcal{I}$ if the evaluation of the SQL query constituting the condition in the CA rule of α returns a nonempty result set. This result set is then used to instantiate α, by non-deterministically picking an answer tuple, and use it to bind the formal parameters of α to actual values. This produces a so-called *ground action* for α. The execution of a ground action amounts to simultaneous application of all its effect specifications, which requires to first manage the service call invocations, and then apply the deletions and insertions. This is done as follows. First, invocations in the ground action are instantiated by resolving the subqueries present in all those insertion effects whose values contain invocation placeholders. Each invocation then becomes a fully specified call to the corresponding service, passing the ground values as input. The result obtained from the call is used to replace the invocation itself, getting a fully instantiated **VALUES** clause for the insertion effect specification. A transactional update is consequently issued on $\mathcal{I}$, first pushing all deletions, and then all insertions. If the resulting DB satisfies the constraints of the data layer, then the update is committed, otherwise it is rolled back.

3   The DAPHNE System

We discuss how ⅾⲁⲡSL has been implemented in a concrete system, called DAPHNE, that provides in-database process enactment and state-space construction for formal analysis. In particular, the first feature is required to address **RQ2** by realizing three main functionalities: *(1)* indicate the executable actions and their parameters; *(2)* manage the invocation of an executable action and the corresponding update; *(3)* handle normal execution vs. execution with logging of historical snapshots transparently to the user.

The core architecture of DAPHNE is depicted in Fig. 2. The system takes as input a representation of a ⅾⲁⲡSL specification (or model) and uses a standard

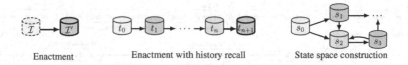

Enactment   Enactment with history recall   State space construction

Fig. 3. The three main usage modalities for DAPHNE, and sketch of the corresponding data structures stored within the DBMS

database management system (DBMS) to support its execution. The DBMS takes care of storing the data relevant to the input dapSL model and supports, through the **DB Engine** of the underlying DBMS, the application of a set of operations that jointly realize the given dapSL actions. The **Flow Engine** constitutes the application layer of the system; it facilitates the execution of a dapSL model by coordinating the activities that involve the user, the DBMS, and the services. Specifically, the **Flow Engine** issues queries to the DBMS, calls stored procedures, and handles the communication with external services through a further module called **Service Manager**.

Next we give a detailed representation of DAPHNE's architecture by describing the stages of each execution step. For the moment we do not consider the concrete encoding of dapSL inside the DBMS. At each point in time, the DBMS stores the current state of the dapSL model. We assume that, before the execution starts, the DBMS contains an initial database instance for the data layer of dapSL model. To start the execution, the **Flow Engine** queries the DBMS about the actions that are enabled in the current state; if one is found, the engine retrieves all possible parameter assignments that can be selected to ground the action, and returns them to the user (or the software module responsible for the process enactment). The user is then asked to choose one of such parameter assignments. At this point, the actual application of the ground action is triggered. The **Flow Engine** invokes a set of stored procedures from the DBMS that take care of evaluating and applying action effects. If needed by the action specification, the **Flow Engine** interacts with external services, through the **Service Manager**, to acquire new data via service calls. The tuples to be deleted and inserted in the various relations of the dapSL model are then computed, and the consequent changes are pushed to the DBMS within a transaction, so that the underlying database instance is updated only if all constraints are satisfied. After the update is committed or rolled back, the action execution cycle can be repeated by selecting either a new parameter assignment or another action available in the newly generated state.

3.1 Encoding a dapSL in DAPHNE

We now detail how DAPHNE encodes a dapSL model $\mathcal{S} = \langle \mathcal{L}, \mathcal{P} \rangle$ with data layer $\mathcal{L} = \langle \mathcal{R}, \mathcal{E} \rangle$ and control layer $\mathcal{P} = \langle \mathcal{F}, \mathcal{A}, \rho \rangle$ into a DBMS. Intuitively DAPHNE represents $\mathcal{L}$ as a set of tables, and $\mathcal{P}$ as a set of stored procedures working over those and auxiliary tables. Such data structures and stored procedures are

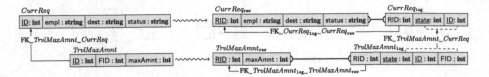

Fig. 4. Relational schemas of *CurrReq* and *TrvlMaxAmnt*, and their historical representation in DAPHNE via two pairs of corresponding tables: $CurrReq_{raw}$ and $CurrReq_{log}$, $TrvlMaxAmnt_{raw}$ and $TrvlMaxAmnt_{log}$.

defined in terms of the native language of the chosen DBMS. These can be either created manually, or automatically instrumented by DAPHNE itself if the user uses the DAPHNE APIs to communicate the definition of $\mathcal{S}$. We employ jOOQ (https://www.jooq.org/) as the basis for the concrete input syntax of dapSL models within DAPHNE. An overview about how jOOQ and the APIs actually work is given in a companion report [5].

Before entering into the encoding details, it is important to stress that DAPHNE provides three main usage modalities. The first modality is *enactment*. Here DAPHNE supports users in the process execution, storing the *current DB*, and suitably updating it in response to the execution of actions. The second modality is *enactment with historical recall*. This corresponds to enactment, but storing all the historical DBs together with information about the applied actions (name, parameters, service call invocations and results, and timestamps). This provides full traceability about how the process execution evolved the initial state into the current one. The last modality is *state space construction for formal analysis*, where DAPHNE generates all possible "relevant" possible executions of the system, using abstract state identifiers instead from timestamps, and using representative DBs to compactly represent (infinitely many) DBs from which $\mathcal{S}$ wold induce the same evolution. This allows DAPHNE to connect back to representative states in case the execution of an action leads to a configuration of the DB that has been already encountered before. Technically, traces of $\mathcal{S}$ are folded into an abstract *relational transition system* (RTS) [4], which faithfully represents not only all possible runs of $\mathcal{S}$, but also its branching structure.

Data Layer. DAPHNE does not internally store the data layer as it is specified in $\mathcal{L}$, but adopts a more sophisticated schema. This is done to have a unique homogeneous approach that supports the three usage modalities mentioned before. In fact, instructing the DBMS to directly store the schema expressed in $\mathcal{L}$ would suffice only in the enactment case, but not to store historical data about previous states, nor the state space with its branching nature. To accommodate all three usages at once, DAPHNE proceeds as follows. Each relation schema R of $\mathcal{L}$ becomes relativized to a *state identifier*, and decomposed into two interconnected relation schemas: *(i)* R_{raw} (*raw data storage*), an inflationary table that incrementally stores all the tuples that have been ever inserted in R; *(ii)* R_{log} (*state log*), which is responsible at once for maintaining the referential integrity of the data in a state, as well as for fully reconstructing the exact content of R

in a state. In details, R_{raw} contains all the attributes A of R that are *not* part of primary keys nor sources of a foreign key, plus an additional surrogate identifier RID, so that $\mathrm{PK}(R_{\mathrm{raw}}) = \langle \mathrm{RID} \rangle$. Each possible combination of values over A is stored only once in R_{raw} (i.e., $R_{\mathrm{raw}}[A]$ is a key), thus maximizing compactness. At the same time, R_{log} contains the following attributes: *(i)* an attribute **state** representing the state identifier; *(ii)* the primary key of (the original relation) R; *(iii)* a reference to R_{raw}, i.e., an attribute RID with $R_{\mathrm{log}}[\mathrm{RID}] \to R_{\mathrm{raw}}[\mathrm{RID}]$; *(iv)* all attributes of R that are sources of a foreign key in $\mathcal{L}$. To guarantee referential integrity, R_{log} must ensure that (primary) keys and foreign keys are now relativized to a state. This is essential, as the same tuple of R may evolve across states, consequently requiring to historically store its different versions, and suitably keep track of which version refers to which state. Also foreign keys have to be understood within the same state: if a reference tuple changes from one state to the other, all the other tuples referencing it need to update their references accordingly. To realize this, we set $\mathrm{PK}(R_{\mathrm{log}}) = \langle \mathrm{PK}(R), \mathsf{state} \rangle$. Similarly, for each foreign key $S[B] \to R[A]$ originally associated to relations R and S in $\mathcal{L}$, we insert in the DBMS the foreign key $S_{\mathrm{log}}[B, \mathsf{state}] \to R_{\mathrm{log}}[A, \mathsf{state}]$ over their corresponding state log relations.

With this strategy, the "referential" part of R is suitably relativized w.r.t. a state, while at the same time all the other attributes are compactly stored in R_{raw}, and referenced possibly multiple times from R_{log}. In addition, notice that, given a state identified by s, the full extension of relation R in s can be fully reconstructed by *(i)* selecting the tuples of R_{log} where $\mathsf{state} = \mathsf{s}$; *(ii)* joining the obtained selection with R_{raw} on RID; *(iii)* finally projecting the result on the original attributes of R. In general, this technique shows how an arbitrary SQL query over $\mathcal{L}$ can be directly reformulated as a state-relativized query over the corresponding DAPHNE schema.

Example 4. Consider relation schemas *CurrReq* and *TrvlMaxAmnt* in Fig. 1. Figure 4 shows their representation in DAPHNE, suitably pairing *CurrReq*$_{\mathrm{raw}}$ with *CurrReq*$_{\mathrm{log}}$, and *TrvlMaxAmnt*$_{\mathrm{raw}}$ with *TrvlMaxAmnt*$_{\mathrm{log}}$. Each state log table directly references a corresponding raw data storage table (e.g., *CurrReq*$_{\mathrm{log}}$[RID] $\to$ *CurrReq*$_{\mathrm{raw}}$[RID]), and *TrvlMaxAmnt*'s state log table, due to the FK in the original DAP, will reference a suitable key of *CurrReq*$_{\mathrm{log}}$ (i.e., *TrvlMaxAmnt*$_{\mathrm{log}}$[state, FID] $\to$ *CurrReq*$_{\mathrm{log}}$[state, ID]). Figures 5, 6 and 7 show the evolution of the DBMS in response to the application of three ground actions, with full history recall.   ◁

We now discuss updates over R. As already pointed out, R_{raw} stores any tuple that occurs in some state, that is, tuples are never deleted from R_{raw}. Deletions are simply obtained by *not* referencing the deleted tuple in the new state. For instance, in Fig. 5, it can be seen that the first tuple of *Pending*$_{\mathrm{raw}}$ (properly extended with its ID, through RID) has been deleted from *Pending* in state 2: while being present in state 1 (cf. first tuple of *Pending*$_{\mathrm{log}}$), the tuple is not anymore in state 2 (cf. third tuple of *Pending*$_{\mathrm{log}}$).

As for additions, we proceed as follows. Before inserting a new tuple, we check whether it is already present in R_{raw}. If so, we update only R_{log} by copying the

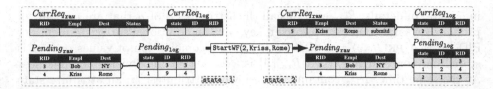

Fig. 5. Action application with two partial DB snapshots mentioning *Pending* and *CurrReq*. Here, StartWF is applied in state 1 with {id = 2, empl = Kriss, dest = Rome} as binding and, in turn, generates a new state 2.

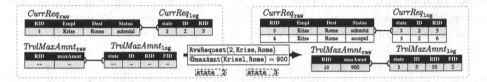

Fig. 6. Action application with two partial DB snapshots mentioning *CurrReq* and *TrvlMaxAmnt*. Here, RvwRequest is applied in state 2 with {id = 2, empl = Kriss, dest = Rome} as binding and 900 resulting from the invocation of service @maxAmnt that, in turn, generates a new state 3.

$R_{\log}$ tuple referencing the corresponding RID in R_{raw}. In the copied tuple, the value of attribute state is going to be the one of the newly generated state, while the values of ID and all foreign key attributes remain unchanged. If the tuple is not present in R_{raw}, it is also added to R_{raw} together with a fresh RID. Notice that in that case its ID and FK attributes are provided as input, and thus they are simply added, together with the value of state, to $R_{\log}$. In the actual implementation, R_{raw} features also a hash attribute, with the value of a hash function computed based on original R attributes (extracted from both R_{raw} and $R_{\log}$). This speeds up the search for identical tuples in R_{raw}.

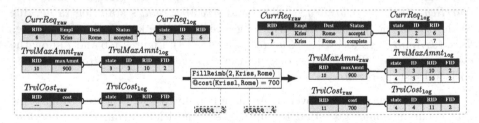

Fig. 7. Action application with three partial DB snapshots mentioning *CurrReq*, *TrvlMaxAmnt* and *TrvlCost*. Here, FillReimb is applied in state 3 with {id = 2, empl = Kriss, dest = Rome} as binding and 700 resulting from the invocation of service @cost that, in turn, generates a new state 4.

Finally, we consider the case of relation schemas whose content is not changed when updating a state to a new state. Assume that relation schema S stays unaltered. After updating R, it is enough to update $S_{\log}$ by copying previous state entries and updating the value of their state id to the actual one. If a FK, whose left-hand side is $S[B]$, belongs to $\mathcal{L}$, the pair $\langle B, \mathtt{state} \rangle$ will reference the most recent versions of the previously referenced tuples. Consider, e.g., Fig. 7. While in his current request Kriss is changing the request status when moving from state 3 to state 4, the maximum traveling budget assigned to this request (a tuple in $TrvlMaxAmnt$) should reference the latest version of the corresponding tuple in $CurrReq$. Indeed, in state 4, a new tuple in $TrvlMaxAmnt_{\log}$ is referencing a new tuple in $CurrReq_{\log}$ that, in turn, corresponds to the one with the updated request status.

Control Layer. Each action α of $\mathcal{P}$, together with its dedicated CA rule, is encoded by DAPHNE into three stored procedures. The encoding is quite direct, thanks to the fact that both action conditions and action effect specifications are specified using SQL.

The first stored procedure, $\alpha\_{\mathtt{ca\_eval(s)}}$, evaluates the CA rule of α in state s over the respective DB (obtained by inspecting the state log relations whose state column matches with s), and stores the all returned parameter assignments for α in a dedicated table $\alpha\_{\mathtt{params}}$. All parameter assignments in $\alpha\_{\mathtt{params}}$ are initially unmarked, meaning that they are available for the user to choose. The second stored procedure, $\alpha\_{\mathtt{eff\_eval(s,b)}}$, executes queries corresponding to all the effects of α over the DB of state s, possibly using action parameters from $\alpha\_{\mathtt{params}}$ extracted via a binding identifier b. Query results provide values to instantiate service calls, as well as those facts that must be deleted from or added to the current DB. The third stored procedure, $\alpha\_{\mathtt{eff\_exec(s,b)}}$, transactionally performs the actual delete and insert operations for a given state s and a binding identifier b, using the results of service calls. It is worth noting that, in our running example, stored procedures that represent an action, all together, in average contain around 40 complex queries. We now detail the DAPHNE action execution cycle in a given state s. *(1)* The cycle starts with the user choosing one of the available actions presented by the **Flow Engine**. The available actions are acquired by calling $\alpha\_{\mathtt{ca\_eval(s)}}$, for each action α in $\mathcal{P}$. *(2)* If any unmarked parameter is present in $\alpha\_{\mathtt{params}}$, the user is asked to choose one of those (by selecting a binding identifier b); once chosen, the parameter is marked, and the **Flow Engine** proceeds to the evaluation of α by calling $\alpha\_{\mathtt{eff\_eval(s,b)}}$. If there are no such parameters, the user is asked to choose another available action, and the present step is repeated. *(3)* If $\alpha\_{\mathtt{eff\_eval(s,b)}}$ involves service calls, these are passed to the **Service Manager** component, which fetches the corresponding results. *(4)* $\alpha\_{\mathtt{eff\_exec(s,b)}}$ is executed. If all constraints in $\mathcal{L}$ are satisfied, the transaction is committed and a new iteration starts from step 1; otherwise, the transaction is aborted and the execution history is kept unaltered, and the execution continues from step 2.

3.2   Realization of the Three Usage Modalities

Let us now discuss how the three usage modalities are realized in DAPHNE. The simple enactment modality is realized by only recalling the current information about log relations. Enactment with history recall is instead handled as follows. First, the generation of a new state always comes with an additional update over an accessory 1-tuple relation schema indicating the timestamp of the actual update operation. The fact that timestamps always increase along the execution guarantees that each new state is genuinely different from previously encountered ones. Finally, an additional binary state transition table is employed, so as to keep track of the resulting total order over state identifiers. By considering our running example, in state 4 shown in Fig. 7, the content of the transition table would consist of the three pairs $\langle 1, 2 \rangle$, $\langle 2, 3 \rangle$, and $\langle 3, 4 \rangle$.

We now discuss state space construction, which is the cornerstone of **RQ3** and that should be ideally realized in a way that adheres to how the enactment engine works. In this way, we ensure that the state space is carried out on the exact same model that is enacted. Due to the presence of external services that may inject fresh input data, there are in general infinitely many different executions of the process, possibly visiting infinitely many different DBs (differing in at least one tuple). In other words, the resulting transition system has infinitely many different states. However, thanks to the correspondence between dapSL and DCDSs, we can realize in DAPHNE the abstraction techniques from [1, 4] to attack the verification of such infinite-state transition systems. The main idea behind such techniques is the following. When carrying out verification, it is not important to observe all possible DBs that can be produced by executing the available actions with all possible service call results, but it suffices to only consider a *meaningful* combination of values, representing all possible ways to relate tuples with other tuples in the DB, in terms of (in)equality of their different components. This is done by carefully selecting the representative values. In [1,4], it has been shown that this technique produces a *faithful* representation of the original RTS, and that this representation is also *finite* if the original system is *state bounded*, that is, has a pre-defined (possibly unknown) bound on the number of tuples that can be stored therein.[1] Constructing the state space is therefore instrumental towards verification of properties such as reachability and soundness, and temporal model checking (in the style of [4]).

State space construction is smoothly handled in DAPHNE as follows. When executed in this mode, DAPHNE replaces the service call manager with a mock-up manager that, whenever a service call is invoked, returns all and only *meaningful* results, in the technical sense described above. E.g., if the current DB only contains string a, invoking a service call that returns a string may only give two interesting results: a itself, or a string different than a. To cover the latter case, the mock-up manager picks a representative value, say b in this example, implementing the representative selection strategy defined in [1,4]. With this mock-up manager in place, DAPHNE constructs the state space by executing

---

[1] Even in the presence of this bound, infinitely many different DBs can be encountered, by changing the values stored therein.

the following iteration. A state s is picked (at the beginning, only the initial state exists). For each enabled ground action in s, and for all *relevant* possible results returned by the mock-up manager, the DB instance corresponding to the update is generated. If such a DB instance has been already encountered (i.e., is associated to an already existing state), then the corresponding state id s' is fetched. Otherwise, a new id s' is created, inserting its content into the DBMS. Recall that s' is *not* a timestamp, but just a symbolic, unique state id. The state transition table is then updated, by inserting $\langle s, s' \rangle$, which indeed witnesses that s' is one of the successors of s. The cycle is then repeated until all states and all enabled ground actions therein are processed. Notice that, differently from the enactment with history recall, in this case the state transition table is graph-structured, and in fact reconstructs the abstract representation of the (RTS) system capturing the execution semantics of $\mathcal{S}$. In [5] we give a few examples of the state spaces constructed for the travel reimbursement process using a special visualizer API implemented in DAPHNE mainly for debugging purposes.

We report here some initial experimental results on state space construction in DAPHNE, demonstrating the complexity in constructing a transition system whose states are full-fledged relational DBs.

Table 1. Experimental results

#(F)	#(States)	#(Edges)	avg(Time)
1	10	10	0.93
2	128	231	4.36
3	1949	5456	114.39
4	32925	128155	6575.95

All experiments were performed on a MacOS machine with a 2.4 GHz Intel Core i5 and 8 GB RAM, encoding and storing the travel management process in PostgreSQL 9.4. Table 1 shows results for the construction of abstract RTSs on randomly generated initial DBs with a number of facts specified in #(**F**). Each experiments come with a time limit of 7200 s, which suffices to generate relatively big abstract RTSs and recognize growth patterns in the conducted experiments. We provide full statistics on the generated abstract RTS: #(**S**) represents the number of states, #(**E**) the number of edges, and **avg(Time)** the average RCYCL execution time. The most critical measures are **Time** and #(**E**), with the latter showing the number of successful action executions, each of which consists in the application of the corresponding SQL code. Such a code consists, for the travel management process, of ~40 complex queries per action. This gives an indication about the feasibility of our approach, but also points out that optimizations have to be studied to handle very large state spaces.

4 Discussion and Related Work

Our approach belongs to the line of research focused on modeling, enactment and verification of data-centric processes. Specifically, DAPHNE directly relates to: *(i)* the declarative rule-based *Guard-Stage-Milestone* (GSM) language [6] and its BizArtifact execution platform; *(ii)* the OMG *CMMN* standard for case handling (https://www.omg.org/spec/CMMN/); *(iii)* the object-aware business process management approach implemented by *PHILharmonic Flows* [12]; *(iv)* the extension of GSM called EZ-Flow [23], with SeGA [22] as an execution platform; *(v)* the declarative data-centric process language RESEDA based on term rewriting systems [19]. These approaches emphasize the evolution of data objects through different states, but often miss a clear representation of the control-flow dimension. For example, GSM provides means for specifying business artifact lifecycles in a declarative rule-based manner, and heavily relies on ECA rules over the data to implicitly define the allowed execution flows. Other examples in *(ii)–(iv)* are rooted in similar abstractions, but provide more sophisticated interaction mechanisms between artifacts and their lifecycle components. dapSL shares with these approaches the idea of "data-centricity", but departs from them since it provides a minimalistic, programming-oriented solution that only retains the notions of persistent data, actions, and CA rules. In this respect, the closest approach to ours is RESEDA. Similarly to dapSL, a RESEDA process consists of reactive rules and behavioral constraints operating over data using the paradigm of term rewriting. RESEDA manipulates only semi-structured data (such as XML or JSON), which have to be specified directly in the tool. dapSL focuses instead on the standard relational model to represent data.

Differently from all such approaches, state-of-the-art business process management systems (BPMSs), such as Bizagi, Bonita BPM, Camunda, Activiti, and YAWL, support an explicit, conceptual representation of the process control flow and the lifecycle of activities, following conventional process modeling notations such as the de-facto standard BPMN. However, such notations tackle only the process logic, and do not provide any conceptual means to address the decision and task logic. Consequently, no conceptual guidelines are given to such BPMSs when it comes to the interplay between the process and the underlying persistent data. The result is that they see the data logic as a "procedural attachment", i.e., a piece of code whose functioning is not captured at the conceptual level, making it difficult to properly understand and govern the so-obtained integrated models [3,8,18]. On the positive side, contemporary BPMSs typically adopt a high-level representation of persistent data, e.g., in the form of object-oriented or conceptual data models. We comment on the relationship and possible synergies between such approaches and dapSL, considering how dapSL could be enhanced with an explicit representation of control-flow, and/or with a conceptual layer for representing the data.

dapSL **with Explicit Control-Flow.** At the modeling level, it is natural to envision an integrated approach where the process logic (including control-flow, event-driven behavior, hierarchical decomposition and activity lifecycle) is specified using conventional notations such as BPMN, the decision logic is specified in standard SQL, and the task logic using dapSL actions. The main question then becomes how the resulting approach can be enacted/analyzed. An option is to apply a translation of the process and decision logic into dapSL rules, and then rely on DAPHNE for enactment and state-space construction. Thanks to the correspondence between dapSL and DCDSs, this can be done by directly implementing the existing translation procedures from process modeling notations to DCDSs, where each control-flow pattern and step in the lifecycle of activities/artifacts becomes a dedicated CA rule. Translations have been defined for: *(i)* data-centric process models supporting the explicit notion of process instance (i.e., case) [14]; *(ii)* Petri nets equipped with resources and tokens with data [15]; *(iii)* recent variants of (colored) Petri nets equipped with a DB storage [7,16]; *(iv)* GSM-based business artifacts [20].

dapSL with Conceptual Data Models. It is often desirable to specify processes at a higher level of abstraction than the database level (e.g., in the form of an object model or ontology). However, if storage stays at the relational level, introducing an intermediate conceptual layer poses key theoretical challenges, not specifically related to our approach, but in general to the alignment between the conceptual and the storage layers. In this respect, the most difficult problem, reminiscent of the long-standing view update problem in database theory [9], is to suitably propagate updates expressed over the conceptual layer on the actual data storage. Some recent works attacked this problem by introducing intermediate data structures [22], or by establishing complex mappings to disambiguate how updates should be propagated [21]. This is not needed if the conceptual layer is a "lossless view" of the data layer, ensuring that high-level updates can always be rewritten into relational updates. This is the approach adopted in Object-Relational Mapping (ORM), such as Hibernate. A conceptual data layer realized as an ORM specification can be directly tackled in DAPHNE. In fact, dapSL can easily be reformulated by using ORM query languages (such as Hibernate HQL) instead of SQL. Then, the back-end of DAPHNE can be simply modified so as to invoke, when needed, the translation of high-level queries into SQL, a functionality natively offered by ORM technologies.

5   Conclusions

We have introduced a declarative, purely relational framework for data-aware processes, in which SQL is used as the core data inspection and update language. We have reported on its implementation in the DAPHNE tool, which at once accounts for modeling, enactment, and state space construction for verification. Since our approach is having a minimalistic, SQL-centric flavor, it is crucial to empirically validate its usability among database and process experts. We also intend to interface DAPHNE with different concrete end user-oriented languages for the integrated modeling of processes and data. As for formal analysis, we plan to augment the state space construction with native temporal model checking capabilities. Finally, given that DAPHNE can generate a log including all performed actions and data changes, we aim at investigating its possible applications to (multi-perspective) process mining.

Acknowledgments. This research has been partially supported by the UNIBZ projects *REKAP* and *DACOMAN*.

References

1. Hariri, B.B., Calvanese, D., De Giacomo, G., Deutsch, A., Montali, M.: Verification of relational data-centric dynamic systems with external services. In: Proceedings of PODS (2013)
2. Belardinelli, F., Lomuscio, A., Patrizi, F.: Verification of agent-based artifact systems. J. Artif. Intell. Res. **51**, 333–376 (2014). https://doi.org/10.1613/jair.4424
3. Calvanese, D., De Giacomo, G., Montali, M.: Foundations of data aware process analysis: a database theory perspective. In: Proceedings of PODS (2013)
4. Calvanese, D., De Giacomo, G., Montali, M., Patrizi, F.: FO μ-calculus over generic transition systems and applications to the situation calculus. Inf. Comp. **259**(3), 328–347 (2018)
5. Calvanese, D., Montali, M., Patrizi, F., Rivkin, A.: Modelling and enactment of data-aware processes. CoRR abs/1810.08062 (2018). http://arxiv.org/abs/1810.08062
6. Damaggio, E., Hull, R., Vaculín, R.: On the Equivalence of incremental and fixpoint semantics for business artifacts with guard-stage-milestone lifecycles. In: Rinderle-Ma, S., Toumani, F., Wolf, K. (eds.) BPM 2011. LNCS, vol. 6896, pp. 396–412. Springer, Heidelberg (2011). https://doi.org/10.1007/978-3-642-23059-2_29
7. De Masellis, R., Di Francescomarino, C., Ghidini, C., Montali, M., Tessaris, S.: Add data into business process verification: bridging the gap between theory and practice. In: Proceedings of AAAI. AAAI Press (2017)
8. Dumas, M.: On the convergence of data and process engineering. In: Eder, J., Bielikova, M., Tjoa, A.M. (eds.) ADBIS 2011. LNCS, vol. 6909, pp. 19–26. Springer, Heidelberg (2011). https://doi.org/10.1007/978-3-642-23737-9_2
9. Furtado, A.L., Casanova, M.A.: Updating relational views. In: Kim, W., Reiner, D.S., Batory, D.S. (eds.) Query Processing in Database Systems. Topics in Information Systems, pp. 127–142. Springer, Heidelberg (1985). https://doi.org/10.1007/978-3-642-82375-6_7
10. Hull, R.: Artifact-centric business process models: brief survey of research results and challenges. In: Meersman, R., Tari, Z. (eds.) OTM 2008. LNCS, vol. 5332, pp. 1152–1163. Springer, Heidelberg (2008). https://doi.org/10.1007/978-3-540-88873-4_17
11. Köpke, J., Su, J.: Towards quality-aware translations of activity-centric processes to guard stage milestone. In: La Rosa, M., Loos, P., Pastor, O. (eds.) BPM 2016. LNCS, vol. 9850, pp. 308–325. Springer, Cham (2016). https://doi.org/10.1007/978-3-319-45348-4_18
12. Künzle, V., Weber, B., Reichert, M.: Object-aware business processes: Fundamental requirements and their support in existing approaches. Int. J. Inf. Syst. Model. Des. **2**(2), 19–46 (2011)
13. Li, Y., Deutsch, A., Vianu, V.: VERIFAS: a practical verifier for artifact systems. PVLDB **11**(3), 283–296 (2017)
14. Montali, M., Calvanese, D.: Soundness of data-aware, case-centric processes. Int. J. Softw. Tools Technol. Transf. **18**(5), 535–558 (2016)
15. Montali, M., Rivkin, A.: Model checking Petri nets with names using data-centric dynamic systems. Formal Aspects Comput. **28**, 615–641 (2016)
16. Montali, M., Rivkin, A.: DB-Nets: on the marriage of colored Petri Nets and relational databases. In: Koutny, M., Kleijn, J., Penczek, W. (eds.) Transactions on Petri Nets and Other Models of Concurrency XII. LNCS, vol. 10470, pp. 91–118. Springer, Heidelberg (2017). https://doi.org/10.1007/978-3-662-55862-1_5

17. Olivé, A.: Conceptual Modeling of Information Systems. Springer, Heidelberg (2007). https://doi.org/10.1007/978-3-540-39390-0
18. Reichert, M.: Process and data: two sides of the same coin? In: Meersman, R., et al. (eds.) OTM 2012. LNCS, vol. 7565, pp. 2–19. Springer, Heidelberg (2012). https://doi.org/10.1007/978-3-642-33606-5_2
19. Seco, J.C., Debois, S., Hildebrandt, T.T., Slaats, T.: RESEDA: declaring live event-driven computations as reactive semi-structured data. In: Proceedings of EDOC, pp. 75–84 (2018)
20. Solomakhin, D., Montali, M., Tessaris, S., De Masellis, R.: Verification of artifact-centric systems: decidability and modeling issues. In: Basu, S., Pautasso, C., Zhang, L., Fu, X. (eds.) ICSOC 2013. LNCS, vol. 8274, pp. 252–266. Springer, Heidelberg (2013). https://doi.org/10.1007/978-3-642-45005-1_18
21. Sun, Y., Su, J., Wu, B., Yang, J.: Modeling data for business processes. In: Proceedings of ICDE, pp. 1048–1059. IEEE Computer Society (2014)
22. Sun, Y., Su, J., Yang, J.: Universal artifacts: a new approach to business process management (BPM) systems. ACM TMIS 7(1), 3 (2016)
23. Xu, W., Su, J., Yan, Z., Yang, J., Zhang, L.: An artifact-centric approach to dynamic modification of workflow execution. In: Meersman, R., et al. (eds.) OTM 2011. LNCS, vol. 7044, pp. 256–273. Springer, Heidelberg (2011). https://doi.org/10.1007/978-3-642-25109-2_17

D²IA: Stream Analytics on User-Defined Event Intervals

Ahmed Awad[1]([✉]), Riccardo Tommasini[2], Mahmoud Kamel[1],
Emanuele Della Valle[2], and Sherif Sakr[1]

[1] University of Tartu, Tartu, Estonia
{ahmed.awad,mahmoud.shoush,sherif.sakr}@ut.ee
[2] Politecnico di Milano, Milan, Italy
{riccardo.tommasini,emanuele.dellavalle}@polimi.it

Abstract. Nowadays, modern Big Stream Processing Solutions (e.g. `Spark`, `Flink`) are working towards ultimate frameworks for streaming analytics. In order to achieve this goal, they started to offer extensions of SQL that incorporate stream-oriented primitives such as windowing and Complex Event Processing (CEP). The former enables stateful computation on infinite sequences of data items while the latter focuses on the detection of events pattern. In most of the cases, data items and events are considered instantaneous, i.e., they are single time points in a discrete temporal domain. Nevertheless, a point-based time semantics does not satisfy the requirements of a number of use-cases. For instance, it is not possible to detect the interval during which the temperature increases until the temperature begins to decrease, nor all the relations this interval subsumes. To tackle this challenge, we present D²IA; a set of novel abstract operators to define analytics on user-defined event intervals based on raw events and to efficiently reason about temporal relationships between intervals and/or point events. We realize the implementation of the concepts of D²IA on top of `Esper`, a centralized stream processing system, and `Flink`, a distributed stream processing engine for big data.

Keywords: Big Stream Processing · Complex event processing · User-defined event intervals

1 Introduction

Streaming data analytics has become a key enabler for organizations' success and sustainability. Data velocity is often too high, and we are forced to process data on-the-fly. To solve this challenge, Stream Processing Engines (SPEs) have been proposed. SPEs are commonly classified into two main categories: Data Stream Management Systems (DSMSs) and complex event processing (CEP) [8].

As streams are infinite sequences of partially ordered data (events), both DSMSs and CEP solutions offer special operators to deal with unboundedness. In

© Springer Nature Switzerland AG 2019
P. Giorgini and B. Weber (Eds.): CAiSE 2019, LNCS 11483, pp. 346–361, 2019.
https://doi.org/10.1007/978-3-030-21290-2_22

particular, DSMSs apply the concepts of temporal windowing that slice streams into finite portions [9] and then applies stateful aggregations, e.g., the average temperature over the last 5 min (Listing 1.1 - Line 1). On the other hand, CEP employs non-deterministic finite-state machines and rule-based languages to define and detect event-patterns on streams [10], e.g., emit fire if a smoke detection is followed by a temperature higher than 40 (Listing 1.1 - Lines 3, 4).

Listing 1.1. DSMS and CEP query in EPL

```
1 select avg(val) from Temperature#time(5 min) output every 5 min;
2
3 insert into Fire
4 select * from pattern [Smoke ->Temperature(val >40)] where timer:within(5 min);
```

In practice, the state-of-the-art of SPEs is vast and includes a variety of DSMSs and CEP languages, as well as hybrid approaches. For instance, EPL is an industrial stream processing language that combines DSMS and CEP features. Esper[1] and OracleCEP[2] are examples of centralized solutions that implement it. Recently, BigSPEs represent a new generation of distributed, scalable and fault-tolerant SPE systems (e.g. Spark, Flink) that have been designed to address the volume and velocity challenges of the Big Data wave. Nevertheless, BigSPEs' focus on scalability goes at the expense of providing less expressiveness. In particular, existing systems provide little expressive Domain Specific Languages (DSL) that do not meet the expectations raised by the centralized solutions [13]. In practice, such expressiveness is crucial in several applications, e.g., healthcare. For example, let us consider the following air traffic scenario where many events are continuously produced during flights, e.g., changes in altitude, speed, and heading of an aircraft. In such scenario, we can be interested in detecting those intervals during which a plane is in cruising mode and performs a change in altitude which is more than 10%.

Listing 1.2. Example encoded in EPL

```
1 create schema AltitudeChange as (starts long, endts long,
2        init_alt long, fin_alt long);
3 create schema CruisePeriod as (onts long, offts long)
4        starttimestamp onts endtimestamp offts;
5 insert into AltitudeChange
6 select minby(ts).value as init_alt, maxby(ts).value as fin_al,
7    maxby(ts).ts as endts, minby(ts).ts as starts
8 from Altitude#time(30 minutes) output every 30 minutes;
9 insert into CruisePeriod select onts, offts from CruiseMode
10 match_recognize ( measures a.ts as onts, b.ts as offts
11 pattern (A B)* defines A as A.value='On', B as B.value='Off');
12 select ac.* from AltitudeChange as ac, CruisePeriod cp
13 where ac.during(cp) and abs(ac.fin_alt - ac.init_alt) / ac.init_alt >= 0.1);
```

If we implement such scenario using EPL (Listing 1.2), we observe that we cannot express it in a single query, however, we need to create a query network. Moreover, the network complexity, i.e., the number of required queries, increases when more conditions are added to the original scenario. On the other hand, if we consider BigSPEs, we observe that they lack the possibility to generate

---

[1] http://www.espertech.com/.

[2] https://docs.oracle.com/cd/E17904_01/doc.1111/e14476/.

and process streams of events with a duration, i.e., interval events. Figure 1 summarizes the spectrum of the streaming language operators extending the CQL model proposed in [5] with three new families of operators, i.e., Event-to-Interval (E2I), Interval-to-Interval (I2I), and Interval-to-Event (I2E) operators.

Among the state-of-the-art stream processing engines, only centralized solutions provide query languages that are expressive enough to process stream of events with durations [4,17].

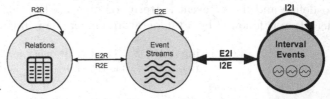

Fig. 1. Stream-Event-IntervalEvent models and operators

However, these queries have to be handcrafted by the application developer connecting several queries, as shown in Listing 1.2. In order to fill this gap, in this paper, we introduce D^2IA (Data-driven Interval Analytics), a *novel* family of operators that enables interval events generation and reasoning. In particular, D^2IA allows generating data-driven event intervals from instantaneous events (**E2I**) by combining event patterns with an extensive collection of aggregation functions. It selects intervals with maximum durations to reduce the complexity of the processing (**I2I**). In addition, it enables efficient reasoning on intervals using Allen's Algebra [3] (**I2E**).

The operators of D^2IA have been designed according to the principles of Codd's language [7,17]:: **Minimality**, i.e., a language should provide only the necessary constructs to avoid multiple ways to express the same meaning. **Symmetry**, i.e., a language construct always expresses the same semantics regardless of the usage context. **Orthogonality**, i.e., meaningful combinations of language constructs should be applicable. We demonstrate the expressiveness and practicality of D^2IA in two ways: (i) we provide an algorithm that translates D^2IA operators to an expressive streaming query language, EPL, that is employed only by centralized solutions. (ii) We implement D^2IA operators on top of Apache Flink[3], a popular distributed stream processing engine.

The remainder of the paper is organized as follows. Necessary background is introduced in Sect. 2. Concepts behind D^2IA are presented in Sect. 3. Section 4 describes the implementation details. Related work is discussed in Sect. 5 before we finally conclude the paper in Sect. 6.

2   Background

2.1   Complex Event Processing

Complex event processing aims at the identification of patterns that represent a complex event over input streams of low-level events [10]. Patterns are analogous to defining regular expressions over strings; they are defined w.r.t. event types

---

[3] https://flink.apache.org/.

and matched against event instances in the streams. Traditionally, events are seen as instantaneous and the timestamp of the last matched event is assigned to the emitted complex event. In the following, we recap these notions.

Definition 1 (Raw Event). *A raw event is an instantaneous and atomic notification of an occurrence of interest at a point in time.*

A raw event has a payload of interest to the application, a timestamp that indicates the point in time when it took place. Moreover, event instances are usually organized in classes or topics. We can represent an event as a triple $<id, payload, ts>$ where id is an identifier of the event source, $payload$ is simply a list of key-value pairs, and ts is the timestamp at which the event was generated. The event type is a determined by id and payload. A complex event is derived from a collection of events using pattern matching, e.g., $FireEvent = SmokeEvent$ *followed-by* $HighTemperatureEvent$.

Definition 2 (Complex Event). *A complex event is a composition of one or more events. The composition is obtained as a result of matching a pattern to streams of composing events. A complex event has a payload and a timestamp which depends on the semantics of the CEP language.*

2.2 Data-Driven Windows

Recently, several types of data-driven windows have been discussed in literature. Traditional window operators [5,9] lack the necessary expressiveness to capture relevant situations. For instance, consider the case of a smart home application. It might be interesting to report only those windows in which temperature goes above a certain threshold. In such case, it is not known ahead when the temperature will rise, i.e. the window width can not be provided. To tackle such use-cases, more expressive window operators have been proposed. Session windows [1] are one example of time-based windows that allows slicing the stream based on user-behavior, e.g., a click stream session. Grossenklaus et al. [12] proposed four types of data-driven windows called frames: (i) **Threshold Frames** report time intervals within a stream where an attribute of a stream element goes higher (lower) than a given threshold. (ii) **Delta Frames** report time intervals within which an attribute of a stream element changes by more than amount x. That is, we can find two elements within the interval such that the difference between their attribute values is higher (lower) than x. (iii) **Aggregate Frames** report time intervals within which an aggregate of an attribute of stream elements remains below a certain threshold. (iv) **Boundary Frames** are time intervals within which an attribute of stream elements remains within one of the predefined boundaries.

3   Operators for User-Defined Intervals Analytics

In this section, we start by defining interval events. Then, we present our D²IA operators for deriving and reasoning about user-defined interval events.

As stated in Definition 2, a complex event has a payload and a timestamp similar to a raw event (Definition 1). However, while it is understandable that the definition of the derived payload is left to the application developer in terms of payloads of the composing events, the reasoning about the timestamp should be more rigorous. The *payload* is a list of key-value pairs. We define two auxiliary functions: (i) *keys* :: payload -> [keys], which returns the keys present in the payload and; (ii) *val* :: *payload, key− > value* to retrieve the value associated to a given key in a payload.

The literature on CEP contains some examples that acknowledge the limitations of an instantaneous temporal model for events. Interval-based models have a richer semantics than traditional point-based ones [4]. Moreover, an interval-based temporal models can represent point events without loss of generality.

Definition 3 (Interval Event). *An interval event is a special event that has a temporal duration which is defined in term of a two time points,* start *and* end.

Interval events, a.k.a. situations, are special kind of events that instead of having a time point-based timestamp, they have a duration, i.e., a temporal interval, within which the event is observed.

Considering Codd's language design principles, introduced in Sect. 1, and inspired by the data frames, discussed in Sect. 2.2, we elicit the following requirements: (R1) **Contextual State Management**, i.e., the target language must allow the definition of contextual variables and partitioning of the state. R1 is required to ensure the feasibility of relative and absolute conditions. (R2)

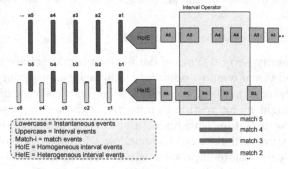

Fig. 2. D^2IA overview: Homogeneous/Heterogeneous Interval Event generators consume events streams and produce interval events.

Analytical Features, i.e., the operators must enable stateful aggregations, for example employing temporal/physical windows. R2 is required to express data-driven windows. (R3) **Pattern Detection**, i.e., the operators must enable interval generation via event detection. R3 is required since complex events can be seen as interval events, considering the timestamp of the initial match and the timestamp of the last match in the provided pattern [4].

In the following sections, we provide details about interval generators and operators. Figure 2 exemplifies a pipeline in which two event streams are transformed into interval events using *interval generators* and fed into an *interval operator* that reasons about the interval events.

3.1 Homogeneous Interval Events Generators

Interval event generators represent a family of D^{2}IA operators which are responsible for creating interval events out of a stream of instantaneous events. In particular, the interval generator transforms the input stream(s) into the output stream based on a pattern specification. If a single input stream is used, the resulting event intervals are *homogeneous*. Otherwise, they are *heterogeneous*.

Definition 4 (Homogeneous Interval Event Generator). *Let E be a raw event from Definition 1. A homogeneous interval event HoIE specification is defined by a tuple* $< E, Occurrence, Value, KeyBy, Condition, Within >$ *where:*

- *Event: refers to the type of the event on which the interval to be defined.*
- *Occurrence: is on the form (min, max) to indicate the minimum and maximum number of event instances to match. Also, wild card * can be used to make no upper-bound on the number of occurrences.*
- *Value: refers to either a constant value, an expression, or an aggregation over the event payload's attribute value. Possible aggregation functions are: min, max, avg, etc. aggregates are computed over the matched raw events.*
- *KeyBy: specifies an attribute in the event's payload to group event instances.*
- *Condition: defines a filter condition over the event instances. Conditions are expressed w.r.t. event's payload attributes and can be either absolute or relative. The former compares the event instance's attribute value with a constant value; the latter compares the event instance's attribute value with an expression over other event instances' attribute values. Relative condition are expressed with the form start(EventInstance.value θ v) $\wedge$ subsequent(EventInstance.value θ Value).*
- *Within: specifies a maximum time interval to wait for the match to validate since the first event arrives. An example is 5 s,*

A homogeneous event interval is generated when one or more (raw) events of the same type are observed in succession. Using analogy with regular expressions, a homogeneous event interval is on the form A{min,max}, where A is the event type. Optionally, the interval definition can be restricted by a temporal window, a condition, or a combination thereof. The temporal window restricts the maximum temporal gap among the occurrences of event instances. The condition puts a restriction on the value of an event instance property to consider it as a match. In D^{2}IA, it is possible to define relative and absolute conditions (Definition 4). The interval event value can be obtained by applying an aggregate on the matching raw events. We use HoIE as an operator to build intervals specification using fluent APIs pattern[4].

Example. Assume a temperature event on the form *Temperature* $<$ *sensor, temp,ts* $>$ which refers to the *sensor* ID that generated the event, the temperature *temp* reading and the timestamp *ts* for the reading. We can define an event interval with absolute condition as

---

[4] https://martinfowler.com/bliki/FluentInterface.html.

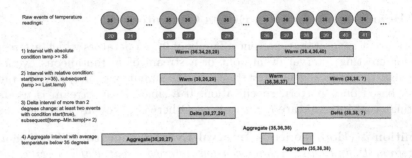

Fig. 3. Homogeneous interval events for the different data-driven frames

Listing 3.1. Warm interval with absolute condition

```
1 WarmAbsolute=HoIE.Event(Temperature).Value(Aggregate.avg(
2 Temperature.temp)).Occurrence(2,5).KeyBy(Temperature.sensor)
3 .Within(5,seconds).AbsoluteCondition(Conditions.greaterOrEqual(
4 Temperature.temp,35))
```

We can also define an event interval with a relative condition on the form.

Listing 3.2. Warm interval with relative condition

```
1 WarmRelative=HoIE.Event(Temperature).Occurrence(2,5)
2 .Value(Aggregate.max(Temperature.temp))
3 .KeyBy(Temperature.sensor).Within(5,seconds).RelativeCondition
4 .Start(Conditions.greaterOrEqual(Temperature.temp,35))
5 .Subsequent(Conditions.greaterOrEqual(Temperature.temp,
6 Last.key(Temperature.temp)))
```

In Listing 3.1, the interval generator is instructed to generate an interval
event of type `WarmAbsolute`. An instance of that interval event is generated upon
observing 2 to 5 instances of the `Temperature` event. These instances have to be
observed within 5 s from each other and each temperature event instance must
have its *temp* value grater than 35. The generated interval instance will have its
value as the **average** of the temperature readings of the matching `Temperature`
event instances. In Listing 3.2, an event interval of type `WarmRelative` is defined
on the same stream of `Temperature` events with the same time window. However, the relative condition indicates that the first matching `Temperature` event
must have its reading greater than 35. Each succeeding matching event must
have its reading greater than or equal to the previously matching event in the
pattern. The value of the generated event interval will be the **maximum** temperature value from the matched raw events. In both cases, **keyBy** is used to group
the raw events, temperature events in these cases, by their sensor id. Figure 3
shows a stream of temperature events on the top, for the same sensor, and the
different matches and event intervals generated for the two cases on rows 1 and
2, respectively.

The ability to define relative conditions on stream elements contributing to a
homogeneous event interval allows D^2IA to cover the four data frames discussed
in Sect. 2.2. To define a threshold frame on temperature events of value 35°, an
interval in D^2IA can be defined much like the `WarmAbsolute` interval definition

from Listing 3.2. Within this context, a delta frame can be defined on the interval within which the temperature reading increases by more than 2°. This can be defined as shown in Listing 3.3.

Listing 3.3. Delta interval

```
1 Delta=HoIE.Event(Temperature).Occurrence(2,Occurrences.Unbounded)
2 .Value(Aggregate.max(Temperature.temp))
3 .KeyBy(Temperature.sensor).RelativeCondition.Start(true)
4 .Subsequent(Conditions.greaterOrEqual((Math.absolute(
5 Math.minus(Temperature.temp,Min.key(Temperature.temp))),2)))
```

In the delta interval definition, we have not used a start condition. Thus, the very first temperature event will start an interval as well as a new temperature event after an interval has been generated. Moreover, we require the minimum number of elements in the interval to be 2. This is to avoid cases where an interval is a singleton. Row 3 in Fig. 3 shows example delta intervals. The first three events were not included because the difference of their values to the minimum value is below 2°. Starting from the event at time 27, the first delta interval begins as the second temperature event satisfies the delta condition. Another interval begins at time 38 and continues.

Listing 3.4. Aggregate interval

```
1 Aggr=HoIE.Event(Temperature).Occurrence(1,Occurrences.Unbounded)
2 .Value(Aggregate.avg(Temperature.temp)).KeyBy(Temperature.sensor)
3 .RelativeCondition.Start(true).Subsequent(Conditions
4 .lessOrEqual(Aggregate.avg(Temperature.temp),35))
```

An aggregate frame of, e.g., average temperature threshold of 35° can be defined shown in Listing 3.4. In this interval definition, we keep adding events to the interval as long as the average of the added elements including the new one makes the condition hold true. Examples of matches to the aggregate interval definition are shown in row 4 in Fig. 3. The first interval spans the time from 20 to 27 as the average of temperature readings was less than or equal to 35. Other two singleton intervals are defined at times 36 and 38 respectively.

The definition of a boundary frame is similar to the threshold frame. Yet, several intervals have to be defined based on the required boundaries to be monitored on the range of attribute values. For example, ranges on the temperature readings of sensors can be defined as *normal*, readings until 25°, *warm* from 26 to 30°, and *hot* if above 30°. This can easily be represented with intervals with absolute conditions as the threshold interval above.

3.2 Heterogeneous Interval Events Generators

In the case of Heterogeneous event intervals, the types of events signifying the start and the end of the intervals are different. Moreover, instances of other event types might be required *not* to be observed within the interval. As an example of a heterogeneous interval, consider the execution of a business process. The whole duration of the process instance is a heterogeneous interval. Even for the individual work items within a process instance, each work item can be seen as a heterogeneous interval [18]. The interval is delimited by a *start* and *end*

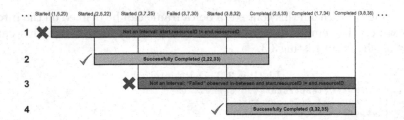

Fig. 4. Heterogeneous interval events

events for the process or the work item. However, the two event instances have to belong to the same process instance. Besides event types identifying the start and the end of the interval, it is possible to refer to other event types within D^2IA. Instances of such event types *must not* be observed within the interval.

Definition 5 (Heterogeneous Interval Event). *Let E be the universe of event types. A heterogeneous interval event HeIE specification is defined by a tuple $< start, end, Exclude, KeyBy, Condition, Within >$ where:*

- *start $\in E$ refers to the type of the start event for the interval,*
- *end $\in E$ refers to the type of the start event for the interval and start $\neq$ end,*
- *Exclude $\subset E$, is the set of event types not to be observed within the interval,*
- *KeyBy: refers to the id attribute of the raw events and/or to any $k \in$ Keys(value) of the raw events to group event instances with the same value together,*
- *Condition: defines the filter condition over the matching events. The condition refers to the properties of the event instances,*
- *Within: is defined by a time span that is defined by the number of time units.*

Example. Consider a process execution engine that emits three different event types to reflect on the evolution of work items (task instances): *Started*, *Failed*, and *Completed*. The three events share the same schema on the form $< workitemID, resourceID, ts >$ with a reference to the work item instance, the resource who would execute the work item and the timestamp ts of the event. We can define an interval for successfully completed work items as:

```
1 SuccessfullyCompleted=HeIE.Start(Started).End(Completed)
2 .Exclude(Failed).KeyBy(workitemID)
3 .Condition(Completed.resourceID =Started.resourceID)
```

Figure 4 shows on top a stream of the instances of the different event types. D^2IA will not consider $Started(1, 5, 20)$ and $Completed(1, 7, 34)$ as an interval because the condition on $resourceID$ is not satisfied, row 1 in the figure. Also, row 3 is not considered as an interval because between $Started$ and $Completed$ an instance of $Failed$ event for the same work item was observed. Only intervals on rows 2 and 4 are valid intervals as per the specification above.

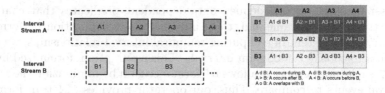

Fig. 5. Interval-interval and interval-point temporal relationships.

3.3 Intervals Temporal Relationships

Event Interval Operators is a family of D^2IA operators which is based on Allen's interval relationships [3]. These operators can efficiently reason about interval temporal relationships occurring between the generated interval events. The interval operator is a binary operator that takes as one input, a stream of interval events and as the other input, either another interval stream or a point-based event stream, but not both. The operator produces point-based *match* events whenever a match is found between two interval events (see **I2E** in Fig. 1).

Unlike stateless stream processing, e.g. [19], where each element is processed independently, the derivation of interval relationships is a stateful operation [2, 14,16]. Thus, this calls for a temporal frame (e.g. windows) to collect a finite subset of stream elements for both inputs. Therefore, we designed our interval operator to work on a tumbling window [9]. The results of the interval operator is a stream of match events. Definition 6 describes the inputs for the interval operator.

Definition 6 (Match Event). *A match event is an instantaneous event resulting from the reasoning about the relationship occurring between two interval events. Match specification is defined by a tuple*
< IntEvent1, IntEvent2, Frame1, Frame2, Relations, TSFunction > where:

- *IntEvent1 and IntEvent2: refer to the interval event types to reason about.*
- *Frame1 and Frame2: refer to the the temporal scope, i.e., the windows required to process (join) the interval event streams.*
- *Relations: refers to a list of temporal relationships to match between the interval events in the scopes.*
- *TSFunction: is a function used to assign a timestamp to the output match event which is instantaneous. Three timestamp function are available: now(), i.e., current system time; earliest (latest), i.e., assign the oldest (most recent) time instant choosing from the start-/end-points of the matched events.*

Listing 3.5 shows an example of an interval operator that works on temperature and smoke interval streams.

Listing 3.5. Interval operator specification

```
1  Match=IntervalOperator.Event1(TemperatureDelta)
2  .Frame1(5 minutes).Event2(SmokeThreshold)
3  .Frame2(5 minutes).Relation([Relations.During])
4  .Timestamp(TimestampFunctions.LATEST)
```

Grossniklaus et al. [12] defined data-dependent predicates that characterize the structure of a frame and, thus, influence the computation performance. Therefore, to the extent of computing temporal interval relationships, we define our frames to consider maximum intervals. This assumption, formalized in Definition 7, is relevant because it allows performance gain by minimizing the number of interval events to compare. Thus, our operator provides I2I transformation as shown in Fig. 1.

Definition 7 (Maximal Interval). *Let I be the set of all possible interval instances generated by an interval Specification. An interval $i \in I$ is maximal iff $\forall j \in I, j \neq i : i < j \vee i > j \vee i \; m \; j \vee i \; mi \; j$.*

As per Definition 7, we can be sure that the temporal relationships between the *sorted* elements of the same interval stream is always $i_j < i_{j+1}$ for $j \geq 0$. The benefit of this property is that we can efficiently calculate temporal relationships between pairs of interval instances of the left *Event1* and the right *Event2* interval streams without having to explicitly compare timestamps of each pair. If contents of each window on the two inputs of the join are sorted by the start timestamp, we can utilize the transitivity of temporal relationships [3] to efficiently compute the temporal inter-relationships between interval instances. For the cases where we have to compare timestamps of intervals, we rely on the efficient set-theoretic approach presented in [11].

Example. Consider the two interval streams A and B in Fig. 5. The dashed rectangles represent the content of a window over each stream. Note that windows width not necessarily should be the same. Within each window, the content is sorted by the timestamp. As per Definition 7, the intervals are either before, after or meet each other. Suppose that we want to define the temporal relationships between contents of the window on stream A and the content of the window on stream B. Namely, we need to find the relationship between $A1, A2, A3, A4$ on the one hand and $B1, B2, B3$ on the other hand. The naïve way to implement that is to perform 12 comparisons. A more efficient way is to infer the type of inter-stream interval relationships utilizing the nature of intra-stream interval relationship. Looking at the right table in Fig. 5, when we compare $A1$ with $B1$, using their start and end timestamps, we can find that $A1$ *contains* $B1$, i.e., $A1$ *di* $B1$. As we learn this relationship, we can deduce the temporal relationship between the other A intervals and $B1$. Since any interval $Ai, i > 1$ will always occur after $A1$, we can deduce the same relationship between those intervals and $B1$. This is represented with gray cells in the table. By comparing $A1$ and $B2$, we find that $A1$ overlaps with $B2$, i.e., $A1$ *o* $B2$. We can not infer an exact relation between other intervals in the A stream and $B2$ because $B2$ ends after $A1$ does. When we compare $A2$ and $B2$, we still find $A2$ *o* $B2$. However, we can find that $A2$ ends after $B2$. Thus, we can deduce that future intervals of A will always occur after $B2$. Finally, we have to compare each A interval with $B3$.

Algorithm 1. HoIE Query Generation

Input: An Event type T; An Occurrence Expression Min,Max; An Absolute Condition Ca;
An Relative Condition Cr; An aggregation function F; An aggregation key K; A
temporal window W

1   *patterns* ← [] *start* ← e0
2   **for** $k \leftarrow 0$ *to Min* **do**
3   ⌊   *start* ← *followedBy start ei*

4   **if** *Max* == *Unbounded* **then**
5 | pattern ← where Ac [followedBy start constrain(Cr, ei)*]
6   ⌊   add pattern patterns

7   **else**
8 | **for** $i \leftarrow min, i<=max, i++$ **do**
9 | | pattern ← start
10 | | **for** $j \leftarrow 0, j<i, j++$ **do**
11 | | ⌊   pattern ← where Ac [followedBy pattern constrain(Cf, ei)]

12 | ⌊   add pattern patterns

13   **foreach** $p \in patterns$ **do**
14   ⌊   output Head as select F (Kp) from p.window(W) where Ca

15   e0...ei with i=Max are of type T

---

4   Proof-of-Concept

In this section, we demonstrate how D^{2}IA fills the gap between scalable streaming data platforms and expressive centralized streaming solutions. In particular, we investigate two complementary proof-of-concepts (i) we demonstrate how we can rewrite D^{2}IA into an expressive CEP languages, i.e., EPL, that supports interval events and Allen's relations, but was not implemented on a scalable infrastructure. (ii) We present our implementation for a scalable version of D^{2}IA on top **Apache Flink**, a popular distributed stream processing engine.

4.1   Translation to EPL

EPL is an industrial stream processing language that combines DSMS and CEP features. The combination of pattern matching and analytical queries relies on the notion of Stream/Event type. I.e., every EPL stream has a schema that corresponds to the type of the items it contains. EPL allows the creation of new streams combing events w.r.t. the order of their appearance. A special operator called "insert into" allows composing queries in a query network. EPL natively supports the relationships of Allen's algebra. Algorithm 1 describes the steps of how HoIE operators can be translated into an EPL query network.

    Algorithm 1 uses the following notations: *output T* places an event of type T to a target stream; *where* applies absolute conditions to a pattern; and *constrain* applies relative conditions to an event. Moreover, it makes use of the following DSMS/CEP operators *window, select, from,* and *followedBy, Kleen's star*(∗), and *not*. Listing 4.1 shows the delta interval from Listing 3.3 translated to EPL.

Listing 4.1. EPL code for the Delta example

```
1 create context PartitionedById
2 partition by sensor from Temperature
3 context PartitionedById
4 insert into Delta select Math.avg(temps), startp, endp
5 from Temperature
6 match_recognize (measures A as temps, A[0].ts as startp, last(A.ts) as endp
7 pattern (A{2,})
8 define A as    Math.abs(A.temp - Math.min(A.temp) >=2));
```

4.2   Implementation on Flink

`Apache Flink` is a scalable stream processing engine. It supports S2R transformation by applying different windowing on data streams. R2R is also supported by manipulation of window contents. It also supports R2S as the results of windowing can be emitted to other streams. In this context, E2E transformations can be achieved using `Flink CEP` library[5]. In particular, `FlinkCEP` is a complex event processing library defined on top of Flink. We use FlinkCEP APIs to realize the interval generator operators, E2I. We use a so-called looping pattern to define the `Occurrence` property of the interval specification. Relative and absolute conditions are implemented via so-called `IterativeConditions`. To compute the aggregate value of the interval, we leverage the feature in Flink-CEP that returns a sequence of all the matched raw events. We use the first and last elements of the sequence to obtain the timestamps that constitute interval's endpoints. Then, we create an instance of the interval type and populate its properties and add it to the respective stream, see Fig. 2. To realize the interval operator, I2E, we use the join operator of Flink. The join operator receives as input two streams. As discussed in Sect. 3.3, we use the time frames, see Definition 6, to bound the number of interval instances to check the match for. To realize I2I transformation, we employ a window operator on the generated interval stream and emit maximal intervals only. Our implementation with example intervals can be found on the project repository[6].

Evaluation. To evaluate our implementation on FlinkCEP, we use a data set of the linear road benchmark[7]. Linear Road is a simulation of a large metropolitan city which is 100 miles wide and long and consists of 10 parallel expressways. Each tuple in the data set describes a vehicle ID, its speed, road, direction and the timestamp of the record. In our evaluation, we created four different homogeneous interval

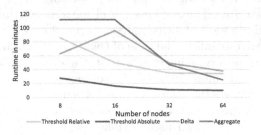

Fig. 6. Different intervals on Flink

---

[5] https://ci.apache.org/projects/flink/flink-docs-stable/dev/libs/cep.html.

[6] https://github.com/DataSystemsGroupUT/ICEP.

[7] http://infolab.stanford.edu/stream/cql-benchmark.html.

specifications, for the different frame types with absolute and relative conditions. We partition the data by vehicle ID and put the conditions on the speed attribute. More details about the interval specifications can be found in the GitHub repository. Figure 6 shows the scalability results in terms of time needed by the different queries to process 1 *million* tuples of the data set under an increasing number of computing nodes in a Flink cluster. Each node is equipped with 30 *GB* of main memory and 16 cores at 2.0 *GHz*. For the different interval specifications, it is clear that Flink scales well as the number of nodes increases. However, for each interval specification, the processing time varies for the same processing capabilities due to the difference in the complexity of the interval specification.

5 Related Work

TPStream [14] introduced a stand alone operator that finds temporal relationships among intervals. TPStream allows defining homogeneous intervals with absolute conditions only. D^{2}IA interval generation operators cover both homogeneous with absolute and relative conditions and heterogeneous intervals.

ISEQ [15] is an operator for reasoning about event intervals using Allen's temporal relationships. ISEQ assumes the existence of intervals and does not provide means to define. Compared to our work, we allow the user to define the intervals from raw (point) events. Moreover, we support both homogeneous and heterogeneous intervals, allow rich conditions on matching events, and calculating aggregations over values of raw events.

CEDR [6] is an event streaming system that embraces an interval-based temporal stream model to unify query language features, handles out-of-order event delivery, and defines correctness guarantees as well as operator semantics. CEDR's events have a validity interval, which indicates the range of time when the tuple is valid from the event provider's perspective. This is used to retrieve events which are still valid at query time. This case can be seen as an example of interval algebra reasoning. However, Allen's operators are not explicit in the language.

ETALIS [4] is an event-driven approach for Complex Event Processing. The language semantics is based on a logic programming. ETALIS represents events as facts and translates complex event patterns into logic rules. Thus, complex events are derived from simpler ones. ETALIS language is very expressive. Although it is possible to express and derive interval relationship across events, ETALIS does not provide any interval event generation mechanism. Events must adopt a two-timestamps temporal model. Moreover, the language does not exploit events ordering for optimizing reasoning about event interval.

Table 1 summarizes the comparison of D^2IA with related work. The implementation of D^2IA on top of Flink supports all operators from Fig. 1. In addition, this implementation leverages the performance scalability provided by Flink. Functionality-wise, EPL supports all the operators. However, this has to be done manually by the developer which is error-prone.

Table 1. Operators coverage and scalability comparison

Feature/System Operator	EPL	TP-Stream	ISEQ	ETALIS	CEDR	Flink	Flink+D2IA
S2R	+	-	-	-	-	+	+
R2R	+	-	-	-	-	+	+
R2S	+	-	-	-	-	+	+
E2E	+	-	+	+	+	+	+
E2I	+	+	-	-	-	-	+
I2E	+	+	+	+	-	-	+
I2I	+	-	-	-	-	-	+
Scalability	-	N/A	-	-	-	+	+

6   Conclusion

In this paper, we presented a family of operators to specify event intervals over data streams and to reason about their temporal relationships (D^2IA). D^2IA supports event intervals derived from single source stream by means of aggregations over timestamped events (homogeneous), and event intervals derived from two or more sources (heterogeneous). D^2IA translates intervals specification into complex CEP specifications; it allows to cover a wide range data-driven intervals as rich conditions regarding events inclusion; and it supports a wide range of aggregations or references to composing events values. We realized a proof of concept using both EPL and on top of Apache Flink. As an interval operator, D^2IA is more expressive than similar approaches as it allows relative conditions which allows defining a wider range of homogeneous intervals than related approaches.

References

1. Akidau, T., et al.: The dataflow model: a practical approach to balancing correctness, latency, and cost in massive-scale, unbounded, out-of-order data processing. PVLDB **8**(12), 1792–1803 (2015)
2. Alharbi, A., Bulpitt, A., Johnson, O.: Improving pattern detection in healthcare process mining using an interval-based event selection method. In: Carmona, J., Engels, G., Kumar, A. (eds.) BPM 2017. LNBIP, vol. 297, pp. 88–105. Springer, Cham (2017). https://doi.org/10.1007/978-3-319-65015-9_6
3. Allen, J.F.: Maintaining knowledge about temporal intervals. Commun. ACM **26**(11), 832–843 (1983)
4. Anicic, D., Rudolph, S., Fodor, P., Stojanovic, N.: Stream reasoning and complex event processing in ETALIS. Semant. Web **3**(4), 397–407 (2012)
5. Arasu, A., Babu, S., Widom, J.: The CQL continuous query language: semantic foundations and query execution. VLDB J. **15**(2), 121–142 (2006)

6. Barga, R.S., Goldstein, J., Ali, M.H., Hong, M.: Consistent streaming through time: a vision for event stream processing. In: CIDR, pp. 363–374 (2007)

7. Codd, E.F.: A database sublanguage founded on the relational calculus. In: Proceedings of the ACM-SIGFIDET Workshops (1971)

8. Cugola, G., Margara, A.: Low latency complex event processing on parallel hardware. J. Parallel Distrib. Comput. **72**(2), 205–218 (2012)

9. Dindar, N., et al.: Modeling the execution semantics of stream processing engines with secret. VLDB J. **22**(4), 421–446 (2013)

10. Etzion, O., Niblett, P.: Event Processing in Action. Manning, Shelter Island (2010)

11. Georgala, K., Sherif, M.A., Ngomo, A.N.: An efficient approach for the generation of Allen relations. In: ECAI, pp. 948–956 (2016)

12. Grossniklaus, M., Maier, D., Miller, J., Moorthy, S., Tufte, K.: Frames: data-driven windows. In: DEBS, pp. 13–24. ACM (2016)

13. Hirzel, M., Baudart, G., Bonifati, A., Valle, E.D., Sakr, S., Vlachou, A.: Stream processing languages in the big data era. SIGMOD Rec. **47**(2), 29 (2018)

14. Körber, M., Glombiewski, N., Seeger, B.: TPStream: low-latency temporal pattern matching on event streams. In: EDBT, pp. 313–324 (2018)

15. Li, M., Mani, M., Rundensteiner, E.A., Lin, T.: Complex event pattern detection over streams with interval-based temporal semantics. In: DEBS (2011)

16. Ostovar, A., Maaradji, A., La Rosa, M., ter Hofstede, A.H.M.: Characterizing drift from event streams of business processes. In: Dubois, E., Pohl, K. (eds.) CAiSE 2017. LNCS, vol. 10253, pp. 210–228. Springer, Cham (2017). https://doi.org/10.1007/978-3-319-59536-8_14

17. Paschke, A.: ECA-RULEML: an approach combining ECA rules with temporal interval-based KR event/action logics and transactional update logics. CoRR (2006)

18. Richter, F., Seidl, T.: TESSERACT: time-drifts in event streams using series of evolving rolling averages of completion times. In: Carmona, J., Engels, G., Kumar, A. (eds.) BPM 2017. LNCS, vol. 10445, pp. 289–305. Springer, Cham (2017). https://doi.org/10.1007/978-3-319-65000-5_17

19. van Zelst, S.J., Fani Sani, M., Ostovar, A., Conforti, R., La Rosa, M.: Filtering spurious events from event streams of business processes. In: Krogstie, J., Reijers, H.A. (eds.) CAiSE 2018. LNCS, vol. 10816, pp. 35–52. Springer, Cham (2018). https://doi.org/10.1007/978-3-319-91563-0_3

Business Process Modeling and Engineering

Extracting Declarative Process Models from Natural Language

Han van der Aa[1(✉)], Claudio Di Ciccio[2], Henrik Leopold[3,4],
and Hajo A. Reijers[5]

[1] Department of Computer Science,
Humboldt-Universität zu Berlin, Berlin, Germany
han.van.der.aa@hu-berlin.de
[2] Institute for Information Business,
Vienna University of Economics and Business, Vienna, Austria
[3] Kühne Logistics University, Hamburg, Germany
[4] Hasso Plattner Institute, University of Potsdam, Potsdam, Germany
[5] Department of Information and Computing Sciences,
Utrecht University, Utrecht, The Netherlands

Abstract. Process models are an important means to capture information on organizational operations and often represent the starting point for process analysis and improvement. Since the manual elicitation and creation of process models is a time-intensive endeavor, a variety of techniques have been developed that automatically derive process models from textual process descriptions. However, these techniques, so far, only focus on the extraction of traditional, imperative process models. The extraction of declarative process models, which allow to effectively capture complex process behavior in a compact fashion, has not been addressed. In this paper we close this gap by presenting the first automated approach for the extraction of declarative process models from natural language. To achieve this, we developed tailored Natural Language Processing techniques that identify activities and their inter-relations from textual constraint descriptions. A quantitative evaluation shows that our approach is able to generate constraints that closely resemble those established by humans. Therefore, our approach provides automated support for an otherwise tedious and complex manual endeavor.

Keywords: Declarative modelling · Natural language processing · Model extraction

1 Introduction

In many business processes the activities are executed in a typical order, without considerable deviations or exceptions. These business processes can be well captured using traditional, imperative business process modeling notations, such as the Business Process Model and Notation (BPMN), because the resulting model specifies which execution orders are allowed. However, other business processes,

© Springer Nature Switzerland AG 2019
P. Giorgini and B. Weber (Eds.): CAiSE 2019, LNCS 11483, pp. 365–382, 2019.
https://doi.org/10.1007/978-3-030-21290-2_23

Table 1. Description and notation of considered DECLARE constraints

Type	Constraint	Explanation	Examples			
Existence	INIT(a)	a is the *first* to occur	✓ acc	✓ abac	✗ cc	✗bac
	END(a)	a is the *last* to occur	✓ bca	✓ baca	✗ bc	✗bac
Relation	RESPONSE(a,b)	If a occurs, then b occurs after a	✓ caacb	✓ bcc	✗ caac	✗bacc
	PRECEDENCE(a,b)	b occurs only if preceded by a	✓ cacbb	✓ acc	✗ ccbb	✗bacc
Mutual rel.	SUCCESSION(a,b)	a occurs if and only if b occurs after a	✓ cacbb	✓ accb	✗ bac	✗bcca
Negative rel.	NOTSUCCESSION(a,b)	a never occurs before b	✓ bbcaa	✓ cbbca	✗ aacbb	✗abb

often referred to as *knowledge-intensive business processes*, are more complex. Their execution orders cannot be fully specified in advance [10]. Such processes are much better captured using declarative process models, since these do not depend on an explicit definition of the allowed behavior [4]. Instead, they use constraints to define the boundaries of the permissible process behavior. This enables declarative models to represent complex processes in a compact way. What both types of process models have in common is their general usefulness for effectively conveying how business processes are executed and for analyzing business processes [13].

Nevertheless, the elicitation and creation of process models does not come without problems. First, many process actors and domain experts lack the knowledge necessary to establish process models themselves [15,30]. Second, the elicitation of process models represents a highly time-consuming task [17]. As a result of both these issues, a wealth of process-related information is often captured in more accessible representation formats, such as textual documents [3,30]. Recognizing the widespread use and relevance of textual documents to capture process information, a variety of techniques have been developed that automatically extract process models from natural language (e.g. [15,16,31]). However, these existing techniques focus solely on *imperative* process models. Therefore, there is currently no technique available that can extract *declarative* process models from natural language text.

To overcome this gap, we use this paper to introduce the first approach for the automatic extraction of declarative process models from natural language. To achieve this, we developed tailored Natural Language Processing (NLP) techniques that identify activities and their inter-relations from textual constraint descriptions. By considering the semantics of these extracted components, we subsequently generate declarative constraints aiming to capture the logic defined in the textual description. A quantitative evaluation shows that our approach is able to generate constraints that show a high resemblance to those established manually. As such, our automated approach supports an otherwise tedious and complex manual endeavor.

The remainder of this paper is organized as follows. Section 2 introduces declarative process modeling and the challenges associated with the automatic extraction of declarative constraints from text. Section 3 presents our proposed approach. Section 4 describes a quantitative evaluation in which we demonstrate the usefulness of our approach. Section 5 elaborates on related work before Sect. 6 provides a conclusion and discusses directions for future research.

2 Problem Illustration

This section provides essential background regarding declarative process modeling (Sect. 2.1) and introduces core challenges associated with the extraction of declarative models from natural language (Sect. 2.2).

2.1 Declarative Modeling

A declarative model represents the behavior of a process by means of *constraints*, i.e., temporal rules that specify the conditions under which activities can or cannot be executed. For the purposes of this paper, we focus on DECLARE, one of the most well-established declarative process modeling languages to date [4].

DECLARE provides a standard library of templates (*repertoire* [9]), which are constraints parametrized over activities. In this paper, we consider five of the most commonly occurring templates [14], depicted in Table 1, focusing in particular on the ones that are topmost in the subsumption hierarchy of DECLARE constraints [9]. *Existence* constraints are *unary* constraints, i.e., predicating on single tasks. For instance, INIT(a) and END(b) establish that all process instances must begin with activity a and terminate with b, respectively. *Relation* constraints are *binary* and relate the execution of an activity to the occurrence of another one in the same instance (i.e., in one particular execution of the process). For example, RESPONSE(a, b)requires that if a is carried out, then b must be eventually performed.PRECEDENCE(a, b) imposes that b cannot be executed if a has not occurred earlier in the process instance. SUCCESSION(a, b) is a so called *mutual relation* constraint that expresses the joint conditions of RESPONSE and

Table 2. Exemplary natural language descriptions and DECLARE constraints

ID	Description	Constraint
S_0	The process starts when a claim is received.	INIT(*receive claim*)
S_1	A claim must be created before it can be approved	PREC.(*create claim, approve claim*)
S_2	Before a claim is approved, it must be created	PREC.(*create claim, approve claim*)
S_3	Creation of a claim should precede its approval	PREC.(*create claim, approve claim*)
S_4	If a claim is approved, then it must have been created first	PREC.(*create claim, approve claim*)
S_5	A claim must be created before it can be approved	PREC.(*create claim, approve claim*)
	or rejected	PREC.(*create claim, reject claim*)
S_6	When an order is shipped, an invoice can be sent	PREC.(*ship order, send invoice*)
S_7	When an order is shipped, an invoice must be sent	RESP.(*ship order, send invoice*)
S_8	When an order is shipped, an invoice must be sent first	PREC.(*send invoice, ship order*)
S_9	An invoice cannot be paid before it is received	NOTSCSN.(*pay invoice, receive invoice*)
S_{10}	An invoice can be paid before it is received	SCSN.(*pay invoice, receive invoice*)
S_{11}	The process ends when the invoice has been paid	END(*pay invoice*)

PRECEDENCE over a and b. Aside from these five templates, we also consider their negative counterparts. For instance, NOTSUCCESSION(a, b) is a *negative relation* constraint which states that if a is executed, then b cannot be carried out any longer.

2.2 Extraction Challenges

To extract declarative constraints from natural language, several challenges must be addressed. These challenges range from identifying sentences that contain constraints to extracting specific constraints from individual sentences. In this work, we primarily focus on challenges related to the latter type. We use the exemplary constraint descriptions from Table 2 as a means to illustrate six core challenges addressed in this work. Note that the majority of these challenges are caused by the flexibility of natural language, which allows the same DECLARE constraint to be described by a wide variety of sentences.

C1: *Synonymous terms and phrases.* Synonyms represents terms that have an equivalent meaning. For instance, the synonymous verbs "*end*", "*complete*", and "*finalize*", can all be used to indicate the final step of a process, such as seen for S_{11}. On a higher level of granularity, entire phrases or sentences may be used to describe the same concept. This requires an extraction approach to analyze and recognize the meaning of a sentence, rather than simply relying on a number of specific terms.

C2: *Description order.* Linguistic variability also manifests itself in the order in which a sentence describes the constraint's components. Some descriptions, such as S_1 and S_3, use a chronological order, first describing the create claim task, whereas S_2 and S_4 use the reverse order. To extract the appropriate constraints from these descriptions, it is therefore key to recognize the semantic relations that exist among the described actions. Crucially, this relation can depend on small textual cues, such as the inclusion of the word "*first*" at the end of sentence S_8. In this case, a single term fully reverses the semantics of the constraint in comparison to S_7.

C3: *Noun-based actions.* Identifying and extracting the actions contained in a textual description represents a core task of process model extraction. State-of-the-art approaches (cf. [15]) that address this task generally assume that activities can be identified by considering verbs in sentences, i.e., *verb-based* activity descriptions such as "*a claim must be created*" in S_1. However, in the case of declarative constraint descriptions, this assumption is often violated. They also describe activities using *noun-based* forms, such as "*creation of a claim*" in S_3. This presents a considerable challenge, since this means that existing extraction techniques cannot be applied in our context.

C4: *Constraint restrictiveness.* The differences between the binary constraints RESPONSE(a, b), PRECEDENCE(a, b), and SUCCESSION(a, b) are considerable from a semantic perspective. However, the differences in their textual descriptions can be minor. Compare, for instance, sentences S_6 and S_7 from Table 2. The term "*can*" in S_6 indicates an optional follow-up to "*ship* *order*," i.e., PRECEDENCE(*ship order*, *send invoice*). By contrast, the term "*must*" in S_7 indicates that *send invoice* has to occur, resulting in a RESPONSE constraint. To be able to appropriately differentiate among these constraint types, an extraction approach should identify terms that indicate how restrictive a constraint is meant to be.

C5: *Negation*. The ability to recognize negation in constraint descriptions is crucial, because the presence of a single negating term can reverse the semantics of the expression. This can, for example, be observed in description S_9, in which the use of "*cannot*" completely changes the meaning of the constraint in comparison to S_{10}.

C6: *Multi-constraint descriptions*. Single sentences may describe more than one declarative constraint. This commonly manifests itself through the use of *coordinating conjunctions*, indicated by terms such as "*and*" and "*or*". These terms can be used to link semantic components of a description that can indicate additional constraints. For example, consider the description S_5. This description is identical to S_1, aside from the conjunction at the end, which reveals that the PRECEDENCE constraint should be applied to both the approval and rejection of a claim.

Next, we describe our extraction approach, which aims to overcome these challenges.

3   Extraction Approach

Figure 1 provides an overview of the three-step approach we propose to extract declarative constraints from textual descriptions. First, linguistic processing is performed to extract *semantic components* from a constraint description. Those components are specifically targeted at the extraction of declarative constraints, e.g., the terms that enable differentiation among the various constraint types. By building on general-purpose NLP techniques, our approach is able to deal with a broad variety of linguistic patterns used in constraints (challenges C1 and C2). Second, our approach analyzes the semantic components in order to identify the activities named in the description. A main novelty in this step is the explicit consideration of noun-based activities, which addresses challenge C3. Finally, in the third step, our approach generates constraints based on identified activities and other semantic information. This step particularly focuses on the identification of subtle semantic differences, which are crucial for the proper differentiation among constraint templates (challenge C4) and negation (C5). The final outcome consists of one or more declarative constraints (challenge C6).

3.1   Step 1: Linguistic Processing

In the first step of our approach, we employ widely-used NLP techniques to identify semantic components that are of specific importance to the extraction of declarative constraints. Figure 2 provides an overview of those components, which are identified as follows.

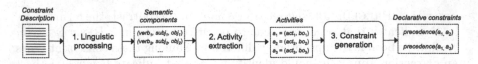

Fig. 1. Overview of the extraction approach

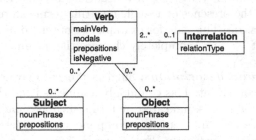

Fig. 2. Main semantic components extracted in the linguistic-processing step

Verbs. Verbs convey *actions*, *occurrences*, or *states* in natural language texts, such as *"to create"*, *"to occur"*, and *"to be"*. So-called *part-of-speech taggers* are well-suited to identify them. They assign a tag indicating a word category to each word in a natural language text [20]. An example of such a tagger is the widely employed *Stanford parser* [21]. To illustrate the usefulness of taggers for the identification of verbs, consider the tags assigned by the Stanford Parser on the words of sentence S_5:

"A/DT manager/NN must/MD create/**VB** a/DT claim/NN before/IN it/PRP can/MD be/**VB** accepted/**VBN** or/CC rejected/**VBN** ./."

Since the explanation of all tags goes beyond the scope of this paper, we focus here on the tags that indicate verbs. In particular, the /VB tag indicates the *base form* of a verb and the /VBN tags indicate the *past participle* of a verb. Therefore, by considering part-of-speech tags we can extract three main verbs from the description: *"create"*, *"accepted"*, and *"rejected"*.

Subjects and Objects. The *subject* of a verb indicates the entity that performs the action. In a process context, the subject typically corresponds to the *actor* executing an activity (e.g., a *manager* who creates a claim). Similarly, the *object* of a verb indicates the entity that is acted upon. In a process context, the object of a verb often corresponds to the *business object* that is affected by an activity, e.g. the *claim* business object being created.

For the identification of subjects and objects, we employ NLP techniques that compute *dependency grammars* for natural language texts. Those grammars capture the grammatical relationships among the words in a sentence using dependency relations. Typed dependency relations, such as the *Stanford relations* [7], describe grammatical relations of a certain type that exist between two words.

For instance, the relation $nsubj(create, manager)$ denotes that *"manager"* is the subject performing the verb *"create"*. Table 3 provides an overview of the dependency relations obtained for constraint S_5.

The most important Stanford relation used to extract subjects is the aforementioned *nsubj* relation. To extract objects, we consider two relations: *dobj* and *nsubjpass*. The *dobj* relation indicates the direct object of a verb, as in the relation $dobj(create, claim)$ from Table 3. The *nsubjpass* relation refers to the *synthetic subject* in a passive clause. However, from a process perspective, this synthetic subject actually fulfils the same role as an object. For example, the phrase *"A claim is created"* contains the relation $nsubjpass(create, claim)$, which is equivalent to the *dobj* relation for active phrases.

Specifiers. We augment the extracted verbs, subjects, and objects with various specifiers. In particular, we focus on the extraction of modal verbs, negations, and prepositions. By employing the previously introduced grammatical dependencies, we identify these as follows:

Modal verbs. Modal verbs are auxiliary verbs that are used to indicate if something is certain, probable, or possible (or not). The principal modal verbs in English are: can/could, may/might, must, will/would and shall/should. Modal verbs play a key role in our approach, because they are an important means to distinguish among various declarative constraints, such as RESPONSE and SUCCESSION (challenge C4). Therefore, we explicitly extract modal verbs and associate them with the related main verbs. For example, in sentence S_5 we use the *aux* relation to relate *"must"* to the verb *"created"*.

Negation. As indicated in challenge C5, the recognition of negations in constraint descriptions is important because failing to do so can lead to the identification of a constraint that is completely the opposite of what is intended. To identify negated verbs, we use the *neg* dependency relation. For example, for constraint description S_9, *"An invoice cannot be paid before it is received"*, the relation $neg(paid, not)$ indicates the negation. By extracting this information, we are able to properly identify negative constraints.

Prepositions. Prepositions are terms used to specify a relationship between a noun and other parts of a sentence. In the context of constraint descrip-

Table 3. Grammatical dependencies for constraint S_5

Relation	Meaning	Relation	Meaning
$det(manager, A)$	determinant	$nsubjpass(accepted, it)$	passive subject
$nsubj(create, manager)$	subject	$aux(accepted, can)$	auxiliary verb
$aux(create, must)$	auxiliary verb	$auxpass(accepted, be)$	passive auxiliary
$det(claim, a)$	determinant	$advcl(create, accepted)$	adverbial clause
$dobj(create, claim)$	object	$cc(accepted, or)$	coordination
$mark(accepted, before)$	marker	$conj(accepted, rejected)$	conjunct

tions, prepositions are commonly used to indicate ordering relations that exist between activities. For instance, in constraint description S_5, the term "*before*" is used to describe a relation between "*a claim is approved*" and "*must create a claim*." In particular, it denotes that the latter part must occur *before* a claim's approval. Thus, we augment nouns with information on their prepositions. To that end, we primarily use the *mark* and *advmod* Stanford dependencies, such as the $mark(accepted, before)$ included in Table 3.

Interrelations. Finally, our approach extracts information regarding two types of interrelations that can exist among verbs in a constraint description: adverbial clauses and conjunctions.

Adverbial clauses. Adverbial clauses are dependent clauses that modify other entities in a text. In the case of constraint descriptions, these can be used to describe relations that exist among verbs. For example, Table 3 shows the relation *advcl(create, accepted)*, which indicates that the phrase containing the former term ("*A manager must create a claim*" represents a specifier for the phrase containing the latter term "*it can be accepted*"). In particular, it specifies a temporal relation between the two phrases. In the remainder, we will denote a relation between two verbs v_1 and v_2 as $rel(v_1, v_2)$.

Coordinating conjunctions. Conjunctions indicate relations between two entities, which are important when handling multi-constraint descriptions (C6). Common conjunctions are indicated by "*and*" and "*or*". For example, in constraint S_5, the term "*or*" indicates that there is a relation between "*accepted*" and "*rejected*". By identifying this relation, we recognize that "*rejected*" is in the same adverbial relations as "*accepted*", i.e., $rel(created, rejected)$ is derived from the adverbial relation $rel(created, accepted)$ and the conjunctive relation $conj(accepted, rejected)$.

After this linguistic processing step, which covers all the linguistic components just discussed, we use the extracted components to identify the activities contained in a constraint description.

3.2 Step 2: Activity Extraction

Activities denote core constructs in any process description, thus also for constraints in declarative process modeling. An activity in a process description generally refers to an *action* that is performed on some *business object*, optionally by a specified *actor*. For example, in constraint S_1, we observe the activities "*create claim*" and "*approve claim*". As indicated by challenge C3, to properly extract activities, we need to consider both *verb-based* and *noun-based* activities.

Verb-Based Activities. For the extraction of verb-based activities, we employ the state-of-the-art technique used by Friedrich et al. [15], which utilizes the semantic components identified in the previous step. The verb corresponds to the action, the verb's subject to the actor, and the verb's object to the activity's business object. For example, in Sect. 3.1, we analysed the verb "*created*", having "*manager*" as a subject and "*a claim*" as the object. This translates to the create claim activity, performed by a manager.

Noun-Based Activities. A noun-based activity is a noun phrase in a constraint description that corresponds to a process activity, such as "*creation of a claim*" and "*its approval*" in constraint S_3. The main concern regarding their extraction is the ability to recognize the situations in which they occur. Therefore, we focus on the identification of verbs that describe the flow of a process, rather than activities. In sentence S_2, for instance, the verb "*precedes*" describes a flow relation between its subject, "*creation of the claim*", and its object, "*its approval*". To recognize such cases, we decided to use an established set of so-called *temporal verbs* [5, p. 39]. This taxonomy includes verbs such as: *to start, to proceed, to end, to finish, to follow, to happen*. We augment this list with some of their synonyms, such as *to occur, to complete*, and *to finish*. When our approach recognizes that an extracted verb corresponds to a temporal verb from the aforementioned list, the approach generates activities based on the subject and object of the verb (if any). For example, the approach would extract the claim creation claim approval activities from sentence S_3. Furthermore, for noun-based activities stemming from verbs with both a subject and an object, we extract a semantic relation between those components. For example, in S_3, we recognize that a relation exists between its activities, i.e., the approach extracts $rel(\text{claim creation, claim approval})$.

3.3   Step 3: Constraint Generation

In the final step of our approach, we generate declarative constraints based on the extracted activities and their semantic interrelations. Algorithm 1 shows the main flow of this generation step. The algorithm takes as input a relation $rel(a, b)$ that exist between two extracted activities. These relations result from the verb interrelations, as identified in Sect. 3.1, and from the noun-based activity extraction, described in Sect. 3.2.

Notably, our approach can handle multi-constraint descriptions (challenge C6) because we apply the algorithm to all relations $rel(a, b)$ identified in a description. For instance, we identify two relations in sentence S_5, namely $rel(\text{create claim, accept claim})$ and $rel(\text{create claim, reject claim})$. As a result, our approach generates two declarative constraints out of a single sentence.

In the remainder of this section, we will describe the core aspects of our algorithm. We examine (i) the generation of unary constraints (lines 3–8), (ii) the determination of the temporal order in binary constraints (lines 9–11), (iii) the differentiation among precedence, response, and succession constraints (lines 12–18), and (iv) the identification of negated constraints (lines 19–20).

Algorithm 1. Declarative constraint generation

```
1: function GENERATECONSTRAINT
2:     Input: rel(a, b)                                    ▷ Relation between actions a and b
3:     metaAct ← ⊥; otherAct ← ⊥;                          ▷ Placeholders for unary constraints
4:     if isMetaAction(a) then metaAct ← a, otherAct ← b;      ▷ Check for meta-activities
5:     if isMetaAction(b) then metaAct ← b, otherAct ← a;
6:     if metaAct ≠ ⊥ then                             ▷ A unary constraint should be generated
7:         if hasStartVerb(metaAct) then return INIT(otherAct)
8:         if hasEndVerb(metaAct) then return END(otherAct)
9:     if reversedDirection(rel(a, b)) then          ▷ Check temporal order of binary constraint
10:         act1 ← b; act2 ← a
11:     else act1 ← a; act2 ← b
12:     template ← ⊥
13:     if isMandatory(act1) ∧ ¬isMandatory(act2) then  ▷ Determine binary constraint template
14:         constraint ← PRECEDENCE(act1, act2)
15:     if ¬isMandatory(act1) ∧ isMandatory(act2) then
16:         constraint ← RESPONSE(act1, act2)
17:     if isMandatory(act1) ∧ isMandatory(act2) then
18:         constraint ← SUCCESSION(act1, act2)
19:     if hasNegation(act1, act2) then                     ▷ Check if template should be negated
20:         constraint ← NOTSUCCESSION(act1, act2)
21:     return constraint
```

Unary Constraint Generation. Unary relations correspond to the INIT(a) and END(a) constraint templates, which identify the start and end points in a process. To identify those types of constraints, we recognize that their constraint descriptions describe activities from the viewpoint of the process itself, rather than from the viewpoint of an actor in the actor. Consider, for instance, the sentence S_0: "*The process starts when a claim is received.*" In this description, the subject, i.e., the actor that performs the *start* activity, is the *process*, rather than, for instance, a *department* or a *manager*.

To generate the unary INIT and END constraints, we identify the involvement of such *process subjects*. We achieve this by checking the actor of an activity against a set of process-related terms (employed by Friedrich et al. [15]), which includes terms such as "*process*", "*instance*", and "*case*". When such a process subject occurs as the *actor* in a description, we establish that the description contains a sort of *meta-action* related to the process flow (lines 3–5). If a meta-action is detected, we then determine if the constraint describes INIT or END by comparing the verb to synonyms of "*start*" and "*end*" in WordNet [25] (lines 7–8). As a result, our approach generates the constraints INIT(*receive claim*) for description S_0.

Binary Constraint Direction. A crucial aspect for the correct extraction of binary constraints, such as RESPONSE(a, b) and PRECEDENCE(a, b), is to recognize which activity in a description corresponds to a and which to b. Such a recognition is not trivial because, considering two activities, the corresponding propositions can be put in different points of the sentence though keeping the same temporal order. For instance, description S_1, "*A claim must be cre-*

ated before it can be approved", describes activity *a* (i.e., create claim) prior to *b* (approve claim). In S_2, propositions are switched but the same constraint is described: *"Before a claim is approved, it must be created"*. We shall name the switch of propositions with respect to the temporal order as *reversed direction*. To properly recognize constraint directions, we consider three aspects that can be present in textual constraint descriptions: *temporal prepositions, temporal verbs,* and *tenses*.

Temporal prepositions. The prepositions that we extracted in step 1 can represent valuable indicators. In particular, prepositions can correspond to a subset of *temporal prepositions*, which indicate different temporal relations that exist between components of a sentence, in our context between activities. For this, we build on an established classification of temporal prepositions.[1] In our approach, we consider the *preceding* and *following* subclasses. The former contains prepositions such as *"ahead of"*, *"before"*, and *"prior to"*, whereas the latter includes *"after"*, *"beyond"*, and *"subsequent to"*.

To illustrate the use of temporal prepositions to our aim, consider again sentence S_2. In step 1 of our approach, it identifies *"before"* as a preposition of *"accepted"* and an interrelation between *"accepted"* and *"created"*. Given that the preposition *"before"* belongs to the class of *preceding* prepositions, our approach is able to recognize that *"accepted"* should be preceded by its related verbs, i.e. by *"create"*. Therefore, it accurately identifies that *a* corresponds to create claim and *b* to accept claim.

Temporal verbs and tenses. For descriptions involving noun-based activities, the *process verbs* identified in Sect. 3.2 can provide valuable indicators of reversed directions. Consider, for example, constraint description S_3, *"Creation of a claim should precede its approval."* In this text, the verb *"precede"* corresponds to a temporal verb from the taxonomy described in Sect. 3.2. This verb specifies that *"claim creation"* should occur before the *"claim approval"*. Conversely, if the text had used the verb *"follow"* rather than *"precede"*, our approach would have identified the reversed direction.

The way in which temporal verbs are used plays a crucial role here. Most importantly, we differentiate between active forms, e.g. *"precede,"* and passive forms, e.g. *"is preceded by."* As an illustration, consider a sentence S_3' that reads *"Creation of a claim is preceded by its approval."* The replacement of an active verb (as seen in S_3) with its infinitive form yields exactly the opposite temporal order between the two activities. The identification and selection of the proper one is included in lines 9–11. Once it has been determined, we finally need to identify the correct constraint *template*.

Binary Constraint Templates. For the binary constraint templates PRECEDENCE, SUCCESSION, and RESPONSE, a key aspect of their accurate elicitation is to recognize what elements distinguishes them. All three constraint templates denote a temporal order between activities *a* and *b*. However, the key

---

[1] See: www.clres.com/db/classes/ClassTemporal.php.

difference is in the restrictions that the constraints impose. PRECEDENCE(a, b) states that b can only occur if a has already been performed. RESPONSE(a, b) indicates the opposite, namely that if a has occurred, then b must follow at some stage. Finally, SUCCESSION(a, b) lies at the intersection of the previous constraints, and enforces that neither a nor b can occur independently from each other.

To identify these different templates in a textual constraint description, we identify indicators of restrictiveness in the text. In particular, we set out to determine whether the tasks involved in a constraint are mandatory or optional (as indicated in lines 12–18). Specifically, we consider the use of modal verbs, as discussed in Sect. 3.1. The modal verbs *can, could, may,* and *might* indicate that something is optional, whereas *must, will, would, shall,* and *should* generally specify that an activity is mandatory. Consider, for instance, the difference between the constraint descriptions S_6 and S_7 from the running example. These descriptions differ because S_6 states that *"an invoice can be sent"* while S_7 states that *"an invoice must be sent"*. For these constraints, the replacement of the *optional* modal *"can"* with the *mandatory* modal *"must"* means that S_7 describes a RESPONSE constraint, rather than PRECEDENCE. We use the presence of modals as follows to determine the template of the constraint.

PRECEDENCE(a,b). If a has an associated mandatory modal, whereas b is associated with an optional modal, then this yields the constraint PRECEDENCE(a, b) because a is a mandatory prerequisite for the optional follow-up b. This is, for instance, seen for constraint S_1, which states that *"A claim must*[mandatory] *be created, before it can* [optional] *be accepted."*

RESPONSE(a,b). If b is accompanied by a mandatory modal whereas a either has an optional or no modal, then the approach recognizes a RESPONSE(a, b) constraint, such as seen for constraint S_7: *"When an order is shipped* [no modal]*, an invoice must* [mandatory] *be sent."*

SUSSESSION(a,b). Finally, using the same reasoning, when both activities are accompanied by mandatory modal verbs, a SUCCESSION(a, b) constraint is generated.

Negation. Finally, we also consider the identification of negation in constraints (lines 19–20). In Sect. 3.1 we described how we identified negated verbs based on dependency relations. For these cases, we return a NOTSUCCESSION constraint, as it is the negative form of SUCCESSION, hence, a fortiori, of RESPONSE and PRECEDENCE. For example, for constraint description S_9 (*"An invoice cannot be paid before it is received"*), our approach recognizes that this is a negative constraint. As a result, our approach returns NOTSUCCESSION(*pay invoice, receive invoice*).

Table 4. Overview of the test collection

Source	INIT	END	PRECEDENCE	RESPONSE	SUCCESSION	Negation	Multi-cons.	Total
DECLARE [26]	1	0	0	3	0	0	0	4
DCR graphs [18,32]	1	1	12	7	2	2	6	22
DECLARE mining [11,24]	2	0	4	4	3	0	1	12
General descriptions [29]	7	3	32	5	2	2	20	49
Syntax variation	0	0	15	0	0	0	0	16
Full collection	11	4	63	19	7	4	27	103

4   Evaluation

To demonstrate the capabilities of our extraction approach, we conduct a quantitative evaluation by comparing automatically extracted declarative constraints to a manually created gold standard. The evaluation goal is to learn how well the automated approach approximates constraints created manually. If our extraction approach can automatically generate definitions that closely resemble those created manually by experts, it seems fair to regard our approach as a viable and efficient alternative to an otherwise time-consuming and complex manual endeavor. The data collection and prototype used in this evaluation are both publicly available.[2]

4.1   Test Collection

To compose the test collection used for our evaluation, we obtained textual constraint descriptions from various industrial and academic sources. The sources can be divided into two sets: (1) sources that specifically describe declarative process models, e.g., works on DECLARE [26] and DCR graphs [18,32], and (2) sources that provide more general, i.e., not specifically declarative, process descriptions, stemming from Sanchez et al. [29]. From these sources, we derived the constraint descriptions that relate to the declarative constraint types included in our scope.

The final collection consists of 103 constraint descriptions, of which Table 4 present the main characteristics. All further details of the collection are publicly available at the aforementioned link. The descriptions included in the collection vary highly in terms of the syntax used to describe constraints. On the one hand, this is because the descriptions stem from different sources and, thus, from different authors. On the other hand, the syntactic differences were intentionally created. A researcher, who is independent of the team involved in the development of the proposed approach, established 15 variations of the constraint PRECEDENCE(*create claim, approve claim*), some of these variations are used as part of the running example in Table 2. Due to these factors, we believe that the test collection is well-suited to achieve a high external validity of the evaluation results.

---

[2] See: https://github.com/hanvanderaa/declareextraction.

4.2   Setup

To be able to compare the generated and manually extracted declarative constraints, we conceptualize the extraction of declarative constraints as a *template* or *slot filling* problem [20]. As a result, each declarative constraint consists of a number of slots, e.g., the constraint SUCCESSION(a, b), contains three slots: (1) a *template* slot, denoting that the template of the constraint is SUCCESSION, (2) a slot for task a (3) a slot for task b. When a constraint description contains multiple constraints, as seen for constraint S_5, the number of slots to be identified increases alongside the number of constraints. Given the nature of a slot filling problem, we can quantify the performance of our approach by computing the well-known *precision* and *recall* metrics. Using A to denote the set of slots filled by our approach and G for the slots filled in the gold standard, precision reflects the fraction of slots that our automated approach filled correctly according to the gold standard ($|A \cap G|/|A|$). Recall represents the fraction of slots filled in the gold standard that were also correctly filled by our approach ($|A \cap G|/|G|$). Furthermore, we report the F_1-score as the harmonic mean of precision and recall.

Table 5. Overview of the evaluation results

Template	Cases	Precision	Recall	F_1-score
INIT	11	0.75	0.82	0.78
END	4	0.88	0.88	0.88
PRECEDENCE	63	0.78	0.71	0.74
RESPONSE	19	0.80	0.77	0.75
SUCCESSION	7	0.68	0.68	0.68
Negation	4	1.00	1.00	1.00
Single-constraint	74	0.79	0.82	0.80
Multi-constraint	27	0.74	0.61	0.67
Type recognition	132	0.86	0.86	0.86
Overall	103	0.77	0.72	0.74

4.3   Results

Table 5 provides an overview of the most important evaluation results. The table shows that our approach achieves an overall precision of 0.77 and a recall of 0.72, yielding an F_1-score of 0.74. In the following, we investigate the results in detail by considering how well our approach deals with the various challenges posed in Sect. 2.

C1, C2: Synonymous terms and description order. Challenges C1 and C2 both relate to the variety of natural language descriptions that can be used to describe a constraint. The ability of our approach to deal with these challenges is, among others, reflected in the results achieved for the 15 constraints we introduced to test syntax variation. For those 15 descriptions, which all describe the same constraint, our approach achieves precision and recall scores of 0.88. This demonstrates that by building on NLP techniques such as parsers, our approach is able to handle linguistic variation well.

C3: Noun-based activities. As described in Sect. 3.2, we have developed a novel approach to extract activities from texts that also extracts noun-based activities. The value of this extraction approach can be determined by comparing our approach's results to those results that would be obtained if we just relied on existing techniques, i.e., if we just identified activities using the extraction approach from [15]. By employing that activity extraction technique, a precision of 0.77 and recall of 0.66 are achieved. By using our approach the recall thus increases from 0.66 to 0.72. This illustrates that the additional consideration of noun-based activities helps to improve performance.

C4: **Constraint restrictiveness.** As shown in Table 5, our approach identifies constraint templates correctly in over 86% of the cases. This means that it is well able to differentiate among the different levels of restrictiveness for constraints. An in-depth analysis of the results also reveals that the template identification errors are largely related to other problems of the approach. For instance, for cases when the activities are not extracted properly, also the constraint template is not identified correctly.

C5: **Negation.** As shown in Table 5, our approach successfully identifies the negation present in constraint descriptions and, furthermore, does not indicate negation when it is not present (i.e., no false negatives). Nevertheless, it should be taken into account that only 4 cases in the test collection contain negated constraints.

C6: **Multi-constraint descriptions.** Finally, we observe that the ability of our approach to deal with multi-constraint descriptions varies. In Table 5, it becomes clear that our approach achieves a lower recall for multi-constraint descriptions than for single-constraint ones (0.61 versus 0.82). However, we also observe that our approach is able to deal with descriptions containing multiple constraints of a single template rather well. Its performance for descriptions that pertain contain multiple templates, e.g. a RESPONSE and a SUCCESSION, is considerably lower. These descriptions are generally longer and, as a result, typically more problematic for the NLP techniques on which we build.

5   Related Work

Textual documents, such as work instructions and process descriptions, represent a valuable source of information in the context of business process management [3]. Their value has led to the recent development of a variety of analysis techniques that focus on process information contained in text, such as techniques that compare process models against textual descriptions [1,29], as well as techniques that consider textual descriptions for process querying [22,23], process matching [6,33], and conformance checking [2]. Closely related to the goal of this paper are existing techniques that focus on the extraction of imperative process models from natural language texts [15,16,27], of which the technique by Friedrich et al. [15] can be regarded as the state-of-the-art in this context [27]. Finally, recent research has focused on the identification and extraction of rules from regulatory documents [12,34].

Our proposed approach provides unprecedented contributions related to the extraction of *declarative* process models from text, specifically the identification of constraint order (Challenge C2), the extraction of noun-based activities (C3), the identification of constraint types (C4), and the handling of multi-constraint descriptions (C6). Though existing techniques are not suitable to fully address them, the integration of the aforementioned advancements [12,34] draws plans for our future work, as discussed in the conclusion.

6   Conclusion

This paper presented the first approach for the automated extraction of declarative process models from textual descriptions. Our approach builds on and significantly extends existing NLP techniques in order to identify process-related information in constraint descriptions and transform these into declarative constraints. A quantitative evaluation demonstrates that our approach achieves a high accuracy when compared to manually established constraints. Therefore, our approach provides automated support for an otherwise complex and tedious manual task, making the declarative modeling paradigm more accessible to a wider audience.

In future work, we aim to extend our approach in several directions. First, we aim to enhance our technique towards a richer repertoire of templates, considering subsumed constraint types such as *alternate* and *chain* templates, as well as by including branched constraints [8]. Second, we intend to augment the control-flow based constraints with other perspectives by focusing on the extraction of data-based and temporal declarative constraints. Finally, we will go beyond the consideration of individual sentences in isolation. Among others, this will involve (i) the extraction of constraints that span multiple sentences, (ii) identifying which sentences actually contain constraints, and (iii) relating extracted constraints to each other. Natural language processing techniques developed in the contexts of requirements engineering [19,28], imperative process model extraction [15], and semantic matching [1] may all help in this regard. As a result, this will enable the extraction of declarative models from full documents, such as process documentations and normative texts.

Acknowledgments. This work has received funding from the EU H2020 programme under MSCA-RISE agreement 645751 (RISE_BPM) and the Alexander von Humboldt Foundation.

References

1. Van der Aa, H., Leopold, H., Reijers, H.A.: Comparing textual descriptions to process models: the automatic detection of inconsistencies. Inf. Syst. **64**, 447–460 (2017)
2. Van der Aa, H., Leopold, H., Reijers, H.A.: Checking process compliance against natural language specifications using behavioral spaces. Inf. Syst. **78**, 83–95 (2018)
3. Van der Aa, H., Leopold, H., van de Weerd, I., Reijers, H.A.: Causes and consequences of fragmented process information: insights from a case study. In: 23rd Americas Conference on Information Systems, AMCIS (2017)
4. Van der Aalst, W.M.P., Pesic, M., Schonenberg, H.: Declarative workflows: balancing between flexibility and support. Comput. Sci. R&D **23**(2), 99–113 (2009)

5. Androutsopoulos, I.: Exploring Time, Tense and Aspect in Natural Language Database Interfaces, vol. 6. John Benjamins Publishing, Amsterdam (2002)
6. Baier, T., Mendling, J.: Bridging abstraction layers in process mining by automated matching of events and activities. In: Daniel, F., Wang, J., Weber, B. (eds.) BPM 2013. LNCS, vol. 8094, pp. 17–32. Springer, Heidelberg (2013). https://doi.org/10.1007/978-3-642-40176-3_4
7. De Marneffe, M.C., Manning, C.D.: The Stanford typed dependencies representation. In: Workshop on Cross-Framework and Cross-Domain Parser Evaluation, pp. 1–8 (2008)
8. Di Ciccio, C., Maggi, F.M., Mendling, J.: Efficient discovery of target-branched declare constraints. Inf. Syst. **56**, 258–283 (2016)
9. Di Ciccio, C., Maggi, F.M., Montali, M., Mendling, J.: Resolving inconsistencies and redundancies in declarative process models. Inf. Syst. **64**, 425–446 (2017)
10. Di Ciccio, C., Marrella, A., Russo, A.: Knowledge-intensive processes: characteristics, requirements and analysis of contemporary approaches. J. Data Semant. **4**(1), 29–57 (2015)
11. Di Ciccio, C., Mecella, M.: On the discovery of declarative control flows for artful processes. ACM Trans. Manag. Inf. Syst. **5**(4), 24:1–24:37 (2015)
12. Dragoni, M., Villata, S., Rizzi, W., Governatori, G.: Combining natural language processing approaches for rule extraction from legal documents. In: Pagallo, U., Palmirani, M., Casanovas, P., Sartor, G., Villata, S. (eds.) AICOL 2015-2017. LNCS (LNAI), vol. 10791, pp. 287–300. Springer, Cham (2018). https://doi.org/10.1007/978-3-030-00178-0_19
13. Dumas, M., La Rosa, M., Mendling, J., Reijers, H.A.: Fundamentals of BusinessProcess Management, 2nd edn. Springer, Heidelberg (2018). https://doi.org/10.1007/978-3-662-56509-4
14. Dwyer, M.B., Avrunin, G.S., Corbett, J.C.: Patterns in property specifications for finite-state verification. In: ICSE, pp. 411–420. ACM (1999)
15. Friedrich, F., Mendling, J., Puhlmann, F.: Process model generation from natural language text. In: Mouratidis, H., Rolland, C. (eds.) CAiSE 2011. LNCS, vol. 6741, pp. 482–496. Springer, Heidelberg (2011). https://doi.org/10.1007/978-3-642-21640-4_36
16. Gonçalves, J.C.d.A., Santoro, F.M., Baiao, F.A.: Business process mining from group stories. In: CSCWD, pp. 161–166. IEEE (2009)
17. Herbst, J., Karagiannis, D.: An inductive approach to the acquisition and adaptation of workflow models. In: IJCAI, vol. 99, pp. 52–57. Citeseer (1999)
18. Hildebrandt, T., Mukkamala, R.R., Slaats, T.: Designing a cross-organizational case management system using dynamic condition response graphs. In: EDOC, pp. 161–170 (2011)
19. Ilieva, M.G., Ormandjieva, O.: Automatic transition of natural language software requirements specification into formal presentation. In: Montoyo, A., Muñoz, R., Métais, E. (eds.) NLDB 2005. LNCS, vol. 3513, pp. 392–397. Springer, Heidelberg (2005). https://doi.org/10.1007/11428817_45
20. Jurafsky, D., Martin, J.H.: Speech & Language Processing. Pearson Education India, Bengaluru (2000)
21. Klein, D., Manning, C.D.: Accurate unlexicalized parsing. In: ACL, pp. 423–430 (2003)
22. Leopold, H., van der Aa, H., Pittke, F., Raffel, M., Mendling, J., Reijers, H.A.: Searching textual and model-based process descriptions based on a unified data format. SoSym **18**(2), 1179–1194 (2019)

23. Leopold, H., van der Aa, H., Reijers, H.A.: Identifying candidate tasks for robotic process automation in textual process descriptions. In: Gulden, J., Reinhartz-Berger, I., Schmidt, R., Guerreiro, S., Guédria, W., Bera, P. (eds.) BPMDS/EMMSAD -2018. LNBIP, vol. 318, pp. 67–81. Springer, Cham (2018). https://doi.org/10.1007/978-3-319-91704-7_5

24. Maggi, F.M., Di Ciccio, C., Di Francescomarino, C., Kala, T.: Parallel algorithms for the automated discovery of declarative process models. Inf. Syst. **74**, 136–152 (2017)

25. Miller, G.A.: WordNet: a lexical database for English. Commun. ACM **38**(11), 39–41 (1995)

26. Pesic, M., van der Aalst, W.M.P.: A declarative approach for flexible business processes management. In: Eder, J., Dustdar, S. (eds.) BPM 2006. LNCS, vol. 4103, pp. 169–180. Springer, Heidelberg (2006). https://doi.org/10.1007/11837862_18

27. Riefer, M., Ternis, S.F., Thaler, T.: Mining process models from natural language text: a state-of-the-art analysis. In: MKWI. Universität Illmenau (2016)

28. Saint-Dizier, P.: Mining incoherent requirements in technical specifications. In: Frasincar, F., Ittoo, A., Nguyen, L.M., Métais, E. (eds.) NLDB 2017. LNCS, vol. 10260, pp. 71–83. Springer, Cham (2017). https://doi.org/10.1007/978-3-319-59569-6_8

29. Sànchez-Ferreres, J., van der Aa, H., Carmona, J., Padró, L.: Aligning textual and model-based process descriptions. Data Knowl. Eng. **118**, 25–40 (2018)

30. Selway, M., Grossmann, G., Mayer, W., Stumptner, M.: Formalising natural language specifications using a cognitive linguistic/configuration based approach. Inf. Syst. **54**, 191–208 (2015)

31. Sinha, A., Paradkar, A.: Use cases to process specifications in business process modeling notation. In: IEEE International Conference on Web Services, pp. 473–480. IEEE (2010)

32. Slaats, T., Mukkamala, R.R., Hildebrandt, T., Marquard, M.: Exformatics declarative case management workflows as DCR graphs. In: Daniel, F., Wang, J., Weber, B. (eds.) BPM 2013. LNCS, vol. 8094, pp. 339–354. Springer, Heidelberg (2013). https://doi.org/10.1007/978-3-642-40176-3_28

33. Weidlich, M., Sheetrit, E., Branco, M.C., Gal, A.: Matching business process models using positional passage-based language models. In: Ng, W., Storey, V.C., Trujillo, J.C. (eds.) ER 2013. LNCS, vol. 8217, pp. 130–137. Springer, Heidelberg (2013). https://doi.org/10.1007/978-3-642-41924-9_12

34. Winter, K., Rinderle-Ma, S.: Detecting constraints and their relations from regulatory documents using nlp techniques. In: Panetto, H., Debruyne, C., Proper, H., Ardagna, C., Roman, D., Meersman, R. (eds.) OTM 2018. LNCS, vol. 11229, pp. 261–278. Springer, Cham (2018). https://doi.org/10.1007/978-3-030-02610-3_15

From Process Models to Chatbots

Anselmo López, Josep Sànchez-Ferreres, Josep Carmona$^{(\boxtimes)}$, and Lluís Padró

Process and Data Science Group, Computer Science Department,
Universitat Politècnica de Catalunya, Barcelona, Spain
{anselmol,jsanchezf,padro,jcarmona}@cs.upc.edu,
http://www.cs.upc.edu/~pads-upc

Abstract. The effect of digital transformation in organizations needs to go beyond automation, so that human capabilities are also augmented. A possibility in this direction is to make formal representations of processes more accessible for the actors involved. On this line, this paper presents a methodology to transform a formal process description into a conversational agent, which can guide a process actor through the required steps in a user-friendly conversation. The presented system relies on dialog systems and natural language processing and generation techniques, to automatically build a chatbot from a process model. A prototype tool – accessible online – has been developed to transform a process model in BPMN into a chatbot, defined in Artificial Intelligence Marking Language (AIML), which has been evaluated over academic and industrial professionals, showing potential into improving the gap between process understanding and execution.

1 Introduction

Formal process modeling notations are ubiquitous in organizations. They precisely describe a business process, using a graphical notation that has a formal execution semantics, amenable for automating certain tasks of the underlying process [3]. These notations, among which Business Process Model and Notation (BPMN) is a prominent example, are not always suitable or understandable by any actor involved in the process. A good example is a logistic processes, where several agents are required, ranging from agents to transport the goods, down to accountants that keep track of the finances of the whole process.

Hence, one cannot assume always that all the actors of a process would be able to understand a BPMN model, in order to know what they need to do for the successful execution of the process. The fact that digital transformation aims at a better maturity and elicitation of an organization' processes [7], would only contribute to increasing the complexity and size of the process repositories in organizations, which in turn causes a pressure on process' actors. The main goal of the work of this paper is to alleviate this pressure. A similar observation and motivation was presented in the seminal work to convert a BPMN model into a textual description [6], from which this paper shares some parts of the methodology proposed.

© Springer Nature Switzerland AG 2019
P. Giorgini and B. Weber (Eds.): CAiSE 2019, LNCS 11483, pp. 383–398, 2019.
https://doi.org/10.1007/978-3-030-21290-2_24

In this paper we are inspired by a trend seen in the last few years in online services. Often, these sites have a section called *Frequently Asked Questions*, where users can read some solutions to common problems. Sometimes, these pages also have guides to execute some complicated processes or tasks. The main problem is that users have to search for their solution through all the web content, which is often a tedious task. That is why companies are using alternatives to help their customers [15]. One of the most implemented options currently is the *conversational bot* or *chatbot*[1].

Chatbots allow a user to query a complex content, so that a more human interaction with it is enabled. Moreover, the user is relieved from the burden of searching for a solution, which is now a task carried out by the chatbot.

In this paper we present a methodology that takes as input a BPMN model, and generates a chatbot aimed to guide a process actor through the modeled business process. The actor can be guided step-by-step through the process, ask questions about who should perform certain task, or to whom should a document be sent, etc. In this way, a more flexible process interaction is envisioned at a very low cost, since using the methodology proposed some of the processes of a process repository can be transformed into chatbots. The methodology has been validated over 33 individuals, both from academy and industry.

The methodology proposed relies on *script-based dialog management* [16], in which the dialog state determines what is the system expecting at a given moment, and the user utterance will determine the system's answer and the transition to a new dialog state. We generate the finite state dialog automaton from the BPMN structure, and the system utterances from the textual components of the model (task labels, pool and swimlane names, ...), and we add additional states and transitions to deal with user questions about actors (e.g. who should do a task) and objects (e.g. to whom a document must be sent).

The organization of this paper is as follows: next section provides a simple example to illustrate the contributions of this paper. Then, in Sect. 3 we provide the necessary background to understand the methodology that will be presented in Sect. 4. In Sect. 5 we describe the prototype tool implementing the methodologys of this paper, which is then validated in Sect. 6. Finally, Sect. 7 summarizes the paper milestones and reports future challenges ahead.

2   Motivating Example

To illustrate the contribution of this paper, Fig. 2 shows an interaction with the chatbot obtained by applying the methodology proposed on the simple process model shown in Fig. 1[2]. The interaction is shown in the following page.

By a careful look at the interaction, one can see the main ingredients of the methodology described in this paper. First, Natural Language Processing (NLP) is required to analyze the text in the different elements of the BPMN model.

---

[1] One can see an example for the case of computer repair at http://www.toshiba.co.uk/generic/yoko-home/.

[2] This example was found in the Signavio Academic Initiative pool of BPMN models.

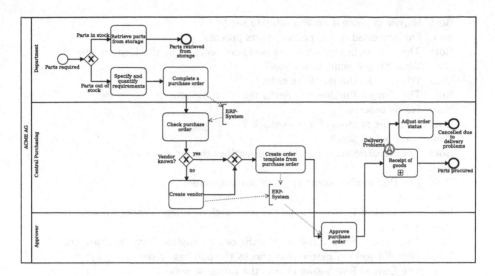

Fig. 1. BPMN representation of the 'procure parts' business process

Second, a tailored finite state automata representation of the underlying process model is used, so that the conversation state is unambiguous depending on the previous questions. Finally, natural language generation is used, so that sentences are created to describe the task to the user in a human-readable manner: see for instance the third-person form when explaining the tasks performed.

3 Preliminaries

3.1 Process Modeling

As it has been already acknowledged in the introduction, formal process notations are an important part of any digitalization initiative, since they open the door to an unambiguous and focused (process) automation. A recent article reports three different process management levels, ranging from multi-process management, to the classical process management level, down to process instance level [8].

Process models can be created using a variety of modeling languages, such as Petri nets, Event-Driven Process Chains (EPCs), and BPMN. Although we focus in BPMN, the contributions of this paper are independent of the specific notation used to define a process model. In particular, we focus on BPMN 2.0, notation created as a standard for business process modeling. BPMN has three different kinds of elements. First, the main elements are the nodes in the diagram, which may belong to three different types: Events, which represent that something happens; Activities, which represents some task that is performed; and Gateways, which split or join flow control. Second, the notation has different edges to connect nodes. A solid line indicates the process workflow, while

Bot: Hi, which process do you want to see?
You: I'm interested in the procure parts process.
Bot: The process begins when the parts are required by the Department. What do you want to do now?
You: Who checks the purchase order?
Bot: The Central Purchasing checks the purchase order.
You: Follow process.
Bot: Parts out of stock/Parts in stock ?
You: Parts out of stock.
Bot: The Department specifies and quantifies the requirements.
You: Next.
Bot: The Department completes the purchase order.
You: Next.
Bot: The Central Purchasing checks the purchase order. Vendor known?
You: Yes.
Bot: The Central Purchasing creates the order template from purchase order.
You: Who did you say before that checks the purchase order?
Bot: The Central Purchasing checks the purchase order.
You: ok.
Bot: The Approver approves the purchase order.
You: Next.
Bot: After that, the Central Purchasing executes process called "receipt of goods".
You: Next.
Bot: Then, the process is finished.

Fig. 2. Example of dialog with the bot generated for the "procure parts" process.

dashed lines represent messages sent between process participants[3]. Finally, there are organization elements such as lanes that contain activities performed by the same participant, and pools, that group several related lanes.

3.2 Dialog Systems

Dialog is the most natural way for humans to communicate, and since the dawn of computers, researchers have aimed to devise ways to communicate with machines as we do with people. From Eliza [19] – the first reactive chatbot – to modern assistants like Siri, Alexa, or Google Assistant, dialog systems construction still strongly rely on large amounts of human intervention, to establish which topics the chatbot should be aware of, and provide useful answers to.

Regardless of whether the dialog interface is oral or written, traditional dialog systems are tailored to a specific task (e.g. helping the user to buy a plane ticket, post a claim for a wrong product, etc.) since the system requires a precise definition of domain concepts and actions to execute depending on the user input. For this reason, they usually are expensive to develop, and not easily customizable to new application domains. This is also the case of modern personal assistants.

---

[3] Dashed lines can also represent data associations.

On the other hand, there are the so-called *recreational* (also known as *conversational*) chatbots which do not target a specific task, but only aim to entertain the user, or to win a Turing's Test competition [18,19].

Dialog systems typically consist of four main components:

- User input processing and understanding: Takes care of processing the user input (which may be speech- or text-based, or even multimodal) and extracting the relevant information and intention.
- Dialog manager: Keeps track of the dialog state, and decides how to update it, and which tasks should be executed at each moment.
- Task Manager: Deals with the back-office operations required for the dialog goal (retrieving information from a database, purchasing tickets, booking reservations, etc).
- Output generator: Produces the appropriate answer or feedback (speech, text, or multimodal) to be sent to user.

Each of this components may be realized at different levels of complexity: Input processing may range from a simple keyword matching on the user text to an advanced Natural Language Processing system. Dialog managers can follow a simple stateless reactive pattern, be based on finite state automata or more complex state-keeping structures, or rely on advanced Machine Learning methods (which require lots of annotated data – actual dialogs – relative to the target domain to be trained). Task Manager – which is missing in non-task oriented dialog systems – is the most domain-dependent component, and must be taylored for each application. And finally, output generation can be approached with techniques ranging from basic pre-written fixed sentences or patterns, up to complete Natural Language Generation systems.

See [1,5] for more details on dialog systems architectures and technologies.

3.3 Natural Language Processing and Generation

Apart from the internal logic or domain-related reasoning that a dialog system must carry out (e.g. access a database to extract available flights matching user's needs, decide which may be most useful, etc.), a crucial part of the dialog is understanding user utterances.

For that, NLP tools are required in order to convert the text spoken or written by the user into structured data that can be used by the system.

In our case, we are generating a chatbot from a BPMN model. For that, we need to extract information from the language components in the model – basically the task labels and pool and lanes descriptions – and for this we also resort to NLP tools to extract the actions being described in the labels, the agents who perform each action, and the objects upon which action is performed. The way we extract this information follows a similar strategy to the one presented in [6].

Another important component in any dialog system is that in charge of generating the system reply that will be sent to the user. Ideally, the system utterance should sound natural, avoid reiteration of already shared information, use a varied set of language structures and lexica, etc. This is addressed by a subfield of NLP known as Natural Language Generation (NLG), that given a semantic representation of the concepts to be expressed, generates the appropriate sentences. NLG is used not only to generate system replies in dialog systems, but also in automatic document generation, either to generate reports from raw from data (*data-to-text* NLG) or from other texts (*text-to-text* NLG) (e.g. automatic summarization).

NLG can be approached at different complexity levels, depending on the task and on the expected results. Simple dialog systems often use pre-canned sentences (which may contain wildcards that are appropriately replaced). A varied set of pre-canned sentences for each situation, from which an answer is randomly chosen when needed, may be enough to avoid a too repetitive user experience.

However, for more advanced NLG applications, complex architectures may be needed. Main steps in a NLG system involve: Determining what to say, planning the structure of the generated text or document, choosing the words to be used, generating the sentences expressing each concept, aggregating or merging several sentences in one to avoid redundancy, introducing pronouns to refer to entities previously mentioned, and finally, realize all that in appropriate and grammatical sentences. More details on NLG techniques can be found in [14].

In our process model scenario, we can not resort to pre-canned text, since each input model may be different. Given that our generated dialog has one state for each model task (see Sect. 4) we apply the *realization* step to obtain a sentence describing the task, and then we use this generated text as a pre-canned pattern at execution time.

4   Chatbot Generation from BPMN

To achieve our goal of generating a dialog agent from a process model in BPMN, we first define which kind of interactions the user is expected to have with the system, namely:

– Ask who is the actor performing any task.
– Ask to who (from who) is a message or a data object sent (received).
– Be guided step-by-step through the process:
   • Find out what is the next task to be executed (or a list of possible tasks, if several are possible) either by a particular actor or in the general process
   • Be asked to provide information when exclusive gateways are reached and be guided into the appropriate branch
   • Be informed when the process ends for a particular actor, or as a whole.

The purpose of these interactions is the use cases that may arise from this work, i.e., helping users to perform tasks of a process model. This type of interactions was required in a short collaboration we had with a process modelling software company. Other types of interactions are left for future work.

Given the expected flows of the dialog, we build a finite state automaton (FSA) that encodes the interactions and conversation flows that we focus in this paper.

The utterances that the system will produce when reaching each state in the FSA are generated analyzing the meaning of the text instances in the BPMN model (task labels and pool/swimlane names), and then feeding this semantic representation into a NLG system.

Also, a variety of patterns to match and interpret user response at each state are generated from model text, plus some general expressions valid for any process (such as "what is the next task?" or "end this conversation").

Once the conversation FSA has been generated, it is encoded into AIML [17], so it can be executed in any available AIML interpretation engine. Figure 3 shows the main steps in the generation process, detailed in the following sections.

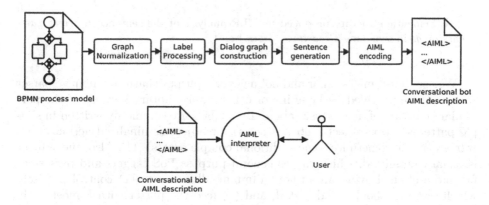

Fig. 3. Chatbot generation process stages (top). Once the chatbot description has been generated, it can be executed by AIML interpreter to interact with the user (bottom).

4.1 Graph Normalization

We start from the BPMN file, and we parse its XML format in order to load the process graph. This graph may require some normalization step, in order to ensure that all blocks in the graph are well-formed. In our case, we aim at having a BPMN that can be partitioned into *Single-Entry Single-Exit* (SESE) components [13]: for instance, the activities P1, P2 and P3 together with the two adjacent parallel gateways form a SESE in Fig. 5(a). Several transformation techniques can be applied in case a process model is not well-formed (e.g., [12]). Hence, in the rest of this paper, we assume the process is well-formed.

4.2   Label Processing

Once the graph is normalized, we have to collect the linguistic information of model labels. We use FreeLing[4] library [10] to desambiguate the part-of-speech of the label text, and to run it through a custom grammar that extracts the action, the object, as well as other complements. The subject is usually ommitted in the task label, so it is retrieved from the pool or swimlane name.

For instance, the label *Retrieve parts from storage* in swimlane *Department* in Fig. 1 would produce the semantic structure in Fig. 4.

[action: *retrieve*,
  subject: *department*,
  object: *parts*,
  complement: *from storage*]

Fig. 4. Semantic structure produced by NLP analysis of the sentence *Retrieve parts from storage* in swimlane *Department* from Fig. 1.

We use a custom grammar and not a general purpose natural language parser such as those provided by FreeLing or other similar library because of the particular structure of model task labels: Task labels are commonly written in simple patterns action-object (*retrieve parts*), or object-nominalized action (*parts retrieval*) with sometimes some additional complement(s) [11]. Also, the subject is usually ommitted, which causes general purpose PoS taggers and parsers to fail more often. Having an ad-hoc grammar allows us to (1) control precisely which patterns should be detected, and (2) feed the parser with k most-likely PoS annotations from the tagger to find out if any of them matches the expected patterns, thus recovering from errors in the tagging step that would lead to wrong parsing results.

4.3   Dialog Graph Construction

Next step is generating the dialog graph, that is, the FSA that encodes all the possible dialog flows. This is a typical architecture followed by many simple chatbots, specially those based on AIML. The dialog graph consists of a set of states and transitions between them. Transition from one state to the next depends on the user utterance.

Definition 1. *A dialog graph FSA is a tuple, $(Q, \mathcal{T}, \delta, A, \Omega)$, where:*

Q *is a finite set of state nodes,*
$\mathcal{T}$ *is the set of all possible text utterances emmited by the user,*
$\delta : Q \times \mathcal{T} \rightarrow Q$ *is a transition function that given the current state $q \in Q$ and a text utterance $t \in \mathcal{T}$ computes the destination state,*

---
[4] http://nlp.cs.upc.edu/freeling.

$A \subseteq Q$ is the set of start state nodes, and
$\Omega \subseteq Q$ is the set of final state nodes.

Note that the transition function δ does not work on a closed alphabet as in normal FSAs. Function δ may range from a simple set of regular expressions performing pattern matching on the user sentence, to a highly sophisticated language analysis system using the latest Artificial Intelligence techniques. In our case, since AIML supports only regular expression based transitions, we restrict ourselves to that approach, though with some extensions provided by the used interpeter (see Sect. 4.5).

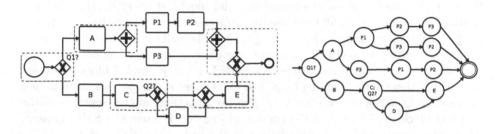

Fig. 5. Initial dialog state graph (right) corresponding to a BPMN model (left). Dotted lines show how split (join) gateways are fused with preceeding (following) elements. Note the expansion of the parallel block into all its possible paths. Self-loops are added later to handle questions or commands valid in any state.

The created dialog graph has a structure that resembles the original BPMN graph, but with some differences to make it suitable for dialog control:

- **Join gateways:** In the BPMN semantics, join gateways describe the point where the branches of a previous split gateway are merged. This kind of node makes no sense in a dialog flow (it would be confusing that the system uttered "Now there is a join. what do you want to do?"). Thus, this kind of nodes are removed from the graph, and its entering edges are associated to the following element.
- **Parallel blocks:** A parallel block consists of the flow elements between a split and a join inclusive gateway. In BPMN, parallel block are interpreted as meaning that the involved tasks may be executed in any order. To account for this behavior in the dialog graph, we create a path in the dialog graph for each valid permutation of the tasks in the parallel branches. In this way, the user can choose the order in which she wants to perform the tasks[5]. Notice that as commented in Sect. 4.1, our strategy to transform parallel blocks (see bellow the formalization of the algorithm for this specific part) assumes that

---

[5] In case of a parallel block consisting on a large amount of parallel tasks, in principle it is not needed to offer all the permutations in the dialog graph, if that contributes to a state-space explosion: the artifact would be that the user only sees a subset of the possibilities offered by the process model, which in some cases can be acceptable.

all parallel blocks in the BPMN are well-structured (a parallel block is *well-structured* when the number of branches going out the split gateway is equal to the number of branches entering the join gateway).

Figure 5 shows a simple example of the transformation of a BPMN model into a graph dialog that guides the user through the process.

The steps performed to recursively expand the parallel blocks and generate the corresponding dialog graph fragment are now overviewed. First of all, a depth-first search traversal is performed to detect split parallel gateways. When one is found, a new parallel block instance is pushed onto a general stack. The stack contains parallel blocks in depth-first order, because we need to guarantee the correct transformation of internal parallel blocks at every depth. Within a particular parallel scope, all the nodes encountered are added to the corresponding parallel branch. If the node is a join gateway, then all the active open branches of the containing parallel block instance are closed, and then the parallel block with the new expanded instance is replaced. For every parallel block detected, we check if there is any parallel block inside. If there is one, we call the function for that node. If there is no block, all the permutations of the branches of the selected block are created in the corresponding newly created FSM fragment. Then, these permutations are connected to the rest of the dialog graph.

Once the control-flow is completely transferred to the dialog graph, the last step of the construction is to also transfer the additional information contained in the BPMN model: messages, actors and data objects. These mainly correspond to self-loops on any conversation state, where information is reported to the user while retaining the conversation state (e.g. the user may ask *who did you say before that checks the purchase order?* even when the conversation is not in the state corresponding to this task).

4.4   Sentence Generation

The dialog graph at this point has the definitive structure, but sentences that will be emmitted by the system at each state have not been generated yet. To generate these sentences, we proceed in consecutive stages.

First, we create the syntactic specifications for each node. This step uses the semantic structures generated during label processing (Sect. 4.2). Using these annotations – and depending on the BPMN element type they correspond to – a syntactic structure is created with the appropriate characteristics (kind of sentence – affirmative, interrogative –, verb features – tense, person, ..., modifiers, etc.) Note that some node types require a special treatment. For instance, at the process start node, the sentence will be headed by the text *The process starts when*, to give the user a better context information. Also, exclusive gateways will be generated as questions and not as affirmative sentences.

Each dialog node can have more than one syntactic structure. Also, the order of the structures can affect the way sentences are generated. The syntactic structures are provided to the *realization engine*, a module that applies syntactic, grammatical and morphological rules to produce a correct phrase with the requested features.

We use the realization engine provided by SimpleNLG[6] library [4], an open-source project that uses basic English lexicon and grammar to transform the input into an appropriate sentence. One of the benefits of SimpleNLG is its potential to be adapted to other languages, using existing linguistic resources and performing some code adaptation.

SimpleNLG provides classes representing different kinds of phrases (verb phrase, noun phrase, prepositional phrase, etc). The calling application can instantiate any phrase specifying the desired features. SimpleNLG engine will build the sentences using grammar rules to properly combine the input phrase instances to form a valid syntactic tree. In our case, we build the phrases using the semantic structures previously created and we use them as required by the node type. Once the phrase instances are created, they are sent to the realization engine to obtain a full sentence.

The realization engine follows several steps to build the final sentence: First, the syntactic rules are applied to obtain the post-syntax tree. This decides, for example, the appropriate order for the words in the target language. Then, the morphological transformations – like selecting the correct determiners or the verb tense – are applied on the obtained tree. Finally, the last step is the orthography function, where sentence punctuation is revised and corrected. If there is some special format required, it is applied after these steps.

Once the sentences for each graph node are generated, we use them as basic information to create the message sentences and the questions:

When the model contains a message element, the user is asked to choose between continuing with the next task in the current lane, or to follow the message and see which task the message recipient will perform[7]. Message information is often encoded in the task originating it, and not in the message element itself, thus the generator needs to check both possibilities and decide which is the right text to use to generate sentences relative to message sending/receiving.

We also generate possible questions about the elements on the process. We resort to the same realization engine to produce questions about who is the responsible for each task, which is the object of an action, or who is the sender/recipient of a message. After some generalization to allow for variations, these questions are included in the set of regular expressions recognized by function δ. Also, this nodes are associated with the related task, so after asking, e.g. *who checks the purchase order* and getting the answer, the user may decide to follow the process from that point, or to remain in the current state.

---

[6] https://github.com/simplenlg.

[7] This can only be done if the information is present in the original BPMN model.

4.5   AIML Encoding

Once the dialog graph is complete and all the needed text has been generated, the dialog can be exported to the desired format to be interpreted by a chatbot engine.

We use *Artificial Intelligence Modeling Language* (AIML) standard because it is the conversational bot definition format most widely used. This XML-based format builds on the concepts of *topics*, which correspond to dialog states, and *categories* to represent the expected transitions from each state. Each category specifies a *pattern* – a regular expression to be matched with the user input, and a *template* providing the answer the bot must emit and the new state to transition to. Since AIML basically describes extended FSAs, it is straightforward to convert our dialog graph into this format. AIML *patterns* allow for the use of wildcards that will match zero or more words in the user input, as well as *sets*, that allow specifying that a word in the user utterance may be any of a given list. We use both this mechanisms to add flexibility to user sentence interpretation, allowing for synonyms, or for extra words inserted in the user input. We pre-encode our *sets* in general synonym dictionaries extracted from WordNet [9].

AIML also supports some features over a pure FSA, such as the possibility of having internal variables to store any relevant information, that may be needed further along in the dialog (e.g. to store some user-provided information such as her name, or some other internal information not encoded in the state). In future versions of our bot generator this could be used, for instance, to ask the user which process role she wants to play, so when describing tasks executed by the selected role, the system would output e.g. *You check the purchase order* instead of *Central Purchasing checks the purchase order.*

4.6   AIML Interpretation

Once the AIML dialog definition file has been generated, it can be executed using any available AIML interpretation engine, so a user can actually interact with the bot.

Among the many open source available options, we use *Program Y*[8]. It is maintained by AIML Foundation (who defines the evolution of the standard), and it is kept in sync with the latest standard updates. Also, it includes some useful additional features, like custom tags o full RegEx support, as well as a variety of front-ends to integrate the dialogs in different environments (standalone, web-based, Telegram, Twitter, Facebook, etc.).

---

[8] https://github.com/keiffster/program-y.

5   Tool Support

The methodology of this paper is available through the NLP4BPM platform [2], accessible at https://bpm.cs.upc.edu/bpmninterface/. Once logged in[9], the user can go to the tab "BPMN to AIML" where a BPMN file can be uploaded and get as a result the AIML corresponding to the created chatbot, applying the methodology of this paper. On the tab "Interpreting AIML" the user can upload the AIML generated to interact with the created chatbot.

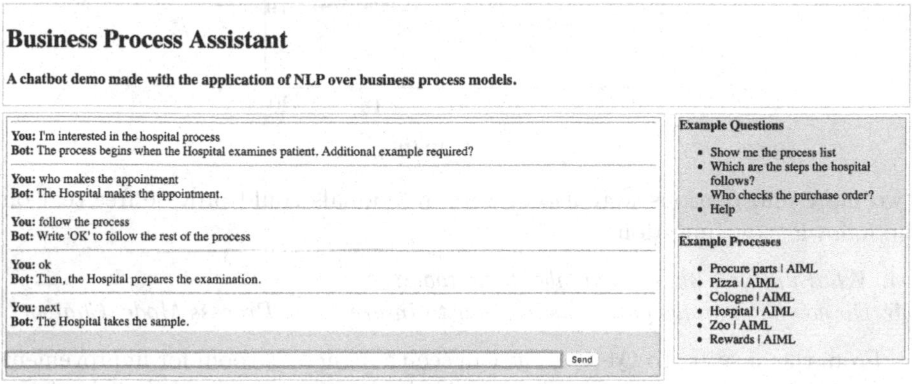

Fig. 6. Example of interpretation for several BPMN process models (available at https://bpm.cs.upc.edu/chatbot).

For a fast insight on the contribution of this paper, we have set up an AIML interpreter demonstrating some generated chatbots for a collection of BPMN models, so that a user can interact with them. Figure 6 shows a screenshot of the environment, accessible at https://bpm.cs.upc.edu/chatbot.

6   Evaluation, Limitations and Use Cases

To evaluate the contribution of this paper, we collected feedback of 33 individuals from academia (27) or industry (6). After interacting with the chatbot for a couple of processes, the following questions were answered:

Q1: *How was your interaction with the chatbot ?* (1: not fluent – 4: very fluent)
Q2: *Did the Process Model Chatbot answer your questions about the process?* (1: it did not – 4: it did)
Q3: *Do you see potential for this kind of application in organizations?* (1: no potential – 4: large potential).

---

[9] An anonymous user is temporarily available for review purposes with the username "demo" and password "caisedemo".

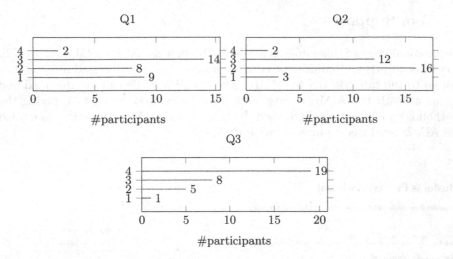

Two more informations were asked, were individuals could provide free text on the following two questions;

Q4: *What did you like/dislike about the tool ?*
Q5: *Do you have any suggestions in order to improve the Process Model Chatbot?.*

From the answers to Q1–Q2, one can see that there is room for improvement in the implementation of our ideas: in both questions, more than half of the answers where on lowest scores. This is an artifact of the limited functionality of the current implementation, which lacks some flexibility and needs to be extended to be able to cover more parts of the process. In spite of this, through the answers to Q3 (81.8% agree on the huge potential of the ideas), we are confident that by improving theses weakness we will be able to come up with a solution that can be of practical use in organizations.

The answers to Q4–Q5 where an interesting source of ideas for improvement and encouragement, but confirmed the limited capabilities of the current implementation. Also, suggestions on use cases where provided, e.g., to help in the training of individuals, to help in the management of process changes, to have a state-aware dialogue between the actors and the process, among others.

7   Conclusions and Future Work

In this paper we have presented a fresh view on the interaction between processes and humans in organizations. By automating the translation between formal model notations like BPMN into conversational agents, a more flexible ecosystem is envisioned. This paper represents the first step towards the ambitious goal of empowering humans in organizations, so that decision-making is facilitated. We foresee multiple directions for future research, among which we highlight:

- Extend the capabilities of the interaction, either by extending the language (in our case, AIML), the types of BPMN constructs to consider, or the interpretation itself. Also, enable the interaction even when the user does not know the main activities of the process.
- Incorporate domain knowledge and/or other perspectives, e.g., data access rights, or security/privacy information.
- Create interactions at the level of process repositories.[10]

Acknowledgments. We would like to thank Gero Decker for drawing our attention to the problem considered in this paper. This work has been supported by MINECO and FEDER funds under grant TIN2017-86727-C2-1-R.

References

1. Chen, H., Liu, X., Yin, D., Tang, J.: A survey on dialogue systems: recent advances and new frontiers. SIGKDD Explor. Newsl. **19**(2), 25–35 (2017)
2. Delicado, L., Sànchez-Ferreres, J., Carmona, J., Padró, L.: NLP4BPM - natural language processing tools for business process management. In: Proceedings of the BPM Demo Track Co-located with 15th International Conference on Business Process Modeling (BPM 2017), Barcelona, Spain, September (2017)
3. Dumas, M., Rosa, M.L., Mendling, J., Reijers, H.A.: Fundamentals of Business Process Management, 2nd edn. Springer, Heidelberg (2018). https://doi.org/10.1007/978-3-662-56509-4
4. Gatt, A., Reiter, E.: SimpleNLG: a realisation engine for practical applications (2009)
5. Jurafsky, D., Martin, J.H.: Speech and Language Processing, 2nd edn. Prentice-Hall Inc., Upper Saddle River (2009)
6. Leopold, H., Mendling, J., Polyvyanyy, A.: Supporting process model validation through natural language generation. IEEE Trans. Softw. Eng. **40**(8), 818–840 (2014)
7. Matt, C., Hess, T., Benlian, A.: Digital transformation strategies. Bus. Inf. Syst. Eng. **57**(5), 339–343 (2015)
8. Mendling, J., Baesens, B., Bernstein, A., Fellmann, M.: Challenges of smart business process management: an introduction to the special issue. Decis. Support Syst. **100**, 1–5 (2017)
9. Miller, G.A.: WordNet: a lexical database for English. Commun. ACM **38**(11), 39–41 (1995)
10. Padro, L., Stanilovsky, E.: FreeLing 3.0: towards wider multilinguality. In: International Conference on Language Resources and Evaluation, pp. 2473–2479, May 2012
11. Pittke, F., Leopold, H., Mendling, J.: Automatic detection and resolution of lexical ambiguity in process models. In: Software Engineering 2016, Fachtagung des GI-Fachbereichs Softwaretechnik, Wien, Österreich, 23–26 Februar 2016, pp. 75–76 (2016)

---

[10] In https://bpm.cs.upc.edu/chatbot we provide very simple queries for detecting processes in a repository. One can think on a more elaborated setting where complex queries can be allowed.

12. Polyvyanyy, A., García-Bañuelos, L., Fahland, D., Weske, M.: Maximal structuring of acyclic process models. Comput. J. **57**(1), 12–35 (2014)
13. Polyvyanyy, A., Smirnov, S., Weske, M.: The triconnected abstraction of process models. In: Dayal, U., Eder, J., Koehler, J., Reijers, H.A. (eds.) BPM 2009. LNCS, vol. 5701, pp. 229–244. Springer, Heidelberg (2009). https://doi.org/10.1007/978-3-642-03848-8_16
14. Reiter, E., Dale, R.: Building Natural Language Generation Systems. Cambridge University Press, New York (2000)
15. Thorne, C.: Chatbots for troubleshooting: a survey. Lang. Linguist. Compass **11**(10), e12253 (2017)
16. Traum, D.R., et al.: Representations of dialogue state for domain and task independent meta-dialogue. Electron. Trans. Artif. Intell. **3**(D), 125–152 (1999)
17. Wallace, R.: The Elements of AIML Style. ALICE AI Foundation (2003)
18. Wallace, R.S.: The anatomy of A.L.I.C.E. In: Epstein, R., Roberts, G., Beber, G. (eds.) Parsing the Turing Test: Philosophical and Methodological Issues in the Quest for the Thinking Computer, pp. 181–210. Springer, Netherlands (2009). https://doi.org/10.1007/978-1-4020-6710-5_13
19. Weizenbaum, J.: ELIZA - a computer program for the study of natural language communication between man and machine. Commun. ACM **9**(1), 36–45 (1966)

Dynamic Role Binding
in Blockchain-Based Collaborative
Business Processes

Orlenys López-Pintado[1(✉)], Marlon Dumas[1], Luciano García-Bañuelos[1,2],
and Ingo Weber[3]

[1] University of Tartu, Tartu, Estonia
{orlenyslp,marlon.dumas}@ut.ee
[2] Tecnológico de Monterrey, Monterrey, Mexico
luciano.garcia@tec.mx
[3] Data61, CSIRO, Sydney, Australia
ingo.weber@data61.csiro.au

Abstract. Blockchain technology enables the execution of collaborative business processes involving mutually untrusted parties. Existing tools allow such processes to be modeled using high-level notations and compiled into smart contracts that can be deployed on blockchain platforms. However, these tools brush aside the question of who is allowed to execute which tasks in the process, either by deferring the question altogether or by adopting a static approach where all actors are bound to roles upon process instantiation. Yet, a key advantage of blockchains is their ability to support dynamic sets of actors. This paper presents a model for dynamic binding of actors to roles in collaborative processes and an associated binding policy specification language. The proposed language is endowed with a Petri net semantics, thus enabling policy consistency verification. The paper also outlines an approach to compile policy specifications into smart contracts for enforcement. An experimental evaluation shows that the cost of policy enforcement increases linearly with the number of roles and constraints.

1 Introduction

Access control is an essential aspect in the design and execution of business processes. Mainstream Business Process Management Systems (BPMSs) rely on static Role-Based Access Control (RBAC) models. In these models, any worker who plays a role is allowed to perform any task associated to this role in any instance of the process, modulo additional constraints such as separation of duties [12]. This approach is unsuitable for collaborative inter-organizational processes involving untrusted actors. For example, a buyer may trust a given carrier but not others, even though they all play the same role.

Blockchain technology enables the execution of collaborative business processes involving untrusted actors [7]. Existing tools such as Caterpillar [6] and

© Springer Nature Switzerland AG 2019
P. Giorgini and B. Weber (Eds.): CAiSE 2019, LNCS 11483, pp. 399–414, 2019.
https://doi.org/10.1007/978-3-030-21290-2_25

Lorikeet [13], support the definition of collaborative processes using high-level notations and their execution on top of blockchain platforms. However, these tools either do not support access control or they adopt a static role binding approach wherein all actors are bound to roles upon process instantiation.

The characteristics of blockchain technology shift the role binding problem in two ways. First, rather than groups or individual users being bound to roles, we need to bind blockchain accounts (or identities) to roles, as shown in Fig. 1. These accounts, in turn, are controlled by users, groups, systems, or (IoT) devices.

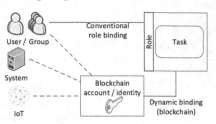

Fig. 1. Relations between tasks, roles, blockchain accounts, and actors (blockchain case vs. conventional case).

Second and more significantly, in open blockchain networks, instances of a collaborative process are created by different actors, and each of these actors trusts one subset of actors but not others. Moreover, the set of actors changes dynamically and so do the trust relations. For example, a buyer may initially trust a carrier and agree to its appointment together with the supplier. But later, the buyer may lose this trust (e.g. if the carrier misses a deadline). Thereafter, the buyer may wish to re-bind the transportation task to another carrier, but this re-binding must be endorsed by the supplier. This example illustrates the need to support *dynamic binding and un-binding of actors to roles* and *collaborative binding of actors to roles* (buyer and supplier both need to agree on the carrier).

This paper proposes a role binding model and a binding policy specification language designed to support collaborative business processes in such open and untrusted environments, as well as an approach to compile policies into executable code. The semantics of the policy specification language is defined via a mapping to Petri nets, which enables the static verification of policies prior to their compilation. The proposed method has been implemented in Caterpillar [6] – a blockchain-based execution engine that supports the Business Process Model and Notation (BPMN). The paper reports on an experimental evaluation aimed at assessing the cost of policy enforcement on the Ethereum blockchain.

The rest of the paper is structured as follows. Section 2 discusses basic concepts of blockchain technology and the limitations of existing role binding models for collaborative processes. Section 3 describes the role binding model and policy language. Section 4 presents the semantics of the policy language and the policy verification approach. Finally, Sect. 5 discusses the implementation and evaluation, while Sect. 6 draws conclusions and sketches future work.

2   Background and Related Work

2.1   Blockchain Technology and Collaborative Processes

A blockchain is a distributed append-only store of transactions distributed across computational nodes and structured as a linked list of blocks, each containing a set of transactions [15]. A blockchain network is made up of nodes, a subset of which holds a replica of the data structure. Clients use a blockchain system (a concrete network) by reading data from and submitting transactions to it. Submitted transactions are grouped into blocks, which are broadcast across the network to be appended to the blockchain. A consensus mechanism ensures tamper-proofness without assuming mutual trust between participants.

A smart contract is a program deployed on the blockchain, which may be invoked via a transaction [15]. In Ethereum, smart contracts are written in the Solidity language, which is compiled into bytecode and executed on the Ethereum Virtual Machine. The computational and data storage consumption of a transaction are measured in *gas*, which translates to monetary costs for the transaction's sender. Each block has a *gas limit* and hence gas directly impacts throughput.

Existing blockchain-based process management tools support the specification of collaborative processes using BPMN [6,13] or domain-specific languages [4], and their execution via smart contracts. These systems focus mainly on the control-flow perspective. Lorikeet [13] implements a static access control mechanism, where roles are bound to accounts upon process instantiation. A method proposed in [10] allows dynamic handoffs of process instances between actors, but does not support the specification and enforcement of permitted handoffs.

2.2 Binding and Delegation Models for Collaborative Processes

The question of dynamic role binding has been considered in the context of Web service composition. For example, in the Business Process Execution Language (BPEL) [1], role binding is supported via *partner links*. A partner link is a variable that holds a reference to a service endpoint. This variable can be modified anytime during an execution of a process. This approach assumes that the whole process is orchestrated by a single actor and that this actor unilaterally decides which actor (i.e. endpoint) should be bound to each role (i.e. partner link). This assumption is also made in [5,9]. These approaches are not applicable in settings where the binding of actors to roles is not determined by a single actor.

Other studies have considered the problem of dynamic role binding in processes that are not orchestrated by a single actor. [11] extracts dynamic authorization policies from service choreographies. These policies are enforced locally by each party, but a central authority specifies all role bindings. BPEL4Chor [3] allows an actor to bind other actors to the roles it has control over. But each role is controlled by a single actor. In other words, collaborative role binding is not supported, e.g. this approach does not support the scenario where both the buyer and seller must agree on the actor who plays the role of carrier. Also, BPEL4Chor does not support role re-binding. In [2,14], dynamic role bindings in decentralized processes are captured via delegations and revocations. This approach supports un-binding (revocation) but does not support collaborative binding (each actor decides on the roles it has control over).

In summary, none of the above studies has addressed the problem of dynamic role binding and un-binding in decentralized processes, where multiple actors must collaboratively agree on each role binding and un-binding decision.

3   Role Binding Model

The starting point of the proposed approach is a (collaborative) business process model where each task is associated with a role. For a given process instance (herein called a *case*), each role may be assigned to at most one actor. An actor has an identity (e.g. a blockchain account) and may represent a user, a group, an organization, a system or a device (cf. Fig. 1). As a running example, Fig. 2 shows a BPMN model of an order-to-cash process. There are six roles represented by numbers below each task label: (1) Customer, (2) Supplier, (3) CarrierCandidate, (4) Carrier, (5) Invoicer and (6) Invoicee. Initially, a customer submits a purchase order (PO) to a supplier. If the PO is rejected the process terminates. Otherwise, the execution continues with the SHIPMENT sub-process, where a supplier requests quotes from multiple carrier candidates (cf. the multi-instance task). Once the shipment completes, two parallel paths are taken to handle the payments. These payments are encapsulated in sub-process INVOICING. This sub-process is called twice: for the supplier's invoice and for the carrier's invoice.

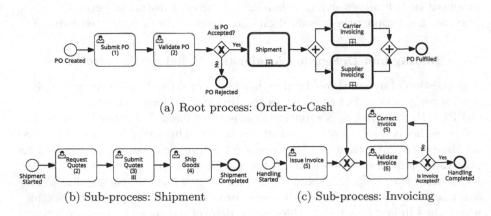

(a) Root process: Order-to-Cash

(b) Sub-process: Shipment   (c) Sub-process: Invoicing

Fig. 2. Running example: (a) an *Order-to-cash* process linked, via call activities, to two reusable sub-processes; (b) *Shipment* and (c) *Invoicing*.

The act of assigning an actor to a role within a case is called *binding*. When a role is not assigned to an actor in a case, we say that the role is unbound. The binding of an actor to a role may happen anytime during a case. Actors may also be unbound from a role – an operation called *release*. A task is performed by the actor bound to the task's role. If a task is enabled when its associated role is unbound, the task waits until the role is bound. Actors may *nominate* themselves or other actors to play a role in a case, or they may request to release themselves or other actors from a role. Given the lack of trust, the nomination/release of an actor to/from a role may require the endorsement of actors playing other roles. If an actor is nominated to a role in a case, this nomination only leads to a binding if the required endorsements are granted. The *binding policy* of a process determines which role(s) are allowed to nominate an actor to a role, to request an actor's release from a role, and to endorse a nomination/release request.

3.1 Binding Policy Specification Language

A policy consists of a set of roles and a set of statements restricting how an actor may be nominated/released to/from a role. A statement is formed by a nominator, a nominee, and optionally a binding and/or an endorsement constraint. The nominator is a role that nominates/releases the actors of another role, namely the nominee. A binding constraint is a boolean expression stipulating that the nominee must be bound (or not) to an actor who is also bound to some other role(s). Binding constraints allow us to implement common resource allocation patterns such as segregation of duties and binding of duties [12]. An endorsement constraint is a boolean expression that determines which roles need to endorse a nomination/release request. A role may be associated with the case-creator, implying that the role is bound upon case creation and does not need a nomination or endorsement. A policy statement applies by default to the root process, but it can be scoped to a sub-process call activity. Figure 3 shows an extract of the grammar of the policy language in Backus Naur form (BNF).[1]

```
⟨statement⟩ ::= [Under ⟨subprocess⟩ ','] ⟨role⟩ ⟨binding_expr⟩ [ ⟨endorse_expr⟩ { ','
                ⟨endorse_expr⟩ } ] ';'
            |   ⟨role⟩ is 'case-creator' ';'

⟨binding_expr⟩ ::= ('nominates' | 'releases') ⟨role⟩ [⟨binding_constraint⟩]

⟨binding_constraint⟩ ::= ('in' | 'not in') ⟨set_expr⟩

⟨endorse_expr⟩ ::= 'endorsed-by' ⟨set_expr⟩

⟨set_exp⟩ ::= ⟨role⟩
          |   ⟨role⟩ ('and' | 'or') ⟨set_expr⟩
          |   '(' ⟨set_exp⟩ ')'
```

Fig. 3. BNF grammar describing the basic statement syntax of a binding policy.

Listing 1 shows a policy for the model in Fig. 2. The policy states that the case creator is automatically bound to the Customer role. The Customer nominates the Supplier (no endorsement needed here). The Supplier, in turn, nominates the Candidate (i.e. the carrier candidate) and the Carrier. The Carrier must be among the actors bound to the Candidate role (cf. binding constraint "Carrier in Candidate"). Note that Candidate is a role associated to a multi-instance task (Submit Quotes), implying that multiple actors may be bound to this role. The Customer must endorse the nomination of the Carrier. Under the Carrier Invoicing call activity, the Invoicer is nominated by the Carrier with endorsement from the Supplier and Customer, and reciprocally for the Invoicee.

---

[1] Some details (e.g. path expressions to refer to nested subprocesses) are omitted for space reasons and can be found at http://git.io/caterpillar.

Meanwhile, under the Supplier Invoicing activity, the **Supplier** nominates the **Invoicer** with **Customer** endorsement, and reciprocally for the **Invoicee**.

This example illustrates the possibilities offered by the policy language to deal with lack of trust. For example, dishonest suppliers could try to derive benefits by not selecting the best carrier candidate but their preferred one. However, the customer would be able to reject such nominations. Also, the policy prevents the supplier from selecting a carrier that has not been a carrier candidate before.

The policy language also allows us to state that the set of actors who endorse a nomination request must fulfill a boolean expression. For instance, the above policy requires that the Invoicer of the carrier services must be endorsed by both the buyer and the supplier. This scenario is relevant in the context of international trade, where both buyers and suppliers need to ensure that they do not deal with black-listed entities or entities in countries banned from trading. The boolean expressions in the endorsement constraint may contain arbitrary combinations of conjunctions and disjunctions. They may not however contain negation, e.g. it is not possible to state that the nomination is approved if a given actor refuses to endorse it. Such scenarios are not applicable in this setting.

```
1 { Customer is case−creator ;
2   Customer nominates Supplier ;
3   Under Shipment , Supplier nominates Candidate ;
4   Under Shipment , Supplier nominates Carrier in Candidate endorsed−by
        Customer ;
5   Under Carrier Invoicing , Carrier nominates Invoicer endorsed−by Supplier
        and Customer ;
6   Under Carrier Invoicing , Customer nominates Invoicee endorsed−by Carrier
7   Under Supplier Invoicing , Supplier nominates Invoicer endorsed−by Customer ;
8   Under Supplier Invoicing , Supplier nominates Invoicee endorsed−by Customer ;
9 }
```

Listing 1. Binding Policy to control the execution of the processes modeled in Fig. 2.

3.2   Runtime Binding Operations

The role binding model relies on three operations. The **nominate** operation allows an actor to request that another actor (or itself) be bound to a role within a process instance (herein called a *case*). Inversely, a **release** operation allows an actor to request that another actor (or itself) be unbound from a role. The **vote** operation allows an actor to accept/reject a nomination or release request.

These operations trigger transitions in the *role lifecycle* depicted in Fig. 4. Within a case, a role is initially UNBOUND. After a **nominate** operation, the role changes to NOMINATED if it requires to be endorsed, otherwise is considered BOUND. A role in NOMINATED state, can transition to the BOUND state after a **vote** operation where the endorser accepts the nomination if, as a result of it, the endorsement constraint of this role is satisfied. On the contrary, a **vote** operation where the endorser rejects the nomination and by doing so makes the role's endorsement constraint unsatisfiable, triggers a transition to the UNBOUND state. If after a `vote` operation, the endorsement constraint remains satisfiable, then the role remains in the NOMINATED state. Symmetrically, a role can transit from BOUND to UNBOUND as a result of a `release` operation, via a RELEASING state, which is specular to the NOMINATED state. If the endorsement constraint associated to a *release* request becomes unsatisfiable, the role goes back to the BOUND state, and if it becomes satisfied, the role moves to the UNBOUND state.

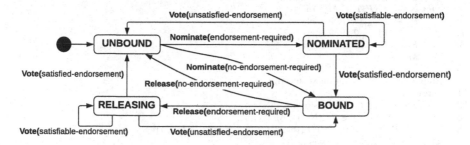

Fig. 4. Lifecycle of a role within a case.

4   Policy Consistency Verification

Nomination and release statements in a policy implicitly induce precedence dependencies in the binding of roles. A statement R1 `nominates` R2 `endorsed-by` R3 implies that for R2 to be bound, R1 and R3 must be bound before. Circular and unresolvable dependencies induced in this way may lead to deadlocks. Accordingly, we define a notion of policy consistency as follows. A policy is *consistent* if, starting from the state where only the roles associated with case-creator are BOUND and after executing any allowed sequence of nomination, release and endorse operations, we always reach a state where all roles will reach the BOUND state via some (other) sequence of nomination, release and endorse operations.

To verify policy consistency, we define a mapping from a policy to a Petri net [8], herein called a *nomination net*. Given the nomination net of a policy, we map the problem of checking policy consistency to a problem of reachability analysis over Petri nets. Algorithm 1 maps a policy to a nomination net. For the sake of conciseness, this algorithm focuses on nomination statements, leaving aside release statements. The mapping of release statements follows a similar structure. For the same reason, the algorithm leaves aside binding constraints.

To illustrate the algorithm, we consider the binding policy in Fig. 5. The algorithm takes as input a symbolic representation of a policy consisting of a set of roles and a set of tuples of the form (nominator, nominee, endorsement-constraint), with $\perp$ denoting an empty constraint. For example, the symbolic representation of the policy in Fig. 5 is given in Fig. 6. Given this input, the algorithm will produce as output the nomination net in Fig. 7.

Algorithm 1. Construction of the Nomination Net for a given Binding Policy

---

1: **function** CONSTRUCTNOMINATIONNET(R, BP)
2:     RNets ← ∅
    ▷ Step 1: Build a Petri net for each role
3:     **for each** role $r \in$ R **do**
4:         RNets ← RNets $\cup \left\{ \left(r \mapsto \left\langle \begin{matrix} \{u_r, n_r, b_r\} & \triangleright P_r \\ \{nm_r, en_r\} & \triangleright T_r \\ \{(u_r, nm_r), (nm_r, n_r), (n_r, en_r), (en_r, b_r)\} & \triangleright F_r \end{matrix} \right\rangle \right) \right\}$

    ▷ Step 2: Merge all role nets to form the nomination net
5:     **let** NNet = $\langle P, T, F, M_0 \rangle$ **in**
6:         $P \leftarrow \bigcup_{r \in R} \mathcal{P}(\text{RNets}[r])$
7:         $T \leftarrow \bigcup_{r \in R} \mathcal{T}(\text{RNets}[r])$
8:         $F \leftarrow \bigcup_{r \in R} \mathcal{F}(\text{RNets}[r])$
9:         $M_0 \leftarrow \emptyset$
10:
    ▷ Step 3: Wire up operation NOMINATE
11:         **for each** $\langle r_{nr}, r_{ne}, \_ \rangle \in$ BP **do**
12:             **select** $b_{nr} \in \mathcal{P}(\text{RNets}[nr])$
13:             **select** $nm_{r_{ne}} \in \mathcal{T}(\text{RNets}[ne])$
14:             $\mathcal{F}(\text{NNet}) \leftarrow \mathcal{F}(\text{NNet}) \cup \{(b_{r_{nr}}, nm_{r_{ne}}), (nm_{r_{ne}}, b_{r_{nr}})\}$

    ▷ Step 4: Wire up operation ENDORSE
15:         **for each** $\langle r_{nr}, r_{ne}, eex \rangle \in$ BP **such that** $eex \neq \perp$ **do**
16:             $\mathcal{P}(\text{NNet}) \leftarrow \mathcal{P}(\text{NNet}) \cup \{disj_{r_{ne}}, eex_{r_{ne}}\}$
17:             $\mathcal{F}(\text{NNet}) \leftarrow \mathcal{F}(\text{NNet}) \cup \{(nm_{r_{ne}}, disj_{r_{ne}}), (eex_{r_{ne}}, en_{r_{ne}})\}$
18:             **for each** conj $\in eex$ **do**
19:                 $\mathcal{T}(\text{NNet}) \leftarrow \mathcal{T}(\text{NNet}) \cup \{eex_{conj}\}$
20:                 $\mathcal{F}(\text{NNet}) \leftarrow \mathcal{F}(\text{NNet}) \bigcup_{r \in conj \wedge b_r \in \mathcal{P}(\text{RNets}[r])} \left\{ \begin{matrix} (b_r, eex_{conj}), (eex_{conj}, b_r), \\ (disj_{r_{ne}}, eex_{conj}) \end{matrix} \right\}$

    ▷ Step 5: Update NNet's initial marking
21:         **let** $r_{cc} \in R$: r_{cc} be case creator **in**
22:             Ps ← $\{u_r \mid r \in R \setminus \{r_{cc}\} \wedge u_r \in \mathcal{P}(\text{NNet}[r])\} \cup \{b_{r_{cc}} \mid b_{r_{cc}} \in \mathcal{P}(\text{NNet}[r_{cc}])\}$
23:             $M_0(\text{NNet})(p) = \begin{cases} 1 & \text{if } p \in Ps \\ 0 & \text{Otherwise} \end{cases}$
24:
25:         **return** NNet

The algorithm proceeds as follows. After initializing variable RNets in line 2, the algorithm builds a Petri net for each node in lines 3–4 (Step 1). Let us consider that we are building the Petri net for role A, which is shown in color blue in Fig. 7. In line 4, the algorithm creates such a Petri net with three places, namely u_A, n_A and b_A, which represent the states of the role's lifecycle UNBOUND, NOMINATED and BOUND, respectively. Similarly, two transitions are added to the Petri net, namely nm_A and en_A, representing the operations 'nominate' and 'endorse'. Finally, four arcs added to complete the Petri net, by connecting the places and transitions. The Petri nets for all the other nodes are created in a similar way. Every Petri net thus created is added to RNets that serves as a map that associates a role to its corresponding Petri net.

In lines 5–9 (Step 2), all the role (Petri) nets are merged to form the initial nomination net, which is held in variable NNet. This is done by taking the union of the elements in the role nets. Also, the initial marking is set to the empty set.

In lines 11–14 (Step 3), the algorithm adds double-headed arcs to the Petri net to synchronize the transition that represents the nomination of roles. To

```
{ A is case-creator;
  A nominates B;
  A nominates C;
  C nominates D, endorsed-by A and B;
}
```

$$R = \{A, B, C, D\}$$
$$BP = \{\langle A, B, \bot \rangle, \langle A, C, \bot \rangle, \langle C, D, A \wedge B \rangle\}$$

Fig. 5. Sample binding policy

Fig. 6. Symbolic representation of the binding policy in Fig. 5

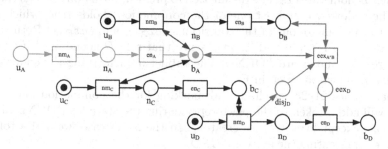

Fig. 7. Nomination net for binding policy in Fig. 5 (Color figure online)

illustrate the idea of nomination, consider the double-headed arc connecting the place b_A and the transition nm_B in Fig. 7, highlighted in red. Simply put, role A will be able to nominate role B when role B is UNBOUND and role A is BOUND (b_A must hold a token). The firing of transition nm_B, that is "nominate B", will change the state of role B from UNBOUND to NOMINATED. The double-headed arc will keep a token in b_A after the nomination of role B.

The encoding of endorsement conditions is handled in lines 15–20 (Step 4). Without loss of generality, we assume that the endorsement conditions are expressed in disjunctive normal form, meaning that there is only one disjunction that relates several conjunctions. We consider two additional cases: (1) no endorsement condition is specified (represented by $\bot$), meaning that no endorsement is required, and (2) only one conjunction is specified. To illustrate this step of the construction of the nomination net, consider the binding policy:

$$D \text{ nominates E, endorsed-by (A and B) or (B and C)};$$

The Petri net in Fig. 8 encodes the endorsement condition in the above policy: $(A \wedge B) \vee (B \wedge C)$. The latter is bound to variable eex in line 15.

In line 16, the algorithm adds two new places: $disj_E$ which encodes the disjunction, and eex_E, which collects the outcome of the endorsement (i.e. it holds a token when one of the endorsement conditions is met). In line 17, these are connected to the transitions of the role: from the nomination nm_E to $disj_E$, and from the out-

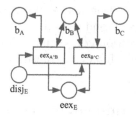

Fig. 8. Net encoding condition $(A \wedge B) \vee (B \wedge C)$

come eex_E to the endorsement en_E (not shown in Fig. 8). Then, in line 18, the algorithm iterates over each one of the conjunctions. In line 19, a new transition, representing the underlying conjunction is added to the net, and the corresponding arc in line 20. For instance, the net in Fig. 8 has transition $eex_{A \wedge B}$ representing conjunction $A \wedge B$, and $eex_{B \wedge C}$ representing $B \wedge C$. Only $eex_{A \wedge B}$ or $eex_{B \wedge C}$ will be able to consume the token held by $disj_E$, which prevents the generation of an arbitrary number of tokens in NNet. $disj_E$ receives a token when nm_E fires, i.e., when D nominates E. The disjunction expressed in this way means that role E can be endorsed if at least one of the conjunctions holds true, which corresponds to the firing of one of the transitions $eex_{A \wedge B}$ and $eex_{B \wedge C}$. Returning to the example in Figs. 5, 6 and 7, we observe that role D is endorsed if and only if both roles A and B are BOUND. The subnet implementing the endorsement condition is shown in green in Fig. 7.

Finally, lines 21–23 set the initial marking for the nomination net. Briefly, line 21 will add a token to the place representing the state UNBOUND of every single role, except for the "case creator". In the latter case, we add a token to the place representing the state BOUND.

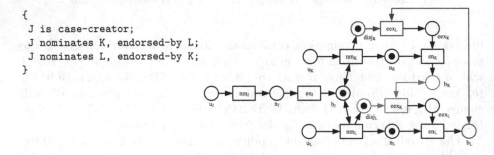

Fig. 9. Binding policy with circular dependency and its nomination net

To verify policy consistency, we use reachability analysis to check if the marking where all roles are bound is always reachable starting from the initial marking where only the roles associated to `case-creator` are bound. In other words, there is no deadlock preventing a role from being bound. Figure 9 shows a binding policy with a circular dependency, leading to a deadlock in the corresponding nomination net. Figure 9 shows the marking where the deadlock occurs. Both roles K and L have been nominated by role J. Hence, $disj_K$ has a token, but transition eex_L cannot fire until b_L has also a token. In order for b_L to have a token, however, transition eex_K needs to fire because it requires b_K to have a token.

5   Implementation and Evaluation

To demonstrate the proposal's feasibility, we developed a compiler that takes as input a policy specification and produces Solidity smart contracts to enforce the policy. This policy compiler is designed to be used in conjunction with the CATERPILLAR BPMN-to-Solidity compiler [6]. The smart contracts generated by the policy compiler manage the association between roles and actors (represented as blockchain accounts), while the smart contracts generated by the BPMN-to-Solidity compiler enforce the control-flow constraints in the process model. When a task is enabled, the *worklist handler* smart contract of CATERPILLAR, checks if the corresponding role is bound to an actor within the current case, and ensures that only this actor can execute the task. The source code of CATERPILLAR, including the binding policy compiler and the examples used in this paper, are available at http://git.io/caterpillar. Below we discuss the generation of smart contracts and evaluate the costs generated by these contracts.

5.1 Compiling Binding Policies into Smart Contracts

Given a process model and a policy specification, the policy compiler generates a smart contract (named BINDINGPOLICY) to encode the policy and a smart contract (TASKROLEMAP) to encode the task-role relations in the process model. The BINDINGPOLICY contract encodes the logic of who can nominate and release each role and the binding and endorsement constraints for each role. A third contract (BINDINGACCESSCONTROL) implements the runtime operations sketched in Sect. 3. BINDINGPOLICY and TASKROLEMAP are singleton contracts – only one instance of each of them is created since these contracts only maintain schema-level data. Meanwhile, the BINDINGACCESSCONTROL contract is instantiated once per case. The BINDINGACCESSCONTROL contract instance of a given case maintains the state of each role, as per the lifecycle in Fig. 4. When a nomination, release, or vote operation is invoked, the BINDINGACCESSCONTROL contract invokes the BINDINGPOLICY contract. The latter checks if this operation is allowed in the current state and computes the new state.

The class diagram in Fig. 10 captures the functionality of the generated smart contracts. Input parameters with no type specification are by default `uint`. As stated above, contract BINDINGACCESSCONTROL implements the runtime operations for nomination, release and voting. Since this contract does not encode anything about a particular policy, it is not generated by the policy compiler, but instead it is hard-coded and deployed once on the target Ethereum blockchain. This contract maintains the state of the role bindings for a given case in a variable called BINDINGSTATE. Given that the cost of a smart contract depends on the amount of data it maintains, we encode the BINDINGSTATE using bitmaps. Similarly, the endorsement constraints are represented as bit arrays. Specifically, we first put these constraints in disjunctive normal form, e.g., (A and B and ...) or (D and ...). Then we implement each conjunction set as a bit array and encode it as a 256-bits unsigned integer – the default word size in Ethereum.

Contract TASKROLEMAP is generated from the process model. This contract is straightforward (it maps tasks to roles), so we do not discuss it further.

The policy specification is compiled into the BINDINGPOLICY contract. Below we discuss how the role binding functions are generated (functions `canNominate`,

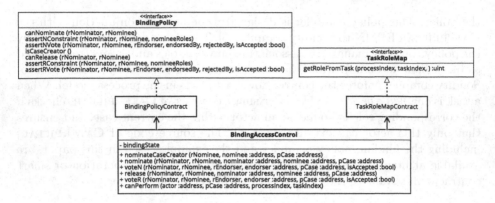

Fig. 10. Class diagram of the smart contracts derived from the policies.

assertNConstraint and assertNVote). The generation of the release functions (canRelease, assertRConstraint and asserRVote) is done in a similar way.

To generate function canNominate, for each distinct nominator in the policy a conditional and bit array, namely nMask, is created with one bit per role such that the presence of a nominee is represented with a *one* and the absence with a *zero*. For example, a nominator with index 3 and nMask = 6 is translated into:

```
function canNominate(uint rNominator, uint rNominee) returns(bool) {
    ...
    if (rNominator == 3)
        return 6 & (1 << rNominee) != 0;
    ...
}
```

Function assertNConstraint verifies if the roles held by a nominee do not contradict the binding constraint. Thus, a conditional instruction per nomination statement including a binding constraint is added. A statement is identified by the union of nominator and nominee, i.e., (1 << rNominator) | (1 << rNominee). Variable nomineeRoles is the bit array encoding the nominee's current roles. Given a constraint of the form (A and B) or (C) or .., the constraint is fulfilled if at least one of the conjunction sets is fully included in nomineeRoles. This is encoded as follows:

```
if ((1 << rNominator) | (1 << rNominee))
    return nomineeRoles & ((1 << A) | (1 << B)) == ((1 << A) | (1 << B))
       || nomineeRoles & (1 << C) == (1 << C) || ...;
```

Function assertNVote checks if an endorser can vote for a nomination and determines the state after this vote. Given the input parameters endorsedBy and rejectedBy, which are bit arrays encoding the roles that already accepted and rejected the nomination, this function determines the resulting state as follows:

1. BOUND if all the roles in at least a conjunction set, namely CS, endorsed the nomination, i.e., (endorsedBy | endorserRole) & CS == CS,

2. UNBOUND if in each conjunction set contains at least one role rejected the nomination, i.e., for each CS, (rejectedBy | endorserRole) & CS != 0,
3. NOMINATED if none of the conditions 1. and 2. are fulfilled yet, i.e., there is at least a conjunction set with no rejections and with roles pending to vote.

5.2   Experimental Setup

We conducted an evaluation to answer the following question: How does the cost (in gas/ether) of enforcing a binding policy increase depending on the size and complexity of the policy statements?[2] We decompose this question into three: (Q1) How do the costs of deploying the generated smart contracts vary with the size of the policy? (Q2) How do the costs of executing the runtime operations vary with the size of the policy? (3) How does the combined cost of enforcing a process model and a binding policy varies with the size of the model?

It follows from Sect. 5.1 that the costs depend on the number of roles to nominate and the number of conjunction sets in the binding/endorsement constraints. Thus, we designed the following experiments: (E1) We varied the number of nomination statements in a policy from 1 to 40, without any binding or endorsement constraints. (E2) We fixed the number of statements to 40, selected one statement, and gradually increased the size of its conjunction set from 1 to 40. (E3) We fixed the number of statements to 40, and gradually added a binding constraint with one conjunction set to each of the 40 statements. (E4, E5) The experiments E3 and E4 were repeated for the endorsement constraint (instead of the binding constraint). (E6) We generated a policy with 40 roles such that each statement includes a binding constraint stipulating that the nominated actor must belong to the role in the previous statement and that the nomination must be endorsed by all actors nominated in previous statements. (E7) Starting from a BPMN model with only one task, we iteratively expanded it by one task at a time (up to 40) and assigned each task to a different role. In this latter experiment, once a role was bound to an actor, we checked that the corresponding task could be performed. Note that the evaluation focuses on nomination statements, but the release statements are symmetric.

We implemented a replayer in Java that generates the policies, triggers their compilation and deployment, and executes the runtime operations via CATER-PILLAR's REST API. For each transaction included in the blockchain, Caterpillar sends some meta-data that includes block number, consumed gas, transaction hash which is collected and assessed by the replayer. For the experimentation we run a *Node.js* based Ethereum client named *ganache-cli*[3] which is widely used to simulate a full client for developing and testing purposes on Ethereum.

---

[2] In Ethereum, gas is linearly related to throughput, see Sect. 2.1. So by answering this question we also indirectly answer the related throughput question.

[3] https://github.com/trufflesuite/ganache-cli.

5.3   Experimental Results

Deployment costs for experiments E1–E5 are plotted in Fig. 11. It can be seen that deployment costs increase quasi-linearly with the size and complexity of the policy. The simplest contract (with a single role bound to case-creator) costs 154,167 gas. As expected, the most pronounced growth in cost occurs for endorsement constraints (E4–E5) as they produce more instructions during code generation. We observe an increase of around 16.0–19.0% when adding a new endorsement constraint and 5.0–6.5% when adding a conjunction set to a constraint. Experiments E2–E3 show that adding a binding constraint increases cost by 4.0–5.7%, while adding a conjunction to a constraint adds 2.4–3.5% overhead. E1 shows that adding one unrestricted statement to nominate a role adds 4.0–4.5% overhead.

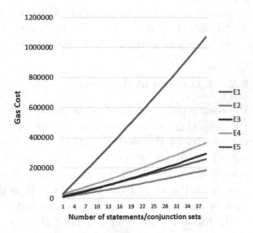

Fig. 11. Growth of deployment costs with size of binding policy.

For the runtime operations, we observed that costs vary depending on the number and the order of statements and conjunction sets in the constraints. The cost to nominate a role is higher when the corresponding policy statement is at the end of the policy. Similar behavior was observed for binding and endorsement constraints. This is because in Ethereum, the gas depends on the number of bytecode instructions executed. Hence, in a function with `if-else-if` instructions, the cost increases with the number of evaluated conditions.

Table 1 shows the min, max, and average costs to perform the nominate and vote operations in experiments E1-E5. Note that voting is less costly than nominating and nomination costs are lower when restricted by binding constraints compared to endorsement constraints.

Table 1. Cost of nominations and votes

		E1	E2	E3	E4	E5
Nom.	Min.	151,586	112,476	111,407	132,417	131,493
	Max.	152,638	152,790	113,447	152,746	153,800
	Ave.	151,948	151,270	112,277	151,738	142,660
Vot.	Min.	-	-	-	76,845	77,184
	Max.	-	-	-	78,136	78,184
	Ave.	-	-	-	77,463	77,541

The combined cost of executing a process model with an associated policy (experiment E6) has several components. First, the contract BINDINGACCESS-CONTROL must be deployed at a fixed cost of 1,340,098 gas, entailing a transaction fee of 0.0067 Ether (ETH)[4]. Next, the contracts generated from the policy must be deployed, with gas ranging from 154,167 (simplest) to 1,803,898 gas (largest policy), corresponding to 0.0007 ETH to 0.0090 ETH. The smart contracts derived from the policies are deployed once and then reused, while the

---

[4] Gas price: 5 Gwei, average from https://ethgasstation.info on 30/11/2018.

contracts handling the process execution are deployed for each case. Thus the policy deployment costs are amortized as more cases are executed. At runtime, roles have to be bound to actors. The costs of executing one nominate operation ranged from 111,407 (0.0005 ETH) to 168,270 (0.0008 ETH), while the `vote` operations cost between 76,845 (0.0003 ETH) and 78,184 (0.0003 ETH). Finally, when an actor performs a task, function `canPerform` is called to check if the actor is bound to the task's role. This function invokes the TASKROLEMAP smart contract to retrieve the task-role relation. We observed a linear growth in the deployment cost of this contract as the number of tasks increased, from 129,539 gas (0.0006 ETH) to 241,114 (0.0012 ETH). The cost of function `canPerform` also grew linearly from 31,693 (0.0001 ETH) to 33,066 (0.0001 ETH).

6 Conclusion

Motivated by the possibilities opened by blockchain-based collaborative process execution, this paper presented a role binding model and a binding policy language that support collaborative binding and unbinding of actors to roles at runtime. The proposal includes a method to verify the consistency of policies defined in the proposed language and an approach to compile the policies into smart contracts. The proposal has been implemented on the CATERPIL-LAR blockchain-based collaborative process execution tool. We evaluated the costs (and therefore throughput) to deploy and execute smart contracts generated from binding policy statements, on the Ethereum platform. The evaluation shows that the deployment and runtime policy enforcement costs grow linearly with the number of roles and the complexity of the constraints. We acknowledge that the evaluation is limited in scope (only one business process and up to 40 roles) and focuses on evaluating cost. An avenue for future work is to further validate the approach via more thorough experiments and case studies.

While the proposed approach has been designed with the goal of supporting collaborative process execution on blockchain, its field of possible applications is wider. Another future work avenue is to study the applicability of this approach to other blockchain applications where dynamic role binding may be required, e.g. in crowdsourcing and computer-supported collaborative work scenarios.

Acknowledgment. This work was funded by the Estonian Research Council (grant IUT20-55) and the European Regional Development Fund (Dora Plus, contract 36.9-6.1/459).

References

1. Andrews, T., et al.: BPEL4WS, Business Process Execution Language for Web Services Version 1.1. IBM (2003)
2. Bussard, L., Nano, A., Pinsdorf, U.: Delegation of access rights in multi-domain service compositions. Identity Inf. Soc. **2**(2), 137–154 (2009)
3. Decker, G., Kopp, O., Leymann, F., Weske, M.: BPEL4Chor: extending BPEL for modeling choreographies. IEEE ICWS **2007**, 296–303 (2007)

4. Frantz, C., Nowostawski, M.: From institutions to code: towards automated generation of smart contracts. In: IEEE FAS*W 2016, pp. 210–215 (2016)
5. Kloppmann, M., et al.: WS-BPEL extension for people - BPEL4People. Joint white paper, IBM and SAP (2005)
6. López-Pintado, O., García-Bañuelos, L., Dumas, M., Weber, I., Ponomarev, A.: CATERPILLAR: a business process execution engine on the ethereum blockchain. CoRR abs/1808.03517 (2018)
7. Mendling, J., et al.: Blockchains for business process management - challenges and opportunities. ACM Trans. Manag. Inf. Syst. **9**(1), 4:1–4:16 (2018)
8. Murata, T.: Petri nets: properties, analysis and applications. Proc. IEEE **77**(4), 541–580 (1989)
9. Pautasso, C., Alonso, G.: Flexible binding for reusable composition of web services. In: Software Composition, pp. 151–166 (2005)
10. Prybila, C., Schulte, S., Hochreiner, C., Weber, I.: Runtime verification for business processes utilizing the Bitcoin blockchain. Futur. Gener. Comput. Syst. **46**, 36–50 (2017)
11. Robinson, P., Kerschbaum, F., Schaad, A.: From business process choreography to authorization policies. In: Data and Applications Security, pp. 297–309 (2006)
12. Russell, N., van der Aalst, W.M.P., ter Hofstede, A.H.M., Edmond, D.: Workflow resource patterns: identification, representation and tool support. In: CAiSE (2005)
13. Tran, A., Lu, Q., Weber, I.: Lorikeet: a model-driven engineering tool for blockchain-based business process execution and asset management. Demo Track at BPM **2018**, 56–60 (2018)
14. Wainer, J., Kumar, A., Barthelmess, P.: DW-RBAC: a formal security model of delegation and revocation in workflow systems. Inf. Syst. **32**(3), 365–384 (2007)
15. Xu, X., Weber, I., Staples, M.: Architecture for Blockchain Applications. Springer, Heidelberg (2019). https://doi.org/10.1007/978-3-030-03035-3

3D Virtual World BPM Training Systems: Process Gateway Experimental Results

Michael Leyer[1,2(✉)], Ross Brown[2], Banu Aysolmaz[3],
Irene Vanderfeesten[4], and Oktay Turetken[4]

[1] University of Rostock, Rostock, Germany
michael.leyer@uni-rostock.de
[2] Queensland University of Technology, Brisbane, Australia
{r.brown, m.leyer}@qut.edu.au
[3] Maastricht University, Maastricht, The Netherlands
b.aysolmaz@maastrichtuniversity.nl
[4] Eindhoven University of Technology, Eindhoven, The Netherlands
{i.t.p.vanderfeesten, o.turetken}@tue.nl

Abstract. It is important for companies that their operational employees have profound knowledge of the processes in which their work is embedded. 3D virtual world (VW) environments are promising for learning, especially for complex processes that have deviations from the standard flow. We design a 3D VW process training environment to improve process learning, particularly for complex processes with alternative flows, represented with gateways in process models. We adopt the method of loci, which suggests the mental traversal of routines for improving learning. Our experiment with 145 participants compares the level of knowledge acquired for a sample process with our 3D VW environment and a 2D depiction. We found that the 3D VW environment significantly increases the level of process knowledge acquired across the typical gateways in processes. Our results contribute to our understanding of how individuals learn knowledge of processes via 3D environments. With a low initial investment, practitioners are encouraged to invest in 3D training systems for processes, since these can be set up once and reused multiple times for various employees.

Keywords: Training · Process model · Virtual worlds · Gateways · Experiment

1 Introduction

For companies, it is important to ensure that employees have a proper knowledge of organizational processes to execute them in an efficient way. Employees knowing the processes they are working in have a better sense on how their work is embedded and invest more time and effort in coordinating with their colleagues [1]. However, such knowledge is often lacking among employees, hence, organizations need ways to enable their employees to get this knowledge [2]. Typical methods used in organizations to make operational employees (employees without leading functions) acquire process knowledge include providing process models before or during operations, organizing training sessions, and lately using technological instruments such as

P. Giorgini and B. Weber (Eds.): CAiSE 2019, LNCS 11483, pp. 415–429, 2019.
https://doi.org/10.1007/978-3-030-21290-2_26

augmented reality glasses [3]. There are difficulties associated with these learning methods, such as process models often requiring too much cognitive effort [4], or augmented reality glasses and trainings being costly and not scalable. Thus, organizations would benefit from alternative training methods to establish process knowledge.

Knowledge acquisition is specifically difficult for complex processes with many alternative paths [5]. In process models, different paths, such as those that are exclusive or parallel, are represented using gateways [4]. Although such models are widely used in organizations for other purposes [4], the high cognitive effort required to investigate the models hamper their use as a knowledge acquisition medium for employees.

One promising way to foster better process learning for employees is to use alternative visualizations for process models [6]. While there has been extensive research on finding a better way to visualize processes, these efforts are mostly on using different notations and representations in a 2D-environment [6]. 3D, however, could provide a better and more realistic experience of processes since humans have difficulties to attach the abstract procedural knowledge to real world objects and experiences [7, 8]. Indeed, as demonstrated by [9] regarding abilities of 3D spaces as engaging educational systems, we see that there is great potential in the use of 3D virtual worlds (VWs) as visual examples of process constructs in a comprehensive training system for processes.

We aim to investigate if 3D VW visualizations help to learn processes better across different gateways, as they are a major cause of complexity in process models. We developed a prototype 3D VW process training environment using the Unity game engine [7]. We use the *method of loci* for designing the environment, suggesting the traversal of the same routine for improving learning in an imagined environment, in our case VWs [10]. Hence, sequences of abstract information can be better memorized by simulating movement through a space with 3D spatial locations mapped to the information that is to be remembered. Experimental results in other disciplines have confirmed the effect of method of loci [11, 12]. Our 3D VW prototype, apart from the time spent on software code development effort, was built for roughly $60 AUD. The approach only needs to read a standard BPMN XML file format, automatically creating activities at the pre-define VW locations of resources defined within the model. This automation makes the return on investment high due to low setup costs.

2   Theoretical Background

2.1   Memory and 3D Virtual Worlds

Via mental or physical actions, humans acquire knowledge and contextual information about the task being performed. This has inspired learning approaches applied in educational settings that draw upon situated learning theory [13] positing that education and training works best when the knowledge is learned in the context of where it will be used (situated), facilitating recall of specific activities primed by the correct context. In addition, there has been extensive research on the role of context in recall and recognition [14, 15] under a number of contexts such as cued recognition and forget scenarios. These studies suggest that the brain uses the 1–2 s in a recall task to store the existing contextual information [16], indicating that viewing scenes in a VW environment may utilize context effects without any need for lengthy viewing.

Several knowledge acquisition and training approaches utilize the method of loci [17, 18]. The approach facilitates laying down of memories of visuospatial routines that are later utilized to remember information by visualizing the traversal of the same routine through the imagined 3D environment [10]. This has been shown to be a superior method for mnemonic memorization of information from behavioral studies [19], also showing its effectiveness in modifying physiological network structures in the brain to enhance recall [10]. Similar brain training effects are enacted by the traversal (as though walking through the environment) of 3D VWs on computers, viz. the human brain undergoes similar changes in the hippocampus as it would when bodily moving in a physical 3D reality, even without moving the body, just from 3D visual input alone [20].

Evidence comes from a number of experiments measuring the effects of embodied context on memory. E.g., airport check-in processes are better remembered with the use of 3D VW representations than using 2D diagrams [8] with virtual reality being superior [21]. Previous studies support the potential benefits of VWs for BPM training, as activity sequences are important knowledge in processes [22]. Such a situated approach should yield good process training results due to aiding recall of task sequences.

VWs are an interactive technology whereby the computer synthesizes a 3D interactive reality, which is "a synchronous, persistent network of people, represented as avatars, facilitated by networked computers" [23]. These VWs may be used via immersive interfaces, such as virtual reality head mounted displays. The use of immersive embodied movement within such VWs has been shown to be superior for training purposes [24]. These results indicate that memory recall and language processing in such environments are strongly affected and may be improved via the stimuli provided. [8] found that, users of a 3D VW in a process elicitation scenario, compared to a normal process editor, provided more correct activity enumeration and naming, and showed evidence of increased confidence in the results, due to less time spent editing the resultant model.

VWs provide a number of learning affordances that can facilitate the transfer of process knowledge to form knowledge structures in a situated context [25]. VWs have been used as learning environments in adult education settings [e.g. 26]. Media features such as representational fidelity, persistence [e.g. 27] and game-like features such as avatars [28] and quest activities [29] are found to promote positive learning outcomes.

This affordances leads us to conclude that 3D VW could be used to impute the memories required in a process training scenario into participants, based upon an abstract process model. The use of method of loci is relevant for designing visuospatial routines of activity flows in VWs. We expect that memory enhancing effects will occur, viz. participants will remember more elements from the process model, and that they would be faster in the process of remembering the information.

2.2 Knowledge Structures of Processes

Processes consist of activities that are connected to each other [4]. The connections define how the elements (activities) are or can be executed in a certain order. Such sequences can be straightforward, i.e., there is always one activity followed by one and only one other activity, or there is a network of activities that allows for various options including parallel or alternative flows.

For effective enactment of organizational processes, employees need to acquire the knowledge structure of their related processes. Such knowledge enables employees to align the execution of their activities in accordance to the other activities in a process and in this way leads to a higher efficiency in process execution [30].

The essential knowledge for employees to foresee the overall process and align the activities is which other activities exist and how they are related to each other rather than how every activity is performed [1]. Thus, the connections between activities and dependencies that define the order in which activities are to be performed need to be learned. The control flow logic indicated by such connections can be ambiguous, i.e., an activity may always follow another activity or one of the many alternative activities can follow. Specifically, divergence and convergence of the control flow logic for decision points and parallel tasks create additional cognitive load, which hinders a formation of knowledge structures [31].

2.3   Related Work

Previously, the use of VWs for BPM has been pioneered by the authors to investigate topics such as remote collaborative modelling [32]. More pertinent to this research has been the positive results from using VWs [8] and immersive virtual reality [21] to elicit process model information from experts. Both these applications have shown successful results in terms of assisting users to collaborate and model more effectively [32] and to provide more accurate and plentiful information.

Other applications of method of loci in VWs and virtual reality include general list memory problems [11, 33–36] and language acquisition [12]. In this work, we take advantage of the representational fidelity and utilize spatial affordances of VWs to create an explicit representation of a process model that supports the method of loci approach. We note that our work aims to be the first to utilise this approach within the field of process training and education.

Amongst industry process simulation systems [37], the closest to our work is OnMap (www.onmap-visual.com), a 2.5D world system for visualising business processes. However, OnMap does not include a theoretical design perspective based on activity types and alternative flows. As far as we are aware, there is no research study to evaluate the learning effects of using OnMap. Additionally, the 2.5D overview provided by OnMap will not enact the loci effect that we utilize in our study.

2.4   Hypotheses

In this study, based on the method of loci, we argue that VWs can be used as an effective way of acquiring knowledge structures of processes [20], since processes are composed of sequential activities related to each other via a set of attributes such as the action, role, and information. By using visual cues of process elements in a real-like space and incremental execution of process steps primed by those elements, VWs can enable the learners to gain experiential memories of processes. Thus, presenting the processes in the form of visuospatial routines with visual cues of process elements should improve learners in acquiring process knowledge of interconnected activities in general. However, we need to distinguish between different connections among activities due to the use of gateways. This is because the knowledge structure to be acquired is different when different gateways are used and the VW needs to be designed differently to show the flow alternatives represented by the gateways. The first goal of the VW is to invigorate the transition between one process activity to another. Thus, as a first hypothesis, we focus on the impact of the VWs for acquiring knowledge of activities directly following each other:

H1. A 3D VW representation of a process leads to better results compared to a 2D representation in identifying direct connections between activities.

The complexity of a process model induced by gateways is among the most influential factors of process model comprehension [5]. Three gateway types are commonly used in process models: XOR split (to cause a flow to two or more mutually exclusive paths), AND split (to depict two or more paths that can be executed concurrently), and OR split (to trigger the execution of one or more paths) gateways [4]. Since these gateways cause alterations in the order of activities in a way that requires the semantic interpretation of the gateways rather than being directly observable from the model itself, they create additional cognitive load [38]. Such extra cognitive load is a major barrier in the formation of knowledge structures of the complete process [39]. VWs can help to overcome the difficulties associated with gateways by depicting such routines in a more representative way, explicating the meaning of the control-flow logic by borrowing real-life concepts and merging them with environment capabilities. Accordingly, we define the following three sub-hypothesis for each gateway type:

H2. A 3D VW representation of a process leads to better results compared to a 2D representation in identifying XOR-connections between activities.

H3. A 3D VW representation of a process leads to better results compared to a 2D representation in identifying AND-connections between activities.

H4. A 3D VW representation of a process leads to better results compared to a 2D representation in identifying OR-connections between activities.

The current body of knowledge in the area of process model understandability suggests that the models with OR-gateways are more difficult to understand than those with XOR or AND-gateways [40]. This can be attributed to the number of mental states that a reader of a model has to build for each gateway in order to understand the control flow of a process. An OR-gateway creates more mental states than an XOR or AND-gateway [41]. Using an OR-gateway increases model's complexity, which in turn hinders its understandability [42]. Furthermore, OR-gateway is associated with high error rates in process models [43]. Accordingly, any means to enhance the comprehension of OR-gateways can have more potential to improve the knowledge acquisition of a process. With traditional process modeling notations, it is difficult to implement visual measures to illustrate the logic behind this gateway and alleviate the high cognitive load associated with it, while a VW environment can be used to explicate its semantics. To gather empirical evidence for this contention, we advance the following hypothesis:

H5. The effect of a VW representation of a process regarding OR-connections is stronger than with other connections.

3   Research Design

3.1   Process Used for the Experiment

For the evaluation, we selected an example process, issue management, which is about dealing with a problem in an organization from its identification to resolution. The complete process model of the selected process in BPMN notation is shown in Fig. 1[1]. This process model depicts the activities performed by the roles Requestor, Ticket Manager, Program Manager, and Developer in an organization when a problem is identified for a corporate IT system. The process consists of 14 activities connected with different gateway types, two IT systems, and 14 information elements.

This process is selected and tailored for the purpose of the experiment for the following reasons. First, it is common in organizations and valid for various domains [44]. Second, the process concepts do not bear technical and domain-specific knowledge. Hence, they are understandable by a wide audience. The process model is designed based on several real-life issue management example processes, and incorporates constructs that makes it suitable for the evaluation of our hypotheses. Therefore, the process model includes divergence from the linear control flow by a decision point indicated by an XOR gateway (the activities of *Register problem as regular* and *Register problem as urgent*), a parallel activity sequence enabled by an AND gateway (the activities of *Prepare verification checklist* and *Develop problem resolution plan with Ticket Manager*), and lastly, an inclusive decision point with an OR gateway (the activities of *Verify problem resolution* and *Verify problem resolution and implementation of plan*). The three different gateways are not combined but only used on the main flow of the process (e.g. an XOR gateway is not placed in one of the parallel paths after the AND gateway). Though this may limit the representability of the example process for real life models, we aimed to control the complexity of the VW and measure the impact of the environment separately for each gateway type.

3.2   Design of the Training Environment

In this section, we describe how we designed the environment to reveal the benefits of VWs for process training[2]. We first start with describing the design to represent a single activity in the VW together with its related elements, then the flow between two activities directly connected to each other, followed by the specifics for each gateway type.

Representation of an Activity and its Related Elements. Following the method of loci, we use the VW environment and the role performing the activity in the form of an avatar to trigger the creation of experiences in a VW as it happens in the physical world [10]. The whole office space and the area in which the activity is performed provide a

---

[1] The model can also be found at: http://www.aysolmaz.com/VWProcessModel.pdf.

[2] The environment can be downloaded from the following links:
    For Windows: http://www.aysolmaz.com/ProbResInfo1Win.zip
    For Mac: http://www.aysolmaz.com/ProbResInfo1Mac.zip.

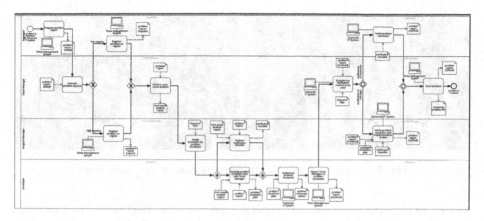

Fig. 1. Example issue management process model used in the experiment.

spatial cue for the users of the training environment [45]. The avatars of the roles create the visual context. The same avatar is depicted when a role is engaged in another activity, and the same desk space is used for the individual tasks s/he performs. In this way, the concepts of visual context and spatial location are used to embody real life concepts and implement visual priming to enhance recall [16]. Other process elements such as IT systems and data elements are represented in an abstract form based on BPMN-style notational elements, since these elements do not have any physical dis-criminatory characteristics. The type of the activity is identified based on the action indicated by its label and the connected process elements. The space in which the activity is performed is set up based on the activity type (e.g. a meeting room or an office desk) [46].

Flow Between Two Directly-Connected Activities. The flow between two activities is depicted by a camera moving along in the office space from the location in which an activity is performed to the next one. An example can be seen in Fig. 2. When the camera approaches the next activity in a third person view, the activity is red (left), indicating the status as *ready to be executed*. When the user interacts with the system by clicking, the status is first updated as *being executed* in amber, and then *completed* in green (right). With the next user click, the camera is moved to the next activity. In this way, the perception of process flow is warranted in a combined stream of activity status and activity changes, triggering the creation of episodic memories [47].

Alternative Flow with an XOR Gateway. An XOR-split is a depiction of a decision point and possible alternative flows based on the given decision in the process. For example, *Evaluate problem urgency* is a decision activity, which leads to a decision of low or high urgency. Given the decision, either the upper activity in Fig. 2 is executed by the role *Requestor*, or the lower one by the *Program Manager*. The process modeling notations lack the ability to inherently represent what the gateway notation means since they use abstractions. Thus, the novice reader relies on the illusory inference to deduce meaning from the symbol [48]. However, VWs have the potential to explicate the flow logic underlying the gateway by harvesting the features of visual

Fig. 2. Example of steps for the representation of alternative flows

priming to physical form and non-physical representation. Exploiting this capability, we invigorate the alternative execution of two activities as in Fig. 2. The two office spaces and roles are shown side by side to allow for the perception of two related activities. The exclusiveness of activities are depicted by initially showing one of the activities as executed, then, with a move of a camera similar to activity transitions, the activity statuses are reset and the alternative activity is shown to be executed. Then, the view switches to a single camera to indicate the convergence of paths and flow of the rest of the activities. The use of BPMN-like gateway symbols and arrows further support the explication of the semantic depicted in physical form.

Parallel Flows with an AND-Split and Join. The AND gateway after the activity *Assign developer for problem resolution* in Fig. 2 divides the flow into two, which leads to activities that needs to be finished before the rest of the process can continue. Thus, our environment design again exploits the depiction of related activities side-by-side with two cameras in the VW. Initially, the office spaces related to two concurrent activities are shown side by side. With each user click, the activities change status together, first both turning to *being executed*, and both *completed* at the end. Then, the camera returns back to single view and the process continues with the next activity.

Inclusive Alternative Flows with an OR Gateway. Among the gateways in process modeling, OR gateway is known to be the most error-prone and difficult to comprehend due to its ambiguous semantics [5]. Accordingly, we expect the highest benefit from the training environment, since it is possible to disentangle the ambiguous semantics of the OR-gateway. Similar to the approach in the other gateways, two camera views are provided side by side for the two activities in the issue management process. Through user clicks, the possible flows of only one of the activities, only the other activity, and both activities are represented consecutively. Since the OR gateway enables the execution of activities exclusively or in parallel, all three options for two activities (only one or the other or both are executed) are depicted in the VW.

3.3   Measures

To analyze if a better formation of knowledge structures can be achieved by means of the designed training environment, we employed a questionnaire to measure how accurate the participants are in remembering the process provided in the training phase[3]. For this, we used the procedure described by Leyer and Strohhecker [39]. Participants received a number of questions each asking for the correctness of the connection between a pair of activities presented in the training environment. Of these pairs being presented, 16 were correct and 17 were wrong pairs to avoid random guessing. We counted the number of correct answers for identifying the 16 correct relationships which resulted in a percentage for each participant. All questions were also characterized by their gateway type according to the process design. The number of questions per gateway are as follows: XOR-splits: 9, AND-splits: 6, OR-splits: 9, No splits: 9.

We additionally used questions to evaluate the cognitive profile (through the Cognitive reflection test (CRT) [49] and Global local thinking style (GLT) test [50, 51]) of participants. This was followed by control questions regarding perceived difficulty, interest, prior modeling experience, job experience as well as age and gender.

3.4 Participants and Procedure

The experiment participants were graduate students in the domain of engineering. These students were enrolled in the same master level course on business process management (BPM), voluntarily participating in the experiment. As a motivation, students were offered 0.5 bonus points (out of 10) to their final course grade. Among 190 students, 145 participated (76.3%) reporting an average interest of 5.7 (SD: 1.97) and a perceived difficulty of 4.07 (SD: 1.97) (Scales 1–9). 69.7% of these participants are male and 30.3% female. Participants' average age is 23.2 years (SD: 1.84 years).

There were two experiment groups: one group received the 2D representation[4] of the issue management process and the other one the 3D VW process visualization. Participants were randomly assigned to a group.

The experiment is formulated as an illustration of a trace through the example process in 2D, represented by BPMN diagram elements shown one at a time on pages. The 3D equivalent is shown as a sequence of 3D activity locations in an office, moving between each one. Both only needed the press of the space bar to traverse the trace to the next element of the process diagram. This keeps the training requirements for our initial prototype to a minimum.

When starting the experiment, participants received instructions on their task. Next, they were presented with the first process visualization (either 2D or 3D depending on their experiment group). The number of pages and 3D-representations was equal to ensure comparability of results. After studying the process through this representation, the students received a questionnaire that consisted of two parts as described in the measurement section: (a) questions on their knowledge structure of the issue management process and (b) questions to evaluate their cognitive profile and to control for

---

[3] The offline version of the questionnaire can be found from the following link:
   http://www.aysolmaz.com/VWQuestionnaire.pdf.

[4] http://www.aysolmaz.com/ProbResInfo/ProbResInfo1.html.

other potential influencing factors. The questions regarding the knowledge structure were directly related to the activities presented in the training phase.

Finally, participants were shown the other representation of the issue management process to allow for a further robustness check in comparing both versions.

4   Results

Table 1 shows the differences between the scores of the 2D vs. the 3D VW and presents the results of the t-tests (unpaired samples) used to check if the differences are significant, as our data is normally distributed (tested with the adjusted K-S test). The scores represent the percentages of correct answers as described in the measurement section. As seen, hypotheses 1 to 4 are supported.

Addressing hypothesis 5, comparing the scores regarding OR-splits with the other connections shows a non-significant result (T(292.9) = .762, p = .78). This result is supported by the confidence intervals (retrieved by applying a bootstrapping procedure) overlapping for each type of splits (XOR-splits: −0.141–0.007; AND-splits: −0.99–0.020; OR-splits: −0.130−−0.015; No splits: −0.129−−.007). Nevertheless, there is some descriptive tendency as the difference between the virtual and the 2D world is the highest one compared to the others and the absolute knowledge structure results show that the lowest values can be found with OR-splits.

Participants perceived both worlds as being statistically similar in terms of difficulty (T(143) = −1.945, ns) and also the interest of participants in both groups was similar (T(143) = −1.392, ns). Age (T(143) = .527, ns), gender (Chi2(1) = 3.886), prior modeling experience (T(143) = .013, ns), job experience (T(143) = .467, ns), CRT (Chi2(3) = 6.238, ns) and GLT (T(143) = .471, ns) do not differ between both groups.

For a further robustness check, participants received the respective other world after answering the questions. Their rating (1–7) of both worlds in comparison reveals that participants of the 2D-group rate the 3D-world (5.37) significantly higher (T (124) = 5.906, p < .001) than the 2D-world (3.64). There is however no difference in this regard with participants of the 3D-group (T(137.98) = .685, ns) with only a slight tendency towards the 3D-world (3D-world: 4.25; 2D-world: 4.04).

Table 1. Comparison of knowledge structure results between both groups (FDRC: false discovery detection)

Construct	2D world	3D VW	Difference (%)	Hypotheses
No splits	.49	.56	14.3	H1: Supported; T(143) = −2.147, p < .05 (FDRC: .028)
XOR-splits	.51	.58	13.7	H2: Supported; T(143) = −1.758, p < .05 (FDRC: .052)
AND-splits	.37	.41	10.8	H3: Supported; T(143) = −1.302, p < .10 (FDRC: .098)
OR-splits	.33	.40	21.2	H4: Supported; T(143) = −2.495, p < .01 (FDRC: .018)

5 Discussion, Implications, and Limitations

Our study sets out to analyze the impact of a 3D VW visualization of processes on understanding the knowledge structure of processes focusing on gateways. The results show a significant positive effect of using a 3D VW visualization compared to a 2D process visualization. These results hold for the representation in general and regarding our hypotheses for the three typical gateways specifically.

However, contrary to our underlying hypothesis, we cannot observe a stronger effect for OR-splits than for the other gateways constructs. In order to search for an explanation, the results can be interpreted that either a different overview is required or that OR-splits are not that complicated to understand. To further analyze the reason for this non-significance, we conduct a post-hoc test, comparing the four types of splits with each other within the 2D and 3D representations separately. The results show that the knowledge structures of the process for both OR-splits and AND-splits are significantly lower than for XOR-splits and no splits ($F(3, 280) = 14.928$, $p < .001$, Games-Howell: OR/XOR, $p < .001$, OR/AND, ns, OR/NO, $p < .001$; $F(3, 292) = 17.160$, $p < .001$, Games-Howell: OR/XOR, $p < .001$, OR/AND, ns, OR/NO, $p < .001$). These results indicate that OR-splits are more difficult, but similar to AND-splits. In order to understand these splits better, different learning mechanisms than addressed with our 3D VW visualization have to be triggered. An approach could be to repeat such sequences more than once or provide additional verbal explanations. Another design consideration comes into play when there are more than two branches within XOR/OR/AND split and joins. More than two camera views would be needed to represent such a structure, which would increase the cognitive load of the reader. A different 3D VW visualization may be developed to represent those structures in a cognitively-efficient way.

Our study has implications for BPM research. First, our results show that 3D VWs can be applied successfully to provide a new way of representing and transferring process knowledge, helping especially to understand complex gateways. While the current literature focuses mostly on notational and personal factors, the need to introduce innovative visualization approaches has been defined [6]. Considering that VWs provide a replication of a real-life setting, typically, a specific instance of a process without considering alternative flows is depicted in a VW. Our results indicate that VWs can be set up to explicate the meaning of gateways in process models, therefore, reflecting the knowledge on the process domain together with notational elements. Thus, while the knowledge captured in a process model is transferred to the learner, the learning process is also improved in VW with respect to gateways. Second, our results contribute to the relevancy of the method of loci in the domain of learning processes. As such, we extend prior work from other domains such as [18] by showing that it is important to design training systems with a 3D VW to ensure a better understanding of processes.

Our research has also practical implications. Although process models are heavily used to communicate process knowledge to diverse process participants [52], specifically for participants from non-technical backgrounds, it is difficult to map real-world concepts to process model elements [7]. To ensure that process knowledge is acquired properly, organizations can provide process trainings to its stakeholders [53]. Various solutions are used for this purpose, such as in-class training, role-playing, or on-the-job training [2], which are costly and may not be always feasible. Specifically as the number of stakeholders to be trained increase and they become geographically diverse, scalability and logistical issues arise. VWs can provide a comprehensive training solution for organizations to overcome such problems. Their current process models can be used as input to easily set up the VW environment [46]. Such a system has to be set up once, but can be distributed among a large number of employees.

Limitations are as follows. First, we pick a sample process in a specific context. While chosen carefully to cover diverse process elements and activity types, there might be differences if other processes with different structures are used. This refers to the complexity in terms of having more or fewer number of connections and gateways, as well as the context. Second, the participants of our experiment are students which have a different behavior from employees having profound experience in understanding processes. Experiments in behavioral operations management have shown that there are no significant differences between managers and students [54] and students are frequently used as proxies to novice professionals in BPM context [42]. Nevertheless, this should be taken into account when interpreting the current results. Third, although an experiment ensures a high internal validity, when using a VW environment in a company, there might be an influence of the perceived and experienced real environment.

6 Conclusion

Our study provides evidence that a 3D VW environment contributes to understanding processes significantly better with different effects for gateways. While the result is encouraging to strive for 3D VW visualization of processes, there are still open questions that require further research.

Future work should analyze whether the effect observed in our study changes with the complexity of the process model used. The complexity can be varied with regard to the number of connections as well as the proportion of the gateways. Such an analysis can potentially result in defining thresholds regarding the effect strength in terms of process model complexity. When there are more than two branches within gateways, there may be better ways of visualizing the activities in multiple branches rather than using camera views side-by-side. Alternative 3D VW visualizations for complex parts of the process model should be developed based on the complexity.

Further work should also concentrate on comparing the 3D VW and the 2D depiction using a regular BPMN notation. While this can be considered as an extra effect, thus, has been excluded in targeting the basic effect as done in this paper, additional insights can be gained regarding the effect of using a specific notation. Such an analysis would also require distinguishing between experts being used to BPMN and novices to determine the effect of the notation and the graphical representation.

Finally, it would be promising to analyze the effect of using a 3D virtual representation on work behavior in a real world environment. Such an analysis not only refers to the knowledge regarding processes, but also regarding the consequences in terms of process efficiency and process-oriented behavior. The effects on work behavior should be observed over a time period of several months to determine whether sustainable effects going beyond using traditional process models can be achieved.

References

1. Babić-Hodović, V., Mehić, E., Arslanagić, M.: The influence of quality practices on BH companies' business performance. Int. J. Manag. Cases **14**, 305–316 (2012)
2. Leyer, M., Hirzel, A.-K., Moormann, J.: Achieving sustainable behavioral changes of daily work practices. The effect of role plays on learning process-oriented behavior. Bus. Process. Manag. J. **24**, 1050–1068 (2018)
3. Ong, S.K., Yuan, M.L., Nee, A.Y.C.: Augmented reality applications in manufacturing. A survey. Int. J. Prod. Res. **46**, 2707–2742 (2008)
4. Dumas, M., La Rosa, M., Mendling, J., Reijers, H.A.: Fundamentals of Business Process Management. Springer, Heidelberg (2018). https://doi.org/10.1007/978-3-662-56509-4
5. Figl, K., Laue, R.: Influence factors for local comprehensibility of process models. Int. J. Hum Comput Stud. **82**, 96–110 (2015)
6. Figl, K.: Comprehension of procedural visual business process models. Bus. Inf. Syst. Eng. **59**, 41–67 (2018)
7. Brown, R., Rinderle-Ma, S., Kriglstein, S., Kabicher-Fuchs, S.: Augmenting and assisting model elicitation tasks with 3D virtual world context metadata. In: Meersman, R., Panetto, H., Dillon, T., Missikoff, M., Liu, L., Pastor, O., Cuzzocrea, A., Sellis, T. (eds.) OTM 2014. LNCS, vol. 8841, pp. 39–56. Springer, Heidelberg (2014). https://doi.org/10.1007/978-3-662-45563-0_3
8. Harman, J., Brown, R., Johnson, D., Rinderle-Ma, S., Kannengiesser, U.: Augmenting process elicitation with visual priming. An empirical exploration of user behaviour and modelling outcomes. Inf. Syst. **62**, 242–255 (2016)
9. Ghanbarzadeh, R., Ghapanchi, A.H., Blumenstein, M., Talaei-Khoei, A.: A decade of research on the use of three-dimensional virtual worlds in health care. A systematic literature review. J. Med. Internet Res. **16**, e47 (2014)
10. Dresler, M., et al.: Mnemonic training reshapes brain networks to support superior memory. Neuron **93**, 1227–1235 (2017)
11. Huttner, J.-P., Robbert, K.: The role of mental factors for the design of a virtual memory palace. In: Twenty-Fourth AMCIS, pp. 2015–2019 (2018)
12. Ralby, A., Mentzelopoulos, M., Cook, H.: Learning languages and complex subjects with memory palaces. In: Beck, D., et al. (eds.) iLRN 2017. CCIS, vol. 725, pp. 217–228. Springer, Cham (2017). https://doi.org/10.1007/978-3-319-60633-0_18
13. Brown, J.S., Collins, A., Duguid, P.: Situated cognition and the culture of learning. Educ. Res. **18**, 32–34 (1989)
14. Godden, D., Baddeley, A.: When does context influence recognition memory? Br. J. Psychol. **71**, 99–104 (1980)
15. Godden, D.R., Baddeley, A.D.: Context-dependent memory in two natural environments. On land and underwater. Br. J. Psychol. **66**, 325–331 (1975)
16. Burgess, N., Hockley, W.E., Hourihan, K.L.: The effects of context in item-based directed forgetting. Evidence for "one-shot" context storage. Mem. Cogn. **45**, 745–754 (2017)
17. Yates, F.A.: The Art of Memory. Routledge & Kegan Paul, London (1966)

18. Huttner, J.-P., Pfeiffer, D., Robra-Bissantz, S.: Imaginary versus virtual loci. Evaluating the memorization accuracy in a virtual memory palace. In: Bui, T. (ed.) Proceedings of the 51st HICSS, pp. 274–282. University of Hawai'i at Manoa Honolulu (2018)
19. Worthen, J.B., Hunt, R.R.: Mnemonology. Psychology Press, New York (2011)
20. Gould, N.F., et al.: Performance on a virtual reality spatial memory navigation task in depressed patients. Am. J. Psychiatry 164, 516–519 (2007)
21. Harman, J., Brown, R., Johnson, D.: Improved memory elicitation in virtual reality: new experimental results and insights. In: Bernhaupt, R., Dalvi, G., Joshi, A., Balkrishan, D.K., O'Neill, J., Winckler, M. (eds.) INTERACT 2017. LNCS, vol. 10514, pp. 128–146. Springer, Cham (2017). https://doi.org/10.1007/978-3-319-67684-5_9
22. van Der Aalst, W.M., Ter Hofstede, A.H., Kiepuszewski, B., Barros, A.P.: Workflow patterns. Distrib. Parallel Databases 14, 5–51 (2003)
23. Bell, M.W.: Toward a definition of "virtual worlds". J. Virtual Worlds Res. 1, 1–5 (2008)
24. Bailenson, J., Patel, K., Nielsen, A., Bajscy, R., Jung, S.-H., Kurillo, G.: The effect of interactivity on learning physical actions in virtual reality. Media Psychol. 11, 354–376 (2008)
25. Dalgarno, B., Lee, M.J.W.: What are the learning affordances of 3-D virtual environments? Br. J. Educ. Technol. 41, 10–32 (2010)
26. Okita, S.Y., Turkay, S., Kim, M., Murai, Y.: Learning by teaching with virtual peers and the effects of technological design choices on learning. Comput. Educ. 63, 176–196 (2013)
27. Choi, B., Baek, Y.: Exploring factors of media characteristic influencing flow in learning through virtual worlds. Comput. Educ. 57, 2382–2394 (2011)
28. Petrakou, A.: Interacting through avatars. Virtual worlds as a context for online education. Comput. Educ. 54, 1020–1027 (2010)
29. Barab, S., Thomas, M., Dodge, T., Carteaux, R., Tuzun, H.: Making learning fun. Quest Atlantis, a game without guns. Educ. Technol. Res. Dev. 53, 86–107 (2005)
30. Leyer, M., Stumpf-Wollersheim, J., Pisani, F.: The influence of process-oriented organizational design on operational performance and innovation. Int. J. Prod. Res. 55, 5259–5270 (2017)
31. Figl, K., Mendling, J., Strembeck, M.: The influence of notational deficiencies on process model comprehension. J. AIS 14, 312–338 (2013)
32. Poppe, E., Brown, R., Recker, J., Johnson, D., Vanderfeesten, I.: Design and evaluation of virtual environments mechanisms to support remote collaboration on complex process diagrams. Inf. Syst. 66, 59–81 (2017)
33. Krokos, E., Plaisant, C., Varshney, A.: Spatial mnemonics using virtual reality. In: Proceedings of the 2018 10th ICCAE, pp. 27–30. ACM, Brisbane (2018)
34. Huttner, J.-P., Pfeiffer, D., Robra-Bissantz, S.: Imaginary versus virtual loci: evaluating the memorization accuracy in a virtual memory palace (2018)
35. Huttner, J.-P., Robra-Bissantz, S.: An immersive memory palace: supporting the method of loci with virtual reality. In: 23rd AMCIS, pp. 1–10 (2017)
36. Huttner, J.-P., Robra-Bissantz, S.: A design science approach to high immersive mnemonic E-learning. In: MCIS 2016 Proceedings, pp. 1–5 (2016)
37. Huang, B., Tang, H.J.: Study of workshop production system based on Petri Nets and Flexsim. In: Proceedings of the 22nd International Conference on Industrial Engineering and Engineering Management 2015, Atlantis Press, Paris, pp. 833–844 (2016)
38. Genon, N., Heymans, P., Amyot, D.: Analysing the cognitive effectiveness of the BPMN 2.0 visual notation. In: Malloy, B., Staab, S., van den Brand, M. (eds.) SLE 2010. LNCS, vol. 6563, pp. 377–396. Springer, Heidelberg (2011). https://doi.org/10.1007/978-3-642-19440-5_25
39. Leyer, M., Strohhecker, J.: Mental models of business processes. Working paper series of the chair of service management, University of Rostock (2017)

40. Sarshar, K., Loos, P.: Comparing the control-flow of EPC and petri net from the end-user perspective. In: van der Aalst, W.M.P., Benatallah, B., Casati, F., Curbera, F. (eds.) BPM 2005. LNCS, vol. 3649, pp. 434–439. Springer, Heidelberg (2005). https://doi.org/10.1007/11538394_36

41. Sánchez-González, L., García, F., Ruiz, F., Mendling, J.: Quality indicators for business process models from a gateway complexity perspective. Inf. Softw. Technol. **54**, 1159–1174 (2012)

42. Dikici, A., Turetken, O., Demirors, O.: Factors influencing the understandability of process models: a systematic literature review. Inf. Softw. Technol. **93**, 112–129 (2018)

43. Mendling, J., Verbeek, H.M.W., Dongen, B.F.V., van der Aalst, W.M.P., Neumann, G.: Detection and prediction of errors in EPCs of the SAP reference model. Data Knowl. Eng. **64**, 312–329 (2008)

44. Aysolmaz, B., Schunselaar, D.M.M., Reijers, H.A., Yaldiz, A.: Selecting a process variant modeling approach: guidelines and application. Softw. Syst. Model. **18**, 1155–1178 (2017)

45. Sauzéon, H., Arvind Pala, P., Larrue, F., Wallet, G., Déjos, M., Zheng, X., Guitton, P., N'Kaoua, B.: The use of virtual reality for episodic memory assessment. Exp. Psychol. **59**, 99–108 (2012)

46. Aysolmaz, B., Brown, R., Bruza, P., Reijers, H.A.: A 3D visualization approach for process training in office environments. In: Debruyne, C., et al. (eds.) On the Move to Meaningful Internet Systems: OTM 2016 Conferences: Confederated International Conferences: CoopIS, C&TC, and ODBASE 2016, pp. 418–436. Springer, Heidelberg (2016). https://doi.org/10.1007/978-3-319-48472-3_24

47. Kimball, D.R., Holyoak, K.J.: Transfer and expertise. In: The Oxford Handbook of Memory, pp. 109–122. Oxford University Press, New York (2000)

48. Khemlani, S., Johnson-Laird, P.N.: Disjunctive illusory inferences and how to eliminate them. Mem. Cogn. **37**, 615–623 (2009)

49. Frederick, S.: Cognitive reflection and decision making. J. Econ. Perspect. **19**, 25–42 (2005)

50. Kimchi, R., Palmer, S.E.: Form and texture in hierarchically constructed patterns. J. Exp. Psychol. Hum. Percept. Perform. **8**, 521–535 (1982)

51. Förster, J., Dannenberg, L.: GLOMOsys: a systems account of global versus local processing. Psychol. Inq. **21**, 175–197 (2010)

52. Melcher, J., Mendling, J., Reijers, H.A., Seese, D.: On measuring the understandability of process models. In: Rinderle-Ma, S., Sadiq, S., Leymann, F. (eds.) BPM 2009. LNBIP, vol. 43, pp. 465–476. Springer, Heidelberg (2010). https://doi.org/10.1007/978-3-642-12186-9_44

53. Indulska, M., Recker, J., Rosemann, M., Green, P.: Business process modeling: current issues and future challenges. In: van Eck, P., Gordijn, J., Wieringa, R. (eds.) CAiSE 2009. LNCS, vol. 5565, pp. 501–514. Springer, Heidelberg (2009). https://doi.org/10.1007/978-3-642-02144-2_39

54. Narayanan, A., Moritz, B.B.: Decision making and cognition in multi-echelon supply chains: an experimental study. Prod. Oper. Manag. **24**, 1216–1234 (2015)

Deriving and Combining Mixed Graphs from Regulatory Documents Based on Constraint Relations

Karolin Winter[1] and Stefanie Rinderle-Ma[1,2(✉)]

[1] Faculty of Computer Science, University of Vienna, Vienna, Austria
{karolin.winter,stefanie.rinderle-ma}@univie.ac.at
[2] Data Science @ Uni Vienna, University of Vienna, Vienna, Austria

Abstract. Extracting meaningful information from regulatory documents such as the General Data Protection Regulation (GDPR) is of utmost importance for almost any company. Existing approaches pose strict assumptions on the documents and output models containing inconsistencies or redundancies since relations within and across documents are neglected. To overcome these shortcomings, this work aims at deriving mixed graphs based on paragraph embedding as well as process discovery and combining these graphs using constraint relations such as "redundant" or "conflicting" detected by the ConRelMiner method. The approach is implemented and evaluated based on two real-world use cases: Austria's energy use cases plus the contained process models as ground truth and the GDPR. Mixed graphs and their combinations constitute the next step towards an end-to-end solution for extracting process models from text, either from scratch or amending existing ones.

Keywords: Regulatory documents · Constraint extraction · Text mining · NLP · Process discovery

1 Introduction

Due to the tremendously increasing amount of regulatory documents the reduction of the manual effort that needs to be put into, e.g., reading and understanding these documents, becomes mandatory [19]. Lately the (semi-)automatic extraction of process model information from natural language text has gained momentum in research and practice [4,11,24]. Inline with this, the goals of this work are to **RG1: generate process model fragments from scratch based on regulatory documents** and **RG2: compare existing process model(s) with process model fragments derived from new regulations.**

Existing approaches [3,6,11] suffer from shortcomings such as the need for structured input describing processes in a sequential manner or the lack of handling noise appropriately. In reality, regulatory documents are often extensive and typically, more than one regulatory document needs to be implemented or the integration of recent ones with already existing regulatory documents must

© Springer Nature Switzerland AG 2019
P. Giorgini and B. Weber (Eds.): CAiSE 2019, LNCS 11483, pp. 430–445, 2019.
https://doi.org/10.1007/978-3-030-21290-2_27

be accomplished. State-of-the-art approaches would create one process model out of each regulatory document and ignore relations and connections between parts of documents or across documents leading to models that cannot directly be employed. Moreover, as pointed out in [2], it is desirable to yield not only a description of processes but also give insights on the context of processes.

Due to these challenges, **RG1** and **RG2** cannot be realized in a one-step solution. In fact, several steps are necessary [24] including pre-processing of the input data and post-processing of the output. Moreover, we argue that a multi-step approach contributes to the understandability of the results and gives users the chance for interaction and inspection of intermediate results which would not be possible with a one-step approach. This also includes valuable insights such as paragraph characterization [26]. We opt for receiving process model information in a rather abstract representation and not directly as, for example, BPMN models. This is motivated by the fact that the process model fragments can be used in different settings and contexts and moreover, can be subject to interpretation by domain experts.

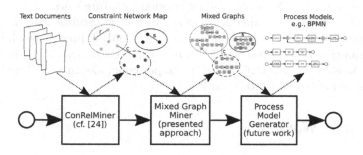

Fig. 1. Overview of the end-to-end approach

Motivated by these design choices, Fig. 1 displays the multi-step approach for tackling **RG1** and **RG2** where the contribution of this work is the *Mixed Graph Miner*.

It takes as input the constraints and their relations that are determined by the ConRelMiner method [24] (step 1). The ConRelMiner enables the grouping of constraints based on, e.g., topics or different stakeholders as well as the detection of redundant, subsumed and conflicting pairs of constraints. The output of the ConRelMiner could be fed into a declarative process model, comparable to mining declarative process models from event logs, e.g., [16]. However, sentences that precede or succeed constraints can provide more detailed information on the order between the constraints resulting in process model fragments (mixed graphs) that can be used for easing the process model generation procedure. The paper at hand opts for deriving such mixed graphs and combining them with the information gained by the ConRelMiner using the underlying regulatory documents and process discovery methods. This provides an *integration of process model fragments into the overall context of the given regulatory documents*, makes the approach *robust against noise* and enables *the analysis of arbitrary as well as multiple regulatory documents*.

For the design of the Mixed Graph Miner, we state sub questions **RQ1: How to extract and present order information within paragraphs from the original text?** and **RQ2: How to put mixed graphs into relation in order to derive contextual information within and across paragraphs?**

For answering **RQ1** our approach re-embeds constraints into their context, i.e., their corresponding paragraphs and within each paragraph connections between the sentences are established which are transformed into arcs indicating control flow paths wherever suitable. The result is one mixed graph per paragraph, i.e., the document collection is represented as a set of mixed graphs. These mixed graphs can be seen as process model fragments and have to be put into relation. For **RQ2**, the additional information provided by the ConRelMiner output is used to set up connections describing relations between constraints which enables a user to recognize inconsistencies or redundancies across the document collection and to retrieve contextual information directly. The final step, i.e., the creation of, e.g., BMPN models will be tackled as future work.

The remainder of the paper is organized as follows. Section 2 outlines related work while Sect. 3 provides fundamentals on the ConRelMiner method. In Sect. 4 the contribution is described in detail and evaluated in Sect. 5. A discussion of the method is given in Sect. 6 before the paper concludes in Sect. 7 with a short summary and outlook of future work.

2   Related Work

Several existing approaches in the business process compliance domain extract information from text. The output ranges from UML models [9,17], over formal models [21], to process models. For the latter, the input varies: [12] investigate BPMN model creation from text artefacts, [6] derive BPMN models based on group stories, and [22] study the creation from use cases. [11] present an approach for BPMN process model generation from natural language text which can be seen the current state-of-the-art. Each of these approaches requires either rather structured input data (sometimes combined with additional information) or produces models that lack precision. This work takes a different approach by using extracted constraints and their relations as vehicle for extracting process models from text. Resolving relations between sentences containing constraints is not discussed in any of the mentioned approaches, but might help to improve derived business rules and process models. Related work on extracting constraints from text includes [7] which extracts SBVR rules from natural language text, but requires a domain specific model. In the information retrieval community there are several approaches targeting the improvement of techniques for deriving contextual information from natural language text. [20], for example, detects discourse and similarity across sentences. In the ConRelMiner this constitutes a part of the relation retrieval between constraints, i.e., sentences need to have a certain similarity as prerequisite. How this similarity is computed is not pre-defined by the approach and can be adapted to other techniques. [18] extracts short text summaries using contextual sentence information by considering sur-rounding sentences within paragraphs. This emphasizes the need for paragraph embedding as presented in this paper. [10] outline a method for extracting rules from legal documents by using logic-based as well as syntax-based patterns. None of these approaches aims at using constraints and text for deriving process mod-els. [23] constructs process models from policies, but not based on text. However, the exploitation of input and output of the constraints as advocated in [23] is adopted by the work at hand.

3 Preliminaries and the ConRelMiner Method

The aim of ConRelMiner (cf. [24]) is to extract constraints from a collection of regulatory documents, to group them by so-called *constraint related subjects*, e.g., topics, departments or stakeholders, and to detect three types of relations (redundancy, subsumption, conflict) between pairs of constraints. This is done by a three step approach. First of all, the documents are pre-processed. This encounters the transformation into plain text format, removing of table of con-tents or copyright forms, chunking into sentences and most important, extracting constraints. A constraint is defined as follows.

Definition 1 (Constraint [24]). *Let S be a set of sentences. A constraint is an element $s \in S$ such that at least one constraint marker is contained in s. The set of all constraints is called C.*

Constraint markers are words indicating explicit instructions, e.g., *should, shall, must*. To further illustrate this, consider a minimal real world example taken from [13] which provides guidelines for pharmaceutical quality risk man-agement. In particular, the paragraphs displayed in Fig. 2 describe how to initiate a quality risk management process, resp. risk review. Constraints in this case are sentences *S1, S7, S8, S9, S10, S11*.

The processing step groups the elicited constraints based on constraint related subjects. This enables users to distinguish between relevant and non-relevant parts of the document collection, i.e., reduce noise. A user can choose among three different methods. The first one uses *term frequencies* and k-means++ clustering, the second one exploits the *structure of sentences* and the third one integrates *external information*, e.g., organigrams or domain knowledge provided by experts.

Afterwards, redundant, subsumed or conflicting constraint pairs are identi-fied (cf. Definition 3 in [24]). A pair of constraints is called redundant, iff both constraints belong to the same group or the similarity of their constraint related subjects is above a user defined threshold, and their actions are similar. Sub-sumed constraint pairs are redundant and the action of at least the first or the second constraint contains additional information. Two constraints are called conflicting iff they belong to different groups or the similarity of constraint

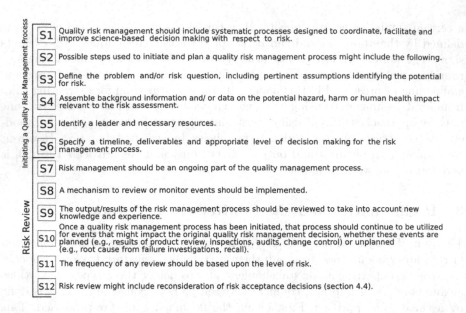

Fig. 2. Running example – textual input

related subjects is below a user defined threshold, but their two actions are similar or iff they are redundant, but contain different time spans.

The result of the ConRelMiner is a *constraint network map* $G_n = (\mathcal{C}, E)$, i.e., a graph whose nodes are constraints, $\mathcal{C}$, and whose edges, E, represent relations between constraints and are labeled as redundant, subsumed or conflicting.

Definition 2 (Constraint Network Map [24]). *A network map is a graph* $G_n = (\mathcal{C}, E)$, *with*

– $\mathcal{C}$ *being a set of nodes where each node* $c \in \mathcal{C}$ *corresponds to one constraint*
– $E \subseteq \mathcal{C} \times \mathcal{C}$ *being the edges.*

Moreover, let $w \colon E \mapsto RL := \{r, s, c\}$ *be a function assigning a label to an edge depending on the corresponding relation between the nodes that span the edge, i.e., redundant (r), subsumed (s), conflicting (c).*

In the running example using term frequencies in combination with k-means++, the constraint network map looks as depicted in Fig. 3. In this case k = 3 was chosen because of the small sample size. Sentences *S1, S7, S9, S10* form the first cluster, *S8* the second one and *S11* the third one. Sentences *S7* and *S9* were detected as being subsumed.

4   Mixed Graph Miner: Deriving Mixed Graphs

The main contribution of the paper is to retrieve a mixed graph for each paragraph, which can be seen as process model fragment, ($\mapsto$ RQ1) and to use the

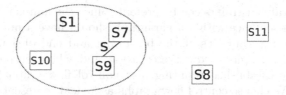

Fig. 3. Running example – output of ConRelMiner

output of the ConRelMiner for combining these graphs ($\mapsto$ RQ2). Each mixed graph consists of control flow paths and, if necessary, of undirected edges. The nodes correspond to sentences which are displayed in a format that represents actors, actions and data elements. Figure 4 displays the overall method which is divided into three phases.

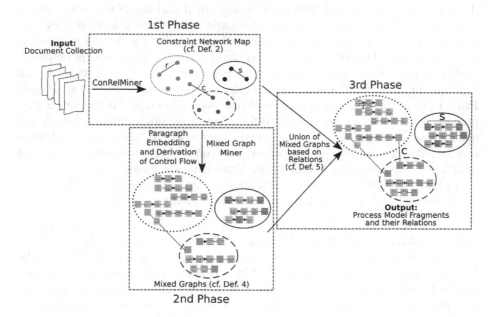

Fig. 4. Overview of method

In the first phase the prepared documents are processed by the ConRelMiner. The output consists of groups of constraints as well as a Constraint Network map describing redundant, subsumed or conflicting constraint pairs, if these are present in the collection. In the second phase, each constraint is embedded into its context, i.e., its corresponding paragraph within the original document and a mixed graph is derived for each paragraph. A user can define the granularity of paragraphs, per default, subsection level is chosen (cf. [26]). For each paragraph a set of sentences S is received which contains at least one constraint. Within each paragraph several constraints can be present. Since the aim is to resolve process fragments, each sentence within a paragraph should have a pre-and succeeding sentence except for sentences at the beginning and end of a paragraph. This corresponds to a graph-based representation and wherever possible, directed edges should be established resulting in a control flow graph (cf. Definition 3 based on [5]). We choose control flow graphs as logical representation which can be transformed into other modeling notations such as BPMN in the sequel.

Definition 3 (Control Flow Graph). *Given a set of sentences $\mathcal{S}$, a control flow graph based on $\mathcal{S}$ is defined as a directed graph $G_f = (\mathcal{S}, A)$, with*

- $\mathcal{S}$ *being a set of nodes that represent the sentences*
- $A \subseteq \mathcal{S} \times \mathcal{S}$ *being the edges that represent control flow paths.*

Control flow paths are established based on (i) sequence markers (cf. [11]) and (ii) input/output relations (cf. [23]). For the latter, within each sentence, the actor(s), action(s) and data must be identified and therefore each sentence is parsed to extract these types of information. As already identified by [11] sentences containing multiple clauses are a challenge. For the further processing, these are split whenever a conjunction or adverbial dependency is detected. Such dependencies can be found by traversing the parse tree provided by an NLP parser, e.g., for the running example, four subclauses in *S10* are found: **Part 1** Once a quality risk management process has been initiated; **Part 2** that process should continue to be utilized for events that might impact the original quality risk management decision, whether these events are planned; **Part 3** (e.g., results of product review, inspections, audits, change control) or **Part 4** unplanned (e.g., root cause from failure investigations, recall).

In this paper, the focus is on extracting sequences, i.e., directly follows relations. Parallel and split relations are considered as future work.

(i) Using Sequence Markers: Markers indicating sequences are, e.g., "then", "after", "afterward", "afterwards", "subsequently", "based on this" or "thus" (cf. [11]). Whenever such a marker is found it is checked whether it is at the beginning or at the end of a sentence. When it is at the beginning, the sentence is linked with its predecessor, otherwise it is linked to its successor. An exception is "after", here the linking is carried out the other way round. Consider the example sentence "After a supervisor has done the assessment, the supervisor must write a report." This sentence is split up by the parser into two subclauses. The marker would be at the beginning of the first subclause and would be linked to the predecessor of this clause, which would be wrong in this case. Considering the reordered sentence "A supervisor must write a report, after the supervisor has done the assessment." leads to an even more complex situation, since the reordering would be wrong again because the second clause containing the "after" must now be linked to its predecessor. Therefore, it must also be considered if "after" is within a sentence containing multiple clauses or not and the linking is not just carried out based on the location of "after" within a clause but also where the clause is located in the original sentence.

(ii) Using Actors and Data Elements: Whenever no explicitly stated sequence can be found, in a second step the input/output technique of [23] is applied. Therefore process elements are derived from the text. In order to reflect process elements, each sentence in S is represented in a structure containing the actor, action, or data elements. This is done by exploiting the NLP tags of a sentence, i.e., an action within a sentence is represented by a verb, the actor is the subject, and data elements are viewed as objects. Challenges like resolving determiners or pronouns like "they" are already tackled during the pre-processing of documents for the ConRelMiner. Determiners or pronouns are replaced by the first preceeding subject that is found within the text and if a sentence contains multiple subjects in multiple clauses it is split into multiple smaller sentences. The ordering of the clauses is hereby maintained. Between two sentences $s_1, s_2 \in S$ a sequence $s_1 \rightarrow s_2$ is established whenever the data element of s_1 becomes the actor of s_2. This technique does not demand a sequential ordering within one paragraph. However, this technique can only be applied when each clause is self-contained, i.e., has an actor, action and data element. If this is not the case, i.e., no reasonable actor, action and data element can be found, the subclause itself is displayed.

Whenever no evidence on a control flow path between sentences can be found, an undirected edge, connecting the sentence with its predecessor and successor is integrated, leading to a so-called mixed graph (cf., e.g., [14]).

Definition 4 (Mixed Graph). *Given a control flow graph $G_f = (S, A)$ on a set of sentences S, a mixed graph $G_m = (S, A, E_s)$ is a graph with*

- *S being the set of nodes*
- *A is the set of directed edges (arcs) representing the control-flow paths between nodes*
- *E_s is the set of undirected edges, in particular, a set of tuples where each element consists of a sentence $s \in S$ and its direct predecessor resp. successor.*

The usage of mixed graphs becomes necessary, since connections within a paragraph shall be established, but it cannot be guaranteed that a paragraph is described in a sequential order, i.e., that the connection is always a control flow path, which is likely to happen for real life documents (for more details, see Sect. 6). Consequently, per paragraph a connected mixed graph is received which corresponds to a process model fragment. ($\mapsto$ RQ1) For reaching RQ2, i.e., the derivation of connections across paragraphs, two or more mixed graphs $\{G_m\}_{i, i \in \mathbb{N}_{>1}}$ and the constraint network graph G_n are combined into one graph (third phase of the approach).

Definition 5 (Union of Graphs based on Constraint Relations). *Let $G_n = (\mathcal{C}, E)$ be the network graph for the given document collection, S_1 and S_2 be two sets of sentences and $G_{m_1} = (S_1, A_1, E_{s_1})$ and $G_{m_2} = (S_2, A_2, E_{s_2})$ be their two mixed graphs. Let $E' \subseteq E$ such that $E' \subseteq S_1 \times S_2$. The union of G_{m_1} and G_{m_2} based on G_n is defined as*

$$(G_{m_1} \cup G_{m_2})_{G_n} := \begin{cases} (\mathcal{S}_1 \cup \mathcal{S}_2, A_1 \cup A_2, E_{s_1} \cup E_{s_2} \cup E') & \text{if } E' \neq \emptyset \\ \emptyset & \text{otherwise.} \end{cases}$$

The label of each edge in E' is preserved.

Definition 5 holds for an arbitrary number of compositions since the union $(G_{m_1} \cup G_{m_2})_{G_n}$ is again a graph.

The overall result is a set of mixed graphs that reflect one process model fragment per paragraph, contain at least one constraint and might be partly connected with each other via the relations retrieved by the ConRelMiner. Figure 5 displays the three possibilities how a redundant, subsumed or conflicting constraint pair can connect nodes of two mixed graphs.

I The constraint pair connects two nodes within the same mixed graph.
II The constraint pair connects the end and start node of two different mixed graphs.
III The constraint pair connects arbitrary nodes of two different mixed graphs.

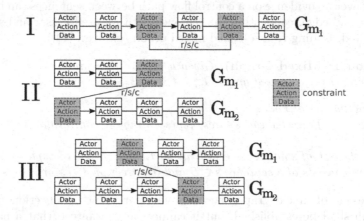

Fig. 5. Possible connections of graphs based on relations

In the case of a `redundant(r)` or `subsumed(s)` relation, case I could indicate a loop. If the relation is `conflicting(c)` a split might be present (cf. [24]) and both branches are described within the paragraph. These relations are in general not considered by state-of-the-art approaches because they are implicitly given in the text. In case II both processes could be combined directly as depicted, i.e., both paragraphs are combined using the constraint pair. In this case for redundant or subsumed relations, this might not indicate a loop but a logic connection between two paragraphs, i.e., processes. For conflicting constraint pairs the situation is like in case I but now both branches are described in separate paragraphs. Note that the paragraphs do not need bo be in a sequential order. Case III is more difficult since it is not possible to directly combine both graphs as in case II since it is unclear how to reorder the nodes before and after the related constraint pair. For conflicting constraint pairs it might mean that the two processes contradict each other because either similar actions are in the scope of different constraint related subjects or similar tasks are within the scope of the same constraint related subject but with different time spans. For redundant or subsumed constraint pairs this case is similar to case II. The reordering of nodes is in each case up to the user.

Figure 6 displays the final result for the running example. It can be seen that almost every edge is undirected in this case due to the missing markers. *S10* was split up into four different parts. The last two parts are not intended by our method, but are produced since the parse tree is searched for each conjunction as well as adverbial clause. In this case no actor, action and reasonable data element can be found and consequently the whole sentence part is returned. However, the method detects that there is a sequence indicated, i.e., directed edges are found between parts of *S10*. These mixed graphs, i.e., process model fragments can serve as input for, e.g., generating process models from scratch. The subsumed relation indicates that the two process elements (*S7* and *S9*) could be combined into one element. For the running example this seems to be only a small benefit but whenever redundancies or subsumptions are detected across several process model fragments the advantages of the approach become evident like it is demonstrated in the evaluation.

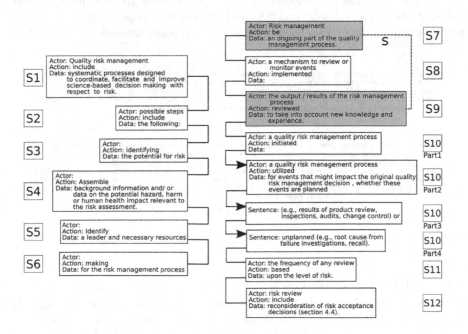

Fig. 6. Mixed graphs – running example

5 Evaluation

The *Mixed Graph Miner* is prototypically implemented on top of the Con-RelMiner using Python 3 in combination with the NLP framework Spacy (https://spacy.io), NLTK [8], and WordNet (https://wordnet.princeton.edu/). The ConRelMiner can group constraints based on three different methods. This paper opts for grouping based on *sentence structure* since this yields the highest precision according to [24]. The first case study on a regulatory document from the energy domain [1] features an end-to-end scenario for **RG1**, i.e., the derivation of a process model from scratch. The second case study on the GDPR (https://bit.ly/2Fa05Kl) tackles **RG1**, i.e., the comparison of existing process models with model fragments stemming from new regulations.

5.1 Austrian Smart Metering Use-Cases

Smart Metering Use-Cases for the Austrian Advanced Meter Communication System [1] contains information on processes w.r.t. smart metering and spans 91 pages. The document is written in German and was translated into English using Google Translate (http://translate.google.com) and a manual refinement. For some processes described within this document manually created and by experts evaluated BPMN models are available, i.e., our results can be compared to those models. The parameters for the ConRelMiner are 0.96 for the overall similarity between sentences and 0.8 for the similarity between constraint related subjects resp. tasks. Two redundant constraint pairs connect Sections 6.3 and

For each relay in the load switching device, an independent, independent of the other relay switching program should be configurable. It should be possible to subdivide the circuit program into daily, weekly, seasonal and annual programs taking into account weekly, holiday and special days. The switching program is managed centrally and transmitted to the load switching device via the communication paths. For control purposes, the circuit program must also be read-back. Any change to the circuit program, regardless of whether it is remotely executed, must be logged in a logbook.

Section 6.3

For each relay in the load switching device, an independent, independent of the other relay switching program should be configurable. It should be possible to subdivide the circuit program into daily, weekly, seasonal and annual programs taking into account weekly, holiday and special days. The service interface (WZ) of the load switching device must be able to change the switching program locally. For control purposes, the circuit program must also be read-back (feedback to the central system via modified circuit program, or also the corresponding note in the logbook, so for example: local switching table change). This state is transmitted to the central system as an ALARM or EVENT when the transmission link (WAN) is available.

Section 6.4

Fig. 7. Textual input – Austria's energy use cases

6.4. The text of these sections is given in Fig. 7 while the output, i.e., union of two mixed graphs, produced by the presented method is given in Fig. 8. For Section 6.3 a BMPN model is available (cf. Fig. 9) which is used for comparison.

It can be seen that within the mixed graph no directed edges were found, i.e., no clear order is given (explicitly) in the text. The first three nodes of the graph for section 6.3 (counted from above) describe general instructions and are reflected as swimlanes by the BPMN model, the fourth node represents the

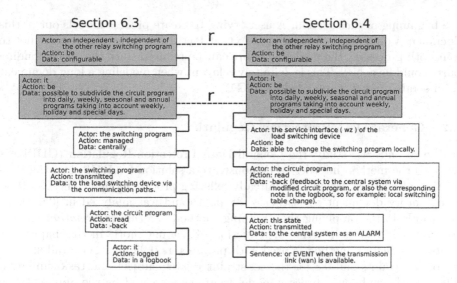

Fig. 8. Mixed graphs – Austria's energy use cases

first message event, the fifth node the second message event. The last node indicates the logbook entry. The actor was not resolved correctly in this case since looking at the original text, the actor should have been "any change in the circuit program". The BPMN model was checked and adapted by a domain expert. Regarding just the textual description, it remains unclear that there should be, e.g., a parallel branch without consulting an expert. Consequently, the BPMN model is ahead in terms of correctness and readability.

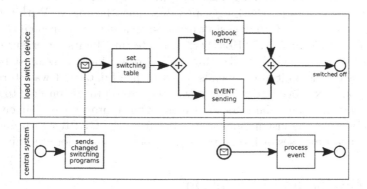

Fig. 9. BPMN model – Austria's energy use cases

However, the benefit of the presented method becomes evident when taking the relations derived by the ConRelMiner into account. With these, a similarity between both graphs is revealed since there are two redundant constraints at the beginning of each section. A user trying to create process models out of this document would be directly pointed to that fact. Even if the user decides not to join both processes, the modeling effort can be reduced since the corresponding parts could be copied. This is definitely relevant when modeling a long document from scratch like it is intended for **RG1**.

5.2   General Data Protection Regulation

In the second case study, the General Data Protection Regulation (GDPR) is fed into the method in order to demonstrate a solution for **RG2**, i.e., the integration of new regulations into already existing process models. The GDPR is a legislatory document consisting of 88 pages and was analyzed in [25], using the ConRelMiner applying the grouping method *external information* leading to promising results in terms of reduction of reading effort. In this paper, the *sentence structure* method is used with parameters 0.95 for the overall similarity of constraints and 0.8 for the constraint related subject and task similarity. The mixed graphs, i.e., process model fragments, created by the approach can be utilized to ensure compliance with the GDPR by integrating additional process tasks into already existing process models. As real-life case, process models describing procedures within the Faculty of Computer Science at the University of Vienna are used (cf. [15]). For this setting, groups referring to, e.g., *data subject* (corresponding to students) or *controller* are of interest, whereas instructions concerning, e.g., *member states* are not directly affecting the processes of the faculty and are disregarded. The approach detected, for example, constraints in Article 15 (Right of access by the data subject) and 17 (Right to erasure) as being subsumed indicating that process steps for these articles might be merged. According to experts, a centralized list containing all services that process student data was introduced and it can be applied in both cases, i.e., for granting information as well as for checking which data must be erased. Within the relevant processes, e.g., the technical staff process, an abstract additional task *delete student data* could be added. However, concrete time limits for erasure are not mentioned within the GDPR. For this task, further documents must be examined and each time limit also depends on the type of data that was stored. This is a very complex procedure and by now, a concrete process on how to erase or communicate the stored data does not exist. Our approach can deliver a structured overview of the instructions stemming from the GDPR which might help to model such processes or integrate single process steps wherever suitable.

6   Discussion and Limitations

Why is it reasonable to not just extract a mixed graph or process model per paragraph using one of the state-of-the-art approaches but to integrate the results of the ConRelMiner? The analysis of regulatory documents, especially when more than one document needs to be considered can be cumbersome. State-of-the-art approaches for extracting process models from natural language text would produce one huge model per document. However, one could argue that each document could be split into paragraphs resulting in several process model fragments. This result is received as an intermediate step by the presented approach (in this case a mixed graph per paragraph). However, connections between these graphs, i.e., the contextual information is still neglected. The presented method overcomes this issue by integrating information on relations between constraints.

What happens if no relations are found? Then each paragraph is viewed separately, which would also be the case for state-of-the-art approaches.

Why should mixed graphs be used, i.e., why is not every edge a control flow path? During the study of several regulatory documents from various domains, we realized that in most cases it can neither be assumed that a process is described sequentially within a paragraph nor be demanded that the ordering of each paragraph is sequential across the document. In contrast, mostly the description resembles an enumeration and therefore no evidence is provided in which order the steps of the process have to be carried out. In this case, it should be up to the user to decide on the order of process steps.

7   Conclusion and Future Work

Extracting process models from regulatory documents is a challenging task. First of all, regulatory documents are not necessarily structured in a process-oriented way and may contain noise. Secondly, process models are rich in information, i.e., contain orderings and may refer to different perspectives such as resources and data. In this work, we opted for constraints as vehicle to extract process fragments, represented as mixed graphs, in combination with paragraph embedding ($\mapsto$ RQ1). The derived mixed graphs are put into context by exploiting relations between constraints that were extracted using the ConRelMiner method ($\mapsto$ RQ2). These mixed graphs can serve as input for either process modeling from scratch or comparing and updating already existing process models. The case studies of Austria's energy use cases and the GDPR in higher education processes assess the approach as promising and illustrate how it could be used towards an end-to-end solution from text documents to process models. Future work will improve on the accuracy for deriving process elements and detect parallel and splits for generating BPMN models.

Acknowledgment. This work has been funded by the Vienna Science and Technology Fund (WWTF) through project ICT15-072.

References

1. Smart metering use-cases für das advanced meter communication system (AMCS), version 1.0. Technical report 1/88, Österreichs Energie (2015)
2. Van der Aa, H., Carmona Vargas, J., Leopold, H., Mendling, J., Padró, L.: Challenges and opportunities of applying natural language processing in business process management. In: Computational Linguistics, pp. 2791–2801 (2018)

3. van der Aa, H., Leopold, H., Reijers, H.A.: Comparing textual descriptions to process models-the automatic detection of inconsistencies. Inf. Syst. **64**, 447–460 (2017)
4. van der Aa, H., Leopold, H., Reijers, H.A.: Checking process compliance against natural language specifications using behavioral spaces. Inf. Syst. **78**, 83–95 (2018)
5. Allen, F.E.: Control flow analysis. In: ACM SIGPLAN Notices, vol. 5, pp. 1–19 (1970)
6. de AR Goncalves, J.C., Santoro, F.M., Baiao, F.A.: Business process mining from group stories. In: International Conference on Computer Supported Cooperative Work in Design, pp. 161–166 (2009)
7. Bajwa, I.S., Lee, M.G., Bordbar, B.: SBVR business rules generation from natural language specification. In: AAAI Spring Symposium, pp. 2–8 (2011)
8. Bird, S., Klein, E., Loper, E.: Natural Language Processing with Python: Analyzing Text with the Natural Language Toolkit. O'Reilly Media, Inc., Massachusetts (2009)
9. Deeptimahanti, D.K., Babar, M.A.: An automated tool for generating UML models from natural language requirements. In: Automated Software Engineering, pp. 680–682 (2009)
10. Dragoni, M., Villata, S., Rizzi, W., Governatori, G.: Combining NLP approaches for rule extraction from legal documents. In: MIning and REasoning with Legal Texts (2016)
11. Friedrich, F., Mendling, J., Puhlmann, F.: Process model generation from natural language text. In: Advanced Information Systems Engineering, pp. 482–496 (2011)
12. Ghose, A., Koliadis, G., Chueng, A.: Process discovery from model and text artefacts. In: Services, pp. 167–174 (2007)
13. Group, I.E.W., et al.: ICH harmonized tripartite guideline, quality risk management q9. In: Technical Requirements for Registration of Pharmaceuticals for Human Use (2005)
14. Hansen, P., Kuplinsky, J., de Werra, D.: Mixed graph colorings. Math. Methods Oper. Res. **45**(1), 145–160 (1997)
15. Kabicher, S., Rinderle-Ma, S.: Human-centered process engineering based on content analysis and process view aggregation. In: Advanced Information Systems Engineering, pp. 467–481 (2011)
16. Ly, L.T., Maggi, F.M., Montali, M., Rinderle-Ma, S., van der Aalst, W.M.P.: Compliance monitoring in business processes: functionalities, application, and tool-support. Inf. Syst. **54**, 209–234 (2015)
17. More, P., Phalnikar, R.: Generating UML diagrams from natural language specifications. Appl. Inf. Syst. **1**(8), 19–23 (2012)
18. Ren, P., Chen, Z., Ren, Z., Wei, F., Ma, J., de Rijke, M.: Leveraging contextual sentence relations for extractive summarization using a neural attention model. In: Research and Development in Information Retrieval, pp. 95–104 (2017)
19. Riefer, M., Ternis, S.F., Thaler, T.: Mining process models from natural language text: a state-of-the-art analysis. Multikonferenz Wirtschaftsinformatik, pp. 9–11 (2016)
20. Saha, T.K., Joty, S., Hassan, N., Hasan, M.A.: Regularized and retrofitted models for learning sentence representation with context. In: Information and Knowledge Management, pp. 547–556 (2017)
21. Selway, M., Grossmann, G., Mayer, W., Stumptner, M.: Formalising natural language specifications using a cognitive linguistic/configuration based approach. Inf. Syst. **54**, 191–208 (2015)

22. Sinha, A., Paradkar, A.: Use cases to process specifications in business process modeling notation. In: Web Services, pp. 473–480 (2010)
23. Wang, H.J., Zhao, J.L., Zhang, L.J.: Policy-driven process mapping (PDPM): discovering process models from business policies. DSS **48**(1), 267–281 (2009)
24. Winter, K., Rinderle-Ma, S.: Detecting constraints and their relations from regulatory documents using NLP techniques. In: On the Move to Meaningful Internet Systems, pp. 261–278 (2018)
25. Winter, K., Rinderle-Ma, S.: Untangling the GDPR using ConRelMiner. arXiv:1811.03399 (2018)
26. Winter, K., Rinderle-Ma, S., Grossmann, W., Feinerer, I., Ma, Z.: Characterizing regulatory documents and guidelines based on text mining. In: On the Move to Meaningful Internet Systems, pp. 3–20 (2017)

A Method to Improve the Early Stages of the Robotic Process Automation Lifecycle

Andres Jimenez-Ramirez[1]([✉]), Hajo A. Reijers[2], Irene Barba[1],
and Carmelo Del Valle[1]

[1] Departamento de Lenguajes y Sistemas Informáticos,
University of Seville, Seville, Spain
{ajramirez,irenebr,carmelo}@us.es
[2] Utrecht University, Utrecht, The Netherlands
h.a.reijers@uu.nl

Abstract. The robotic automation of processes is of much interest to organizations. A common use case is to automate the repetitive manual tasks (or processes) that are currently done by back-office staff through some information system (IS). The lifecycle of any Robotic Process Automation (RPA) project starts with the analysis of the process to automate. This is a very time-consuming phase, which in practical settings often relies on the study of process documentation. Such documentation is typically incomplete or inaccurate, e.g., some documented cases never occur, occurring cases are not documented, or documented cases differ from reality. To deploy robots in a production environment that are designed on such a shaky basis entails a high risk. This paper describes and evaluates a new proposal for the early stages of an RPA project: the analysis of a process and its subsequent design. The idea is to leverage the knowledge of back-office staff, which starts by monitoring them in a non-invasive manner. This is done through a screen-mouse-key-logger, i.e., a sequence of images, mouse actions, and key actions are stored along with their timestamps. The log which is obtained in this way is transformed into a UI log through image-analysis techniques (e.g., fingerprinting or OCR) and then transformed into a process model by the use of process discovery algorithms. We evaluated this method for two real-life, industrial cases. The evaluation shows clear and substantial benefits in terms of accuracy and speed. This paper presents the method, along with a number of limitations that need to be addressed such that it can be applied in wider contexts.

Keywords: Robotic process automation · Process discovery ·
Business process outsourcing

1 Introduction

The term Robotic Process Automation (RPA) refers to a software paradigm where robots are programs which mimic the behavior of human workers

© Springer Nature Switzerland AG 2019
P. Giorgini and B. Weber (Eds.): CAiSE 2019, LNCS 11483, pp. 446–461, 2019.
https://doi.org/10.1007/978-3-030-21290-2_28

interacting with information systems (ISs) and whose objective is to perform structured and repetitive tasks quickly and profitably [12,22,27]. Significant cost savings, agility, and quality improvement are associated to a successful RPA project [6]. Nonetheless, not all processes are suitable for automation. The following criteria need to be met [12]: the process (1) must be highly frequent, (2) with a low level of exceptions, (3) involving an enclosed cognitive scope, and (4) susceptible to human errors. According to these criteria, the best candidates to be subjected to RPA projects are processes found within the back-offices of a company [13].

In general, an RPA project follows the following lifecycle:

1. An analysis of the context to determine which processes – or parts of them – are candidates to be robotized, considering the criteria mentioned earlier.
2. The design of the selected processes, which involves the specification of the actions, data flow, etc., which must be developed.
3. The development of each designed process.
4. The deployment of the robots in their individual environments (e.g., virtual machines) to perform their jobs.
5. A testing or control phase in which the performance of each robot is analyzed and errors are detected. Noted that within the traditional software development lifecycle testing precedes deployment, RPA is characterized by lacking a testing environment; only the production environment is available.
6. The operation and maintenance of the process, which takes into account each robot's performance and error cases; the outcomes of this phase enable a new analysis & design cycle to enhance the robots.

When considering state-of-the-art RPA technology, specifically solutions like UIPath [25] or WorkFusion [29], it is apparent that these mostly focus on the later stages of the lifecycle, i.e, the actual development and deployment stages. They provide very limited support to detect candidates of tasks or processes to automate. To date, there are also no established methods to carry out these analysis and design phases. As a result, current RPA projects mainly rely on the analysis of documentation, which may be of poor quality and may require substantial effort to understand. Considering that designed robots are typically deployed in production environments, where they interact with operational ISs, there is much risk involved with building on an inaccurate analysis.

Interestingly, in companies that have adopted RPA, people and robots typically work side by side within their back-offices. People are in charge of managing the processes that are either not suitable for RPA or which still need to be robotized. To carry out their work, these human employees receive formal training on how to deal with the cases that belong to the process under their control, but also receive training-on-the-job: they experience exceptions, process deviations, and undocumented cases on a daily basis. We will leverage their domain knowledge and analyze their behavior as the main ingredients of a method that improves and speeds up the early stages of the RPA lifecycle.

Against this backdrop, we propose in this paper a method that starts by monitoring the computers of the back-office staff in a non-invasive manner by recording the screen, mouse and key events. Next, we apply a set of mechanisms (e.g., image similarity and frequency analysis) to transform this information into a standardized event log [1] including UI information, i.e., the sequence of raw images is converted to a set of shorter sequences of events each one corresponding to a process instance that the back-office staff has performed. The generated log is then used to automatically discover the underlying process. As widely acknowledged [3, 13, 16], the process mining paradigm [2] provides efficient and suitable analytic techniques to address this step.

To evaluate our proposal, it has been applied to two industrial cases. We chose the domain of business process outsourcing (BPO) to select these cases since they provide a particularly challenging setting. When a process is outsourced, various companies are involved in carrying it out and the ISs in this process context may be geographically dispersed. What is more, the use of secured connections (e.g., Citrix) is the standard in outsourced scenarios, which only permits raw images to be gathered from the monitored screen instead of the structure of the information that is being processed. The results of our evaluation show clear benefits in the early phases of RPA projects in the BPO domain by (1) improving accuracy and (2) saving time. In addition, our evaluation shows that the insights generated during the analysis phase are also beneficial during further stages of the RPA lifecycle.

The rest of the paper is organized as follows. Section 2 motivates the need for leveraging human knowledge to foster better RPA analysis and design in a BPO context. Section 3 presents the details of our proposed method. Section 4 reports the results for the cases we used for our evaluation. Section 5 presents related work on RPA. Finally, Sect. 6 concludes the paper with a summary and description of future work.

2   Context

In a BPO scenario (cf. Fig. 1), back-office tasks are carried out both by teams of humans and teams of robots. For both types of teams, documentation of the prescribed process is a crucial ingredient. This documentation covers the various case situations in a mix of formal and informal descriptions, typically containing some sort of ambiguity or uncertainty (e.g., lacking information related to the software ecosystem beyond the ISs which are used). We will take a look at the role that documentation plays in more detail first.

As far as the human staff is concerned, documentation is used as the basis for training them. While human performers are expected to be able to deal with a particular process on the basis of this training, they are likely to encounter non-documented scenarios. Humans are expected to make decisions under such circumstances, which they are usually capable of by applying a cognitive effort – probably by applying common sense (i.e., *on-the-job training*). Typically, such new decision-making behavior is then incorporated into a knowledge database, which is shared across the team.

As explained earlier, the deployment of a robot team emerges from following the common RPA lifecycle, i.e., by going through the phases of analysis, design,

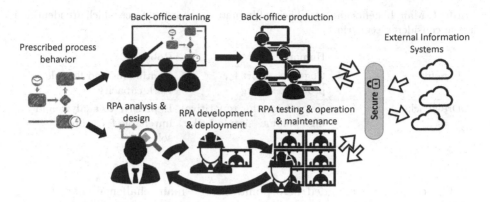

Prescribed process behavior

Back-office training

Back-office production

External Information Systems

RPA analysis & design

RPA development & deployment

RPA testing & operation & maintenance

Secure

Fig. 1. Current situation of the business.

development, deployment, testing, operation, and maintenance. In the analysis and design phases, a significant effort is spent on formalizing the process to be carried out in such a way that ambiguity and uncertainty are reduced about the way various cases should be dealt with. Selected parts of the prescribed process are formally documented and delivered to the developers of the robots. These developers produce the robot code, which is then gradually deployed such that the robots can execute the related processes while their behavior is monitored and tested. After a period of time, a full team of robots will be ready to execute the process in question. However, robots tend to be rigid and do not behave well under unexpected circumstances. When an unexpected situation occurs, two things happen: (1) the involved robot gets stuck and a human operator must bring the process to a situation where the robot can go on – typically, the starting point of a new case, and (2) the RPA lifecycle starts again to analyze the newly encountered situations to decide which of these must be included in the design to deploy an updated version of the robot team.

From a company's perspective, each team – human or robotic – has its own benefits and drawbacks, which can be seen in Table 1. While robots can work 24/7 and can be flexibly spawned to deal with heavy workloads, they are expensive to analyze and have a low accuracy when dealing with judgment-based tasks, e.g., deciding what to do based on unstructured data. Therefore, they require the supervision of humans, which are typically engaged with knowledge-intensive tasks and relieved of repetitive, simple tasks [5].

As stated before, analyzing a process that is to be robotized is a time-consuming task and only a small portion of the process can be robotized initially, i.e., the most structured and repeated parts [3]. During the lifetime of such a process, new scenarios and corrections are detected and included in the robotized set. Eventually, only the most unstable and judgment-based parts of a process remain separated from the cases that can be handled by robots. The human team will stay in charge to deal with these. The sooner this eventual situation is reached, the more profitable the RPA project is.

Table 1. Main benefits and drawbacks of human vs robot taskforce which are identified in the considered scenario.

	Human	Robot
Benefits	Cognitive effort for problem solving	Continuous and flexible work capacity
Drawbacks	Not efficient for repetitive, high volume, simple tasks	Expensive to analyze and unreliable for problem solving

The context we provided here points at the main challenge that is being addressed in this paper: to reduce the effort to analyze the actual system. As the reader may have noticed, this effort is done twice: (1) when the human team is trained or *trained-on-the-job*, and (2) when new documentation is received or when errors are detected, which trigger a new analysis of the robots. Although managers of the human teams and managers that are concerned with the development of robots communicate with each other, the flow of knowledge that is available in the human teams to that of the development teams is far from ideal. To mend this, the current paper tries to automate this flow.

3   Method

In this section, we will describe our proposal to deal with the challenges that exist in an RPA setting. Essentially, this method leverages the knowledge of back-office staff for improving the early stages of the RPA lifecycle. This method starts with behavioral monitoring (cf. Sect. 3.1), after which a set of configuration cycles are conducted over the monitored information (cf. Sect. 3.2). Each cycle produces a process model that is related to such behavior (cf. Sect. 3.3). Figure 2 depicts an overview of this proposal.

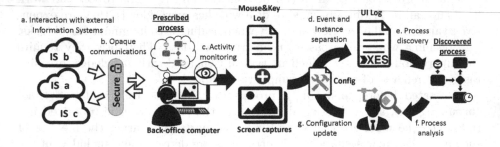

Fig. 2. Overview of the proposal.

3.1   Behavioral Monitoring

As can be seen in Fig. 2, in a BPO setting, a back-office employee interacts with different ISs (e.g., proprietary ERP systems cf. Fig. 2a) to perform a number of repetitive, administrative processes. The interaction with these ISs is done through secured connections (e.g., Citrix cf. Fig. 2b), which makes it difficult to perform a transparent analysis of the user interaction by means of tree-like structures (e.g., HTML DOM or Windows UI). Therefore, only raw images on the one hand and mouse and keyboard events on the other can be monitored from someone's computer during their interactions with an IS. Our method starts by recording these back-office interactions through non-intrusive monitoring software (i.e., it is invisible for the user, cf. Fig. 2c). This software captures a single long trace of events with the information depicted in Table 2.[1] Such events may be related to several traces (or instances) of the same process.

3.2   Configuration Cycles

A specific algorithm is executed to identify events and traces/instances to generate a UI Log (cf. Fig. 2d, Definition 1, Algorithm 1). For this step, a default configuration (i.e., a set of pairs $key - value$) is used with the information shown in Table 3.

Definition 1. *An **UI Log** is a XML file whose grammar is an extension of the standard XES [1]. This extension incorporates the* concept standard [1] attributes *(i.e.,* concept:name *for traces and events) and the attributes of Table 2.*

Algorithm 1. From raw log to UILog

---

input : Log l, Config c
output: UILog uiL

1 $uiL \leftarrow createBasicLog(l)$
2 $uiL.groupEventsByFingerprint(c.similarity\_th)$

3 $uiL.deleteEventsByTemplates(c.templates)$
4 $uiL.deleteEvents(c.rm\_events)$
5 **foreach** $(source, targets) : c.join\_events)$ **do**
6 $\quad \lfloor \ uiL.joinEvents(source, targets)$

7 **if** $c.st\_event$ *is not defined* **then**
8 $\quad \lfloor \ c.st\_event \leftarrow uiL.mostReapeatedEvent()$

9 $uiL.divideLogInTracesByStartEvent(c.st\_event)$

---

[1] These event attributes are considered necessary for different use cases. However, not all of them are useful for the current paper.

Table 2. Event attributes captured from the UI.

Name	Description	Name	Description
app_name	Name of the application which is being used. Not useful in secured systems	*keystrokes*	Sequence of keystrokes pressed. Only if *event_type* is keystroke
focus	Indicates if the application has just gained the focus	*start_ts*	Start timestamp
event_type	$\{click, keystroke\}$	*end_ts*	End timestamp
click_type	$\{left, right, middle\}$. Only if *event_type* is click	*img_name*	Name of the file with the screen capture
click_coords	Coordinates of the click. Only if *event_type* is click	*img_fingerprint*	Quasi-unique string summarizing the image

Table 3. Configuration attributes.

Key	Description
similarity_th	Threshold to use for grouping images. If it increases, it will be more likely that two images are considered the same event
st_events	Set of event to be considered the alternative starts of the instances
rm_events	Set of events to be removed from the log
rm_templates	Set of images to remove the events which contains any of them
join_events	Set of pairs $(source, target)$ to join the source with the target events
sp_processes	Set of processes to be considered *special or exceptional* and, thus, to be separated from the final model

In a first step (cf. line 1 of Algorithm 1), the UI Log is created using the basic information of the input log i.e., the data of Table 2. Next, the images are used to identify repeated events (i.e., atomic process activities) and divide the long trace into different smaller traces.

First of all, repeated events are identified through an image-similarity algorithm which groups similar images (e.g., a log-in window with two different user names will be grouped together). In this step (cf. line 2 of Algorithm 1), the Hamming distance [14] of image fingerprints (e.g., pHash or Image-match [28]) is used to check whether two images correspond to the same activity or event, i.e., if such a distance is below the configured threshold, then both images are grouped together. As a result, each event of the log now contains the event *concept* : *name*. As the log may contain noise, some mechanisms are enabled to clean the log from it (cf. lines 3–6 of Algorithm 1):

1. Some events can be deleted if they contain some configured templates (e.g., a social network or email icon, cf. Table 3 *rm_templates*).
2. Some detected events can be directly deleted (e.g., the log-in window of an ERP system, cf. Table 3 *rm_events*).
3. Some events can be considered to be the same although they look different (cf. Table 3 *join_events*).

Secondly, to separate the one-trace log into different traces, an event (i.e., the most repeated or a configured set, cf. lines 7–8 of Algorithm 1, Table 3 *st_events*) is used to split this long trace into smaller traces, each of which corresponds to a different instance (cf. line 9).[2] Therefore, in the resulting UI log, traces with different *concept* : *name* are created containing their corresponding events.

3.3   Process Discovery

The generated UI log is used as input of a process discovery algorithm (cf. Fig. 2e). The purpose of this step is to generate graphical process models that capture the behavior of the back-office employee. It is here that a business analyst becomes involved. First, the processes which meet a configured specification are marked as special (cf. Table 3 *sp_processes*). These relate to less relevant processes, which either obscure the main process or convert it into a spaghetti model. What is more, this mechanism can be used to exclude undesired processes, e.g., when the employee deals with multiple procedures on a daily basis. Second, the main process that is cleaned from the special cases is captured too.

Although the aforementioned steps (cf. Fig. 2d and e) are automatic, there are some parts where errors may be introduced. For example, the back-office employee may introduce noise in the UI log if she performs personal activities, the image-similarity algorithm may group images together that actually correspond to different events, and a wrong event may be selected to divide the cases. To deal with this, our proposal includes a manual activity by a business analyst to analyze the generated models (cf. Fig. 2f). In this step, the business analyst can perform a deep review of both the special model and the main model. In case she considers this necessary, any process model may be refined by providing a new configuration setting for a next iteration of the process discovery stage (cf. Fig. 2g). The process model that results from a number of iterations exactly captures how the back-office employee applies her know-how.

The outcomes of this approach can be used to improve different phases of the RPA lifecycle, as follows:

---

[2] Note that considering an event for dividing the traces implies that this selected event may not appear in the middle of a trace.

1. The final process model represents a key element for the analysis and design phases since it includes (1) information about the real process – which may differ from the documented one–, (2) figures on the frequency of the cases – which is relevant to decide which cases should be robotized–, and (3) the human effort that is still required to be allocated to the process – which is necessary to evaluate the potential performance of the RPA deployment.
2. The additional UI log information, which is associated to the activities of the process model, provides strong support for the development phase since it includes the actions that have been done (i.e., keystrokes and clicks) that lead one activity to other for the different instances of each case type. Furthermore, testing the developed robots will become easier since the UI logs can be used to generate test scenarios.

In the evaluation that follows, we will focus on our primary objective, the optimization of the analysis and design phases.

4   Evaluation

To evaluate our method, we worked together with Servinform S.A.[3], which is active in the BPO domain. To be more precise, we carried out the analysis and design phases for RPA scenarios within two companies. We compared the outcomes with those that resulted from the conventional analysis and design activities of Servinform for the same scenarios. Section 4.1 describes the set-up that underlies our evaluation; Sect. 4.2 provides the data analysis and summarizes the results of the evaluation.

4.1   Set-Up

To enable our evaluation, a software infrastructure is developed and deployed (cf. Fig. 3) to support the following use case:

1. A back-office computer is monitored for some time through non-intrusive software written in the AutoIT scripting language [7]. The software sends all events (cf. Table 2) to a central server using JSON messages.
2. A central server, coded using Java and the Spring Cloud framework [23], exposes a REST API for receiving the events of the monitored computer and storing both the images and the UI events into a MySQL database. The fingerprint of the images is calculated by a Python component[4].
3. After the observation period, an analyst requests a process model that is based on the monitored events to the central server. For this purpose, a configuration (cf. Table 3) is sent through a custom-made ProM plugin.

---

[3] Serviform is a Spanish BPO company with an IT consulting area.
[4] There are several alternatives for computing a fingerprint of an image, in this paper we based on [28].

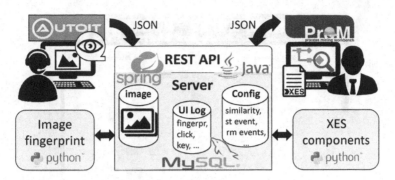

Fig. 3. Developed infrastructure.

4. The central server stores the configuration and applies it to the collected event log using specific components written in Python. Such components take care of grouping events, separating instances, etc. to eventually generate a XES document (cf. Definition 1) which is sent back to the ProM plugin.
5. The analyst could in principle select any process mining algorithm that is available in the ProM interface to discover the process model behind the XES document. Nonetheless, due to this special evaluation context, we developed a simple algorithm based on [21], which generates EPC models [4] by merging the process instances of the log. Such models are shown in the ProM interface (cf. Fig. 4) to be reviewed by the analyst. The analyst may either decide to finish the discovery cycle or generate a new configuration, thus going back to step 3 of the use case.

This use case has been applied to two outsourced processes, which are carried out by two different companies. These companies, a major Spanish bank and a telecommunication company, consented to cooperate for the sake of this evaluation, but did not authorize the disclosure of their names. Therefore, we will refer to them as *company*1 and *company*2. The processes of interest are well known by Servinform and have been in production for months. For the purpose of this evaluation, we obtained the results from an *a priori* analysis and design for each process, as carried out by Servinform. We will refer to the models that describe the behavior of the two processes as the *a priori* models. These models provide us with the insight into the understanding of the processes on the basis of a conventional, document-oriented analysis and design phases. The *a priori* model for *company*1 contains 5 alternative paths (i.e., different sequences of process activities); for *company*2, there are 9 different paths. Note that the relative simplicity of the complexity of these models is precisely the reason that they were considered as candidates for RPA.

Our method has been deployed, which means in particular that our software was installed and was executed on two back-office computers, one for each company. The software has been actively gathering and analyzing events for a period of one week. In general, an appropriate logging involves a trade-off between reach-

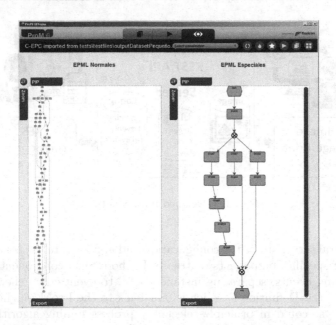

Fig. 4. Main (left) and special (right) processes visualization in the ProM plugin.

ing a proper size of the log and working towards a reasonable time to start the process analysis. We considered one week to be appropriate since it guaranteed us to observe, at least, 200 completely logged cases for both processes. This amount of cases for processes with an a priori complexity of approximately 10 alternative paths seemed adequate. After one week of observation, a business analyst with general knowledge of the underlying, outsourced processes started working with the ProM plugin to go through different configuration cycles for each process. For the sake of explaining our evaluation results, we will only consider (1) the *initial model* (i.e., the first model that is automatically created on the basis of a default configuration, cf. Sect. 3.2), and (2) the *final model* (i.e., the last model that is discovered after going through some configuration cycles and a considerable cognitive effort). These two models are stored with the goal of being analyzed by the company staff.

To compare for each process the *a priori* model with the discovered models, we used different measures:

1. *#paths a priori*, *#paths initial* and *#paths final*: the number of process paths which are included in the *a priori* model, initial model, and final model respectively,
2. *%new*: the percentage of paths that are present in the final model but cannot be found in the *a priori* model,
3. *%non-discovered*: the percentage of paths that are present in the *a priori* model that cannot be found in the final model.

4.2   Results and Conclusions

Table 4 shows the values that we obtained for the measures we introduced. As can be seen from this table when considering the *#paths a priori* and *#paths final* columns, both scenarios show that our method discovers a greater variety of paths than the conventional approach. This difference is mainly due to the fact that new paths are discovered. Specifically, in both cases more than 30% of the paths within the final models are new. This means that the monitored employees have dealt with cases in ways that were not *a priori* modelled yet exist in real life. When considering the *non-discovered* column, it is interesting to note that the final model totally captures the paths in the *a priori* model for the process within the first company, but that there is one path out of the 9 in total in the *a priori* model for the second company (11%) that is not found back in the final model. This can be interpreted in different ways. It could hint at the event log to be too small (and the observation period to be too short) to identify all paths. However, given the low complexity of the path in question, it could also be seen as an indication that this particular path is actually not considered so relevant by the business analyst.

Table 4. Result regarding the *a priori* and the final models.

Company	#Paths a priori	#Paths initial	#Paths final	%New	%Non-discovered
#1	5	46	12	7/12 (**58%**)	0/5 (**0%**)
#2	9	60	13	5/13 (**38%**)	1/9 (**11%**)

It is also interesting to briefly review the *#paths initial* column, i.e. the ones that are generated on the basis of default configuration settings. When analyzing these models, many more paths can be seen – 46 in *company*1 and 60 in *company*2. Yet, many of them are of poor quality since they are based on noise and irrelevant events. This gives us the insight that it is essential to combine the automatic steps of our proposal with the cognitive effort of the business analyst: this combination transforms the big sets of *bad* paths within the initial models into smaller numbers of *high quality* paths within the final models.

Finally, we also present here some additional insights that we collected from the feedback from the business analyst who was involved in this evaluation on the overall method:

1. The increase in the covered process behavior in the final models is significant and relevant. Moreover, some of the new paths may not belong only to the outsourced processes (i.e., the interaction with the external ISs) but to company's own internal computer ecosystem, e.g., the process to solve a common network connection problem which is not related to the outsourced process. Therefore, the proposal may also detect paths that are unlikely to appear in any *a priori* model based on documentation.

2. The tools that are part of our method appear useful to clean the initial models from noise and to decide on which paths are relevant. When it happens that some relevant paths correspond to small repetitive patterns, like exceptions that may happen in different longer paths (e.g., closing an unexpected pop-up and then continue with the normal path), it does mean that the analyst must decide between throwing out the full path or making a stronger cognitive effort to separate such patterns and capture this knowledge.

3. The final models include additional, relevant data about process paths when compared with the *a priori* models (e.g., path frequency, mouse actions, time, etc.). In our evaluation, we only focused on the use of the frequency of paths since this was acknowledged to be most relevant for the analyst.

4. Although time has not been measured in this evaluation, discovering the final model by the analyst turned out to be a matter of hours, i.e., the time between the first configuration is done until the final process model is generated. To compare: in the opinion of the analyst, the conventional, document-based analysis and design of the *a priori* model is a matter of days or even weeks. This provides preliminary indications that this proposed method can indeed help to also speed up the analysis and design phases.

In summary, this evaluation clearly shows the improved accuracy of analyzing processes using our tool-supported method in comparison with extracting knowledge process knowledge from documents. We also obtained some tentative insights on additional benefits, most importantly about shortening the time required to discover the relevant parts of processes that can be robotized.

5 Related Work

In recent years, other authors have also proposed techniques that can be applied in the early stages of an RPA project. Specifically, [15] summarizes a number of best practices and provides guidance to prioritize processes for the analysis phase. However, this work lacks any technical support for this phase. From a more technical point of view, [17] proposes the use of natural language processing and machine learning for detecting candidate activities from a textual description of processes. Unlike [17], our proposal analyzes the actual behavior of the system instead of what is available in the documentation. In that sense, we provide a new perspective of relevant information that seems worth considering. In turn, the authors of [18] introduce the concept of *desktop activity mining*. Similar to our method, this work combines monitoring techniques with process mining [2]. However, it would not be feasible to apply this in complex settings such as the BPO domain we considered since it requires access to actual UI elements. Similarly, [16] suggests that using process mining for discovering local process models (i.e., frequent patterns) from UI logs may be useful to train robots. Also, [3] describes how RPA may leverage techniques from process mining paradigm. Unlike our proposal, [3,16] focus on a characterization of the problems involved and only suggest in abstract terms how they can be addressed.

There are other research areas related to our approach. On the one hand, the human-computer interaction community also faces the problem of understanding user behavior using logs [11]. Instead of discovering the underlying process, [19] proposes a method to check the alignment between the user log and a Petri Net which model the expected interaction of the user. In turn, [10] analyzes event logs to group events in frequent and meaningful tasks. Similarly, [26] proposes a grouping approach to differentiate the kind of users that interact with an interface. However, [10, 26] rely on a previous identification of click operations while our approach is based on low-level clickstreams.

On the other hand, the process mining community pays special attention to event log preprocessing for enhancing log quality. It is recognized that real world logs are often noisy because some of their traces are duplicated, incomplete, inconsistent, or reflect some other incorrect behavior [8]. The presence of noise in the event log leads to unnecessarily complex discovered models that do not accurately reflect the underlying process [24]. Within the process mining community, various techniques have been proposed to discover and remove noise (e.g., [9,20]) that can be adapted to be a part of the cleaning mechanisms that are part of our approach.

6   Conclusion

This paper presents a method for improving the analysis and design phases of the RPA lifecycle in a BPO context. This context is specially challenging since, in general, it implies using secured connections in a way that the ISs to interact with are seen as black box systems: the inputs are mouse and keyboard events and the output is a raw image related to the screen of the ISs.

To address such a complex scenario, we described our main idea: to leverage the knowledge of back-office staff who interact with the ISs on a daily basis. To do so, their computers are monitored and this information is then transformed into a UI log using a series of image-analysis algorithms. Next, this UI log is refined and used to discover the underlying process model using techniques from the process mining paradigm.

This paper describes the steps and the tools that are part of the proposed method. It has been applied to two real-life processes, which form the basis of our evaluation. The results indicate that the proposed method is suitable for the considered problems. Principally, it improves the accuracy of the process analysis. Among the additional benefits, there are indications that this method would considerably speed up the early stages of an RPA analysis as well.

Nonetheless, the approach presents some limitations that are planned to be mitigated as future work. First, the proposed method considers a log regarding a single-user interaction. In case that multiple back-office computers are monitored, a variety of solutions may exist, but each of these need to be evaluated. For instance, a procedure could be to discover each single-user process model first and then merge them into a single process model. Second, this paper generates a process model that mimics the behavior of a user including possible errors or inefficiencies. Although some of these may be identified and cleaned from the log by using our approach, others may require further improvements and optimizations that are out of the current scope. Third, the behavior which is analyzed only covers the events which are observable, i.e., performed through the back-office computer. Identifying such non-observable events is useful since the existence of them in a path indicates that such a path is not a good candidate to be robotized.

As further future work, we plan (1) to investigate how further phases can be enhanced on the basis of logged events and automated discovery techniques, (2) to evaluate the current method in a controlled experiment that, on the one hand, considers experts' opinions regarding the paths discovered and, on the other hand, focuses on measuring time gains since the current conclusions about time may not be generalizable to other scenarios, (3) to analyze the impact of using different process discovery algorithms for generating the final model, and (4) to investigate further mechanisms to clean and enhance the UI log, e.g., identifying activities using screen-scraping algorithms.

Acknowledgments. This research has been supported by the Pololas project (TIN2016-76956-C3-2-R) of the Spanish Ministerio de Economía y Competitividad. Special thanks to Rafael Cabello from Serviform S.A. for providing his invaluable support and access to the case data.

References

1. IEEE standard for extensible event stream (XES) for achieving interoperability in event logs and event streams. IEEE Std 1849–2016, pp. 1–50 (2016)
2. van der Aalst, W.M.P.: Process Mining: Data Science in Action. Springer, Heidelberg (2016). https://doi.org/10.1007/978-3-662-49851-4
3. van der Aalst, W.M.P., Bichler, M., Heinzl, A.: Robotic process automation. Bus. Inf. Syst. Eng. **60**(4), 269–272 (2018)
4. van der Aalst, W.: Formalization and verification of event-driven process chains. Inf. Softw. Technol. **41**(10), 639–650 (1999)
5. Aguirre, S., Rodriguez, A.: Automation of a business process using robotic process automation (RPA): a case study. In: Figueroa-García, J.C., López-Santana, E.R., Villa-Ramírez, J.L., Ferro-Escobar, R. (eds.) WEA 2017. CCIS, vol. 742, pp. 65–71. Springer, Cham (2017). https://doi.org/10.1007/978-3-319-66963-2_7
6. Asatiani, A., Penttinen, E.: Turning robotic process automation into commercial success - case opuscapita. J. Inf. Technol. Teach. Cases **6**(2), 67–74 (2016)
7. Autoit (2018). https://www.autoitscript.com/site/autoit/. Accessed 1 Mar 2019
8. Cheng, H.J., Kumar, A.: Process mining on noisy logs - can log sanitization help to improve performance? Decis. Support. Syst. **79**, 138–149 (2015)
9. Conforti, R., La Rosa, M., ter Hofstede, A.H.: Noise filtering of process execution logs based on outliers detection (2015)
10. Dev, H., Liu, Z.: Identifying frequent user tasks from application logs. In: Proceedings of the 22nd International Conference on Intelligent User Interfaces, pp. 263–273 (2017)

11. Dumais, S., Jeffries, R., Russell, D.M., Tang, D., Teevan, J.: Understanding user behavior through log data and analysis. In: Olson, J.S., Kellogg, W.A. (eds.) Ways of Knowing in HCI, pp. 349–372. Springer, New York (2014). https://doi.org/10.1007/978-1-4939-0378-8_14

12. Fung, H.P.: Criteria, use cases and effects of information technology process automation (ITPA). Adv. Robot. Autom. **3**(3), 1–10 (2014)

13. Geyer-Klingeberg, J., Nakladal, J., Baldauf, F., Veit, F.: Process mining and robotic process automation: a perfect match. In: International Conference on Business Process Management, pp. 1–8 (2018)

14. Gusfield, D.: Algorithms on Strings, Trees, and Sequences: Computer Science and Computational Biology. Cambridge University Press, Cambridge (1999)

15. Le Clair, C.: Digitization Leaders Share Robotic Process Automation Best Practices. Forrester Research Inc., Cambridge (2016)

16. Leno, V., Dumas, M., Maggi, F.M., La Rosa, M.: Multi-perspective process model discovery for robotic process automation. CEUR Work. Proc. **2114**, 37–45 (2018)

17. Leopold, H., van der Aa, H., Reijers, H.A.: Identifying candidate tasks for robotic process automation in textual process descriptions. In: Gulden, J., Reinhartz-Berger, I., Schmidt, R., Guerreiro, S., Guédria, W., Bera, P. (eds.) BPMDS/EMMSAD -2018. LNBIP, vol. 318, pp. 67–81. Springer, Cham (2018). https://doi.org/10.1007/978-3-319-91704-7_5

18. Linn, C., Zimmermann, P., Werth, D.: Desktop activity mining - a new level of detail in mining business processes. In: Workshops der INFORMATIK 2018 - Architekturen, Prozesse, Sicherheit und Nachhaltigkeit, pp. 245–258 (2018)

19. Marrella, A., Catarci, T.: Measuring the learnability of interactive systems using a petri net based approach. In: Proceedings of the 2018 Designing Interactive Systems Conference, pp. 1309–1319. ACM (2018)

20. Mǎruşter, L., Weijters, A.T., Van Der Aalst, W.M., Van Den Bosch, A.: A rule-based approach for process discovery: dealing with noise and imbalance in process logs. Data Min. Knowl. Discov. **13**(1), 67–87 (2006)

21. Rosa, M.L., Dumas, M., Uba, R., Dijkman, R.M.: Business process model merging: an approach to business process consolidation. ACM Trans. Softw. Eng. Methodol. (TOSEM) **22**, 11 (2012)

22. Slaby, J.R.: Robotic automation emerges as a threat to traditional low-cost outsourcing. Horses for Sources (2018)

23. Spring cloud (2018). https://spring.io/projects/spring-cloud. Accessed 1 Mar 2019

24. Suriadi, S., Andrews, R., ter Hofstede, A.H., Wynn, M.T.: Event log imperfection patterns for process mining: towards a systematic approach to cleaning event logs. Inf. Syst. **64**, 132–150 (2017)

25. Uipath (2018). http://www.uipath.com. Accessed 1 Mar 2019

26. Wang, G., Zhang, X., Tang, S., Zheng, H., Zhao, B.Y.: Unsupervised clickstream clustering for user behavior analysis. In: Proceedings of the 2016 CHI Conference on Human Factors in Computing Systems, pp. 225–236. ACM (2016)

27. Willcocks, L., Lacity, M., Craig, A.: Robotic process automation: strategic transformation lever for global business services? J. Inf. Technol. Teach. Cases **7**(1), 17–28 (2017)

28. Wong, C., Bern, M.W., Goldberg, D.: An image signature for any kind of image. In: International Conference on Image Processing, pp. 409–412 (2002)

29. Workfusion (2018). http://www.workfusion.com. Accessed 1 Mar 2019

Generation and Transformation of Compliant Process Collaboration Models to BPMN

Frederik Bischoff[1], Walid Fdhila[2], and Stefanie Rinderle-Ma[3(✉)]

[1] Cronn GmbH, Bonn, Germany
[2] SBA-Research, Vienna, Austria
[3] Faculty of Computer Science, University of Vienna, Vienna, Austria
stefanie.rinderle-ma@univie.ac.at

Abstract. Collaboration is a key factor to successful businesses. To face massive competition in which SMEs compete with well established corporates, organizations tend to focus on their core businesses while delegating other tasks to their partners. Lately, Blockchain technology has yet furthered and eased the way companies collaborate in a trust-less environment. As such, interest in researching process collaborations models and techniques has been growing. However, in contrast to BPM research for intra-organizational processes, where a multitude of process models repositories exist as a support for simulation and work evaluation, the lack of such repositories in the context of inter-organizational processes has become an inconvenience. The aim of this paper is to build a repository of collaborative process models that will assist the research in this area. A top-down approach is used to automatically generate constrained and compliant choreography models, from which public and private process models are derived. Though the generation is partly random, it complies to a predefined set of compliance rules and parameters specified by the user.

Keywords: Process collaboration · Process models · Compliance rules

1 Introduction

Digitalization, blockchain and Industry 4.0 have created an environment in which organizations cooperate with more ease and efficiency. This open environment enabled Small and Medium Enterprises (SMEs) to collaborate more efficiently and compete with more established organizations. Therefore, research in process collaborations has become primordial [9]. Academic and industrial research include standards, infrastructure, and solutions that range from management and modeling of process collaborations, to enabling monitoring and improving security, compliance and privacy in such constellation [7]. However, in contrast to Business Process Management (BPM) research for intra-organizational processes where repositories of process models exist to support simulation and evaluation

© Springer Nature Switzerland AG 2019
P. Giorgini and B. Weber (Eds.): CAiSE 2019, LNCS 11483, pp. 462–478, 2019.
https://doi.org/10.1007/978-3-030-21290-2_29

of research techniques [13], such repositories (synthetic and real-world models) are entirely missing in the context of inter-organizational processes.

This paper provides a parametric framework to build a repository of process collaboration models which would serve for testing and evaluating research approaches. As real world models are hard to obtain due to privacy issues, this framework generates synthetic models, whose execution can result in distributed logs of synthetic data useful for mining techniques. The generation must ensure the consistency, compatibility and compliability of such models [7]. A set of compliance rules that follow specific patterns could be specified along with a set of parameters regarding the number or type of tasks or gateways per model. The approach follows a top-dow approach where a compliable choreography model is generated, from which public and private processes are derived. Such models are internally represented as Refined Process Structure Tree (RPST) [17], which are transformed into BPMN models to ensure their executability. The resulted repository could be used to support research simulation such as change propagation [6], compliance checking [7] or mining [1] of collaborative processes.

The paper is structured as follows. In Sect. 2 , fundamentals of process collaborations are presented. Section 3 elaborates the conceptual approach that is implemented in Sect. 4. In Sect. 5 related approaches are discussed in Sect. 6 the paper concludes.

2   Fundamentals

In an inter-organization setting, partners combine their core businesses to provide an added value service, dynamically or statically, at runtime or design time respectively [14]. Process collaborations comprise different but overlapping models [6]. A **private model** describes the internal logic of a partner including its *private activities* and *interactions*. *Private activities* are tasks that are not visible to other participants. In the private model of Fig. 1(a), *Check Inventory* is a private activity, whereas *Receive Order* involves message exchange with another participant and therefore is an interaction. A **public model** is a restricted view on the private model, and shows all *interactions* of one single partner. Private activities which are not relevant for other partners are omitted deliberately. Public activities might also be non-interaction tasks made visible to partners [4,5]. In this paper, public activities are solely interactions but can easily be extended through model enriching. Figure 1(b) presents the public model of the *distributor* process. A **collaboration model** is the interconnection of all participants public models. In BPMN, participants are represented as pools that contain their corresponding public models and the message exchanges as arrows that connect them. Figure 1(c) shows an example of a collaboration model. A **Choreography model** represents a high level view on the sequencing of all interactions between the involved partners. Each message exchange is represented as an interaction (i.e, choreography activity) with an initiating partner, a receiving partner (shaded in grey) and the message exchanged (c.f. Fig. 1(d)).

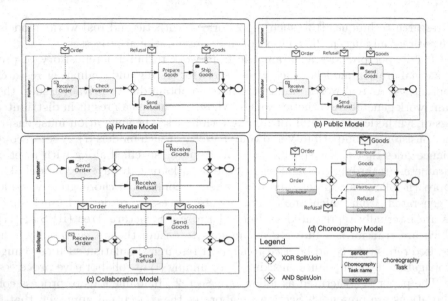

Fig. 1. Choreography model example

In collaborative processes, there are different level of correctness within and across the models [7,11]. **Consistency** means that the private model is consistent with its corresponding public model. **Compatibility** involves the collaboration model and ensures that the public models are compatible with each others. This means that there exist no flaws in the communication between participants (e.g., deadlocks, livelocks). While behavioral compatibility focuses on the correctness of behavioral dependencies between participants (i.e., control flow), structural compatibility requires that for every message that may be sent, the corresponding participant is able to receive it. We also distinguish between three types of compliance: (i) global compliance rules (GCR) that constrain the choreography model, (ii) local compliance rules (LCR), which constrain the private model of a particular participant but not visible to other partners, and finally (iii) assertions, which are agreements between two or more partners, where a partner guarantees that its private/public process complies with the constraint [7]. **Compliability** ensures that a choreography model does not conflict with GCRs [7]. As the aim of the paper is to produce collaborative models that comply with pre-specified GCRs, then the generation should ensure the correctness of the resulted models with respect to the aforementioned aspects. Compliance patterns supported in this work will be discussed in Sect. 3.1.

3   Model Generation and Transformation to BPMN

3.1   Parametrization and Compliance Specification

The process collaboration generator conceptualized in this work generates all four different model types and follows a *top-down approach* [7]. In a *top-down*

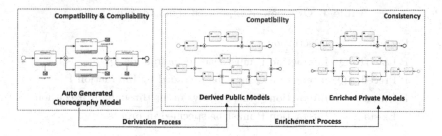

Fig. 2. Top-Down approach

approach (cf. Fig. 2), first the choreography model is build, then the public and private models of each partner are derived and defined consistently. Thereby, each interaction (choreography task) of the choreography model is converted into a send and receive tasks in the corresponding public process models. In turn, each private model is derived from its corresponding public model by enriching the latter with abstract private tasks. The collaboration model is build by interconnecting all public models. As depicted in Fig. 2, during model generation, all the aforementioned correctness criteria are considered. In particular, the approach ensures that only model specific flow objects are used to build the processes and that they are connected appropriately (structural compatibility). It also guarantees the absence of deadlocks and livelocks (behavioral compatibility) and offers the possibility to define global compliance rules GCR, to which the generated collaboration should comply (compliability). Deriving public models from a choreography model offers the advantage that if the latter is implemented correctly, the *compatibility* of the derived public models is automatically ensured.

Constraining the Collaboration. Despite the premise that the process collaborations should be generated randomly, it is reasonable to set some boundaries within which the random generation takes place. The implemented generator provides two different ways to influence the resulting choreography model and hence the whole collaboration. The first one provides the possibility to constrain the choreography model in terms of the employed flow objects and their exact quantity by specifying several input parameters. The second one enables the user to impose global compliance rules based on compliance patterns to which the resulting model must comply.

Parametric Constraints. The following input parameters are specified to influence the random generation of the choreography model and subsequently the derived models:

- Number of partners: determines the number of collaboration participants.
- Number of interactions: determines the number of messages exchanges.
- Number of exclusive gateways per model.
- Number of parallel gateways per model.

Table 1. Overview of supported compliance patterns

Pattern	Description
P LeadsTo Q	Interaction P must lead to Interaction Q
P Precedes Q	Interaction Q must be preceded by Interaction P
P Universal	Interaction P must always occur throughout execution
P Exists	Interaction P must be specified in process

– Maximum branching: determines the maximum possible number of paths created for each gateway.

Compliance Constraints. To specify GCRs, the pattern-based approach is utilized [16]. In [16], a repository of *process control patterns* is introduced, which are high-level templates used to represent process properties which the process specification must satisfy. In this work, only compliance rules that constrain the sequence and occurrence of interactions are considered. Compliance patterns that involve data, time and resource perspectives are future work. Table 1 summarizes the supported compliance patterns. Note that the *P LeadsTo Q* pattern does not imply immediate succession of interaction Q to interaction P.

3.2 Process Collaboration Generation

The generation of compliant collaboration processes follows the principle *'first build then check'*, which means that after a random choreography model has been generated, it will then be checked whether the interactions defined within the compliance rules can be assigned to the already built model in such a way that the resulting interaction sequence complies to the imposed rules. If the interaction allocation is not possible without violating the compliance rules, new random models will be build until a compliant model has been generated. If the checking of the compliance rules fails repeatedly, it's an indicator that the amount of interactions in the model is too small in comparison to those specified within the compliance rules. To overcome this, the number of interactions might be increased by the user. After a successful assignment of the compliance rules, the remaining public and private models are derived out of the generated choreography model. At last, all models will be translated into a valid BMPN/XML. Algorithm 1 illustrates the generation process of process collaborations, with all major steps explained in the following subsections.

Random Choreography Model Generation. Throughout the generation process, it is essential to keep track of the current model state at every point to ensure structural and behavioral correctness. Therefore a *Model Tracking* component is necessary, which provides control flow logic and a corresponding data

---

Algorithm 1. Overall Collaboration Generation Controller

```
 1  buildSuccess = false;
 2  while buildSuccess ≠ true do
 3      Generate Random Choreography Model;
 4      if compliance rules are defined then
 5          Compliance Rules Assignment;
 6          if assignment successful then
 7              buildSuccess = true;
 8          else if number of interaction mod increase_percentage ≡ 0 then
 9              increase number of interactions by factor increase_factor;
10          end
11      else
12          buildSuccess = true;
13      end
14  end
15  Derive Public and Private Models;
16  Transform Models to BPMN;
```

---

model, and uses graph decomposition concept using RPST [17] to ensure structured process models. In [17], a parsing algorithm for *two-terminal graphs*[1] is introduced that results in a unique graph decomposition represented as a hierarchical tree of *modular* and *objective fragments*. In the *Model Tracking* component of this work, the equivalent of a modular and objective fragment is called a *split*. A split is created for each gateway fork that is put into the model. Each split contains several *branches* that represent the different paths created by a parallel or exclusive gateway. Again, each branch holds the set of nodes that are on the path of a particular branch, whereas a path and therefore a split is limited by the merge node of its corresponding fork gateway node. In terms of a choreography model, nodes are limited to interactions and gateways. Figure 3 illustrates the concept of the *Model Tracking* component. There exist three splits with the split nodes: start event (blue), exclusive gateway#1 (red) and parallel gateway #1 (green). The split with the start event as the split node and the end event as the merge node has always only one branch, the root branch. Technically, this is not a split in the sense of the terminology. But because of the underlying control flow logic and data model that defines that every branch must be related to a split, this pseudo-split is necessary to keep track of the root branch. Note that branches and therefore also splits, contain other splits, e.g. split #2 contains split #3 in branch #3. Additionally, each branch has a status, which indicates whether the branch is *open, split* or *closed. Open* defines that the branch is not yet enclosed by the merge node of its corresponding split node and can further evolve by putting more nodes on its path. *Closed* means that the branch is finalized and can not further evolve. Within the *Model Tracking* component, a branch gets closed by putting the corresponding gateway merge node to the parent's branch and marking the branch as closed. A branch can also be in *split* state if it contains another split and none of this split branches are yet closed, thus there exists no merge node for this split. In this case, a branch cannot evolve

---

[1] A directed graph that has a unique source node s and a unique sink node $t \neq s$ with all other nodes V are on a path from s to t.

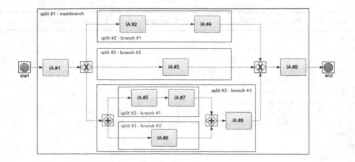

Fig. 3. Model tracking component - concept (Color figure online)

until one of it's child split's branches is in state *closed* and a merge node is placed on the branch. Then, the state changes to *open*. When closing a branch, first it is necessary to determine if a branch is allowed to be closed without violating the correctness of the choreography models. This depends on the split node type of the branch. The premise is that if the split node type is a parallel gateway, the branch is determined as *closable* only if there is an interaction on all its enclosed paths. This means, that if a branch has a child split, it does not necessary imply that an interaction is on the parent branch, but might be on the branches of its child split or even on a deeper nested branch.

Tracking branches status is crucial for satisfying structural and behavioral correctness. Because of the parametric limitation on the number of interactions in the build process or even directly at the beginning, interactions are not always allowed to be selected as next node type. Similarly, not every open branch is allowed to be randomly selected for putting the next node into the model as this might violate the correctness of the model or exceeding the number of defined interactions. In order to determine whether this situation applies to a current build state, the *Model Tracking* component monitors the amount of *free* and *reserved interactions*. Reserved interactions are a subset of the remaining interaction that have either predetermined positions in the current model (resInteractionBranches) or will be needed in further paths created by not yet employed gateways (resInteractionsGateways). The exact amount of these reserved interactions depends on the number of non-closable branches of the current model and the number of gateways that are not yet put into model. Free interactions are interactions which are not yet used nor reserved for the model.

Definition 1. *Let x be the number of branches which are open and non-closable, remainingInteractions be all interactions not yet put into the model and remainingXOR and remainingAND the number of gateways not yet put into the model. Then,* resInteractionBranches $= x$

resInteractionAndGateways $= remainingAND + 1$

resInteractionXORGateways $= If\ remainingAND > 0\ Then\ 0\ Else\ 1$

resInteractionGateways $= resInteractionAndGateways$

$$+resInteractionXORGateways$$

$$resInteractionsTotal = resInteractionBranches + resInteractionGateways$$
$$freeInteractions = remainingInteractions - resInteractionsTotal$$

Regarding the current model, each open and non closable branch increases the amount of *resInteractionBranches* by one. Parallel gateways that are not yet placed into the model will later create at least two new branches, which then again need at least one interaction on each of it's paths. Considering that a gateway node is allowed to be immediately followed by another gateway node without an interaction in between, the minimum amount of *resInteractionAndGateways* is *remainingAndGateways* + 1. This premise also influences the impact of remaining exclusive gateways on the number of *resInteractionsGateways*. Each remaining exclusive gateways only increases the number of *resInteractionsGateways* by 1 if there is no more remaining parallel gateways. Indeed, if there exist a remaining parallel gateway, the exclusive gateway could be put on a branch of the parallel gateway directly after the split, and therefore the one needed interaction of the exclusive gateway is already considered in the calculation of *resInteractionAndGateways*. After the amount of *reserved interactions* is calculated, the number of *free interactions* is determined by the difference between the amount of *remaining interactions* and the number of *reserved interactions*. Based on the values of the specified variables defined in Definition 1, the node type of the next node to be put in the model and the corresponding position can be randomly selected without resulting in an incorrect model. For example, if the amount of *free interactions* is less than 1, the random branch selection (position in the model) for putting the next node is limited to the branches that are not yet closable. On the other hand, if the amount of *free interactions* is superior to 0, then all open branches can be selected for putting the next node. When selecting the next possible node type, interactions are only allowed to be randomly chosen if the amount of *free interactions* is superior to 0 or not all remaining interactions are reserved by not yet consumed gateways.

The overall procedure for generating random choreography models is shown in Algorithm 2. Note that the step of random branch closing is necessary to obtain balanced choreography models with respect to nested branches. If there would be no random branch closing mechanism, the resulting models would be very similar. A mechanism that closes branches whenever they are closable would only result in models with lesser nested branches whereas a mechanism that never closes branches would result in models that have highly nested branching. By the time a branch is not randomly closed, a node of the predefined node type gets instantiated. In case of an interaction, only the plain object without any sender, receiver or message gets instantiated. Is the selected node type a gateway, the number of branches is determined by randomly selecting a number between 2 and the current maximum branching amount. The maximum branching amount is generally limited by the user specified max branching parameter. But again, due to the limitation of interactions, the specified maximum amount of branches can not be adducted as the upper border without considering the current amount of free interactions. The possible upper limit is determined dynamically each time

---

Algorithm 2. Generate Choreography Model

```
 1  begin
 2  │    while remainingInteractions > 0 do
 3  │    │    nextNodeType ← getRandomNodeType()
 4  │    │    selectedBranch ← getRandomBranch()
 5  │    │    if selectedBranch is closable then
 6  │    │    │    close branch by random
 7  │    │    │    if closed then
 8  │    │    │    │    continue
 9  │    │    │    end
10  │    │    else
11  │    │    │    nextNode ← instantiate node of nextNodeType
12  │    │    │    if nextNodeType is Gateway then
13  │    │    │    │    branchCount ← getRandomBranchCount()
14  │    │    │    │    split ← instantiate new split
15  │    │    │    │    for i ← 0 to branchCount do
16  │    │    │    │    │    branch ← instantiate new branch
17  │    │    │    │    │    split.branches ← branch
18  │    │    │    │    │    i ← i + 1
19  │    │    │    │    end
20  │    │    │    end
21  │    │    │    selectedBranch.nodes ← selectedBranch.nodes ∪ nextNode
22  │    │    │    decrease remainingNodes of nextNodeType
23  │    │    end
24  │    end
25  │    close still open splits
26  │    add end event to root branch
27  │    enrich interactions with reasonable sender and receiver sequence
28  end
```

---

a gateway node is put into the model by taking the minimum branching amount, which is always two, and adding the amount of free interactions.

After a random number of branches is determined, the gateway node is added to the assigned branch and the corresponding split and branches are instantiated within *Model Tracking*. Finally, the amount of the selected node type is decreased by one and the loop starts over by selecting a random node type for the next node to be put into the model. To achieve behavioral correctness in choreography models, beside a correct sequence flow, a message flow must be incorporated. Therefore, a sender and receiver must be assigned to each interaction in order to form a valid sender-receiver sequence. Thereby, the sender of a succeeding interaction Q must always be either the sender or receiver of the directly preceding interaction P on the path. If this rule is not considered and the sender of a directly succeeding interaction Q is neither the sending nor the receiving participant of the directly preceding interaction P, a flawless execution of the process is not possible, because the sender of interaction Q will never know if the directly preceding interaction P has been performed yet. For gateways, it is additionally ensured that all branches of that split terminate with interactions that have the same participant in common. This helps to determine a possible sender for the succeeding interaction after the merge. Note that because the sequence flow is first build without considering the corresponding message flow, it is likely that at some points, an additional interaction must be inserted into the model to satisfy the above stated rules of sender-receiver sequences.

Compliance Rules Assignment. Instead of considering the imposed compliance rules during the generation, a *first build then check* approach was favored to allow users to specify compliance rules, which can be applied to existing choreography models to check if the latter complies to them. When specifying global compliance rules, it must be checked whether the imposed rules are consistent with one another. In the context of the four supported patterns, this applies only to the the the patterns 'LeadsTo' and 'Precedes'. For instance, consider the following set of compliance rules: {**C1**: P LeadsTo Q, **C2**: Q LeadsTo S **C3**: S Precedes P}. In this example, the rules *C1* and *C2* conflict with *C3* because *C1* and *C2* imply that the involved activities must occur in the order P-Q-S, whereas in *C3*, S must occur before P. Algorithm 3 shows the conflict checking procedure. The result of this procedure is a set of conflict free compliance rules, which determines a specific order sequence between the involved interactions. The specific interactions of the compliance rules are then eventually assigned to the existing interactions within the previously generated model in a way that it complies to the interaction order and the compliance rules. Therefore, the first step is to determine all possible positions within the model for each compliance rule. The result is a set of possible position combinations (interactions placed in the model during initial choreography generation) for the compliance rule specified for Interactions P and Q. For each possible position of P there has to be at least one possible position for Q. The rules that determine applicable positions for the four implemented compliance patterns are shown in Definitions 2–5.

Definition 2. *Possible position assignments for the interactions P and Q of a compliance pattern P LeadsTo Q are as follows.*

- *Interaction P should have reachable interactions on its subsequent paths.*
- *Interaction Q should be reachable if Interaction P has been reached.*

Definition 3. *Possible position assignments for the interactions P and Q of a compliance pattern P Precedes Q are as follows.*

- *Interaction P is always reached prior to Interaction Q.*
- *Interaction Q has interactions on its preceding path that are always reached prior to Interaction Q.*

Definition 4. *Possible position assignments for the interaction P of a compliance pattern P Universal are as follows.*

- *Interaction P = An interaction that will always be reached.*

Definition 5. *Possible position assignments for the interaction P of a compliance pattern P Exists are as follows.*

- *Interaction P = An interaction that can be reached.*

Algorithm 3. Adding Compliance Rules

```
    Input  : compliance rule cr
             dictionary orderDependencies of Interactions P and their succeeding Interactions S
 1  begin
 2    if cr is order pattern then
 3        p ← preceding interaction of cr
 4        s ← succeeding interaction of cr
 5        if !orderConflictCheck(p, s) then
 6            add cr to complianceRules
 7            if p ∈ P of orderDependencies then
 8            |   add s to succeeding interactions S of p
 9            else
10            |   add p to orderDependencies
11            |   add s to succeeding interactions S of p
12            end
13        else
14        |   add cr to conflictedRules
15        end
16    end
17  end
18  Function orderConflictCheck(p, s)
19    if s ∈ P of orderDependencies then
20        foreach s ∈ S of p do
21            if s == p then
22            |   return true
23            else if orderConflictCheck(s, p) then
24            |   return true
25        end
26    else
27    |   return false
28    end
```

If the interactions used for specifying the rules are disjoint between all the compliance rules, the sets of assignment combinations are already sufficient to assign the involved interactions to positions that result in a model that is compliant with the opposed rules. But if there are particular interactions that are used in more than one compliance rule specification, the intersection of the interaction's possible assignments of all involved compliance rules represents the set of possible assignments for this particular interaction. The assignment procedure iterates over the interaction order and for each interaction, the intersection of the possible assignments of all affected compliance rules is calculated. Is the current interaction specified as the succeeding interaction of an affected order compliance rule, the possible model positions of this rule are limited to the succeeding model positions of the corresponding, already assigned, preceding interaction. Is the resulting intersection of the sets of possible assignments empty, then there is no valid position in the model where the interaction could be assigned to. In this case, the whole assignment process fails and results in a failed choreography build process. Is the intersection of possible model positions not empty, the procedure choses the interaction that has the most interactions on it's succeeding path. This ensures, that the assignment process does not fail because of higher ranked interactions being assigned to positions at the end of the model, so that there are no valid positions left for lower ranked ones.

Algorithm 4. Transform Private and Public Model to BPMN

```
    Input  : edges ← edges of RPST
             collaboration ← internal collaboration representation
 1  begin
 2  │   xmlDoc ← initialize BPMN XML collaboration document
 3  │   foreach edge ∈ edges do
 4  │   │   nodes ← edge.getSource() ∧ edge.getTarget()
 5  │   │   sequenceFlows ← create new sequenceFlow XML-Element for edge
 6  │   │   foreach node ∈ nodes do
 7  │   │   │   if node == SendTask then
 8  │   │   │   │   processNodes ← create new sendTask XML-Element
 9  │   │   │   │   messages ← create new message XML-Element
10  │   │   │   │   messageFlows ← create new messageFlow XML-Element
11  │   │   │   else if node == ReceiveTask then
12  │   │   │   │   processNodes ← create new receiveTask XML-Element
13  │   │   │   │   messages ← create new message XML-Element
14  │   │   │   │   messageFlows ← create new messageFlow XML-Element
15  │   │   │   else if node == PrivateActivity then
16  │   │   │   │   processNodes ← create new task XML-Element
17  │   │   │   else if node == ParalellGateway then
18  │   │   │   │   processNodes ← create new paralellGateway XML-Element
19  │   │   │   else if node == ExclusiveGateway then
20  │   │   │   │   processNodes ← create new exclusiveGateway XML-Element
21  │   │   │   else if node == Event then
22  │   │   │   │   if node == startEvent then
23  │   │   │   │   │   processNodes ← create new startEvent XML-Element
24  │   │   │   │   else
25  │   │   │   │   │   processNodes ← create new endEvent XML-Element
26  │   │   │   │   end
27  │   │   end
28  │   end
29  │   xmlDoc ← add sequenceFlows, processNodes, messages and messageFlows
30  │   Export xmlDoc
31  end
```

Deriving the Collaboration Models. In the process of deriving the models, each interaction of the choreography model results in a send and receive task in the corresponding public models of the involved partners. For an interaction, in the initiating and receiving participant public models, a send task and a corresponding receiving tasks are inserted respectively. Additionally, for each public model, a reduction of the model's sequence flow is enabled, without violating the choreography model sequence flow. Thereby, each gateway of the choreography model is checked for interactions within its subsequent paths involving the current participant. If there are none, the gateway and it's subsequent paths are not put into the public model of this participant. In order to derive the private models from the public models, the public models are randomly enriched with private tasks as well as some additional sequence flow elements (gateways) without violating the predefined sequence flow. The public models are used as a basis for private models, which then enriched with private tasks.

3.3 BPMN Transformation

In order to translate the RPST representation of the models to BPMN/XML, the internal model elements for events, tasks, gateways, edges and participants must be mapped to the corresponding BPMN elements of the different model types. Therefore the procedure loops recursively through all the graphs edges, extracts all the necessary information from the fragments (source, target) and generates the corresponding BPMN elements. In Algorithm 4, the procedure for transforming private and public models is outlined. As input serves the RPST and the internal collaboration representation, which includes necessary informations about the public task relationships. Collaboration, public and private models share the same XML structure, which is initialized in the first step (initialize BPMN XML collaboration document). In collaboration models all participant public models are described, whereas the public models only contain the described process of one participant and only a black box process for the others, which is necessary for referencing to public activities. When creating public activity elements (send/receive task), the necessary partner references are available in the internal collaboration model representation.

4   Implementation

The presented work was implemented and integrated within the C3Pro framework[2] [6]. The latter provides techniques for defining, propagating and negotiating changes in the context of collaborative processes. The framework already provides functionalities for importing and transforming BPMN process models into RPST representation (but not vice versa) and calculating change effects on the different models. The current work complements the framework by automatically generating repositories of collaborative models that would serve as a testbed for assessing and simulating change propagation techniques. As this work also supports the specification of compliance rules to which the generated models should comply, the resulted repository is also being used for evaluating approaches for compliance checking in the context of process collaborations. Even though the implementation is integrated within the C3Pro framework, it still represents an independent component that could be used for several research purposes; e.g., faults prediction [2], mining. The component for transforming RPST models to BPMN enables their simulation and executability.

Figure 4 represents a simplified class structure of the implemented components, that are necessary for generating process collaborations, starting with the generation of the Choreography Model that complies to imposed compliance rules, leading to deriving the public, private as well as the collaboration models, and finishing with the translation to BPMN/XML. The numbers indicate the order in which the components are instantiated.

The logic of coordinating the entire generation process (see Algorithm 1) is implemented in the *Collaboration Generation Controller* component. The *Choreography Model Generator* comprises the algorithm for generating random models (see Algorithm 2). Thereby it utilizes the *Model Tracking* component constantly, which represents the actual model and provides the necessary functionalities to ensure the correctness of the resulting model. The introduced logic of specifying

---

[2] Source code available at: http://gruppe.wst.univie.ac.at/c3pro/repo.zip.

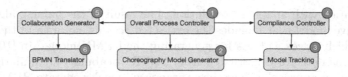

Fig. 4. Prototype architecture

and imposing GCRs is implemented within the *Compliance Controller* component. It also utilizes the same instance of the *Model Tracking* class in order to find possible assignments for the imposed interaction order. The *Collaboration Generator* provides the functionalities of deriving the public and private models from the generated choreography model. At last, the translation of the internal model representation to BPMN, is encapsulated within the *BPMN Translator* component (see Algorithm 4). The prototype has been tested and already served as input for research on change propagation and compliance checking in collaborative processes. The execution of generated BPMN models[3] might be automated to enable logging and process collaborations mining. Models were generated to test the influence of the parameters "number of parallel/exclusive gateways" and "maximum branching" on the effort for model generation (without compliance rules) and the interrelation of number of imposed compliance rules, gateways, and successful generation of models.

Results and lessons learnt: The time to generate the models increases linearly with the number of gateways, independently whether parallel or exclusive gateways are used. The same holds for the "maximum" branching parameter. The reason is that the number of branches in the generated models increase and hence the algorithm has to check for more branches when creating the models. The number of parallel gateways does not influence the success of model generation for any number of compliance rules (1–100 compliance rules were tested). The existence of exclusive gateways greatly influences the model generation success; independently of the number of compliance rules (in the simulation 1–100) 76% of the model generations fail. Another simulation run tested the number of successful model generations depending on the number of exclusive gateways (for 60 compliance rules). For 0 and 1 exclusive gateways 100% of the generations are successful. The number of successful generations then drops in an inverse exponential way; for more than 50 exclusive gateways no generation attempt is successful anymore. Here also the effect of compliance rules that are depending on each other and hence impose strict sequence order on the models kicks in.

5   Related Works

Several research methods have been proposed, which generate process models from natural language text [8,10]. In [8], BPMN models are produced from natural language texts by utilizing syntax parsing and semantic analyzing mechanism

---

[3] Data available at: http://gruppe.wst.univie.ac.at/c3pro/data.zip.

in combination with anaphora resolution. The result of the parsing algorithm is a declarative model that includes the extracted actions, actors and their dependencies, which serves as basis for generating the BPMN model. In [10], BPMN and DMN models are constructed from SBVR vocabulary[4]. Similarly, several transformation approaches have been proposed, which generate BPMN models from existing UML use cases [12,19] or sequence diagrams [15].

In comparison to this work, the aforementioned approaches require the original specification as text or UML diagram to generate the business models. This is limited by the availability of such resources, and also do not deal with compliance constructs or choreography models.

In [18], process models are generated using semi-structured information about process activities along with their execution conditions. This specification is then formalized as a constraint satisfaction problem (CSP) and fed to a constraint solver that generates synthetic execution logs, which in turn, serve as input for process mining techniques. This again, requires a data collection phase, in which participants have to provide valid specifications to be merged. Also, it does not deal with choreography models nor differentiate between public or private models. In [3], BPMN process models are generated randomly. In contrast to this work, the latter focuses on intra-organizational process models. It also supports user-defined parameters to influence the model outcome in terms of number of node types and degree of branching. In, [14] a bottom-up approach has been proposed, which combines existing private processes to build process collaborations using adaptors. This assumes the availability of such models and requires a preselection of the models that will be composed (e.g, consumer, provider). The approach does not support compliance rules and does not allow much control over the complexity of the output models (e.g., number of exclusive gateways).

6   Conclusion

This work provided an approach that generates repositories of constrained process collaborations while ensuring their correctness in terms of compatibility, consistency and compliability. Such repositories are useful for simulating and evaluating research works in the context of inter-organizational processes. The approach is implemented and the resulted repositories are already exploited for simulating change propagation, compliance checking and faults prediction in collaborative processes. Future work includes generating distributed logs for mining and considering more compliance patterns.

Acknowledgment. This work has been funded by the Vienna Science and Technology Fund (WWTF) through project ICT15-072 and COMET SBA-K1.

---

[4] Semantics of Business Vocabulary and Business Rules.

References

1. van der Aalst, W.M.P.: Process Mining: Discovery Conformance and Enhancement of Business Processes, 1st edn. Springer, Heidelberg (2011). https://doi.org/10.1007/978-3-642-19345-3
2. Borkowski, M., Fdhila, W., Nardelli, M., Rinderle-Ma, S., Schulte, S.: Event-based failure prediction in distributed business processes. Inf. Syst. **81**, 220–235 (2017)
3. Burattin, A.: PLG2: multiperspective process randomization with online and offline simulations. In: BPM Demo Track, pp. 1–6 (2016)
4. Cabanillas, C., Norta, A., Resinas, M., Mendling, J., Ruiz-Cortés, A.: Towards process-aware cross-organizational human resource management. In: Bider, I., et al. (eds.) BPMDS/EMMSAD -2014. LNBIP, vol. 175, pp. 79–93. Springer, Heidelberg (2014). https://doi.org/10.1007/978-3-662-43745-2_6
5. Eshuis, R., Norta, A., Kopp, O., Pitknen, E.: Service outsourcing with process views. IEEE Trans. Serv. Comput. **8**(1), 136–154 (2015). https://doi.org/10.1109/TSC.2013.51
6. Fdhila, W., Indiono, C., Rinderle-Ma, S., Reichert, M.: Dealing with change in process choreographies: design and implementation of propagation algorithms. Inf. Syst. **49**, 1–24 (2015)
7. Fdhila, W., Rinderle-Ma, S., Knuplesch, D., Reichert, M.: Change and compliance in collaborative processes. In: SCC, pp. 162–169 (2015)
8. Friedrich, F., Mendling, J., Puhlmann, F.: Process model generation from natural language text. In: Mouratidis, H., Rolland, C. (eds.) CAiSE 2011. LNCS, vol. 6741, pp. 482–496. Springer, Heidelberg (2011). https://doi.org/10.1007/978-3-642-21640-4_36
9. Grefen, P., Rinderle, S., Dustdar, S., Fdhila, W., Mendling, J., Schulte, S.: Charting process-based collaboration support in agile business networks. IEEE Internet Comput. 1 (2018). https://doi.org/10.1109/MIC.2017.265102547
10. Kluza, K., Honkisz, K.: From SBVR to BPMN and DMN Models. Proposal of translation from rules to process and decision models. In: Rutkowski, L., Korytkowski, M., Scherer, R., Tadeusiewicz, R., Zadeh, L.A., Zurada, J.M. (eds.) ICAISC 2016. LNCS (LNAI), vol. 9693, pp. 453–462. Springer, Cham (2016). https://doi.org/10.1007/978-3-319-39384-1_39
11. Knuplesch, D., Reichert, M., Fdhila, W., Rinderle-Ma, S.: On enabling compliance of cross-organizational business processes. In: Daniel, F., Wang, J., Weber, B. (eds.) BPM 2013. LNCS, vol. 8094, pp. 146–154. Springer, Heidelberg (2013). https://doi.org/10.1007/978-3-642-40176-3_12
12. Lubke, D., Schneider, K., Weidlich, M.: Visualizing use case sets as BPMN processes. In: 2008 Requirements Engineering Visualization, pp. 21–25 (2008)
13. Rosa, M.L., et al.: Apromore: an advanced process model repository. Expert Syst. Appl. **38**, 7029–7040 (2011)
14. Seguel, R., Eshuis, R., Grefen, P.W.P.J.: Architecture support for flexible business chain integration using protocol adaptors. Int. J. Coop. Inf. Syst. **23**, 1450008 (2014)
15. Suchenia (Mroczek), A., Kluza, K., Jobczyk, K., Wiśniewski, P., Wypych, M., Ligęza, A.: Supporting BPMN process models with UML sequence diagrams for representing time issues and testing models. In: Rutkowski, L., Korytkowski, M., Scherer, R., Tadeusiewicz, R., Zadeh, L.A., Zurada, J.M. (eds.) ICAISC 2017. LNCS (LNAI), vol. 10246, pp. 589–598. Springer, Cham (2017). https://doi.org/10.1007/978-3-319-59060-8_53

16. Turetken, O., Elgammal, A., van den Heuvel, W.J., Papazoglou, M.P.: Capturing compliance requirements: a pattern-based approach. IEEE Softw. **29**, 28–36 (2012)
17. Vanhatalo, J., Voelzer, H., Koehler, J.: The refined process structure tree. Data Knowl. Eng. **68**(9), 793–818 (2009)
18. Wisniewski, P., Kluza, K., Ligeza, A.: An approach to participatory business process modeling: BPMN model generation using constraint programming and graph composition. Appl. Sci. **8**(9), 1428 (2018)
19. Zafar, U., Bhuiyan, M., Prasad, P.W.C., Haque, F.: Integration of use case models and BPMN using goal- oriented requirements engineering. JCP **13**, 212–221 (2018)

GameOfFlows: Process Instance Adaptation in Complex, Dynamic and Potentially Adversarial Domains

Yingzhi Gou, Aditya Ghose$^{(\boxtimes)}$, and Hoa Khanh Dam

Decision Systems Lab, School of Computer Science and Software Engineering,
University of Wollongong, Wollongong, Australia
{yg452,aditya,hoa}@uow.edu.au

Abstract. Business processes often need to be executed in complex settings where a range of environmental factors can conspire to *impede* the execution of the process. Gou et al. [1] view process execution as an *adversarial game* between the *process player* and the *environment player*. While useful, their approach leaves open the question of the role of the original process design in the story. Process designs encode significant specialist knowledge and have significant investments in process infrastructure associated with them. We provide a machinery that involves careful deliberation on when and where to deviate from a process design. We conceive of a process engine that frequently (typically after executing each task) re-considers the next task or sequence of tasks to execute. It performs trade-off analysis by comparing the following: (1) the likelihood of successful completion by conforming to the mandated process design against (2) the likelihood of success if it were to deviate from the design by executing a *compensation* (i.e., an alternative sequence of tasks that takes the process from the current state to completion).

Keywords: Process execution · Compensation · Robustness · Adaptation

1 Introduction

It is generally recognized that business processes need to be executed in complex settings where a range of environmental factors can conspire to *impede* the execution of the process. The impediments thrown up by the environment can be deliberate or unintentional. The impediments might work to prevent the achievement of the functional goals of a process or its non-functional targets or key performance indicators. For example, an outsourced search for past buying behaviour of a customer in a credit check process might return no results, or results of a wrong customer, thus preventing the successful execution of an instance of this process. An automated process for maintaining the ambient temperature inside a building might be impeded by a non-functioning air-conditioner, by a faulty sensor that reports incorrect temperature reading, or by a heater that is turned

© Springer Nature Switzerland AG 2019
P. Giorgini and B. Weber (Eds.): CAiSE 2019, LNCS 11483, pp. 479–493, 2019.
https://doi.org/10.1007/978-3-030-21290-2_30

on by a person in a room who feels that the auto-maintained temperature is too low. A clinical process might have to face obstacles caused by a patient who forgets (or deliberately ignores) to ingest a prescribed pill left at his/her bedside by a nurse.

Gou et al. [1] present the first steps towards an approach that leverages game tree search techniques to enable process execution in such environments. They key idea is to view process execution as an *adversarial game* between the *process player* and the *environment player* (which encapsulates possibly many actual agents in the operating context of the process, including competitors, suppliers, customers, market regulators, legislative bodies and so on). They assume that in the worst case, the behaviour of the environment player will be *maximally adversarial*. In other words, they assume that the environment player will seek to make it as difficult as possible for the process player to execute a process to successful conclusion. They formulate the process execution problem as a two-player turn-taking game of perfect information. They show that game tree search techniques such as Minimax search and Monte Carlo Tree Search (MCTS) can be used to effectively compute workarounds to the adversarial behaviour of the environment player.

The question they leave open is the role of the original process design in the story. They propose machinery that can be consulted by the process engine at each step in process execution to answer the question: what is the best task (or sequence of tasks) to execute next? This is a critical shortcoming, since process designs represent the outcome of considerable careful deliberation, and encode significant domain knowledge and expert insight. Process designs often have significant investments in process infrastructure associated with them. Frequent and ad hoc deviations from process designs can render much of this investment pointless. Instead, they can require fresh (and often on-the-fly) investments in new infrastructure.

This paper addresses this gap. We provide a machinery that involves careful deliberation on when and where to deviate from a process design. We conceive of a process engine that frequently (typically after executing each task) re-considers the next task or sequence of tasks to execute. It performs trade-off analysis by comparing the following: (1) the likelihood of successful completion by conforming to the mandated process design against (2) the likelihood of success if it were to deviate from the design by executing a *compensation*, i.e., an alternative sequence of tasks that takes the process from the current state to completion (the term *compensation* describes how we compensate for some event that requires deviation from the mandated process design). To compute the likelihood of the current process design completing successfully (in the face of an adversarial environment player whose behaviour is captured in an *environment model*), we use Monte Carlo sampling of simulated executions of the process. To compute an alternative process compensation (and to compute the likelihood of success of that compensation), we use game tree search.

Traditional conceptions of process designs that rely on task IDs to represent information about the *effects* of the task are not easily amenable to the kinds of analysis that would reveal whether a given state of affairs impedes the achievement of process goals. Indeed, a conception of state is essential for any form of goal-oriented analysis. If we limit ourselves to process task IDs, then the only conception of state available to us would be in the form of sequences of tasks executed. Goals, on the other hand, are typically articulated in the form of states, or conditions that must hold. However, this analysis is significantly simpler if tasks are annotated with their expected and/or desired outcomes (i.e. post-conditions or effects). For instance, a given state of the environment, after a task, would impede the process if it negated any of the desired post-conditions. A large body of reported work leverages semantic annotation of business process designs [2–10]. A number of proposals also address the problem of semantic annotation of web services in a similar fashion [11–14]. Our framework, therefore, leverages semantically annotated process model (i.e., process models where each task is annotated with post-conditions).

Our approach is predicated on the following assumptions. We assume that the complex organizational context within which a business process is executed can be abstracted and modelled as a single *environment player*. We assume that the actions taken by this environment player can be sensed and recognized (i.e., the process player has a pre-existing vocabulary of the possible actions - and their post-conditions - that the environment player might take). The conception of *adversariality* that we use admits both *intentional* and *unintentional* adversariality. Adversarial actions of the environment player will be of the latter kind in most business process execution contexts. Modelling these as adversarial behaviour is nonetheless useful since they ultimately impede the successful execution of a process. *Uncertainty* about the behaviour of the environment plays an important role in this account but we need to deal with the uncertainty associated with actions leading to both positive and negative consequences for the process player (hence adversariality does not reduce to uncertainty).

The paper is structured as follows. Section 2 formalizes the process execution as a two-player game and describes how the execution outcomes of process instances are predicted and how instances are redesigned/compensated. Section 3 provides a detailed experimental implementation and evaluation. Section 4 discusses how our approach is compared with existing works while Sect. 5 provides concluding remarks.

2 Process Execution

The overall machinery for process execution operates as follows:

- At every step in the process, we perform Monte Carlo sampling to determine the likelihood that the process will execute to a goal-satisfying state. This involves a simulation (or symbolic execution) of the specified process design. In the spirit of turn-taking games, we assume that after the execution of every process task, the environment player makes a move. The *environment model* is a function that takes a state as input (the current state of the process and its operating context) and generates a set of states as output (each output state corresponding to a possible move by the environment player). Each ⟨*InputState, OutputState*⟩ pair is associated with a probability (these ultimately inform the computation of the probability of achieving a goal-satisfying state for the process instance). The *process player* learns by observation, continually updating these probabilities as more instances are executed.

- If this probability is below a user-specified threshold, the search for a *compensation*, i.e., an alternate suffix for the currently executed process instance is initiated. This involves game tree search, where the capabilities of the organization executing the process represent the moves the *process player* can make while the *environment model* determines the moves the environment player can make.
- This search of the space of adversarial moves helps us generate a *complete* or *partial compensation*. A complete compensation provides a complete suffix, i.e., the complete sequence of tasks to be executed to process completion. Since game tree search can be computationally complex, we often specify *depth cutoffs* (in the same spirit as what is done with games like chess and Go). In these settings, we obtain a partial compensation which tells what sequence of tasks to execute for part of the remainder of the process (since these steps are iterated over later process tasks, future calls to the game tree search module will give us progressively more complete compensations).
- We perform Monte Carlo sampling with the compensation thus computed to determine its likelihood of leading us to a goal-satisfying state (for trees with depth cutoffs, we apply a *heuristic evaluation function* as is standard practice for games like chess or Go.
- Ultimately, the goal of this exercise is to decide whether to conform to the process design, or whether to deploy a compensation as computed above.
- We repeat this procedure after every task in the process.

Definition 1 (The Decision Problem). *Given:*

- *A process model* $\mathcal{P}$
- *A capability library* $\mathcal{A}$ *for the organization (the* process player*) consisting of tasks with post-conditions.*
- *A set of* exogenous states, *i.e., states brought about by the environment player. By contrast,* endogenous states *are brought about via the execution of process tasks (including compensation tasks) by the process player. The* environment behaviour model $\mathcal{E}$ *is a function that takes as input the current state of the process and operating context and generates as output a set of pairs of the form* $\langle s', pr_{s,s'}$ *where* s' *is an exogenous state and* $pr_{s,s'}$ *is the probability that the environment player will bring about state* s' *when the current state of the process and its operating context is* s.
- *A set of goal states* G, *the achievement of any of which indicates successful process execution.*
- *The current state* $s_{observed}$ *of the process and its operating context.*

– *A state update operator $\oplus$ where $\oplus : S, \mathcal{A} \to S$ that updates the given state $s \in S$ to a new state $s' \in S$ to incorporate the post-conditions generated by executing an action $a \in \mathcal{A}$ in s.*

Compute:

1. *The probability p that the current process instance will reach a goal state by conforming to the current process model $\mathcal{P}$, and*
2. *An alternative process model $\mathcal{P}'$ (if one exists) such that from the current state, it has a probability $p' > p$ to reach a goal state.*

There are many realizations of the $\oplus$ operator in the literature on reasoning about action, such as the Possible Worlds Approach (or PWA) [15] (which takes the post-conditions of the most recent action plus as many assertions from the prior state description as can be consistently added to create the resulting state description, while bringing to bear a domain knowledge base while checking consistency). We use this in our experimental evaluation.

Brief Example: Consider a manufacturing process that needs to take into account the likelihood of equipment breakdowns/failure. At any point, the process execution machinery can choose to: (1) continue to execute the mandated manufacturing process, or (2) temporarily suspend the manufacturing process and perform maintenance activities or (3) order/install/replace new parts or new equipment. Options (2) and (3) admit further variations, such as scheduling maintenance after a certain time interval (as opposed to immediate maintenance) or scheduling the installation of replacement parts or equipment after a certain period of time. The GameOfFlows process engine would periodically (which could even be after every process step), reconsider the process design. Using failure probabilities for equipment and parts supplied by manufacturers, the engine would perform Monte Carlo sampling of the space of alternative completions of the process, with the transition probabilities in the environment model obtained from these manufacturer-supplied failure probabilities. It would adjust these transition probabilities in the environment model over time by observing actual equipment failure rates (which might be at variance with the manufacturer-supplied data). In computing compensations, it would have available the capabilities of the organization (the know-how, or the set of tasks the organization is capable of executing—this would include options (1), (2) and (3) above, as well as their variants). Depending on the results of the analysis we describe, the process engine might choose to continue following the task sequence specified in the process design, or deploy compensations which might involve the scheduling of preventative maintenance activities or the installation of replacement equipment.

In the following, we describe 2 key algorithms used by the GameOfFlows engine via examples: the algorithm for computing the likelihood of success using Monte Carlo sampling and the algorithm for computing compensations.

Monte Carlo Sampling Example: Consider an extension of the manufacturing process example above, shown in Fig. 1, where A, B, C and D are regular

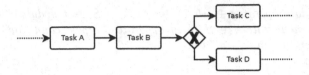

Fig. 1. A (partial) manufacturing process

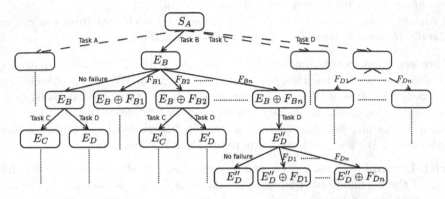

Fig. 2. Possible scenarios of execution from the state after Task A

manufacturing tasks. Figure 2 shows the states that can accrue after the execution of each task. We assume that we have just executed Task A, and the current state is S_A. E_B is the expected state that accrues after executing Task B in state S_A. After executing Task B, we permit the environment player to make a move. If that move, in the restricted viewpoint of this example, leads to no failure, we remain in E_B. We now introduce the notion of *failure type*. Let Task B involve the use of a lathe to make a bolt. The failure type associated with F_{B1} leads to the production of bolts with a diameter larger than the specification, while the failure type associated with F_{B2} leads to the production of bolts with a diameter smaller than the specification. F_{B1} and F_{B2} formally denote the post-conditions (or effects) or the corresponding failure types. State $E_B \oplus F_{B1}$ is obtained by performing state update on state E_B with the failure post-conditions F_{B1}. States $E_B \oplus F_{B2}$, $E_B \oplus F_{Bn}$ etc. are similarly obtained. From the perspective of Monte Carlo sampling, Fig. 2 lays out the tree of possible futures over which we execute random playouts. If we were to assume that the leaf nodes in the tree in Fig. 2 were indeed the leaf nodes of the tree obtained via the execution of a complete process, then we would check leaf node for *goal compliance* (for instance, we would check whether $E_D'' \models g$ for some goals state g in the set of goal states of interest G). A random playout would take us from the current state to a leaf state by making random choices of successor states. The overall probability of success is computed by dividing the number of successful (i.e., goal compliant) playouts by the total number of playouts executed.

Adversarial Tree Search Example: For computing compensations (when the probability of success falls below a user-specified threshold), we perform game tree (or adversarial tree) search. For Monte Carlo sampling, we use only that part of the tree in Fig. 2 that involves task sequences mandated by the current process model (what constitutes the current process model changes every time we compute a compensation, but we start with the original user-specified process model). In computing compensations, we consider the full set of capabilities in the *capability library* discussed above (the resulting nodes are connected to their parent nodes by dashed lines in Fig. 2. In the next section, we report results from the use of two distinct game tree search algorithms: minimax search with α-β cutoffs and Monte Carlo Tree Search (MCTS). Viewing the tree in Fig. 2 as a *game tree* the moves of the process player and the environment player are represented in alternating levels. In minimax search, we usually cutoff the game tree at a pseudo-leaf level (i.e., at a level of the tree higher than the actual leaf nodes) to deal with the limited time available for computing each move. We then apply a *heuristic evaluation function* which computes a reasonable "guess" on the likelihood of a given leaf node leading to a win state for the maximizing player. We then propagate these numbers up the tree (a higher value denoting a higher likelihood of a win) while performing minimax reasoning (the maximizing player always selects a node with the highest likelihood of a win while the minimizing player always selects a node with the lowest likelihood of a win). Once we have numbers labelling each of the options available at the current root node, we are able to make a choice of move (using the same minimax logic). The α-β cutoffs provide the basis for a version of branch-and-bound search (we omit details due to space constraints). We can use game tree search of this kind to both compute the next move (the next task to execute in the current process instance) or the next sequence of moves (i.e., the next sequence of tasks). By expanding the scope of this reasoning, we can effectively compute a complete *suffix* for the process instance, starting from the point where we decide to re-consider the process design.

In a simplified account of MCTS, we use random playouts (in the sense of our discussion above) to compute the likelihood of a win from a given pseudo-leaf node (thus replacing the heuristic evaluation function used in minimax search).

The environment model is updated whenever an exogenous state is observed (i.e., whenever the environment player makes a move). Environment model update (specifically the update of transition probabilities) can be done in a variety of different ways. For instance failure probabilities supplied by a manufacturer of a piece of equipment can be updated as more instances of a manufacturing process are executed (we increase the numerator by 1 every time a failure is observed and increase the denominator by 1 every time a new instance is executed). Obviously, the more observations of exogenous states are made (e.g. the more process instances are executed), the better the environment model would reflect the true behaviour of the environment.

Without any prior knowledge on the behaviour of the environment, it is safe to assume that all the exogenous states are equally likely to occur. However, in a realistic setting, the probabilities of all possible exogenous states are not uniformly distributed but some of the states may be more likely to occur to the others. It is also possible the probabilities of exogenous states changes over time. For example, a call center may lass staffed in off-hours thus the exogenous states that caused by limited staff are more likely to happen.

The outcome of the process is predicted using Monte-Carlo method, where a number of symbolic simulations of the remainder of the process is run against the environment model in a 2-player game. The ratio of the success (goal compliant) simulations over the total simulations are collected as the approximate probability of success for the instance. The point of departure to classic Monte-Carlo method is that the process player always acts following its process model, while the environment player free to select its actions (limited by the environment model). The prediction algorithm considers the randomness and uncertainty of the environment (we only know what may happen but never know what actually happens) by running multiple symbolic simulations and collecting the win-loss statistics.

Here we propose to use game-tree search as the basis of our process redesign and compensation machinery since the classical planning algorithms only consider one player (not suitable for adversarial game). The adaptation of the game-tree search for compensation is very simple. Instead of taking the child at the root of the search tree (which is how it is done in classic game-tree search), we recursively select the best child of the current node from the root to horizon of the search to create a sequence of best moves for the process player as the new process (remainder of the current process instance) to follow. One may notice the meaning of "the best" are different to players, where the best moves for the process will be the part of the compensation that maximize the chance of reaching a goal state, while the best moves for the environment leads to the worst state for the process. Note also that this assumption of *extreme adversariality* is simply a conservative strategy, akin to Murphy's law which states that if something can go wrong, it will. Therefore, the compensation selected using this method is equivalent to worst-case reasoning as the sequence of action is planned under the assumption that the environment is always trying to maximize damage.

3   Experimental Evaluation

All of the evaluation reported in this section was executed on an Intel® Core™ i5–4440 machine with 16 GB memory in Ubuntu 16 and Java SE 8.

We deem a process instance to be successful if it is goal-compliant under the available resource bounds. An instance is deemed to be a failure if it fails to achieve a goal-compliant state by executing k tasks (where k is a user-specified parameter) or if it fails to arrive at a goal-compliant state within a "execution budget" (which, in our evaluation, is set to be double the number of tasks in the longest task trace admitted by the process model). These bounds are necessary to prevent situations where the predict-evaluate-redesign cycle runs indefinitely.

Table 1. Summary of process models evaluated

Model ID	Number of Unique Tasks	Number of Distinct Task Sequences	Length of Distinct Task Sequences	Size of Post-Conditions	Number of Clauses in Domain Knowledge Base (in CNF)	Size of Clauses
Process01	4	1	[4,4]	[1,2]	3	[2,3]
Process02	4	2	[3,3]	[1,2]	2	[3,3]
Process03	10[†]	1	[5,5]	[1,7]	3	[3,3]
Process04	7	3	[4,5]	[2,4]	7	[2,3]
Process05	7	3	[4,5]	[2,4]	7	[2,3]
Process06	9	9	[5,5]	[1,3]	2	[3,3]
Process07	10	9	[5,5]	[1,7]	6	[3,4]
Process08	11	12	[6,7]	[0,6]	9	[2,4]
Process09	8	3	[3,6]	[1,2]	0[‡]	[0,0][‡]
Process10	9	3	[5,6]	[1,1]	0[‡]	[0,0][‡]

[†]There are 5 tasks that are not used in the process model but are available in compensation.
[‡]All propositional variables are independent from each other, that is, there is no constraint between any of these variables.

We use 10 process models with different complexities (summarized by Table 1), where the Process09[1] and Process10[2] are "real world" process models. We measure the complexity of a process using 6 different properties, listed below. The *number of unique tasks* describes the size of the *capability library*, and thus the number of alternative tasks available for computing process compensations. The *number of distinct task sequences* counts the distinct task traces admitted by the process model. The *length of distinct task sequences* is represented by a pair of natural numbers $[j, k]$, where j represents the smallest task sequence length and k represents the length of the longest task sequence. The *size of post-conditions* is also represented by a pair of natural numbers $[p, q]$ where p represents the smallest number of distinct propositions in any task post-condition in that process while q represents the largest number of distinct propositions in any task post-condition in that process. The *number of clauses in the domain knowledge base* (represented in CNF) is self-explanatory. The *size of clauses* is another pair of natural numbers $[r, s]$ where r is the number of propositions in the smallest length clause in the domain knowledge base and s is the number of propositions in the longest clause.

Each process was simulated 2000 times continuously (2000 process instances) in a dynamic environment. The first 1000 instances were "vanilla" simulations in

---

[1] The example process, "Customer Onboarding", from http://workflowpatterns.com/.
[2] A process describing Australian Student Visa Application.

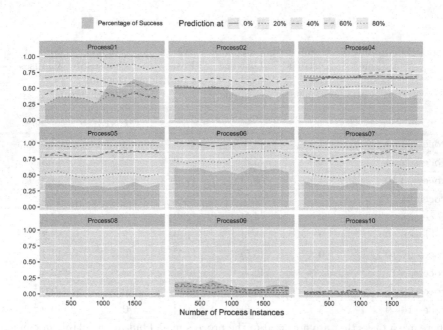

Fig. 3. Predicted process outcomes and the average success rate

the adversarial environment, where there was no redesign done to the instance. The second 1000 instances were simulated with run-time redesign enabled, where half of the processes instances (500) were redesigned using MCTS and others using minimax tree search.

Figure 3 illustrates the average predicted probabilities of success at the start of process instances (0% completion), and at points where the process is 20%, 40%, 60% and 80% complete. The pink shaded area shows the percentage of the successful instances.

Insights: Unsurprisingly, the first 1000 instances where the compensation machinery is disabled, the prediction is the most accurate towards the end of the execution. Some of the processes start with a high probability of success, then the probability decreases (*Process*01, *Process*05, *Process*06, and *Process*07), while some others start with a low probability of success and then the probability increases (*Process*09 and *Process*10 (there is no clear pattern in the rest). This observation may be caused by the structure of the process model and the importance or criticality of the tasks. For example, if a task that contributes the most to the goal were executed early in the process, the effect of it may more likely be overwritten by the environment over the time of execution. If the part of the effect of a task is unique that no other tasks after it does the same, the process is less likely to recover from any exogenous state to the effect of the task. We also notice that the percentage of goal realization of the simulated instances are model-dependent, which shows some models are not robust in an adversarial environment. It can be concluded that some of the process models are not

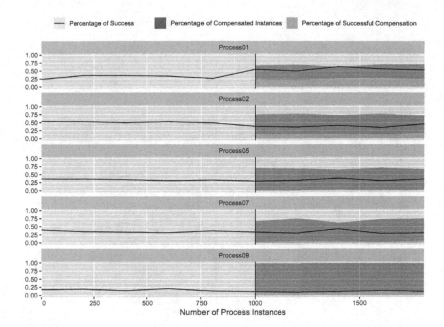

Fig. 4. Percentage of success without and with compensation (redesign)

designed for adversarial environment (such as the real-word models *Process*08, *Process*09 and *Process*10).

Computing Compensations: The redesign of the process is done using game-tree search. We evaluate both minimax search with α-β cut-offs and MCTS. The tree search algorithms explore new task sequences that are not limited by the process model whenever the predicted probability drops below the threshold (0.5). Due to the large branching factor of the game-tree search, the minimax algorithm takes advantage of the heuristic evaluation function (Eq. 1) that returns the minimum of normalized shortest distances of the state description s at a pseudo-leaf node to any known states S_k in the original process. In the equation below, $Cn(s)$ stands for the set of all logical consequences of a set of sentences s.

$$h(s, S_k) = \min_{s_k \in S_k} \frac{|Cn(s) \cap Cn(s_k)|}{|Cn(s_k)|} \tag{1}$$

We also limit the "search budget" to 100 samples for MCTS. The sequence of tasks is then selected according to the most valuable branch in the search tree (i.e. the branch where every node holds the highest value amongst its siblings). The new sequence of task is then used as the new, redesigned process if it has higher chance of success compared with the current prediction. This redesign routine takes places whenever the predicted probability of success of the current process model dropped below threshold.

Insights: With compensation, successful instances of *Process*01 increased from 25% to 60%, where there are more than 75% of the instances are com-

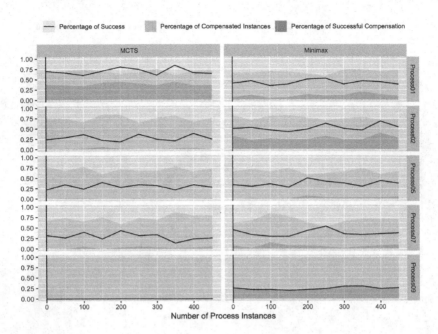

Fig. 5. Percentage of success compensation using MCTS or Minimax search

pensated and 25% compensated instances realizing the process goal (Fig. 4). *Process*02, *Process*04, *Process*05 and *Process*06 is robust enough at threshold 0.5 (however their actual rates of success are lower), and need a higher threshold in order to trigger compensation more frequently) However, the success rate of compensated instances of *Process*02 and *Process*06 are low, possibly due to the limited capabilities that do not provide enough options to find any better alternatives. The percentages of compensated cases appear to be negatively correlated with the percentage of success, which is expected as the number of compensation increases only when the predicted success rate is low.

In Fig. 4 we compared the proportion of successful instances with and without compensation. In Fig. 5, we plot the proportion of successful compensations computed with MCTS on the one hand and minimax tree search on the other hand.

Insights: The results in Fig. 5 suggest that MCTS only out-preforms minimax tree search on *Process*01 whereas the minimax tree search generally produce better redesigns (with the respect to success rate). This is probably because of the 100-sample limit on MCTS that restrict the search capability too much on large problems (see Fig. 5) thus the task sequence found is unlikely to be better than the current sequence executed. Overall, it is impossible to find a single design and redesign that will always succeed in an adversarial environment unless the goal of the process is empty (in which nothing can be done by the environment to impede the execution). If we allow infinite resources for a process instance, it is possible to always achieve a goal in our setting as it is always possible to keep doing other tasks until a goal state is reached. Our experiment also highlights the fact that not all process models are designed to be robust in an adversarial environment, where some of the processes are more resistant to failures than others. There are many domain specific variables that affect our approach, to maximize the effectiveness of our prediction and compensation, the compensation-starting threshold, the budget for the search algorithm (in terms of the depth of search to minimax tree search and the number of sampling for MCTS), tasks that can be used in compensation, etc.

Insights: Computation time was also evaluated (detailed results omitted due to space constraints). Overall, the prediction of the likelihood of success using Monte Carlo sampling and the computation of compensations could both be done in reasonable time. In computing compensations, MCTS was in general much faster than minimax search (consistent with a number of studies comparing these two algorithms).

4 Related Work

Process flexibility has been the focus of considerable research attention. Prominent amongst these are the work of Reichert et al. [16] (and the various successors to the original ADEPT framework), but also others [17–21]. Some approaches focus on the design [22], while others focus on exception handling by design [20,23]. In this paper, we have not explicitly discussed exception handling because we do not require any pre-defined conditions or rules to detect and handle runtime exceptions. Instead, we prevent exception from occurring by compensating early.

Some proposals address flexibility in process execution, such as by taking into account of risks [24], by generating optimized enactment plans according to multiple optimization objectives [25], by following a checklist where the processes are human-driven [26], or by allowing minimal deviation from a design during execution [27]. Generally speaking, in this literature, changing or augmenting the process instances according to the execution context involves either following predefined guidelines [20,22] or generating new process model for the instances at the runtime with some form of predefined objectives either automatically or by human actors [25–27].

Additionally, there are proposals that utilize agent technologies to create more flexible process models (since intelligent agent architectures are designed to deal with a flexible environment) [18]. Automatic planning can also be applied to process planning [28]. Our work does not involve the explicit use of automated planning techniques, but planning implicitly occurs as a by-product of adversarial search.

To the best of our knowledge, nothing exists in the literature that involves the application of game tree search to the problem of achieving process flexibility, robustness or resilience.

5 Conclusion

This paper provides a novel conception of process execution machinery that combines frequent reconsideration of the currently planned sequence of tasks with the use of Monte Carlo sampling of simulated process completions to compute the likelihood of success and the use of game tree search to compute process compensations. Our experimental evaluation suggests that this is a promising approach.

References

1. Gou, Y., Ghose, A., Dam, H.K.: Leveraging Game-tree search for robust process enactment. In: Dubois, E., Pohl, K. (eds.) CAiSE 2017. LNCS, vol. 10253, pp. 461–476. Springer, Cham (2017). https://doi.org/10.1007/978-3-319-59536-8_29
2. Fensel, D., Facca, F., Simperl, E.: Web service modeling ontology. In: Fensel, D., Facca, F., Simperl, E., Toma, I. (eds.) Semantic Web Services, pp. 107–129. Springer, Heidelberg (2011). https://doi.org/10.1007/978-3-642-19193-0_7
3. Fensel, D., et al.: Enabling Semantic Web Services: The Web Service Modeling Ontology. Springer, Heidelberg (2006). https://doi.org/10.1007/978-3-540-34520-6
4. Hepp, M., Leymann, F., Domingue, J., Wahler, A., Fensel, D.: Semantic business process management: a vision towards using semantic Web services for business process management. In: IEEE International Conference on e-Business Engineering, pp. 535–540. IEEE (2005)
5. Hinge, K., Ghose, A., Koliadis, G.: Process SEER: a tool for semantic effect annotation of business process models. In: Proceedings of the 13th IEEE International EDOC Conference. IEEE Computer Society Process (2009)
6. Di Pietro, I., Pagliarecci, F., Spalazzi, L.: Model checking semantically annotated services. IEEE Trans. Softw. Eng. **38**, 592–608 (2012)
7. Smith, F., Proietti, M.: Rule-based behavioral reasoning on semantic business processes. In: Proceedings of the 5th International Conference on Agents and Artificial Intelligence, pp. 130–143. SciTePress (2013)
8. Weber, I., Hoffmann, J., Mendling, J.: Beyond soundness: on the verification of semantic business process models. Distrib. Parallel Databases **27**, 271–343 (2010)
9. Di Francescomarino, C., Ghidini, C., Rospocher, M., Serafini, L., Tonella, P.: Semantically-aided business process modeling. In: Bernstein, A., Karger, D.R., Heath, T., Feigenbaum, L., Maynard, D., Motta, E., Thirunarayan, K. (eds.) ISWC 2009. LNCS, vol. 5823, pp. 114–129. Springer, Heidelberg (2009). https://doi.org/10.1007/978-3-642-04930-9_8
10. Ghose, A., Koliadis, G.: Auditing business process compliance. In: Krämer, B.J., Lin, K.-J., Narasimhan, P. (eds.) ICSOC 2007. LNCS, vol. 4749, pp. 169–180. Springer, Heidelberg (2007). https://doi.org/10.1007/978-3-540-74974-5_14
11. Martin, D., et al.: Bringing semantics to web services: the OWL-S approach. In: Cardoso, J., Sheth, A. (eds.) SWSWPC 2004. LNCS, vol. 3387, pp. 26–42. Springer, Heidelberg (2005). https://doi.org/10.1007/978-3-540-30581-1_4
12. Meyer, H.: On the semantics of service compositions. In: Marchiori, M., Pan, J.Z., Marie, C.S. (eds.) RR 2007. LNCS, vol. 4524, pp. 31–42. Springer, Heidelberg (2007). https://doi.org/10.1007/978-3-540-72982-2_3

13. Montali, M., Pesic, M., van der Aalst, W.M.P., Chesani, F., Mello, P., Storari, S.: Declarative specification and verification of service choreographiess. ACM Trans. Web **4**, 3:1–3:62 (2010)

14. Smith, F., Missikoff, M., Proietti, M.: Ontology-based querying of composite services. In: Ardagna, C.A., Damiani, E., Maciaszek, L.A., Missikoff, M., Parkin, M. (eds.) Business System Management and Engineering. LNCS, vol. 7350, pp. 159–180. Springer, Heidelberg (2012). https://doi.org/10.1007/978-3-642-32439-0_10

15. Ginsberg, M.L., Smith, D.E.: Reasoning about action I: a possible world approach. Artif. Intell. **35**(2), 165–195 (1988)

16. Reichert, M., Dadam, P.: Adeptflex—supporting dynamic changes of workflows without losing control. J. Intell. Inf. Syst. **10**(2), 93–129 (1998)

17. Van Der Aalst, W.M.P., Jablonski, S.: Dealing with workflow change: identification of issues and solutions. Comput. Syst. Sci. Eng. **15**(5), 267–276 (2000)

18. Buhler, P.A., Vidal, J.M.: Towards adaptive workflow enactment using multiagent systems. Inf. Technol. Manag. **6**(1), 61–87 (2005)

19. Heinl, P., Horn, S., Jablonski, S., Neeb, J., Stein, K., Teschke, M.: A comprehensive approach to flexibility in workflow management systems. ACM SIGSOFT Softw. Eng. Notes **24**, 79–88 (1999)

20. Klein, M., Dellarocas, C.: A knowledge-based approach to handling exceptions in workflow systems. Comput. Support. Coop. Work. (CSCW) **9**(3–4), 399–412 (2000)

21. Reijers, H.A.: Workflow flexibility: the forlorn promise. In: Proceedings of the Workshop on Enabling Technologies: Infrastructure for Collaborative Enterprises, WETICE, pp. 271–272 (2006)

22. Hermann, T., Hoffman, M., Loser, K.U., Moysich, K.: Semistructured models are surprisingly useful for user-centered design. In: Designing Cooperative Systems. Proceedings of COOP 2000, pp. 159–174 (2000)

23. Nepal, S., Fekete, A., Greenfield, P., Jang, J., Kuo, D., Shi, T.: A service-oriented workflow language for robust interacting applications. In: Meersman, R., Tari, Z. (eds.) OTM 2005. LNCS, vol. 3760, pp. 40–58. Springer, Heidelberg (2005). https://doi.org/10.1007/11575771_6

24. Conforti, R., de Leoni, M., La Rosa, M., van der Aalst, W.M.P.: Supporting risk-informed decisions during business process execution. In: Salinesi, C., Norrie, M.C., Pastor, Ó. (eds.) CAiSE 2013. LNCS, vol. 7908, pp. 116–132. Springer, Heidelberg (2013). https://doi.org/10.1007/978-3-642-38709-8_8

25. Jiménez-Ramírez, A., Barba, I., del Valle, C., Weber, B.: Generating multi-objective optimized business process enactment plans. In: Salinesi, C., Norrie, M.C., Pastor, Ó. (eds.) CAiSE 2013. LNCS, vol. 7908, pp. 99–115. Springer, Heidelberg (2013). https://doi.org/10.1007/978-3-642-38709-8_7

26. Baumann, M., Baumann, M.H., Schönig, S., Jablonski, S.: Enhancing feasibility of human-driven processes by transforming process models to process checklists. In: Bider, I., et al. (eds.) BPMDS/EMMSAD -2014. LNBIP, vol. 175, pp. 124–138. Springer, Heidelberg (2014). https://doi.org/10.1007/978-3-662-43745-2_9

27. Gou, Y., Ghose, A., Chang, C.-F., Dam, H.K., Miller, A.: Semantic monitoring and compensation in socio-technical processes. In: Indulska, M., Purao, S. (eds.) ER 2014. LNCS, vol. 8823, pp. 117–126. Springer, Cham (2014). https://doi.org/10.1007/978-3-319-12256-4_12

28. Schuschel, H., Weske, M.: Integrated workflow planning and coordination. In: Mařík, V., Retschitzegger, W., Štěpánková, O. (eds.) DEXA 2003. LNCS, vol. 2736, pp. 771–781. Springer, Heidelberg (2003). https://doi.org/10.1007/978-3-540-45227-0_75

Information System Security

Security Vulnerability Information Service with Natural Language Query Support

Carlos Rodriguez[1]($\boxtimes$), Shayan Zamanirad[1], Reza Nouri[1,2], Kirtana Darabal[1], Boualem Benatallah[1], and Mortada Al-Banna[1]

[1] UNSW Sydney, Sydney, NSW 2052, Australia
{crodriguez,shayanz,boualem,mortadaa}@cse.unsw.edu.au
[2] QANTAS Airways, Sydney, NSW 2020, Australia
{s.nouri,kirtana.darabal}@unswalumni.com

Abstract. The huge data breaches and attacks reported in the past years (e.g., the cases of Yahoo and Equifax) have significantly raised the concerns on the security of software used and developed by companies for their day-to-day operations. In this context, becoming aware about existing security vulnerabilities and taking preventive actions is of paramount importance for security professionals to help keep software secure. The increasingly large number of vulnerabilities discovered every year and the scattered and heterogeneous nature of vulnerability-related information make this, however, a non-trivial task. This paper aims at mitigating this problem by making security vulnerability information timely available and easily searchable. We propose to enrich and index security vulnerability information collected from publicly available sources on the Web. To make this information easily queryable we propose a natural language interface that allows users to query this index using plain English. The evaluation results of our proposal demonstrate that our solution can effectively answer questions typically asked in the security vulnerability domain.

Keywords: Security vulnerability · Indexing ·
Natural language interfaces · Information integration

1   Introduction

In July 2017, one of the most notorious cyber security attacks was discovered in Equifax's dispute portal servers, which resulted in a breach of personal information of approximately 145 million individuals[1]. The attack was possible due to a known and unpatched vulnerability found in their servers running Apache

---

[1] https://www.gao.gov/assets/700/694158.pdf.

R. Nouri and K. Darabal—This work was done while the authors were at UNSW Sydney.

© Springer Nature Switzerland AG 2019
P. Giorgini and B. Weber (Eds.): CAiSE 2019, LNCS 11483, pp. 497–512, 2019.
https://doi.org/10.1007/978-3-030-21290-2_31

Struts (https://struts.apache.org). Reports[1] estimate a breach-related cost of $439 million through the end of 2018.

While events like these have significantly raised the concern regarding software security, the ever increasing reliance on software systems to support business operations and the rising numbers of new vulnerabilities reported every year make the task of keeping software systems secure a very difficult one [19]. Recent cybersecurity reports[2] show that in year 2017, approximately 21,000 vulnerabilities were discovered and reported. This value is 31% larger than what was discovered in the year before. Furthermore, as of mid-2018, more than 10,000 vulnerabilities were disclosed[3], of which 16.6% have high severity scores (CVSSv2[4]) ranging between 9 and 10.

In order for security professionals to become aware and informed about security vulnerabilities, an integrated access to such information is needed. However, while much of the security vulnerability information is publicly available (e.g., Vulners (https://vulners.com), NVD (https://nvd.nist.gov) and OWASP (https://owasp.org)), such information is in many cases scattered across different, heterogeneous and complex information silos that have low or no integration [7]. For example, while NVD provides a curated and uniquely identified list of vulnerabilities, finding the list of software affected, exploits and patches for a given vulnerability requires in most cases querying separately multiple, disparate sources. Moreover, accessing such information may require different forms of query mechanisms including manual keyword search, the use of domain-specific languages (DSLs), REST API calls, among other mechanisms.

This paper aims at mitigating the problems above by providing an integrated source of vulnerability information that leverages on publicly available information about security vulnerabilities. More specifically, we propose to leverage on multiple, heterogeneous and complementary sources, which we further enrich using state-of-the-art Knowledge Graphs (KGs) [17] and vector representation of words (word embeddings) [12] to enable a richer representation of vulnerability information. Such integrated and enriched information is thus capable of not only providing information about vulnerabilities alone, but also affected software and vendors, associated exploits, attacks and patches, which jointly can help understand and mitigate the risks posed by security vulnerabilities. In order to overcome the complexity of querying such heterogeneous information, we propose a Natural Language Interface (NLI) that allows security professionals to seamlessly query security vulnerability information. Such NLI does not require learning ad-hoc languages for query purposes, nor it needs familiarity with the underlying information schema. In summary, the contributions of this paper are:

---

[1] https://www.reuters.com/article/us-equifax-cyber/equifax-breach-could-be-most-costly-in-corporate-history-idUSKCN1GE257.

[2] https://pages.riskbasedsecurity.com/2017-ye-vulnerability-quickview-report.

[3] https://www.riskbasedsecurity.com/2018/08/more-than-10000-vulnerabilities-disclosed-so-far-in-2018-over-3000-you-may-not-know-about/.

[4] https://www.first.org/cvss/v2/guide.

- We propose an approach and architecture to (i) *collect* and *integrate* security vulnerability information from multiple, heterogeneous and disparate sources, (ii) *enrich* the integrated information with existing KGs and word embeddings, (iii) *index* such information, and (iv) *query* with support for natural language (NL) expressions.
- We devise an NLI that is able to translate NL expressions into queries that are executable by the underlying index and search engine.
- We evaluate our proposed approach and demonstrate that our solution is able to effectively answer questions typically asked in the security vulnerability domain using NL queries.

The rest of the paper is organized as follows. Section 2 discusses related work. Section 3 presents the security vulnerability information model used for our index. Section 4 presents our architecture and discusses the collection, enrichment and indexing of security vulnerability information. Section 5 discusses how NL queries are translated into the underlying search engine's query language. Next, Sect. 6 presents the evaluation of our proposal. We conclude the paper with Sect. 7.

2   Related Work

We explore related work from two perspectives that are key to our work: Security vulnerability information sources and information querying with NL support.

Security Vulnerability Information Sources. The cybersecurity domain have traditionally relied on multiple sources when it comes to inquiring about security vulnerabilities. One of the most widely used sources is the National Vulnerability Database (NVD) (https://nvd.nist.gov), a U.S. government repository of security vulnerability information. NVD provides a list of vulnerabilities dating back to year 1988, where each vulnerability is uniquely identified by its CVE ID (Common Vulnerabilities and Exposures). Another example is the Zero Day Initiative or ZDI (https://www.zerodayinitiative. com), which allows security researchers to privately report 0-day vulnerabilities to vendors. Vulnerabilities are collaboratively made public by ZDI and the affected vendor through a joint advisory. Other useful sources of vulnerability-related information include security bulletins and advisories created and managed by vendors. Examples include Mozilla's security advisory (https://www.mozilla.org/en-US/security/advisories/), Redhat's product security center (https://access.redhat.com/security/) and the Apache Security Team (https://www.apache.org/security/). Further sources exist that provide useful archives of exploits (https://www.exploit-db.com), breach reports (https://breachlevelindex.com), vendor-specific patches (https://portal.msrc.microsoft.com) and crowd-sourced vulnerability reports (https://www.hackerone.com). Vulners (https://www.vulners.com) aims at partly mitigating the heterogeneity and complexity of security vulnerability information by normalizing and aggregating the available sources above. However, in the current version, there is no integration among the difference sources and the query interface is still at the complexity level of the DSL of the underlying indexing and search engine.

Information Querying with NL Support. The use of NL for querying information sources has been largely enabled thanks to the research carried out mainly in the intersection of areas such as Natural Language Processing (NLP) [5], database systems [2] and Semantic Web technologies [6]. Among the works that combine NLP with Semantic Web, Tablan et al. [18] propose QuestIO, an NLI that allows for querying structured information in a domain independent fashion. The work leverages both NLP techniques and semantic web technologies to help query structured information stored in ontologies. In the same line, Lopez et al. [10] propose PowerAcqua, a Q&A system for querying information stored in heterogeneous, semantic resources. Its main contribution lies in the ability to combine multiple, large and heterogeneous information sources, which helps empower their Q&A system. Kaufmann et al. [8] propose Querix, a system that allows for asking users for clarification whenever ambiguities emerge while querying ontologies using NL.

On a different front, other works looked into providing NLIs to query more traditional database systems. In this context, Li and Jagadish [9] propose NaLIR, an NLI that is able to translate NL queries written in English into SQL statements. Similarly, PRECISE [13] is a system that translates NL queries into SQL queries using a lexicon, which helps expand the NL query vocabulary. TiQi [14] proposes an NLI that leverages on previous work (PRECISE [13]) to help query traceability information in software repositories. In our paper, we do not aim at advancing the field of NLIs. However, we do leverage on some of the techniques discussed above to provide NL query support over security vulnerability information. To the best of our knowledge, our work is the first to provide unified, integrated, enriched and indexed security vulnerability information with NL query capabilities.

3   Security Vulnerability Information Model

Building an integrated source of security vulnerability requires, first of all, the identification of useful information sources that will meet the information needs of users inquiring about security vulnerability. Several such information sources exist as previously discussed in the related work section. However, *what are the concrete elements users inquire about in the context of security vulnerablities?* In an empirical study on questions asked while diagnosing security vulnerabilities, Smith et al. [16] identified a total of 78 questions typically asked in this context, which are categorized into (i) vulnerabilities, attacks and fixes (e.g., *"how can I prevent this attack"*), (ii) code and applications (e.g., *"where is this method defined?"*), (iii) individual questions (e.g., *"have I seen this before"*), and (iv) problem solving support (e.g., *"can my team members/resources provide me with more information?"*).

The study above provides a useful guide into typical, vulnerability-related questions. It is worth noting, however, the wide range of questions asked in relation to security vulnerabilities, many of which go beyond inquiring strictly about security vulnerability information. For example, category (ii) focuses mostly on questions related to the programming code being analyzed, while category (iii) involves developers' self-reflection, understanding and expectation questions. In our work, we leverage on the results of this study and exclusively focus on questions related to *inquiring about security vulnerability information* that is publicly available on the Web. Table 1 shows an excerpt of questions as emerged from [16].

Table 1. Sample of questions asked when diagnosing security vulnerabilities (extracted from [16]). Terms that are relevant for the security vulnerability domain are underlined.

Security vulnerability questions
Q1: "Is this a real vulnerability?"
Q2: "What are the possible attacks that could occur?"
Q3: "How can I prevent this attack?"
Q4: "How can I replicate an attack to exploit this vulnerability?"
Q5: "What is the problem (potential attack)?"
Q6: "What are the alternatives for fixing this?"
Q7: "How do I fix this vulnerability?"
Q8: "How serious is this vulnerability?"
Q9: "Are all these vulnerabilities the same severity?"

The questions listed in Table 1 emphasize on five main information elements (see the underline words), namely, *vulnerabilities/weaknesses, attacks, fixes* and *exploits*. Leveraging on our experience and results from previous research [1,3] on security vulnerability discovery, exploration and understanding, we derive the model shown in Fig. 1(a), which aims at capturing the information elements listed above. In this model, the *vulnerability* entity represents a reported vulnerability, which is characterized by properties such as an *id* (i.e., the CVE of the vulnerability), *publishedDate, description*, among other properties. A vulnerability typically exists in a *software* that is developed by a *vendor*. Moreover, a vulnerability is typically reported by a *discoverer* (e.g., a white hat hacker). Vulnerabilities are further characterized by a *weakness* that is uniquely identified by an identifier known as CWE (Common Weakness Enumeration) (https://cwe.mitre.org). Besides the information above, we also consider additional entities such as *exploits, attacks* and *patches*. An *exploit* is a piece of software or data that can take advantage of an existing vulnerability. An exploit can be used to *attack* a software containing a vulnerability. Finally, a *patch* is a fix to a software that can help mitigate the risks of being attacked due to a vulnerability.

The information model presented in Fig. 1(a) integrates different entities that jointly provide a fuller and richer picture about security vulnerabilities. In the next section, we discuss in more details how existing, disparate information silos publicly available on the Web can be integrated, enriched and indexed for providing a unified access to security vulnerability information.

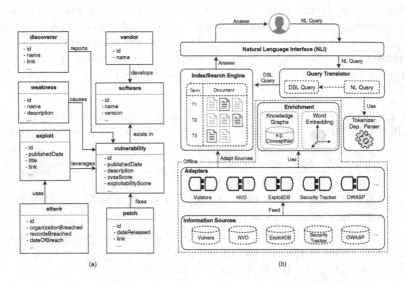

Fig. 1. (a) Security vulnerability information model (we show just an excerpt of the properties for each entity). (b) Architecture for collecting, enriching, indexing and querying security vulnerability information. The bottom part of the architecture operates offline, while the upper part does it online.

4 Collecting, Enriching and Indexing Security Vulnerability Information

The approach proposed in this paper consists of three phases, namely, (i) information source collection, adaptation and enrichment, (ii) information indexing, and (iii) information querying with NL query support. This section presents the first two (we discuss the latter separately in Sect. 5). We show the overall architecture of our proposed solution in Fig. 1(b) and use it as a reference to elaborate on each of the phases above.

4.1 Security Vulnerability Information Collection, Adaptation and Enrichment

At the bottom of Fig. 1(b), we show examples of various, publicly available *information sources* that can be used to collect security vulnerability information.

The collection of such information can be done through various mechanisms, including REST API calls and web data extraction. For example, while the information provided by Vulners is represented as JSON documents and accessible through REST APIs, SecurityTracker's information is available mainly as HTML web pages, which requires for web data extraction techniques [4]. The tasks of accessing, collecting, adapting and integrating the information sources to the target representation (which is presented in the next section) require, therefore, the creation of dedicated adapters for each of the information sources of interest. A list of adapters is exemplified in the *Adapters* component at the bottom of Fig. 1(b).

In order to have a richer representation of the integrated information resulting from the previous step, we propose to enrich such information with semantics from the security vulnerability domain (see the *Enrichment* component in Fig. 1(b)). Such enrichment will allow us to provide more flexibility in expressing NL queries. Consider, for example, an NL query such as *what vulnerabilities are there in Internet Explorer?*. In this query, a user may choose to ask the same question using different mentions for *Internet Explorer*, such as *IE* or simply *Explorer*. The enrichment of the original security vulnerability information aims at enabling the possibility of using alternative mentions for such entities, thus, allowing for more flexibility in NL expressions.

Security vulnerability information enrichment is performed at two levels. First, at the **attribute level**, we store the various mentions that can be used to refer to an attribute in our information model (see Fig. 1(a)). For example, for the attribute *vulnerability.publishedDate* (we use the dot notation, *entity.attribute*, to refer to attributes of an entity), we store other mentions such as {*publication date, release date, announcement date, ...*}. In this way, whenever a user uses any of these mentions in an NL query (e.g., *release date*), we can associate it to the target attribute (i.e., *vulnerability.publicationDate*). Second, at the **value level**, we store mentions of attribute values for relevant attributes within this domain. For example, one relevant attribute is *weakness.name*. A possible weakness (i.e., attribute value) in the context of security vulnerabilities is *Improper Neutralization of Input During Web Page Generation*. This weakness is, however, also commonly referred to as *CWE-79*, *XSS* and *Cross-Site Scripting*[5]. With this enrichment we can therefore refer to weakness *CWE-79* by using any of its alternative mentions.

The enrichments above are performed by leveraging on named-entity recognition [11], KGs [17] and word embeddings [12] (see the *Enrichment* component in Fig. 1(b)). Named-entity recognition is used to recognize named-entities appearing in attributes of the security vulnerability information. In this work, we focus on three main entity types that are relevant in this domain, namely, *software*, *weakness* and *vendor*. Examples of such named-entities include *Internet Explorer* (software), *Microsoft* (vendor) and *XSS* (weakness). The named-entity recognizers (we use Stanford's NER [11]) are trained using a combination of publicly available lists of named-entities (e.g., for software, NVD's Common Platform

---

[5] https://cwe.mitre.org/data/definitions/79.html.

Enumeration (CPE) list[6]), which are extended with alternative mentions using existing KG. Such mentions are obtained from ConceptNet [17] through its APIs, by leveraging its *synonym relation*. In addition, for enrichment at the schema level, we use word embeddings [12] trained on data from Information Security Stack Exchange (https://security.stackexchange.com), which allows us to enrich attribute mentions with semantically-related terms from the security domain. Next, we show how we represent this information for indexing purposes and how we extend it with the enrichments discussed in this section.

4.2   Security Vulnerability Information Indexing

The majority of security vulnerability information available on the Web is of unstructured or semi-structure nature [7]. Much of such information consists of textual descriptions of vulnerability-related artifacts such as exploits, patches, breaches and security advisory bulletins. In order to efficiently query this information, we therefore propose to rely on existing indexing and searching technologies that are capable of efficiently dealing with such unstructured and semi-structured information. More specifically, in this work we rely on ElasticSearch (https://www.elastic.co) (see the *Index/Search Engine* component in Fig. 1(b)), an open-source index and search engine based on Apache Lucene (https://lucene. apache.org).

In ElasticSearch, indexes are flat collections of documents represented as JSON. In order to represent our information model shown in Fig. 1(a), we therefore need to translate that model into JSON documents while still keeping the relationships among the different entities of the model[7]. We do so by denormalizing (flattening) the model in Fig. 1(a). The result is shown in Fig. 2(a). In this representation, we have one document per each vulnerability. This document is self-contained (and vulnerability-centric) meaning that all *related* entities (as shown in Fig. 1(a)) are contained within the same document. As an example, Fig. 2(b) shows a document for vulnerability *CVE-2009-1295*, which also includes related entities such as software affected (e.g., *Ubuntu*) and weaknesses (e.g., *Configuration*) involved. This representation will allow us to effectively retrieve documents from our index to answer queries such as *Vulnerabilities in Ubuntu, with weakness CWE-16*, which involves relationships (encoded in our JSON representation) found in our security vulnerability information model (Fig. 1(a)).

In addition to the attributes of our original information model (Fig. 1(a)), we add to each document the *enrichments* discussed in the previous section (see the shaded attributes in Fig. 2(a) and (b)). More specifically, we extend the original information model with additional attributes that contain mentions of named-entities that are relevant in this domain. As explained before, in this paper we focus on the entity types *software*, *vendor* and *weakness*. Figure 2(b) shows examples of alternative mentions for the named-entities *Ubuntu OS* (the software), *Ubuntu* (the vendor) and *CWE-16* (weakness).

---

[6] https://nvd.nist.gov/products/cpe.
[7] https://www.elastic.co/guide/en/elasticsearch/guide/current/relations.html.

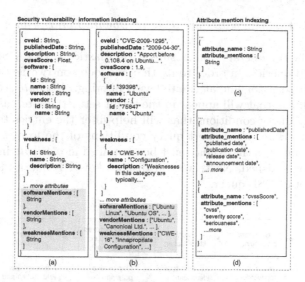

Fig. 2. Index-ready JSON representation of our security vulnerability information model (introduced in Fig. 1(a)): (a) JSON schema of our information model (shaded attributes correspond to enrichments), (b) Example of a single document containing vulnerability information, (c) JSON schema for storing attribute mentions, (d) example of two attributes and their possible mentions

Finally, besides indexing security vulnerability information, we also keep a separate index in which we store different mentions of the attributes of our information model. The mentions are stored using the schema shown in Fig. 2(c), where each JSON document stores the name of an attribute (as used in the main index schema) and its alternative mentions. Figure 2(d) shows an example JSON document for the attribute *publishedDate*. In the next section, we show how the enrichments (i.e., entity and attribute mentions) discussed above are used by our NLI.

5 Security Vulnerability Information Querying with NL Support

In order to be able to answer NL queries on top of the index introduced in the previous section, we first need to understand the intent of users as expressed in their NL queries. In this section we discuss how this translation takes place (see the *Query Translator* component in Fig. 1(b)). Since this work uses ElasticSearch for indexing and searching, we show how we do this translation into ElasticSearch's own DSL[8]. Figure 3 summarizes the steps of the translation process. For illustration purposes, we use in this section the following exemplary

---

[8] https://www.elastic.co/guide/en/elasticsearch/reference/current/query-dsl.html.

NL query: *What vulnerabilities are there in Ubuntu Linux, with a severity score of 10?*

Our translation operates on a subset of ElasticSearch's DSL to support attribute-based queries. In order to do this, we focus on two features from this DSL: Attribute selection and attribute-based filtering. *Attribute selection* is used to select attributes that will appear in the result set. Attribute-based filtering is used to specify query conditions that will help filter the entries to be retrieved from the index. Here, we support query conditions of the form *attribute:value*, where the semantics is that *value* must be contained in *attribute* in order for the condition to be satisfied. Next, we will discuss how NL queries are translated into this subset of DSL query.

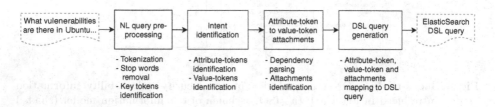

Fig. 3. Steps for NL to ElasticSearch's DSL query translation.

NL Query Pre-processing. The first step toward translating our exemplary NL query consists in dividing the query into tokens that carry the semantics of the user's NL expression. We use Stanford Core NLP Parser [11], which helps us identify tokens in the query. Once tokenization is performed, we proceed with removing stop words that do not contribute to the semantics of the NL expression. In our exemplary query, we remove the tokens *What, are, there, in, with, a* and *of*. This leaves us with the tokens *vulnerablities, Ubuntu Linux, severity score* and *10*, which we call *key tokens* (see Fig. 4). These key tokens are used for identifying the intent expressed in the NL query.

Intent Identification. Once key tokens are identified, the next task consists in recognizing the intent of the NL query. We consider two types of intents: (i) attribute selection, and (ii) attribute-value based filtering. In the first case, the user expresses his information needs by indicating the information item (attribute) he/she is interested in. For example, in our exemplary NL query, the user is asking about *vulnerabilities* in a software, which can be thought of as the list of *CVEs* (see the *cveId* attribute in Fig. 2(a) and (b)) of vulnerabilities affecting such software. We address this intent by matching key tokens to attributes in our index. In the second case, we consider intents related to filter conditions that a user may express in an NL query. For instance, in our exemplary query, the user does not want just any vulnerability, but only the ones affecting the software *Ubuntu Linux*. We address this intent by identifying key tokens that refer to values stored in our index, which can be used as filtering conditions.

We identify the intents above by first focusing on intent type (i). We take each key token and try to match it to each of the attributes' mentions stored in our index (see, e.g., Fig. 2(d)). If we find a match between a key token and an attribute mention (e.g., the key token *severity score* matches one of the mentions for the attribute *cvssScore*), we save the corresponding attribute name (e.g., *cvssScore*) for latter use and designate that key token as an *attribute-token* [13].

When a key token cannot be matched to any attribute mention, we try to match it to an attribute value of the index (thus, focusing on intent type (ii)). For example, the key token *Ubuntu Linux* does not match any attribute mention. However, it does match one of the mentions of the (enrichment) attribute *softwareMention* (see, e.g., Fig. 2(b)). Since a mapping could be found to one of the attribute values, we designate *Ubuntu Linux* as a *value-token*, and we associate it to the corresponding attribute (*softwareMention*). As a result, the *overall* intent identification task will yield a mapping of attribute-tokens to attributes names (e.g., *severity score → cvssScore*) and a mapping of value-tokens to attributes names (e.g., *Ubuntu Linux → softwareMentions*).

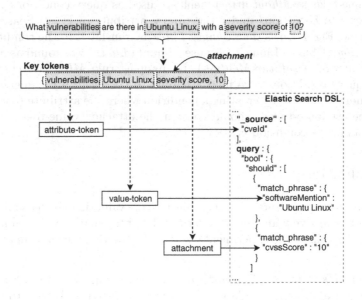

Fig. 4. Translating NL queries into ElasticSearch's DSL query.

Attribute-Token to Value-Token Attachments. In some cases, users may indicate the intent of finding items that satisfy a condition explicitly expressed in the NL query. In our exemplary query, the user is asking about vulnerabilities in Ubuntu Linux, where such vulnerabilities have a given severity score (*severity score of 10*). In order to identify such conditions, we need to detect if any of the attribute-tokens is related to a value-token [13]. To do so, we use dependency parsing [11] techniques to detect such relations (also referred to as *attachments* [13]). In our exemplary NL query, the dependency parsing results indicate that the attribute-token *severity score* is attached to the value-token *10*. From this attachment, we infer that the attribute corresponding to the attribute-token *severity score* (the attribute is *cvssScore* in this case) should contain the value-token *10* (i.e., *cvssScore:10*). We use this attachment next to build query conditions using the search engine's DSL query.

DSL Query Generation. Given the mappings and attachments identified in the previous steps, we are now ready to generate the DSL query to be executed by the search engine. Figure 4 shows how we generate ElasticSearch's DSL query for our exemplary NL query. We follow three mapping rules for generating such DSL. In mapping rule *MR1* (attribute-tokens are used for attribute selection in ElasticSearch's DSL), we map the attribute names corresponding to attribute-tokens (without attachments) to the _source attribute of the DSL (see the mapping of *vulnerabilities* to *cveId* in Fig. 4). Attribute names listed here are going to appear in the result set returned by ElasticSearch (this can be thought of as the *projection* operation in relational databases). In mapping rule *MR2* (value-tokens *without* attachment are used as query conditions), we map value-tokens to conditions under the **query** attribute of ElasticSearch's DSL. For example, Fig. 4 shows that *Ubuntu Linux* is translated to the condition *softwareMention*:"Ubuntu Linux" (because *"Ubuntu Linux"* was found as one of the values of attribute *softwareMention*). In mapping rule *MR3* (attachments are used as query conditions), we map attribute-tokens (*with* attachments) to the DSL's **query** attribute by creating a condition where the attribute (corresponding to the attribute-token) should contain the attached value-token. In Fig. 4, this results in the condition *cvssScore:10*.

6   Evaluation

We conducted experiments with the objective of evaluating the feasibility of our approach to effectively answer NL queries related to security vulnerabilities. We present the details of the experimental setting, evaluation mechanism and results below.

Questions Used in the Evaluation. We use the questions from Smith et al. [16] for our evaluation. We adapted the questions listed in Table 1 to questions that are more contextualized to the information model supported by our solution (see the examples in Table 2). This adaptation is necessary in order to turn questions that make references to generic or vague information items into more concrete questions that can be answered with the information we support. For example, the reference to *"this vulnerability"* in question Q8 cannot be answered with our solution without providing a reference to a vulnerability (e.g., by using a CVE identifier or similar). We created variants for each of the AQs (e.g., using references to different vulnerabilities and software), which gave us a total of 65 variants (a mean of approximately 7 variants per AQ). We use these variants for the purpose of our evaluation.

Table 2. Examples of adapted questions. The questions in bold font are the original questions (Q) from [16], while questions in regular font are examples of adapted questions (AQ). We used a total of 65 variants of these AQs for the evaluation.

Examples of adapted security vulnerability questions
Q1: "Is this a real vulnerability?"
AQ1: "What are the details of vulnerability CVE-2004-1305?"
Q2: "What are the possible attacks that could occur?"
AQ2: "What are the possible attacks on Firefox?"
Q3: "How can I prevent this attack?"
AQ3: "How can I prevent attacks exploiting shellshock?"
Q4: "How can I replicate an attack to exploit this vulnerability?"
AQ4: "Is there any exploit for vulnerability CVE-2004-1305?"
Q5: "What is the problem (potential attack)?"
AQ5: "What's the weakness in HeartBleed?"
Q6: "What are the alternatives for fixing this?"
AQ6: "Is there a workaround to protect against Dirty COW?"
Q7: "How do I fix this vulnerability?"
AQ7: "What are the patches to remediate CVE-2017-3561?"
Q8: "How serious is this vulnerability?"
AQ8: "What's the severity of shellshock?"
Q9: "Are all these vulnerabilities the same severity?"
AQ9: "What's the severity of vulnerabilities CVE-2017-3561 and CVE-2017-3563?"

Dataset. We collected security vulnerability information from Vulners and NVD (for vulnerabilities, weaknesses, discoverer, software and vendors), ExploitDB (for exploits), Breach Level Index (for attacks), and SecurityTracker (for patches). The dataset we use for evaluation consisted of a sample of approximately 102K vulnerabilities, 25K exploits, 33K patches, 21K software and 12K vendors affected, and 124 weaknesses. These sources were integrated and enriched as discussed in previous sections.

Implementation. The proposed solution was implemented based on the architecture shown in Fig. 1(b). The adapters for the sources listed above were implemented using Python 2.7. For enrichment, we leveraged on ConceptNet (as explained earlier) and word embeddings trained on Information Security Stack Exchange. We trained the model using Word2Vec [12] and a skip-gram model with negative sampling (sampling rate of 10 words), 300 dimensions and context word window of 5. We used ElasticSearch 5.5.2 as our index and search engine. Tokenization, dependency parsing and named-entity recognition were done using Stanford Core NLP 3.8. The NLI and query translator were implemented using Python 2.7.

Expert Evaluation. We fed the 65 AQs discussed before to our solution and obtained the corresponding answers. Such answers were evaluated by a domain expert in the area of cybersecurity who judged whether the answers provided by our solution satisfy the NL query in input. Since the results returned by ElasticSearch are ranked using a TF/IDF-based scoring system, we use the metrics R-Precision and Precision@n (or precision at level n), which are typically used in Information Retrieval [15]. R-precision is computed as $TP/|Rel|$, where TP is

Table 3. Evaluation results. We report on average values for $|Rel|$, R-Precision and P@10. P@10 is computed only for questions with a potentially large $|Rel|$ [15].

Question	|Rel|	R-Precision	P@10
AQ1	1.30	1.00	
AQ2	265.40	0.93	1.00
AQ3	1.60	0.85	
AQ4	1.00	1.00	
AQ5	1.17	1.00	
AQ6	1.60	0.85	
AQ7	1.10	1.00	
AQ8	1.17	1.00	
AQ9	2.00	1.00	
Avg.		**0.96**	

the number of true positives and $|Rel|$ is the total number of relevant results for a given query (here, TP is computed only for the top $|Rel|$ answers). For queries with a potentially large number of results we employ Precision@n. This metric is used to compute relevant results on the top n answers, which is useful in scenarios where end-users are typically interested only on the top results (e.g., web search) [15]. Precision@n is computed as $P@n = TP/n$, where TP is the true positives and n corresponds to the number of top results to be considered (here, TP is computed only for the top n results). In this evaluation we consider the top-10 results and therefore compute Precision@10.

Results and Discussion. The results of our evaluation is presented in Table 3. Most questions have a low $|Rel|$, except for question Q2. High $|Rel|$ values were observed whenever an NL query contained value-tokens that can appear among the values of attributes inside entries that are not relevant to an NL query. In AQ2 the expert expected to get vulnerabilities related to Firefox browser only. The system returned, however, also vulnerabilities affecting Mozilla Firefox OS. Yet, Table 3 reports a Precision@10 of 1.00. Questions AQ1, AQ4-5 and AQ7-9 report high R-Precision values. This stems from the nature of the corresponding questions, which inquire information about specific vulnerabilities, attacks and exploits (e.g., *CVE-2004-1305* and *ShellShock*) without much ambiguity (as opposed to AQ2). Questions AQ3 and AQ6 ask, essentially, the same question, but using different terminology. We obtained the same results and thus we report the same $|Rel|$ and R-precision values. The R-precision have in both cases the lowest values across the various AQs.

The proposed solution and evaluation come with their own *limitations*. Range queries (e.g., *vulnerabilities with severity between 7 and 10*) and questions that imply *Yes/No* answers are not supported in the current version. While our solution cannot provide answers for the former, in the latter case the answer provided is either an empty result set (for "No" answers) or a list of results (for "Yes" answers). In addition, questions involving aggregate functions such maximum/minimum values (e.g., *what's the latest vulnerability in Ubuntu?*) and sums/counts (e.g., *how many vulnerabilities are there in FreeBSD?*) are not currently supported. The same applies for comparison operators such as > and <. In addition, our evaluation focuses only on the set of questions obtained from [16] and involves only one expert evaluator. More thorough evaluations are needed with a larger and more varied set of questions, involving also pilot users and additional evaluators. We plan to expand our evaluation in this direction.

7   Conclusion and Future Work

This paper proposes an approach and architecture for supporting the exploration and understanding of security vulnerabilities. Our approach stems from the pressing needs for a unified, integrated and easy-to-query security vulnerability information platform that helps businesses mitigate the threats from the growing number of security vulnerabilities. The NL query capability of the proposed solution makes it a good candidate for integration into productivity tools used in software development and devops environments (e.g., through chatbots), which can help bring security vulnerability information seamlessly into context and while performing core development and devops tasks.

Directions for future work include the development of domain-specific ontologies and knowledge graphs for supporting more complex queries beyond attribute-based queries (e.g., relationship-based queries), further enrichments using intelligent information taggers that leverage on advancements in NLP and AI, and the use of alternative sources (e.g., Twitter) for obtaining updates on the latest cybersecurity developments (e.g., 0-day vulnerabilities and attacks).

Acknowledgement. We acknowledge Data to Decisions CRC (D2D-CRC) for funding this research.

References

1. Al-Banna, M.: Crowdsourcing software vulnerability discovery: expertise indicators, organizations perceptions and quality control. Ph.D. thesis, Computer Science and Engineering, Faculty of Engineering, UNSW (2018)
2. Coronel, C., Morris, S.: Database Systems: Design, Implementation, & Management. Cengage Learning, Boston (2016)
3. Darabal, K.: Vulnerability exploration and understanding services. Master thesis, Computer Science and Engineering, Faculty of Engineering, UNSW (2018)
4. Ferrara, E., De Meo, P., Fiumara, G., Baumgartner, R.: Web data extraction, applications and techniques: a survey. Knowl. Based Syst. **70**, 301–323 (2014)
5. Hirschberg, J., Manning, C.D.: Advances in natural language processing. Science **349**(6245), 261–266 (2015)
6. Hitzler, P., Krotzsch, M., Rudolph, S.: Foundations of Semantic Web Technologies. CRC Press, Boca Raton (2009)
7. Kampanakis, P.: Security automation and threat information-sharing options. IEEE Secur. Priv. **12**(5), 42–51 (2014)
8. Kaufmann, E., Bernstein, A., Zumstein, R.: Querix: a natural language interface to query ontologies based on clarification dialogs. In: ISWC, pp. 980–981 (2006)

9. Li, F., Jagadish, H.V.: NaLIR: an interactive natural language interface for querying relational databases. In: ACM SIGMOD, pp. 709–712. ACM (2014)

10. Lopez, V., Fernández, M., Motta, E., Stieler, N.: PowerAqua: supporting users in querying and exploring the semantic web. Semant. Web **3**(3), 249–265 (2012)

11. Manning, C., Surdeanu, M., Bauer, J., Finkel, J., Bethard, S., McClosky, D.: The Stanford CoreNLP natural language processing toolkit. In: ACL, pp. 55–60 (2014)

12. Mikolov, T., Sutskever, I., Chen, K., Corrado, G.S., Dean, J.: Distributed representations of words and phrases and their compositionality. In: Advances in Neural Information Processing Systems, pp. 3111–3119 (2013)

13. Popescu, A.M., Etzioni, O., Kautz, H.: Towards a theory of natural language interfaces to databases. In: IUI 2003, pp. 149–157. ACM (2003)

14. Pruski, P., Lohar, S., Goss, W., Rasin, A., Cleland-Huang, J.: TiQi: answering unstructured natural language trace queries. Requirements Eng. **20**(3), 215–232 (2015)

15. Schütze, H., Manning, C.D., Raghavan, P.: Introduction to Information Retrieval, vol. 39. Cambridge University Press, Cambridge (2008)

16. Smith, J., Johnson, B., Murphy-Hill, E., Chu, B., Lipford, H.R.: Questions developers ask while diagnosing potential security vulnerabilities with static analysis. In: ESEC/SIGSOFT FSE 2015, pp. 248–259. ACM (2015)

17. Speer, R., Havasi, C.: Representing general relational knowledge in ConceptNet 5. In: LREC, pp. 3679–3686 (2012)

18. Tablan, V., Damljanovic, D., Bontcheva, K.: A natural language query interface to structured information. In: Bechhofer, S., Hauswirth, M., Hoffmann, J., Koubarakis, M. (eds.) ESWC 2008. LNCS, vol. 5021, pp. 361–375. Springer, Heidelberg (2008). https://doi.org/10.1007/978-3-540-68234-9_28

19. Zhao, M., Grossklags, J., Liu, P.: An empirical study of web vulnerability discovery ecosystems. In: ACM SIGSAC, pp. 1105–1117. ACM (2015)

Automated Interpretation and Integration of Security Tools Using Semantic Knowledge

Chadni Islam[1,2,3]([⊠]), M. Ali Babar[1,2]([⊠]), and Surya Nepal[3]([⊠])

[1] School of Computer Science, University of Adelaide,
Adelaide, SA 5005, Australia
{chadni.islam,ali.babar}@adelaide.edu.au
[2] CREST Centre, Adelaide, SA 5005, Australia
[3] Data61, CSIRO, Sydney, NSW 2122, Australia
surya.nepal@data61.csiro.au
http://crest-center.net

Abstract. A security orchestration platform aims at integrating the activities performed by multi-vendor security tools to streamline the required incident response process. To make such a platform useful in practice in a Security Operation Center (SOC), we need to address three key challenges: interpretability, interoperability, and automation. In this paper, we proposed a novel semantic integration approach to automatically select and integrate security tools with essential capability for auto-execution of an incident response process in a security orchestration platform. The capability of security tools and the activities of the incident response process are formalized using ontologies, which have been used for NLP based approach to classify the activities for the emerging incident response processes. The developed ontologies and NLP approaches have been used for an interoperability model for selection and integration of security tools at runtime for the successful execution of an incident response process. Experimental results demonstrate the feasibility of the classifier and interoperability model for achieving interpretability, interoperability, and automation of security tools integrated into a security orchestration platform.

Keywords: Security orchestration · Ontological model · Self-adaptive · Automation and interoperability · Security automation

1 Introduction

The Security Operation Center (SOC) of an organization uses a variety of security tools, developed by different vendors, to protect an organization's Information and Communication Technology (ICT) infrastructure and Business Application (BA) [1–3]. Examples of such tools are Intrusion Detection System (IDS), Firewall, Endpoint Detection and Response (EDR), and Security Information and Event Management (SIEM). According to a recent report by Enterprise Strategy Group [4], on average a SOC has 25 different security tools, and this number goes up to 100 for some SOCs. Most of these tools work independently. The security experts of a SOC are expected to monitor and analyze the activities (i.e., validate alerts, correlate log, and remove malware) of these security tools to respond to an incident [1, 5–7]. The continuous

© Springer Nature Switzerland AG 2019
P. Giorgini and B. Weber (Eds.): CAiSE 2019, LNCS 11483, pp. 513–528, 2019.
https://doi.org/10.1007/978-3-030-21290-2_32

process of monitoring and analyzing the security activities are time-consuming, tedious and repetitive [5, 8].

Most SOC in recent years uses Security Orchestration Platform (SecOrP) to orchestrate the activities of security tools and automate the repetitive tasks manually performed by security experts [5–7]. Deployment of a SecOrP requires an organization to assess their existing security tools' capabilities (e.g., intrusion detection, log management, packet sniffing, and log correlation) and prepare an Incident Response Plan (IRP) [5–8]. An IRP is a sequence of activities that are performed by various security tools. Based on the assessment of an organization's existing tools and requirements, APIs or plugins are developed for integrating security tools into SecOrP and rules are defined to orchestration and automate the IRP [1, 5, 9].

Emerging threat behaviors and variations in organization's infrastructure cause experts to change the deployment and execution environment of SecOrP, such as the integration of new tools, updates of tools capability or modification of an IRP [3, 7, 10]. Existing SecOrPs, however, are not adaptive towards such changes [3, 7, 10]. Experts must sufficiently understand the APIs and rules of SecOrP to make it adaptive to the changes by defining new rules or developing new APIs [5, 11, 12]. Human intervention is required to adjust the changes because security tools are not *interoperable* and SecOrP cannot *interpret* security tools' activities and their input and generated data [12, 13]. A recent study by the SANS Institute *(Escal Institute of Advanced Technologies)* has revealed that the integration of security tools is the third most challenging task of SOC [14].

SecOrP requires the semantic knowledge to formalize various inputs, outputs, and activities of security tools. The formalized concepts enable a SecOrP to *interpret* the changes in runtime environment and *automate* the execution of modified or new IRP without any human intervention. Ontologies can be used to provide the required formal specification to support *interoperability* and *semantic integration* of security tools in a SecOrP without any human involvement [15, 16]. Semantic integration refers to the ability of SecOrP to understand the semantics of the input or output of security tools. A SecOrP can semantically interpret the activities of security tools when the formalization incorporates semantic integration of security tools.

The process of defining a suitable ontology is not straightforward [17]. A well-built ontology depends on domain expertise. Formalizing various security tools and the activities of IRP are challenging due to the ambiguity of the terminology used by different vendors. The features of security tools and activities are defined using Natural Language; same activity is defined using different terms in different IRP. The development of ontology is an incremental process. Domain experts require to perform manual tasks to keep ontologies updated as per the new knowledge.

We propose an integration framework for SecOrP that integrates the data generated by different security tools to automate the execution of an IRP by making security tools *interoperable*. The proposed *integration framework* consists of an *ontological model*, a *prediction module* and an *annotation module*. We have formalized the core concepts of SecOrP in an ontology that are required to automate the execution of an IRP. We have followed a systematic approach to define the classes of our ontology and the relationships among the classes.

We have designed and developed a prediction module utilizing the existing Natural Language Processing (NLP) and Machine Learning (ML) techniques to automatically classify the activities with text description according to the ontology. For a new activity description in an IRP, we have performed a text-based similarity measure with the existing list of activity description. We have defined a threshold for the similarity measure that is used to invoke the prediction module when the similarity score is above the threshold. For a similarity score below the threshold, we have designed an annotation module to generate and recommend the possible classes to experts and automatically annotate the new classes in ontology after an expert selects the classes.

We have designed and implemented an interoperability model to select the best suite of tools that have the required capability to execute an IRP. We check the compatibility of the set of selected tools for interoperability based on their capabilities in terms of their input, output and execution environment. In this paper, we do not show the development and evaluation of the ontology; instead, we demonstrate the use of the ontology by the prediction module and interoperability model for auto-execution of IRPs. Following are the key contributions of our work expected in this paper.

- An ontological model to formalize the diverse activities and capabilities of security tools (ref. Sect. 4.1).
- A prediction module to automatically classify activities according to the ontology and an annotation module to annotate the unmatched activities with the existing ontology (ref. Sect. 4.2 & 4.3).
- An interoperability model to select the security tools to automate the sequence of activities in an IRP (ref. Sect. 5).

2 Related Work

A large-scale SecOrP requires formalization of the concepts of different security tools and their respective activities. Most of the existing literature on SecOrP only focuses on providing APIs or plugins for multi-vendor tools without considering the importance of formalizing the standard features or concepts used by different tools [1, 5–7]. STIX[1], CyBox[2], and Unified Cybersecurity Ontologies (UCO) are the examples of some of the known ontologies for the security domain. UCO combines the existing ontologies. However, it does not provide an ontology for security tools and their activities; nor does UCO support an IRP's activities, which are required by a SecOrP. A few studies formalize various concepts of information security, threats and attacks related information for sharing the information among security community [15, 16, 18]. Though, none of these studies focuses on formalizing the concepts of IRP or diverse nature of security tools.

One recent study has developed ontologies for enabling tool-as-service (TSPACE) for cloud-platform [17]. Based on stakeholder's requirements and tools artifacts, the

---

[1] https://stixproject.github.io/about/.
[2] https://cyboxproject.github.io/.

required tools are selected using the ontologies, which help stakeholder to alleviate the semantic conflict while integrating multiple tools. The proposed ontology in TSPACE cannot automate the execution of the activities or enable interoperability among security tools. Moreover, TSPACE does not capture the capabilities of tools essential for *interpretability* and *interoperability*. Our proposed ontological model provides the capabilities of security tools to support *interpretability* and *interoperability* of security tools in a SecOrP. Our work supports the *interoperability* issue by mapping the capabilities of the security tools with the activities of an IRP. Using the ontological model, a SecOrP is able to *interpret* the diverse security tools capabilities for making them work together to *automate* the execution of security tools' activities without any human intervention.

Besides a general lack of *interpretability* and *interoperability* among multi-vendor security tools, we also did not find any work that addresses the issues with changing IRP due to emerging threat behavior. Our proposed prediction module supports the auto-classification of new activity description according to the ontology for automatic execution of IRP. To the best of our knowledge, this is the first work that has enabled *auto-integration* of security tools in a SecOrP and developed a prediction module to classify activity description based on ontology. The *automation* is achieved by enabling *interpretability* and *interoperability* among a variety of security tools from different vendors and *auto-classification* of activity description according to the ontology.

3 Motivation Scenario

An incident is any unwanted event that violates specific security objectives (confidentiality, integrity, and availability) of an organization's assets. An IRP aims to provide the best sequence of activities that are necessary to perform in response to an incident, e.g., alerts for the *phishing email*, *DDoS attack*, and so forth. Table 1 shows an IRP for one such incident, spear phishing email. A phishing email is used to obtain sensitive information by disguising as a trustworthy entity in electronic communication.

Table 1. The incident response plan for a phishing attack

#	Response	Activity Description
ac_1	*Is this* a phishing attack?	*Validate* if this is a phishing attack
ac_2	*Scan* endpoint – malware found?	After running a *scan*, *determine* whether malware was found
ac_3	*Remove* malware – success?	*Determine* whether the malware was successfully removed
ac_4	*Wipe* and *reimage*	If you did not successfully *remove* the malware found, this task instructs you to perform a *wipe* and *reimage* the infected computer
ac_5	*Update* email protection software	If it was determining as phishing attack, you are prompted to *update* email protection software accordingly
ac_6	*Remove* unread phishing email	Perform the steps necessary to *remove* unread phishing email still in the queue

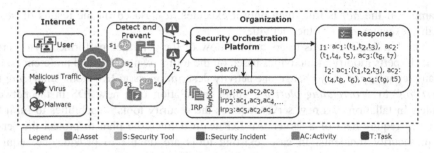

Fig. 1. Overview of a security orchestration platform

Figure 1 shows a scenario of SecOrP where it collects the details of an incident, checks in the playbook for the corresponding IRP and rules therein, select the tools to perform the activities based on the rules, orchestrates the activities and automates the execution of an IRP. Most SecOrPs have a playbook as shown in Fig. 1 where a SOC defines rules based on their respective IRPs. SecOrP shows the scan and ongoing operation through its dashboard based on which a SOC team makes the required decisions, defines new rules in the playbook and performs complex analysis. We refer to the activities that are performed by SecOrP to orchestrate and automate an IRP as *Task*. To address the interoperability issue, an existing SecOrP offers APIs or plugins to communicate with different security tools. Most of these APIs or plugins are not vendors or tools agnostic and fail when updates or changes are required [1, 5, 9]. There are several challenges associated with existing SecOrP; however, in this work, we only focus on the challenges mentioned below. We use the example of Table 1 to illustrate the challenges that arise during the auto-execution of IRP by SecOrP.

First, the IRP of Table 1 is written in text and does not follow a formal structure. There exists ambiguity among different words. Different words are used to define the same types of activities. For example, both *Response* and *Activity Description* of Table 1, i.e., *"Is this a Phishing attack?"* and *"Validate if this is a phishing attack"* are referring to the same activity. A SOC does not follow any specific structure while defining the activities of an IRP. The similar types of activities performed for different security incidents require different tools. For example, *"remove malware"* and *"remove phishing email"* both refer to activity *"remove"* although the execution of these activities requires two different types of security tools. A SecOrP cannot automatically *interpret* the abovementioned similarities or ambiguity.

Second, a SecOrP needs to deal with different tools that are not interoperable to automate the execution of an IRP's activities. For example, to execute an activity ac_1 of Table 1, a threat intelligence platform, e.g., *Malware Information Sharing Platform (MISP[3])*, is needed. A *MISP* is used by a SecOrP to validate the incident. The execution of ac_2 requires an *EDR* tool to scan endpoints and a *SIEM* to identify the malware from *EDR* logs. Each activity has one or multiple rules associated with it. A SecOrP uses these rules to orchestrate and automate an IRP by using different security tools. For

---

[3] https://www.misp-project.org/.

example, if the ac_1 is true, then only it executes ac_2. Based on the results of ac_2, it further executes ac_3 or other activities.

Third, a SecOrP needs to control the flow of the activities performed by different tools. Experts modify the activities based on the tool's availability and preferences. For example, an expert may change one activity description in an IRP from "*analyzing the alert log*" to "*correlating alert log*" after installation of a new IDS in the network router. Installation of a new server requires the security tools' capabilities to fulfil the security requirement of a server. An IRP team defines the plan to protect the server from security incidents. In case, existing tools are unable to provide the required capability; a SOC integrates new security tools to protect the server.

Fourth, there may be multiple tools available for execution of a single activity. For example, different *EDR* tools and dedicated malware detection tools are used to perform "*scan endpoint for malware.*" There is a lack of systematic approach that can be followed to perform the selection of interoperable security tools.

Considering the changing activities in IRP that needs integration of new tools, the challenge is how to provide an interoperability model for a variety of security tools to automatically execute different sets of IRP. In the next sections, we first propose the semantic integration framework and then the interoperability model that uses the component of the integration framework to address the abovementioned challenges.

4   Integration Framework for Security Orchestration Platform

4.1   Ontological Model to Enable Semantic Integration

A SecOrP deals with various types of data produced by heterogeneous security tools. These data can be structured, semi-structured, or unstructured. Data produced by one tool are not always interpretable by another tool. Therefore, these heterogeneous security tools are not *interoperable*. We develop an *ontological model* to represent multi-sourced data and enable semantic-based data integration among heterogeneous security tools in a SecOrP [15, 16]. We define the classes of the required ontology by following a structured approach to keep consistency among the classes.

Design and Development of an Ontology Class. We follow a bottom-up approach to develop the main concepts of our ontology that contains three main classes: *SecurityTool*, *Capability*, and *Activity*. These classes are defined to formally represent heterogenous security tools from different vendors. We leverage the TSPACE work [17] to design the capabilities of security tools in-terms of their functional and non-functional features. The functional feature is the ability of a security tool to execute an activity such as *packet capturing*, *intrusion detection* and so forth. The non-functional features include input and output data structures, and configuration details required to execute an activity. For example, a network-based IDS takes *network traffic* or *packet* (i.e., *tcpdump*), where a host-based IDS works with *system logs (i.e., syslog)*. Even though both types of IDSs produce alerts as an output, the *output format (i.e., PCAP, CSV)* and data (i.e., *IP address, URL*) also vary depending on SOC's preferences.

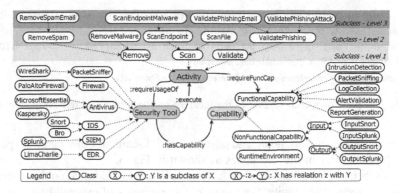

Fig. 2. Excerpt of our ontology (For better quality see at https://github.com/Chadni-Islam/Security-Ontology/blob/master/Ontology.jpeg)

The *Capability* class of the ontology consists of the two subclasses *FunctionalCapability* and *NonFunctionalCapability* to capture the features of security tools as shown in Fig. 2. The diversity among input and output data structures is apprehended using three subclasses under *Non-FunctionalCapability* class: *Input*, *Output*, and *RuntimeEnvironment*. The input and output of the security tools need to be explicitly defined to be analyzed by a SecOrP. A well-designed *Capability* class enables SecOrP to auto-generate the APIs between security tools by retrieving the information about required input commands and produced output. The ability of a SecOrP to deconstruct the output of one tool and then to use the output to formulate the input of another tool enables *interoperability* between isolated security tools.

We analyze the functional capabilities of multiple security tools to identify the subclasses of the *SecurityTool* class, where each tool has more than one functional capability. The *SecurityTool* class is categorized based on the main functionalities of the security tools. We define the first level of the subclass of the security tool based on the types of activities (e.g., *detect, monitor, scan, validate* and so on) they provided. For example, *IDS, SIEM, Antivirus,* and *Firewall* are different types of security tools that are defined as the subclass of the *SecurityTool* class. The available commercial and open source security tools are categorized under each of these subclasses based on the benchmark of their functional capabilities. For example, different types of SIEM, i.e., *Splunk*[4] and *RSA NetWitness*[5], are subclasses of SIEM.

We define and categorize different types of activities as the subclass of the *Activity* class. The activities are associated with the detection, prevention, recovery and remediation actions of a threat defense and response life-cycle. We follow a systematic set of guidelines to define the subclasses of the Activity class manually. First, we only use the verb and noun of the sentence of activity description to define the subclasses of the Activity class. For example, for the activities of Table 1, *Validate, Remove, Scan, Wipe, Reimage* and *Update* are the subclasses of level 1 of the Activity class. Then, we

---

[4] https://www.splunk.com/.

[5] https://www.rsa.com/en-us/products/threat-detection-response/ .

ac_1: Is **(Verb)** this **(Det)** a **(Det)** phishing **(Verb)** Attack **(Noun)** ? **(Punc)** = Is **(Validate)** Phishing Attack
Subclass: Validate → Validate Phishing → Validate Phishing Email
ac_2: Determine **(Verb)** whether **(Adp)** the **(Det)** data **(Noun)** associated **(Verb)** with **(Adp)** this **(Det)**
is **(Verb)** sensitive **(Adj)** = Determine Data Sensitivity
Subclass: Determine → Determine Data → Determine Data Sensitivity

Fig. 3. The parts of speech tagging of the incident response plan and removing stop words

combine the adjacent verb, noun, and adjective and discard all other parts-of-speech to define the categories of the subclasses as shown in Fig. 3.

Each subclass of the Activity class has multiple subclasses based on the capabilities required to execute the activity. For example, the execution of two validation activities: *validation of a phishing email* and *validation of exposure of confidential information* require different capabilities; therefore, they are categorized under different subclasses: *ValidatePhishingAttack* and *ValidateDataExposure*. We also consider the activity "*Is this a phishing attack?*" under the class *Validate*, as this is more similar to validating whether an alert/attack is phishing or not. We consider a different sentence with similar meaning into the same class. For example, the activity "*scan endpoint for malware*" and "*scan host for malware*" requires the same types of capabilities and thus are categorized under the same class *ScanEndpointMalware*. These subclasses can have more subclasses depending on the requirements to execute the activities. Figure 2 shows part of the subclasses of the *Activity* class that we have built following the abovementioned process.

Defining Relationships and Constraints. We define the relationship between the classes to select the tools with appropriate capabilities to execute an activity. The relationships between the classes are shown in Fig. 2. We define a set of reasoning rules to enhance the relationships between different classes for error-free integration. These rules enable us to express conditions about the occurrence or non-occurrence of the required activities, the creation of instances, tracking and managing activities of a SecOrP. For example, each security tool must have at least one functional capability associated with threat defense and incident response to execute an activity. The security tools must satisfy the capabilities associated with a class to be part of that class.

Execution of each activity depends on the availability of the relevant security tools and preference of an organization's security requirements. An auto-execution of an activity requires at least one tool with the required functional capability to execute a desired activity. We impose different types of restrictions for creating the instance of a class that must satisfy the relationship it holds with other classes. The defined rules enable a SecOrP to avoid ambiguity while creating an instance of a class. A SecOrP executes the activities sequentially; as a result, the security tool that is selected to execute ac_{i+1} must have access to the output of a security tool that executes ac_i. For example, if *Splunk* requires to analyze the alert log produce by *Snort*[6], it must have

---

[6] https://www.snort.org/.

access to the output file of *Snort*. Similarly, a SecOrP needs to have the authorization to run and stop every security tool that is integrated into it.

The proposed ontological model enables a SecOrP to interpret activities and security tools capabilities. Retrieving the information of the non-functional capability class, SecOrP can *interpret* the data generated in various forms and also formulate the input command to invoke a particular tool for auto-execution of the activity.

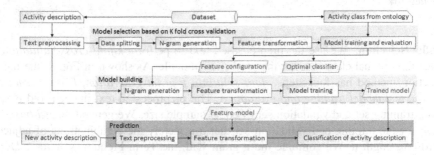

Fig. 4. Development of the prediction module

4.2 Classification of Activities Based on Text Similarity

A SOC adds new types of activities or updates the existing IRP to keep playbook updated for emerging threat. Considering the available tools to execute IRPs, we leverage existing NLP and ML techniques to automatically classify the new activity description according to the activity ontology. It makes SecOrP capable of analyzing an IRP and transforming the data into a representation that gives both an analyst and machine insights about the data. We consider the classes of Activity class in different level separately (Fig. 2). An example of a class on each level includes: level 1 {*Remove, Scan, Validate*}, level 2 {*RemoveSpam, RemoveMalware, ScanFile*}, and level 3 {*RemovePhishingEmail, ValidatePhishingEmail*}. From the perspective of ML, this problem is designed as a multiclass supervised text classification problem.

Given a new activity description in an IRP, we design the prediction module to classify the activity description according to the classes of the ontology. The overall workflow of building an ML-based *prediction module* is given in Fig. 4. The dataset is consist of the activity descriptions labeled according to the ontology. Table 2 shows examples of the labels that correspond to the activity described in each level of the ontology for *Activity* class. Initially, the dataset is divided into training and testing set. The key components of building the ML model includes *text preprocessing, model selection, model building*, and *prediction*. The model selection and model building processes work on the training set and the prediction process work on the testing set or with new activity description.

Text Preprocessing. We start with a corpus of activity description and follow the standard process of text wrangling and pre-processing. During the preprocessing step, we remove the null-value, punctuation, stop words, and meaningless words for the analysis. We perform parts-of-speech tagging of the text before removing the stops words and only keep the verb, adjective, and noun.

Table 2. Activity description and corresponding class label

Activity description	Level 1	Level 2	Level 3
Scan endpoint to see whether malware was found	*Scan*	*ScanEndpoint*	*ScanEndpointMalware*
Is this a phishing email	*Validate*	*ValidatePhishing*	*ValidatePhishingEmail*
Isolate the malicious node from the network	*Isolate*	*IsolateMalicious*	*IsolateMaliciousNode*

Model Selection. We use the preprocessed text to perform *k-fold cross-validation* to select the optimal classifiers for the prediction module. As shown in Fig. 4, the model selection method has four steps: *data splitting, n-gram generation, feature transformation*, and *model training and evaluation*. The preprocessed text in each fold is split in the training set and validation set of equal sample size. We generate *word-based n-gram* for the training and validation set that are merely the combinations of adjacent words of length n. We combine the n-gram with the Term Frequency-Inverse Document Frequency (TF-IDF) for each activity description.

The ML-based classifiers cannot directly process the text documents. Most of them expect numerical feature vector of fixed size whereas the raw text documents are of variable length. The features generated from n-gram are presented into *Document-Term Matrix (DTM)* where each row corresponds to an activity description and each column correspond to a word in the term.

In the model training and evaluation steps, we train the four classifiers (*Random Forest, Linear Support Vector, Multinomial Model* of *Naïve Bayes*, and *Logistic Regression*) on the training set and then evaluates the model on the validation set using different evaluation metrics (*accuracy, recall, precision*, and *f1-score*). The classifier with the highest average cross-validation score is selected as an optimal classifier. The process is repeated for each level (level 1, 2 and 3). The optimal classifiers and feature representations are returned for all three levels.

Model Building. The model building process uses the whole set of preprocessed training set to generate the word n-gram. Here n-gram generation and feature transformation are based on the identified feature configuration for each level of class. The generated n-gram vocabularies are combined with the feature configuration to create the feature model. The feature model has been saved to transform the data for future prediction. The extracted features are trained with the optimal classifiers returned in the model selection process to build the prediction model for each level.

Prediction. The prediction process is used for both testing the trained model and classifying the new activity description. In this process, the activity descriptions are first preprocessed and then using the saved feature model transformed to a feature set. Finally, the features set is used by the saved trained model to determine the class of the activity description in terms of the ontology for each level.

The prediction module reduces the manual analysis of the activity description by classifying the activities according to the ontology.

4.3 Design and Development of the Annotation Module

The new activity description may not always fall in any of the existing activity class of the ontology. In this context, we are considering these types of description as an outlier. To identify the outlier description, we perform text-based similarity checking of the updated or new description with the existing activity description and measure the cosine similarity. We define a threshold for considering whether the description is an outlier in terms of the existing set of activity description. If the new description is not an outlier, then only the description is sent to the prediction module. If the new description is considered as an outlier, we develop the annotation module to automate the generation of the possible list of classes following same set of guideline that is proposed to design the *Activity* class in Sect. 4.1. The generated classes are matched with the existing set of classes, and if none of the classes are found in the ontology, the annotation module recommends the possible list of the classes to a user. Once a user selects the corresponding classes, it creates new classes for the activity description and if required requests for additional details about the classes from the user to keep the ontology consistent.

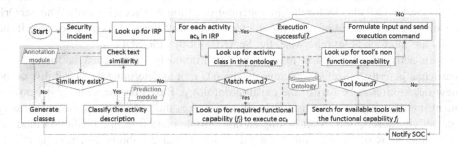

Fig. 5. Workflow of the proposed solution

5 Interoperability Model for Execution of IRP

A SecOrP may need to invoke a different set of security tools in a different order to execute a variable sequence of IRPs. For example, one IRP may include an activity *scan endpoint*, followed by another activity *correlate alerts log*, whereas another IRP may include *correlating alerts logs* followed by *scan endpoint*. Both of these IRPs require the same security tools in different orders. We provide the interoperability model for auto-execution of the required IRPs, where one tool can understand the output of other tools. The model also helps SecOrP to interpret the output and input of different security tools. For example, a SIEM tool needs an output of alerts produced by IDS and a system log produced by EDR to perform correlation. Figure 5 shows the overall workflow of the interoperability model starting from gathering a security incident to notify a SOC. Two key tasks of the interoperability model are: select the desired tools based on their functional and non-functional capabilities and invoke the tools to execute an IRP. The key components of the integration framework (*ontological model, prediction* and *annotation module*) as shown in Fig. 5 are used to design the interoperability model.

We have designed a Query Engine (QE) to retrieve the information from the ontology. Given a set of Security tools $S = \{s_1, s_2, ..., s_m, ...\}$, a list of the required activities $AC = \{ac_1, ac_2, ..., ac_k ...\}$ and a list of capability, $F = \{f_1, f_2, ..., f_j, ...\}$, a SecOrP looks up for the corresponding IRP for each security incident. For each activity ac_k of *IRP*, SecOrP invokes the QE to search for the corresponding *Activity* class. If the activity is found in the ontology, the SecOrP invokes QE to retrieve the capability required to execute the activity. Considering f_j is the required functional capability, a SecOrP queries to retrieve the security tool that has the functional capability, f_j. In case, multiple tools are available, the SecOrp selects the right tool from the list. In the next step, the SecOrP retrieves the non-functional capability of the selected security tool to formulate the input command for instructing the tool to execute the activity. The QE extracts the necessary information from the ontology to formulate the input for the tool. After constructing the input command, a SecOrP calls the tool's corresponding routine to execute the activities. If the execution is successful, the next activity in the IRP is executed by following the same sequence of tasks (performed by SecOrP).

Considering the output produced by one tool s_m is provided as an input to another tool s_p, a SecOrP checks for the interoperability of the two security tools. The SecOrP deconstructs the output of s_m to formulates the input of the s_p. It is only possible if the tools are interoperable; otherwise, the SecOrP notifies the SOC.

An activity's description may change continuously; if no class is found for a particular activity, a SecOrP first invokes the AU unit to determine the possibility of the new description to be part of the existing ontology. Based on the similarity measurement it either generates the list of classes or invokes the prediction module to classify the activity description. After getting an appropriate class from the prediction module, the same steps of looking for the required functional capability and non-functional capability to execute the activity are carried out.

Following the abovementioned process, a SecOrP can automate the sequence of activities in an IRP even when changes occur in the underlying execution environment. The interoperability model enhances the capability of a SecOrP to automate the execution of an IRP by interpreting the activity, required capability, and tools interoperability.

6   Experiments and Results

We carried out a set of experiments to assess the feasibility of the proposed prediction module and interoperability model.

Preparing the Dataset for Prediction Module: Our experimental dataset is based on the IRP crawled from the website of *ServiceNow*[7] that resulted in 1080 activity

---

[7] https://docs.servicenow.com/: offers on-demand, cloud-based IT service management solution, forms-based workflow application development, automation workflow, productivity tool for business user and so forth.

descriptions. For each activity description, we manually labeled the classes according to the ontology as shown in Table 2. We have *34 categories* under level 1, *67 categories* under level 2 and *74 categories* under level 3.

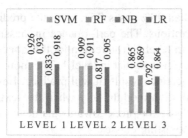

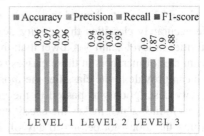

(a) Validated Weighted average of F1-Score   (b) Testing results of Random Forest classifier

Fig. 6. Bar plot of (a) validated weighted average of F1-score for optimal configuration of different classifiers and (b) testing results of random forest for three levels of class

Implementing the Prediction Module: We used the *sci-kit-learn, NLTK* and *spaCy* package of python to build a classifier. For each level, we first separately implemented four classification algorithms with different hyper-parameter settings. We performed k-fold cross validation for each configuration by splitting the data set into different training and validation sets. We used the function *GridSearchCV()* to select the optimal configuration and perform cross-validation for each classifier. For both *Support Vector Machine (SVM)* and *Linear Regression (LR)*, we considered different values for the regularization parameter (i.e., 0.01., 0.1, 1, 10, and 100). For *Multinomial Naïve Bayes (NB)*, we considered prior probability of class True and False. For *Random Forest (RF)*, we considered different values for estimators (i.e., 10, 100, 20, 200, 50, and 500) and the maximum number of leaves (i.e., 10, 50, 100, and 200). Figure 6(a) shows the results of different classifiers for the optimal configuration. We examined the performance of the classifiers in terms of accuracy and F1-score [19]. F1 score is considered more reliable than accuracy. *Accuracy* reflects the total of the correct predictions divided by the total number of cases. F-1 score is the harmonic mean of the Precision and Recall. *The precision* represents the total of the correct predictions for each class divided by the total number of activities predicted for that class. The *recall* is the correct prediction for each category divided by the total number that belongs to this category. Comparing the results of the classifier, we found that RF outperformed other classifiers. We built the final model with the RF classifier. The optimal configuration for *RF* (estimators, maximum leaf) for levels 1, 2 and 3 are (50, 100), (100, 100) and (10, 200), respectively. We used 70% of the activities for each level as the training data and 30% as the testing data. Figure 6(b) shows the results of the RF for different evaluation metrics.

Developing the Interoperability Model: We implemented a Proof of Concept (POC) system using seven security tools (*Snort, Splunk, LimaCharlie, Wireshark, WinPcap, Microsoft essential,* and *MISP*) to study the viability of the interoperability model. We described their capabilities in terms of the ontological model and used a list of IRPs with different activities. We used the network traffic and system logs as the input to identify the security incidents. The experimental study used 21 different capabilities and 9 IRPs with 17 activities. We only considered the activities for which the capabilities were available. We changed the activities and observed the corresponding changes in the operation's execution.

Discussion: The results showed that in more than 90% cases (Fig. 6(b)) the prediction module accurately classified the activity descriptions. The performance in classifying the activities in level 2 and 3 is lower than that in level 1. The reason for this appears to be the number of members in these classes is lower than that in level 1. The more input data we can provide to the classifier the more accurate results it will produce. Besides, the activity description was passed to the prediction module only when the text similarity was found, which makes the classifiers less error-prone towards the new activity description that does not belong to any of the existing classes.

Out of the 17 IRPs, the POC was able to automate 15 IRPs successfully and 2 IRPs partially. While modifying the activity descriptions, there were two activities (update email protection software and detect phishing email) for which security tools were not available. For these two activities, the interoperability model was unable to find suitable security tools, thus failed to automate the execution of that particular IRPs. Except for these two activities, the POC automatically (a) retrieved the information from the developed ontology; (b) generated the configuration details to call the desired security tools; and (c) thus enabled *interpretability* and *interoperability* among different security tools and SecOrP.

Threats to Validity: We developed the ontology based on freely available and open source security tools' capabilities, and activity descriptions, which might not fully represent the situations of scenarios of an organization. Considering the development of an ontology is an incremental process, a human expert can easily extend the ontology to incorporate the tools used in an organization. The selected optimal may not guarantee the highest performance for classifying the new and updated activity descriptions since an infinite number of configurations are available to tune the hyper-parameters of ML classifiers. The selected classifiers might not be the best one, but it provides a learning-based approach to classify the activity description which can be further improved and extended with different classifiers and configurations. The model we built is retrainable and can be easily trained with the new dataset.

7   Conclusion

Given the widespread adoption of SecOrP over the last couple of years, there is an increasing demand for self-adaptive SecOrPs. Our research purports to devise a solution that can enhance the *interpretability* and *interoperability* of security tools integrated into a SecOrP. The proposed approach allows a SecOrP to select the required security tools that are interoperable for auto-execution of an IRP. We have introduced an ontological model to formalize the security tools, their capabilities, and the activities of an IRP. A learning-based prediction module is proposed to reduce the manual work of security staff to define the classes for activity in a playbook. The proposed interoperability model successfully automates the execution of most of the IRPs at runtime.

In future work, we will extend the system to automate the generation of the APIs from the ontology. We also aim to use the semantic definition of tools capabilities to auto-create the APIs when new security tools with new capability are integrated, and design a probabilistic model for selecting and integrating security tool.

Acknowledgment. This work is partially supported by Data61/CSIRO, Australia. We acknowledge the contributions of the shepherd reviewer Professor Andreas L. Opdahl from the University of Bergen, Norway who provided insightful comments with continuous engagement to improve the paper.

References

1. Demisto.   https://www.demisto.com/wp-content/uploads/2017/04/MH-Demisto-Security-Automation-WP.pdf. Accessed 11 Oct 2017
2. Koyama, T., Hu, B., Nagafuchi, Y., Shioji, E., Takahashi, K.: Security orchestration with a global threat intelligence platform. NTT Tech. Rev. **13**, 1–6 (2015)
3. Luo, S., Salem, M.B.: Orchestration of software-defined security services. In: 2016 IEEE International Conference on Communications Workshops, ICC 2016, pp. 436–441 (2016)
4. Enterprise Strategy Group. https://www.esg-global.com/research/esg-research-report-cybersecurity-analytics-and-operations-in-transition. Accessed 25 Feb 2019
5. McAfee. https://www.mcafee.com/au/solutions/orchestration.aspx. Accessed 20 Oct 2017
6. Komand. https://www.komand.com/. Accessed 21 Oct 2017
7. Feitosa, E., Souto, E., Sadok, D.H.: An orchestration approach for unwanted internet traffic identification. Comput. Netw. **56**, 2805–2831 (2012)
8. SIEMPLIFY. https://www.siemplify.co/security-orchestration-automation. Accessed 1 Nov 2017
9. SWIMLANE.   https://swimlane.com/use-cases/security-orchestration-for-automated-defen se/. Accessed 20 Nov 2017
10. Yu, T., Fayaz, S.K., Collins, M., Sekar, V., Seshan, S.: PSI: precise security instrumentation for enterprise networks. In: Network and Distributed System Security Symposium (NDSS), San Diego, CA, USA (2017)
11. SWIMLANE. https://swimlane.com/ebook-sao-capabilities/. Accessed 20 Oct 2017
12. FireEye. https://www.fireeye.com/solutions/security-orchestrator.html. Accessed 11 Jan 2018
13. Microsoft. https://www.microsoft.com/en-us/windowsforbusiness/windows-atp. Accessed 21 Jan 2018
14. Crowley, C., Pescatore, J.: The Definition of SOC-cess? SANS 2018 Security Operations Center Survey. SANS (2018)
15. Evesti, A., Ovaska, E.: Ontology-based security adaptation at run-time. In: 2010 4th IEEE International Conference on Self-Adaptive and Self-Organizing Systems (SASO), pp. 204–212. IEEE (2010)
16. Syed, Z., Padia, A., Finin, T., Mathews, M.L., Joshi, A.: UCO: a unified cybersecurity ontology. In: AAAI Workshop: Artificial Intelligence for Cyber Security (2016)
17. Chauhan, M.A., Babar, M.A., Sheng, Q.Z.: A Reference architecture for provisioning of tools as a service: meta-model, ontologies and design elements. Future Gener. Comput. Syst. **69**, 41–65 (2017)

18. Krauß, D., Thomalla, C.: Ontology-based detection of cyber-attacks to SCADA-systems in critical infrastructures. In: 2016 6th International Conference on Digital Information and Communication Technology and Its Applications, DICTAP 2016, pp. 70–73 (2016)
19. Dua, S., Du, X.: Data Mining and Machine Learning in Cybersecurity. Auerbach Publications, Boca Raton (2016)

An Assessment Model for Continuous Security Compliance in Large Scale Agile Environments
Exploratory Paper

Sebastian Dännart[1,2](✉), Fabiola Moyón Constante[2], and Kristian Beckers[2]

[1] Infodas GmbH, Cologne, Germany
s.daennart@infodas.de
[2] Siemens Corporate Technology, Munich, Germany
{fabiola.moyon,kristian.beckers}@siemens.com

Abstract. Compliance to security-standards for engineering secure software and hardware products is essential to gain and keep customers trust. In particular, industrial control systems (ICS) have a significant need for secure development activities. The standard IEC 62443-4-1 (4-1) is a novel norm that describes activities required to engineer secure products. However, assessing if the norm is still fulfilled in continuous agile software engineering environments is difficult. It often remains unclear how the agile and the secure development process have to intertwine. This is even more problematic when changes on the basis of assessment results of 4-1 or other secure development activities have to be applied. We contribute a novel assessment model that contains a baseline process for secure agile software engineering compliant to 4-1. Our assessment results show precisely where in the development process activities or artifacts have to be applied. Moreover, it contains a refinement into goals and metrics that allow the evaluator to present the evaluate with a precise 'shopping list' of where to invest to achieve compliance. Afterwards, management can include precise compliance expenditure estimates in their business models.

Keywords: IT security · Agile development ·
Compliance assessment · Security standard

1 Introduction

Agile software engineering provides the basis for faster software development aligned with a close cooperation with the customer and is a de-facto standard for software engineering in numerous domains [18]. Nevertheless, software engineering for domains with a high demand for security, such as industrial control systems (ICS), has several obstacles to overcome before agile methodologies can be largely applied. In particular, software for security critical systems often has to

© Springer Nature Switzerland AG 2019
P. Giorgini and B. Weber (Eds.): CAiSE 2019, LNCS 11483, pp. 529–544, 2019.
https://doi.org/10.1007/978-3-030-21290-2_33

be engineered compliant to security standards, which demand numerous security analysis and risk management activities, as well as strict documentation. Today software engineering methods are missing to provide compliance to these standards and large scale agile methodologies, e.g. the Scaled Agile Framework (SAFe) [16]. The ICS domain is regulated by security-standard family IEC 62443 and the secure software engineering process by IEC 62443-4-1 [5] (4-1) in terms of cybersecurity. Current research [14] contains an approach that analyzed and modeled this standard and the agile software engineering processes SAFe. The result is a set of BPMN processes that shows the activities and artifacts required to fulfill both standards. Furthermore, some proposals were made how to merge the 4-1 standard and SAFe. To meet specific agile requirements, such as lean processes with high flexibility, all conformance actions are consequently integrated in the existing agile development cycle without bloating processes.

Our contribution is an assessment methodology for agile security compliant processes based on the SAFe and 4-1 models. Process maturity assessment can answer the question, how repeatable and optimized the agile development process is, while security-standard assessment methods provide details of nonconformance with the norms. Transferring the agile mindset into the assessment, not only the process is measured, but conformance can be monitored during repeated agile-specific characteristics, such as sprints. Currently, these assessments have to be done separately. We propose to combine these assessments into one method provides both answers. For that end, we re-use the established Capability Maturity Model Integration for development (CMMI-dev) to assess process maturity and we add a model for measuring artifact quality because security standard compliance assessments are largely based on documentation. Furthermore, we designed this tool to support security compliant management decisions. Therefore, we provide the means to create a detailed 'shopping list' of which activities and artifacts need to be created to achieve security compliance. This list can be enhanced with costs so the management can weight the cost of security compliance versus the expected revenue it generates.

We evaluated our exploratory approach with one of Germany's largest industrial actors in the field of ICS. For that purpose, we interviewed in total 21 senior industrial experts from the fields of software development, security engineering and security management. Interviews with those experts were used to evaluate practical applicability and the utility of our work.

2   Background and Related Work

Security-Standard Compliant SAFe. *IEC 62443* constitutes a series of standards for network and system security published by the International Electrotechnical Commission (IEC). Group 4 focuses on requirements for component providers for industrial automation and control systems, part 4-1 describes process requirements for secure product development [5]. We refer to this part of the standard as "4-1" or "4-1 standard". The *Scaled Agile Framework (SAFe)* is a widely used process framework that scales lean and agile development to large organizations with multiple levels and that defines corresponding roles, responsibilities, activities, and artifacts [10]. For such environments Security-standard compliant SAFe (S^2C-SAFe) aims to bridge the gap between lean and agile development, practical security, and compliance [14]. S^2C-SAFe is one solution for the well-known research problem of integrating security into lean and agile methods [1,3,19] and the only solution for integrating 4-1 and SAFe.

Maturity Models for Security and Agile. Measuring maturity of development processes is a well-known field that contains common frameworks like the Capability Maturity Model Integration for development (CMMI-dev) [2], the ISO/IEC 15504 SPICE-framework [15], or the COBIT5 Process assessment model [6]. All of them focus on processes and define several maturity levels for assessing the processes maturity. Concerning agile development, current models do not focus on security but aspects like velocity, estimated effort, or sprint planning [8]. Furthermore, security requirements are hard to measure and very specific for each case, the range of assessment models in this field is narrow [7]. Considering the individual requirements of assessment of the combination of both, security and agile development, there are no common models.

Related Work. A common theme in security requirements engineering is modeling aspects of socio technical systems (STS). For example, Lamsweerde [9] investigates security requirements for software, Mouratidis [13] and Liu [12] analyze organizational security issues, and Herrmann [4] focuses on business processes. The work of Li [11] considers all aspects of STS in one holistic model. These approaches have in common that they often analyze security concerns in separate models. This leads to a gap in knowing where to conduct which security activity in a large scale agile process.

3   Security-Standard Compliance Assessment Model

As a first step, we set up on Moyons [14] work and completed S^2C-SAFe by injecting requirements of all practices of the 4-1 standards into the agile development processes of SAFe; a framework of about 80 single models arose. Of course, by just merging all the processes there is no evidence of compliance until particular implementation has been reviewed. For stating compliance with the requirements of 4-1, the norm demands one or more of the following conditions per requirement:

1. processes named by the requirement shall be specified, employed or enforced
2. certain aspects shall be defined, identified, characterized, tracked or documentation shall be created.

Following this segmentation, 4-1 requirements can be divided into two dimensions of requirements - *processes* and *artifacts*. Within the processes certain IT security measures shall be implemented within the development process. Artifacts represent outputs and deliverables needed to prove compliance. Those can be embodied as code snippets, log files or other sort of documentation. Hence a model which aims to assess compliance has to factor both, *process maturity* and *artifact quality*, in.

The Security-standard Compliance Assessment Model (S²C-AM) presented in this paper combines both dimensions to deliver a consolidated state of compliance for each requirement of the 4-1 standard.

3.1   Process Maturity

There are several models to assist assessing the maturity of processes (see Sect. 2). The 4-1 itself proposes CMMI-dev [2] to measure maturity of required processes. Moreover, the 4-1 [5] delivers a mapping between CMMI-devs maturity levels and the expectations on processes by the 4-1 standard itself. S²C-AM utilizes this mapping for the process dimension of compliance assessment.

Furthermore, the proposed approach delivers specific metrics for every process the 4-1 requires. Due to the major focus of agile development on processes and the ability of S²C-SAFe to keep processes lean in spite of additional security tasks, the proposed approach delivers metrics for those goals as well. Those metrics are part of the requirement cards described in Sect. 3.4 of this paper.

3.2   Artifact Quality

In contrast to process maturity methods for measurement of artifact quality is hardly prevalent. Therefore, we propose a new model based on maturity levels as well to keep needed skill adaption down.

Basically, two aspects describe the quality of artifacts: completeness and timeliness. The quality of an artifact arises of the combination of both (Table 1).

Levels and descriptions have been designed iteratively and were discussed and optimized in cooperation with process and security experts.

As mentioned above the quality of artifacts is based on the two aspects of completeness and timeliness. To support decision making on which level fits best, we deliver a support matrix (shown in Fig. 1) which combines both aspects to a certain artifact quality level. Basically, the single aspect has to be rated from 0 - none/worst to 2 - complete/best. The two grey fields logically can not be true: if there is no documentation, it cannot be up-to-date.

3.3   Compliance Matrix

After process maturity and artifact quality for a single requirement have been elicited, the requirement can be placed in the compliance matrix as shown in Fig. 2. The vertical axis displays the level of process maturity described in Sect. 3.1, the horizontal one covers the level of artifact quality in Sect. 3.2.

Four example requirements have been placed in Fig. 2 representing the requirements of 4-1 standards *Practice 3 Secure Design*. Focusing on displayed

Table 1. Profile groups and count of interviewees each.

Level	Quality level	Description
1	None	There is no documentation available
2	Partial	Documents and output of processes comply to certain requirements of 4-1 standard. Possibly information is available in different sources but has to be consolidated to meet requirements completely. Potentially some artifacts are not up-to-date
3	Complete	All necessary artifacts to proof compliance are available in a structured form. Potentially some artifacts are not up-to-date
4	Up-to-date	To reach this level, creation and update of artifacts are fully integrated in the employed S^2C-SAFe processes. Processes are lived and updates on a regular basis are verifiably warranted Note: To reach this level, usually there is a process maturity of level 3 necessary

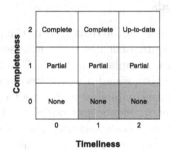

Fig. 1. Support matrix for categorization of artifacts

requirement *SD-1* it seems that the required process has a process maturity of "2 - Managed" and the artifact quality of the artifacts demanded by 4-1 in this single requirement is "2 - partial".

During workshops with 4-1 experts they pointed out that an auditor or evaluator would expect certain minimum process maturity and artifact quality to see the 4-1 requirements as fulfilled: a minimum of level 3 for each of the compliance dimensions is necessary. Therefore, the green coloured area of the matrix in Fig. 2 represents 4-1 standard compliance. The orange area is not completely compliant and has some specific deficits. The red area is not compliant, while

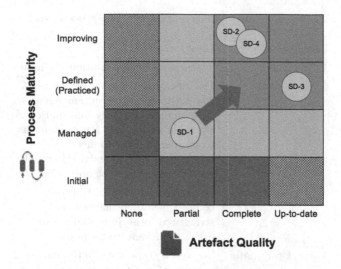

Fig. 2. Compliance matrix with exemplary requirements

the shaded area is logically not possible: if there is a defined process according to S^2C-SAFe, there cannot be no artifact, as well as an up-to-date artifact is impossible with just having an initial process.

3.4   Requirement Cards

Before the level of compliance can be displayed in the proposed model, the compliance to a certain 4-1 requirement has to be assessed. Therefore, we designed requirement cards as shown exemplarily in Fig. 3. Besides a summary of the original text from the 4-1 standard, we added expected input artifacts and expected output artifacts. To facilitate compliance assessment we derived particular practice goals from the 4-1 requirements and enriched them with related metrics to enable precise assessment of achievements. The subsumption of those assessments allows a placement of the requirement in the S^2C-AM matrix.

Using the same identifiers as used in S^2C-SAFe a direct link into the agile processes is possible. Thereby, input and output artifacts can be determined precisely and for every metric relevant tasks and artifacts are assigned. With this, both, product supplier and auditors, for instance can easily identify where in the agile development process improvements have to take place and which processes struggle. Focusing on artifacts, a cross-reference for related metrics to every output artifact was added.

As the arrow in Fig. 2 indicates, for requirement *SD-1* process maturity as well as artifact quality have to be improved to become compliant. To identify potential improvements the requirements card points on possible weak points and proposes tasks and artifacts to focus on to expunge them.

use of externally accessible interfaces (for example, by users and third-parties) reduces the potential for accidental misuse.

Practice Goals and Metrics				
Practice Goals	Related Metrics		Related tasks	Related artifacts
SD-1-G1	SD-1-G1-a	Number of interfaces characterized	SD-t4; SD-t5	SD-a4
Product's interfaces are characterized	SD-1-G1-b	All interfaces characterized	SD-t4; SD-t6; SD-g1	SD-a5
Viewing interfaces within the setting prov... including both protections offered by the product security c...	SD-1-G1-c	Secure interface design included in secure design	SD-t6 ...ple, where it can be open to attack. [...]Finally, preparing documentation for the	SD-a5; SD-a3
SD-1-G2	SD-1-G2-a	Threat model has been used consequently	SD-t5	SD-a4; SR-a6
Identification of relevant interface data per interface	SD-1-G2-b	Interfaces are characterized by interaction types	SD-t5	SD-a4
Practice Goals	SD-1-G2-c	Specification of users and roles to use interface	SD-t5; SD- t17	SD-a4
SD-1-G1	SD-1-G2-d	Relevance of interface is adequately described	SD-t12; SD-t13; SD-t14; SD-t15; SD-t20; SD-t21	SD-a4
Product's interfaces are characterized	SD-1-G2-e	External accessibility is documented adequately	SD-t5	SD-a4
	SD-1-G3-a	Mitigation of the threats identified in the threat model are described	SD-t5; SD-t16; SD-t17; SD-t18; SD-t19; SD-t22;	SD-a4; SD-a5
SD-1-G2	SD-1-G2-a	Threat model has been used consequently	SD-t5	SD-a4; SR-a6

• • •

Practice Artefacts and Metrics		
Artifact		Related Metrics
SD-a3	Secure Design	SD-1-G1-c
SD-a4	Secure design of selected interface	SD-1-G1-a; SD-1-G2-a; SD-1-G2-a; SD-1-G2-c; SD-1-G2-d; SD-1-G2-e; SD-1-G3-a; SD-1-G3-b
SD-a5	Secure design of all interfaces	SD-1-G1-b; SD-1-G1-c; SD-1-G3-a

Fig. 3. Excerpts of the requirement card for the *Secure Design* requirement *SD-1 Secure design principles*

3.5 From Assessment to Process Improvement

Combining the components, namely the S^2C-SAFe, the bi-dimensional compliance matrix and the requirement cards as well as the method to use them, there appears a direct path to particular improvement of certain practice goals. Figure 4 drafts this process. Sticking to the same example as in Sect. 3.3 and Fig. 2 Requirement *SD-1* is still in deficit. As shown in Fig. 4 the requirement card of *SD-1* suggests metrics for the practice goal and points on related tasks and artifacts responsible for the performance concerning this metric. The next step leads directly into the S^2C-SAFe development process as shown in the process excerpt in Fig. 4. Thus, the highlighted elements of the process model have a direct impact on the compliance.

4 Support of Business-Relevant Security Choice

One major goal, besides the pure assessment of security-standard compliance, was the ability to integrate the S^2C-AM results in common management frameworks. Delivering security demands through well-known methods will make it easier for management to include security in their daily thoughts. Enabled through the design of the requirement cards this component of the proposed approach facilitates refinement of business goals, justification of security spendings and a steering tool.

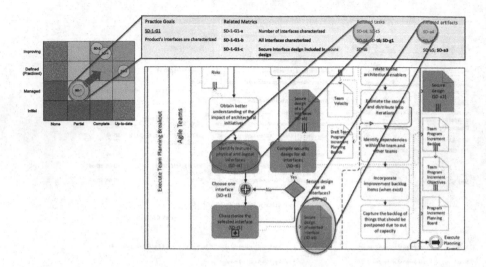

Fig. 4. Connection of multiple elements: compliance matrix (top left); excerpt of the *SD-1* requirement card (top right); excerpt of S²C-SAFe (bottom right), showing parts of *SD-1* integration.

4.1   Refinement of Business Goals

COBIT5 derives its processes from IT-related goals which cascade from enterprise goals and stakeholder needs [6]. Following this method, the design of the requirement cards is based on process description in COBIT5. Moreover, COBIT5s goal cascade can be extended by the requirements of the 4-1 standard. As shown in Table 2 we developed cross-reference tables, which assign the practice goals, introduced in Sect. 3.4, to COBIT5s IT-related goals. Just as in COBIT5, the practice goals are marked as primary (P) or secondary (S) influencing the referenced IT-related goal.

Via this reference, practice goals can be connected directly to IT-related goals and their reference to enterprise or business goals, thus, their business relevance can be illustrated. Vice versa business goals can be refined down to the level of practice goals for secure development and - in connection with the requirement cards - down to security tasks in the agile development process.

4.2   Justification of Security Spendings

Security spendings are hard to justify because measures and projects often do not offer a clear return on investment (ROI) and so security budgets stay narrow. By building a causal chain between enterprise goals and particular security processes, investments can be linked up to actual business strategies.

As process tasks and creation of artifacts need a certain amount of time and money, a particular assumption of costs for improvement of the identified process parts. Therefore, through the proposed approach, not only a assessment of compliance can be made but costs for compliance improvement can be specifically

Table 2. Example of COBIT5 IT-related goals cross-reference matrix for practice goals of 4-1 requirement *SD-1 Secure design principles*. (P = primary influence; S = secondary influence)

Practice 3 Secure Design SD-1 Secure Design Principles	IT compliance	IT-related risk	Transparency of IT costs	Security of information	Secure IT product development
	02	04	06	10	18
SD-1-G1 Products interfaces are characterized	P	S	P	P	P
SD-1-G2 Identification of relevant interface data	P	S		S	P
SD-1-G3 Mitigation of vulnerability of interfaces	P	S		S	P

calculated. By utilizing the connection to the COBIT5 goal cascade (see Fig. 2) those costs can be assigned to certain enterprise goals and strategic alignment.

With this approach, management can decide which costs the more of compliance causes and if adjustments are worth it.

4.3 Management Steering Tool

While the proposed metrics help to assess compliance, process maturity and artifact quality, they are an opportunity to enable managers fine-tune their processes. Having a look at the compliance matrix of Sect. 3.3, it shows not only the compliance level but offer starting points for improvement or change processes. Taking a look on a special goal from a certain practice goal, particular tasks can be identified in the agile development process and chosen for improvement projects. While a certain objective should be reached with those projects, possible consequences for other IT-related, and enterprise goals can be derived from the cross-reference tables. This enables managers to choose whether to improve a single requirement with a single focus or to earn low hanging fruits by improving requirements with multiple effects.

5   Evaluation

To evaluate the proposed assessment model and the method to use it, we conducted a qualitative expert interview series. During 21 semi-structured interviews with experts, working as cybersecurity specialists and managers at one of Germany's largest industrial actors, our main focuses were the needs of practitioners and how the S2C-AM can solve them. Moreover, we asked for practical benefits the S2C-AM delivers and the potential limitations of the approach. After all, we tried to figure out if the experts would use the model in there daily work. Therefore, the following research questions (RQ) guided our evaluation and where asked among others during the interviews[1]:

RQ 1 Does S^{2}C-AM cover all relevant aspects for compliance assessments?
RQ 2 From management perspective, does the model deliver the information managers demand for?
RQ 3 Which challenges exist when assessing security-standard compliance in this way?

5.1 Subject Selection

The S^{2}C-AM will mainly touch three different fields in practice: security, agile development and management. The model can potentially either bring benefits or barriers for players in all three areas.

To collect necessary needs and opinions from all the necessary fields, connected with security compliance, we asked security experts and agile development experts as well as governance and management experts. They cover for instance internal security process consultants, IT-infrastructure security specialists, developers and project leaders in agile environments, security governance consultants as well as managers from different business units. Additionally, among our interviewees there were IEC committee members for the IEC 62443 standard and an active contributor to SAFe.

Table 3 lists expert profiles, characterizes them and shows the number of interviewees associated with that group. Each interviewee was associated to only one group. We distinguish between different senior security experts, according to their main expertise and current area of responsibility.

5.2 Survey Instrument

Due to our goal to receive new ideas, valuable input and important expertise besides the singular appraisal of our method, we selected semi-structured interviews as the technique to conduct the interviews [17]. Meeting the interviewees in insulated environments, the interviews lasted between 60 and 90 min. One or two interviewers conducted the interviews with one to a maximum of two experts.

Each interview started with a quick briefing of the interview flow, followed by of a short explanation of the subjacent S^{2}C-SAFe and a detailed introduction in the S^{2}C-AM, containing the models elements, its possible application and the management integration approach. Afterwards the semi-structured interview was based on an interview guideline which consisted of five areas based on the research questions defined above.

---

[1] For the complete interview questionnaire visit https://sites.google.com/view/s2c-am-evaluation.

Table 3. Profile groups and count of interviewees each.

Profile	Characterization	Interviews	Count
SAFe Contributors	Contribute to improve SAFe. Companies ultimate experts concerning scaled agile	#8	1
IEC 62443 Contributors	Contributed to and evaluated the IEC 62443 norm for the IEC. Companies ultimate experts concerning for IEC 62443	#16, #17	2
Senior experts for IT security (management position)	Experienced and accepted experts for IT security. Holding a management position in the company	#9, #10, #13, #18, #21	5
Senior experts for security in IT infrastructure	Experienced and accepted experts for IT security. Responsible for IT security concerning IT infrastructure in their company	#14, #15	2
Senior experts for IT security governance	Experienced and accepted experts for IT security governance in their company, including IT governance, maturity models and frameworks	#1, #2 #20	3
Senior experts for IT security processes	Experienced and accepted experts for IT security processes. Responsible for IT security process assessment in their company	#4, #5 #19	3
Senior experts for agile development	Experienced and accepted experts for agile methodology and development. Responsible for agile development processes in their company	#3, #7 #11, #12	4
Experts for IT security	Experts for IT security in others than the areas above	#6	1
Overall count			21

5.3 Evaluation Results

As we analyzed the opinions of all experts in a qualitative manner, the following section summarizes all answers and interprets the results according to our research questions. Answers of particular interviewees will be pointed out by referencing the interview number (e.g. #13).

Section 5.3 Process maturity model, 5.3 Artifact quality model and 5.3 Compliance matrix discuss the basic elements of the model and answer on research question 1 (RQ1). Section 5.3 Management deals with RQ2 and Sect. 5.3 Practical use answers RQ3.

In addition, we asked if process maturity and artifact quality level description as well as the compliance matrix is intuitive and easy to understand. As Fig. 5 shows, the opinion of the interviewees is for all three aspects satisfying. The newly developed levels of the artifact quality are for 85 percent of the inter-

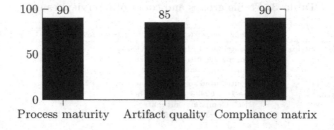

Fig. 5. Percentage of interviewed experts, who find the mentioned elements of the model intuitive and easy to understand.

viewees intuitive and easy to understand. 90 percent described the combined representation of both dimensions in the compliance matrix like this as well.

Process Maturity Model. For the design of the process maturity dimension we adopted the CMMI-dev-based model the 4-1 proposes. Interviewees encouraged us to do so and titled this as a good basis for acceptance in practice.

"Applying this, we would be way ahead." - *IEC 62443 Contributor (#16)*

Three interviewees (*#8, #18, #21*) mentioned using CMMI-dev as a baseline means a lack of agile aspects. The levels adopted from 4-1 standard do not clearly require the process to be lived, four of the interviewees (#1, #5, #7, #10) pointed out. Finally three experts (#12, #13, #14) mentioned that a questionnaire or any other support for conduction the assessment might be helpful.

Artifact Quality Model. While most experts (17 out of 21) agree that the two major aspects for a good artifact are completeness and timeliness, a few more aspects to consider were named: for instance correctness of content (*#7, #8*), traceability (*#18*) and understandability (*#10*). Moreover, four interviewees (*#4, #12, #14, #20*) demanded templates for each required artifact, to deliver precise information on required structure and content. Only one participant (*#19*) called the artifact dimension "understandable but unnecessary".

"This seems to be a very good method." - *IEC 62443 Contributor (#17)*

Although one interviewee (*#2*) was in doubt if timeliness is really measurable, another expert (*#6*) said that "the use of the support matrix illustrates the path to certain levels very comprehensible". Finally, an *IT infrastructure expert (#14)* presumed that "the model might be much more valuable than just to use it for agile development."

Compliance Matrix.

"If we only get those two dimensions under control, we are fine!" - *Agile development expert (#7)*

The conjunction of process maturity and artifact quality was appreciated by all experts but one (#19) who thought it was too complex. Two interviewees (#12, #18) missed roles and responsibilities in this representation and another one (#17) supposed to put in a third dimension of "multiple projects in a row". First and foremost the simplicity of this representation and the good level of abstraction for the management is emphasized by the interviewed experts.

> "Especially for representing conformity, that model is perfectly comprehensible." - *Senior expert IT security in management position (#18)*

Management Focus.

> "The matrix is a really good representation, this is exactly what they want." - *IEC 62443 Contributor (#16)*

Regarding RQ1, we asked all experts, if the model delivers all necessary information demanded by the management for compliance insights and control decisions - 95 percent agreed completely. Although some raised that only the matrix should find its way into management summaries due to complexity of the requirement cards. Their granularity might be to detailed but could be abstracted.

Moreover, one *IEC 62443 contributor* mentioned (#16) that the complete model might be a enormous help for auditors as well. An *IT security expert in management position* highlighted the expedient value of cascading from enterprise goals down to practice goals and vice versa. Two-thirds appreciate the link-ability to COBIT5s goal cascade and the adoption of its process description for the requirement cards, as it is a well known IT government framework.

> "Until now we did not find an appropriate bridging between business an IT - this seems to be a good one." - *Senior expert IT security in management position (#18)*

Practical Use.

> "This approach perfectly fits to our manner of depicting and living processes." - *IEC 62443 Contributor (#16)*

About 80% of the experts would like to try the approach directly in their division. The others concerned that it might be to heavy to integrate ad hoc and would wait until pilot projects worked out. Regarding RQ2 the main challenges the participants see are the regulation of process overhead and therefore the acceptance of the higher workload for development teams. Moreover, some demand for a road map and trainings for developers as well as project leaders to introduce the model.

The rising relevance of compliance and its verification in the future makes this model a valuable asset, a *senior expert IT security in management position* (#21) stated. Some experts see more than an assessment tool in this approach by now. Although an *expert for security in IT infrastructure (#15)* complained that in his sense most managers trust their guts instead of rational criteria.

Finally, the concluding tenor of almost all interviews was: "please, can we give it a try?"

6   Conclusion and Future Work

Our contribution provides a foundation for business-driven security compliance management. It is currently tailored to the security-standard IEC 62443-4-1 (4-1) for secure product development in the industrial control system (ICS) domain and the Scaled Agile Framework (SAFe). However, they are currently provided in BPMN models, these can be exchanged with little effort and therefore allow our approach to be used with other standards and frameworks as well.

In particular, we showed how the precision of process models in combination with security maturity assessment based on the 4-1 standard can be utilized to detect non-conformance, precisely describe what activities and artifacts have to be improved or introduced. By this, our method delivers compliance by default. Moreover, it enables to estimate the costs of security compliance. Note that costs can be expressed in time, which the activities add to the overall development effort, in the amount of money these extra hours cost, and in the costs for creating and maintaining the additional artifacts. These numbers provide management with an estimation of how much they have to spend for security compliance. Therefore, management can decide if the costs for compliance justifies the improvement in product quality.

Results of our evaluation with numerous key stakeholder of a major industry player in the field of ICS confirm the usefulness and applicability of our work.

6.1   Limitations and Threats to Validity

We discuss the threats to validity using the four validity classes proposed by Wohlin et al. [20].

Construct Validity. The measurements of the experiment include the process maturity standard CMMI-dev, which is an internationally established method to assess process quality. Therefore, we believe this measure to be appropriate for our study. The artifact quality approach adopts the same method. Combination of two dimensions in a matrix is a common, intuitive method to aggregate. However, findings are based on opinions of experts, which did neither have hands-on experience with the model nor the method.

Conclusion Validity. The experiment was conducted by using one particular part of the security standard IEC 62443-4-1 and SAFe. We decided not to show the entire models and assessment tool in order to avoid lengthy processes and too much complexity. Moreover, the participants were interviewed individually, to avoid that they talk to each other.

Internal Validity. We selected practitioners in this experiment who hold leading positions in software engineering and security engineering in a large German company, active in the field of ICS. To assess expert status, we asked the participants for a self-assessment of their knowledge and skills in the knowledge areas of security and software engineering.

References

1. Ahola, J., et al.: Handbook of the Secure Agile Software Development Life Cycle. University of Oulu, Finland (2014)
2. CMMI Product Team: CMMI for Development, version 1.2 (2006)
3. Fitzgerald, B., Stol, K.J.: Continuous software engineering: a roadmap and agenda. J. Syst. Softw. **123**, 176–189 (2017)
4. Herrmann, P., Herrmann, G.: Security requirement analysis of business processes. Electron. Commer. Res. **6**(3), 305–335 (2006)
5. IEC: 62443-4-1 Security for industrial automation and control systems Part 4–1 Secure product development life-cycle requirements. IEC (2016)
6. Isaca, P.A.M.: Using COBIT 5. ISACA, Rolling Meadows (2013)
7. Jaquith, A.: Security Metrics: Replacing Fear, Uncertainty, and Doubt. Pearson Education, London (2007)
8. Kupiainen, E., Mäntylä, M.V., Itkonen, J.: Using metrics in agile and lean software development - a systematic literature review of industrial studies. Inf. Softw. Technol. **62**, 143–163 (2015)
9. van Lamsweerde, A., Letier, E.: Handling obstacles in goal-oriented requirements engineering. IEEE Trans. Softw. Eng. **26**(10), 978–1005 (2000)
10. Leffingwell, D., Yakyma, A., Jemilo, D., Oren, I.: SAFe Reference Guide. Pearson, London (2017). (2017 edn.)
11. Li, T., Horkoff, J.: Dealing with security requirements for socio-technical systems: a holistic approach. In: Jarke, M., et al. (eds.) CAiSE 2014. LNCS, vol. 8484, pp. 285–300. Springer, Cham (2014). https://doi.org/10.1007/978-3-319-07881-6_20
12. Liu, L., Yu, E., Mylopoulos, J.: Security and privacy requirements analysis within a social setting. In: Proceedings of the 11th IEEE International Conference on Requirements Engineering, RE 2003, Washington, DC, USA, pp. 151. IEEE Computer Society (2003)
13. Mouratidis, H., Giorgini, P.: Secure Tropos: a security-oriented extension of the Tropos methodology. J. Auton. Agents Multi-Agent Syst. (2005)
14. Moyon, F., Beckers, K., Klepper, S., Lachberger, P., Bruegge, B.: Towards continuous security compliance in agile software development at scale. In: Proceedings of RCoSE. ACM (2018)
15. Pino, F.J., Baldassarre, M.T., Piattini, M., Visaggio, G.: Harmonizing maturity levels from CMMI-DEV and ISO/IEC 15504. J. Softw. Maintenance Evol.: Res. Pract. **22**(4), 279–296 (2010)
16. Scaled Agile Inc.: Safe reference guide (2017). http://www.scaledagileframework.com/
17. Shull, F., Singer, J., Sjøberg, D.I.: Guide to Advanced Empirical Software Engineering. Springer, London (2007). https://doi.org/10.1007/978-1-84800-044-5
18. TechBeacon: Survey: is agile the new norm? (2017). https://techbeacon.com/survey-agile-new-norm

19. Turpe, S., Poller, A.: Managing security work in scrum: tensions and challenges. In: Proceedings of SecSE (2017)
20. Wohlin, C., Runeson, P., Höst, M., Ohlsson, M.C., Regnell, B., Wesslén, A.: Experimentation in Software Engineering. Springer, Berlin (2012). https://doi.org/10. 1007/978-3-642-29044-2

Learning and Mining in Information Systems

Proactive Process Adaptation Using Deep Learning Ensembles

Andreas Metzger(✉) ⓘ, Adrian Neubauer, Philipp Bohn, and Klaus Pohl

paluno – The Ruhr Institute for Software Technology,
University of Duisburg-Essen, Essen, Germany
{andreas.metzger,adrian.neubauer,philipp.bohn,
klaus.pohl}@paluno.uni-due.de

Abstract. Proactive process adaptation can prevent and mitigate upcoming problems during process execution. Proactive adaptation decisions are based on predictions about how an ongoing process instance will unfold up to its completion. On the one hand, these predictions must have high accuracy, as, for instance, false negative predictions mean that necessary adaptations are missed. On the other hand, these predictions should be produced early during process execution, as this leaves more time for adaptations, which typically have non-negligible latencies. However, there is an important tradeoff between prediction accuracy and earliness. Later predictions typically have a higher accuracy, because more information about the ongoing process instance is available. To address this tradeoff, we use an ensemble of deep learning models that can produce predictions at arbitrary points during process execution and that provides reliability estimates for each prediction. We use these reliability estimates to dynamically determine the earliest prediction with sufficient accuracy, which is used as basis for proactive adaptation. Experimental results indicate that our dynamic approach may offer cost savings of 27% on average when compared to using a static prediction point.

Keywords: Business process monitoring · Proactive adaptation · Prediction · Accuracy · Earliness

1 Introduction

Proactive process adaptation can prevent the occurrence of problems and it can mitigate the impact of upcoming problems during process execution [1,18,31] by dynamically re-planning the flow of a running process instance [19,28,37]. Proactive process adaptation thereby can avoid contractual penalties or time-consuming roll-back and compensation activities.

Proactive process adaptation relies on predictive process monitoring to predict potential problems. Predictive process monitoring predicts how an ongoing process instance (a.k.a. case) will unfold up to its completion [8,16,22]. If a potential problem is predicted, adaptation decisions are taken at run time

© The Author(s) 2019
P. Giorgini and B. Weber (Eds.): CAiSE 2019, LNCS 11483, pp. 547–562, 2019.
https://doi.org/10.1007/978-3-030-21290-2_34

to prevent or mitigate the predicted problem. As an example, a delay in the expected delivery time for a freight transport process may incur contractual penalties [11]. If during the execution of such freight transport process a delay is predicted, faster transport services (such as air delivery instead of road delivery) can be proactively scheduled in order to prevent the delay.

With respect to predictions, there are two important requirements for proactive process adaptation. On the one hand, predictions must have high accuracy, as, for instance, false negative predictions mean that necessary adaptations are missed. On the other hand, predictions should be produced early during process execution, as this leaves more time for adaptations, which typically have non-negligible latencies. However, there is an important tradeoff between these two requirements. Later predictions typically have a higher accuracy, because more information about the ongoing process instance becomes available.

We address the aforementioned tradeoff by using ensembles of deep learning models. Ensemble prediction is a meta-prediction technique where the predictions of m prediction models are combined into a single prediction [30]. We use deep learning ensembles to produce predictions at arbitrary points during process execution. In addition we compute reliability estimates for each prediction by computing the fraction of prediction models that predicted the majority class [19]. A high reliability indicates a high probability that the ensemble prediction is correct. We use these reliability estimates to dynamically determine the earliest prediction with sufficiently high reliability and use this prediction as basis for proactive adaptation. Experimental results based on four real-world data sets suggests that our dynamic approach offers cost savings of 27% on average when compared to using a fixed, static prediction point.

Section 2 provides a detailed problem statement and analysis of related work. Section 3 describes our approach. Section 4 provides its experimental evaluation.

2   Problem Statement and Related Work

2.1   Prediction Accuracy and Reliability

Problem. As mentioned above, one key requirement for proactive process adaptation are accurate predictions. Informally, prediction accuracy characterizes the ability of a prediction technique to forecast as many true violations as possible, while generating as few false alarms as possible [33]. Prediction accuracy is important for two main reasons [21]. First, accurate predictions deliver more true violations and thus trigger more required adaptations. Each missed required adaptation means one less opportunity for preventing or mitigating a problem. Second, accurate predictions mean less false alarms, and thus triggering less unnecessary adaptations. Unnecessary adaptations incur additional costs for executing the adaptations, while not addressing actual problems.

Previous research on predictive process monitoring (see [16] for an overview) focused on aggregate accuracy, such as precision or recall. Even though a high aggregate accuracy is beneficial, it does not provide direct information about the accuracy of an *individual* prediction. Knowing the accuracy of an individual prediction is important, because some predictions may have a higher probability of being correct than others. Proactive adaptation decisions are taken on a case by case basis. Therefore, the information about whether an individual prediction may be correct provides additional support for decision making [18, 19].

Prediction techniques traditionally used for predictive process monitoring (such as decision trees, k-nearest-neighbors, support vector machines, and multi-layer perceptrons [8, 16]) can provide probabilities to indicate whether an individual prediction is correct (e.g., in the form of class probabilities of a decision tree). Yet, probabilities estimated by most of these prediction techniques are poor [38]. In contrast, so called *reliability estimates* (e.g., computed from ensembles of prediction models) can provide better estimates of the probability that an individual prediction is correct [2].

Related Work. To improve aggregate prediction accuracy, deep learning techniques are being employed for predictive process monitoring [5, 9, 17, 26, 27, 34]. In particular, Recurrent Neural Networks (RNNs) are employed, which are a special type of artificial neural network, where each neuron also feeds back information into itself [5, 10]. Empirical evidence indicates that RNNs provide significant accuracy improvements for predictive process monitoring [5, 20, 34]. As an example, the empirical results of our previous work on using RNNs show an accuracy improvement of 36% when compared to multi-layer perceptrons [20]. Yet, the aforementioned approaches only consider aggregate accuracy and do not consider the accuracy of individual predictions for proactive adaptation decisions.

In the literature, some authors considered the probability that an individual prediction is correct. Maggi et al. [15] use decision tree learning for predictive process monitoring. As a follow up, Francescomarino et al. [7] employ random forests (an ensembles of decision trees) for prediction. Both use class probabilities of decision trees. They analyze how selecting predictions using class probabilities impacts on aggregate prediction accuracy. They observe that using class probabilities may improve aggregate accuracy, but at the expedient of loosing predictions that are below a given probability threshold. Yet, they do not analyze in how far using these class probabilities may improve proactive process adaptation and whether it may offer cost savings.

In our earlier work, we used reliability estimates computed from ensembles of multi-layer perceptrons to decide on proactive adaptation [18, 19]. If the reliability for a given prediction is equal to or greater than a predefined threshold, the prediction is used to trigger a proactive adaptation. In [19] we considered reliabilities computed from ensembles of classification models, which led to cost savings of up to 54% (14% on average). In [18] we also included the magnitude of a predicted violation (computed from ensembles of regression models) into the adaptation decision, which led to additional cost savings of up to 31% (14.8% on average). Yet, we used a fixed point for our predictions (the 50% mark of process execution), and thus did not consider the aspect of prediction earliness.

2.2 Prediction Earliness

Problem. Predictions can be made at different points during the execution of a process instance. The point during process execution for which a prediction is made is called *checkpoint* [13,22]. When determining checkpoints, there is an important tradeoff to be taken into account between prediction accuracy and the earliness of the prediction [13]. This is particularly important when predictions at a given checkpoint are used as basis for proactive process adaptation.

Typically, prediction accuracy increases as the process unfolds, as more information about the process instance becomes available. As an example, between the 25% mark and the 75% mark in process execution, accuracy may increase by 44% (as reported in [36]) and even by 97% (as reported in [22]). This means later predictions have a higher chance to be correct predictions, and thus one should favor later checkpoints as basis for proactive process adaptation.

However, waiting for the predictions of later checkpoints also means that the remaining time for proactively addressing problems becomes shorter [13]. This can be important as adaptations typically have non-negligible latencies, i.e., it may take some time until they become effective [23]. As an example, dispatching additional personnel to mitigate delays in container transports may take several hours. Also, the later a process is adapted, the fewer options may be available for adaptation. As an example, while at the beginning of a transport process one may be able to transport a container by train instead of ship, once the container is on-board the ship, such adaption may no longer be feasible. Finally, if an adaptation is performed late in the process and turns out not to be effective, not much time may remain for any remedial actions or further adaptations. This means one should choose a rather early checkpoint.

Related Work. In the literature, the tradeoff between prediction accuracy and earliness was approached from different angles. Several authors use prediction earliness as a dependent variable in their experiments. This means they evaluate their proposed predictive process monitoring techniques by considering prediction earliness in addition to prediction accuracy. As an example, Kang et al. [12], Teinemaa et al. [36], and we in our earlier work [20,22] measured the accuracy of different prediction techniques for the different checkpoints along process execution. Results presented in the aforementioned works clearly show the tradeoff between prediction earliness and accuracy. However, how to resolve the tradeoff between accuracy and earliness was not further addressed.

To increase the earliness of accurate predictions, several authors proposed new variants of prediction techniques. As an example, Teinemaa et al. investigate whether unstructured data may increase prediction earliness and accuracy [35]. Similarly, Leontjeva et al. exploit the data payload of process events to increase prediction earliness [14]. Finally, Francescomarino et al. investigate in how far hyper-parameter optimization [7] and clustering [6] can improve earliness. A similar tradeoff between accuracy and earliness was investigated for time series classification, i.e., for predicting the class label of a temporally-indexed set of data points. The aim is to predict the final label of a time series with sufficiently high accuracy by using the lowest number of data points. Being able to accurately classify a time series early on facilitates early situation detection and thus may help to timely respond to risks and failures [24]. An additional motivation is to reduce the computational effort when compared with using the whole time series for prediction, which is of particular concern for resource- or power-constrained devices [25, 29]. As an example, Mori et al. use probabilistic classifiers to produce a class label for a time series as soon as the probability at a checkpoint exceeds a class-dependent threshold [25]. The aforementioned works address different needs of earliness and accuracy by setting the available parameters, such as prediction reliability thresholds. However, they did not examine in how far the techniques have found a good trade-off between earliness and accuracy. Doing so, requires quantifying the utility of the achieved trade-off, as comparing the techniques solely based on earliness and accuracy may not provide a fair comparison. To quantify such utility, we thus measure how choosing the actual checkpoint for adaptation decisions impacts on overall costs of process execution.

3   Deep Learning Ensembles for Proactive Adaptation

To find a trade-off between earliness and accuracy, we exploit the fact that reliability estimates can provide information about the accuracy of an individual prediction. The key idea of our approach is to (i) dynamically determine, for each process instance, the earliest checkpoint that delivers a sufficiently high reliability, and (ii) use this checkpoint to decide on proactive adaptation.

We compute predictions and reliability estimates from ensembles of deep learning models, specifically RNN models. Ensemble prediction is a meta-prediction technique where the predictions of m prediction models, so called *base learners*, are combined into a single prediction [30].

Ensemble prediction is primarily used to increase aggregate prediction accuracy, while it also allows computing reliability estimates (see Sect. 2.1). Computing reliability estimates is the main reason why we use ensembles of RNN models in our approach. As added benefit, predictions computed via such ensembles provide higher prediction accuracy than using a single RNN model. As an example, RNN ensembles provide an 8.4% higher accuracy when compared with a single RNN model (as used in [20]).

Figure 1 provides an overview of the main activities of our approach.

The ensemble of RNN models creates a prediction T_j at each potential checkpoint j. In addition, it provides the reliability estimate ρ_j for this prediction. If the ensemble predicts a violation at checkpoint j, a proactive adaptation may be needed in order to prevent or mitigate the predicted violation. However, we only act on this prediction if its reliability ρ_j is equal to or greater than a predefined threshold, i.e., we only act if we consider the prediction reliable enough. Thereby, our approach dynamically determines the earliest checkpoint with sufficient reliability that is used as basis for proactive adaptation. This implies that the actual checkpoint chosen for a proactive adaptation decision will vary among the different process instances, in the same way the reliability estimates may be different for each prediction and each process instance.

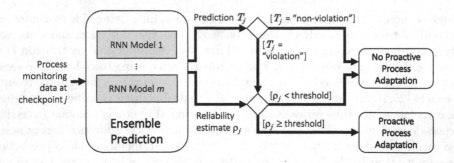

Fig. 1. RNN ensemble for dynamically deciding on proactive process adaptation

3.1 RNNs as Base Learners

We use RNNs as base learners, i.e., as the individual models in the ensemble, as RNNs can handle arbitrary length sequences of input data [10]. Thus, a single RNN can be employed to make predictions for business processes that have an arbitrary length in terms of process activities. In contrast, other prediction techniques (such as random forests or multi-layer perceptrons) either require training a prediction model for each of the checkpoints or they require the special encoding of the input data to train a single model [16,22,36]. However, these encodings entail information loss and thus may limit prediction performance.

RNNs also facilitate the scalability of our dynamic approach. Assume we have c checkpoints in the business process. A single RNN model can make predictions at any of these c checkpoints [5,34]. If we want to avoid information loss, other prediction techniques would require the training of c prediction models, one for each of the c checkpoints. Our exploratory performance measurements indicate a training time of ca. 8 min per checkpoint for multi-layer perceptrons on a standard PC, while the training time for an RNN was 25 min[1]. This means that RNNs provide better scalability for our approach if the process has many potential checkpoints ($c > 3$ in our case).

We use RNNs with Long Short-Term Memory (LSTM) cells as they better capture long-term dependencies in the data [17,34]. Our implementation of these RNN base learners is available online[2]. It exploits the Keras library[3] running on top of TensorFlow[4].

However, RNNs also face specific challenges when used for predictive process monitoring. Even though the data that is fed into an RNN is sequential, i.e., a sequence of events, these events represent the execution of business processes which may include loops and parallel regions. Such non-sequential control flows

---

[1] Further performance speedups are possible via special-purpose hardware and RNN implementations. RNN training time reduced to 8 min on GPUs (using CuDNN), and further to 2 min on TPUs (Tensor Processing Units).

[2] https://github.com/Chemsorly/BusinessProcessOutcomePrediction.

[3] https://keras.io/; Version 2.2.4.

[4] https://github.com/tensorflow/; Version 1.9.

can make prediction with RNNs more difficult [5,9,34], as RNNs were conceived for natural language processing, which is sequential by nature [10].

To address these difficulties, we employ the following two solutions (presented in earlier work [20]). First, instead of incrementally predicting the next process event until we reach the final event and thus the process outcome (such as proposed in [5,9,34]), we directly predict the process outcome. Thereby, we avoid the problem RNNs may have in predicting the next process activity when process execution entails loops with many repeated activities [9,34]. Second, we encode parallel process activities by embedding the branch information as an additional attribute of the respective process activity. Thereby, we address the problem that parallel process activities can make the prediction task more difficult [5].

3.2 RNN Ensembles

We use bagging (bootstrap aggregating [4]) as a concrete ensemble technique to build the base learners of our RNN ensemble. Bagging generates m new training data sets from the whole training set by sampling from the whole training data set uniformly and with replacement. For each of the m new training data sets an individual RNN model is trained. We use bagging with a sample size of 60% to increase the diversity of the RNN ensembles. Generating the ensembles using bagging also contributes to the scalability of our approach, as the training of the base learners can happen in parallel.

For computing the ensemble predictions T_j and reliability estimates ρ_j for each checkpoint j, we employ the strategies defined in [18,19], because these strategies showed reasonably good results for a fixed checkpoint. Let us assume that at each checkpoint j, each of the m base learners of the ensemble delivers a prediction result $T_{i,j}$, with $i = 1, \ldots, m$, where $T_{i,j}$ is either of class "violation" or "non-violation".

The **ensemble prediction** for checkpoint j is computed as a majority vote:

$$T_j = \begin{cases} \text{"violation"}, & |i : T_{i,j} = \text{"violation"}| \geq m/2 \\ \text{"non-violation"}, & \text{otherwise.} \end{cases}$$

The **reliability estimate** ρ_j for prediction T_j is computed as the fraction of base learners that predicted the majority class:

$$\rho_j = max_{i=1,\ldots,m}\left(\frac{|i : T_{i,j} = \text{"violation"}|}{m}, \frac{|i : T_{i,j} = \text{"non-violation"}|}{m}\right)$$

4 Experimental Evaluation

4.1 Cost Model

We aim to answer the question in how far determining checkpoints based on reliability estimates (our *dynamic* approach) compares to determining checkpoints based on aggregate accuracy (the *static* approach). To this end, we quantify and compare the costs of process execution and adaptation of these approaches.

We employ a cost model used in our previous work [19], which incorporates two cost factors of proactive process adaptation as shown in Fig. 2. The first cost factor is *adaptation costs*, as an adaptation of a running processes typically requires effort and resources, and thus incurs costs. The second cost factor is *penalties*, which may be faced in two situations. First, a proactive adaptation may be missed. This can be due to a false negative prediction (i.e., a non-violation is predicted despite an actual violation), or because the reliability threshold was not reached, even though it was an actual violation. Second, a proactive adaptation may not be effective, i.e., the violation may persist after the adaptation.

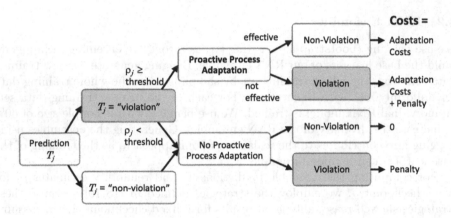

Fig. 2. Cost model for proactive process adaptation

4.2   Experimental Variables

We consider *cost* as the **dependent variable** in our experiments. For each process instance, we compute its individual costs according to the cost model defined in Sect. 4.1. The total costs are the sum of the individual costs of all process instances in our test data set. The test data set comprises 1/3 of the process instances of the overall data set.

We consider the following **independent variables** (also shown in Table 1):

Reliability threshold $\theta \in [.5, 1]$. As introduced in Sect. 3, a proactive adaptation is triggered only if the reliability of a predicted violation is equal to or greater than a pre-defined threshold, we name θ.

Relative adaptation costs $\lambda \in [0, 1]$. To be able to concisely analyze and present our experimental results, we assume constant costs and penalties (like we did in [19]). Thus, the costs of a process adaptation, c_a, are expressed as a fraction of the penalty for process violation, c_p, i.e., $c_a = \lambda \cdot c_p$. We thereby can reflect different situations that may be faced in practice concerning how costly a process adaptation in relation to a penalty may be. Choosing $\lambda > 1$ would not make sense, as this leads to higher costs than if no adaptation is performed.

Adaptation effectiveness $\alpha \in (0, 1]$. If an adaptation results in a non-violation, we consider such an adaptation effective (cf. Fig. 2). We use α to represent the fact that not all adaptations might be effective. More concretely, α represents the probability that an adaptation is effective. We do not consider $\alpha = 0$ as this means that no adaptation is effective. To reflect the fact that earlier checkpoints may be favored as they provide more options and time for proactive adaptations (see Sect. 2.2), we vary α in our experiments in such a way that α linearly decreases over the course of process execution. This means that the probability for effective proactive adaptations diminishes towards the end of the process. To model this, we define α_{max} as the α for the first checkpoint in the process instance, and α_{min} as the α for the last checkpoint.

Table 1. Variation of independent variables

Variable		Lower bound	Upper bound	Increment
Rel. adaptation costs	λ	0.0	1.0	.1
Reliability threshold	θ	.5	1.0	.005
Adaptation effectiveness	α_{max}	.1	1.0	.1
	α_{min}	.1	α_{max}	.1

4.3 Data Sets

We use four data sets from different sources. The *Cargo2000* transport data set[5] is the one we used in our previous work. The other three data sets are among the ones frequently used to evaluate predictive process monitoring approaches [3,5, 32,34,36]. Table 2 provides key characteristics of these data sets, including the number of checkpoints we used in our experiments.

Table 2. Data sets used in experiments

Name	Pos. class	Pos. class ratio	Process instances	Process variants	Check-points
Cargo2000	Delayed air cargo delivery	27%	3,942	144	7
Traffic	Unpaid traffic fine	46%	129,615	185	4
BPIC2012	Unsuccessful credit application	52%	13,087	3,587	23
BPIC2017	Unsuccessful credit application	59%	31,413	2,087	23

4.4 Experimental Results

Using two of the data sets as an example, Fig. 3 gives a first impression of the effect of our dynamic approach. The figure shows the costs of the dynamic approach (bold) and the costs of the static approach for each of the possible

---

[5] Available from https://archive.ics.uci.edu/ml/datasets.

checkpoints (dashed). The right hand side of each chart shows the costs without any adaptation (expressed by $\theta > 1$). These costs also serves as baseline. We chose $\alpha_{\max} = .9$ and $\alpha_{\min} = .5$, reflecting the fact that early on in the process there is a high chance that adaptation is effective, whilst at the very end, this chance is only 50%. Also, we show the results for two values of λ (relative adaptation costs). A $\lambda = .1$ reflects the situation where adaptation is rather cheap, whereas $\lambda = .4$ a situation where it is more expensive.

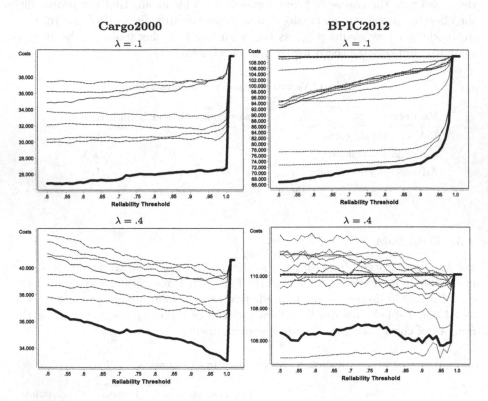

Fig. 3. Costs of dynamic approach (**bold**) vs. static approach (each dashed line represents one checkpoint); $\alpha_{\max} = .9$; $\alpha_{\min} = .5$

The charts in Fig. 3 indicate that the dynamic approach provides cost benefits when compared to the static approach, in particular when adaptations are not too expensive ($\lambda = .1$). The charts for more expensive adaptations ($\lambda = .4$) show that cost savings may become less, and may even be negative, such as for BPIC2012, where the static approach performs better for three checkpoints.

Also – independent of the static or dynamic approach – it can be observed that if adaptation costs get higher, a higher threshold (and thus more conservative stance in taking adaptation decisions) offers cost savings. While costs for $\lambda = .1$ are lowest for small thresholds, the situation is exactly opposite for $\lambda = .4$. The reason is that if adaptation costs are low (smaller λ) carrying out unnecessary adaptations is not so costly and thus it pays off not being too conservative (i.e., setting a lower threshold). However, if adaptation costs are high (greater λ), unnecessary adaptations can quickly become very costly, and thus being more conservative (i.e., setting a higher threshold) pays off.

To further explore the situations in which the dynamic approach offers cost savings, we performed a full-factorial experiment, combining all parameter settings of our independent variables as shown in Table 1. The results for all four data sets are presented in Table 3 for different, selected values of λ. For each λ, 6666 different situations were explored.

Table 3. Number of situations (and fraction of all situations in %)

λ	A Cost(proactive) < Cost(no adapt.)		B Cost(dynamic) < Cost(static)		$A-B$	A Cost(proactive) < Cost(no adapt.)		B Cost(dynamic) < Cost(static)		$A-B$
	Cargo2000					BPIC2012				
.05	5720	85.8%	5496	82.4%	3.4%	5043	75.7%	4892	73.4%	2.3%
.25	4303	64.6%	4053	60.8%	3.8%	3443	51.7%	3189	47.8%	3.8%
.45	2353	35.3%	2030	30.5%	4.8%	1529	22.9%	1210	18.2%	4.8%
.65	704	10.6%	436	6.5%	4.0%	398	6.0%	137	2.1%	3.9%
.85	86	1.3%	14	.2%	1.1%	96	1.4%	0	0.0%	1.4%
	Traffic					BPIC2017				
.05	5696	85.4%	5282	79.2%	6.2%	5996	89.9%	5948	89.2%	.7%
.25	4385	65.8%	3971	59.6%	6.2%	5078	76.2%	5027	75.4%	.8%
.45	2673	40.1%	2280	34.2%	5.9%	3618	54.3%	3552	53.3%	1.0%
.65	560	8.4%	168	2.5%	5.9%	1739	26.1%	1661	24.9%	1.2%
.85	51	.8%	0	0.0%	.8%	31	.5%	0	0.0%	.5%

Column A shows the number of situations for which proactive adaptation leads to lower costs than the baseline costs when not performing an adaptation. This is an important metric to contextualize our results, as proactive adaptation may not be beneficial in all situations. In particular, when adaptation costs are high and the chances for a successful adaptation are low, proactive adaptation may not help (e.g., see [19]). As can be seen in column A, the relative number of situations, where proactive adaptation helps saving costs diminishes as λ increases. As an example, while for a $\lambda = .05$, proactive adaptation is beneficial in 85.4% of situations for Traffic and 75.7% for BPIC2012, this goes down to .8% and 1.4% respectively for $\lambda = .85$.

Column B shows the number of situations where the dynamic approach has lower costs than the static approach. This indicates that the dynamic approach indeed offers additional cost savings in many situations when compared to the static approach. As can be seen from the last column, the situations in which the static approach has less costs than the dynamic approach, are not very high (at around 3% on average). Again, the dynamic approach offers the highest number of savings for smaller values of λ, where the number of situations reach 82.4% for Cargo2000 and even 89.2% for BPIC2017 to give an example.

The actual cost savings of the dynamic approach compared with the static one are shown in Table 4 for different values of λ and θ. Gray cells highlight where costs of the dynamic approach are less than the costs of the static one ('0' indicates that the costs of proactive adaptation are higher than the costs of not performing an adaptation). The table shows the cost savings for selected values of θ, averaged over all combinations of α.

Table 4. Average savings of dynamic vs. static approach in %

λ	Threshold θ											Threshold θ										
	.5	.55	.6	.65	.7	.75	.8	.85	.9	.95	1.0	5	.55	.6	.65	.7	.75	.8	.85	.9	.95	1.0
	Cargo2000											BPIC2012										
.05	24	24	23	21	21	19	19	18	17	17	16	52	52	50	49	46	45	44	43	41	34	0
.25	14	14	14	13	13	12	12	11	11	11	11	24	24	23	23	22	22	22	22	21	19	0
.45	8.1	8.4	8.6	8.4	8.4	7.7	7.6	7.4	7.3	7.2	7.3	11	12	12	12	12	12	12	12	12	11	0
.65	-14	6	6.1	6.7	6.5	5.7	4.6	4.3	4.4	4.2	4.3	2.3	3.4	3.6	4.1	4	4.2	4.8	3.6	4.1	4.6	0
.85	-20	-18	-16	-14	-12	-12	-11	-9.4	-8.3	-5.8	2.1	-28	-28	-28	-28	-27	-27	-26	-25	-23	-13	0
	Traffic											BPIC2017										
.05	98	94	90	85	80	72	68	62	55	46	30	110	110	100	100	91	87	82	79	77	74	60
.25	33	33	32	32	31	30	30	29	27	25	19	44	44	43	42	40	39	38	37	36	35	30
.45	22	22	22	21	21	20	20	19	19	17	13	33	33	32	32	31	30	28	27	26	24	18
.65	-19	-18	-18	-16	-16	4.9	4.9	5.2	7.2	6	7	30	29	26	26	26	24	23	21	20	17	8.4
.85	-29	-28	-27	-26	-25	-24	-23	-22	-20	-15	-7.6	-14	-14	-14	-14	-14	-14	-13	-12	-11	-9.8	-7.2

Higher thresholds imply that cost savings are achieved for higher values of λ. As an example, for Traffic a threshold of $\theta = .6$ allows cost savings up to $\lambda = .45$, while a $\theta = .8$ allows cost savings up to $\lambda = .65$. The reason is that a higher threshold means that adaptation decisions are take more conservatively. They are taken only if a prediction is highly reliable, which in turn implies that the number of unnecessary (and costly) adaptations are reduced.

However, being conservative comes at a risk. The cost savings for higher thresholds can become smaller than the cost savings for lower thresholds. As an example, while for Cargo2000 a threshold of $\theta = .5$ leads to cost savings of up to 24%, this goes down to savings of only up to 16% for $\theta = 1$. And it may even mean that the cost of proactive adaptation is higher than not performing any adaptation, as can be seen for $\theta = 1$ for BPIC2012.

Overall (i.e, considering all possible situations), the average savings are 9.2% for Cargo2000, 27.2% for Traffic, 15.1% for BPIC2012, and 35.8% for BPIC2017. Across all four data sets, average savings are 27%. We conclude that the dynamic approach can deliver cost savings compared to the static approach, with a high chance that it is better than not performing any proactive adaptation at all.

In addition, the dynamic approach comes with the benefit that there is no need for an up-front decision on which checkpoint to use as basis for proactive adaptation, which is required in the static approach. In particular this means, that there is no need for a testing phase during which aggregate accuracies are computed in order to select a suitable static checkpoint.

4.5   Threats to Validity

Internal Validity. To minimize the risk of bias, we explored different ensembles sizes (ranging from 2 to 100). Literature indicates that smaller ensembles might perform better than larger ensembles ("many could be better than all" [38]). In our experiments, however, the size of the ensemble did not lead to different principal findings. Yet, by using a larger ensemble, we gain more fine-grained reliability estimates than by using a smaller ensemble.

External Validity. To cover different situations that may be faced in practice, we specifically chose different reliability thresholds, different probabilities of effective process adaptations, as well as different slopes for how these probabilities diminish towards the end of process execution. In addition, we used four large, real-world data sets from different application domains, which differ in key characteristics. For the sake of generalizability, we used a naïve approach to select data from the event log, i.e., we used whatever data is available and did not perform any manual feature engineering or selection. For non-numeric data attributes a categorical encoding (one-hot) was used.

Construct Validity. We took great care to ensure we measure the right things. In particular, we used a cost model that was tested in our previous work. However, we have only used constant cost functions for adaptation costs and penalties. Yet, as we showed in our previous work [18], the shape of the cost functions can have an impact on savings. We aim to investigate the impact of such non-constant cost functions as part of our future work.

Conclusion Validity. As our experiments indicate, the choice of cost model parameters (such as λ and α) impacts on whether proactive adaptation has a positive impact on cost. To address this threat, we have carefully identified influencing variables and varied them over the whole range of permissible values.

5   Conclusions and Perspectives

Dynamically determining which prediction along the process execution to use for proactive adaptation can offer cost savings. Our experimental results indicate average cost savings of 27% when compared to using a static prediction point. Such a dynamic approach thereby effectively addresses the tradeoff between prediction accuracy and prediction earliness. Also, the dynamic approach does not require a testing phase during which aggregate accuracies are computed in order to select a suitable static prediction point.

As part of our future work, we will extend our dynamic approach towards non-constant cost models. In particular, we will consider different shapes of penalties and different costs of adaptations. To this end, we will employ regression models to predict continuous indicators in order to quantify, for instance, the extent of deviations. Regression models will also facilitate computing more complex reliability estimates (e.g., ones that use the variance of the ensemble).

Acknowledgments. We cordially thank the anonymous reviewers for their constructive comments and Richard Späker for sharing his insights of the BPIC2012 data set. Research leading to these results received funding from the EU's Horizon 2020 R&I programme under grant 731932 (TransformingTransport).

References

1. Aschoff, R., Zisman, A.: QoS-driven proactive adaptation of service composition. In: Kappel, G., Maamar, Z., Motahari-Nezhad, H.R. (eds.) ICSOC 2011. LNCS, vol. 7084, pp. 421–435. Springer, Heidelberg (2011). https://doi.org/10.1007/978-3-642-25535-9_28
2. Bosnic, Z., Kononenko, I.: Comparison of approaches for estimating reliability of individual regression predictions. Data Knowl. Eng. **67**(3), 504–516 (2008)
3. Breuker, D., Matzner, M., Delfmann, P., Becker, J.: Comprehensible predictive models for business processes. MIS Q. **40**(4), 1009–1034 (2016)
4. Dietterich, T.G.: Ensemble methods in machine learning. In: Kittler, J., Roli, F. (eds.) MCS 2000. LNCS, vol. 1857, pp. 1–15. Springer, Heidelberg (2000). https://doi.org/10.1007/3-540-45014-9_1
5. Evermann, J., Rehse, J., Fettke, P.: Predicting process behaviour using deeplearning. Decis. Support Syst. **100**, 129–140 (2017)
6. Di Francescomarino, C., Dumas, M., Maggi, F.M., Teinemaa, I.: Clustering-based predictive process monitoring. IEEE Trans. Serv. Comput. (2018, early access)
7. Di Francescomarino, C., Dumas, M., Federici, M., Ghidini, C., Maggi, F.M., Rizzi, W.: Predictive business process monitoring framework with hyperparameter optimization. In: Nurcan, S., Soffer, P., Bajec, M., Eder, J. (eds.) CAiSE 2016. LNCS, vol. 9694, pp. 361–376. Springer, Cham (2016). https://doi.org/10.1007/978-3-319-39696-5_22
8. Di Francescomarino, C., Ghidini, C., Maggi, F.M., Milani, F.: Predictive process monitoring methods: which one suits me best? In: Weske, M., Montali, M., Weber, I., vom Brocke, J. (eds.) BPM 2018. LNCS, vol. 11080, pp. 462–479. Springer, Cham (2018). https://doi.org/10.1007/978-3-319-98648-7_27
9. Di Francescomarino, C., Ghidini, C., Maggi, F.M., Petrucci, G., Yeshchenko, A.: An eye into the future: leveraging a-priori knowledge in predictive business process monitoring. In: Carmona, J., Engels, G., Kumar, A. (eds.) BPM 2017. LNCS, vol. 10445, pp. 252–268. Springer, Cham (2017). https://doi.org/10.1007/978-3-319-65000-5_15
10. Goodfellow, I., Bengio, Y., Courville, A.: Deep Learning. MIT Press, Cambridge (2016)
11. Gutiérrez, A.M., Cassales Marquezan, C., Resinas, M., Metzger, A., Ruiz-Cortés, A., Pohl, K.: Extending WS-agreement to support automated conformity check on transport and logistics service agreements. In: Basu, S., Pautasso, C., Zhang, L., Fu, X. (eds.) ICSOC 2013. LNCS, vol. 8274, pp. 567–574. Springer, Heidelberg (2013). https://doi.org/10.1007/978-3-642-45005-1_47
12. Kang, B., Kim, D., Kang, S.: Real-time business process monitoring method for prediction of abnormal termination using KNNI-based LOF prediction. Expert Syst. Appl. **39**(5), 6061–6068 (2012)

13. Leitner, P., Ferner, J., Hummer, W., Dustdar, S.: Data-driven and automated prediction of service level agreement violations in service compositions. Distrib. Parallel Databases **31**(3), 447–470 (2013)
14. Leontjeva, A., Conforti, R., Di Francescomarino, C., Dumas, M., Maggi, F.M.: Complex symbolic sequence encodings for predictive monitoring of business processes. In: Motahari-Nezhad, H.R., Recker, J., Weidlich, M. (eds.) BPM 2015. LNCS, vol. 9253, pp. 297–313. Springer, Cham (2015). https://doi.org/10.1007/978-3-319-23063-4_21
15. Maggi, F.M., Di Francescomarino, C., Dumas, M., Ghidini, C.: Predictive monitoring of business processes. In: Jarke, M., et al. (eds.) CAiSE 2014. LNCS, vol. 8484, pp. 457–472. Springer, Cham (2014). https://doi.org/10.1007/978-3-319-07881-6_31
16. Marquez-Chamorro, A.E., Resinas, M., Ruiz-Cortes, A.: Predictive monitoring of business processes: a survey. IEEE Tran. Serv. Comput. **11**(6), 962–977 (2017)
17. Mehdiyev, N., Evermann, J., Fettke, P.: A multi-stage deep learning approach for business process event prediction. In: Conference on Business Informatics (CBI 2017), Thessaloniki, Greece, 24–27 July 2017 (2017)
18. Metzger, A., Bohn, P.: Risk-based proactive process adaptation. In: Maximilien, M., Vallecillo, A., Wang, J., Oriol, M. (eds.) ICSOC 2017. LNCS, vol. 10601, pp. 351–366. Springer, Cham (2017). https://doi.org/10.1007/978-3-319-69035-3_25
19. Metzger, A., Föcker, F.: Predictive business process monitoring considering reliability estimates. In: Dubois, E., Pohl, K. (eds.) CAiSE 2017. LNCS, vol. 10253, pp. 445–460. Springer, Cham (2017). https://doi.org/10.1007/978-3-319-59536-8_28
20. Metzger, A., Neubauer, A.: Considering non-sequential control flows for process prediction with recurrent neural networks. In: 44th Euromicro Conference on Software Engineering and Advanced Applications (SEAA 2018), Prague, Czech Republic, 29–31 August 2018. IEEE Computer Society (2018)
21. Metzger, A., Sammodi, O., Pohl, K.: Accurate proactive adaptation of service-oriented systems. In: Cámara, J., de Lemos, R., Ghezzi, C., Lopes, A. (eds.) Assurances for Self-Adaptive Systems. LNCS, vol. 7740, pp. 240–265. Springer, Heidelberg (2013). https://doi.org/10.1007/978-3-642-36249-1_9
22. Metzger, A., et al.: Comparing and combining predictive business process monitoring techniques. IEEE Trans. Syst. Man Cybern. Syst. **45**(2), 276–290 (2015)
23. Moreno, G.A., Cámara, J., Garlan, D., Schmerl, B.R.: Flexible and efficient decision-making for proactive latency-aware self-adaptation. ACM Trans. Auton. Adapt. Syst. **13**(1), 3:1–3:36 (2018)
24. Mori, U., Mendiburu, A., Dasgupta, S., Lozano, J.A.: Early classification of time series by simultaneously optimizing the accuracy and earliness. IEEE Trans. Neural Netw. Learn. Syst. **29**(10), 4569–4578 (2018)
25. Mori, U., Mendiburu, A., Keogh, E., Lozano, J.A.: Reliable early classification of time series based on discriminating the classes over time. Data Min. Knowl. Discov. **31**(1), 233–263 (2017)
26. Navarin, N., Vincenzi, B., Polato, M., Sperduti, A.: LSTM networks for data-aware remaining time prediction of business process instances. In: Symposium Series on Computational Intelligence, Honolulu, USA, 27 November–1 December 2017, pp. 1–7. IEEE (2017)
27. Nolle, T., Seeliger, A., Mühlhäuser, M.: BINet: multivariate business process anomaly detection using deep learning. In: Weske, M., Montali, M., Weber, I., vom Brocke, J. (eds.) BPM 2018. LNCS, vol. 11080, pp. 271–287. Springer, Cham (2018). https://doi.org/10.1007/978-3-319-98648-7_16

28. Nunes, V.T., Santoro, F.M., Werner, C.M.L., Ralha, C.G.: Real-time process adaptation: a context-aware replanning approach. IEEE Trans. Syst. Man Cybern. Syst. **48**(1), 99–118 (2018)

29. Petitjean, F., Forestier, G., Webb, G.I., Nicholson, A.E., Chen, Y., Keogh, E.J.: Dynamic time warping averaging of time series allows faster and more accurate classification. In: Kumar, R., Toivonen, H., Pei, J., Huang, J.Z., Wu, X. (eds.) 2014 IEEE International Conference on Data Mining (ICDM 2014), Shenzhen, China, 14–17 December 2014, pp. 470–479. IEEE Computer Society (2014)

30. Polikar, R.: Ensemble based systems in decision making. IEEE Circ. Syst. Mag. **6**(3), 21–45 (2006)

31. Poll, R., Polyvyanyy, A., Rosemann, M., Röglinger, M., Rupprecht, L.: Process forecasting: towards proactive business process management. In: Weske, M., Montali, M., Weber, I., vom Brocke, J. (eds.) BPM 2018. LNCS, vol. 11080, pp. 496–512. Springer, Cham (2018). https://doi.org/10.1007/978-3-319-98648-7_29

32. Rogge-Solti, A., Weske, M.: Prediction of business process durations using non-markovian stochastic petri nets. Inf. Syst. **54**, 1–14 (2015)

33. Salfner, F., Lenk, M., Malek, M.: A survey of online failure prediction methods. ACM Comput. Surv. **42**(3), 10:1–10:42 (2010)

34. Tax, N., Verenich, I., La Rosa, M., Dumas, M.: Predictive business process monitoring with LSTM neural networks. In: Dubois, E., Pohl, K. (eds.) CAiSE 2017. LNCS, vol. 10253, pp. 477–492. Springer, Cham (2017). https://doi.org/10.1007/978-3-319-59536-8_30

35. Teinemaa, I., Dumas, M., Maggi, F.M., Di Francescomarino, C.: Predictive business process monitoring with structured and unstructured data. In: La Rosa, M., Loos, P., Pastor, O. (eds.) BPM 2016. LNCS, vol. 9850, pp. 401–417. Springer, Cham (2016). https://doi.org/10.1007/978-3-319-45348-4_23

36. Teinemaa, I., Dumas, M., Rosa, M.L., Maggi, F.M.: Outcome-oriented predictive process monitoring: review and benchmark. CoRR abs/1707.06766 (2017)

37. Weber, B., Sadiq, S.W., Reichert, M.: Beyond rigidity - dynamic process lifecycle support. Comput. Sci. R&D **23**(2), 47–65 (2009)

38. Zhou, Z.H.: Ensemble Methods: Foundations and Algorithms. Chapman and Hall/CRC, Boca Raton (2012)

Using Machine Learning Techniques for Evaluating the Similarity of Enterprise Architecture Models
Technical Paper

Vasil Borozanov[1], Simon Hacks[1(✉)], and Nuno Silva[2]

[1] Research Group Software Construction, RWTH Aachen University,
Aachen, Germany
borozanov@gmail.com, hacks@swc.rwth-aachen.de
[2] Department of Computer Science and Engineering, Technical University of Lisbon,
Lisbon, Portugal
nuno.silva@inov.pt

Abstract. Enterprises Architectures (EA) are facilitated to coordinate enterprise's business visions and strategies successfully and effectively. The practitioners of EA (architects) communicate the architecture to other stakeholders via architecture models. We investigate the scenario where accepted architecture models are stored in a repository. We identified the problem of unnecessary repository expansion by adding model components with similar properties or behavior as already existing repository components. The proposed solution aims to find those similar components and to notify the architect about their existence.

We present two approaches for defining and combining similarities between EA model components. The similarity measures are calculated upon the properties of the components and on the context of their usage. We further investigate the behavior of similar architecture models and search for associations in order to obtain components that might be of interest. At the end, we provide a prototype tool for both generating requests and obtaining a result.

Keywords: Enterprise architecture · Model · Graph · Machine learning

1 Introduction

Enterprises without centralized management of their strategic plans and business processes lack the possibility of providing consistency and direction for their activities. To avoid this, a mechanism for coordinating the integrated development and use of shared information systems and data is required [15]. Enterprise Architecture (EA) refers to both definition and representation of a high-level view of the business processes and IT systems within an organization [22]. It

P. Giorgini and B. Weber (Eds.): CAiSE 2019, LNCS 11483, pp. 563–578, 2019.
https://doi.org/10.1007/978-3-030-21290-2_35

is a well-defined practice that applies architecture principles and practices in a standardized way to execute their strategies, in order to determine how an organization can most effectively achieve its current and future objectives. Their goal is to optimize across processes into an integrated environment that is responsive to change and supportive of the delivery of the business strategy [23].

The Enterprise Architecture Management (EAM) is a discipline consisting of functions related to EA, such as maintenance or providing information gathered from the EA [24]. EAM is a management practice that sets and maintains a set of guidelines and architecture principles that guide the design and development of EA to achieve its vision and the strategy [2].

The practitioners of EA, called enterprise architects, are inter alia responsible for modeling the EA using architecture *models*. The fundamental building blocks of the models are the *components* and the *relations* between them. For easier understanding and communicating of the architecture to the stakeholders, the architects can develop a set of representations of the overall architecture called *views*.

We investigate the scenario of a company that uses a *repository* of all accepted models. In time, the repository can grow into one complex structure of components and relations. Adding a new model can cause unnecessary expansion in the repository if they are not checked beforehand. Components with similar attributes, or components used in the same context but with different names will be treated as newly introduced components and added again in the repository. Elaborating on this problem of repository pollution, we state our research question:

How can machine learning techniques enable enterprise architects to avoid adding duplicates to the repository?

The pollution of the repository is critical for two reasons. First, the repository expanses with respect to its total number of contained components. This leads to a higher complexity of the whole repository and, thus, makes it for the enterprise architects harder to understand. However, the second reason is much more critical: all reports on the repository are distorted, probably resulting in wrong decisions of EA's stakeholders.

To elaborate on our research question, next we give a concrete example, which allows the reader to better understand the problem. Afterwards, we describe the theoretical background, which is needed to answer our research question. In Sect. 5, we show how we apply these theories on our concrete problem, before we discuss our implementation. Section 7 outlines our conducted evaluation, followed by related work and our conclusion.

2   Exemplary Problem

To enable a better understanding of the problem of repository pollution and how it occurs, we take a simple illustration. The models provided in Figs. 1a and 1b are developed independently. After the acceptance of both, the two models form the initial state of the repository, depicted in Fig. 2a.

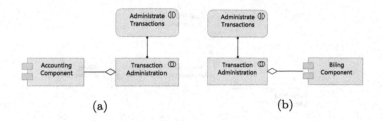

Fig. 1. Different EA models example

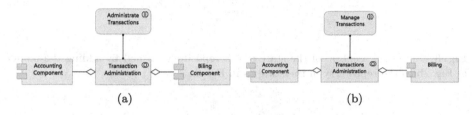

Fig. 2. (a) Simplified scenario of the state of the repository (b) Model Containing redundant components

In the repository, *Transaction Administration* aggregates both *Accounting* and *Billing* components from different models, while retaining only one instance of *Transaction Administration*. An architect decides to implement the similar financial scenario in a different model (Fig. 2b). The system proceeds to integrate this model in the repository, which results in several replicated components (see Fig. 3):

- *Billing*: The architect supplied a shorter name for the component *Billing Component*.
- *Transactions Administration*: Providing behavior for administrating several transactions can possibly be replaced by the already existing *Transaction Administration*.
- *Manage Transactions*: Although the name differs from the *Administrate Transactions*, they provide same functionality.

Currently, there is no mechanism for redundancy check. Components with similar attributes and purpose can be stored multiple times, which in turn introduces management issues due to the increased complexity of the repository data. This also makes it difficult for architects to reuse certain components.

3   Research Method

To formalize our research method, we use the Design Science Research Methodology (DSRM) [14]. According to DSRM, there are several steps to apply this

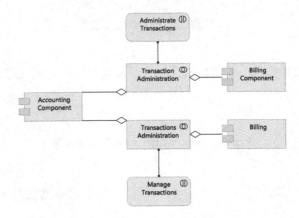

Fig. 3. Simplified scenario of the state of the repository formed by adding the model in Fig. 2b to the repository in the state as in Fig. 2a

process successfully. Having defined and formulated the problem, we proceed with the following:

Objectives and Solution: The objective was to develop a solution that will identify all new components, evaluate the model against the repository, and return a list of components already stored in the repository that can be reused in the given project. The final decision whether the suggested components will be incorporated or not is left to the architect. This ensures that the architecture model retains its correctness.

Design and Development: The solution we proposed was a machine learning model. The data on our disposal was unlabeled - we did not have any information on what the correct substitution for the specific component should be. Therefore, we focused on the unsupervised approaches, combining them into one suitable model.

Demonstration and Evaluation: We tested our solution with a simulated repository and architecture models where we knew in advance the correct substitutions for every newly introduced component. This allowed us to evaluate the correctness of the recommended components on labeled data.

Communication: The solution was distributed to the architects as a software service. It consisted of two parts: a server-side module where we performed the evaluation, and a client-side module which allowed the architects to select the architecture model that they wanted to evaluate.

4   Theoretical Background

This section describes the theory behind our approach. First, we define similarity and distance in the scope of our research. Then, we present the fundamental aspects of graph theory used in our proposed solution. Finally, we formalize association rules and a set of parameters used for association analysis.

4.1 Similarity and Distance

With the use of complex objects, we identify the need of fundamental operation for similarity assessment between two objects. If we consider the following spaces: $\mathbb{F}$, which denotes the feature space of an object and $\mathbb{R}^{\mathbb{F}}$, the space of all feature representations, then such function maps the feature space to a score $s : \mathbb{R}^{\mathbb{F}} \times \mathbb{R}^{\mathbb{F}} \to \mathbb{R}$.

Similarity function is the measure which determines how closely related two objects are based on their representation, following the given properties [17]:

– Symmetry: $\forall x, y \in \mathbb{R}^{\mathbb{F}} : s(x,y) = s(y,x)$ - the order of the objects in the input should not affect the output score
– Maximum self-similarity: $\forall x, y \in \mathbb{R}^{\mathbb{F}} : s(x,x) \geq s(x,y)$ - nothing can be more similar than the object itself

If two objects are similar, then the similarity function will have a high positive score.

In contrast to similarity, the *dissimilarity* is a measure defined by a distance function that quantifies how different two objects are. For function $d : \mathbb{R}^{\mathbb{F}} \times \mathbb{R}^{\mathbb{F}} \to \mathbb{R}$ to qualify as distance, in needs to fulfill the following constraints [6]:

– Non-negativity: $\forall x, y \in \mathbb{R}^{\mathbb{F}} : d(x,y) \geq 0$
– Reflexivity: $\forall x \in \mathbb{R}^{\mathbb{F}} : d(x,x) = 0$
– Symmetry: $\forall x, y \in \mathbb{R}^{\mathbb{F}} : d(x,y) = d(y,x)$

Both dissimilarity and similarity models express the closeness between objects. The conversion from the first to latter is essentially converting from distance to similarity function. Since they are negatively correlated, any monotonically decreasing transformation can be applied to convert similarity measures into dissimilarity. Consequently, any monotonically increasing transformation can be applied to convert the similarity to distance. If the similarity values are normalized in the range from 0 to 1, then the corresponding dissimilarity (distance) can be expressed as:

$$d(x,y) = 1 - s(x,y) \tag{1}$$

4.2 Graph Theory

In order to search for similarities between the EA models, a proper representation is needed. We find that representing the models as labeled graphs is the most acceptable solution [5].

A **labeled graph** is defined by a the tuple $G = (V, E, r_V, r_E)$ such that:

– V is a finite set of vertices,

- E is a finite set of edges between the vertices,
- $r_V \subseteq V \times L_V$ is the function that assigns labels to vertices,
- $r_E \subseteq V \times V \times L_E$ is the function that assigns labels to edges.

In this manner, we can represent the EA components as vertices and the connections between them as graph edges.

To calculate the similarity between vertices in a graph, both the labels of the vertices and the edges in the graph need to be considered. The SimRank [10] algorithm takes this into consideration. It accepts a labeled graph G as input and compares each vertex of the graph with the rest. Two vertices are considered similar if they are referenced by other similar vertices in the graph, or formally expressed with by Eq. 2:

$$s^{SR}(p,q) = \frac{C}{|I(p)||I(q)|} \sum_{i=1}^{|I(p)|} \sum_{j=1}^{|I(q)|} s^{SR}(I_i(p), I_j(q)) \qquad (2)$$

The constant $C \in \mathbb{R}$ is a user given value from 0 to 1 called the decay factor, $I(p)$ and $I(q)$ are the set of all predecessor vertices of p and q (other nodes who point to p and q) with the total count of $|I(p)|$ and $|I(q)|$ accordingly, and $I_i(p)$ and $I_j(q)$ are the i-th and j-th predecessor of the nodes p and q. Dividing by the total number of predecessors pairs allows us to obtain normalized value: a range between 0 (maximum dissimilarity) to 1. For any vertex v that has no predecessors ($I(v) = \emptyset$), the similarity is set to zero. Alternatively this can be expressed using the set of successors $O(p)$ and $O(q)$ of the nodes p and q (vertices pointed by p and q), or (as shown later in our approach) both $I(p)$ and $O(p)$ combined.

SimRank is calculated recursively: two score between two vertices is dependent of the pre-calculated similarity of their neighbours. The initial similarity score is calculated using the binary similarity:

$$s_0^{SR}(p,q) = \begin{cases} 1 & \text{if } p = q \\ 0 & \text{else} \end{cases} \qquad (3)$$

4.3   Association Analysis

Association rule mining [9] searches for recurring relationships in a given data set. More specific, it discovers the associations and correlations between two set of items (item set).

An association rule is indicated as $\{A_1, A_2, ..., A_m\} \Rightarrow \{B_1, B_2, ..., B_n\}$, where $\forall i,j \mid i \leq m, j \leq n$, A_i and B_j are non-empty *item sets*. In order to select only the rules that are interesting for evaluation, we use the *support* and *confidence* parameters. Support *supp* for the rule $A \Rightarrow B$ indicates the fraction of transactions that contain both A and B:

$$supp(A \Rightarrow B) = P(A \cup B) \qquad (4)$$

Support filters out rules that occurred by chance. Confidence $conf$ for the rule $A \Rightarrow B$ indicates the fraction of items contained in B that are also contained in A. It measures the reliability made by a rule:

$$conf(A \Rightarrow B) = P(B|A) \tag{5}$$

Rules with $supp \geq minsup$ and $conf \geq minconf$ are called *strong rules*. For generating rules that satisfy the minimal support and confidence, we use the *Apriori* algorithm [1]. This approach considers only the frequent items as basis for generating candidates and extends them to larger item sets with other frequent items.

5 Research Proposal

In this section we give an overview how the similarity models were applied to suit our needs.

5.1 Prerequisites

For a given EA project model, we make the following assumptions:

- The architecture model is complete: the response we are calculating is based on the assumption that all the necessary components and relations are there.
- The project architecture is correct: the types of the components are correct, and the relations between the components are all present and correct.
- The views in the architecture projects are clearly defined: this allows successful application of the association mining. Since there is no explicit notion for a transaction, we rely on the views - every component that is a part of the view belongs in the same transaction.

To categorize a component from the model as a newly introduced, we check if a component with the exact name and type does not exist in the repository. We ignore the description attribute since it is not a required field.

5.2 Feature Extraction and Similarity Models

The underlying representation of the given EA model and the repository is a labeled directed graph. Each node of the graph presents a component with the features: *name* (or title), *type* and *description*, whereas the relations between them are modeled as edges. The same model applies to the repository data. For two labeled directed graphs, we combine **attribute based** and **structure based** similarities.

Attribute-based similarities calculate the similarity score between two features while ignoring the graph structure. For evaluating the similarity between the names of the components, we apply the *String Edit Distance(d^{EDIT})* [12]. The edit distance is very robust when it comes to comparing single words, but results in large distance score if the strings contain words in different order. To overcome this, we apply the distance measure on pairs of words [11]. We introduce word tokenization, remove any digit characters from the words and discard the words that do not contribute to semantic meaning, such as personal pronouns and definite or indefinite articles.

Let p and q be two components and p_words and q_words be the tokenized and processed titles of the first and second component respectively. For each word from p_words, we apply the String Edit distance to measure the difference with every word from q_words, convert it to a similarity score and record only the highest word–wise similarity that occurred for that given word. In the case of difference in the number of words, we compare each word from the input string that has more words to avoid any loss of information. To achieve normalization between 0 and 1, we divide the similarity value by the larger the number of words for the given titles. This is shown in Algorithm 1.

Algorithm 1. Name-based similarity

1: **procedure** s^{NAME}(p,q)
2: p_words = tokenize(p)
3: q_words = tokenize(q)
4: less_words = min(p_words, q_words)
5: more_words = max(p_words, q_words)
6: total_similarity ← 0
7: **for each** m **in** more_words:
8:     word_similarity ← 0
9:     **for each** l **in** less_words **do**:
10:        current_similarity = $1 - d^{EDIT}$(m,l) / max(size(m),size(l))
11:        **if** current_similarity > word_similarity **then**
12:            word_similarity = current_similarity
13:     total_similarity = total_similarity + word_similarity
14: **return** total_similarity / size(more_words)

For evaluating the similarity between the types of components, we apply the binary similarity. This is a very restrictive similarity that suits the assumption that the EA models are correct and the components have the right type. For two given components p and q with their respective types t_p and t_q, the type similarity is:

$$s^{TYPE}(p,q) = \begin{cases} 1 & \text{if } t_p = t_q \\ 0 & \text{else} \end{cases} \tag{6}$$

For calculating the similarity based on the description of components, we rely on the semantic meaning of the text. The description of the text is converted to a *Term Frequency - Inverse Document Frequency* (TF-IDF) vector [13]. This metric was motivated by the length of the text: the String Edit Distance will not be able to perform well since it relies on the syntactic matching of the words. TF-IDF emphasizes the importance of a word based on how frequent it appears for the given component's description (term frequency) and how rarely it appears throughout other component's description (document frequency).

Let t be a word from the description d, N the total number of documents and D the number of documents where t appears. The TF-IDF score for t is calculated as:

$$tf\_idf(t, d, D) = word\_count(t, d) \log \frac{N}{1 + D},\qquad(7)$$

where $word\_count(t,d)$ returns the number how many times the word t has appeared in the document d.

After obtaining the TF-IDF vector for each word in the description $desc_p$ and $desc_q$ of the components p and q, the description similarity is calculated using the cosine distance:

$$s^{DESC}(p, q) = 1 - d^{COS}(tf\_idf(desc_p, D), tf\_idf(desc_q, D))\qquad(8)$$

where $tf\_idf(desc_p, D)$ returns a TF-IDF vector for every word from $desc_p$.

To combine all the different similarities into one, we use a weighted average function from the similarity models:

$$s^{ATTR}(p, q) = \frac{w_1 s^{NAME}(p, q) + w_2 s^{TYPE}(p, q) + w_3 s^{DESC}(p, q)}{w_1 + w_2 + w_3}\qquad(9)$$

The **context-based** similarity is calculated based on the graph structure of the EA models. For this, we change the input to accept two graphs: $s^{SR}(p, q)$. For the initial cases $s_0^{SR}(p, q)$, we assign maximal similarity if the titles are a complete match and the components have the same type.

To come up with **combined** context– and attribute–based similarity, we integrate the attribute similarity in the SimRank approach. We call this model *Extended SimRank* (Eq. 10). To achieve this, we relax the initial similarity s_0^{ESR} by assigning a score calculated from the attribute similarity model, if the score is above a given threshold t (Eq. 11). We also check both the predecessors and the successors of any node v for the context-based similarity: $D(v) = I(v) \cup O(v)$.

$$s^{ESR}(p, q) = \frac{C}{|D(p)||D(q)|} \sum_{i=1}^{|D(p)|} \sum_{j=1}^{|D(q)|} s^{ESR}(D_i(p), D_j(q))\qquad(10)$$

$$s_0^{ESR}(p, q) = \begin{cases} s^{ATTR}(p, q) & \text{if } s^{ATTR}(p, q) > t \\ 0 & \text{else} \end{cases}\qquad(11)$$

Inspecting every pair of vertices between graphs with n and m nodes leads into generating $n * m$ candidates. To speed up the process of evaluation, we skip the nodes which do not have any incoming and outgoing edges, since such nodes cannot contribute to the structural similarity when using s^{ESR}. For such nodes, we rely only on the s^{ATTR}.

6   Implementation

The implementation of our solution is dependent on several technologies. The **server side** is built using the Java technology. The acceptance of the EA models is realized with POST requests with the following parameters:

- file: mandatory field which contains the ArchiMate (XML) file that needs to be evaluated.
- k: a number of maximum returned components for a single query component (optional).

The ArchiMate files and the repository are read and converted to directed labeled graphs using the JGraphT library [20] and its *DirectedGraph* class. For the repository we are interested in the content of the *Architecture* section and the *Types* section. Each XML node represents either an ArchiMate component, if located under the "Components" section, or an ArchiMate relation, if located under the "Relations" section.

To get a better understanding of the structure of the repository as a graph, we use *Gephi* - a tool for analytics and detailed visualization of graphs [4]. The total size of the graph is 3922 nodes with 9657 edges. Out of those, 1147 are isolated nodes (no incoming and outgoing edges). The diameter is 7, and the average path length is 4.79. The average degree per node (both incoming and outgoing considered) is 4.93. Given graph size, we consider the repository graph as a weakly connected. This is also confirmed by the low value of 0.001 for the density.

Before calculating any similarity, we filter out any unnecessary replicated information which might affect the prediction outcome at the end. The repository is cleaned up by discarding all the replicated components, i.e. components with the same *name* and *type* (the *description* feature is not mandatory, therefore not considered a factor). This results in a reduction of 28 components.

The description of every component is converted into a TF-IDF vector. For this, a corpus needs to be built where each description of a component is considered as a document. Every word (term) gets evaluated using Eq. 7. For tokenization of the title of the components, we use the *WordTokenizer* class from the WEKA library[1] for Java. For the association mining we use the statistical programming language R and the package *arules*[2]. The chosen value for minimal support was 0.17 was the largest value where rules were still generated. Combined with the minimum confidence value of 0.75, the algorithm resulted in the generation of 77 rules.

The **client side** was realized as a plug-in for the Archi tool[3], which is an Eclipse-based IDE. The plugin provides a button on the toolbar of the IDE that allows the architect to select the desired ArchiMate model file. Afterwards, the file is uploaded to our server and the module waits for a response back. The

---

[1] https://www.cs.waikato.ac.nz/ml/weka.
[2] https://cran.r-project.org/web/packages/arules/index.html.
[3] https://www.archimatetool.com.

response contains a JSON list of components that are not part of the repository and their most similar components from the repository. The result is presented as a dialog with a tabular view inside Archi.

7 Evaluation

The similarity models we applied are unsupervised, meaning we do not have the true output available. To successfully evaluate them, we manually created a simulation and architecture model. The repository data consisted of 327 nodes and 275 edges and the model of 35 nodes and 23 edges. The model components were provided from two sources chosen pseudo-randomly from the repository and inserted without any relations to the repository.

A subset of 16 model components were subject to manual change of the attributes, so that different scenarios for similarity can be tested based on a title, description, type, structural similarity and combination of all. Only the nodes that did not appear in the repository were tested. There were 20 unidentified nodes in total, out of which four did not have any substitution. For every evaluation test, the k value was set to the lowest value of 1, which evaluates the shortest result list.

We also set up a simulation of an ArchiMate model for creating transactions. The simulation transaction file consisted of the same number of components and edges as the previous simulation model file, distributed in the same number of views. We replaced each unidentified component with its counterpart from the repository if such existed. Using the approach of creating transaction per view level, we created a set of five transactions with 18 items. Finally, we discarded newly introduced components without substitution as well as the components that did not belong to any view.

For evaluating the correctness of the similarity models, we compared three different metrics: accuracy, precision, and recall [19]. For the association rule mining, we focused only on the accuracy, since the results were returned in the form of "if the components on the left–side of the rule exist, then the components on the right–side of the rule might be of interest". Therefore we could not make the connection which result components belong to which query components. All metrics range from 0 (the lowest value) to 1 (highest value).

We evaluated the similarity models each one separately, as well as the combination between them. The overview is given in Fig. 4. The first evaluation was performed on each feature similarity model separately. We set the number of returned components to one ($k=1$). The title and type similarity showed poor performance in every metric. The description similarity model showed maximum precision value and better values for accuracy and recall. However, since the description is optional for the components, it cannot be taken as a single metric. The usage of a single feature similarity model is not recommended as they do not provide an effective recommendation service.

Next, for the evaluation of the weighted similarity combination s^{ATTR} we configured the similarity using the values 0.5, 0.1 and 0.4 for the weights w_1,

w_2, and w_3 respectively. The weights were provided from a domain expert and reflected the importance of each feature. To avoid results with components with low similarity score, we introduced a threshold t = 0.5. The weighted combination performed better than any separate feature similarity model if the number of suggested components is taken into account as well, which was 17 for the given threshold.

Next, we evaluated the SimRank approach, using the combined in- and out-degree. We noticed the improvement in the score compared to the weighted combination, so we incorporated the two methods together as the *SimRank Extended* s^{ESR} with a threshold of 0.5. The *SimRank Extended* showed the higher accuracy, recall, and the highest F1 score. Increasing the number of returned components k to higher number did not affect the score in our simulation.

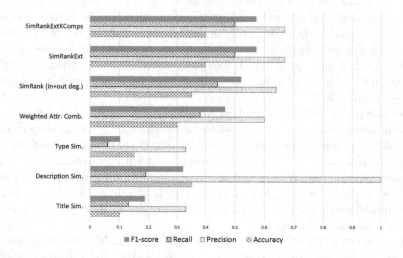

Fig. 4. Comparison of all similarity models

We performed the association mining with the following input: minimal support of 0.2 (the highest support value that still returns results), and confidence of 1 (the maximal possible value). This generated a set of 293 rules. Out of those, for the model that we evaluated, 13 components were returned. We identified a total of 7 correctly suggested components that were a suitable replacement, with an accuracy of 0.54. The rules had a low support value, which means that the component sets did not often appear in transactions. However, confidence had the highest value, thus giving a high level of certainty concerning the truth of the association rules. This method is highly dependent on the data set provided by the architects.

The threats of validity are mainly situated in our prerequisites. First, we assume that the basic model is complete. If we relax this assumption, our approach might propose components which are wrong or even no components.

Nonetheless, our approach proposes only components and the final decision is taken by a human. Therefore, the consequences of relaxing this prerequisite are manageable. The same argumentation holds for our second prerequisite that the project architectures are correct. Last, we assume that views represent the changes made by the projects. However, this prerequisite is based only on the technical issue that we need to know what has been changed and, consequently, does not threat our results.

8   Related Work

Previous research [8,16,18,21] was motivated by analyzing EA models as a network graph and applying different ML concepts on EA models by providing decision support for enterprise architects. The work of [8] focuses on representing the complexity of information systems architecture in social network terms and then capturing insights from the graph representation, where components of the architecture are interpreted as nodes, and the dependencies between the components as links.

Different similarity approaches, as well as metrics, have been proposed in the literature to identify the similarity and the differences between models to be matched. The work of Dijkman et al. [7] presents three similarity metrics in order to investigate matching of similar business process models in a given repository namely (i) structural similarity that compares element labels by considering topology structure of business process models; (ii) behavioural similarity that compares element labels by considering behavioural semantics of process models; and (iii) label matching similarity that compares elements based on words in the labels of business process model elements (string edit distance).

Compared to Dijkman et al. [7], our work elaborates on structural similarity (i) and label matching similarity (iii). Dijkman et. al. use Graph Edit Distance as an underlying method for (i). We find that this approach fails when comparing graphs of significantly different sizes (e.g. a model and a repository), as the returned score will always be of high value. We also expand the knowledge in (iii) as we not only consider the labels of the elements but also their attributes. To research behavioural similarity (ii) did not make sense in our case, because our model did not contain elements with behavioural semantics. Nonetheless, e.g. ArchiMate contains elements to model processes and, consequently, future research can take behavioural similarity for EA models also into account.

The work of Aier and Schönherr [3] presents a clustering approach in determining the structure of Service Oriented Architectures (SOA). The paper shows the application of clustering algorithms in supporting the design of a SOA. However, their approach does not present evaluation criteria in comparing different clustering methods. We try to apply different community detection algorithms on EA models which can group similar kinds of connected components.

9   Conclusions

Modeling an EA can result in a complex graph-like structure with many components (vertices) and relations between them (edges) in a repository. We recognized the problem that adding a model to the repository which contains components with similar attributes and behavior as some other repository components, but with different name, leads to repository pollution. To solve this, we inspected two approaches. The first approach relied on finding patterns between two enterprise architecture models. The second approach adopted a collaborative way of recommending components that might be of interest.

For evaluating the architecture models, similarity and collaborative approach were used. The result was formatted to give a list of k closest components for each component that cannot be found in the repository. The evaluation showed that the similarity models have high precision and low recall characteristics. The generated association rules have low support and high confidence value, which means that the item sets of the rules appear rarely, but we are confident that the generated rule will be true.

Our research was realized in two parts: as a server solution able to perform the evaluations and as a plug-in for the Archi tool able to generate requests and notify the architects for the results. Although our implementation is targeted for EA, the solution we propose is generic and can be applied to any domain that can be modeled as a graph with nodes and edges.

As we rely on a graph-like presentation of the EA model, our approach can be generalized and applied also to other models which can be presented as graphs. We assume that, for instance, our approach might also work for UML models as ArchiMate and UML class diagrams are quite similar.

The current limitations are the constraints we impose before evaluating the EA models. The EA models have to be complete and correct, which means that the tool cannot be used as a recommendation system (suggesting components as the model is in the process of creation). This limitation may be solved in future by incorporating techniques from the model recommendation domain. Also the approaches are not optimized: as the size of the repository increases, recommending a list of components takes more time. Consequently, we will elaborate on this point in future. Lastly, our approach cannot be fully automatized since we rely on a human expert to confirm that the recommended components are the right substitution. We do not see any possibilities to overcome with this issue.

References

1. Agrawal, R., Srikant, R.: Fast algorithms for mining association rules in large databases. In: Proceedings of the 20th International Conference on Very Large Data Bases, VLDB 1994, pp. 487–499. Morgan Kaufmann Publishers Inc., San Francisco (1994)
2. Ahlemann, F., Stettiner, E., Messerschmidt, M., Legner, C.: Strategic Enterprise Architecture Management: Challenges, Best Practices, and Future Developments. Springer, Heidelberg (2012). https://doi.org/10.1007/978-3-642-24223-6

3. Aier, S., Schoenherr, M.: Integrating an enterprise architecture using domain clustering. In: Lankhorst, M.M., Johnson, P. (eds.) Proceedings of the Second Workshop on Trends in Enterprise Architecture Research, pp. 23–30, June 2007
4. Bastian, M., Heymann, S., Jacomy, M.: Gephi: An open source software for exploring and manipulating networks. In: ICWSM (2009)
5. Champin, P.-A., Solnon, C.: Measuring the similarity of labeled graphs. In: Ashley, K.D., Bridge, D.G. (eds.) ICCBR 2003. LNCS (LNAI), vol. 2689, pp. 80–95. Springer, Heidelberg (2003). https://doi.org/10.1007/3-540-45006-8_9
6. Deza, M.M., Deza, E.: Encyclopedia of Distances. Springer, Heidelberg (2009). https://doi.org/10.1007/978-3-642-00234-2
7. Dijkman, R., Dumas, M., Van Dongen, B., Käärik, R., Mendling, J.: Similarity of business process models: Metrics and evaluation. Inf. Syst. **36**(2), 498–516 (2011)
8. Dreyfus, D., Iyer, B.: Enterprise architecture: a social network perspective. In: Proceedings of the 39th Annual Hawaii International Conference on System Sciences (HICSS 2006), vol. 8 (2006)
9. Han, J.: Data Mining: Concepts and Techniques. Morgan Kaufmann Publishers Inc., San Francisco (2005)
10. Jeh, G., Widom, J.: SimRank: a measure of structural-context similarity. In: Proceedings of the Eighth ACM SIGKDD International Conference on Knowledge Discovery and Data Mining, pp. 538–543. ACM, New York (2002)
11. La Rosa, M., Dumas, M., Uba, R., Dijkman, R.: Business process model merging: an approach to business process consolidation. ACM Trans. Softw. Eng. Methodol. **22**(2), 11:1–11:42 (2013)
12. Navarro, G.: A guided tour to approximate string matching. ACM Comput. Surv. **33**(1), 31–88 (2001)
13. Neto, J.L., et al.: Document clustering and text summarization (2000)
14. Peffers, K., Tuunanen, T., Rothenberger, M., Chatterjee, S.: A design science research methodology for information systems research. J. Manag. Inf. Syst. **24**(3), 45–77 (2007)
15. Rood, M.A.: Enterprise architecture: definition, content, and utility. In: Proceedings of 3rd IEEE Workshop on Enabling Technologies: Infrastructure for Collaborative Enterprises, pp. 106–111 (1994)
16. Santana, A., Souza, A., Simon, D., Fischbach, K., De Moura, H.: Network science applied to enterprise architecture analysis: towards the foundational concepts. In: 2017 IEEE 21st International Enterprise Distributed Object Computing Conference (EDOC), pp. 10–19. IEEE (2017)
17. Santini, S., Jain, R.: Similarity measures. IEEE Trans. Pattern Anal. Mach. Intell. **21**(9), 871–883 (1999)
18. Schoonjans, A.: Social network analysis techniques in enterprise architecture management. Ph.D. thesis, Ghent University (2016)
19. Shani, G., Gunawardana, A.: Evaluating recommendation systems. In: Ricci, F., Rokach, L., Shapira, B., Kantor, P.B. (eds.) Recommender Systems Handbook, pp. 257–297. Springer, Boston, MA (2011). https://doi.org/10.1007/978-0-387-85820-3_8
20. Sichi, J., Kinable, J., Michail, D., Naveh, B., Contributors: JGraphT - Graph Algorithms and Data Structures in Java (Version 1.1.0) (2017). http://www.jgrapht.org
21. Simon, D., Fischbach, K.: IT landscape management using network analysis. In: Poels, G. (ed.) CONFENIS 2012. LNBIP, vol. 139, pp. 18–34. Springer, Heidelberg (2013). https://doi.org/10.1007/978-3-642-36611-6_2

22. Tamm, T., Seddon, P., Shanks, G., Reynolds, P.: How does enterprise architecture add value to organisations? Commun. Assoc. Inf. Syst. **28**, 141–168 (2011)
23. The Open Group: TOGAF Version 9.1. Van Haren Publishing, Zaltbommel (2011)
24. van der Raadt, B., van Vliet, H.: Designing the enterprise architecture function. In: Becker, S., Plasil, F., Reussner, R. (eds.) QoSA 2008. LNCS, vol. 5281, pp. 103–118. Springer, Heidelberg (2008). https://doi.org/10.1007/978-3-540-87879-7_7

Efficient Discovery of Compact Maximal Behavioral Patterns from Event Logs

Mehdi Acheli[1]([✉])([iD]), Daniela Grigori[1], and Matthias Weidlich[2]

[1] Univ. Paris-Dauphine, CNRS UMR[7243], LAMSADE, 75016 Paris, France
{mehdi.acheli,daniela.grigori}@dauphine.fr
[2] Humboldt-Universität zu Berlin, Berlin, Germany
matthias.weidlich@hu-berlin.de

Abstract. Techniques for process discovery support the analysis of information systems by constructing process models from event logs that are recorded during system execution. In recent years, various algorithms to discover end-to-end process models have been proposed. Yet, they do not cater for domains in which process execution is highly flexible, as the unstructuredness of the resulting models renders them meaningless. It has therefore been suggested to derive insights about flexible processes by mining behavioral patterns, i.e., models of frequently recurring episodes of a process' behavior. However, existing algorithms to mine such patterns suffer from imprecision and redundancy of the mined patterns and a comparatively high computational effort. In this work, we overcome these limitations with a novel algorithm, coined COBPAM (COmbination based Behavioral Pattern Mining). It exploits a partial order on potential patterns to discover only those that are compact and maximal, i.e. least redundant. Moreover, COBPAM exploits that complex patterns can be characterized as combinations of simpler patterns, which enables pruning of the pattern search space. Efficiency is improved further by evaluating potential patterns solely on parts of an event log. Experiments with real-world data demonstrates how COBPAM improves over the state-of-the-art in behavioral pattern mining.

Keywords: Behavioral patterns · Process discovery · Pattern mining

1 Introduction

Process mining connects the research areas of data mining with process modeling and analysis [1]. Specifically, the analysis of information systems may be supported by exploiting the event logs recorded during their execution. Techniques for process discovery use such event logs and construct a model of the underlying end-to-end process. Recently, a plethora of process discovery algorithms has been proposed [3]. These algorithms impose varying assumptions on the event log used as input, e.g., in terms of the event model [17]; adopt different target languages, e.g., Petri-nets [18], process trees [14], or BPMN [8]; and differ in

© Springer Nature Switzerland AG 2019
P. Giorgini and B. Weber (Eds.): CAiSE 2019, LNCS 11483, pp. 579–594, 2019.
https://doi.org/10.1007/978-3-030-21290-2_36

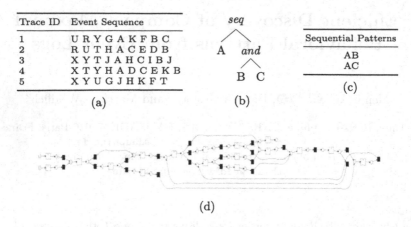

Trace ID	Event Sequence
1	U R Y G A K F B C
2	R U T H A C E D B
3	X Y T J A H C I B J
4	X T Y H A D C E K B
5	X Y U G J H K F T

(a)

seq
A   and
B   C

(b)

Sequential Patterns
AB
AC

(c)

(d)

Fig. 1. (a) Event log; (b) behavioral pattern; (c) 2-length sequential patterns extracted with PrefixSPAN [16]; (d) end-to-end model mined by FHM [23].

how they cope with noise and incompleteness, e.g., avoiding over-fitting [24] or filtering noise [6].

Most existing discovery algorithms, however, aim to unify *all* the behavior observed in the log into an end-to-end model. As such, they are not suited for domains in which process execution is highly flexible, as the resulting models are unstructured and are subject to over-generalization [1]. The reason being that there is a large variability of the behavior of different process instances and a model capturing all variations tends to be complex. It was therefore suggested to derive insights about flexible processes by mining behavioral patterns [21, 22]. These patterns are formalized as process models, yet they capture only comparatively small episodes of a process' behavior that occur frequently. The basic idea is illustrated in Fig. 1. For the example log, given as a set of traces, i.e., sequences of events that denote the executions of different activities, a traditional discovery algorithm such as the Flexible Heuristics Miner (FHM) [23] would yield a complex model. However, one may observe that the traces show a specific behavioral pattern: An execution of activity A is followed by B and C in parallel. Detecting such a pattern provides a general understanding of the regularities in process execution. Note though, that such a pattern cannot be detected using standard techniques for sequential pattern mining, such as PrefixSPAN [16], as those would miss complex behavioral dependencies such as concurrency and exclusive choices.

Existing algorithms [21,22] to mine behavioral patterns suffer from imprecision and redundancy of the mined patterns, and a comparatively high computational effort. That is, even though certain behavior is frequent, patterns may capture (i) only a part of the frequent behavior (i.e., they are not maximal), or (ii) a combination of frequent behavior with infrequent behavior (i.e., patterns are not compact). For instance, in Fig. 1, the pattern *seq(a, and(b,c))* is frequent. Arguably, discovery of further patterns *seq(a,b))* and *seq(a, xor(b,k))* would not lead to any new insights on the process, so that it is sufficient to discover the former one. At the same time, existing algorithms suffer from high run-times since pattern candidates are evaluated based on the complete event log.

In this paper, we overcome the above limitations with COBPAM, a novel combination-based algorithm to mine behavioral patterns that are formalized as process trees. It identifies all trees of which the behavior can be found in a certain number of traces of the event log, which takes up the well-established notion of support for patterns in sequence databases [10]. Moreover, we consider a notion of language fitness to assess how strongly a tree materializes. Based thereon, the contributions of COBPAM are threefold:

(1) It defines a partial order on pattern candidates to discover only those that are maximal and compact, thereby improving effectiveness of pattern mining.
(2) It efficiently explores the pattern search space by pruning strategies, exploiting that complex patterns are combinations of simpler patterns.
(3) It further improves efficiency by considering only a subset of traces, when evaluating the support and language fitness of a pattern candidate.

The paper is structured as follows. Section 2 reviews related work on process discovery and pattern mining. Preliminaries are given in Sect. 3. We then define algebraic operations and structures on potential behavioral patterns in Sect. 4, while quality metrics for them are presented in Sect. 5. Our novel mining algorithm for behavioral patterns, COBPAM, is introduced in Sect. 6. We evaluate the algorithm in experiments with real-world event logs in Sect. 7, before we conclude and discuss future research directions in Sect. 8.

2   Related Work

The discovery of behavioral patterns defined with respect to their frequency in a log connects two research areas: sequential pattern mining and process mining. In this section, we will mention the algorithms in the former area that inspired our work and then proceed with an overview of process mining algorithms that aim to derive insights for event logs that have been recorded for flexible processes.

GSP [20] is a sequential pattern mining algorithm that combines pairs of sequential patterns of length k to obtain patterns of length $k + 1$. As it will be discussed later, we adopt this principle for COBPAM when generating behavioral patterns. We also borrow the concept of a projected database in the form of log projections from the PrefixSPAN algorithm [16] to evaluate the pattern candidates on the minimal number of traces possible. Moreover, we adopt the maximality principle as discussed for sequential patterns in [10].

Trace clustering is an active research area concerned with inferring insights from logs of flexible processes [4,5,11,19]. These techniques group traces into homogeneous clusters, so that process discovery is applied to each cluster to obtain comparatively structured models. Such techniques are well-suited if a log contains few groups of similar traces. Yet, they do not cater for scenarios, where a partitioning of a log into groups of similar traces is not possible.

Targeting flexible processes, the Fuzzy miner [12] discovers abstract models that describe only the most significant behavior of a log. It enables control of the level of aggregation and abstraction of events and relations between them. Yet, it fails to mine certain behavioral structures, such as concurrency.

The Declare Miner [15] discovers a set of rules that are satisfied by a certain share of traces. These rules come in the form of relations between activities, e.g., two activities being always executed together in a trace, potentially in a fixed order. These rules relate to the presence or the absence of behavior. Each rule, however, is limited to a relation between at most two activities, while our approach considers patterns with an arbitrary number of activities.

The Episode Miner [13] is another algorithm that discovers frequent patterns. The results are partial orders over activities. The method, however, does not support loops and choice constructs.

Our work is inspired by the discovery of Local Process Models (LPMs) [22]. Specifically, we also adopt the notion of process trees to represent behavioral patterns that are observed in event logs in unstructured domains. However, existing algorithms for LPM discovery limit the size of patterns and are not grounded in the traditional definition of support, as known from sequence databases. Rather, when mining LPMs, a trace may account for multiple occurrences of a pattern. Moreover, the algorithm of [22] follows a generate-and-test approach, where only frequent trees are expanded by replacing an activity with some structured behavior. This way, a single tree may be evaluated multiple times in the discovery process. Also, the discovery neglects certain types of patterns, e.g., two infrequent trees that become frequent when joined by a choice operator. Moreover, the existing discovery algorithm relies on the computation of alignments on the entire log, which turns out to be computationally heavy for large-scale event logs.

Compared to the mining of LPMs, our COBPAM algorithm adopts a well-established definition of support for behavioral patterns. COBPAM further provides several innovations. Mined patterns are guaranteed to show desirable properties (maximality and compactness), while the discovery algorithm also leverages pruning strategies and explores pattern candidates solely on a subset of the traces of a log. Note that the initial approach to discover LPMs [22] has been extended with goal-driven strategies to mine patterns based on notions of utility and constraint satisfaction [21]. Yet, these extensions are orthogonal to our work.

3   Preliminaries

This section presents basic definitions. We begin with the notion of an event log.

Definition 1. *Let A be a set of* activity identifiers *(activities), and A^* the set of all sequences over A. A* trace $\sigma \in A^*$ *is a finite sequence of activities. An* event log L *is a multiset of traces.* $|L|$ *denotes its size, i.e., the number of traces it contains.*

A process discovery technique takes as input an event log and constructs process models. Process trees [7] are a language to capture such process models.

Definition 2. *A* process tree *is an ordered tree structure, such that leaf nodes represent activities and non-leaf nodes represent operators. Considering a set of activities A, a set of binary operators $\Omega = \{seq, and, loop, xor\}$, a process tree is recursively defined as follows:*

- *$a \in A$ is a process tree.*
- *considering an operator $x \in \Omega$ and two process trees P_1, P_2, $x(P_1, P_2)$ is a process tree having x as root, P_1 as left child, and P_2 as right child.*

The language of a process tree $\Sigma(P)$ is the set of traces it generates. The language is also defined recursively. We exemplify the language of each operator for two activities $a, b \in A$: $\Sigma(seq(a, b)) = \{\langle a, b\rangle\}$; $\Sigma(and(a, b)) = \Sigma(and(b, a)) = \{\langle a, b\rangle, \langle b, a\rangle\}$; $\Sigma(xor(b, a)) = \{\langle a\rangle, \langle b\rangle\}$; and $\Sigma(loop(a, b)) = \{\langle a\rangle, \langle aba\rangle, \langle ababa\rangle, \ldots\}$. Since the language associated with a loop operator is infinite, we define the n-language of a tree $\Sigma_n(P)$ as the set of traces obtained when traversing each loop n-times, e.g., $\Sigma_1(loop(a, b)) = \{\langle a\rangle, \langle aba\rangle\}$.

4   Algebraic Operations and Structures on Process Trees

We now devise a method for constructing process trees incrementally. We propose to combine two process trees composed of n activities to derive process trees of $n + 1$ activities. The process trees combined must be identical except for a single leaf node. We further impose conditions on these leaves, as follows:

Definition 3. *Given a process tree P of depth i, a leaf node a of depth d is called* potential combination leaf, *if $d \geq i - 1$ and there is no leaf b of depth d' on the left of a such that $d' > d$.*

Two process trees that can be combined are called seeds.

Definition 4. *Process trees P_1 and P_2 are called* seeds, *if they contain two potential combination leaves, a in P_1 and a' in P_2, such that by replacing a in P_1 with a', we obtain P_2.*

The above notion requires that both process trees are identical except at the level of the leaves a and a'. For instance, *seq(a, b)* and *seq(a, c)* are seeds. Next, we formally define the algebraic operation of combination.

Definition 5. *A* combination *of two seeds P_1 and P_2 through an operator x is an operation generating two process trees. Starting from P_1, the combination leaf a is replaced by the operator x, whose children are set to a and a'. a becomes the left child in one resulting tree, and the right child in another one. a and a' are called the* combination leaves *and x is called the* combination operator.

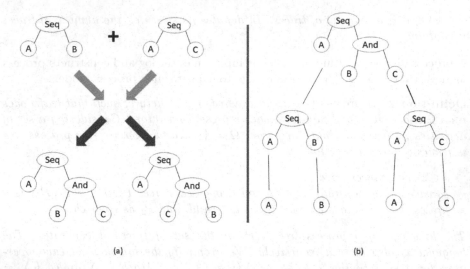

Fig. 2. (a) a combination operation of two process trees (b) the construction tree of the process tree *seq(a, and(b,c))*

Figure 2a shows an example of a combination of two process trees *seq(a, b)* and *seq(a, c)* through the concurrency operator, which results in two trees: *seq(a, and(b,c))* and *seq(a, and(c,b))*.

Thanks to the conditions characterizing the potential combination leaves, the following theorem holds true:[1]

Theorem 1. *For a process tree P of depth i ≥ 1, there is a unique pair of seeds P_1 and P_2, whose combination through an operator x results in P. P_1 and P_2 are called 'the' seeds of P and x is called the defining operator of P.*

Given that every process tree of depth larger than zero results from the combination of two unique seeds, we introduce additional structures.

Definition 6. *Given a process tree P of depth i ≥ 1, we define its* construction tree. *The nodes of this tree are process trees: The root is P, the leaves are trees with single activity nodes; the children of a non-leaf node are its seeds.*

Figure 2b exemplifies the construction tree of the process tree *seq(a, and(b,c))*.

Definition 7. *We define the* construction graph *over the set of activities A. It is a directed acyclic graph. Its (infinite) set of nodes is given by all possible process trees. An edge is defined between nodes n_1 and n_2, if n_1 is a seed of n_2. We say that n_2 contains n_1 through the defining operator of n_2.*

To identify a tree, COBPAM uses the concept of representative word.

---

[1] The proof can be found in the accompanying technical report at: http://www.lamsade.dauphine.fr/~macheli/behavioralPatterns/paper.pdf.

Definition 8. *Each process tree P is assigned a* representative word $RW(P)$, *a sequence of characters. It is constructed by pre-order traversal of its nodes, outputting activities and operators.*

For example, the representative word of $seq(a, and(b, c))$ is '(a (b c and) seq)'.

5   Quality Metrics

This section defines metrics to evaluate the quality of a behavioral pattern that is formalized as a process tree. These metrics rely on a Boolean function $\epsilon(\sigma, P)$ that returns one, if $\sigma \in \Sigma(P)$, i.e., trace σ fits the process tree P; otherwise, it returns zero. To determine whether this predicate holds true, we compute an alignment [2] between the trace and the process tree. Such an alignment is a sequence of steps that are defined for the trace σ and one of the traces of the process tree P. Each step in the alignment is either a synchronous move (both traces show the same activity) or an asynchronous move (only one of the traces shows an activity, while a placeholder is introduced for the other one). These steps need to be defined such that the sequence of moves yields the original traces when ignoring placeholders introduced as part of asynchronous moves. Techniques for alignment computation strive for the construction of an optimal alignment, i.e., a sequence of steps of minimal costs, where costs are assigned solely to asynchronous moves.

Following the reasoning given in [22], we consider solely alignments with asynchronous moves that introduce placeholders for the trace of the process tree P. As such, the exact behavior exhibited by the trace σ among all the traces of the process tree P is identified. We capture this by a function $v(\sigma, P)$. For example, in Fig. 1, the behavior exhibited by the trace 1 is $\langle ABC \rangle$, while trace 2 exhibits $\langle ACB \rangle$. Both traces are part of the language of the discovered pattern.

We employ these functions to define the concept of projection and several quality metrics that provide the foundation for the COBPAM algorithm.

Definition 9. *A* projection *is a subset of an event log associated with a process tree P that contains the traces that can be aligned with P:*

$$proj(P) = \{\sigma \in L \mid \epsilon(\sigma, P) = 1\}.$$

Definition 10. *Given an event log L, the* frequency *of a process tree P is the number of traces that exhibit its behavior:*

$$frequency(P) = \sum_{\sigma \in L} \epsilon(\sigma, P) = |proj(P)|.$$

Its support *is the frequency over the size of the log:*

$$support(P) = \frac{frequency(P)}{|L|}.$$

Definition 11. *Given an event log L, the* language fitness *of a process tree P is the ratio of the behavior seen in the log and all the behavior allowed for by the model. If P does not contain loop operators, it is defined as:*

$$language\_fitness(P) = \frac{|\{v(\sigma, P) | \sigma \in L \wedge \epsilon(\sigma, P) = 1\}|}{|\Sigma(P)|}.$$

If P contains loop operators, its language will be infinite, so that its language fitness will tend to zero. In this case, we use the n-language of P:

$$language\_fitness(P) = \frac{|\{v(\sigma, P) | \sigma \in L \wedge \epsilon(\sigma, P) = 1\}|}{|\Sigma_n(P)|}$$

6 Behavioral Pattern Discovery with COBPAM

This section presents a new algorithm to discover process trees that represent frequent behavior in a log. Our idea is to explore a construction graph, starting from process tress of single activities. Each process tree is evaluated against a part of the log that may exhibit its behavior to calculate the aforementioned quality metrics. We also introduce projection and pruning rules to limit the number of process trees to evaluate and the number of traces used for evaluation.

In Sect. 6.1, we discuss a monotonocity property that is later exploited in our pattern search. We then define what we consider compact and maximal process trees in Sect. 6.2, and introduce optimization based on projections in Sect. 6.3. In Sect. 6.4, a detailed view of the algorithm is given.

6.1 A Monotonicity Property

The combination operation introduced in Sect. 4 replaces a potential combination leaf with a sub-tree representing a portion of a behavior that either extends the behavior of the original tree (when using the choice operator) or constrains it (when using a sequence, loop, or concurrency operator). When evaluating a process tree whose defining operator is a constraining operator (sequence, loop, concurrency), we essentially want that the trace exhibits all the behavior of its seeds except at the position of the combination leaf. At this position, additional behavior shall replace the appearance of an activity in the trace. The shared behavior between a process tree and its seeds represents a context to which the additional behavior is joined. Hence, if a trace does not exhibit the context, there is no need to evaluate the added behavior.

From the above, it follows that, if one of the seeds is not frequent, there is no need to evaluate the tree, as it will be infrequent too. This is a monotonicity property of the support metric. Based thereon, we specify a **first pruning rule**: If a seed is infrequent, it should not be combined using a constraining operator.

6.2   Compact and Maximal Process Trees

We further direct our search for behavioral patterns towards process trees that are useful from an analysis point of view. We therefore define compactness of process trees, as follows:

Definition 12. *Given an event log L, a process tree P is* compact, *if it satisfies all of the following conditions:*

(1) P does not exhibit the choice operator as a root node. If this condition is violated, the process tree would be the union of completely separate behaviors. While this may result in a frequent tree, the tree is arguably of little interest.

(2) P does not result from a combination through a choice operator, where, given L, one of the seeds is frequent. This is motivated as follows: If a tree P_1 is frequent, combining it with any other tree P_2 through the choice operator results in a frequent tree. Yet, P_2 adds complexity by means of behavior that may not even appear in the log.

(3) P does not contain a loop operator $loop(P_1, P_2)$, such that only the behavior of P_1 appears in L. While having only the behavior of P_1 yields a valid trace of the respective process tree, the derivation of an operator $loop(P_1, P_2)$ is not meaningful, if L does not contain the behavior of P_2.

Note that from condition (2), we immediately derive a **second pruning rule** for the exploration of candidate patterns: When performing a combination through the choice operator, both seeds must be infrequent.

In addition to compactness, there is a second property that is desired for behavioral patterns. It is motivated by the monotonicity property. The latter states that a frequent process tree P whose defining operator is a constraining operator must have two frequent seeds. Hence, we shall return solely P, as the seeds can simply be derived from P and are known to be frequent. In other words, we consider P to be the representative of its seeds. Furthermore, by transitivity, P is a representative of the paths in the construction tree composed solely of trees defined by constraining operators. As a consequence, discovery shall be limited to the largest representatives, which we call maximal behavioral patterns.

Definition 13. *Considering all behavioral patterns of at most depth i, a behavioral pattern is* maximal, *if it is frequent and not contained through a constraining operator in another frequent process tree of depth smaller or equal to i.*

In the example of Fig. 1, the trees $seq(a,b)$ and $seq(a,c)$ are frequent, but not maximal, since they are contained in $seq(a, and(b,c))$ as shown through the construction tree in Fig. 2b. When $seq(a, and(b,c))$ is discovered, all the frequent trees it represents, such as $seq(a,c)$, can be deduced.

6.3   Optimization Based on Projections

Recall that we aim at the discovery of frequent process trees. The runtime complexity of a method to solve this problem is governed by the size of the construction graph, which increases exponentially when the number of activities increases, and by the size of the log used to evaluate the quality of the trees. To cope with the latter, we present an optimization that complements the two pruning rules introduced in Sects. 6.1 and 6.2. Our optimization uses projections to assess the frequency of a tree based on a small number of traces:

- When performing a combination through a constraining operator, the behavior associated with the resulting trees may only appear in the intersection of the projections of the seeds. As a result, quality metrics are calculated solely based on the said intersection. Moreover, the size of the intersection of the seeds projections represents an upper bound for the frequency of the resulting trees. This yields a **third pruning rule**: If the upper bound is less than the frequency threshold, the combination is not considered further.
- When performing a combination using the choice operator, the projection associated with the resulting trees is the union of the projections of the seeds. Moreover, the frequency of the resulting trees can be precisely derived and corresponds to the size of the union of the seed projections. On another hand, the language of the new trees is the union of the languages of the seeds.

6.4   The COBPAM Algorithm

Now we are ready to present COBPAM, an algorithm that strives for efficient discovery of behavioral patterns that are frequent, compact and maximal. In order to achieve high efficiency, it largely neglects infrequent activities. More precisely, it discovers process trees that are built from frequent activities as well as frequent combinations of two infrequent activities through the choice operator. Here, a frequent combination of two infrequent activities is considered as a single activity in the remainder of the algorithm.

Note that pruning of infrequent trees, in general, implies a certain loss of patterns. Due to the choice operator, trees that are infrequent at some point can be combined to frequent ones at a later stage. Hence, pruning infrequent trees potentially leads to missing some frequent patterns that comprise a choice operator. Despite this, COBPAM applies the respective pruning, since without it, a large number of infrequent process trees would need to be evaluated. Moreover, the loss of frequent behavioral patterns in the discovery process is limited to process trees that comprise the choice operator. Completeness of the discovery result for trees built of constraining operators is not affected.

The idea of the COBPAM algorithm is to incrementally build up sets of process trees. In the light of the pruning rules, we maintain two sets, containing only frequent and infrequent trees, respectively. The former set serves as the basis for combinations through the constraining operators, whereas the latter set serves for choice-based combinations. All trees inside either set are identical except for a single leaf node. In fact, any two trees in a set are seeds and can be combined. Moreover, since the difference between two seeds is a single leaf, we associate each set with an identifier in the form of a representative word that applies to any of the representative words of the contained trees. Take, for example, the tree $seq(a,b)$. Its representative word is $(a\ b\ seq)$. The process

---

Algorithm 1. COBPAM: Function *addFreq*

input : P, a process tree; Γ, set of frequent process trees;
Θ, a set of frequent compact maximal process trees;
τ_S, a support threshold; τ_L, a language fitness threshold.

1 $\Gamma' \leftarrow \emptyset$;
2 **for** $P' \in \Gamma$ **do**
3 $\quad \lfloor \ \Gamma' \leftarrow$ combine P, P' through operators $\{and, loop, seq\}$ with pruning rules;

4 **for** $R \in \Gamma'$ **do**
5 $\quad$ **if** $\tau_S < support(R)$ *(Definition 10)* **then**
6 $\quad\quad$ **if** $\tau_L < language\_fitness(R)$ *(Definition 11)* **then**
7 $\quad\quad\quad$ $\Theta \leftarrow \Theta \cup R$;
8 $\quad\quad\quad$ $\Theta' \leftarrow$ trees on constraining operat. paths in construction tree of R;
9 $\quad\quad\quad$ $\Theta \leftarrow \Theta \setminus \Theta'$;
10 $\quad\quad$ **for** *each potential combination leaf a in R* **do**
11 $\quad\quad\quad$ $RW \leftarrow$ create representative word, replace a with '$\_$' in $RW(R)$;
12 $\quad\quad\quad$ $\Gamma_{RW} \leftarrow$ set containing frequent trees identified by RW;
13 $\quad\quad\quad$ $addFreq(R, \Gamma_{RW}, \Theta, \tau_S, \tau_L)$;

14 $\quad$ **else**
15 $\quad\quad$ **for** *each potential combination leaf a in R* **do**
16 $\quad\quad\quad$ $RW \leftarrow$ create representative word, replace a with '$\_$' in $RW(R)$;
17 $\quad\quad\quad$ $\gamma_{RW} \leftarrow$ set containing infrequent trees identified by RW;
18 $\quad\quad\quad$ $addInfreq(R, \gamma_{RW}, \Theta, \tau_S, \tau_L)$;

19 $\Gamma \leftarrow \Gamma \cup P$;

---

tree can be added to the set defined by *(a _ seq)*, where the underscore is a placeholder for any activity. So, any other tree, e.g., *seq(a,c)*, can be added to the set by replacing the placeholder with an activity. The placeholder is always at the position of a potential combination leaf. This way, any two trees in the set can be combined.

The algorithm revolves around two functions, *addFreq*, defined in Algorithm 1, that adds the process tree P to a set Γ containing only frequent trees; and *addInfreq*, defined in Algorithm 2, that adds P to a set γ containing only infrequent trees. By Θ, we further denote the set of frequent compact maximal trees, which represents the actual result of our algorithm. As such, the respective trees must satisfy a given language fitness threshold. Moreover, since the result shall contain only maximal trees, each time a frequent tree defined by a constraining operator is added to it, parts of its construction tree are deleted.

The COBPAM algorithm starts by creating the set of frequent process trees identified by the word '$\_$', i.e., any frequent tree with a single activity is added to it. We apply function *addFreq* on this set for each frequent activity. The algorithm then proceeds recursively, switching between *addFreq* and *addInfreq*. Note that one may use a maximum recursion depth d, which then also limits the maximum depth for the discovered trees to force termination.

Algorithm 2. COBPAM: Function *addInfreq*

---

input : P, a process tree; γ, set of infrequent process trees;
Θ, a set of frequent compact maximal process trees;
τ_S, a support threshold; τ_L, a language fitness threshold.

1 $\gamma' \leftarrow \emptyset$;
2 **for** $P' \in \gamma$ **do**
3    $\lfloor$ $\gamma' \leftarrow$ combine P and P' through *choice* operator;

4 **for** $R \in \gamma'$ **do**
5   **if** $\tau_S < support(R)$ *(Definition 10)* **then**
6   **if** $\tau_L < language\_fitness(R)$ *(Definition 11)* **then**
7       $\lfloor$ $\Theta \leftarrow \Theta \cup R$;

8   **for** *each potential combination leaf a in R* **do**
9       $RW \leftarrow$ create representative word, replace a with '_' in $RW(R)$;
10       $\Gamma_{RW} \leftarrow$ set containing frequent trees identified by RW;
11       $addFreq(R, \Gamma_{RW}, \Theta, \tau_S, \tau_L)$;

12   **else**
13   **for** *each potential combination leaf a in R* **do**
14       $RW \leftarrow$ create representative word, replace a with '_' in $RW(R)$;
15       $\gamma_{RW} \leftarrow$ set containing infrequent trees identified by RW;
16       $addInfreq(R, \gamma_{RW}, \Theta, \tau_S, \tau_L)$;

17 $\gamma \leftarrow \gamma \cup P$;

---

7 Experimental Evaluation

In this section, we evaluate the efficiency and effectiveness of COBPAM by comparing it to LPM discovery on real-life datasets. We first present details on the used datasets and the experimental setup. We then compare the algorithms in terms of their efficiency and effectiveness (quantitative and qualitative).

7.1 Setup and Datasets

COBPAM has been implemented as a plugin in the ProM framework [9] as the package *BehavioralPatternMining*. We ran the experimental evaluation on a PC with an i5-1.8 Ghz processor, 8 GB RAM and MacOS High Sierra.

We ran COBPAM and LPM discovery [22] on four real-world event logs. COBPAM was parameterized with a value of 0.7 for the support and language fitness thresholds, and a value of 2 for the maximal depth. The implementation of LPM discovery in ProM has a single parameter, i.e., the bound for the number of LPMs to discover. We set this bound to 500, the maximal possible value.

We used the following event logs, which are publicly available:[2]

- Sepsis: A log of a treatment process for Sepsis cases in a hospital. It contains 1050 traces with 15214 events that have been recorded for 16 activities.

---

[2] https://data.4tu.nl/repository/collection:event_logs_real.

- Traffic Fines: A log of an information system managing road traffic fines, containing 150370 traces, 561470 events, and 11 activities.
- Hospital: A log of a dutch hospital containing 1143 traces, 150291 events, and 624 activities.
- WABO: A log of a building permit application process in the Netherlands. It contains 1434 traces with 8577 events, recorded for 27 activities.

7.2   Results

Efficiency. Running both algorithms for behavioral pattern discovery, we observed the execution times reported in Table 1. They depend on the size of the log, the number of activities and events, and the complexity of the behavioral patterns in the log. COBPAM generally turns out to be more efficient.

Table 1. Execution times of COBPAM and LPM discovery

	Sepsis	Traffic fines	Hospital	WABO
COBPAM	22 min	28 min	6 h	75 s
LPM discovery	88 min	68 min	>48 h	26 h

Quantitative Effectiveness. Next, we assess the relevance of patterns discovered by our algorithm and LPM discovery. While COBPAM guarantees that discovered patterns are compact and maximal, we check how many patterns derived by LPM discovery also satisfy these properties. Given the above execution times, we focus on three logs: Sepsis, Traffic fines, and WABO.

The results are summarized in Table 2. For instance, for the Sepsis log, among the 500 patterns mined by the LPM discovery, 336 patterns satisfy the support and language fitness thresholds set by COBPAM. Among these, 194 are not compact and 17 are not maximal. So, only 125 of the patterns derived by LPM discovery are maximal and compact, whereas COBPAM discovered 386 such patterns. Similar results are obtained for the other datasets. We conclude that the patterns derived by LPM discovery contain much redundant information, whereas COBPAM yields many more relevant patterns.

Qualitative Effectiveness. Lastly, we conducted a qualitative analysis on the patterns derived by COBPAM and LPM discovery for the Sepsis log. This log is well-suited for our analysis as its end-to-end process model obtained with the FHM algorithm shows that the process is highly unstructured with intertwined execution paths, a high number of choice and loop constructs, and many edges.

In Fig. 3, we show some patterns derived by LPM discovery that satisfy the thresholds set to COBPAM. Patterns found by COBPAM are shown in Fig. 4. We notice the difference in the trees derived by the two algorithms. For instance, the tree (12) was not extracted by COBPAM, because it is not maximal. In fact,

Table 2. Pattern statistics of LPM discovery and COBPAM

	COBPAM	LPM discovery		
		Relevant	Non-maximal	Non-compact
Sepsis	386	125	17	194
Traffic fines	4	1	0	0
WABO	28	21	5	235

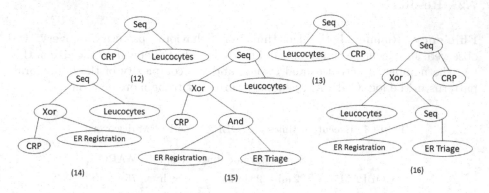

Fig. 3. Behavioral patterns mined by LPM discovery

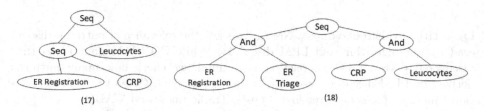

Fig. 4. Behavioral patterns mined with COBPAM

it is contained in tree (17). Knowing that (17) is frequent, one knows that *"ER Registration"* followed by *"CRP"* followed by *"Leucocytes"* is frequent. Hence, it follows that *"CRP"* followed by *"Leucocytes"*, as in tree (12), is frequent, too.

The trees (14), (15), and (16) are not discovered by COBPAM either, as they are not compact. Trees (14) and (15) are obtained from (12) by replacing activity *"CRP"* by a choice that includes activity *"CRP"* and some other behavior. Then, knowing that tree (12) is frequent, one concludes that the trees (14) and (15) are also frequent. Hence, they do not give new information. Similarly, tree (16) can be constructed from tree (13). The construction and evaluation (support, language fitness) of such trees lead to execution time being wasted without gaining further information about the process.

8   Conclusion

In this paper, we proposed COBPAM, an efficient algorithm for behavioral pattern mining. Potential patterns are obtained by combining simpler patterns using algebraic operations on process trees. Compared with an exhaustive search, the efficiency of the algorithm is improved by pruning the search space, evaluating the candidates solely on parts of the event log (using projections), and exploiting calculations already done for smaller trees. Moreover, the algorithm exploits a partial order on potential patterns to discover only those that are maximal while respecting a compactness property. An experimental evaluation with real-world event logs demonstrated how COBPAM improves over the state-of-the-art in behavioral pattern mining in terms of execution time and relevance of extracted patterns.

In a future work, we plan to investigate the relation between operators in terms of their semantics. For instance, if $and(a,b)$ is infrequent then $seq(a,b)$ is also infrequent. That is because the behavior of the sequence operator is included in that of the concurrency operator. Moreover, we intend to further improve efficiency by using frameworks for parallel computing.

References

1. Van der Aalst, W.: Process Mining: Data Science in Action. Springer, Berlin (2016). https://doi.org/10.1007/978-3-662-49851-4
2. Adriansyah, A.: Aligning observed and modeled behavior. Ph.D. thesis (2014)
3. Augusto, A., et al.: Automated Discovery of Process Models from Event Logs: Review and Benchmark (2018)
4. Bose, R.P.J.C., van der Aalst, W.M.: Context aware trace clustering: towards improving process mining results. In: 2009 SIAM International Conference on Data Mining (2009)
5. Bose, R.P.J.C., van der Aalst, W.M.P.: Trace clustering based on conserved patterns: towards achieving better process models. In: Rinderle-Ma, S., Sadiq, S., Leymann, F. (eds.) BPM 2009. LNBIP, vol. 43, pp. 170–181. Springer, Heidelberg (2010). https://doi.org/10.1007/978-3-642-12186-9_16
6. vanden Broucke, S.K., De Weerdt, J.: Decis. Support Syst. Fodina: a robust and flexible heuristic process discovery technique **100**, 109–118 (2017)
7. Buijs, J.C., Van Dongen, B.F., Van Der Aalst, W.M.: A genetic algorithm for discovering process trees. In: CEC 2012, June, pp. 1–8. IEEE (2012)
8. Conforti, R., Dumas, M., García-Bañuelos, L., La Rosa, M.: BPMN miner: automated discovery of BPMN process models with hierarchical structure. Inf. Syst. **56**, 284–303 (2016)
9. van Dongen, B.F., de Medeiros, A.K.A., Verbeek, H.M.W., Weijters, A.J.M.M., van der Aalst, W.M.P.: The ProM framework: a new era in process mining tool support. In: Ciardo, G., Darondeau, P. (eds.) ICATPN 2005. LNCS, vol. 3536, pp. 444–454. Springer, Heidelberg (2005). https://doi.org/10.1007/11494744_25
10. Fournier-Viger, P., Chun, J., Lin, W., Kiran, R.U., Koh, Y.S., Thomas, R.: A survey of sequential pattern mining. Ubiquit. Int. **1**(1), 54–77 (2017)
11. Greco, G., Guzzo, A., Pontieri, L., Saccà, D.: Discovering expressive process models by clustering log traces. IEEE TKDE **18**, 1010–1027 (2006)

12. Günther, C.W., van der Aalst, W.M.P.: Fuzzy mining – adaptive process simplification based on multi-perspective metrics. In: Alonso, G., Dadam, P., Rosemann, M. (eds.) BPM 2007. LNCS, vol. 4714, pp. 328–343. Springer, Heidelberg (2007). https://doi.org/10.1007/978-3-540-75183-0_24

13. Leemans, M., van der Aalst, W.M.P.: Discovery of frequent episodes in event logs. In: Ceravolo, P., Russo, B., Accorsi, R. (eds.) SIMPDA 2014. LNBIP, vol. 237, pp. 1–31. Springer, Cham (2015). https://doi.org/10.1007/978-3-319-27243-6_1

14. Leemans, S.J.J., Fahland, D., van der Aalst, W.M.P.: Discovering block-structured process models from event logs - a constructive approach. In: Colom, J.-M., Desel, J. (eds.) PETRI NETS 2013. LNCS, vol. 7927, pp. 311–329. Springer, Heidelberg (2013). https://doi.org/10.1007/978-3-642-38697-8_17

15. Maggi, F.M., Mooij, A.J., Van Der Aalst, W.M.: User-guided discovery of declarative process models. In: CIDM 2011, April, pp. 192–199. IEEE (2011)

16. Pei, J., et al.: Mining sequential patterns by pattern-growth: the PrefixSpan approach. IEEE Trans. Knowl. Data Eng. **16**, 1424–1440 (2004)

17. Senderovich, A., Weidlich, M., Gal, A.: Temporal network representation of event logs for improved performance modelling in business processes. In: Carmona, J., Engels, G., Kumar, A. (eds.) BPM 2017. LNCS, vol. 10445, pp. 3–21. Springer, Cham (2017). https://doi.org/10.1007/978-3-319-65000-5_1

18. Solé, M., Carmona, J.: Process mining from a basis of state regions. In: Lilius, J., Penczek, W. (eds.) PETRI NETS 2010. LNCS, vol. 6128, pp. 226–245. Springer, Heidelberg (2010). https://doi.org/10.1007/978-3-642-13675-7_14

19. Song, M., Günther, C.W., van der Aalst, W.M.P.: Trace clustering in process mining. In: Ardagna, D., Mecella, M., Yang, J. (eds.) BPM 2008. LNBIP, vol. 17, pp. 109–120. Springer, Heidelberg (2009). https://doi.org/10.1007/978-3-642-00328-8_11

20. Srikant, R., Agrawal, R.: Mining sequential patterns: generalizations and performance improvements. In: Apers, P., Bouzeghoub, M., Gardarin, G. (eds.) EDBT 1996. LNCS, vol. 1057, pp. 1–17. Springer, Heidelberg (1996). https://doi.org/10.1007/BFb0014140

21. Tax, N., Dalmas, B., Sidorova, N., van der Aalst, W.M., Norre, S.: Interest-driven discovery of local process models. Inf. Syst. **77**, 105–117 (2018)

22. Tax, N., Sidorova, N., Haakma, R., van der Aalst, W.M.: Mining local process models. J. Innov. Digit. Ecosyst. **3**(2), 183–196 (2016)

23. Weijters, A.J.M.M., Ribeiro, J.T.S.: Flexible heuristics miner (FHM). In: CIDM 2011, pp. 310–317 (2011)

24. van Zelst, S.J., van Dongen, B.F., van der Aalst, W.M.P.: Avoiding over-fitting in ILP-based process discovery. In: Motahari-Nezhad, H.R., Recker, J., Weidlich, M. (eds.) BPM 2015. LNCS, vol. 9253, pp. 163–171. Springer, Cham (2015). https://doi.org/10.1007/978-3-319-23063-4_10

Discovering Responsibilities with Dynamic Condition Response Graphs

Viktorija Nekrasaite, Andrew Tristan Parli, Christoffer Olling Back[(✉)], and Tijs Slaats

Department of Computer Science, University of Copenhagen,
Emil Holms Kanal 6, 2300 Copenhagen S, Denmark
viktorijanekrasaite3@gmail.com, drewparli@gmail.com,
{back,slaats}@di.ku.dk

Abstract. Declarative process discovery is the art of using historical data to better understand the responsibilities of an organisation: its governing business rules and goals. These rules and goals can be described using declarative process notations, such as Dynamic Condition Response (DCR) Graphs, which has seen widespread industrial adoption within Denmark, in particular through its integration in a case management solution used by 70% of central government institutions. In this paper, we introduce PARNEK: a novel, effective, and extensible miner for the discovery of DCR Graphs. We empirically evaluate PARNEK and show that it significantly outperforms the state-of-the-art in DCR discovery and performs at least comparably to the state-of-the-art in Declare discovery. Notably, the miner can be configured to sacrifice relatively little precision in favour of significant gains in simplicity, making it the first miner able to produce understandable DCR Graphs for real-life logs.

Keywords: Declarative process discovery · Declarative models · Dynamic Condition Response Graphs · DCR Graphs · DCR discovery

1 Introduction

Automating knowledge intensive processes offers unique challenges: the problems faced by knowledge workers are highly heterogeneous and tend to require unique solutions. In municipal government, for example, no two citizens are exactly the same: when dealing with long-term unemployment or illness, solutions will be tailored to each citizen's individual needs. These unique solutions are to a large degree determined by the case workers themselves, in sharp contrast to

This work is supported by the Hybrid Business Process Management Technologies project (DFF-6111-00337) funded by the Danish Council for Independent Research, and the EcoKnow project (7050-00034A) funded by the Innovation Foundation. First and second author listed alphabetically.

P. Giorgini and B. Weber (Eds.): CAiSE 2019, LNCS 11483, pp. 595–610, 2019.
https://doi.org/10.1007/978-3-030-21290-2_37

traditional production processes where the worker is usually expected to strictly follow the instructions of the system. At the same time, organisations and their workers do have many responsibilities: goals need to be met, laws need to be adhered to and business practices followed. Information systems should ensure that these responsibilities are met, and therefore some form of control over the activities of the workers is still required.

Because of this high degree of flexibility, it can be problematic to focus on the *how* of knowledge work: defining all possible paths through a process becomes cumbersome as the number of variations increases, and often it is impossible to exactly predict what variations may occur in the future. Instead, it can be helpful to focus on the *what* of knowledge work: the goals we aim to achieve, and the rules to which must adhere. It can then be left to the information system to derive possible paths from these goals and rules.

Imperative process notations such as BPMN and Petri nets are used to capture the how of a process by using a flow-based paradigm: when executing the model, one follows the flow of the model, usually indicated by arrows, executing the activities of the model along the way. Such notations are poorly suited to capturing the what of the process: rules are not defined explicitly, but instead encoded as allowed paths. One rule may affect many different paths, and each path could result from many different rules interacting with each other. *Declarative* process notations such as Declare and Dynamic Condition Response (DCR) Graphs are better suited to capturing rules. They describe a process as a set of constraints which can be mapped directly to specific business rules or goals. An execution semantics is usually achieved by either mapping the declarative model to a flow-based model (e.g. transition systems), or by introducing an operational semantics that reasons over the state of the different constraints and/or activities of the model.

Instead of requiring process consultants to design all rules upfront based on requirement specifications and interviews with users, it can be helpful to use data describing the historical execution of processes, represented as event logs, to automatically derive possible rules in the form of formal constraints. Finding and proposing constraints automatically reduces the workload of the consultants and ensures the resulting models are grounded in practice, instead of an ideal – but not fully realistic – world envisioned by the users.

Such declarative process discovery algorithms can produce models in various notations. Although Declare [15], the first declarative notation introduced exclusively for describing business processes, is most prevalent in academia, there is no documented usage of the notation in industry, leaving it as a mostly academic pursuit. DCR Graphs [9] is a more recent declarative notation that has been more successful commercially. It was picked up by a Danish developer of case management systems, leading to the creation of a commercial modelling tool [18]. More recently, 70% of Danish central government institutions adopted a case management solution that uses a DCR process engine, including the police, military, tax authorities and largest public universities[1].

---

[1] http://www.kmd.dk/indsigter/fleksibilitet-og-dynamisk-sagsbehandling-i-staten.

DCR Graphs' success notwithstanding, process discovery based on this nota-tion is still in its infancy: there currently exists a single algorithm, which first generates a model with all possible constraints and then removes constraints until the model allows all behaviour seen in the event log. We posit that this approach is inconsistent with the declarative paradigm: if the goal of declara-tive models is to support flexibility, then it is counter-productive to start from an assumption that the process should be fully constrained. This intuition is supported by a closer look at the generated models: they are precise, but lack simplicity and often appear to mimic flow-based diagrams in structure.

In this paper, we introduce the PARNEK miner, a novel discovery algorithm for DCR Graphs, with a more methodologically sound basis than existing DCR Graphs miners: we start from a fully unconstrained model and, based on the event log, propose constraints that should be introduced to reasonably restrict behaviour. We show that PARNEK significantly outperforms the state-of-the-art in DCR Graphs discovery and that our results are at minimum comparable to that of MINERful, a state-of-the-art miner in declarative process discovery. We also discuss advantages of PARNEK in terms of configurability and extensibility.

The paper continues as follows: we first discuss related work in Sect. 2 and introduce DCR Graphs in Sect. 3. In Sect. 4, we explain the core algorithms underlying the PARNEK miner. We empirically evaluate PARNEK against the state-of-the-art in DCR Graphs and Declare mining in Sect. 5 and conclude in Sect. 6.

2   Related Work

Declarative notations were first introduced to the BPM community through the work on Declare [15], which proposed mapping an extensive number of control flow patterns to linear temporal logic constraints. The first process discovery algorithm for Declare was the Declare Miner [13], which suffered from being a brute-force approach, leading to poor run-time performance. A significant improvement was proposed in [12]. Another Declare-based miner, MINERful [2], has been developed as an alternative, focusing on run-time efficiency and a high degree of customisation. A multi-perspective approach to Declare discovery, including data, time and resource constraints, was introduced in [17].

Several alternative declarative notations have been proposed [11,21]. Two stand out in particular for having led to the development of corresponding pro-cess discovery algorithms. The guard-stage-milestone model [10] provides a more artifact-centric, rather than constraint-centric, view on processes, but integrates declarative aspects and has become the basis of the recent CMMN standard [14]. A process mining approach for GSM was proposed in [16] as a multi-step process that first discovers artifact life-cycles in an event log and then maps these to a GSM schema.

DCR Graphs offers several advantages over Declare, namely stronger formal expressiveness [5], an operational semantics defined directly on the model with a corresponding visual representation and active adoption by industry [18]. Several

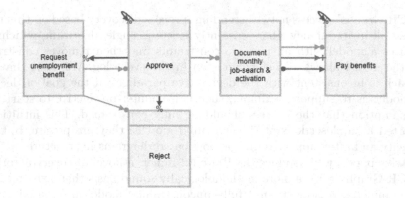

Fig. 1. DCR graph of a basic unemployment process.

extensions have been proposed, such as data [19], time [8] and subprocesses [3]. The work on process discovery for DCR Graphs has not advanced to the stage of considering these extensions yet, as finding a suitable base algorithm is the first priority.

3   Modelling Responsibilities with DCR Graphs

In this section we describe the structure and semantics of DCR Graphs in more detail and illustrate their use for modelling casework by using a simplified running example of a municipal unemployment process.

Example 31 (Unemployment Process). *A citizen starts the unemployment process by filing a request for unemployment benefits. Until it is approved, they can update this request at any time to correct it or provide additional information. Once a request has been submitted, a municipal caseworker can approve or reject the request. It is possible to approve a request that was previously rejected, for example because additional information was provided, or a mistake was made. However, it is not possible to reject a request that has already been approved (cancellation of benefits is handled by its own separate process). Once the request is approved, the citizen should submit monthly documentation of the progress of their job-search. Once documentation is provided, the municipality is required by law to pay their benefits.*

Figure 1 shows the unemployment process modelled as a DCR Graph.

The *activities* of the process are represented as boxes. In formal DCR terminology these are referred to as *events*, which can represent anything that can happen, such as an activity executing, but also data changing or deadlines being reached. Note that these are different from the *log events* used in process discovery, as they can represent more than one occurrence of something happening. In process discovery terminology they are closer to *event classes*.

An unconstrained activity can happen at any time, any number of times. This means that in a graph with no constraints, anything can happen at any time, making it equivalent to the flower model often encountered in flow-based notations.

To constrain the behaviour of the process, we introduce *relations*. The *condition relation*, denoted as `Request unemployment benefit →• Reject`, indicates that we cannot reject a request before it has been submitted. Conditions do not alternate: after the first request, one can reject it any number of times, even if no new requests are submitted. This befits the declarative paradigm which stresses only adding constraints when absolutely required. In this case it may, for example, be convenient to update a rejection with additional reasons. Similarly, `Request unemployment benefit` is a condition for `Approve`, which is a condition for `Document monthly job-search`, which is a condition for `Pay benefits`.

The *exclusion relation*, denoted as `Approve —% Reject`, indicates that after doing `Approve`, it is no longer possible to `Reject` the request because it has been removed from the process. `Approve` similarly removes `Document monthly job-search`. Events can also exclude themselves, meaning that after they have been executed, they are no longer a part of the process. This is the case for `Approve` and `Pay benefits`.

Exclusion of events is *dynamic*: it can be undone by re-including the event through the *inclusion relation*, denoted as `Document monthly job-search →+ Pay benefits`. Including an event adds it back into the process, allowing it to be executed again. In the example, each time monthly documentation is submitted, pay benefits will be included and can be executed again.

The final *response relation* is used to indicate future requirements or goals. It is denoted as `Document monthly job-search •→ Pay benefits` and ensures that when monthly documentation is submitted, benefits will eventually be paid.

While timed constraints [8] could be used to further specify the model, for example by stating that `Document monthly job-search` can only happen once per month, we only consider control-flow constraints in this paper and leave the discovery of other perspectives to future work.

4   Discovery of Dynamic Condition Response Graphs

Given that we aim to mine flexible declarative models, we start from the least restrictive DCR Graph, containing all activities seen in the event log and no relations, allowing for any trace over these activities. PARNEK implements a number of algorithms for adding relations to this unrestricted model. These algorithms are largely orthogonal, each finding relations independently that can be combined to form the final model. According to the declarative paradigm exceptional behaviour should be embraced and therefore all algorithms have been designed to guarantee perfect fitness. The miner can be configured by the user to select which algorithms should be used. Through experimentation, we identified a number of promising configurations.

4.1   The Base ParNek algorithm

The base algorithm is inspired by a subset of the constraint templates used by the MINERful [2] algorithm, however we do not always map these precisely. Instead we aim for a balance between simplicity and precision where we allow for small amounts of additional behaviour in cases where this means introducing significantly fewer relations. We consider the following constraints:

- AtMostOne(A): All such activities can be represented as a self-excluding activity in a DCR graph, i.e., A $\rightarrow\!\%$ A
- Response(A, B): We utilise this constraint template to add response relations to the model i.e., A $\bullet\!\!\rightarrow$ B
- Precedence(A, B): We utilise this constraint template to add condition relations to the model i.e., A $\rightarrow\!\bullet$ B
- ChainPrecedence(A, B): We map this constraint to A includes B and B is a self-excluding activity, i.e., A $\rightarrow\!+$ B and B $\rightarrow\!\%$ B

The base algorithm will often find redundant condition and response relations. For example, for a DCR Graph containing only the conditions A $\rightarrow\!\bullet$ B, B $\rightarrow\!\bullet$ C and A $\rightarrow\!\bullet$ C, the relation A $\rightarrow\!\bullet$ C is redundant because the other two conditions already ensure that C can not happen before A has happened. We use this transitive property to remove unnecessary conditions. The same form of transitivity can be applied to response relations. It should be noted that this transitivity does not always hold: when an event is dynamically excluded, its outgoing relations are also considered excluded. For example, if we remove the condition A $\rightarrow\!\bullet$ C and add the exclusion D $\rightarrow\!\%$ B to the previous example, one would be allowed to execute D, excluding not only the event B, but also the condition B $\rightarrow\!\bullet$ C, allowing C to be executed afterwards. However, removing conditions and responses will never lower the fitness of the model: it will at worst lower precision by allowing additional traces not seen in the log. Experiments showed that this loss of precision was heavily offset by a gain in simplicity, for example for the BPIC-2012 event log we can reduce the number of condition relations from 160 to 30 in return for a decrease in precision of 0.0003.

In the next step of the base algorithm we first build Predecessor and Successor sets for each activity. The Predecessor set contains all the activities which can happen before the *last* occurrence of a specific activity in a trace. Similarly, the Successor set contains the activities that can happen after the *first* occurrence of a target activity in a trace. We leverage these sets to discover two types of exclusions. The first type is based on the observation that an activity can exclude its predecessors which are absent in the Successor set, i.e., B $\in$ Predecessor(A, log)\Successor(A, log). Moreover, it is possible to skip activities in the model with a self exclusion, i.e., B $\notin$ SelfExclusions. This is because self exclusion relations are either the result of AtMostOne or ChainPrecedence, meaning this extra exclude relation would be redundant. The second type of exclusions addresses mutually exclusive activities: an activity can exclude activities not present in Predecessor(A, log) $\cup$ Successor(A, log).

To ensure that we keep the model simple, we also apply an optimisation step to exclusions. Each time we wish to add an exclusion A $\rightarrow\!\%$ B, we first check if there is already a predecessor of A that excludes B, in which case we do not add the additional exclusion. Similarly to the previous optimisation step, this approach may lead to a slight decrease in precision, but is guaranteed to keep the model fully fitting and leads to a large reduction in the number of constraints.

4.2 Mining Additional Conditions

The optional COND algorithm is aimed at mining more complex condition patterns. In the base algorithm we only discover a condition A $\rightarrow\!\bullet$ B when A always precedes B in the log. However, because of the possibility of dynamically excluding conditions, there may exist relevant conditions where this is not the case.

To discover such conditions, we follow these steps:

1. Mine a graph by using one variation of PARNEK
2. Take a union of activities that come before the last occurrence of a specific activity (remove those which already have a condition)
3. Examine the resulting activities in every trace using three sets:
   - POSSIBLECONDS: Activities that may have a condition relation to a target activity. In the beginning, the set consists of all the activities that occur before the last occurrence of the target activity except those which already have a condition relation to it
   - IGNORE: All the activities in POSSIBLECONDS before the first occurrence of the target activity in a current trace
   - CHECK = POSSIBLECONDS \ IGNORE, i.e., activities for which we need to execute the trace, keeping track of whether the activity is included or excluded from the current trace every time we want to execute the target activity. We stop the verification process if:
     - the activity gets executed
     - we reach the last target activity in the current trace
     - the activity is included when we want to execute the target activity
   If the process gets terminated because of the third condition, then we remove the activity from POSSIBLECONDS since it is not possible to have a condition from it.

By the end of step 3 we are left with the additional conditions. Our experiments showed that the COND algorithm tends to add a few conditions at most. The precision increase from these conditions varied largely per log, with some logs seeing no increase and one log seeing an increase from 0.59 to 0.87.

4.3 Improvements for Long, Similar Sequences, Repeated Activities

The presence of activities in the event log that repeat themselves non-trivially or long sequences of activities that are highly similar significantly decreases the precision of the models that the base PARNEK algorithm is capable of mining. To increase precision, we developed an optional CHECKFOLLOW algorithm which discovers dynamic include and exclude relations that help guide the local execution of the model.

We define NOTDIRECTLYFOLLOWS(A) as the set of activities that occur after, but not directly after A and not including A. Next we add exclusion relations from A to each activity in NOTDIRECTLYFOLLOWS. We repeat this for all activities in the log. To make sure that these activities are included in the graph again, we need to define the set DIRECTLYPRECEDES(B, A). This is the set of all activities that directly precede B in the event after the execution of A and not including B. Here we can equate B to one of the activities the A dynamically excluded above. This means that adding inclusion relations to B from all the activities in its corresponding DIRECTLYPRECEDES(B, A) set will ensure the perfect fitness of the mined model.

In order to balance between model simplicity and precision, CHECKFOLLOW takes a threshold parameter that is compared against the cardinality of DIRECT-LYPRECEDES before introducing any new constraints. By keeping the threshold low, one lowers the number of constraints found, prioritising simplicity over precision. Through experimentation, we noticed that the effect of the threshold is most noticeable when set to either 1 or ∞. In general, we observed that the CHECKFOLLOW algorithm greatly improved the precision of the model, but at the cost of adding a large amount of additional constraints. We discuss this difference in more detail in Sect. 5.

4.4   Running Example

Let us consider our running example and abbreviate the five activities as follows: Request unemployment benefit (U), Approve (A), Reject (R), Document monthly job-search (D), Pay benefits (P).

Table 1. A log which consists of 8 traces.

U	U, R	U, R, R, A	U, R, A, D, P
U, U	U, R, U	U, A, D, P	U, A, D, P, D, P

If we provide PARNEK, in particular the base algorithm, with the event log in Table 1 then we observe that A happens at most once in every trace, i.e., it excludes itself. Moreover, every time D happens, it is followed by P, i.e., we have a response relation. Also, D and P follow the CHAINPRECEDENCE pattern, where P is always directly preceded by D. Therefore we discover an inclusion from D to P and a self-exclusion for P. Furthermore, U is the first activity in every trace. As a result, it has conditions to A and R. Additionally, we have A →• D since D can only happen after A was executed. In other words, in order to proceed with an unemployment process, first an application needs to be approved. On top of that, there is another condition D →• P because P never occurs before the first D in any trace. Finally, if we look at activity A, its PREDECESSOR set contains {U, R} while SUCCESSOR set consists of D and P. If we take the difference of these two sets, we are left with {U, R}. Since neither U nor R has a self-exclusion, we can add exclusion relations from A to them. This results in the DCR Graph shown in Fig. 1.

5 Evaluation

We evaluate the PARNEK miner by comparing its performance against two declarative miners: the DCR miner from [4], referred to as baseline, and MINERful, which returns models based on the Declare modelling language. Aside from running time, we evaluate the degree of under- and overfitting using a notation-agnostic precision metric, and fitness-based cross-validation, respectively.

5.1 Methodology

Metrics. Process mining is generally framed as a *descriptive* data mining task: the aim is to accurately describe training data [7]. To this end, quality metrics such as precision and fitness computed on the *in-sample* data set are most often reported. In regards to precision we follow this paradigm, since the formulation of precision we employ cannot be computed on traces which cannot be replayed on the model (as are likely to be present in out-of-sample data). We also present an estimate of *out-of-sample* performance in terms of fitness using cross-validation.

Precision. The most widely adopted precision metrics in the process mining literature are defined on Petri nets and cannot be applied to declarative models. A formulation of precision defined on the underlying state-transition system has been proposed in [20] and was implemented for the evaluation proposed in [1]. This formulation allows for comparison across all modelling notations.

Let $\mathcal{E}$ denote the set of unique events in an event log with $e \in \mathcal{E}$. Let $\text{en}_L(e)$ denote the set of activities sharing the same context (i.e., prefix) as event e in log L. Let $\text{en}_M(e)$ denote the set of activities enabled in the state of model M immediately *prior* to executing e. The precision of M w.r.t. log L is given by

$$P_L(M) = \frac{1}{|\mathcal{E}|} \sum_{e \in \mathcal{E}} \frac{|\text{en}_L(e)|}{|\text{en}_M(e)|} \tag{51}$$

This metric captures the degree to which more behaviour is allowed by the model than has been observed in the log.

Normalised Precision. The above formulation of precision is a function of the log as well as the model, and we would like to establish a normalised formulation by establishing a lower and upper bound for the log. This will allow us to better understand the relative difference between miners based on what the worst and best case results are for a particular log.

Let P_L^l and P_L^u denote the lower and upper bound for precision, respectively. The normalised precision is given by

$$P_L^n(M) = \frac{P_L(M) - P_L^l(M)}{P_L^u - P_L^l} \tag{52}$$

We take as P_L^l the precision of the *flower* model, in which any activity encountered in the log is enabled in every context. The only models resulting in a lower estimate of P_L^l are those which allow *more activities than encountered in the log* to be enabled. We base P_{upper} on the maximum formal expressiveness of the modelling notations used. We know that DCR Graphs capture all regular languages and therefore for each event log there exists a DCR Graph representing it with a precision of 1. Thus $P_L^u = 1$.

Cross-validation. Precision gives an indication of the degree to which a model may be *underfitting* the data. Unless we assume that an event log represents all of the behaviour we can expect to encounter, we should also investigate the generalisability of our model: the degree to which it may be *overfitting* the training data.

Traditional supervised learning tasks define an error metric, e.g. the number of correctly classified instances in classification tasks, or a distance-based metric, such as the residual sum of squares, for regression tasks. Cross-validation is one approach to estimating the error of a given model on *out-of-sample* data.

We take as our error metric simple trace fitness: the percentage of out-of-sample traces able to be replayed on the model. If we interpret process mining as a binary classification problem (in which traces either fall into acceptable or unacceptable classes), with event logs containing only positive examples, then fitness can be interpreted as *recall*, i.e. the ratio of traces accepted by the model to the total number of traces in the validation log:

$$\text{fitness} = \frac{|\text{true positives}|}{|\text{true positives}| + |\text{false negatives}|} \tag{53}$$

We employ k-fold cross-validation, splitting the original logs into k partitions of equal size. The nth partition is then held out as a validation set, the miner run on the remaining $k - 1$ partitions, and the resulting model evaluated on the validation set. This is repeated for $n \in \{1, \ldots, k\}$. We report the mean fitness across all k validation sets. Traces are ordered chronologically by the timestamp of the first event prior to partitioning.

We report results for lower k than the standard $k = 10$, having observed that lower k are more informative in that most miners produce almost perfectly fitting models when trained on 90% of the log. Note that computing (normalised) precision of a model mined from the training data and evaluated on the validation data is possible, but problematic since these metrics become skewed by the fact that precision can only be computed for fitting traces. For this reason, we report normalised precision for the whole log.

Logs. We base log selection on the criterion of public availability, drawing upon (i) the IEEE Task Force on Process Mining Real-life Event Log Collection[2], (ii) two additional logs also published by the 4TU Center for Research Data[3,4], and (iii) one real-life log originating from our own industrial contacts [6].

For logs containing activities with more than one *lifecycle transition* such as A.start and A.complete, we present results both for the log in which this distinction is ignored, and a modified log in which these are considered distinct activities. No other preprocessing has been performed.

Miner Configuration. We evaluate two variants of the PARNEK miner: the base algorithm described in Sect. 4.1 with the improvement for mining additional conditions described in Sect. 4.2; and a variant which includes all of the improvements described in Sect. 4.3. Internal experiments showed that the first variant produced simpler models with a reasonable number of constraints. The second variant produced more precise, but more complex models.

MINERful has three parameters: a minimum threshold for *support, confidence*, and *interest factor*. We set support to 1.0 to ensure perfect fitness on training data. The remaining two parameters are set such that the resulting model is as close in size to the corresponding PARNEK variant. Parameters are determined automatically by a divide and conquer parameter tuning algorithm, with a step resolution of 0.1. MINERful is allowed to consider all constraints in the Declare language, including negative constraints. Finally, before the size of the mined model is evaluated, inconsistency checking is applied using the setting HIERARCHYCONFLICT with constraint sorting policy: ACTIVATIONTARGETBONDS, FAMILYHIERARCHY, SUPPORTCONFIDENCEINTERESTFACTOR. Redundancy checking does not finish for all logs and therefore not applied.

5.2   Implementation

The aforementioned evaluation metrics have been implemented in a stand-alone CLI application[5]. All mining and evaluation processes were performed on a Lenovo Thinkpad P50 with a 64-bit Intel Xeon E3-1535M v3 2.90 GHz CPU and 32 GB of RAM running Windows 10 Enterprise 64-bit edition. The PARNEK miner and its source code are available publicly for research purposes[6].

5.3   Results and Discussion

The bottom half of Table 3 shows aggregated results across logs, we make the following observations:

---

[2] http://data.4tu.nl/repository/collection:event_logs_real.
[3] https://doi.org/10.4121/uuid:6df27e59-6221-4ca2-9cc4-65c66588c6eb.
[4] https://doi.org/10.4121/uuid:5a9039b8-794a-4ccd-a5ef-4671f0a258a4.
[5] https://github.com/backco/qmpm.
[6] https://github.com/viktorija-nek/ParNek.

1. PARNEK is able to find significantly simpler models than the baseline (ratio of 0.14), while sacrificing relatively little precision (ratio of 0.58).
2. An extended version of PARNEK is able to find equally precise models (ratio of 1.00), using noticeably fewer constraints (ratio of 0.68).
3. When aiming for comparable model sizes, PARNEK finds more constraints than MINERful (ratio of 1.58 and 1.47 on respectively small and large models), but leads to a relatively larger increase in precision (ratio of 2.12 and 1.53 on respectively small and large models).

Table 2. Median mining time in milliseconds across 20 runs. The MINERful values to the right of either PARNEK variant are the result of confidence and interest factor thresholds (adjacent) which produce models of a size comparable to the PARNEK variant. Log names suffixed by LT have the lifecycle transition included in the event name, so that they will be interpreted as instances of distinct activities.

	PARNEK (COND)	MINER-ful	Conf./Int. Fac.	PARNEK (FULL)	MINER-ful	Conf./Int. Fac.	Base line
BPI Challenge 2012	1281	5108	$0.5/0.2$	2433	4614	$0.2/0.1$	1975
BPI Challenge 2012 LT	2089	6713	$0.5/0.3$	4951	6238	$0.2/0.0$	2864
BPI Challenge 2013	65	1410	$0.0/0.9$	151	1107	$0.0/0.0$	173
BPI Challenge 2013 LT	124	1992	$0.1/0.0$	340	1296	$0.0/0.0$	350
BPI Challenge 2017	5164	25409	$1.0/0.5$	9964	25657	$0.1/0.0$	7807
Activities Daily Living	72	1185	$0.3/0.2$	224	872	$0.0/0.0$	432
Activities Daily Liv. LT	115	2515	$0.7/0.1$	1127	2094	$0.1/0.0$	1497
Document Processing	189	2999	$1.0/0.2$	253	2478	$0.7/0.6$	220
Document Proc. LT	272	3558	$1.0/0.2$	274	3558	$1.0/0.2$	166
Dreyer Foundation	34	917	$0.4/0.2$	114	655	$0.1/0.0$	145
Electronic Invoicing	163	3345	$1.0/0.8$	294	2983	$1.0/0.5$	202
Electronic Invoicing LT	177	4048	$1.0/0.8$	301	3461	$1.0/0.5$	218
Hospital Billing	307	7662	$0.4/0.0$	507	6652	$0.0/0.0$	425
NASA CEV	497	3919	$0.5/0.2$	3370	3276	$0.0/0.0$	1832
NASA CEV LT	1310	7444	$0.5/0.4$	11381	6978	$0.1/0.0$	7948
Production	34	1809	$0.1/0.0$	359	1741	$0.0/0.0$	1205
Production LT	76	4931	$0.1/0.0$	1656	5349	$0.0/0.0$	10075
Sepsis Cases	112	887	$0.6/0.0$	225	562	$0.1/0.0$	229
Traffic Fines Mgmt.	623	7289	$0.3/0.3$	742	6270	$0.2/0.0$	647
WABO Receipt Phase	32	483	$0.8/0.0$	90	963	$0.8/0.0$	95

Looking at individual logs gives further insights. Some of the most notable logs include (multiples are w.r.t. to corresponding MINERful or PARNEK variant, respectively, unless otherwise stated):

BPIC 2012. PARNEK(COND) almost doubles precision by adding only 3 relations.

BPIC 2013. MINERful achieves the same precision with only 2 constraints.

BPIC 2017. PARNEK(COND) more than doubles precision with *fewer* relations.

Document Proc. PARNEK(COND) almost triples precision with just 2 extra relations.

D. Proc. (LT). PARNEK(FULL) gets 0.99 prec. with 150 relations vs. Baseline's 558.

Table 3. TOP: Comparison of miners based on normalised precision (PN), generalisation (GEN), and model size. Generalisation to *out-of-sample* data is estimated as mean trace fitness on hold-out data in 5-fold cross-validation. Normalised precision and model size are based on the complete log. Two variants of the ParNek miner are reported: the base algorithm with the additional conditions improvement from Sect. 4.2 (COND), and the algorithm with all improvements (FULL). To the right of the results for each ParNek variant are results for models produced by MINERful when restricted to a model size comparable to that produced by ParNek. Baseline refers to the DCR miner from [4]. Size refers to the number of constraints/relations. Log names suffixed by LT have the lifecycle transition included in the event name, so that they will be interpreted as instances of distinct activities. (*) Due to computational limitations, this value was computed using 2-fold cross-validation.
BOTTOM: Relative improvement of miners against other miners or their own variant. Each number represents the mean increase in size and precision, respectively.

Logs	ParNek(COND)			MINERful			ParNek(FULL)			MINERful			Baseline		
	SIZE	PN	GEN	SIZE	PN	GEN	SIZE	PN	GEN	SIZE	PN	GEN	SIZE	PN	GEN
BPIC 2012	68	0.28	≈1	65	0.15	1.0	343	0.36	≈1	235	0.22	≈1	762	0.42	≈1
BPIC 2012 LT	99	0.26	≈1	83	0.14	≈1	1066	0.5	≈1	838	0.27	≈1	1668	0.51	≈1
BPIC 2013	7	0.49	1.0	0	0.51	1.0	11	0.51	1.0	9	0.51	1.0	17	0.51	1.0
BPIC 2013 LT	32	0.22	≈1	31	0.23	≈1	138	0.29	≈1	101	0.28	≈1	170	0.29	≈1
BPIC 2017	75	0.18	≈1	87	0.08	1.0	594	0.32	≈1	566	0.22	≈1	865	0.34	≈1
Activities	90	0.02	0.75	78	≈0	0.62	994	0.08	0.44	803	0.07	0.48	1084	0.07	0.48
Activities LT	228	0.04	0.75	226	0.16	0.77	3288	0.45	0.44	3247	0.42	0.51	4594	0.46	0.46
Doc. Proc.	34	0.44	1.0	32	0.16	1.0	101	0.51	1.0	70	0.23	1.0	156	0.51	1.0
Doc. Proc. LT	83	0.88	1.0	72	0.26	1.0	132	0.99	1.0	72	0.26	1.0	540	0.99	1.0
Dreyer Found.	123	0.12	0.98	120	0.17	0.98	887	0.54	0.94	431	0.3	0.96	1148	0.56	0.95
Elec. Inv.	24	0.36	1.0	49	0.2	1.0	83	0.49	1.0	65	0.2	1.0	130	0.49	1.0
Elec. Inv. LT	57	0.61	1.0	131	0.5	1.0	134	0.82	1.0	187	0.51	1.0	440	0.98	1.0
Hosp. Billing	56	0.45	≈1	38	0.46	≈1	297	0.72	≈1	209	0.71	≈1	337	0.72	≈1
NASA CEV	137	0.14	≈1	125	0.04	≈1	3144	0.54	0.86	2157	0.39	0.71	2415	0.43	0.86
NASA CEV LT	298	0.31	0.98	281	0.25	≈1	7018	0.82	0.86	6451	0.71	0.84	9996	0.88	0.86
Production	720	0.02	0.87	123	≈0	0.78	2916	0.09	0.63	2765	0.11	0.57	3120	0.08	0.65
Production LT	1123	0.03	0.90	763	0.01	0.66	9287	0.12	0.54	11967	0.14	0.47*	13363	0.12	0.54
Sepsis Cases	83	0.21	0.99	77	0.19	0.98	194	0.25	0.96	106	0.2	0.97	284	0.21	0.97
Traffic Fines	22	0.79	1.0	21	0.62	1.0	70	0.93	≈1	44	0.79	1.0	150	0.93	≈1
WABO Receipt	93	0.61	0.99	90	0.39	0.99	388	0.7	0.99	90	0.39	0.99	873	0.81	0.99

$\frac{1}{N}\sum(\cdot)$	$\frac{\text{ParNek(COND)}}{\text{MINERful(COND)}}$	$\frac{\text{ParNek(FULL)}}{\text{MINERful(FULL)}}$	$\frac{\text{ParNek(FULL)}}{\text{ParNek(COND)}}$	$\frac{\text{MINERful(FULL)}}{\text{MINERful(COND)}}$	$\frac{\text{ParNek(COND)}}{\text{Baseline}}$	$\frac{\text{ParNek(FULL)}}{\text{Baseline}}$
SIZE	1.579	1.474	7.324	7.751	0.144	0.679
PRECISION	2.117	1.526	2.610	5.142	0.576	1.003

Elec. Inv. (LT). For both versions of this log, PARNEK makes significant improvements, often with *fewer* relations.

Traffic. PARNEK outperforms, the COND variant doing so with one extra relation.

WABO. PARNEK(COND) increases precision by 56.4% with just 3 extra relations.

PARNEK is often able to improve precision at the expense of only a small number of additional relations, and in some cases even *fewer* relations than MINERful. The converse is also true for MINERful for a handful of logs, implying that the combination of modelling language and mining algorithm are best suited for certain types of processes, being able to capture behaviour which is more *meaningful* in the given context. The aggregated results across logs, however, indicate that PARNEK has an overall advantage.

From Table 2 we can see that PARNEK outperforms both the Baseline algorithm and MINERful on several, though not all, of the logs we evaluated. Notably, its running time is often markedly faster, the only exceptions being for the most computationally intensive, i.e. FULL, variant of PARNEK which is somewhat slower on a few logs.

Finally, PARNEK(COND) returns models with higher or near equal generalisability, as measured by 5-fold cross-validation, compared to all other miners.

6   Conclusion

In this paper we introduced the PARNEK miner, a novel discovery algorithm for DCR Graphs. We compare the miner to the state-of-the-art in DCR (baseline) and Declare (MINERful) discovery and show that PARNEK significantly outperforms the state-of-the-art in DCR discovery. In addition, it performs at least comparably to the state-of-the-art in Declare discovery. While a precise comparison between DCR Graphs and Declare is difficult to make, it can be argued that Declare relations carry more semantic meaning, making them more complex to reason about, leading to an argument in favour of PARNEK outperforming the state-of-the-art in declarative mining in general. However, this would require a more thorough study on the relative complexity of the different notations.

In addition to these empirical observations, we note that because of the compositional architecture of PARNEK it allows for better configurability and leaves room for future extensions, features that are not clearly present in the baseline algorithm. We believe that this makes PARNEK much more suitable for practical applications, a notion that is supported by expressed stakeholder interest in the integration of the algorithm into commercial DCR tools.

Future Work. In the future, we hope to take advantage of the fact that PARNEK is both easily configurable and extensible by developing an interactive user-guided discovery approach. This will require research into the use of negative sample data, ranking of constraints based on relevance and the use of partial domain models to guide the discovery. In addition, we are considering further extensions to the algorithm for finding models of even higher quality, for example by supporting more complex uses of the response relation.

References

1. Back, C.O., Debois, S., Slaats, T.: Towards an empirical evaluation of imperative and declarative process mining. In: Woo, C., Lu, J., Li, Z., Ling, T.W., Li, G., Lee, M.L. (eds.) ER 2018. LNCS, vol. 11158, pp. 191–198. Springer, Cham (2018). https://doi.org/10.1007/978-3-030-01391-2_24
2. Di Ciccio, C., Mecella, M.: On the discovery of declarative control flows for artful processes. ACM Trans. Manag. Inf. Syst. **5**(4), 24:1–24:37 (2015)
3. Debois, S., Hildebrandt, T., Slaats, T.: Hierarchical declarative modelling with refinement and sub-processes. In: Sadiq, S., Soffer, P., Völzer, H. (eds.) BPM 2014. LNCS, vol. 8659, pp. 18–33. Springer, Cham (2014). https://doi.org/10.1007/978-3-319-10172-9_2
4. Debois, S., Hildebrandt, T.T., Laursen, P.H., Ulrik, K.R.: Declarative process mining for DCR graphs. In: SAC 2017, pp. 759–764 (2017)
5. Debois, S., Hildebrandt, T.T., Slaats, T.: Replication, refinement & reachability: complexity in dynamic condition-response graphs. Acta Informatica **55**(6), 489–520 (2018)
6. Debois, S., Slaats, T.: The analysis of a real life declarative process. In: 2015 IEEE Symposium Series on Computational Intelligence, pp. 1374–1382 (2015)
7. Goedertier, S., Martens, D., Vanthienen, J., Baesens, B.: Robust process discovery with artificial negative events. J. Mach. Learn. Res. **10**(Jun), 1305–1340 (2009)
8. Hildebrandt, T., Mukkamala, R.R., Slaats, T., Zanitti, F.: Contracts for cross-organizational workflows as timed dynamic condition response graphs. J. Logic Algebraic Program. (JLAP) **82**, 164–185 (2013)
9. Hildebrandt, T.T., Mukkamala, R.R.: Declarative event-based workflow as distributed dynamic condition response graphs. In: PLACES (2010)
10. Hull, R., et al.: Introducing the guard-stage-milestone approach for specifying business entity lifecycles. In: Bravetti, M., Bultan, T. (eds.) WS-FM 2010. LNCS, vol. 6551, pp. 1–24. Springer, Heidelberg (2011). https://doi.org/10.1007/978-3-642-19589-1_1
11. Ly, L.T., Rinderle-Ma, S., Dadam, P.: Design and verification of instantiable compliance rule graphs in process-aware information systems. In: Pernici, B. (ed.) CAiSE 2010. LNCS, vol. 6051, pp. 9–23. Springer, Heidelberg (2010). https://doi.org/10.1007/978-3-642-13094-6_3
12. Maggi, F.M., Bose, R.P.J.C., van der Aalst, W.M.P.: Efficient discovery of understandable declarative process models from event logs. In: Ralyté, J., Franch, X., Brinkkemper, S., Wrycza, S. (eds.) CAiSE 2012. LNCS, vol. 7328, pp. 270–285. Springer, Heidelberg (2012). https://doi.org/10.1007/978-3-642-31095-9_18
13. Maggi, F.M., Mooij, A.J., van der Aalst, W.M.P.: User-guided discovery of declarative process models. In: 2011 IEEE Symposium on Computational Intelligence and Data Mining. IEEE (2011)
14. Object Management Group: Case Management Model and Notation, Version 1.0. Webpage, May 2014. http://www.omg.org/spec/CMMN/1.0/PDF
15. Pesic, M., van der Aalst, W.M.P.: A declarative approach for flexible business processes management. In: Eder, J., Dustdar, S. (eds.) BPM 2006. LNCS, vol. 4103, pp. 169–180. Springer, Heidelberg (2006). https://doi.org/10.1007/11837862_18

16. Popova, V., Fahland, D., Dumas, M.: Artifact lifecycle discovery. Int. J. Coop. Inf. Syst. **24**, 1550001 (2015)
17. Schönig, S., Di Ciccio, C., Maggi, F.M., Mendling, J.: Discovery of multi-perspective declarative process models. In: Sheng, Q.Z., Stroulia, E., Tata, S., Bhiri, S. (eds.) ICSOC 2016. LNCS, vol. 9936, pp. 87–103. Springer, Cham (2016). https://doi.org/10.1007/978-3-319-46295-0_6
18. Slaats, T.: Flexible process notations for cross-organizational case management systems. PhD thesis, IT University of Copenhagen, January 2015
19. Slaats, T., Mukkamala, R.R., Hildebrandt, T., Marquard, M.: Exformatics declarative case management workflows as DCR graphs. In: Daniel, F., Wang, J., Weber, B. (eds.) BPM 2013. LNCS, vol. 8094, pp. 339–354. Springer, Heidelberg (2013). https://doi.org/10.1007/978-3-642-40176-3_28
20. Van der Aalst, W., Adriansyah, A., van Dongen, B.: Replaying history on process models for conformance checking and performance analysis. Wiley Interdisc. Rev.: Data Min. Knowl. Discovery **2**(2), 182–192 (2012)
21. Zeising, M., Schönig, S., Jablonski, S.: Towards a common platform for the support of routine and agile business processes. In: 10th IEEE International Conference on Collaborative Computing: Networking, Applications and Worksharing, October, pp. 94–103 (2014)

Fifty Shades of Green: How Informative is a Compliant Process Trace?

Andrea Burattin[1]($\boxtimes$), Giancarlo Guizzardi[3], Fabrizio Maria Maggi[2], and Marco Montali[3]

[1] Technical University of Denmark, Kgs. Lyngby, Denmark
andbur@dtu.dk
[2] University of Tartu, Tartu, Estonia
[3] Free-University of Bozen-Bolzano, Bolzano, Italy

Abstract. The problem of understanding whether a process trace satisfies a prescriptive model is a fundamental conceptual modeling problem in the context of process-based information systems. In business process management, and in process mining in particular, this amounts to check whether an event log conforms to a prescriptive process model, i.e., whether the actual traces present in the log are allowed by all behaviors implicitly expressed by the model. The research community has developed a plethora of very sophisticated conformance checking techniques that are particularly effective in the detection of non-conforming traces, and in elaborating on where and how they deviate from the prescribed behaviors. However, they do not provide any insight to distinguish between conforming traces, and understand their differences. In this paper, we delve into this rather unexplored area, and present a new process mining quality measure, called *informativeness*, which can be used to compare conforming traces to understand which are more relevant (or informative) than others. We introduce a technique to compute such measure in a very general way, as it can be applied on process models expressed in any language (e.g., Petri nets, Declare, process trees, BPMN) as long as a conformance checking tool is available. We then show the versatility of our approach, showing how it can be meaningfully applied when the activities contained in the process are associated to costs/rewards, or linked to strategic goals.

Keywords: Conformance checking · Business value · Process mining · Goals

1 Introduction

The increasing availability of event data recorded by information systems, electronic devices, web services, and sensor networks provides detailed information about the actual processes in a wide range of systems and organizations. Process mining techniques [1] can use such event data to discover and enhance processes,

P. Giorgini and B. Weber (Eds.): CAiSE 2019, LNCS 11483, pp. 611–626, 2019.
https://doi.org/10.1007/978-3-030-21290-2_38

check the conformance of actual with expected behaviours, and ultimately provide insights on how processes are executed in reality.

The typical starting point for process mining algorithms is an event log. Each event in a log refers to an activity (i.e., a well-defined step in a process) and is related to a particular case, in turn identifying a process instance. The events belonging to a case are ordered and can be seen as one "run" of the process (often referred to as a trace of events). Event logs may store additional information about events such as the resource (i.e., person or device) responsible for the execution or triggering of the activity, the timestamp of the event, or additional data attributes recorded with the event. Typically, three types of process mining techniques can be distinguished [1]: *(i)* process discovery (learning a model from example traces in an event log), *(ii)* conformance checking (comparing the observed behavior in the event log with the expected behaviors expressed by a process model), and *(iii)* model enhancement (extending models based on additional information in the event logs, e.g., to highlight bottlenecks).

In particular, conformance checking has lately attracted a lot of attention both from the research community and the industry, being instrumental to understand the presence, extent, and nature of *deviations* separating the actual and expected courses of execution of the process [4]. In an organizational context, such deviations are key towards a better governance, risk management, and compliance, since they may reveal legal/normative issues, or opportunities to further improve and optimize processes. In this respect, virtually all approaches in the conformance checking spectrum focus on the detection of behaviors that do not comply with a prescriptive process model, and in turn on the fine-grained analysis of the resulting deviations. Interestingly, *no fine-grained insight is instead provided in the case of compliant behaviors.*

In this paper, we delve into this unexplored area, arguing that analyzing, classifying, and better understanding compliant behaviors is as important as in the case of non-compliant ones. To do so, we appeal to the fact that business processes intimately relate to the value chain of an organization, and hence activities in a process are executed because they ultimately *contribute to value.* This, in turn, provides a conceptual basis to measure compliant traces, which makes some traces more *informative* about the process than others.

We propose a novel notion of *informativeness* of a trace. Informativeness should not be confused with standard measures used to classify traces based on the value, or reward, they produce. Instead, it directly relates to conformance, in the following sense: a trace is informative if it conforms to the process model of interest, and, in addition, it contains behavior that: *(i)* is not necessary to achieve conformance, and *(ii)* such behavior impacts (positively or negatively) to the resulting value. These two aspects single out behaviors that could have been skipped according to the process, but that proved meaningful when ascribing value to the course of execution. Let us substantiate this with a very simple example. The payment phase of a shop selling process consists of a sequence of tasks where a clerk performs the payment using the data of the customer and, if the payment is accepted, puts the paid items in a bag, inserts the receipt in the bag, and optionally also includes a discount badge for future purchases. Consider two compliant executions, performed by John and Jane. John strictly follows the sequence of mandatory tasks. Jane instead decides to also put a discount badge in the customer bag. If we ascribe value to this process depending on the customer satisfaction, both executions positively contribute to it, as the customer gets the items they wanted. However, the trace produced by Jane is more informative, as she exhibited a behavior that is not strictly required to conform to the process prescriptions, but that positively contributes to the customer satisfaction. Notice that the trace produced by Jane would have remained informative even if she performed some optional behavior negatively impacting on the customer satisfaction, such as inserting advertisement sheets in the customer bag.

Starting from this intuition, we formalize informativeness into a parameterized, model-agnostic *metric* that can be effectively used to measure informativeness, and classify traces on this basis. The metric is model-agnostic in the sense that it can be applied on process models expressed in any language (e.g., Petri nets, Declare, process trees, BPMN) as long as a conformance checking tool is available. A proof-of-concept implementation to compute this metric is available as a plug-in for the well-established ProM process mining framework.

To show the effectiveness and versatility of our approach, we ground it within two scenarios. In the first scenario, prescriptive processes emerge from the sophisticated requirement models introduced in [7]. Such models contain hard and soft goals, which can be decomposed into more specific goals and ultimately tasks, possibly marked as optional. In this setting, informativeness provides a tool to compare traces based on the presence of optional behaviors that achieve or prevent the achievement of soft goals. In the second scenario, we consider standard BPMN processes whose tasks are associated to costs/rewards.

The rest of the paper is structured as follow: Sect. 2 introduces the notion of informativeness, framing it in the context of conceptual modeling. It then provides the two scenarios used throughout the paper. Section 3 shows how the informativeness of a process trace can be actually computed, demonstrating that it reconstructs the intuitive understanding of informativeness as discussed in Sect. 2. Section 4 tackles related work and Sect. 5 concludes the paper and spells out directions for future work.

2   On the Notion of Informativeness

In this section, we introduce the notion of informativeness from the point of view of conceptual modeling of processes and we show, via realistic yet to-the-point examples, how such problems can impact typical scenarios.

2.1   Intended, Allowed, Compliant and Informative Traces

Modeling is the activity of representing the physical and the social world for the purposes of communication, understanding, problem solving, controlling and automation [10]. As discussed in depth in [5], according to this view, *models* are representations of *conceptualizations* of reality. Conceptualizations are the result of cognitive operations created by abstracting (filtering out) certain features of states of affairs of reality. These conceptualizations, in a sense, delimit the set of *abstractions* that can be carved out of reality, i.e., the abstractions that are deemed acceptable according to that conceptualization. So, for example, if we have a proper conceptualization of genealogy, the concepts of ancestor, descendent, father, mother, offspring and their ties allow us to build individual abstractions representing particular states of affairs (e.g., John is the father of Paul and Mary is an ancestor of John), which are constructed by abstracting from a number of features of reality according to these concepts (e.g., from the weight and hair color of John, Paul and Mary). Moreover, this conceptualization proscribes a number of abstractions that represent states of affairs unacceptable according to that conceptualization (e.g., John being his own ancestor, John having two biological fathers, John's biological father changing with time).

If a model is a representation of a conceptualization, an adequate model of a conceptualization is one that accepts as valid instances (or *allowed model instances*) exactly those that represent the state of affairs deemed acceptable by that conceptualization [5]. We call these instances *intended model instances*. Models, however, are frequently *under-constrained*, thus, accepting as allowed, instances that are non-intended. Frequently, they are also *over-constrained*, thus, excluding as valid (i.e., as allowed) intended instances. In the case of process modeling, model instances are execution traces, i.e., possible executions of a process model.

In Fig. 1, we contrast the set of intended instances (traces) of a process model with the set of allowed traces delimited by a given process specification. As we can observe, there are traces that are intended according to the underlying conceptualization of reality, but are excluded by the process model (the difference between intended and allowed traces). Moreover, we have traces that are allowed by the model, but do not correspond to intended traces (the difference between allowed and intended traces). Furthermore, as shown in Fig. 1, a subset of the intended traces (i.e., executions that are actually enacted in reality) can be recorded in event logs. The difference between the set of intended traces present in a log and the set of allowed ones delimits the set of *non-compliant traces*. In other words, a non-compliant trace is one that is intended by a given conceptualization (as evidenced by the event log), but is not prescribed by the process model that aims at capturing that conceptualization. In contrast, the intersection between the set of allowed traces and those recorded in the log is called the set of compliant traces.

Many authors in the literature of process mining have proposed metrics for characterizing and ranking non-compliant traces (according to different degrees of non-conformance). But what about the set of compliant traces? Traditionally, all compliant traces are thought of as standing in the same footing and, as such, are thought as having equal importance for the process analyst. As previously mentioned, in this paper, we defend the notion of *informativeness* of a trace, i.e., how informative that trace is for the process analysis. As we elaborate in the sequel, how informative a trace is depends on the relation between the activities constituting a process and the value-based elements outside the process, namely, the goals (and anti-goals) of suitable stakeholders. Specifically, the important aspect to consider is the value that is brought by the execution of activities that are not strictly required to make the trace compliant: these are the ones that make the execution interesting if they impact on value.

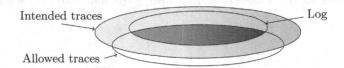

Fig. 1. Representation of the traces involved in the scenario presented in this paper. The color indicates the informativeness (light green: not informative; dark green: very informative) of intended traces. We aim at "giving colors" (i.e., assign informativeness) to compliant traces (i.e., traces in the log also allowed by the process model). (Color figure online)

The main ingredients of process models are actions (intentional events). As discussed in [6], actions are manifestations of intentions inhering in the stakeholders. Goals (as expressed in frameworks such as i* [6,7,14]) are the propositional content of the stakeholders's intentions. In other words, every action is caused by a certain intention of a stakeholder, whose propositional content is formulated as a goal. Goals can be either mandatory or optional for specific stakeholders. Mandatory top goals (i.e., mandatory goals that are not components of other goals) are termed *hard goals*. Optional top goals are called *soft goals*.[1] Optional goals in general (i.e., "nice-to-have" goals) are also called *preferences*. Moreover, goals relate to each other via decomposition (or refinement) relations. These can be either OR-decompositions (representing that the satisfaction of any sub-goal is sufficient for satisfying the composed goal) or AND-decompositions (meaning the satisfaction of the composed goal requires the joint satisfaction of all mandatory sub-goals). Moreover, goals (both optional and mandatory) can relate to each other via contribution relations. These contributions can be either positive (e.g., the satisfaction of a goal A implies the satisfaction of another goal B - called a make contribution) or negative (e.g., the satisfaction of a goal B is incompatible with the satisfaction of a goal C - termed a break contribution). Analogously, the execution of actions can, while addressing a goal, exert positive or negative contributions to other goals.

Process models are designed to explicitly coordinate the execution of action types that together afford the satisfaction of the stakeholder's goals. So, all

---

[1] We are fully aware of the different senses in which the term soft goal is employed in the literature [6], namely, alternatively as a synonym to non-functional requirement, fuzzy propositional content, or propositional contents without a generally accepted satisfaction criteria. Here, as in [7], we use the term in the specific sense just defined.

intended and compliant traces of a process model should *satisfy all the mandatory goals* that motivated the creation of that process. However, compliant traces can differ wrt. their informativeness, i.e., *the degree to which they positively or negatively contribute to the satisfaction of optional goals*. The stronger is the contribution that a trace makes wrt. these goals, the more value (positive or negative)[2] it adds to the stakeholder(s) at hand. In other words, the informativeness of a trace is a measure of how much value (either negative or positive) a trace brings to the stakeholder(s) whose goals motivate the design of that process.

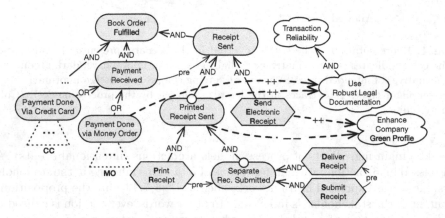

Fig. 2. Fragment of the wholesale book seller requirement model from [7].

2.2 Running Examples

To better introduce the problem tackled in this paper, let us analyze some realistic examples. We start by introducing a language where the goals are explicitly reported in the formalism and then we move to another scenario where goals need to be manually elicited.

Example 1. We consider the setting of [7], where business processes implicitly emerge from the representation of requirements. In particular, [7] puts forward a sophisticated goal-oriented modeling framework. It uses, as a basis, the classical goal-oriented approach described before, where *(i)* both hard and soft goals are considered; *(ii)* goals are subject to AND/OR decomposition into sub-goals and ultimately tasks; *(iii)* hard goals achieve or prevent the achievement of soft goals. In addition, [7] adopts: *(i)* *optional goals*, to express goals that should

---

[2] As discussed in [12], even though people intuitively assume a positive connotation of the term value, value emerges from events that impact goals either positively or negatively. More specifically, the value ascribed to an event consists of *benefits* (positive value contributions) or *sacrifices* (negative value contributions).

not necessarily be achieved towards the achievement of their parent goals; *(ii)*
preference goals, to capture the relative importance of certain soft goals; *(iii)*
temporal constraints on the executability of tasks, in a way that is reminiscent
of declarative, constraint-based processes. For self-containedeness, we depict in
Fig. 2 an excerpt of the case study from [7], which tackles a wholesale book seller.
Goals are represented as rounded rectangles, tasks as hexagons. Hard goals are
colored, whereas soft goals are white. Optional goals are marked with a circle on
top. Cloud-shaped soft goals denote preference goals. Beside AND/OR contribution arcs, we have dashed arcs labeled with "++" (resp., "−−") to indicate that
when the source goal is achieved (or the source task is executed) then the target
goal is also achieved (resp., cannot be achieved); thin arcs labeled with "pre'
indicate that the target element cannot be achieved/executed until the source
one is achieved/executed. The **CC** and **MO** goals do not contain optional parts.

The presence of *optional goals that are sub-goals of hard goals* in the model,
which in turn underlies the presence of optional tasks, is the basis to understand
how informative different traces are. Informativeness depends on how behavior
that is exhibited, but is not essential towards conformance, actually impacts
(either negatively or positively) on the overall, resulting value.

Consider, for example, the soft goal *Transaction Reliability* as the main focus
to understand the overall, produced value. Consider now the following four conforming scenarios:

Scenario Book-CC. The book order is paid via credit card, and then the
corresponding receipt is sent by executing the Send Electronic Receipt task.

Scenario Book-CC-PR. Similar to the previous scenario, with the addition
that also a printed receipt is sent, by executing the Print Receipt task.

Scenario Book-CC-2PR. Extension of the previous scenario, ensuring that a
separate printed receipt is submitted. This is done by executing, after Print
Receipt, the two tasks that Submit and Deliver the Receipt.

Scenario Book-MO-PR. An alternative scenario where payment is done using
a money order, and then the corresponding receipt is sent both electronically
and physically, by respectively performing the Print Receipt and Send Electronic Receipt tasks.

Scenario **Book-CC** is not particularly informative (when compared to other
compliant traces), since it conforms to the requirements but does not include
any non-mandatory behavior with the purpose of satisfying the *Transaction
Reliability* soft goal. Scenario **Book-CC-PR** is more informative: the execution
of Print Receipt could be removed without jeopardizing conformance, but its
presence ensures the reliability of the overall transaction. Scenario **Book-CC-
2PR** is as informative as scenario **Book-CC-PR**: the presence of the additional
tasks for submitting and delivering the receipt is not essential to guarantee conformance, but at the same time does not interact with reliability of the transaction, which is already implicitly achieved by the fact that the receipt has been
previously printed. Finally, scenario **Book-MO-PR** is not informative. In fact,
it consists of an initial behavior that achieves the hard goal *Payment Done via
Money Order*, and has also the effect of guaranteeing reliability of the overall

transaction. This initial portion of the entire scenario is essential towards conformance, since its removal would jeopardize the achievement of the *Payment Received* goal, in turn preventing the fulfillment of the book order. The fact that this essential part satisfies the reliability of the transaction makes the execution of the Print Receipt task irrelevant, and hence not informative, as opposed to scenarios **Book-CC-PR** and **Book-CC-2PR**.

Interestingly, scenario **Book-MO-PR** would actually become informative if the scope of the analysis covers all soft goals, not just *Transaction Reliability*. In such a case, in fact, the optional execution of Print Receipt prevents the company to enhance its green profile, which would not happen if such a task was not present in the scenario. This is an example of informativeness arising from a negative impact to the overall produced value.   ◁

For the next example, we consider a BPMN process model. In this case, the goals (i.e., the values) are not explicit so different interpretations are possible.

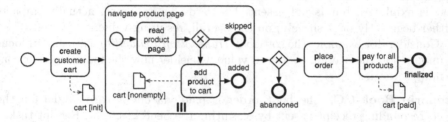

Fig. 3. Fragment of an e-commerce, order-to-delivery process.

Example 2. Consider the fragment of an online order-to-delivery process shown in Fig. 3. Each process instance relates to a *cart* case object, which is manipulated by the customer. When the process starts, the cart is *initialized*. Then, the customer may navigate through multiple product pages by browsing the e-commerce website. For each navigated page, after accessing the page itself, the customer may possibly decide to add the accessed product to her own cart (in this case, the cart enters into the *nonempty* state). When all pages of interest have been navigated, the customer may decide to quit, or to finalize the order.[3] This, in turn, amounts to placing the order and then paying for all the products in the cart, which has the effect of moving the cart into the *paid* state.

We consider now 4 scenarios, accounting for different instances of this process:

Cart-Empty. The customer visits the pages of some products, but does not add any product to the cart, and consequently abandons the process.

Cart-Abandon. The customer visits the pages of some products, and adds a product to her cart costing 20 euros. Then, the customer decides not to finalize the cart, and so simply abandons.

---

[3] For simplicity, we model this as a deferred choice, but in reality we should also ensure that the customer cannot proceed to the order finalization if the cart is empty.

Cart-Pay. As the previous scenario, but now the customer finalizes the order, going through the placement task, and paying 20 euros.

Cart-PayMore. An extended version of the previous scenario, where the customer adds two products to the cart, one costing 20 euros and another costing 30 euros, finally paying a total amount of 50 euros.

All scenarios contain optional behaviors: the only mandatory task is Create Customer Cart, while all the others denote optional, possibly informative behavior.

We now analyze informativeness by considering, as value, the impact of each scenario on the evolution of the carts, considering that potentially informative traces should make the cart *nonempty*, and then possibly also *paid*. With this objective in mind, scenario **Cart-Empty** is not informative, since the cart simply stays in the *init* state. Scenario **Cart-Abandon** is instead informative: the customer adds an item to the cart making it *nonempty*, through the execution of the optional Add Product to Cart task. Scenario **Cart-Pay** is more informative than **Cart-Abandon**: the cart is further moved to the *paid* state through the execution of the optional process fragment consisting of the sequence of Place Order and Pay for All the Products tasks. Scenario **Cart-PayMore** is as informative as **Cart-Pay**: more items are added to the cart, but in terms of state evolution of the cart, this has the same overall effect than in **Cart-Pay**. In particular, the second execution of Add Product to Cart is not informative, as it was preceded by another instance of the same task that made the cart *nonempty*.

An alternative assignment of values (and hence informativeness) is by considering the potential/concrete monetary gain associated to the tasks involved in the process. In particular, assume that the Add Product to Cart task gets associated to the potential gain of the added products, and that the Pay for All Products task gets associated to the overall, paid amount. The other tasks do not come with any gain instead. With this objective in mind, scenario **Cart-Empty** is not informative, as it does not contain any optional behavior involving any gain. Scenario **Cart-Abandon** is instead informative: the customer decides to add a product to the cart for a potential gain of 20 euros. Scenario **Cart-Pay** is more informative than **Cart-Abandon**, because of the presence of a second optional task, in particular Pay for All Products, also coming with a concrete gain of 20 euros. Scenario **Cart-PayMore** is, in this interpretation of value, even more informative as **Cart-Pay**: it contains the execution of three optional tasks that come with positive gains: the two executions of Add Product to Cart, and the execution of Pay for All Products, incurring respectively in a gain of 20 (potential), 30 (potential), and 50 (concrete) euros.

Notice that various ways to aggregate such task-related costs into a single value may be singled out. Depending on such aggregation, different values for informativeness may be obtained, giving more weight to traces that end up with an actual gain (possibly for orders containing few items), or to traces with a cart containing very costly products that in the end are however not paid.   ◁

The examples provided in this section can help to better understand the general concept and the aim of informativeness and, at the same time, they can serve as a guide to the actual realization of the metric.

3   Informativeness Metric

In this section, we present a possible realization of the informativeness metric. We formally define the metric and then investigate how it can be instantiated to the two examples previously described. Additionally, we report about a proof-of-concept implementation for the computation of the metric.

3.1   Realization and Formal Definition

Let us first define the basic elements that are needed to compute how informative a process trace is. Given a set of unique event identifiers U (e.g., $U \subseteq \mathbb{N}$), a set of attribute names A_n and a set of attribute values[4] A_v, an *event* $e = (id, f)$ is a tuple made of a unique event identifier $id \in U$ and a key-value relation $f : A_n \to A_v$ mapping attribute names to the corresponding values. Common attributes contained in events are *name*, *timestamp*, and *originator*. With a projection operator π on events it is possible to extract specific values of specific attributes from the attribute key-value relation, i.e., $\pi_a((id, f)) = f(a)$. For example, consider event $e = (42, \{name = \text{'purchase'}, timestamp = \text{2019-06-03}, cost = 100\})$, then $\pi_{name}(e) = purchase$ and $\pi_{cost}(e) = 100$. If the key-value relation does not contain any mapping for the given attribute name, then the default value 1 is returned, i.e., $\pi_\perp(e) = 1$. Additionally, the event identifier can be extracted with $\pi_{id}(e) = 42$. For readability purposes, in the rest of the paper, we assume that no attribute in f is named id, thus π_{id} is always unambiguous.

The set of all events is denoted with E, the set of all possible sequences of events is called $T = E^*$, and a sequence of events $t \in T$ is called *trace*. Single events of $t = \langle e_1, e_2, \dots, e_n \rangle$ are accessed by the corresponding index, e.g., $t(1) = e_1, t(2) = e_2$. The length of a trace is denoted as $|t| = n$. Given a trace $t = \langle e_1, e_2, \dots, e_n \rangle$, the deletion of some events from it (without perturbing the order of the remaining ones) generates a so-called *sub-sequence*[5] of the original trace. Note that a sub-sequence is also a trace. The set of all possible sub-sequences of t, which are not empty and not equal to t itself, is denoted with $S(t)$ and contains $2^{|t|} - 2$ traces.[6]

Given a trace t and a sub-sequence $s \in S(t)$, we define the diff operator, which returns the sequence of events to be removed from t to generate s:

$$\text{diff}(t, s) = \langle e_i \mid e_i \in t \wedge e_i \notin s \rangle.$$

The actual implementation of the diff operator can use the unique event identifier (i.e., $\pi_{id}(e)$) to establish if an event belongs to the original trace or not.

---

[4] In this context, *value* denotes a symbolic/numeric constant.

[5] Sub-sequences should not be confused with sub-strings.

[6] Consider the set I of indexes of events in trace t: $I = \{1, 2, \dots, |t|\}$. By taking only events from a subset of I, we can generate a possible sub-sequence of t. Therefore, the set of all possible sub-sets of I, also called power-set $\mathcal{P}(I)$, contains the indexes of all possible sub-sequences and $|\mathcal{P}(I)| = 2^{|I|} = 2^{|t|}$. From this value, we need to remove two special sub-sequences: the empty and the original ones. Therefore, we end up with $2^{|t|} - 2$ possible sub-sequences.

In order to define the informativeness of a sub-sequence $s \in S(t)$, it is necessary to know which attributes bring value and how to aggregate them. Therefore, given an attribute name a, a value adapter m, and an aggregation operator $\odot$, we define:

$$\text{informativeness}(s, t, a, m, \odot) = m \bigodot_{e \in \text{diff}(t,s)} \pi_a(e). \tag{1}$$

The simplest implementation of informativeness just counts the number of removed events and is realized with $a = \bot$ (recall $\pi_\bot(e)$ always returns 1), $m = 1$ and $\odot = \Sigma$. In this case, we obtain the definition $\sum_{e \in \text{diff}(t,s)} 1 = |\text{diff}(t, s)|$. Another example of informativeness function is the inverse of the costs of the tasks present in the original trace but not in the sub-sequence, i.e., $a = cost$, $m = -1$, $\odot = \Sigma$, thus obtaining $-\sum_{e \in \text{diff}(t,s)} \pi_{cost}(e)$.

With these definitions in place, it is possible to obtain the informativeness of a trace t wrt. a model M as the maximal informativeness among all sub-sequences in $S(t)$ that are compliant with M. Algorithm 1 reports a possible way of computing the metric. The algorithm takes as input the trace t, the model M and a conformance function C. Additional inputs are a, m and $\odot$, as previously mentioned in Eq. 1, to configure the informativeness function. The first check performed by the algorithm is to verify that the trace is indeed compliant with the model (lines 1–3). After that, all possible sub-sequences are iterated (line 6) and, for the compliant ones (line 7), the corresponding informativeness is computed (line 8). The best informative score is kept with the sub-sequence producing it (lines 9–12). Finally, the best informativeness, together with the tasks involved in its computation are returned to the user (line 15). If the trace does not contain any optional behavior, then no sub-sequence is compliant and therefore the maximal informativeness is never re-assigned, with 0 being returned.

The computational complexity of the algorithm is controlled by two main factors: the number of sub-sequences and the complexity of the conformance checking technique (the informativeness function has linear complexity on the number of events of the sub-sequence). Such complexity could represent a limitation for using this formalization in complex scenarios. However, in this paper, we prefer to focus on conceptual aspects, consciously leaving out all possible optimizations, to not sacrifice understandability.

3.2   Example of Measure Calculation

It is interesting to observe how the informativeness measure can be calculated on the previous examples (cf. Sect. 2.2). For Example 1, let us denote by **CC** and **MO** the traces that respectively achieve the two goals *Payment Done via Credit Card* and *Payment Done via Money Order* (recall that they contain all mandatory tasks). We use the following notation to represent task executions: $T(i_r, i_g)$, where T is a task (compactly denoted using the bold initials of its description, as shown in Fig. 2), while i_r and i_g are two boolean (0/1) attributes respectively indicating whether the task impacts (in a positive or a negative way) on the achievement of soft goals *Transaction Reliability* and *Enhance Company*

Algorithm 1. Trace informativeness

Input: $t \in \mathcal{T}$: a trace;
$\quad\quad$ $M \in \mathcal{M}$: the reference model;
$\quad\quad$ $C : \mathcal{M} \times \mathcal{T} \rightarrow \{true, false\}$: a conformance function which, given a model
$\quad\quad$ and a trace, returns '$true$' if the trace is compliant, '$false$' otherwise;
$\quad\quad$ $a, m, \odot$: configuration of the informativeness function as in Eq. 1.

Output: The informativeness of the trace and the activities bringing it

$\quad$ ▷ Check that the current trace is compliant with the model
1 **if** $C(M, t) = false$ **then**
2 $\quad$ | $\quad$ **return** error ▷ The initial trace must be compliant
3 **end**

$\quad$ ▷ Initialize structures to keep maximal informativeness
4 $s_{max} \leftarrow 0$
5 $t_{max} \leftarrow t$

$\quad$ ▷ Iterate over all possible sub-sequences of t
6 **foreach** $t' \in S(t)$ **do**
7 $\quad$ | $\quad$ **if** $C(M, t') = true$ **then** ▷ Continue if the sub-sequence is compliant
8 $\quad$ | $\quad$ | $\quad$ $s \leftarrow$ informativeness$(t', t, a, m, \odot)$
9 $\quad$ | $\quad$ | $\quad$ **if** $s > s_{max}$ **then**
10 $\quad$ | $\quad$ | $\quad$ | $\quad$ $s_{max} \leftarrow s$
11 $\quad$ | $\quad$ | $\quad$ | $\quad$ $t_{max} \leftarrow t'$
12 $\quad$ | $\quad$ | $\quad$ **end**
13 $\quad$ | $\quad$ **end**
14 **end**

15 **return** $(s_{max}, \text{diff}(t, t_{max}))$ ▷ The difference between t and t_{max} contains
$\quad\quad$ the most informative activities. If no sub-sequence is compliant,
$\quad\quad$ then the informativeness is 0

Green Profile. We can then compactly indicate, with a slight abuse of notation, **CC**$(0, 0)$ and **MO**$(1, 0)$. These two boolean attributes, if not natively present in the trace, can be computed by pre-processing the trace, e.g., by relying on the planning technique from [7]. To compute informativeness, we also need a conformance function that accepts the traces and the model, and that judges the trace compliant if and only if it achieves the top, hard goal *Book Order Fulfilled*. This, again, can be directly computed using the planning technique from [7].

We consider $a = i_r$, $m = 1$, and the aggregation operator $\odot = \Sigma$. Then the scenarios correspond to the following informative traces:

Scenario Book-CC: trace $\langle \mathbf{CC}(0, 0), \mathsf{SER}(0, 1) \rangle$ with informative value 0, since no sub-sequence is compliant.

Scenario Book-CC-PR: trace $\langle \mathbf{CC}(0, 0), \mathsf{SER}(0, 1), \mathsf{PR}(1, 1) \rangle$ with informative value 1, since PR can be removed without threatening conformance, and it brings a value of 1 for i_r (since it achieves the corresponding soft goal).

Scenario Book-CC-2PR: trace $\langle \mathbf{CC}(0,0), \mathsf{SER}(0,1), \mathsf{PR}(1,0), \mathsf{SR}(0,0), \mathsf{DR}$ $(0,0)\rangle$ with informative value 1, since the sub-sequence $\langle \mathsf{PR}(1,0), \mathsf{SR}(0,0),$ $\mathsf{DR}(0,0)\rangle$ can be safely omitted, and only PR brings value (as in the previous scenario).

Scenario Book-MO-PR: trace $\langle \mathbf{MO}(1,0), \mathsf{SER}(0,1), \mathsf{PR}(0,1)\rangle$ with informative value 0. Notice that, in this case, PR has $i_r = 0$, since the corresponding soft goal has been already achieved via **MO**, which constitutes an essential, non-omittable behavior. Informativeness would become 2 if we consider $a = i_g$ instead, since both tasks SER and PR actually interact with the corresponding soft goal (the first by temporarily achieving it, the second by reverting the achievement).

For Example 2, let us adopt the following notation for representing task executions: $T(g_p, g_c)$, where T is a task (compactly represented using the bold initials of the task descriptions, as shown in Fig. 3), g_p is the potential gain associated with the execution of the activity, and g_c is the concrete gain of the task. If the activity does not bring any gain, the values are omitted. For example, scenario **Cart-Abandon** is described as $\langle \mathsf{CC}, \mathsf{RP}, \mathsf{RP}, \mathsf{AP}(20,0), \mathsf{RP}\rangle$.

As reported in the example, we can think on several value definitions. We consider here valuable executions with expensive items in the cart, or with paid items. To achieve that, we assume $m = 1$, $\odot = \Sigma$, and $a = g_p$ or $a = g_c$, respectively. Then we obtain:

Cart-Empty: $\langle \mathsf{CC}, \mathsf{RP}, \mathsf{RP}, \mathsf{RP}\rangle$ with informative value 0 in both cases (despite there are activities which are not needed).

Cart-Abandon: $\langle \mathsf{CC}, \mathsf{RP}, \mathsf{RP}, \mathsf{AP}(20,0), \mathsf{RP}\rangle$ with informative values 20 and 0 (an item is added to the cart, but no payment is done).

Cart-Pay: $\langle \mathsf{CC}, \mathsf{RP}, \mathsf{RP}, \mathsf{AP}(20,0), \mathsf{RP}, \mathsf{PO}, \mathsf{PP}(0,20)\rangle$ with informative values 20 and 20 (the added item is then paid).

Cart-PayMore: $\langle \mathsf{CC}, \mathsf{RP}, \mathsf{RP}, \mathsf{AP}(20,0), \mathsf{RP}, \mathsf{AP}(30,0), \mathsf{PO}, \mathsf{PP}(0,50)\rangle$ with informative values 50 and 50 (using the same line of reasoning of **Cart-Pay**).

We might derive new attributes combining values from others, e.g., $g_{tot} = g_p + 2g_c$, where we assign some value for having products in the cart but, when these are paid, the value significantly increases. Clearly, domain knowledge as well as specific goals are needed to define what the actual attribute is meant to capture.

A similar line of reasoning could be carried out when informativeness has to be calculated considering the impact of tasks to the cart states, assuming that the information about the state transitions of the cart is readily available in the trace (or that the trace has been pre-processed accordingly).

3.3 Implementation

A proof-of-concept implementation of the technique is available as a ProM plug-in (see https://github.com/delas/informativeness). The plug-in considers models represented as process trees and relies on existing conformance checking plug-ins. Nevertheless, as mentioned before, extending the technique to cope with other modeling languages is merely a trivial implementation exercise (as conformance checking techniques are already available in ProM). Our implementation uses, as parameters, $a = \perp$, $m = 1$ and $\odot = \Sigma$, grounding the informativeness function as in Eq. 1 to $\sum_{e \in \text{diff}(t,s)} 1 = |\text{diff}(t,s)|$.

4   Related Work

In [7], Liaskos et al. propose an approach for representing and reasoning about goal prioritization in Goal-Oriented Requirements Engineering (GORE). In particular, they employ a version of i* models with optional goals, preferences and preference priority markers (weights). In addition, they use an existing preference-based planner over that extended i* model to search for alternative plans that best satisfy a given set of mandatory and preferred requirements. Their notion of a "preferred plan" addresses a similar issue as the notion of informativeness proposed here. However, their approach differs from ours in important ways. Given that their main focus is requirements engineering, their contribution addresses exclusively design-time (type-level) plans. Here, in contrast, given our emphasis on process mining, the focus is on the informative compliant (token-level) traces. As such, while their approach compare alternative plans defined over a model, we focus on comparing informative values of different variants of particular compliant traces by identifying the added value of optional parts of that trace. Furthermore, despite dealing with a similar notion, the author did not explicitly propose a precise value-based metric for measuring how informative process traces are.

Within process mining [1], many techniques have been proposed for model-to-log comparison, i.e., analyze the relationships between a log and a process model [4]. For example, to investigate the quality of a discovered model it is possible to compute three quality measures [3]: fitness [2,11] (answering the question: "is the model able to replay the log?"), precision [8,9] ("is the model underfitting the log?"), and generalization [13] ("is the model overfitting the log?"). These three measures are typically combined with a fourth one, called simplicity, which quantifies the "complexity" of the structure of the model (this measure is not particularly related to a specific log but measures specific properties of the model). As argued before though, conceptually speaking, all these measures are detecting the extent to which a model and a log "deviate". Therefore, traces that are compliant with the model cannot be distinguished between each other. Historically, process mining researchers always focused on quantifying the extent to which a trace is problematic (e.g., not fitting the model). Though, no effort has been put in establishing *how informative* a trace is.

5   Final Considerations and Future Work

We have presented a metric, namely informativeness, to identify compliant executions of business processes which are of particular interest. Such executions can be used to gain better understanding of the process and to trigger further investigations, such as improvement or redesign initiatives. Informativeness summarizes the performed behavior that goes beyond the necessary tasks required by the reference model and that impact on value. This non-trivially combines the employed definition of value and that of non-mandatory behavior. It is worth pointing out that in imperative languages non-mandatory behavior is typically observed in the presence of optional tasks or repetitions. Considering BPMN models, for example, optional tasks are realized with inclusive and exclusive gateways (i.e., OR and XOR), which are also involved in the construction of loops. To realize loops it is also possible to use task markers (i.e., loop and multiple instance markers). In the context of declarative languages, non-mandatory behavior can be caused by the presence of such control-flow structures (i.e., loops or optional tasks), but also by the fact that the model is under-constrained. Under-constrained models are fairly common in the declarative domain and, by using the informativeness metric presented in this paper, it is possible to highlight undesired, compliant behaviors.

Many future works are conceivable, starting from a proper realization of the metric: the algorithm reported in this paper aimed solely to understandability, but for practical purposes it is inefficient. Specific implementations, tailored to concrete modeling languages, can leverage the corresponding semantic properties to drastically reduce the computational requirements.

Acknowledgements. The work is supported by Innovation Fund Denmark project EcoKnow.org (7050-00034A). The authors would like to thank Marlon Dumas for providing the inspiration for Fig. 1.

References

1. van der Aalst, W.M.: Process Mining, 2nd edn. Springer, Heidelberg (2016). https://doi.org/10.1007/978-3-662-49851-4
2. Adriansyah, A., van Dongen, B., van der Aalst, W.M.: Conformance checking using cost-based fitness analysis. In: Proceedings of EDOC, pp. 55–64. IEEE (2011)
3. Buijs, J.C.A.M., van Dongen, B.F., van der Aalst, W.M.P.: On the role of fitness, precision, generalization and simplicity in process discovery. In: Meersman, R., et al. (eds.) OTM 2012. LNCS, vol. 7565, pp. 305–322. Springer, Heidelberg (2012). https://doi.org/10.1007/978-3-642-33606-5_19
4. Carmona, J., van Dongen, B.F., Solti, A., Weidlich, M.: Conformance Checking - Relating Processes and Models. Springer, Cham (2018). https://doi.org/10.1007/978-3-319-99414-7
5. Guizzardi, G.: On ontology, ontologies, conceptualizations, modeling languages. In: Frontiers in Artificial Intelligence and Applications, Databases and Information Systems. IOS Press (2007)
6. Guizzardi, R.S.S., Franch, X., Guizzardi, G.: Applying a foundational ontology to analyze means-end links in the i* framework. In: Proceedings of RCIS, pp. 1–11 (2012)
7. Liaskos, S., McIlraith, S.A., Sohrabi, S., Mylopoulos, J.: Representing and reasoning about preferences in requirements engineering. Requirements Eng. **16**(3), 227–249 (2011)

8. Munoz-Gama, J.: Conformance Checking and Diagnosis in Process Mining. LNBIP, vol. 270. Springer, Cham (2016). https://doi.org/10.1007/978-3-319-49451-7
9. Muñoz-Gama, J., Carmona, J.: A fresh look at precision in process conformance. In: Hull, R., Mendling, J., Tai, S. (eds.) BPM 2010. LNCS, vol. 6336, pp. 211–226. Springer, Heidelberg (2010). https://doi.org/10.1007/978-3-642-15618-2_16
10. Mylopoulos, J.: Conceptual modelling and telos. In: Conceptual Modelling, Databases, and CASE, pp. 49–68 (1992)
11. Rozinat, A., van der Aalst, W.M.: Conformance checking of processes based on monitoring real behavior. Inf. Syst. 33(1), 64–95 (2008)
12. Sales, T.P., Guarino, N., Guizzardi, G., Mylopoulos, J.: An ontological analysis of value propositions. In: Proceedings of EDOC, pp. 184–193. IEEE Press (2017)
13. Vanden Broucke, S.K., De Weerdt, J., Vanthienen, J., Baesens, B.: Determining process model precision and generalization with weighted artificial negative events. IEEE Trans. Knowl. Data Eng. 26(8), 1877–1889 (2014)
14. Yu, E., Giorgini, P., Maiden, N., Mylopoulos, J.: Social Modeling for Requirements Engineering. MIT Press, Cambridge (2011)

Solution Patterns for Machine Learning

Soroosh Nalchigar[1]($\boxtimes$), Eric Yu[1], Yazan Obeidi[2], Sebastian Carbajales[2],
John Green[2], and Allen Chan[2]

[1] Department of Computer Science, University of Toronto, Toronto, Canada
{soroosh,eric}@cs.toronto.edu
[2] IBM Canada Ltd., Markham, Canada
yazan.obeidi@ibm.com, {sebastia,green,avchan}@ca.ibm.com

Abstract. Despite the hype around machine learning (ML), many organizations are struggling to derive business value from ML capabilities. Design patterns have long been used in software engineering to enhance design effectiveness and to speed up the development process. The contribution of this paper is two-fold. First, it introduces solution patterns as an explicit way of representing generic and well-proven ML designs for commonly-known and recurring business analytics problems. Second, it reports on the feasibility, expressiveness, and usefulness of solution patterns for ML, in collaboration with an industry partner. It provides a prototype architecture for supporting the use of solution patterns in real world scenarios. It presents a proof-of-concept implementation of the architecture and illustrates its feasibility. Findings from the collaboration suggest that solution patterns can have a positive impact on ML design and development efforts.

Keywords: Conceptual modeling · Machine learning ·
Advanced analytics · Business analytics · Design patterns

1 Introduction

Despite the hype around machine learning (ML), many organizations are struggling to derive business value from ML capabilities [25]. Development of ML solutions have inherent complexities. It requires understanding what ML can and cannot do for organizations [7], specifying a well-defined business case and problem [24], translating and decomposing it into ML problem(s) [28], data preparation and feature selection [14], ML algorithm selection and trade-offs [18], and finding linkages between ML models and business processes [23], among others. Tackling these complexities requires not just a specialized ML skillset and talent (which are hard to obtain and retain) but also executives and stakeholders who know about ML technology and how to use it [12,15].

Design patterns have long been used in software engineering to enhance the design effectiveness and to speed up the development process. By offering collections of well-proven solutions to commonly occurring design problems, design

© Springer Nature Switzerland AG 2019
P. Giorgini and B. Weber (Eds.): CAiSE 2019, LNCS 11483, pp. 627–642, 2019.
https://doi.org/10.1007/978-3-030-21290-2_39

patterns have facilitated software development efforts and streamlined the communication between developers [8].

In earlier work, a conceptual modeling framework for requirement elicitation, design, and development of advanced analytics and ML solutions had been introduced [19–22]. The contribution of this paper is two-fold. *First,* it introduces solution patterns as an explicit way of representing well-proven ML designs for commonly-known and recurring business analytics problems. A solution pattern is comprised of a number of parts, including stakeholders, their decision activities, business questions, ML algorithms, metrics and parameters, contextual information, quality requirements, datasets, and data preparation workflows. It is an artifact, in the form of a conceptual model, that represents generic ML solution designs tailored to particular business contexts or situations. Through several instantiations, the paper illustrates that solution patterns can organize, store, and present knowledge on various aspects of ML solution design, such as:

- What can ML offer, given a business context?
- What type of analytics is applicable to the problem at hand?
- What algorithms belong to that category?
- When to use what algorithm and how to configure different algorithms?
- How to evaluate and compare alternative algorithms?
- What non-functional requirements (NFRs) are critical and relevant?
- How different algorithms are known to influence the NFRs?
- What data is relevant for the problem at hand?
- How to transform and prepare the raw data for different ML algorithms?

By providing reusable answers to these questions, solution patterns tackle a wide range of complexities that one would face in the development of ML solutions.

Second, it reports on the feasibility, expressiveness, and usefulness of solution patterns, in collaboration with an industry partner in the context of business process management. It provides a prototype architecture for using solution patterns in real world scenarios. It presents a proof-of-concept implementation of the architecture and illustrates its feasibility. Moreover, it provides evidence collected during the collaboration, suggesting that solution patterns can have a positive impact on ML design and development efforts.

Organization. Section 2 presents illustrations of solution patterns. Section 3 introduces modeling concepts and their semantic relationships. Section 4 reports on feasibility, expressiveness, and usefulness of solution patterns. Section 5 reviews related work and Sect. 6 concludes the paper.

2   Illustrations

This section illustrates solution patterns for three common business processes, namely: loan approval, fraud detection, and task assignment processes. The content and the knowledge in these models are accumulated from survey papers

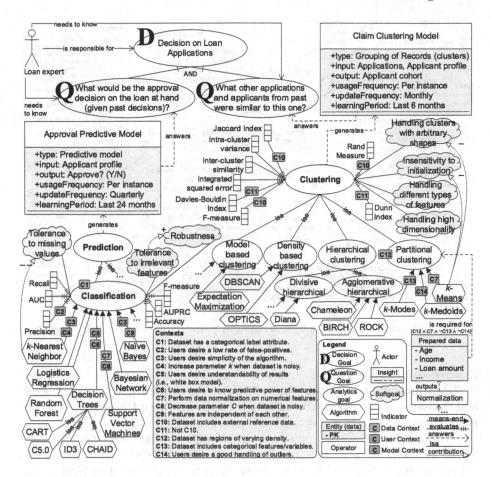

Fig. 1. A portion of loan approval solution pattern. Not all Contexts and Contribution Links are shown due to space limitations.

and textbooks (e.g., [9,13,14,17,29]) supplemented with collective experience of authors from real world advanced analytics projects.

A solution pattern starts with a characterization of the business problem and needs toward which the pattern is targeted. These are represented in terms of *Actors, Decision Goals, Question Goals*, and *Insights*. Figure 1 shows the pattern for loan approval business process. It shows that a Loan expert, as part of the loan application approval process, is responsible for making the Decision on Loan Applications. Decision Goals are decomposed into one or more Question Goals. What would be the approval decision on the loan at hand (given past decisions)? is an example of a Question Goal. The pattern indicates that in order to make the Decision on Loan Applications, a Loan expert needs to know what will be the (ML-generated) recommendation on a new case, given the past decisions. Question Goals are answered by Insight elements. Figure 1 shows that a Predictive model

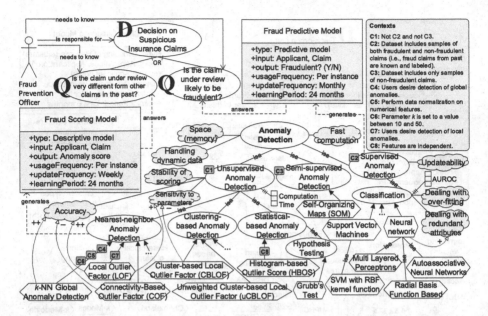

Fig. 2. A portion of fraud detection solution pattern. Refer to Fig. 1 for legend.

that receives Applicant profile as input and generates a binary value of Approve? (Y/N) as output, can answer the Question Goal at hand. By linking actors and decisions to questions and insights, a solution pattern translates a business problem into a (set of) well-defined ML problem(s).

Having defined the ML problem, the pattern then provides solution design(s) for it. It describes what type of analytics is applicable and what algorithms belong to that category. This is represented in terms of *Analytics Goals*, *Algorithms*, and *Means-End* links. Figure 1 shows that in order to generate an Approval Predictive Model, one need to accomplish a Prediction type of Analytics Goal, where Classification goal is a sub-type. The pattern shows that *k*-Nearest Neighbor, Naïve Bayes, and Support Vector Machines are among alternative algorithms for performing Classification.

Every ML algorithm has certain assumptions that limit its applicability to certain contexts. An essential part of a solution pattern provides knowledge on when to use and how to configure different algorithms. These are represented in terms of *User Contexts*, *Data Contexts*, and *Model Contexts*. In Fig. 1, User Context C3 shows that the *k*-Nearest Neighbor algorithm is applicable when Users desire simplicity of the algorithm. On the other hand, Data Context C9 states that the Naïve Bayes algorithm is applicable when Features are independent of each other. In addition, Model Context C8 says that for using the Support vector machines algorithm, one should Decrease parameter *C* when dataset is noisy.

A critical aspect of ML solution design is numerical evaluation and comparison of algorithms. Solution patterns describe what metrics are applicable for the problem at hand and when to use which metric. These are represented in terms of *Indicators* and *Evaluates* links. The pattern in Fig. 1 shows that Accuracy and Precision are among other metrics that can be used for evaluating the Approval Predictive Model. Data Context C2 states that Precision should be used for evaluation when Users desire a low rate of false-positives.

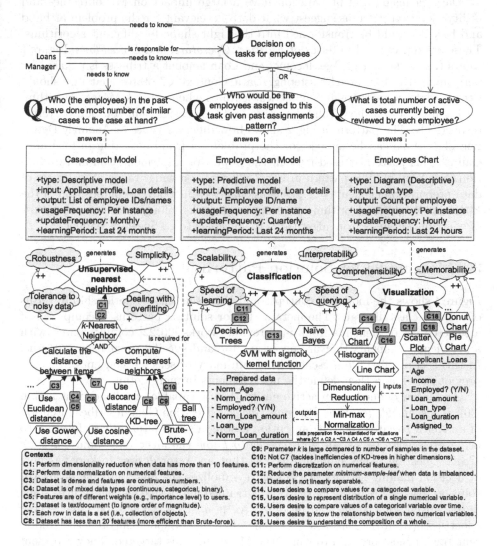

Fig. 3. A portion of task assignment solution pattern. Refer to Fig. 1 for legend.

Designing ML solutions includes taking into account the qualities that are desired by users and trade-offs among them (e.g., interpretability, speed, memory). Towards this, a solution pattern shows what NFRs are relevant to the domain and problem at hand. It also reflects the knowledge on how different algorithms are generally known to perform with respect to those requirements.

These are represented in terms of *Softgoals* and *Contribution* links. Figure 1 shows that Tolerance to missing values is a Softgoal that needs to be considered in performing Classification. It reflects that *k*-Nearest Neighbor would break (−−) this quality.

Data cleansing and preparation have a large impact on ML outcomes and utility. Solution patterns suggest what data is relevant for the problem at hand and how it should be transformed into the right shape for different algorithms. These are represented in terms of *Entities, Operators*, and *Data Flows*. Figure 1 shows that a dataset of Age, Income, and Loan amount attributes is required for performing the Partitional clustering. Data Context C7 states that one should Perform data normalization on numerical features when using *k*-Means algorithm.

Figures 2 and 3 show fraud detection and task assignment solution patterns, respectively. The pattern in Fig. 2 shows how different types of Anomaly Detection algorithms can be applied for the problem of fraud detection in insurance claims. This pattern is used later in the paper for implementation and evaluation (See Sect. 4). The pattern in Fig. 3 illustrates a wider range of instances of data preparation elements (e.g., Dimensionality Reduction), decomposition of the *k*-Nearest Neighbor algorithm into finer-grain tasks, along with more instances of contribution links from algorithms to softgoals (e.g., Speed of learning).

3   Metamodel for Solution Patterns

Figure 4 shows the modeling concepts and their semantics relationship in terms of a UML class diagram. The metamodel for solution patterns is comprised of a selected set of elements from our previous works [20, 22] complemented with a set of new elements that are necessary for and specific to solution patterns. In this section, first we present a brief summary of selected concepts from our previous work and then define the new elements in more detail.

An *Actor*, defined as an active entity that is capable of independent action [30], *is responsible for* some *Decision Goals*. A Decision Goal describes intention of an Actor towards choosing an option among a set of alternatives. In order to achieve Decision Goals, an Actor *needs to know* the answer to some *Question Goals*. Question Goals symbolize things that an Actor desires to know as part of decision making activity. An *Insight* symbolizes the final outcome of an ML solution (e.g., a *Predictive Model* that is trained and tested) which returns some *output* given some *input* and by doing so, it *answers* a Question Goal. These constructs (from the Business View part of the metamodel [20]) together represent the business problem to which the ML solution is targeted. They represent who (Actor) needs what (Insight), and why (Decision and Question goals).

An *Analytics Goal* symbolizes the high-level intention of extracting Insights from datasets, e.g., *Prediction Goal*. An *Algorithm* is a procedure or task that carries an Analytics Goal. An Algorithm is linked to an Analytics Goal via a *Means-End* link, representing an alternative way of accomplishing that goal. *Indicators* represent ML metrics that evaluate algorithms' performance, while *Softgoals* represent non-functional requirements that are critical in design of

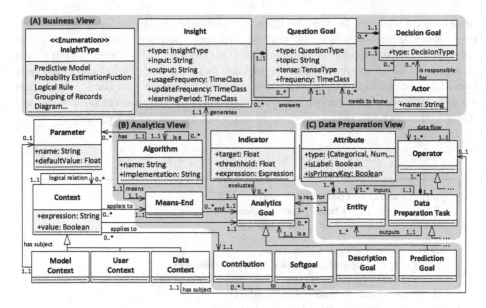

Fig. 4. Metamodel for solution patterns (partial). The gray-shaded areas denote a selected set of elements from our precious works [20,22].

the solution. These constructs (from the Analytics View part of the metamodel [20]) together capture the design of ML solution for the business problem. They represent what ML algorithms are applicable for the problem at hand and how one would compare and select among them.

A *Data Preparation Task* represents some transformation (e.g., *Dimensionality Reduction*) on a dataset. It consists of one or more *Operators* that are connected via *Data Flows*. Formed by a set of *Attributes*, an *Entity*, symbolizes a dataset. These constructs (from the Data Preparation View part of the metamodel [20]) together describe what data preparation workflows are needed to transform the data into the right shape for execution of ML algorithms.

More details and examples of the three views are provided in our previous works [19–22]. The rest of this section focuses on modeling elements that are specific to solution patterns.

Contexts. To define this construct, we use and extend the proposal by Ali et al. [5]. A context is a partial state of the world that is relevant to analytical requirements. It is expressed as a formula of predicates about the domain. Contexts need to be verified. Three kinds of contexts are distinguished here, based on their source of verification. *User Contexts* are contexts that need to be verified based on information from actors (i.e., solution users). *Data Contexts* are contexts that can be verified based on information about the dataset (e.g., size, feature distributions, types). They can also represent certain recommendations on how to transform and prepare dataset for the problem at hand. *Model Contexts* are contexts that can be verified based on algorithm configurations and parameter values. They can also represent certain recommended configurations to be taken into account in experiments and solution design. This differentiation serves as a way to facilitate representation of knowledge on under what data and user conditions, a solution design (including algorithm choice and data preparation steps) is applicable for the problem at hand and how parameters need to be set. Table 1 shows the structure of context expressions in EBNF formalism.

Table 1. EBNF grammar for context expressions

$\langle user\_context \rangle$:- $\langle User\_Predicate \rangle$
  | $\langle user\_context \rangle$ 'and' $\langle user\_context \rangle$
  | $\langle user\_context \rangle$ 'or' $\langle user\_context \rangle$;

$\langle data\_context \rangle$:- $\langle Data\_Predicate \rangle$
  | 'Perform' $\langle operation \rangle$ 'when' $\langle Data\_Predicate \rangle$
  | 'Perform' $\langle operation \rangle$ 'on' $\langle data\_type \rangle$ '**features.**'
  | $\langle data\_context \rangle$ 'and' $\langle data\_context \rangle$
  | $\langle data\_context \rangle$ 'or' $\langle data\_context \rangle$;

$\langle operation \rangle$:- '**normalization**' | '**dimensionality reduction**' | '**discre...**'

$\langle data\_type \rangle$:- '**numerical**' | '**categorical**' | '**datetime**' | '**binary**' | ...;

$\langle model\_context \rangle$:- $\langle Model\_Predicate \rangle$
  | $\langle Model\_Predicate \rangle$ 'when' $\langle data\_context \rangle$
  | $\langle model\_context \rangle$ 'and' $\langle model\_context \rangle$
  | $\langle model\_context \rangle$ 'or' $\langle model\_context \rangle$;

Contexts may apply to the Means-End, Contribution, and Evaluation links, as well as to the Analytics Goals. A context applied to a Means-End link shows that the corresponding Analytics Goal (i.e., the end) can be achieved by the Algorithm (i.e., the means) only if the context holds. When a context is applied to a Contribution link, it represents situations under which the Algorithm contributes (positively or negatively) to the Softgoal. On the other hand, contexts applied to Evaluation links represent knowledge on when the Indicator is applicable for evaluating the associated Analytics Goal. Lastly, a context that is applied to an Analytics Goal represents the activation rule of the goal towards generating Insights for the business questions at hand. A context can be defined in terms of other contexts via some logical relations. For example, in Fig. 2, $C1$ is defined as $\neg(C2 \wedge C3)$. Multiple contexts applied to a single element is equivalent to a conjunction of those contexts.

Parameters. This element (not shown in the graphical notation) represents configuration values that are required as input by an Algorithm. An Algorithm can have zero to many Parameters. The meta-attribute *defaultValue* captures information on default or recommended values for parameters. A Parameter can be the subject of some Model Contexts.

4 Implementation and Evaluation

In this section we report on the feasibility, expressiveness, and usefulness of the proposed approach in this paper. In particular, we have attempted to answer the following questions: (Q.i) Can ML solution patterns be implemented and used in real world scenarios?, (Q.ii) Are the modeling concepts adequate for expressing the solution patterns?, and (Q.iii) What are the benefits of using solution patterns when applying machine learning to business problems?

We first devised a prototype architecture for using the patterns in real world scenarios. We implemented the architecture for the fraud detection solution pattern to test its applicability over sample datasets. In the findings section, we report our observations and lessons learned through the course of these steps.

This study was conducted in collaboration with an industry team within a large information technology company. The high level objective of this collaboration was to embed a ML component within a business process management platform. The metamodel, pattern instances, and a prototype architecture were developed by the academic team (first two authors) and then implemented by developers from the industry partner. The industry team had deep expertise in developing and supporting workflow solutions, but was incorporating a ML component for the first time. This allowed us to obtain feedback and collect observations about ML solution patterns in real world scenarios. The feedback was obtained through a questionnaire and follow-up discussions.

4.1 Prototype Architecture

The prototype architecture is composed of nine logical components that together provide semi-automated support for using solution patterns (Fig. 5).

Pattern Repository. This component stores a collection of solution patterns (such as those in Figs. 1, 2 and 3). Following the semantics defined in the metamodel (Fig. 4), patterns can be expressed in standard, machine understandable formats (e.g., XML) so that the content can be queried and retrieved at run-time.

Data Extractor. It collects the raw data file(s) along with metadata information (e.g., variable types, label attribute flags). The component serves the Data Preparator and Data Context Monitor components.

Context Analyzer. This component is responsible for providing the status of context elements. It depends on the Pattern Repository to provide relevant context elements to be investigated. Given a pattern, this component parses the structure and generates a context analysis workflow (depending on structure of the graph). This allows for systematic discovery of alternatives for applying ML

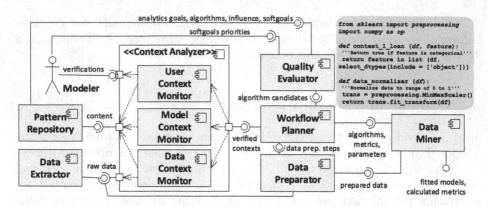

Fig. 5. UML component diagram of prototype architecture (partial). The gray shaded area shows sample codes, in Python, for the Data context monitor and Data preparator components.

algorithms to the problem at hand, depending on which contexts hold. Figure 6 presents two samples of workflows generated from the loan approval and fraud detection patterns. For each context, a binary status value is generated, representing if the contexts holds true or not. The *User Context Monitor* verifies User Contexts, which needs input from the Modeler. The *Data Context Monitor* parses the raw dataset, which comes from the Data Extractor, and analyzes the Data Context elements against data types, feature distributions, and values. The *Model Context Monitor* verifies model configurations and parameter values. Results of these components are provided to the Workflow Planner component.

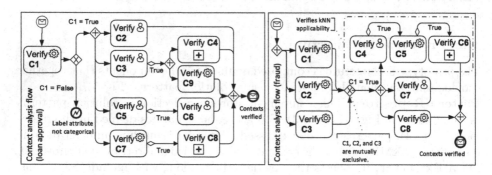

Fig. 6. Examples of context analysis workflows generated by the Context Analyzer from loan approval and fraud detection patterns (partial).

Quality Evaluator. This component is responsible for analyzing the influences of algorithms on (hierarchies of) softgoals. It recommends a list of algorithms to be included in or excluded from the workflow based on their influences on non-functional requirements. It depends on the Pattern Repository component to retrieve the list of relevant softgoals and also to retrieve the knowledge on how each algorithm is known to perform with respect to those softgoals. It also receives the importance and priority of softgoals from the Modeler.

Workflow Planner. This component is responsible for suggesting analysis scenarios to be performed on the dataset. It interprets the verified contexts along with candidate algorithms and specifies the order of actions to be executed by the Data Preparator and Data Miner components. It also ensures that the necessary data preparation and model configurations (e.g., parameter values) are collected and transmitted for the execution.

Data Preparator. This includes an implementation of a wide range of data preparation tasks and techniques such as data cleansing, noise removal, missing values treatment, data normalization, and data integration. It performs common data preparation and transformation tasks and generates the prepared data table that is ready to be consumed by the Data Miner component. This component depends on the Workflow Planner component to provide the list and order of the necessary preparation steps to be performed on the data. It also received the raw data from the Data Extractor component.

Data Miner. It includes an implementation of a wide range of ML algorithms and is responsible for executing algorithms on an input dataset, storing the fitted models, and reporting on evaluation metrics. This component depends on the Workflow Planner to provide a list of algorithms to be executed and metrics to be calculated. It receives the prepared dataset(s) from the Data Preparator.

4.2   Implementation

We have developed a proof-of-concept implementation of the architecture to test its feasibility and to identify potential logical shortcomings (Q.i). The implementation is written in Python programming language which offers a wide range of libraries for data manipulation (e.g., Pandas[1]), scientific computing (e.g., NumPy[2] and SciPy[3]), and machine learning functions (e.g., Scikit-learn[4]). The graphical user interface was developed in IBM Business Automation Workflow. The focus of implementation was the fraud detection solution pattern (Fig. 2).

A randomly generated dataset of 1,000,000 insurance claims was prepared in two steps. First, a set of claims following a typical distribution was created to represent the non-fraudulent samples. Then, a small number of anomalies were manually inserted into the dataset. This included applicants with unusual claim amounts for certain policies, compared to the rest of population. The dataset included attributes such as applicant's age, claim amount, employment status, policy cost, claim type, among others.

---

[1] https://pandas.pydata.org/.

[2] https://www.numpy.org/.

[3] https://www.scipy.org/.

[4] https://scikit-learn.org/.

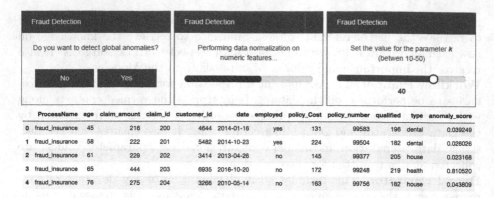

Fig. 7. User views from prototype implementation of fraud detection solution pattern.

Figure 7 shows screen shots from the implementation of the above data scenario. In the top-part, the dialog boxes show that design choices were led by the status of various contexts. It shows that the system verifies contexts $C4, C5$, and $C6$ from Fig. 2, following the process model in Fig. 6. At the bottom, it shows a sample of anomaly scores generated for a sample of claims.

4.3 Findings

Through the course of the collaboration with the industry partner, the academic team has collected some feedback and observations about expressiveness and usefulness of solution patterns. The findings suggest that solution patterns can have a positive impact on design and development of ML solutions.

Regarding adequacy of concepts (Q.ii), the academic team found that *the primitive concepts of the metamodel can capture various aspects of ML design knowledge*. The semantics and expressiveness of the three solution patterns were discussed with and reviewed by the industry team during regular meetings. The feedback received from the industry partner was generally positive, reflecting that solution patterns encapsulate a large and critical body of ML design knowledge. An important outcome of the collaboration with industry partner was some enhancements to the metamodel, such as classification of the Context element into the Data, User, and Model Context sub-types. Before this collaboration, there was only a general context element, with no grammar for expressions.

Regarding usefulness of the approach (Q.iii), some feedback was reported by the industry team as follows: (a) Solution patterns *offer an efficient way of transferring ML design knowledge among developers*. In particular, the industry team was able to gain a useful amount of ML design knowledge by reviewing the content of patterns. This included the content of data contexts (e.g., how to prepare the dataset?), user contexts (e.g., what do I need to discuss with end-users?), model contexts (e.g., what should be the range of parameters?), algorithms (e.g., what algorithms are relevant for my problem?) and their influences on softgoals (e.g., how would each algorithm influence quality requirements?). By using the fraud detection pattern, the project team quickly realized that depending on the data availability, some anomaly detection approaches might be more suitable than others. In particular, if both fraud and non-fraud samples are available, a supervised anomaly detection approach should be used; but if only examples of non-fraud claims were present, a semi-supervised approach is appropriate.

(b) Solution patterns can *potentially reduce time and cost of ML development efforts.* When tasked with the problem of fraud detection for insurance claims, rather than starting out from scratch, solution patterns enabled the project team to start with algorithms and techniques that have been shown to work for the problem at hand. This reduced the exploration and experimentation efforts at the early phases of the project. Also, the patterns simplified the coding phase by pointing developers to existing libraries and implementations of ML algorithms.

(c) The patterns offer *a way to constrain the solution space into a narrower scope based on qualities that are deemed critical by the modeler and end-users.* For example, in the fraud detection pattern, if dealing with redundant attributes is critical, the pattern recommends neural network techniques as a means for satisfying that requirement (See Fig. 2).

(d) Visual representations of patterns was *a convenient and easy to understand encapsulation of ML design.* The development team, initially not familiar with goal-oriented modeling languages, was able to comprehend and consume the produced patterns after a quick tutorial on the notation.

As a result of prototype implementation, certain improvements and extensions to the proposal were deemed necessary. During implementation, the team encountered situations where there is a conflict between softgoals and the contexts that system has verified. Certain mechanisms need to be developed for handling such situations. From an extensibility perspective, there needs to be specific guidelines and procedures on how one can create new and extend existing patterns. The current graphical format of presenting a pattern can be extended with a structured template or domain-specific language that allows for effective retrieval, connection to existing ML libraries, and linking patterns to each other.

There are several threats to validity of the findings and results in this work. The content of patterns presented in this work are mainly drawn from survey papers and textbooks, supplemented with authors' practical experience. Such content would require further validations and extensions by ML experts with practical experiences. Moreover, a formal and structured approach could be developed and used for developing the patterns. The current study was conducted in collaboration with a single industry team. Stronger evidences towards adequacy of concepts (i.e., Q.ii) could be obtained by involving a group of ML experts for evaluating the approach and sufficiency of modeling elements. In addition, stronger evidences about benefits of solution patterns (i.e., Q.iii) could be collected by comparing the approach against ML development without solution patterns (e.g., relying on current professional practice or literature searches). Quantitative research methods could be leveraged to measure the time and costs saved as a result of using solution patterns.

5   Related Work

Related to our work are those that provide best practices, catalogues and patterns for analytics and ML solution development. Chen et al. [10,11] provide a reference architecture and technology catalogue for big data system development. Sculley et al. [26] provide a set of anti-patterns to be avoided while designing ML systems. Zinkevich [31] provides a set of best practices for engineering ML solutions. Breck et al. [6] offers a range of test cases for ensuring reliability of ML systems. The approach in this paper is different in that it offers an explicit and systematic way of representing business requirements and linking them to relevant ML algorithms, while capturing user-, data-, and model-contexts.

A range of machine learning services on cloud platforms are offered by various providers such Microsoft (Azure ML Studio [3]), Google (Cloud AI [4]), and Amazon (SageMaker [1]). They offer (semi) automated tool support for data preparation, model training, testing, and deployment tasks. These platforms come with documentation, guidelines, and community support (e.g., [2]). The work in this paper is different in that business questions and decisions play a critical role in deriving solution design. Furthermore, quality requirements (Softgoals), user preferences (User Contexts), data characteristics (Data Contexts), and parameter configurations (Model Contexts) influence the solution design.

A number of data mining formal ontologies have been developed (e.g., [27]), some with the goal of offering intelligent assistance to domain users during the analytics process (e.g., [16]). Differently, the approach in this paper starts from business decisions and questions and link them to alternative ML algorithms and data preparation techniques, while considering quality requirements.

The choice of the term solution patterns is intended to convey the differences between the approach in this paper and existing software design patterns (e.g., [8]). Patterns in this paper are more problem-domain specific and are less-generic compared to design patterns. They are (conceptually) closer to a working solution and hence for adopters to use them as starting point of implementation.

6   Conclusions

This paper introduced solution patterns as an explicit and systematic way of representing well-proven ML designs for business problems. It illustrated that, by representing ML design knowledge in a reusable form, patterns can address a wide range of complexities that one would face in designing ML solutions. Based on an industry collaboration, the paper reported on the feasibility, expressiveness, and usefulness of the patterns. Further empirical studies are under way to evaluate the benefits and limitations of the overall framework as well as the solution patterns work presented in this paper. This includes involving a group of ML experts for evaluating adequacy of concepts, validating and expanding the content of the patterns, assessing benefits of the approach against a baseline, and experiments and case studies with real-world datasets.

References

1. Amazon SageMaker. http://aws.amazon.com/sagemaker/. Accessed 11 Mar 2018
2. Azure AI Gallery. http://gallery.azure.ai/. Accessed 11 Oct 2018
3. Azure Machine Learning Studio. http://azure.microsoft.com/en-us/services/machine-learning-studio/. Accessed 11 Mar 2018
4. Google Cloud AI products. http://cloud.google.com/products/ai/. Accessed 11 Mar 2018
5. Ali, R., Dalpiaz, F., Giorgini, P.: A goal-based framework for contextual requirements modeling and analysis. Requirements Eng. 15(4), 439–458 (2010)
6. Breck, E., Cai, S., Nielsen, E., Salib, M., Sculley, D.: The ML test score: a rubric for ML production readiness and technical debt reduction. In: 2017 IEEE International Conference on Big Data, pp. 1123–1132. IEEE (2017)
7. Brynjolfsson, E., McAfee, A.: The business of artificial intelligence: what it can –and cannot– do for your organization. Harv. Bus. Rev. 7, 3–11 (2017)
8. Buschmann, F., Henney, K., Schimdt, D.: Pattern-Oriented Software Architecture, vol. 5. Wiley, Hoboken (2007)
9. Chandola, V., Banerjee, A., Kumar, V.: Anomaly detection: a survey. ACM Comput. Surv. 41(3), 15 (2009)
10. Chen, H.-M., Kazman, R., Haziyev, S.: Agile big data analytics for web-based systems: an architecture-centric approach. IEEE Trans. Big Data 2, 234–248 (2016)
11. Chen, H.-M., Kazman, R., Haziyev, S., Hrytsay, O.: Big data system development: an embedded case study with a global outsourcing firm. In: Proceedings of the First International Workshop on BIG Data Software Engineering, pp. 44–50. IEEE Press (2015)
12. Davenport, T.H., Ronanki, R.: Artificial intelligence for the real world. Harv. Bus. Rev. 96(1), 108–116 (2018)
13. Goldstein, M., Uchida, S.: A comparative evaluation of unsupervised anomaly detection algorithms for multivariate data. PloS ONE 11(4), e0152173 (2016)
14. Han, J., Pei, J., Kamber, M.: Data Mining: Concepts and Techniques. Elsevier, Amsterdam (2011)
15. Henke, N., et al.: The Age of Analytics: Competing in a Data-Driven World, vol. 4. McKinsey Global Institute, New York (2016)
16. Keet, C.M., et al.: The data mining optimization ontology. Web Seman. Sci. Serv. Agents World Wide Web 32, 43–53 (2015)
17. Kotsiantis, S.B.: Supervised machine learning: a review of classification techniques. Informatica 31, 249–268 (2007)
18. Luca, M., Kleinberg, J., Mullainathan, S.: Algorithms need managers, too. Harv. Bus. Rev. 94(1), 20 (2016)
19. Nalchigar, S., Yu, E.: Conceptual modeling for business analytics: a framework and potential benefits. In: 19th IEEE Conference on Business Informatics, pp. 369–378 (2017)
20. Nalchigar, S., Yu, E.: Business-driven data analytics: a conceptual modeling framework. Data Knowl. Eng. 117, 359–372 (2018)
21. Nalchigar, S., Yu, E.: Designing business analytics solutions: a model-driven approach. Bus. Inf. Syst. Eng. (2018)
22. Nalchigar, S., Yu, E., Ramani, R.: A conceptual modeling framework for business analytics. In: Comyn-Wattiau, I., Tanaka, K., Song, I.-Y., Yamamoto, S., Saeki, M. (eds.) ER 2016. LNCS, vol. 9974, pp. 35–49. Springer, Cham (2016). https://doi.org/10.1007/978-3-319-46397-1_3

23. Ng, A.: What artificial intelligence can and can't do right now. Harv. Bus. Rev. **9** (2016)
24. Ransbotham, S., Gerbert, P., Reeves, M., Kiron, D., Spira, M.: Artificial intelligence in business gets real. MIT Sloan Manag. Rev. (2018)
25. Schreck, B., Kanter, M., Veeramachaneni, K., Vohra, S., Prasad, R.: Getting value from machine learning isn't about fancier algorithms – it's about making it easier to use. Harv. Bus. Rev. (2018)
26. Sculley, D., et al.: Machine learning: the high interest credit card of technical debt. In: SE4ML: Software Engineering for Machine Learning (2014)
27. Vanschoren, J., Soldatova, L.: Exposé: an ontology for data mining experiments. In: International Workshop on Third Generation Data Mining: Towards Service-Oriented Knowledge Discovery, pp. 31–46 (2010)
28. Veeramachaneni, K.: Why you're not getting value from your data science. Harv. Bus. Rev. **12**, 1–4 (2016)
29. Xu, R., Wunsch, D.: Survey of clustering algorithms. IEEE Trans. Neural Netw. **16**(3), 645–678 (2005)
30. Yu, E.: Modelling strategic relationships for process reengineering. Soc. Model. Requirements Eng. **11**, 2011 (2011)
31. Zinkevich, M.: Rules of machine learning: best practices for ML engineering (2017)

Managing and Simplifying Cognitive Business Operations Using Process Architecture Models

Zia Babar[1(✉)], Eric Yu[1], Sebastian Carbajales[2], and Allen Chan[2]

[1] University of Toronto, Toronto, Canada
zia.babar@mail.utoronto.ca, eric.yu@utoronto.ca
[2] IBM Canada, Markham, Canada
{sebastia,avchan}@ca.ibm.com

Abstract. Enterprises increasingly rely on cognitive capabilities to enhance their core business processes by adopting systems that utilize machine learning and deep learning approaches to support cognitive decisions to aid humans responsible for business process execution. Unlike conventional information systems, for which the design and implementation is a much-studied area, the design of cognitive systems and their integration into existing enterprise business processes is less well understood. This results in long drawn-out implementation and adoption cycles, and requires individuals with highly specialized skills. As cognitively-assisted business processes involve human and machine collaboration, non-functional requirements, such as reusability and configurability that are prominent for software system design, must also be addressed at the enterprise level. Supporting processes may emerge and evolve over time to monitor, evaluate, adjust, or modify these cognitively-enhanced business processes. In this paper, we utilize a goal-oriented approach to analyze the requirements for designing cognitive systems for simplified adoption in enterprises, which are then used to guide and inform the design of a process architecture for cognitive business operations.

Keywords: Business process management · Goal modeling ·
Cognitive computing · Cognitive business operations ·
Requirements engineering

1 Introduction

Enterprises are increasingly taking advantage of cognitive computing to improve their business operations, resulting in greater operational efficiencies through better decision making and ongoing cycles of learning and improvement [1]. However, cognitive services are difficult to implement within the current technological landscape and require significant effort. By cognitive systems, we mean application systems which have certain critical characteristics that help distinguish them from other enterprise information systems [2]; these include functioning with a degree of autonomy, demonstrating continuous learning behavior, perceiving events in the surrounding environment, and showing ongoing adaptation to evolving circumstances.

© Springer Nature Switzerland AG 2019
P. Giorgini and B. Weber (Eds.): CAiSE 2019, LNCS 11483, pp. 643–658, 2019.
https://doi.org/10.1007/978-3-030-21290-2_40

Designing cognitive systems for simplified integration into complex enterprise process environments can be difficult as it needs to factor in the following,

- Reduce the cost and duration of implementation while minimizing the need to engage highly skilled individuals for extended periods of time.
- Ongoing changes to business processes and cognitive systems behavior that enterprises routinely undergo; changes which are unknown at design time.
- The adaptive nature of engagement between human business users and the evolving and self-learning capabilities of cognitive systems.

Any solution needs to be multi-dimensional and consider the design of the cognitive systems, their integration in business processes, and their usage by human users - while considering the changing nature of business, human engagements, and systems complexity. At design-time these are often unknown, so it is difficult to design the business process integration and simultaneously being able to achieve non-functional requirements of simplifying the cost and complexity of the overall solution.

In this paper, we consider how enterprises can analyze different alternatives for simplified adoption and maintenance of cognitively-enhanced business operations. In Sect. 2 we introduce a motivating example to illustrate key aspects of the problem. In Sect. 3 we elaborate on process architectural models for the domain under study whereas in Sect. 4 we discuss how the NFR framework can be used to determine multiple ways of configuring the domain's system and processes. In Sect. 5 we propose a method that organizations can follow to come up with a to-be process architecture configuration that considers non-functional enterprise requirements and stakeholder objectives while allowing for handling ongoing enterprise transformations. In Sect. 7 we refer to related work and in Sect. 8 we outline future research directions and conclude the paper.

2 Motivating Example: Simplified Cognitive Business Operations

To illustrate and discuss some key concepts of this paper, we consider an enterprise about to adopt cognitive services as part of its routine business operations, thus moving towards *Cognitive Business Operations* (or CBO). By CBO we mean the spectrum of enterprise business operations and their involved processes, decision making activities using insights from available data, and the engagements between business operations users and cognitive systems [3]. Incorporating cognitive systems in existing business processes would enable faster, more uniform, and consistent decision-making despite changing contextual and situational factors, and staff rotation. Traditional human-based decision making rely on intuition and experience which are subject to personal biases and have variations in the accuracy and speed of decision-making.

The challenge in designing and deploying CBO in any enterprise is in how to minimize the overall cost of the solution, reduce the need for individuals with specialized skillsets (such as data scientists and business analysts), and shorten the overall duration of any project engagement. There has to be a management of ongoing changes without re-engaging these individuals or undergoing expensive redesigns at both a system and process level. Further, as the enterprise is dynamic, there could be changes in engagements between the human users and the cognitive systems, while including self-learning requirements from the cognitive solution, managing evolving contexts and adaptation etc. The range of possible changes, and the need to minimize the impact and cost of managing them, is essential. Thus, any solution that an enterprise selects should not focus only on functional requirements but must also ensure that non-functional goals of simplified CBO adoption are addressed.

This *Simplified CBO* can be characterized by the following non-functional requirements (NFRs).

- **(High) Learnability:** Learnability implies feedback and higher-order analysis of options by applying previous experience. Considering this, business operations powered by cognitive systems should be dynamically reconfigured in response to evolving enterprise requirements and environmental factors. The changes could take many forms, from the manner in which human users engage with cognitive systems, to changes in surrounding context that necessitates some response, etc.
- **(High) Reusability:** A fundamental premise in cognitive solutions is the ability to have reusable knowledge artifacts that provide best practices and patterns-based solutions to commonly occurring problems. Such a reusable knowledge base could be built over time in the form of knowledge catalogues with the cognitive solution being designed to leverage these so as to reduce the effort of solving known problems and handling situations.
- **(High) Configurability:** While any cognitively-enhanced solution being proposed for an enterprise would require an initial setup, ongoing reconfigurations are necessary to support evolving enterprise requirements and changing circumstances. Thus, ability to reconfigure aspects of the solution is essential to reduce continuous project cost and human involvement (at both deployment time and post-deployment).
- **(High) Developability:** Any cognitively-enhanced solution needs to be customized to intelligently handle different environments, requirements and changing circumstances. Hence the product should allow for some form of development to extend, enhance or modify functionality after it has been released. Due to the variability in the business and technical requirements and contexts for cognitive systems, it is impractical to identify all possible configurations required for different organizations.

By identifying and prioritizing the NFRs [4] for the domain under study, we are better able to devise a to-be solution that encompasses the interplay of systems, processes, and user engagements. Such a solution would ideally (a) reduce the cost, time and complexity of integration of cognitive systems in business processes, and (b) minimize the process reconfiguration and systems reimplementation as the enterprise environment changes.

3   Modeling Simplified CBO As-Is Using Process Architectures

We need a modeling notation to be able to express different design configurations of process architectures, so that we can reason about the pros and cons of alternative designs. Here alterative designs are therefore different ways of modifying the architecture. Process architecture models depict relationships between multiple business processes that exist in a domain, while abstracting away from process-level details. Detailed models and over-specifications are best avoided in favour of highlighting relationships and process aspects that facilitate enterprise transformation with corresponding tradeoffs being considered.

We have previously proposed hiBPM [5–8], a conceptual modeling framework for process architecture modeling and analysis. It emphasizes the existence of various decision-making points and offers sufficient expressiveness so as to allow relevant architectural properties to be analyzed, for contrasting among alternative process architecture design options. Figure 1 presents an As-Is hiBPM Process Architecture Model (or just hiBPM model) of a loan approval scenario, with the loan approval/rejection decision being the focus of analysis. The figure illustrates a traditional deployment solution that emphasizes the attainment of functional goals, while neglecting to consider the non-functional requirements of Simplified CBO.

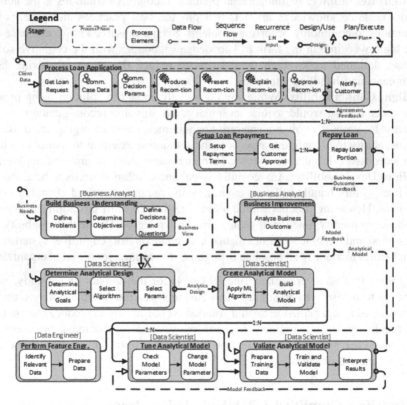

Fig. 1. As-Is process architecture model for the loan application process

The hiBPM model comprises of several constructs. Process Element (PE) is a basic activity unit that produces some output or outcome. Repositioning a PE within a process architecture results in variable behaviour and characteristics to support transformation objectives. Process Stages (PS) are collections of PEs that are to be executed collectively as part of the same execution cycle. Process stages are generally structured in a manner where they deliver some enterprise functionality. In the figure, the domain-specific process stages (**Process Loan Application, Setup Loan Repayment,** and **Repay Loan**) are centrally shown as process stages, with the cognitive system-specific process stages (e.g., **Create Analytical Model, Tune Analytical Model,** and **Validate Analytical Model**) producing the software artifacts necessary for enabling cognitive decision making. The relationships (data flows and sequence flows) that exist between process stages are also shown. The **1:N** annotation on outgoing flows indicates a *recurrence* relationship. Process Phases (PP) are sections within a PS that produce the same result irrespective of the arrangement of PEs within, i.e. the reordering of PEs does not result in any change in the outcome of the PP. **Process Loan Application** contains a single process phase that pertains to the collection of decision-making PEs that produce and present a recommendation.

The process architecture can be configured in multiple ways while still accomplishing the same enterprise functional goals and simultaneously trading off between enterprise NFRs. A PE can either be executed before or after other PEs. Postponing a PE provides the benefit of executing it with the latest context while advancing a PE (earlier than other PEs) reduces process execution complexity, uncertainty and cost. By moving a PE from a stage with a lower recurrence to one with a higher recurrence, enterprises can ensure that activities are performed using the latest data. Conversely, moving a PE to a lower recurrence results in a reduced execution cost as the PEs are executed less frequently.

The domain-specific business processes rely on different systems artifacts to help with processing a loan application. **Analytical Model** is a design artifact that is "used" as part of the **Process Loan Application** processing. Thus, there exists a Design-Use relationship (indicated by the "U") between the **Validate Analytical Model** and the **Process Loan Application** process stages. PEs can also be moved from a design stage to a use stage (and vice versa), with such a repositioning either leading to an increased design or to trading the design effort for run-time usage control. **Build Business Understanding** produces a plan that is executed by the **Determine Analytical Design**. Thus there exists a Plan-Execute relationship between these two process stages (indicated by the "X"). PEs can be moved from an execution stage to a planning stage (and vice versa). Such movements create variations in the plan-execute behavior and allow either increased pre-planning or shifting more responsibility to the execution side. The hiBPM notation is explained in greater detail in [5–8].

While not part of the modeling notation, some process stages are annotated with process participants responsible for their execution to indicate different domain actors and their involvement. Several process stage requires the involvement of **Data Scientist**, who performs manual operations to execute the activities within that process stage; this incurs time and cost, with the **Analytical Model** produced generally being custom developed for a particular situation.

4 Using the NFR Framework to Analyze the As-Is

Goal models [9] can provide the means to analyze and guide possible configurations of the process architecture to help satisfy both functional and non-functional objectives of Simplified CBO. This is done through constructing and navigating the goal graphs and seeing how a goal structure can be applied to an appropriate configuration of the process architecture model where the promise of Simplified CBO is possible. However, this does not imply a one-to-one mapping between the two modeling approaches, as goal models and hiBPM models can be at different levels of granularity and detail. Rather, the goal models are used as a guide for determining additional process structures and alternative process configurations that may need to be present in the hiBPM model. The goal model in Fig. 2 permits such an analysis showing Alternatives A and B that indicate two possible ways of configuring the system and processes for attaining Simplified CBO. These goals are linked to process actions, each of which achieves a certain functional goal. The goal model in Fig. 2 is not meant to be comprehensive but is limited to a subset of use cases.

Alternative A shown is for the as-is situation at an enterprise that has attained its functional requirements for CBO by utilizing a traditional analytical model-based solution. The NFRs for Simplified CBO are decomposed down to their operational goals with the roles required for their attainment annotated in blue. For example, we see that a **Data Scientist** is responsible for a number of operationalized goals, which include **Select Algorithms**, **Develop Analytical Models**, etc. Similarly, the **Business Analyst** is responsible for studying the enterprise space and helping **Develop Business Solutions** for that particular organization. These collectively help convey the significant involvement of these high-skilled individuals in the overall project activities which prevents the attainment of the NFRs of **Learnability** and **Reusability**. We use a goal satisfaction analysis technique [10] to qualitatively assess whether the softgoals can be satisfied (✓) or denied (✗). Weakly satisfied or weakly denied conditions are shown using the same symbols, but with a "dot" added. As can be seen in Fig. 2, the primary softgoal of Simplified CBO for the Line-of-Business is not satisfied, thus Alternative A is not ideal, despite attaining the functional goals.

The branch marked Alternative B in Fig. 2 pertains to the incorporation of a *Cognitive Business Advisor* (CBA) that helps attain the NFRs of **Learnability**, **Reusability Developability** and **Configurability**. . The CBA leverages recommendation systems [11] to aid and assist with decision making (e.g. loan approved, loan rejected etc.) for the business users. The business users here are internal staff who are responsible for, or involved in, repetitive business process execution. The CBA alternative is qualitatively analyzed against the same set of NFRs however the solution provided in this alternative contributes to the NFRs differently. In order to achieve **Reusability**, there is a reliance on creating reusable knowledge nuggets and artifacts as part of pre-deployment activities. **Learnability** is achieved through ongoing **Sense Context** and **Detect Change**; based on which suitable actions are performed to process context changes and selection configurations.

For both Alternative A and Alternative B, **Configurability** is managed at runtime and pre-runtime through having configurable settings. By runtime we mean reconfiguring the CBA (or **Analytical Model**) to behave differently during the execution of business operations, which can be done through changing application or database parameters. Pre-runtime configuration is achieved through configuration settings done at either build or deploy time. There are advantages and disadvantages to both approaches, discussion of which is beyond the scope of this paper. Finally, **Developability** of the product is attained through having modular components, no-code/low-code and codeable architecture for extending product features.

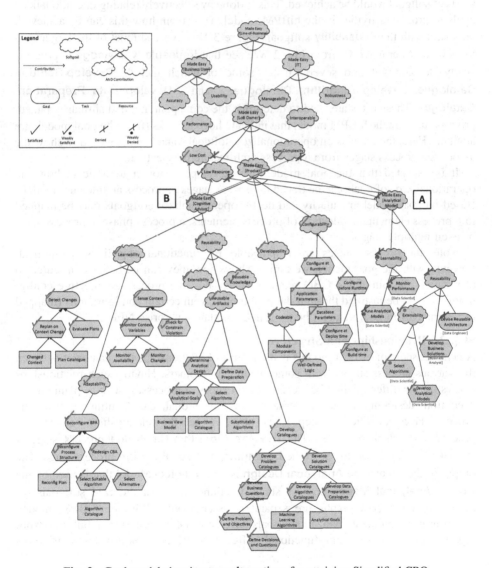

Fig. 2. Goal model showing two alternatives for attaining Simplified CBO

5   A Method to Determine Supporting Process Structures

As part of the research contribution of this paper, a multi-step method is proposed below that allows for a structured determination of supporting processes required to attain Simplified CBO NFR objectives without cycles of trial and error. This method is better illustrated by selecting a narrow example, such as the case of **Develop Catalogue** for Alternative B.

Step 1 – Determine Process Stages

In the first step, the intention is to explore and depict how the attainment of a certain kinds of softgoal would be achieved. This is done by selectively relating operationalized goals to process activities in the hiBPM model. To explain how this can be achieved, let's start with the **Reusability** softgoal. Figure 3(1) shows a snippet of the larger goal model (for Alternative B) from Fig. 2. We see that **Reusable Knowledge** is progressively decomposed into several tasks, some of which include **Develop Solution Catalogue, Develop Algorithm Catalogue,** and **Develop Data Preparation Catalogue**. These tasks are used to determine the corresponding, and similarly named, process stages in the hiBPM model that indicate how the tasks (from the goal model) are attained. Here, the focus is on operationalized softgoals, and these are used to show the associated process stages from a process architecture perspective.

It is expected that the goal models are developed enough to indicate how the operationalized softgoals can be traced to process stages in process architecture models. Based on goal model granularity and detail, operationalized softgoals may be mapped to a process element, a collection of process elements, a process phase, a process stage or even multiple stages.

Note, the process stages are responsible for functional objectives' attainment, however with the goal model, we aim to show how they can be better configured to also satisfy the Simplified CBO requirements. Thus, the process architecture configuration would be justified through the goal model, with certain configurations (mapped to alternatives in goal models) better suited to attain enterprise NFRs.

Step 2 - Relationships and Structure

A central aspect of hiBPM models is the nature of relationships that can exist between the various process stages, with some feeding into others. Having such relationships allows for the differentiation between different types of processes, such as planning vs. execution, designing vs. using, strategic vs. operational, etc. Continuing from the process stages identified in Step 1, we now can see the relationships between the processes stages in Fig. 3(2). The **Develop Algorithm Catalogue** process stage is shown to have relationship with the **Determine Analytical Design** process stage. The output of the **Determine Analytical Design** is an **Analytical Model** that is used by the **Create Analytical Model** process stage. Conjunctive operationalized softgoals (or tasks) from the goal graphs are separately operationalized in the hiBPM model, meaning that the operationalized softgoals have separate process stages, but they work together to attain some non-functional softgoal. AND de-compositions in the goal model from Fig. 3(1) are reflected in the hiBPM models where the AND relationship means that two process stages need to work together to collectively attain the upper-level softgoal.

It should be clarified that the goal graph is not meant to be a precise definition of the multi-level process stage relationship in process architecture models. Rather, the goal model interdependency structure is used as a guide to understand the relationships between different process stages.

Step 3 – Process Stage Internals

For each process stage, the internal process phases and process elements need to be determined to better understand how the process stage can attain the functional objectives that it is responsible for, while supporting non-functional objective attainments. Take the example of **Develop Analytical Catalogue** as this process stage is essential to ensure the **Reusability** NFR. Again, the goal model provides a useful starting point for the determining the internal details for the hiBPM model. In the goal model of Fig. 3(1), we see that **Develop Analytical Catalogue** is decomposed into several tasks (**Organize ML Algorithms, Evaluate Algorithm Performance, Map ML Algorithms to Analytical Goals**). Depending on the granularity of the operationalized goals, these tasks (from the goal model) can be used to show either process elements or process phases in hiBPM. This can be seen in Fig. 3(3) as the **Develop Algorithm Catalogue** process stage and the three internal process elements being executed in sequence to produce the **Algorithm Catalogue** output.

The process elements or process phases are shown as a sequence of activities within a process state, which when executed on being provided some input, produce an output that is then used by downstream process stages. As the emphasis of the hiBPM is on architectural relationships between business processes, the internals of process stages

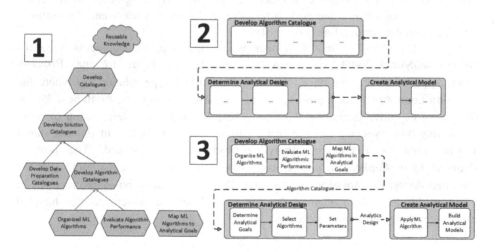

Fig. 3. Determining process stages and their internals

are usually only defined at a level where they show sufficient detail on how the functional requirements are attained, including the activities required to produce the necessary output for those process stages.

Step 4 - Resource Dependencies

In hiBPM, there are information flows, plans and designs which can be considered as being analogous to resources in goal models. These incoming flows (i.e. information flow, plans or designs) to a process stage help that process stage attain its goals. The identification of these resources can be done using the goals models, which are then used to show the inputs to various process stages (or process elements); further defining the relationships between the process stages. For example, as shown in the goal model in Fig. 4(1), the **Develop Algorithm Catalogue** task has certain resource dependencies (shown as **Machine Learning Algorithms** and **Analytical Goals**). These map to the similarly named process stage of **Develop Analytical Catalogue**. The resource dependencies of **Machine Learning Algorithms** and **Analytical Goals** would be inputs to the **Develop Analytical Catalogue** process stage. While not shown, it's easy to extend this reasoning and see that the **Analytical Catalogue** would be the output of the **Develop Analytical Catalogue** and the input to the **Determine Analytical Design** downstream process stage.

At the end of step 4, most of the supporting process stages, their relationships, including inputs and outputs (as data flows or systems artifacts) have been discovered using the selected alternative from the goal model. These additional processes are expected to help attain the Simplified CBO non-functional objectives.

Step 5 – Integration of Supporting Processes

In this step, we need to consider how the previously identified supporting and surrounding process stages are to be integrated in the primary cognitive enhanced business process as part of the overall to-be process architecture. By integration, we mean the various relational inflows that go into the primary business process and the outflows that feed into the surrounding process stages.

Figure 4(2) shows a model snippet where the supporting process stage of **Create Analytical Model** is shown to provide an input to the **Process Loan Application** process stage. This is a Design-Use type relationship where the **Process Loan Application** process stage is repeatedly "using" the **Analytical Model** design for cognitive decision-making purposes. Through the determination of these supporting processes, we can see that changing inputs to upstream process stages would result in a different **Analytical Model** being designed. The primary **Process Loan Application** process stage would not need to change, rather just the modified **Analytical Model** would be used. Thus, the primary business processes in CBO are insulated from ongoing changes in environment, which are then handled elsewhere in the supporting processes.

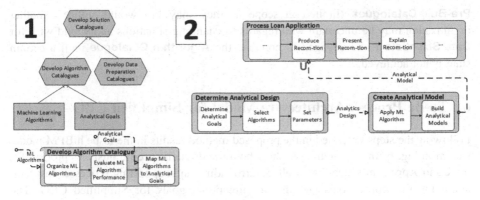

Fig. 4. Determining resource dependencies and process integration

Step 6 - Alternatives to Process Design

In the discussions so far, we've proceeded on the assumption that there is only one desired process configuration that helps attain non-functional goals along with the prerequisite functional goals of CBO. However, in reality, there may be several possible alternative process configurations. While each alternative will satisfy the CBO functional goals, there may be trade-offs when it comes to satisfying the non-functional goals. These alternatives are represented as OR decompositions in the goal model.

In Fig. 5 we reconsider the **Develop Analytical Solution** task which is achieved through either having **Pre-Built Catalogues** or having runtime catalogues populated by a **Data Scientist** (these are labeled as "A" and "B" in the goal model). The former approach helps reduce the cost and time of deployment however the latter approach is better able to handle unforeseen post-deployment situations that are not part of the catalogue. These two alternatives are represented in the hiBPM model as two possible process configurations. The selection of either one is done based on the priority and preference of the enterprise (as ascertained through goal analysis). For example, one enterprise may feel that there is no unpredictable situation expected and thus

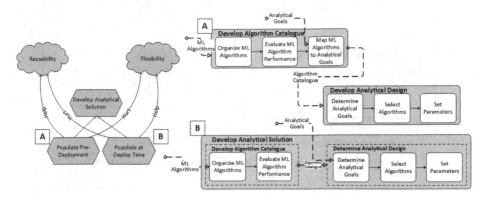

Fig. 5. Determining alternative process architecture configurations

Pre-Built Catalogues (limited in scope as they may be) would suffice. Another organization may be uncertain with regards to changing situations and would wish for **Data Scientists** to be engaged to populate the **Algorithm Catalogue** until a certain state is not achieved.

6 To-Be Process Architecture Model for Simplified CBO

Following the steps proposed in the proposed method results in the to-be hiBPM model shown in Fig. 6. In this figure, we show both the domain specific business process for the **Loan Approval** process, as well as surrounding and supporting processes that help attain the functional goals and the non-functional goals for Simplified CBO. The

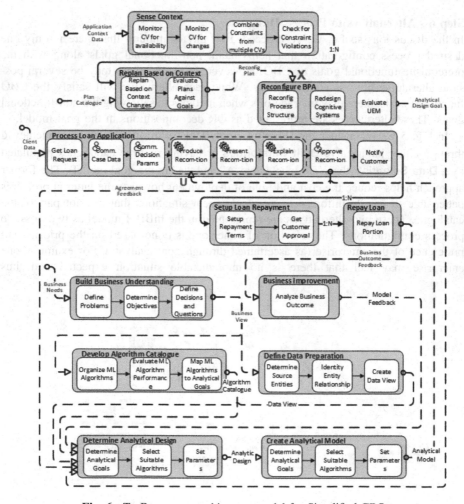

Fig. 6. To-Be process architecture model for Simplified CBO

additional process stages particularly help with the satisfying of the **Learnability** and **Reusability** Simplified CBO NFRs. The **Reusability** NFR was achieved by determining the process configuration as explained in the previous section. Although not similarly explained, it is easy to follow that the **Learnability** NFR can be achieved through sending and managing external context changes, as determined by following the provided method. These (the overall process architecture for enabling these NFRs) collectively come together as the CBA solution that encompasses both process-level and systems-level reconfigurations.

7 Related Work

Process architectures are used to provide abstract representation of multiple processes that exist in an enterprise [12]. Additional processes relationships are proposed in [13]. Process architectures can also be seen as a means for developing a more holistic view of the organization by associating business process modeling and enterprise architecture, while additionally decomposing processes into higher level of granularity that provide increasing visibility on the constituent parts of the integrated processes [14]. Our notion of process architecture differs from these as we are focused on the need for ongoing change in the enterprise and use process architectures to model those changes and analyze possible variants of process architecture configurations that exist.

Traditional business process modeling notations, such as BPMN [15], rely on an imperative approach where the process model represents (in great detail) the process state of the system and all permitted actions. However, capturing such detailed specifications of the system-under-study is challenging, particularly as the underlying processes may be ever changing. Declarative process modeling notation (such as BPMN-D) allows the capturing of constraints on activity flows [16]; any flow is permitted as along as the constraints are upheld. Other approaches in BPM have focused on the role of "artifacts" within process design and execution; the argument being made that without having an understanding of the information context, business participants often are too focused on execution of process activities without understanding the reasons for the execution, thus limiting opportunities for operational efficiency and process innovation [17]. Here a business artifact is self-contained, trackable "instance of a flow entity in the network" and has a unique identity. In our case, we consider the artifacts to demonstrate evolving capabilities and be flexible in both design and execution, thus requiring the introducing of Design-Use and Plan-Execute relationships.

The impact of cognitive computing on business process management (BPM) is covered in [18] where multiple types and levels of business processes are discussed; these include transaction-intensive, judgement-intensive, and design & strategy support processes. These processes result from the incorporation of cognitive capabilities within an enterprise and how cognitive processes enablement can be attained. Notions of business process architecture also exist in the enterprise architecture area. For example, in ArchiMate, business process cooperation includes causal relationships between business processes, mapping of business processes onto business functions, realization of services by business processes, and the use of shared data [19], and can also imply the type of relationships among business processes. Some enterprise architecture frameworks (e.g., ADM in TOGAF) do allow for phase-based ongoing change [20], but do not cover the full range of periodic and variable enterprise transformation considerations when deciding among multiple alternate configurations.

8 Conclusions and Future Work

This paper focuses on the issues of designing and configuring process architectures when non-functional requirements (NFRs) for enterprises need to be considered. Specifically, we considered the NFRs for ensuring the management and simplification of Cognitive Business Operations (CBO) and how process architecture reconfiguration (s) are needed for their satisficing. We used a domain example for which the process architecture model was constructed in a manner that would ensure the attainment of functional goals associated with the cognitive-enhanced business processes. However, this as-is model did not consider or satisfies the Simplified CBO NFRs. Additional processes needed to be introduced, including design abstractions for cognitive systems, which allowed the attainment of Simplified CBO objectives. Determining these supporting processes is difficult and can take iterative experimentation and trial-and-error exercises. Goal modeling allowed for the determination of a to-be alternative, with the proposed method (introduced in Sect. 5) providing a structured and methodological approach to uncovering additional supporting processes, including system design abstractions. These collectively provide the required pre-requisites to attain Simplified CBO objectives.

This approach is part of our ongoing effort for the development of a comprehensive method aimed at simplifying enterprise adoption of cognitive systems. Overall, this is aimed at supporting a systematic and controlled introduction of automation into organizations. Future research in this area will focus on:

- Introduction of cognitive systems in enterprises usually results in increased automation, resulting in changes in responsibility assignments among humans and automated systems. The modes of engagement between users and systems was initially covered in [3], however we plan to study this change dimension in more detail.
- The design of cognitive systems is considered at an abstract level (as explained using design-use relationships), without discussing the details on how these systems would evolve to conform to the changes in process architecture. These design implications need to be better understood.
- Solutions to problems are to be collectively stored in *design catalogues*. The expectation is that these catalogues would contain commonly accepted patterns for solving problems from an enterprise configuration perspective. We wish to see how these catalogues can be populated with some initial patterns.

Finally, we are evaluating this approach by applying it in several domains, each which have differing characteristics. These domains have high rates of evolution and change and have sections in the enterprise which change at different rates. Further, the practicality and usefulness of the proposed approach is being evaluated with an industrial partner. The purpose of this is to ensure that the hiBPM framework contains sufficient expressiveness to capture the domain characteristics for analysis.

Acknowledgements. This work was partially funded by IBM Canada Ltd. through the Centre for Advanced Studies (CAS) Canada (Project #1030).

References

1. Ogiela, L., Ogiela, M.R.: Advances in Cognitive Information Systems, vol. 17. Springer, Heidelberg (2012)
2. Vernon, D.: Artificial Cognitive Systems: A Primer. MIT Press, Cambridge (2014)
3. Lapouchnian, A., Babar, Z., Yu, E., Chan, A., Carbajales, S.: Designing process architectures for user engagement with enterprise cognitive systems. In: Poels, G., Gailly, F., Serral Asensio, E., Snoeck, M. (eds.) PoEM 2017. LNBIP, vol. 305, pp. 141–155. Springer, Cham (2017). https://doi.org/10.1007/978-3-319-70241-4_10
4. Chung, L., Nixon, B.A., Yu, E., Mylopoulos, J.: Non-functional Requirements in Software Engineering, vol. 5. Springer, New York (2012). https://doi.org/10.1007/978-1-4615-5269-7
5. Lapouchnian, A., Yu, E., Sturm, A.: Re-designing process architectures towards a framework of design dimensions. In: International Conference on RCIS, pp. 205–210. IEEE (2015)
6. Lapouchnian, A., Yu, E., Sturm, A.: Design dimensions for business process architecture. In: Johannesson, P., Lee, M.L., Liddle, Stephen W., Opdahl, Andreas L., López, Ó.P. (eds.) ER 2015. LNCS, vol. 9381, pp. 276–284. Springer, Cham (2015). https://doi.org/10.1007/978-3-319-25264-3_20
7. Lapouchnian, A., Yu, E.: Exploiting emergent technologies to create systems that meet shifting expectations. In Proceedings of 24th Annual International Conference on Computer Science and Software Engineering, pp. 371–374. IBM Corporation (2014)
8. Babar, Z., Lapouchnian, A., Yu, E.: Modeling DevOps deployment choices using process architecture design dimensions. In: Ralyté, J., España, S., Pastor, Ó. (eds.) PoEM 2015. LNBIP, vol. 235, pp. 322–337. Springer, Cham (2015). https://doi.org/10.1007/978-3-319-25897-3_21
9. Van Lamsweerde, A.: Goal-oriented requirements engineering: a guided tour. In: Proceedings of Fifth IEEE International Symposium on Requirements Engineering, pp. 249–262. IEEE (2001)
10. Horkoff, J., Yu, E.: Comparison and evaluation of goal-oriented satisfaction analysis techniques. Requirements Eng. **18**(3), 199–222 (2013)
11. Ricci, F., Rokach, L., Shapira, B.: Introduction to recommender systems handbook. In: Ricci, F., Rokach, L., Shapira, B., Kantor, P. (eds.) Recommender Systems Handbook, pp. 1–35. Springer, Boston (2011). https://doi.org/10.1007/978-0-387-85820-3_1
12. Dumas, M., La Rosa, M., Mendling, J., Reijers, H.: Fundamentals of Business Process Management (Chap. 2). Springer, Heidelberg (2013). https://doi.org/10.1007/978-3-662-56509-4
13. Eid-Sabbagh, R.-H., Dijkman, R., Weske, M.: Business process architecture: use and correctness. In: Barros, A., Gal, A., Kindler, E. (eds.) BPM 2012. LNCS, vol. 7481, pp. 65–81. Springer, Heidelberg (2012). https://doi.org/10.1007/978-3-642-32885-5_5

14. Malinova, M., Leopold, H., Mendling, J.: An empirical investigation on the design of process architectures. In: 11th International Conference on Wirtschaftsinformatik, pp. 1197–1211 (2013)
15. Business process Model and Notation, v2.0. http://www.omg.org/spec/BPMN/2.0/PDF/
16. De Giacomo, G., Dumas, M., Maggi, F.M., Montali, M.: Declarative process modeling in BPMN. In: Zdravkovic, J., Kirikova, M., Johannesson, P. (eds.) CAiSE 2015. LNCS, vol. 9097, pp. 84–100. Springer, Cham (2015). https://doi.org/10.1007/978-3-319-19069-3_6
17. Bhattacharya, K., Gerede, C., Hull, R., Liu, R., Su, J.: Towards formal analysis of artifact-centric business process models. In: Alonso, G., Dadam, P., Rosemann, M. (eds.) BPM 2007. LNCS, vol. 4714, pp. 288–304. Springer, Heidelberg (2007). https://doi.org/10.1007/978-3-540-75183-0_21
18. Hull, R., Motahari Nezhad, H.R.: Rethinking BPM in a cognitive world: transforming how we learn and perform business processes. In: La Rosa, M., Loos, P., Pastor, O. (eds.) BPM 2016. LNCS, vol. 9850, pp. 3–19. Springer, Cham (2016). https://doi.org/10.1007/978-3-319-45348-4_1
19. ArchiMate 3.0 Specification. http://pubs.opengroup.org/architecture/archimate3-doc/
20. TOGAF® Version 9.1. http://pubs.opengroup.org/architecture/togaf9-doc/arch/index.html

A Constraint Mining Approach
to Support Monitoring
Cyber-Physical Systems

Thomas Krismayer[✉], Rick Rabiser, and Paul Grünbacher

CDL MEVSS, Institute for Software Systems Engineering,
Johannes Kepler University Linz, Linz, Austria
{thomas.krismayer,rick.rabiser,paul.gruenbacher}@jku.at

Abstract. The full behavior of cyber-physical systems (CPS) emerges during operation only, when the systems interact with their environment. Runtime monitoring approaches are used to detect deviations from the expected behavior. While most monitoring approaches assume that engineers define the expected behavior as constraints, the deep domain knowledge required for this task is often not available. We describe an approach that automatically mines constraint candidates for runtime monitoring from event logs recorded from CPS. Our approach extracts different types of constraints on event occurrence, timing, data, and combinations of these. The approach further presents the mined constraint candidates to users and offers filtering and ranking strategies. We demonstrate the usefulness and scalability of our approach by applying it to event logs from two real-world CPS: a plant automation software system and a system controlling unmanned aerial vehicles. In our experiments, domain experts regarded 74% and 63%, respectively, of the constraints mined for these two systems as useful.

Keywords: Constraint mining · Runtime monitoring ·
Cyber-physical systems

1 Introduction

The behavior of complex cyber-physical systems (CPS) [10] emerges fully only during operation, when the systems interact with their environment. Runtime monitoring is thus needed to detect when CPS deviate from their requirements. Different research communities have been developing monitoring approaches for various kinds of systems and diverse types of checks [18], e.g., requirements monitoring, complex event processing, and runtime verification. Many of these approaches express the expected behavior formally in a form of (temporal) logic [22] or as constraints in a domain-specific language (DSL) [19]. However, for industrial CPS, manually writing such constraints is error-prone and tedious due to the systems' size, complexity, and heterogeneity. Further, the continuous evolution of such systems requires frequently defining new and updating existing

© Springer Nature Switzerland AG 2019
P. Giorgini and B. Weber (Eds.): CAiSE 2019, LNCS 11483, pp. 659–674, 2019.
https://doi.org/10.1007/978-3-030-21290-2_41

constraints. Automatically mining constraints based on information extracted from the systems during operation is thus desirable.

In this paper we introduce an approach to automatically mine constraint candidates from events and data recorded from CPS to support runtime monitoring. Our mining approach supports different types of constraints: temporal constraints checking the occurrence, timing, and order of events; value constraints checking the correctness of attached event data values; and hybrid constraints combining the former two. These constraint types have been identified as essential in two projects on monitoring CPS of plant automation software systems [19] and systems controlling unmanned aerial vehicles [2]. In a short paper [9] we discussed initial ideas and presented a first algorithm for constraint mining. Here, we present our significantly refined and extended approach, including a thorough evaluation of its usefulness and scalability with two different real-world CPS. In particular, our approach now also allows processing events produced by distributed systems, and multiple instances of the same types of systems running in parallel, which is common in CPS. Specifically, our approach automatically mines constraints from event logs recorded in CPS and represents them in an existing constraint DSL [19], which enables their immediate use in a monitoring tool. We use event logs from two real-world CPS, a plant automation system and a drone control system. We demonstrate that our approach can mine constraints for these CPS and that a significant share of the mined constraints are assessed as useful (and often as critical) for monitoring these systems by the developers of the two systems. We also show that our approach scales to large event logs.

2   Background and Running Example

Our constraint mining approach works with events and data produced by a CPS and produces candidates for constraints that can be used to check the compliance of these systems at runtime.

We use the Dronology CPS [2] as a **running example**. Dronology provides a framework for controlling and coordinating the flights of unmanned aerial systems (drones) to support applications such as search-and-rescue, surveillance, and scientific data collection. Ensuring that the drones remain functional and operate as expected during their missions calls for a runtime monitoring system checking requirements such as: (R1) Drones have to complete the routes they are assigned in a given time; (R2) While a drone is flying on a route, its altitude has to be within a certain range to prevent it from crashing; (R3) When a new drone connects to the system, it has to be on the ground – waiting for commands. Such requirements can be expressed as constraints (cf. Table 1) and checked at runtime by a monitoring system. We use the REMINDS constraint DSL [19] to represent constraints. All constraints contain a specific trigger event type to initialize their evaluation. A constraint is checked at runtime, whenever an event of this type is encountered in the event stream of the monitored system.

Event Logs. The basis for our mining approach are *event logs* that comprise events and associated data produced by a system, usually resulting from runs of different systems or the completion of different tasks. Each event has a certain type. Logs contain multiple *event sequence types* (patterns of multiple event types that have to occur in a given order) and *event sequence instances* (concrete events matching an event sequence type). In our running example, when a new drone connects to the system, a `handshake` event is sent containing the coordinates. Dronology then can assign routes to the connected drones, which are executed one after the other. During these flights the drone sends approximately one `state` event per second to report its position, speed, attitude, battery status, flight mode, etc. The `startRoute` and `endRoute` events represent the start and end of the execution of a route. A `waypoint` event is sent whenever the drone reaches one of the defined points of the current route. One basic event sequence type in our running example is `startRoute–waypoint–endRoute`.

The information stored in event logs also has implications for the **constraint types** that can be mined. The minimal input needed for our mining approach is an event log containing timestamped events. Event logs can be produced by monitoring tools, but also through standard logging tools used in most software systems today. Our DSL supports the following constraint types [19]:

Temporal constraints define a sequence of events that has to occur in a given or arbitrary order and (optionally) within a certain time. Such constraints typically describe a specific task of the monitored system that consists of several individual steps. For instance, requirement *R1* can be expressed as the temporal constraint #3 shown in Table 1. Temporal constraints can be mined from an event log containing timestamped events without any further input.

Value constraints specify the valid content of one event data element – either as one explicit value (e.g., "state.armable = true") or with thresholds (e.g., "waypoint.location/z >= 5m"). Often such data elements are grouped hierarchically, e.g., the three coordinates of the current position of a drone (X, Y, Z) are grouped into an element `location`. Value constraints can be mined from event logs that contain event data elements attached to some of the events. Requirement *R2* given above can be formulated as constraint #2 shown in Table 1.

Hybrid constraints combine temporal and value constraints to define further restrictions on event sequences. They include multiple events that have to occur in a given order and/or time, like in a temporal constraint, and additionally check event data elements of at least one of these events, like in a value constraint. For instance, requirement *R3* can be expressed as constraint #5 shown in Table 1. Hybrid constraints can also check the relation between multiple event data elements, potentially related with multiple different events, e.g., to ensure that a certain ID remains unchanged for all events of one particular sequence. Mining hybrid constraints requires timestamps and event data in the log.

Scopes. As our mining approach is intended to mine constraints for monitoring complex CPS, information about the provenance of the events is needed. If

Table 1. Examples of ranked (1–5) and filtered (F) constraints mined for the Dronology CPS.

Number	Constraint
1	**if event** state **occurs** data(armable) = true
2	**if event** waypoint **occurs** data(location/z) $\geq$ 5 **and** data(location/z) $\leq$ 30
3	**if event** startRoute **occurs event** endRoute **occurs within** 147 seconds
4	**if event** handshake **occurs event** state **occurs within** 2 seconds
5	**if event** handshake **occurs event** state **occurs with** state.data(status) = 'STANDBY' **within** 2 seconds
F_1	**if event** state **occurs** data(status) = 'STANDBY'
F_2	**if event** handshake **occurs event** state **occurs with** state.data(armable) = true **within** 2 seconds

available, we therefore use information on the *scope* of the events in a complex system architecture for our mining process. Scopes can represent both hardware and software components of the CPS. Depending on the level of detail of the available instrumentation a scope may represent, e.g., an entire system in the CPS or an individual process or machine. It is further possible that certain systems (and thus scopes) exist multiple times within a CPS. For instance, D_1 may be the scope of all events that represent actions and messages of drone D_1, while events produced by a second drone D_2 may have the scope D_2. In this example, each drone will produce the same types of events and data. However, their instances still have to be analyzed individually during constraint mining. Our mining approach can also deal with event logs that do not contain scopes. In this case, we either assume a default scope for events or derive scope information from event names.

3   Constraint Mining Approach

Our mining approach takes event logs as input and produces temporal, value, and hybrid constraints. The approach can be split into five steps (cf. Algorithm 1):

Step 0 – Creating a Uniform Event Representation. In this preparatory step the input event log files are parsed to facilitate further processing of the data. We use an event object structure to make our approach independent of the type and format of the inputs. Our parser supports event log files recorded with our monitoring tool REMINDS [23] but can easily be adapted to new file types, event types, and event data elements. We also check if all events and event data elements are valid and contain an event type and a timestamp. In addition events can contain scope information and event data elements of different types.

Algorithm 1. Constraint mining approach.

```
 1: function MINECONSTRAINTS(LogFiles)
 2:     EventLog ← parse(LogFiles)                                                    ▷ step 0
 3:     SequenceTypes, Constraints ← detectSequenceTypes(EventLog)                    ▷ step 1
 4:     for all s ∈ SequenceTypes do
 5:         Instances ← getInstances(EventLog, s)        ▷ extract sequence instances matching s
 6:         Vectors, Constraints ← createFeatureVectors(Instances, Constraints)       ▷ step 2
 7:         Constraints ← analyze(Vectors, Constraints)                              ▷ step 3
 8:     end for
 9:     return filterAndRank(Constraints, EventLog)                                   ▷ step 4
10: end function
```

Algorithm 2. Detecting sequences (approach: step 1).

```
 1: function DETECTSEQUENCETYPES(EventLog)
 2:     SequenceTypes ← ∅, Constraints ← ∅
 3:     for all s ∈ Scopes do
 4:         Events ← {e | e ∈ EventLog ∧ e.scope = s}
 5:         F ← extractFragments(Events)                                    ▷ cf. Algorithm 3
 6:         SeqT_s ← combineFragments(F)                    ▷ sequence types of s; cf. Algorithm 4
 7:         SeqT_s ← SeqT_s ∪ extend(SeqT_s, EventLog) ▷ extend with event types from other scopes
 8:         for all seq ∈ SeqT_s do
 9:             Constraints ← Constraints ∪ createTemporalConstraint(seq)
10:         end for
11:         EventTypes_s ← {e.type | e ∈ Events ∧ |{a | a ∈ Events ∧ a.type = e.type}| ≥ 5}
12:         SequenceTypes ← SequenceTypes ∪ F ∪ SeqT_s ∪ EventTypes_s
13:     end for
14:     return (SequenceTypes, Constraints)
15: end function
```

Step 1 – Detecting Event Sequence Types. Our mining approach detects event sequence types within an event log, as described in Algorithm 2, thereby mining temporal constraints (line 9). For each scope `extractFragments` (cf. Algorithm 2 line 5 and Algorithm 3) extracts pairs of event types (a, b), where a is followed by b at a configurable rate θ (in our experiments it was set to 95% based on previous tests). Examples for such sequence fragments mined for Dronology include `startRoute–waypoint` and `startRoute–endRoute`.

Distinguishing different instances of a scope becomes essential in cases such as Dronology, where multiple drones of the same type concurrently produce events. The different drones, i.e., scope instances, execute routes simultaneously, meaning, that Dronology receives events from multiple drones, e.g., two `startRoute` events before the first `endRoute` event. Assigning these events correctly to the different scope instances is thus necessary to avoid incorrectly mined constraints. Our mining approach calls `extractFragments` (Algorithm 2 line 5) for each scope instance of the current scope s and merges the extracted co-occurrence information, before executing `combineFragments` (line 6). As a result events belonging to different scope instances do not interfere with each other and constraints are extracted using the combined information from all scope instances.

The sequence fragments are then combined in `combineFragments` (cf. Algorithm 2 line 6 and Algorithm 4) such that the average time of the resulting sequence is minimal. After extracting the sequence types from one scope, our algorithm searches for events from other scopes that can be fit into the already

Algorithm 3. Extracting sequence fragments (approach: step 1).

1: **function** EXTRACTFRAGMENTS(*Events*)
2:    $F \leftarrow \varnothing$
3:    $EventTypes \leftarrow \{e.type \mid e \in Events\}$
4:    **for all** $(a, b) \in \{(x, y) \mid (x, y) \in EventTypes \times EventTypes \wedge x \neq y\}$ **do**
5:       $E_a \leftarrow \{e \mid e \in Events \wedge e.type = a\}$
6:       $E_b \leftarrow \{e \mid e \in Events \wedge e.type = b\}$
7:       $ConseqE \leftarrow \{(e_{a1}, e_{a2}) \mid (e_{a1}, e_{a2}) \in E_a \times E_a$
             $\wedge \, (\exists e_b \mid e_b \in E_b \wedge e_{a1}.timestamp < e_b.timestamp < e_{a2}.timestamp)$
             $\wedge \, (\nexists x \mid x \in E_a \wedge e_{a1}.timestamp < x.timestamp < e_{a2}.timestamp)\}$
             ▷ Two consecutive events of type a with at least one event of type b in between
8:       **if** $\dfrac{|ConseqE|}{\max(1, |E_a|-1)} > \theta$ **then**   ▷ Configurable threshold θ
9:          $F \leftarrow F \cup \{(a, b)\}$
10:      **end if**
11:   **end for**
12:   **return** F
13: **end function**

Algorithm 4. Combining sequence fragments (approach: step 1).

1: **function** COMBINEFRAGMENTS(F)
2:    $SequenceTypes \leftarrow \varnothing$
3:    **while** $F \neq \varnothing$ **do**
4:       $seq \leftarrow f \mid (f \in F \wedge (\nexists x \mid x \in F \wedge x.duration < f.duration))$
5:       **while** $\exists a \mid a \in F \wedge \text{combine}(seq, a) \neq \varnothing$ **do**   ▷ seq can be extended further
6:          $n \leftarrow a \mid a \in F \wedge \text{combine}(seq, a) \neq \varnothing \wedge (\nexists b \mid b \in F \wedge \text{combine}(seq, b).duration <$
             $\text{combine}(seq, a).duration)$
7:          $seq \leftarrow \text{combine}(seq, n)$ ▷ extend the sequence type with fragment n
8:          $F \leftarrow F \setminus \{b \in F \mid b.partOf(seq)\}$
9:       **end while**
10:      $SequenceTypes \leftarrow SequenceTypes \cup seq$
11:   **end while**
12:   **return** $SequenceTypes$
13: **end function**

---

extracted sequences. For each pair of subsequent event types A and B within the sequence, we thus determine the frequency f of events from other scopes to appear between these two events. If f exceeds a (configurable) threshold – in our experiments the threshold was set to 0.9 as it yielded the best results – the event type is added between A and B. In addition to event sequence types also event types with at least five instances are extracted and analyzed in the following steps (cf. line 11 in Algorithm 2).

After detecting the (abstract) event sequence types, we extract the individual event sequence instances (i.e., events that together match the event sequence type pattern) from the recorded event log (getInstances in line 5 in Algorithm 1). Additionally, we compute the time between the first and the last event of each sequence instance to estimate the maximum time for the respective temporal constraint. When estimating the maximum time, we remove outliers, i.e., event sequence instances that take much longer than the majority of the instances. Constraint #3 shown in Table 1 is an example of a constraint that is mined in the first step.

Step 2 – Creating Feature Vectors. For each extracted event sequence instance i our approach generates a feature vector as $\{f \mid f \in e.fields \wedge e \in i.events\}$. We extract data fields that have the same value in all feature vectors as value constraints. If the data field does not belong to the the trigger event, it is additionally extracted as hybrid constraint candidate, as the event might also occur independent from this sequence – possibly with different values for this data element. Constraints #1 and F_1 shown in Table 1 are an example of a value and a hybrid constraint mined from one sequence (`handshake-state`) for the same data element (`state.armable` indicating that the drone is ready for take off). For the same sequence also constraints #5 and F_2 are mined for field `state.status`. The status for a drone that just connected to the system, i.e., right after the handshake, is always reported as 'STANDBY' – indicating that the drone is currently waiting to be assigned a route. However, when a drone is currently executing a route, the status is reported as 'ACTIVE'.

Step 3 – Analyzing Feature Vectors. We next analyze the feature vectors as shown in Algorithm 5. For numeric event data elements we extract an interval that contains all observed values (cf. line 7). An example for this is constraint #2 in Table 1. We also extract all event data elements that have a constant value for a majority of all sequences (cf. line 10). The threshold for the extraction is set to $1 - \epsilon$, which is also used during filtering in step 4. If the data element does not belong to the first event of the sequence, the constraint is mined both as a value constraint and a hybrid constraint referring to the first event of the sequence, as also done for constant values in step 2.

Additionally, our algorithm detects multiple data elements that have the same value in each feature vector and extract them as a hybrid constraint, if the fields belong to two different events, or as a value constraint, if they belong to the same event (cf. line 15). For instance, in the event sequence type `handshake-state` the two events always report the same coordinates (event data element `location`), because the handshake is complete when the drone is still on the ground and therefore not moving.

Step 4 – Filtering and Ranking Constraints. Constraints that violate very often (evaluate to false) are typically not realistic and thus unlikely to be selected by the user. Therefore, our algorithm filters all constraints that violate more often than a defined error rate ϵ for all event sequences from the complete event log to reduce the number of false positives. However, a strict threshold would overly limit the number of available constraint candidates – especially considering that the user might adapt the constraint candidates to better fit the actual behavior of the system. In our experiments we set ϵ to one third. As a result, for example, the constraint candidate F_1 in Table 1 that is only fulfilled for 23% of all `state` events in the event log is removed from the list.

Our algorithm also detects and filters duplicate constraints or constraints referring to the same event data element. Duplicates are created, e.g., if a constraint for a data element is mined for both an event sequence type and the

Algorithm 5. Analyzing feature vectors (approach: step 3).

```
 1: function ANALYZE(Vectors, Constraints)
 2:     Fields ← {f | f ∈ v.fields ∧ v ∈ Vectors}              ▷ all fields of all feature vectors
 3:     Names ← {f.name | f ∈ Fields}
 4:     for all fieldName ∈ Names do
 5:         Values ← {f.value | f ∈ Fields ∧ f.name = fieldName}
 6:         if ∀x ∈ Values | x ∈ ℝ then
 7:             Constraints ← Constraints ∪ createValueConstraint(fieldName, min(Values),
                    max(Values))
 8:         end if
 9:         if ∃val ∈ Values | ( |{v ∈ Vectors | v.fieldName = val}| / |Vectors| > 1 − ϵ ) then    ▷ error rate ϵ
10:             Constraints ← Constraints ∪ createValueConstraint(fieldName, val) ∪
                    createHybridConstraint(fieldName, val)
11:         end if
12:     end for
13:     for all {x, y} ∈ Names × Names | x ≠ y do
14:         if |{v ∈ Vectors | v.x = v.y}| / |Vectors| > 1 − ϵ then
15:             Constraints ← Constraints ∪ createValueOrHybridConstraint(x, y)
16:         end if
17:     end for
18:     return Constraints
19: end function
```

individual event. If multiple instances of the constraint contain the same value for the event data element, the duplicates can simply be removed. However, if multiple constraints containing different values remain (e.g., one constraint with a constant and one with an interval), the algorithm keeps constraints based on the constraint type – keeping more general constraints – and the percentage of positive evaluations – keeping constraints with a higher accuracy. For example, in Table 1 both the first and the last constraint refer to the field `armable` of the event `state`. In this case the more general value constraint (#1) is kept over the more specific hybrid constraint (F_2). Additionally, our algorithm supports users in completely filtering constraint candidates matching particular rules, e.g., to only consider temporal constraints. Our algorithm then ranks the remaining constraints by accuracy and number of evaluations: $\frac{|\#\text{fulfilled}|}{|\#\text{evaluated}|} + \frac{|\#\text{evaluated}|}{|\max(\#\text{evaluated})|}$.

4   Evaluation

We evaluate our approach regarding its usefulness and scalability to address the following two research questions:

- *RQ 1.* How useful are the temporal constraints, value constraints, and hybrid constraints automatically mined by analyzing event logs recorded from CPS?
- *RQ 2.* Does the proposed approach scale to large event logs recorded from real-world CPS?

We followed the research process depicted in Fig. 1 to evaluate our approach by applying it to two real-world systems (cf. Sect. 4.1), which are available to us as part of ongoing research collaborations. Domain experts instrumented these systems to produce event logs, which we then used as input for our constraint

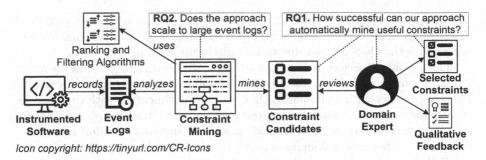

Fig. 1. Research process.

mining approach. Domain experts further gave us feedback on the mined constraints. The resulting datasets are of realistic size, and are thus a good basis for evaluating both the usefulness and scalability of our approach.

We obtained feedback from the main developers of each system on the usefulness of the constraint candidates. This was done in two steps: (1) In a pilot phase we sent a first subset with different types of constraints to the domain experts to get quick feedback on the mined results, primarily for identifying potential problems of parsing the event logs. We also configured the mining approach to their needs by applying type filters. Specifically, the domain expert for the first system was primarily interested in temporal and hybrid constraints, while all types of constraints were considered as relevant for the second system. (2) We then applied the mining approach and sent the full set of mined constraints to the domain experts. We asked the domain experts to assess each constraint using one of the following options: *yes*, i.e., select this mined constraint for monitoring; *yes with minor changes*, i.e., select this constraint after small adjustments (e.g., of certain parameters or operators defined in the constraint); and *no*, i.e., don't further consider this constraint. We also motivated experts to add comments providing a rationale for their decisions and asked them to assess the criticality of each constraint: while highly critical constraints help to detect major errors during monitoring, constraints of low importance can provide useful warnings. We used a follow-up questionnaire with open questions to get qualitative feedback on possibly missing constraints, ideas for new constraints, and how surprising the experts found the mined constraints.

4.1 Systems and Datasets

The first dataset includes events monitored from an industrial plant automation system of our industry partner Primetals Technologies. Engineers of Primetals Technologies used the REMINDS monitoring tool [23] to record a 24-hour event log from an automation system running in a metallurgical plant in China during production. Specifically, the events were recorded from the Quality Control System (QCS) system that collects and analyses data from different processes within a metallurgical plant. The dataset contains a total of 18,239 events with

35 different event types from four different scopes. Data on process identifiers, descriptions, sensor values, etc. is attached to about 90% of the events. We cannot publish the QCS dataset due to non-disclosure agreements.

The second dataset contains events from a CPS controlling drones using the Dronology framework [2], already used in simplified form as a running example. Dronology comes with a simulator, that allows experimenting with drones using exactly the same control software system, but not the actual hardware. To create our dataset, we used two pre-defined and simultaneously running scenarios – designed together with a domain expert – in which five drones performed a total of 105 flights in the simulator. In the first scenario two drones are used to deliver items from one central warehouse to one of ten different customer locations and return back to the warehouse. In the second scenario three drones perform random aerial maneuvers at a flight field. The Dronology dataset contains a total of 15,200 events with five different event types from five different scopes (i.e., the five different drones). 14,560 of these events are state events that are sent approximately once every second by each of the five drones capturing status values the drones report, such as position, direction, and speed. The Dronology dataset can be downloaded from http://mevss.jku.at/?attachment_id=3056.

4.2   Constraint Mining Results (RQ1)

To address *RQ1*, we analyzed, for each dataset, the number of *yes, yes with minor changes*, and *no* options the domain expert selected; the expert's comments regarding criticality; and the qualitative feedback. Constraints rated with *yes* and *yes with minor changes* can be used for monitoring and are therefore regarded as useful in this evaluation. However, constraints rated with *no* might still give valuable insights, e.g., by revealing unintended behavior or as basis for new constraints. Following our research process we initially showed a subset of different constraint candidates mined for the datasets to the respective domain expert and asked for initial feedback. We included rather diverse constraint candidates to illustrate the different types of constraints that can be mined by the algorithm. We used this initial feedback to define constraint type filters for the different datasets, but not for the actual evaluation. In a second round we used the approach to create a full list of constraint candidates for each of the systems.

Quality Control System. Our approach could mine a total of 34 temporal and hybrid constraint candidates from the QCS dataset. Following the feedback from the initial round, we excluded all value constraints for the final candidate list. Out of the 34 mined constraints, the domain expert rated 25 as useful: two constraints were rated as *yes* and 23 were rated as *yes with minor changes*. The domain expert added comments to eleven yes-with-minor-changes constraint candidates to indicate high similarity with already selected constraints. Only nine out of the 34 constraints were marked with *no*. Overall, the domain expert thus regarded 74% (25/34) of the mined constraints as useful, 41% (14/34) can be regarded as immediately usable in the monitoring infrastructure.

The domain expert rated 15 of the 25 useful constraint candidates as *important* (i.e., could result in problems but would not lead to a crash) and ten as *interesting* (i.e., provides useful warnings or information). While no constraint was rated as *critical* (i.e., would lead to a system crash), this could be expected, as the system under investigation is a quality control system that collects information and does not directly influence the metallurgical process.

The overall feedback we received was very positive stating that "important relations between events are detected" and that some of the mined constraint candidates can be used as inspiration for writing new constraints. However, although meaningful, some of the constraint candidates were highly similar, differing only in the data elements they check, and so probably only some of them would be selected in practice. The expert did not report about any constraints that he expected, but were not found by our algorithm.

Dronology. From the Dronology dataset our approach mined a total of 50 constraint candidates – six temporal constraints, 18 hybrid constraints, and 26 value constraints. Of these 50 constraint candidates, the domain expert rated nine as *yes*, 18 as *yes with minor changes*, and 16 as *no*. The remaining seven constraints could not be rated, because they check values for which the domain expert could not assess the correctness of the thresholds. These constraints are therefore neglected in the remainder of the evaluation. The domain expert rated eight constraints as *critical*, ten as *important*, and six as *interesting*. For three constraint candidates, the domain expert defined the criticality as *sanity check*, i.e., these constraints check the correct setup of the control system and the drones. Overall, 27/43 constraints, i.e., 63%, were regarded as useful by the domain expert for the Dronology system.

A strength of our approach is that it can mine temporal, value, and hybrid constraints. The domain expert provided feedback that for Dronology value constraints are more useful than temporal constraints. This feedback shows a fundamental difference to the QCS, for which value constraints were regarded as less relevant. We also received feedback that some of the constraint candidates could be used as a basis for developing further checks – also based on data that is not yet logged by the drones, such as proper compass calibration.

4.3   Performance of Mining (RQ2)

To address *RQ2*, we instrumented our mining algorithms to measure the execution time of our overall approach for different event logs of different size. We used subsets of the two datasets – starting with 500 events and incrementing the size up to the full set. We additionally created larger sets containing up to 100,000 events by combining multiple instances of the original datasets. All experiments were performed using the same computer, equipped with an Intel® Core™ i7-6700 processor and 16 GB RAM, with 8 GB of memory given to the evaluation runs. To balance out variations in the runtime we repeated the process 100 times for both datasets. To reduce the influence of the warm-up time we excluded the

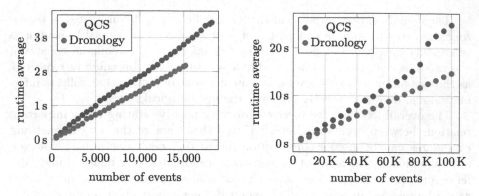

Fig. 2. Average runtime of the constraint mining algorithm (RQ2).

first run for each experiment and report the average for the remaining 99 runs. For each of the subsets we used our constraint mining approach and recorded the time required for the mining. The runtime for the QCS dataset is on average 39% higher than the runtime for the Dronology subsets. This difference can be explained with the higher number of distinct event types (35 in the QCS dataset vs. five in the Dronology dataset) and the higher amount of data (data per event in the QCS dataset is nine times the size of the data per event in the Dronology dataset).

Figure 2 shows the average runtime for mining for both datasets. The results show that the runtime of our approach grows almost linearly in relation to the number of events in the input for the system. The QCS dataset containing events recorded in 24 h is a very realistic use case and more than fit to evaluate our approach. Therefore it is a very positive result that even for the entire dataset our mining approach is completed within an average runtime of 3.4 s. For the (slightly smaller) Dronology dataset the algorithm completes in 2.2 s. Also the results for the experiments with multiple instances of the datasets shifted in time grows almost linearly – with only one discontinuity between 80,000 and 85,000 events for the QCS. This discontinuity results from the additional instances of certain event types. The runtime for the sets with 100,000 events is still very reasonable with 14.8 s for the Dronology set and 24.9 s for the QCS dataset. We can thus conclude that our approach scales well to large event logs recorded from real-world cyber-physical systems.

4.4   Threats to Validity

We evaluated our approach on two diverse datasets from two very different CPS. The results showed that our approach is useful for detecting different types of constraints in these cases. While we obviously cannot guarantee that our approach would work equally well in other domains or for other types of systems, the selected systems are representative examples of complex, distributed CPS. Furthermore, we had access to domain experts and developers, which gives our results higher credibility. Also, neither the domain experts instrumenting the systems nor the developers providing feedback on the mined constraints were involved in the development of the mining approach described in this paper.

Our evaluation also included qualitative feedback from domain experts. This is of course subjective and relies on their and our interpretations. Also, only one domain expert provided feedback for each dataset. However, we involved the lead developers of each system, who are best qualified to provide feedback on the usefulness of the mined constraints. Additionally, we checked the plausibility of the results by presenting them to multiple other experts during meetings. Overall, we regard such expert feedback as important to complement the otherwise quantitative data.

5   Related Work

The problem of automatically or semi-automatically extracting information such as specifications, constraints, invariants or validity rules by analyzing source code or output of software systems has been investigated in various research areas and for different purposes.

Specification mining [12] can be divided into static and dynamic approaches. Static mining analyzes the source code of a program to detect invariants, while dynamic mining uses the output of the program to compute specifications. Example applications of static specification mining include the detection of bugs [25] and the mining of correct API usage [20]. Both approaches extract the program behavior in the form of finite state machines (FSM). A combined approach is presented by Grant et al. [7], who integrate static and dynamic specification mining to extract and analyze the states of distributed applications.

Dynamic specification mining is closer related to our own approach, as we also analyze the event logs of software systems. For instance, our approach for detecting event sequences (cf. step 1) follows a similar idea as the approach presented by Gabel and Su [6], i.e., both approaches extract short sequences and combine them. Pattern mining approaches, e.g., the one by Lo et al. [11], classify software behaviors based on recorded system runs. Typically, repetitive series of events are used as a basis to define recurring behavior and to detect deviations from this behavior.

Several approaches have been proposed to mine different types of constraints. Ernst et al. [5] mine value constraints that hold at certain points in a program. Narayan et al. [17] mine temporal constraints extended with further restrictions on the execution time. The complex event processing approach by Margara et al. [16] aims to learn temporal constraints from event logs by collecting all constraints fulfilled for different event sequences and extracting those constraints fulfilled in all sequences.

Some dynamic specification mining approaches extract both temporal and value constraints. For instance, Lo and Maoz [13] extract temporal constraints in the form of scenarios and additionally extract value constraints that are fulfilled during these scenarios. Ammons et al. [1] semi-automatically construct finite state machines representing temporal program execution patterns and additionally capture attributes that have to remain constant throughout the execution. Similarly, Lorenzoli et al. [14] and Walkinshaw et al. [24] extract extended finite state machines that additionally contain value constraints for the edges.

Process mining approaches [21] also aim to find temporal constraints as part of creating models of existing processes. The modeled processes are not necessarily software executions, but can come from very different domains, such as workflow in hospitals or banks. Di Ciccio and Mecella [4] discover multiple different types of temporal processes from event traces. Debois et al. [3] create a process model from Dynamic Condition Response graphs. Maggi et al. [15] additionally use data attached to events to extract rules between pairs of events expressed in temporal logic that include checks on related data items.

Compared to existing work, our approach supports mining value constraints, temporal constraints, and hybrid constraints by combining different techniques. We further represent the constraints in an integrated manner using a constraint DSL, making their immediate use in a tool for monitoring CPS possible.

6   Conclusion and Future Work

We presented an approach to mine constraints from event logs recorded from CPS. Our approach is capable of mining different types of constraints in an integrated manner. The resulting constraints can be directly used in a monitoring tool. We have shown that our approach mines useful constraints for two CPS: a plant automation system and a system controlling drones. Domain experts reported that 74% and 63%, respectively, of the constraint candidates can be used for monitoring their systems. The performance analysis of the constraint mining algorithm showed that it scales well for both datasets. We are currently developing more specialized ranking and grouping approaches supporting users in selecting and adjusting useful constraints [8]. As part of our future work, we are planning to use our approach with event logs from other systems, especially from further application areas.

Acknowledgments. The financial support by the Austrian Federal Ministry for Digital and Economic Affairs, the National Foundation for Research, Technology and Development, and Primetals Technologies is gratefully acknowledged.

References

1. Ammons, G., Bodík, R., Larus, J.R.: Mining specifications. ACM SIGPLAN Not. **37**(1), 4–16 (2002)
2. Cleland-Huang, J., Vierhauser, M., Bayley, S.: Dronology: an incubator for cyber-physical systems research. In: Proceedings of the 40th International Conference on Software Engineering: New Ideas and Emerging Results, pp. 109–112. ACM (2018)
3. Debois, S., Hildebrandt, T.T., Laursen, P.H., Ulrik, K.R.: Declarative process mining for DCR graphs. In: Proceedings of the 32nd ACM SIGAPP Symposium on Applied Computing, pp. 759–764. ACM (2017)
4. Di Ciccio, C., Mecella, M.: A two-step fast algorithm for the automated discovery of declarative workflows. In: Proceedings of the 2013 IEEE Symposium on Computational Intelligence and Data Mining, pp. 135–142. IEEE (2013)
5. Ernst, M., et al.: The Daikon system for dynamic detection of likely invariants. Sci. Comput. Program. **69**(1), 35–45 (2007)
6. Gabel, M., Su, Z.: Javert: fully automatic mining of general temporal properties from dynamic traces. In: Proceedings of the 16th ACM SIGSOFT International Symposium on Foundations of Software Engineering, pp. 339–349. ACM (2008)
7. Grant, S., Cech, H., Beschastnikh, I.: Inferring and asserting distributed system invariants. In: Proceedings of the 40th International Conference on Software Engineering, pp. 1149–1159. ACM (2018)
8. Krismayer, T., Kronberger, P., Rabiser, R., Grünbacher, P.: Supporting the selection of constraints for requirements monitoring from automatically mined constraint candidates. In: Knauss, E., Goedicke, M. (eds.) REFSQ 2019. LNCS, vol. 11412, pp. 193–208. Springer, Cham (2019). https://doi.org/10.1007/978-3-030-15538-4_15
9. Krismayer, T., Rabiser, R., Grünbacher, P.: Mining constraints for event-based monitoring in systems of systems. In: Proceedings of the 32nd IEEE/ACM International Conference on Automated Software Engineering, pp. 826–831. IEEE (2017)
10. Lee, E.A.: Cyber physical systems: design challenges. In: 11th IEEE International Symposium on Object-oriented Real-Time Distributed Computing, pp. 363–369. IEEE (2008)
11. Lo, D., Cheng, H., Han, J., Khoo, S.C., Sun, C.: Classification of software behaviors for failure detection: a discriminative pattern mining approach. In: Proceedings of the International Conference on Knowledge Discovery and Data Mining, pp. 557–566. ACM (2009)
12. Lo, D., Khoo, S.C., Han, J., Liu, C.: Mining Software Specifications: Methodologies and Applications. CRC Press, Boca Raton (2011)
13. Lo, D., Maoz, S.: Scenario-based and value-based specification mining: better together. Autom. Softw. Eng. **19**(4), 423–458 (2012)
14. Lorenzoli, D., Mariani, L., Pezzè, M.: Automatic generation of software behavioral models. In: Proceedings of the 30th International Conference on Software Engineering, pp. 501–510. ACM (2008)
15. Maggi, F.M., Dumas, M., García-Bañuelos, L., Montali, M.: Discovering data-aware declarative process models from event logs. In: Daniel, F., Wang, J., Weber, B. (eds.) BPM 2013. LNCS, vol. 8094, pp. 81–96. Springer, Heidelberg (2013). https://doi.org/10.1007/978-3-642-40176-3_8
16. Margara, A., Cugola, G., Tamburrelli, G.: Learning from the past: automated rule generation for complex event processing. In: Proceedings of the 8th ACM International Conference on Distributed Event-Based Systems, pp. 47–58. ACM (2014)

17. Narayan, A., Cutulenco, G., Joshi, Y., Fischmeister, S.: Mining timed regular specifications from system traces. ACM Trans. Embed. Comput. Syst. **17**(2), 46:1–46:21 (2018)
18. Rabiser, R., Guinea, S., Vierhauser, M., Baresi, L., Grünbacher, P.: A comparison framework for runtime monitoring approaches. J. Syst. Softw. **125**, 309–321 (2017)
19. Rabiser, R., Thanhofer-Pilisch, J., Vierhauser, M., Grünbacher, P., Egyed, A.: Developing and evolving a DSL-based approach for runtime monitoring of systems of systems. Autom. Softw. Eng. **25**(4), 875–915 (2018)
20. Shoham, S., Yahav, E., Fink, S.J., Pistoia, M.: Static specification mining using automata-based abstractions. IEEE Trans. Soft. Eng. **34**(5), 651–666 (2008)
21. van der Aalst, W., et al.: Process mining manifesto. In: Daniel, F., Barkaoui, K., Dustdar, S. (eds.) BPM 2011. LNBIP, vol. 99, pp. 169–194. Springer, Heidelberg (2012). https://doi.org/10.1007/978-3-642-28108-2_19
22. Vardi, M.Y.: An automata-theoretic approach to linear temporal logic. In: Moller, F., Birtwistle, G. (eds.) Logics for Concurrency. LNCS, vol. 1043, pp. 238–266. Springer, Heidelberg (1996). https://doi.org/10.1007/3-540-60915-6_6
23. Vierhauser, M., Rabiser, R., Grünbacher, P., Seyerlehner, K., Wallner, S., Zeisel, H.: ReMinds: a flexible runtime monitoring framework for systems of systems. J. Syst. Softw. **112**, 123–136 (2016)
24. Walkinshaw, N., Taylor, R., Derrick, J.: Inferring extended finite state machine models from software executions. Empirical Softw. Eng. **21**(3), 811–853 (2016)
25. Weimer, W., Necula, G.C.: Mining temporal specifications for error detection. In: Halbwachs, N., Zuck, L.D. (eds.) TACAS 2005. LNCS, vol. 3440, pp. 461–476. Springer, Heidelberg (2005). https://doi.org/10.1007/978-3-540-31980-1_30

Behavior-Derived Variability Analysis: Mining Views for Comparison and Evaluation

Iris Reinhartz-Berger[✉], Ilan Shimshoni, and Aviva Abdal

Department of Information Systems, University of Haifa, Haifa, Israel
{iris,ishimshoni}@is.haifa.ac.il,
avivaab@bezeqint.net

Abstract. The large variety of computerized solutions (software and information systems) calls for a systematic approach to their comparison and evaluation.
Different methods have been proposed over the years for analyzing the similarity
and variability of systems. These methods get artifacts, such as requirements,
design models, or code, of different systems (commonly in the same domain),
identify and calculate their similarities, and represent the variability in models,
such as feature diagrams. Most methods rely on implementation considerations
of the input systems and generate outcomes based on predefined, fixed strategies
of comparison (referred to as *variability views*). In this paper, we introduce an
approach for mining relevant views for comparison and evaluation, based on the
input artifacts. Particularly, we equip SOVA – a Semantic and Ontological
Variability Analysis method – with data mining techniques in order to identify
relevant views that highlight variability or similarity of the input artifacts
(natural language requirement documents). The comparison is done using
entropy and Rand index measures. The method and its outcomes are evaluated
on a case of three photo sharing applications.

Keywords: Software Product Line Engineering · Variability analysis ·
Requirements specifications · Feature diagrams

1 Introduction

Analyzing similarities and differences between computerized solutions (software and
information systems) is important for different purposes, e.g., effective and efficient
software development and maintenance, market analysis of competing products, and
more. The field of Software Product Line Engineering (SPLE) [7, 19] introduces
different variability analysis methods whose purpose is to identify and determine the
precise similarities and differences among a family of software products (called Software Product Lines – SPL), as well as to specify and model the analysis outcomes.
A well-known variability modeling notation is feature diagrams [17], in which similarities and differences are organized in trees (sometimes graphs): the nodes represent
features – user-visible aspects, qualities, or characteristics of a system or systems, and
the edges represent dependencies among features (e.g., mandatory vs. optional features,
XOR - vs. OR-grouped features).

© Springer Nature Switzerland AG 2019
P. Giorgini and B. Weber (Eds.): CAiSE 2019, LNCS 11483, pp. 675–690, 2019.
https://doi.org/10.1007/978-3-030-21290-2_42

Different variability analysis methods may use various types of artifacts, such as requirements, design & architecture, and code [1]. In this work we focus on variability analysis based on natural language requirements, which is widely studied [3] and enables comparison and evaluation at early development stages. Moreover, requirements-based methods support analyzing the variability of systems which may be differently implemented but yet provide solutions to similar problems. Most methods use fixed, predefined strategies of comparison, which we call from now on *variability view* or *view* for short. The views are commonly inherited from the selected similarity metrics and do not reflect differences in stakeholders' preferences, tasks' characteristics, and input systems. Examples include methods which concentrate on similarities and differences in objects, components, or sub-systems (i.e., *structural views*), and methods that focus on variability in functions, methods, or services (i.e., *functional views*) [13].

In order to demonstrate the problems with fixed, predefined variability views, consider the two requirements of e-shop applications presented in Table 1. Variability analysis methods which follow a functional view will find similarities between the requirements, as both refer to client ordering. Variability analysis methods that consider a structural view, on the other hand, will find no similarities between these requirements (one refers to the inventory and the other to customer preferences). Thus, using the latter on requirements whose similarities are mainly functional is useless.

Table 1. Requirements of e-shop products

#	Requirement
1	When the customer orders a product, the system will update the inventory accordingly
2	The user can order up to 10 products in a single order. The system will record customer preferences

The above example illustrates the need to define variability views in a more flexible way, based on the input artifacts (requirements in our case). In this paper, we introduce a method that mines appropriate, relevant views based on characteristics of the compared systems and recommends how to analyze variability. Particularly, we extend SOVA – a Semantic and Ontological Variability Analysis [11–13], which supports different behavior-related views, with data mining techniques in order to explore how to compare and evaluate a given set of systems based on their requirements.

The rest of this paper is structured as follows. Section 2 reviews existing requirements-based variability analysis methods and elaborates on SOVA. Section 3 introduces our approach, while Sect. 4 presents preliminary results and discusses advantages and limitations. Finally, Sect. 5 summaries the work and suggests future research directions.

2   Related Work

Variability analysis in general and variability modeling in particular serve different purposes (and various stakeholders). These include management of existing variability, product   configuration,   requirements   specification,   derivation   of   product, design/architecture, planning of variability, domain modeling, software deployment, documentation, QA/testing, and marketing feature scoping [5]. For each such task, the required variability information may be different or differently represented. For example, variability modeling for planning purposes use feature-based representation, as the coarser and more abstract notion of features (as opposed to lower-level decisions or variation points) facilitates planning [5]. Design and architecture may concentrate on the variability of components, whereas marketing and QA tasks are more likely to be interested in the variability of functions, actions, and services [12]. However, most (requirements-based) variability analysis methods do not support such flexibility in views. We next review requirements-based variability analysis methods in Sect. 2.1 and elaborate in Sect. 2.2 on a specific method, SOVA – Semantic and Ontological Variability Analysis [13], which is extended in this work.

2.1 Requirements-Based Variability Analysis

Recent studies systematically review or map variability analysis methods. The work in [1] points on 55 primary resources of requirements-based methods, making it the second largest group (after source code-based methods). Examples of requirement artifacts used by these methods are specifications, feature descriptions, customer requests, test suites, and documentation. Concentrating on natural language requirements, the work in [3] identifies four main phases in variability analysis: (1) Requirement assessment, which involves scrapping product descriptions and retrieving legacy documents; (2) Term extraction, which uses text processing techniques; (3) Feature identification, where similarity measures and clustering algorithms are used for extracting features; and (4) Formation of feature diagrams (or other variability models). As the two aforementioned systematic reviews do not explicitly refer to variability views, we briefly review here existing requirements-based variability analysis methods and their main relevant characteristics (see Table 2 for a summary).

FENL [2] is an approach for Feature Extraction for reuse of Natural Language requirements. It extracts phrases that can represent software features from software reviews and uses combinations of nouns, verbs, and/or adjectives to identify objects and actions that expose software functionalities. Latent Semantic Analysis (LSA) with Singular Value Decomposition (SVD) [9] is used for calculating similarity.

BUT4Reuse [15] supports bottom-up adoption of SPLs from different artifact types. With respect to requirements, it uses Requirements Interchange Format (ReqIF) [18] and Wu and Palmer (WUP) natural language comparison technique [24].

The method in [8] analyzes variability based on a set of informal and incomplete product descriptions. The process includes extracting and naming features, mining feature associations and implications, extracting feature hierarchy and identifying cross-tree constraints and OR-grouped features. The similarity is computed as the inner product of the corresponding descriptor vectors (tf-idf – term frequency-inverse document frequency – is used to assign weights).

The method in [4] introduces an approach to automatically extract product comparison matrices (PCM) from a set of informal product descriptions written in a natural language. The process includes term recognition, contrastive analysis, information extraction, clustering, and syntactical heuristic similarities (namely, edit distance and other metrics based on words' morphology).

In [10], a method is suggested for mining common and variant features from publicly available documents of competitors (brochures). The method is based on contrastive analysis [6] which aims at detecting terms (conceptually independent linguistic units, which are composed of single or multiple words) that are specific for the domain of the documents under consideration. Commonality (i.e., identity similarity) refers to the domain-specific terms that are common to all the documents.

Table 2. Requirements-based variability analysis methods

Source	Input format	Similarity metric	Description
FENL [2]	Textual software reviews	LSA with SVD	The approach supports extracting software functionalities from key phrases and combinations of nouns, verbs, and/or adjectives
BUT4Reuse [15]	ReqIF files	WUP	The framework provides support for extracting a common internal representation of the artifact variants, identifying blocks, identifying and locating features, and discovering constraints
Davril et al. [8]	Product descriptions	Vectors product + tf-idf	The method supports building feature diagrams from informal and incomplete product descriptions
Ben Nasr [4]	Product descriptions	Syntactical heuristics	The method synthesizes product comparison matrices (PCM) from a set of product descriptions utilizing term recognition, information extraction, clustering, and syntactical heuristic similarities
Ferrari et al. [10]	Brochures	Identity	Employing contrastive analysis, the method supports extracting domain-specific terms and their comparison.
Niu et al. [17]	Software Requirements Specifications (SRS)	Identity	The method extracts (action-oriented) Functional Requirements Profiles (FRP) and use them for generating Orthogonal Variability Models (OVM)
SOVA [12]	Textual (functional) requirements	MCS	The method uses ontological and semantic considerations to compare behaviors (initial state, external events, and final states) extracted from functional requirements. A set of weights and thresholds enables generation of different feature diagrams, reflecting different views

The method in [17] suggests extracting Functional Requirements Profiles (FRP) from Software Requirements Specifications (SRS). The FRPs are defined to be action-oriented (represented by "verb–DO" pairs). The validated extraction constructs are amenable to semantic case analysis and Orthogonal Variability Modeling (OVM) [19], so as to uncover the variation structure and constraints.

The approaches reviewed above and summarized in Table 2 support specific variability views, which are commonly inherited from the used similarity metrics. Acknowledging the existence of different ways to compare systems in general and requirements in particular, the suitability of these methods for different variability analysis tasks is limited. SOVA, described next, tries to tackle this concern by supporting a variety of behavior-related views.

2.2 SOVA

SOVA – Semantic and Ontological Variability Analysis [11–13, 21] – analyzes the similarity and variability of functional software requirements written in a natural language. This is done in a three-step process: behavior extraction, similarity calculation, and variability analysis. First, the method extracts the behaviors specified in the requirements and represents them as triplets: the *initial state* of the system before the behavior occurs (the pre-condition), the *external event* that triggers the behavior, and the *final state* of the system after the behavior occurs (the post-condition or outcomes). Each *behavioral component* (i.e., initial state, external event, final state) is further represented by *behavioral vectors* of the form (actor, action, object), where *actor* refers to *who* performs the behavior, *action – what* is performed, and *object – on what* it (the action) is performed[1]. The behavioral component of a requirement may be composed of multiple behavioral vectors. Table 3 exemplifies the results of the behavior extraction step in SOVA on the two requirements from Table 1.

Second, the method calculates similarity by comparing the behaviors component-wise: behaviors with similar initial states, similar external events, and similar final states are the most similar ones. The similarity of two requirements is calculated as the weighted average of similarities of their behavioral components, whereas the similarity of two behavioral components is calculated as the weighted average of the similarities of their corresponding roles (actor, action, and object). Role-level similarity is calculated based on Mihalcea-Corley-Strapparava (MCS) method [16], which combines corpus-based and knowledge-based semantic measures. More details on the similarity calculations in SOVA can be found in [13].

Finally, the variability among the input files (requirements documents) is analyzed to identify optionality and common combinations of requirements. To this end, SOVA uses a variant of the hierarchical agglomerative clustering algorithm [22], which is a "bottom-up" approach: each element (requirement in our case) starts in its own cluster, and pairs of "similar" clusters are iteratively merged until similarity goes beyond a pre-defined threshold (0.7 in our case). For defining similarity of clusters, we used *complete*

---

[1] SOVA refers to a fourth role – instrument – *how* is the action performed? Due to the absence of this part in our example, we exclude it from the discussion.

linkage: the distance between two clusters is defined as *the longest distance (the lowest similarity)* between two elements in these clusters. The outcomes of this step are represented in feature diagrams [14], where the compared requirements are at the leaves level and inner nodes represent clusters of similar requirements.

The similarity calculation (step #2) can be manually tuned by six weights (three for the different roles and three for the different behavioral components). The weight vectors may represent different variability views. A *structural view*, for example, concentrates on differences in objects in the initial and/or final states of the behaviors, whereas a *functional view* focuses on variability in actions of external events. Table 4 presents the results of comparing the two requirements from Table 1 using: (1) a structural view where the weights of the object role and the final state behavioral component is 1, and (2) a functional view where the weight of the external event behavioral component is 1 and the weights of the action and object roles are 0.7 and 0.3 respectively (as functionality is mainly determined by the action but also by the object on which the action is performed). We observe high differences between the similarity calculations of the same two requirements, which are highly similar with respect to structure (0.9 out of 1.0) and poorly similar with respect to functionality (0.22 out of 1.0). Note that different weight vectors can represent similar views. Moreover, additional structural, functional, and other behavior-related views exist, each of which realizes a different way to compare the same set of requirements. We refer to these observations in a more formal way in Sect. 3.

Table 3. Extraction of behaviors of the requirements from Table 1 in SOVA; each behavioral component is represented via vectors of the form (actor, action, object)

	Initial state	External event	Final state
#1	—	(customer, order, product)	(system, update, inventory)
#2	—	(user, order, up to 10 products)	(system, record, customer preferences)

Table 4. Example of comparison options for the requirements from Table 1

	Component level weights			Role level weights			Overall similarity
	Initial state	External event	Final state	Actor	Action	Object	
Final state structure	0	0	1	0	0	1	0.22
Event functionality	0	1	0	0	0.7	0.3	0.9

Empirically evaluating the usefulness of SOVA [13], it appears to create outputs that are comprehensible to humans. However, it seems that the selection of the variability view may help or confuse the users in performing certain tasks, e.g., performing functionality-related variability tasks via structural views or vice versa. Moreover, currently the decision on variability views in SOVA is not guided and requires ad hoc setting of values to the different weights, where the consequences are not clear upfront. To tackle these obstacles, we suggest a systematic approach which analyzes the input requirements and recommends on relevant variability views.

3 Mining Variability Views from Software Requirements

The suggested approach utilizes data mining techniques. Figure 1 provides an overview. First, variability analysis is performed in SOVA using different *settings* (namely, weight vectors). The analysis includes behavior extraction and similarity calculation & clustering[2]. Then, the variability mining phase is introduced. We next elaborate in Sect. 3.1 on its first step – intra-view evaluation, and in Sect. 3.2 on its second step – cross-view evaluation. Although the method is applied to requirements-based variability analysis and SOVA, it can be used with other methods and artifact types. Hence, the method is specified and discussed for the general case and exemplified on SOVA.

3.1 Intra-view Evaluation

The inputs for the variability mining phase in general and for the intra-view evaluation in particular are the comparison results of the variability analysis phase and specifically the similarity results. We represent them as quadruplets as follows.

Definition 1. A *comparison result* is a quadruplet of the form (r_1, r_2, s, sim), where r_1, r_2 are the compared requirements, s is the setting used for the comparison (typically defined by values to weights, parameters, and thresholds), and sim is the similarity value indicating the degree of similarity of requirements r_1, r_2, under setting s.

Table 4 exemplified two comparison results, $(r_1, r_2, s_1, 0.22)$ and $(r_1, r_2, s_2, 0.9)$ which refer to the same pair of requirements r_1, r_2, but different settings and similarity values.

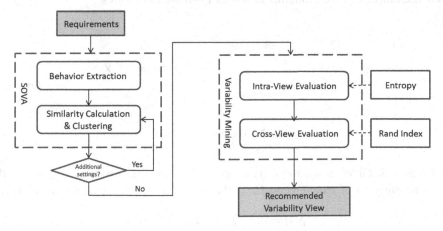

Fig. 1. An overview of the suggested method

---

[2] Clustering is done as part of the third step in SOVA – variability analysis; the other part of this step – feature diagram generation – is not required for the current work.

To evaluate the "relevance" of a particular setting to compare a given set of requirements, we need to measure the amount of "disorder" in order to identify settings according to which the requirements can be considered similar, but still variability can be observed. In other words, we aim to avoid cases in which all requirements are clustered in a single cluster ("too similar") or each requirement appears in a separate cluster ("too different"). To this end, we use the notion of *entropy*, which is well known in the field of machine learning. Below we define and explain entropy in our context.

Definition 2. Given a setting s and a set of clusters $\{C_1, C_2, \ldots C_n\}$ grouping the comparison results of s, the *entropy* of s is calculated as follows.

$$\Omega(s) = -\sum_{i=1..n} p_i \log_2 p_i,$$

where: p_i is the fraction of requirements in cluster C_i (in setting s).

As noted, both minimal and maximal values of entropies for a given set of requirements are not desirable. The minimal value of entropy (Ω_{min}) is obtained when all requirements appear in the same cluster. In this case, $\Omega_{min} = 0$. This means that the setting could not "properly" differentiate between the input requirements. The maximal value of entropy (Ω_{max}) is obtained when each requirement appears in a different cluster. If M is the overall number of requirements, $W_{max} = -\log_2 1/M$. Such a setting is "irrelevant" for comparing the given requirements because it highlights requirements' uniqueness and finds no similarities. Thus, the settings we would like to recommend are those that are not close to the boundaries ($\Omega_{min}, \Omega_{max}$), e.g., settings s2, s3, and s4 in Fig. 2. In order to achieve this, the method orders the settings according to their relevance, i.e., their minimal distances from the boundaries.

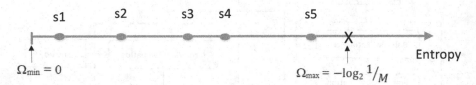

Fig. 2. The axis of entropy

Definition 3. Given a setting s, its entropy $\Omega(s)$ and the maximal entropy of the corresponding set of requirements Ω_{max}, the *relevance* of s is calculated as follows:

$$\rho(s) = \min(\Omega(s), \ \Omega_{max} - \Omega(s))$$

The higher the relevance score is, the more relevant the setting may be for comparing the given set of requirements. In Fig. 2, the intra-view evaluation step results in the following (partially) ordered list of settings: (1) S3; (2) S4; (3) S2; (4) S1, S5. The top K settings are passed to the next step – cross-view evaluation.

3.2 Cross-View Evaluation

The previous step separately evaluates the relevance of each setting. Yet, it should be noted that the settings may be related to each other. In SOVA, for example, different settings may represent similar variability views. Table 5 demonstrates seven possible settings: setting #1 represents a mixed view, in which similar weights are given to the behavioral components (namely, initial state, external event, and final state) and there is a preference of action and object similarities over actor similarity; settings #2 to #4 specify functional views which clearly prefer similarities in actions and events (the differences in these settings refer to the weight of object similarity); finally, settings #5 to #7 specify structural variability views which clearly prefer similarities in states and objects (the differences here refer to the weights of initial vs. final state similarities).

To perform cross-view evaluation, we use the notion of Rand-index [20], which is known in data clustering for measuring the similarity between two clustering outcomes. Rand index in our context is defined as follows.

Definition 4. Given two settings, s1 and s2, Rand index, R, is calculated as:

$$R(s1, s2) = \frac{a+b}{\binom{n}{2}} = \frac{a+b}{\frac{n(n-1)}{2}},$$

where:

- a is the number of requirement pairs that are in the same cluster in s1 and in the same cluster in s2.
- b is the number of requirements pairs that are in different clusters in s1 and in different clusters in s2.
- n is the overall number of requirements.

Table 5. Examples of possible settings in SOVA

#	Initial state	External event	Final state	Actor	Action	Object	Comment
1	0.33	0.34	0.33	0.2	0.4	0.4	Mixed
2	0.0	1.0	0.0	0.0	0.5	0.5	Functional
3	0.0	1.0	0.0	0.0	0.7	0.3	Functional
4	0.0	1.0	0.0	0.0	1.0	0.0	Functional
5	0.0	0.0	1.0	0.0	0.0	1.0	Structural
6	1.0	0.0	0.0	0.0	0.0	1.0	Structural
7	0.5	0.0	0.5	0.0	0.0	1.0	Structural

We chose Rand index rather than other clustering comparison measures, since it does not require the existence of a base ("correct") clustering (as opposed to F-Measure or confusion matrix). However, it takes into consideration only the leaves level, neglecting the structure of the generated feature diagrams. In the future we intend to explore the integration of tree similarity measures to support comparison of clustering refinements.

Rand index ranges between 0 and 1. The higher Rand index is, the more similar the settings are. This may indicate that they represent the same or similar variability views. When evaluating the quality of a clustering (with respect to similarity to the expected outcomes), the following heuristics have been suggested [23]: (a) Rand index values greater than 0.90 are viewed as excellent clustering, (b) values greater than 0.80 are considered good clustering, (c) values greater than 0.65 reflect moderate clustering, and (d) values smaller than 0.65 reflect poor clustering. We use these heuristics for defining *variability views* which are sets of similar settings, namely provide similar clustering outcomes.

Definition 5. A *variability view* is a set of settings S, such that the Rand index of each pair of settings in S is greater than 0.80, i.e., for each $s_i, s_j \in S$, $R(s_i, s_j) > 0.80$.

The introduction of 'variability view' allows recommending on a shorter list of settings for inspection: rather than exploring all individual settings, similar settings are examined as a single view. We next demonstrate this step, as well as the whole method.

4   Preliminary Results

4.1   Design and Execution

For evaluation purposes, we implemented the whole method and used a set of three variants of a photo sharing application. Two of the variants are based on the known application of Picasa, and follow a cloning scenario (namely, one variant was created from the other by copying and adapting). The third variant specify the requirements of another application, but still refer to functions such as opening and managing albums, editing and viewing photos/pictures, managing users and setting sharing options. Overall we had 315 requirements which differ in their functional aspects, as well as in their structural ones (e.g., the properties and possible states of users, photos/pictures, albums, labels, and watermarks)[3].

Basically, SOVA supports a large range of settings (6 weights with non-discrete values). We ran the method with the seven settings presented in Table 5, which exemplify a scenario in which the user has doubts whether the comparison should be structural, functional, or a mixture of both.

---

[3] The requirements used for the evaluation can be found at https://sites.google.com/is.haifa.ac.il/corereq/tool-data/generated-outputs.

4.2   Results

For the three photo sharing applications, we received the results presented in Table 6. The maximal entropy of 315 requirements is 8.30. Thus, the outcomes of the intra-view evaluation indicate on settings #1 to #4 as potentially relevant. Particularly, the functional settings (#2 to #4) got medium entropies (4.01-4.41) and high relevance scores (3.89–4.01). The mix setting (#1) also seems relevant with a score of 3.25 for both entropy and relevance. The structural settings, on the other hand (#5 to #7) are not recommended for exploration as their entropies and relevance scores are low, indicating that comparison in this direction may be useless for the given input.

Among the four settings recommended by the first step, the Rand index values, calculated while performing cross-view evaluation, show that the functional settings (#2, #3, #4) belong to the same variability view (Rand index between 0.89 and 1.00). Hence it is recommended to explore only one of them. Another setting that deserves exploration is the mix setting (#1) that is different from the functional settings and hence represents another variability view that considers both functional and structural aspects, as well as the performers (i.e., agents) of behaviors.

Figure 3 depicts the feature diagrams of settings #1, #3, #4, and #6 (note that the method recommends exploring only settings #4/#3 and #1, in this order). The roots of the feature diagrams appear to the left of each diagram. Similar requirements are grouped under the same inner node, introducing new levels to the right of the diagram root. Feature diagrams in which all or most leaves appear under the root represent irrelevant settings, namely, settings whose entropy is close to the boundaries (the rectangles illustrate the places in the diagrams where grouping of similar requirements occurs according to the given setting). As can be seen, setting #6 (representing the "best" structural setting) is very poor for evaluating the similarity and variability of the given set of requirements (the rectangle surrounding the potentially similar requirements is quite small). In this case, it does not mean that the requirements are very different, as the mix setting (#1) and especially the functional view (represented by settings #2 to #4) give better results that enable comparison to some extent (illustrated by relatively large rectangles). This leads to the conclusion that the requirements highlight functional (rather than structural) aspects of the behaviors in the corresponding systems and thus they should be compared and evaluated according to those aspects.

Table 6. Preliminary evaluation results (the entropy and relevance scores of the individual settings appear along with the column headings, Rand index values appear in the cells)

# $(\Omega, \rho) \rightarrow$	1 (mix) (3.31, 3.31)	2 (fnc1) (4.41, 3.89)	3 (fnc2) (4.41, 3.89)	4 (fnc3) (4.01, 4.01)	5 (str1) (1.81, 1.81)	6 (str2) (2.34, 2.34)	7 (str3) (0.94, 0.94)
1 (mix)		0.76	0.76	0.74	0.54	0.62	0.36
2 (fnc1)			1.00	0.89	0.51	0.60	0.32
3 (fnc2)				0.89	0.51	0.60	0.32
4 (fnc3)					0.54	0.63	0.33
5 (str1)						0.73	0.48
6 (str2)							0.58
7 (str3)							

4.3   Discussion and Limitations

The suggested method assumes that a given set of requirements can be compared for similarity and variability in different ways. Note that we do not deal with the "correctness" of the variability analysis outcomes, acknowledging the existence of different ways to perform the analysis, each of which may be relevant to different sets of variability tasks (see the discussion at the beginning of Sect. 2). However, as the number of possibilities may be very large, and setting of parameters (e.g., weights and thresholds) may be arbitrary and irrelevant to the input set of requirements (recall the example in Table 1 and its results in Table 4), the method recommends on settings and variability views that may be relevant to the given input requirements. Figure 4 is a partial example based on the comparison results achieved following setting #4 (fnc3). The right-most nodes are leaves in the feature diagram shown in Fig. 3(c) and represent requirements (each requirement appears as rsova_<*requirement-document-name*>_<*reuiqrement-id-in-the-document*>). The left-most nodes depict how the requirements are grouped according to the given setting (#4): tag addition, box corners dragging, photos sharing, and new label creation. These (inner) nodes may further be grouped with similar requirements (leaves) and/or groups of similar requirements (inner nodes), introducing an upper level to the feature diagram. The differences between the outcomes of setting #4 and setting #3 (or #2) originate from considering (to some extent) object similarity. For example, requirements that refer to "album generation" and "user creation" will be considered similar in setting #4 due to the relatively high semantic similarity between their actions: generation and creation. These requirements will be considered less similar in setting #3 (and setting #2) because of the low similarity between the objects (album and user) and since the actions of generation and creation differ to some extent (i.e., are not identical).

Fig. 3. Feature diagrams representing variability analysis outcomes for (a) setting #1 (mix), (b) setting #3 (fnc2), (c) setting #4 (fnc3), (d) setting #6 (str2)

It should be noted that currently the method recommends on relevant variability views taking into consideration *all* requirements and their similarities with respect to the recommended settings. In cases of heterogonous aspects, e.g., some requirements focus on structural aspects while others – on functional aspects, it may be reasonable to consider several settings (rather than a single one) on the same input. Returning to our example in Fig. 3(c), we see that there are non-comparable requirements with respect to setting #4 (fnc3) – all the requirements that appear above the rectangle. It may be the case that those requirements are completely different, but it may turn out that there is a good (different) way to compare them, e.g., considering structural aspects.

Another important issue that requires further investigation is the mapping between the different variability views and types of variability tasks. It was shown in [13] that presenting variability according to different views may affect performance of humans when conducting variability-related tasks (in terms of both correctness and efficiency). Currently, the method recommends on relevant views based on the input requirements only, neglecting the task at hand. It is important to improve the method such that the recommendation will consider the task at hand, besides the input requirements.

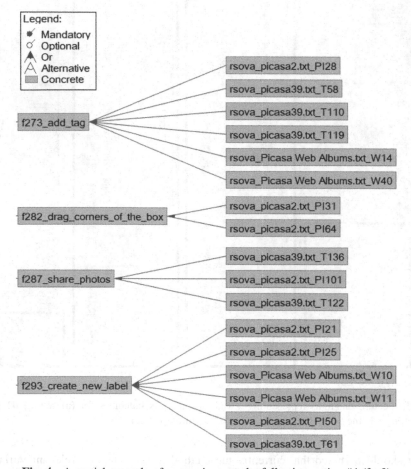

Fig. 4. A partial example of comparison results following setting #4 (fnc3)

5 Summary and Future Work

Comparison and variability analysis of systems may be done considering different aspects and development artifacts. In this work, we propose a method for recommending on relevant ways (variability views) to compare and evaluate the similarity of systems based on functional requirements expressed in a natural language. The method considers the characteristics of the behaviors extracted from the input requirements and utilizes data mining techniques in order to perform intra-view evaluation based on the entropies of each setting and cross-view evaluation based on Rand index values of different settings.

Although implemented to a specific requirements-based variability analysis method – SOVA (Semantic and Ontological Variability Analysis), the suggested approach is much more general and can be applied to other methods and other types of artifacts (e.g., design models and code). Future directions of the research include applying the approach to additional methods, as well as considering multi-settings comparison and supporting task-oriented recommendation, as discussed at the end of Sect. 4.3. We further intend to extend the evaluation of the method in terms of usability of the approach and usefulness of its outcomes. Machine learning and deep learning algorithms may also be considered to improve the intra-view and cross-view evaluations.

References

1. Assunção, W.K., Lopez-Herrejon, R.E., Linsbauer, L., Vergilio, S.R., Egyed, A.: Reengineering legacy applications into software product lines: a systematic mapping. Empirical Softw. Eng. **22**(6), 2972–3016 (2017)
2. Bakar, N.H., Kasirun, Z.M., Salleh, N., Jalab, H.A.: Extracting features from online software reviews to aid requirements reuse. Appl. Soft Comput. **49**, 1297 (2016)
3. Bakar, N.H., Kasirun, Z.M., Salleh, N., Jalab, H.A.: Feature extraction approaches from natural language requirements for reuse in software product lines: a systematic literature review. J. Syst. Softw. **106**, 132–149 (2015)
4. Ben Nasr, S., et al.: Automated extraction of product comparison matrices from informal product descriptions. J. Syst. Softw. **124**, 82–103 (2017)
5. Berger, T., et al.: A survey of variability modeling in industrial practice. In: Proceedings of the Seventh International Workshop on Variability Modelling of Software-intensive Systems, p. 7. ACM, January 2013
6. Bonin, F., Dell'Orletta, F., Montemagni, S., Venturi, G.: A contrastive approach to multiword extraction from domain-specific corpora. In: Proceedings of the Seventh Conference on International Language Resources and Evaluation (LREC 2010) (2010)
7. Clements, P., Northrop, L.: Software Product Lines: Practices and Patterns, vol. 3. Addison-Wesley, Reading (2002)
8. Davril, J.M., Delfosse, E., Hariri, N., Acher, M., Cleland-Huang, J., Heymans, P.: Feature model extraction from large collections of informal product descriptions. In: Proceedings of the 2013 9th Joint Meeting on Foundations of Software Engineering, pp. 290–300. ACM, August 2013
9. Deerwester, S., Dumais, S.T., Furnas, G.W., Landauer, T.K., Harshman, R.: Indexing by latent semantic analysis. J. Am. Soc. Inf. Sci. **41**(6), 391–407 (1990)

10. Ferrari, A., Spagnolo, G.O., Dell'Orletta, F.: Mining commonalities and variabilities from natural language documents. In: Proceedings of the 17th International Software Product Line Conference, pp. 116–120. ACM, August 2013

11. Itzik, N., Reinhartz-Berger, I.: SOVA-a tool for semantic and ontological variability analysis. In: CAiSE (Forum/Doctoral Consortium), pp. 177–184 (2014)

12. Itzik, N., Reinhartz-Berger, I.: Generating feature models from requirements: structural vs. functional perspectives. In: Proceedings of the 18th International Software Product Line Conference: Companion, Workshops, Demonstrations and Tools, vol. 2, pp. 44–51. ACM, September 2014

13. Itzik, N., Reinhartz-Berger, I., Wand, Y.: Variability analysis of requirements: considering behavioral differences and reflecting stakeholders' perspectives. IEEE Trans. Softw. Eng. **42**(7), 687–706 (2016)

14. Kang, K.C., Cohen, S.G., Hess, J.A., Novak, W.E., Peterson, A.S.: Feature-oriented domain analysis (FODA) feasibility study (No. CMU/SEI-90-TR-21). Software Engineering Institute, Carnegie-Mellon University, Pittsburgh, PA (1990)

15. Martinez, J., Ziadi, T., Bissyandé, T.F., Klein, J., Le Traon, Y.: Bottom-up adoption of software product lines: a generic and extensible approach. In: Proceedings of the 19th International Conference on Software Product Line, pp. 101–110. ACM, July 2015

16. Mihalcea, R., Corley, C., Strapparava, C.: Corpus-based and knowledge-based measures of text semantic similarity. In: AAAI, vol. 6, pp. 775–780, July 2006

17. Niu, N., Savolainen, J., Niu, Z., Jin, M., Cheng, J.R.C.: a systems approach to product line requirements reuse. IEEE Syst. J. **8**(3), 827–836 (2014)

18. OMG: The Requirements Interchange Format Specification – Version 1.2. https://www.omg.org/spec/ReqIF/

19. Pohl, K., Böckle, G., van Der Linden, F.J.: Software Product Line Engineering: Foundations, Principles and Techniques. Springer, Heidelberg (2005). https://doi.org/10.1007/3-540-28901-1

20. Rand, W.M.: Objective criteria for the evaluation of clustering methods. J. Am. Stat. Assoc. **66**(336), 846–850 (1971)

21. Reinhartz-Berger, I., Itzik, N., Wand, Y.: Analyzing variability of software product lines using semantic and ontological considerations. In: Jarke, M., et al. (eds.) CAiSE 2014. LNCS, vol. 8484, pp. 150–164. Springer, Cham (2014). https://doi.org/10.1007/978-3-319-07881-6_11

22. Steinbach, M., Karypis, G., Kumar, V.: A comparison of document clustering techniques. In: KDD Workshop on Text Mining, vol. 400, no. 1, pp. 525–526, August 2000

23. Steinley, D.: Properties of the Hubert-Arable adjusted Rand index. Psychol. Methods **9**(3), 386 (2004)

24. Wu, Z., Palmer, M.: Verbs semantics and lexical selection. In: Proceedings of the 32nd Annual Meeting on Association for Computational Linguistics, pp. 133–138. Association for Computational Linguistics, June 1994

CAiSE 2019 Tutorials

Building Data Warehouses in the Era of Big Data

An Approach for Scalable and Flexible Big Data Warehouses

Carlos Costa[1] and Maribel Yasmina Santos[2(✉)]

[1] Centre for Computer Graphics – CCG, Guimarães, Portugal
carlos.costa@dsi.uminho.pt
[2] ALGORITMI Research Centre, Department of Information Systems,
University of Minho, Guimarães, Portugal
maribel@dsi.uminho.pt

Abstract. During the last few years, the concept of Big Data Warehousing gained significant attention from the scientific community, highlighting the need to make design changes to the traditional Data Warehouse (DW) due to its limitations, in order to achieve new characteristics relevant in Big Data contexts (e.g., scalability on commodity hardware, real-time performance, and flexible storage). The state-of-the-art in Big Data Warehousing reflects the young age of the concept, as well as ambiguity and the lack of common approaches to build Big Data Warehouses (BDWs). Consequently, an approach to design and implement these complex systems is of major relevance to business analytics researchers and practitioners. In this tutorial, the design and implementation of BDWs is targeted, in order to present a general approach that researchers and practitioners can follow in their Big Data Warehousing projects, exploring several demonstration cases focusing on system design and data modelling examples in areas like smart cities, retail, finance, manufacturing, among others.

Keywords: Big Data · Data Warehousing · Big Data Warehousing · Analytics

1 Topic Relevance and Novelty

Nowadays, the community is studying the role of the DW in Big Data environments [1], thus the concept of BDW is emerging, with new characteristics and design changes. Currently, research on this topic is scarce and the state-of-the-art shows that the design of BDWs should focus both on the physical layer (infrastructure) and on the logical layer (data models and interoperability between components) [2]. Moreover, in general terms, a BDW can be implemented by leveraging the capabilities of Hadoop, NoSQL, or NewSQL to either complement or fully replace traditional relational databases. The existing non-structured practices and guidelines are not enough. The lack of prescriptive research on the topic of Big Data Warehousing is alarming, as there is no common approach to design and implement BDWs, as formerly existed in the

© Springer Nature Switzerland AG 2019
P. Giorgini and B. Weber (Eds.): CAiSE 2019, LNCS 11483, pp. 693–695, 2019.
https://doi.org/10.1007/978-3-030-21290-2

realm of traditional DWs, and the community needs a rigorously evaluated approach to design and build BDWs, according to recent and improved characteristics and data structures [3, 4].

The shift to a use case driven approach and the young age of Big Data as a research topic result in ambiguity regarding BDWs, but, as [5] claims, it would be a mistake to discard decades of architectural best practices based on the assumption that storage for Big Data is not relational nor driven by data modelling. The SQL-on-Hadoop movement [6] proves that data structures known for many years are more relevant than ever, although modified and optimized, as will be seen in this tutorial.

2   Goal and Objectives

The main goal of this tutorial is to disseminate an approach that can be prescribed for BDW design and implementation, providing to practitioners and researchers a structured and evaluated way of building these complex systems. This approach intends to avoid the risk of uncoordinated data silos frequently seen in today's environments, due to a "lift and shift" strategy and an excessive focus on trying to find the best technology to meet the demands. Considering this context, this tutorial will help the audience understand the purpose and characteristics of BDWs, and it will also demonstrate how to use a general approach for the design and implementation of BDW that can be replicated for several real-world applications. The tutorial objectives are as follows:

1. Understand the role of the BDW in the vast Big Data landscape, and clearly identify the technologies suitable for this context;
2. Define the logical components and data flows of the Big Data Warehousing system, using appropriate and replicable design philosophies and constructs;
3. Plan adequate data pipelines to collect, prepare, and enrich batch and streaming data;
4. Learn how to apply a data modelling method for BDWs, in order to avoid different ad hoc approaches applied in each project or use case;
5. Learn how to design a system for a real-world Big Data Warehousing application domain, focusing on data modelling and data visualization capabilities;
6. Apply the data modelling method in several real-world applications (e.g., smart cities, retail, finance, and manufacturing), exercising different modelling guidelines.

References

1. Krishnan, K.: Data Warehousing in the Age of Big Data. Morgan Kaufmann Publishers Inc., San Francisco (2013)
2. Russom, P.: Evolving Data Warehouse Architectures in the Age of Big Data. The Data Warehouse Institute (2014)
3. Costa, C., Santos, M.Y.: Evaluating several design patterns and trends in big data warehousing systems. In: Krogstie, J., Reijers, H. (eds.) CAiSE 2018. LNCS, vol. 10816, pp. 459–473. Springer, Cham (2018). https://doi.org/10.1007/978-3-319-91563-0_28

4. Costa, C., Andrade, C., Santos, M.Y.: Big data warehouses for smart industries. In: Sakr, S., Zomaya, A. (eds.) Encyclopedia of Big Data Technologies. Springer, Cham (2018)
5. Clegg, D.: Evolving data warehouse and BI architectures: the big data challenge. TDWI Bus. Intell. J. **20**, 19–24 (2015)
6. Floratou, A., Minhas, U.F., Özcan, F.: SQL-on-Hadoop: full circle back to shared-nothing database architectures. Proc. VLDB Endow. **7**, 1295–1306 (2014). https://doi.org/10.14778/2732977.2733002

Semantic Modeling of Performance Indicators for Collaborative Information Systems

Claudia Diamantini[✉], Domenico Potena, and Emanuele Storti

Department of Information Engineering, Polytechnic University of Marche,
Ancona, Italy
{c.diamantini,d.potena,e.storti}@univpm.it

1 Overview

Performance Indicators (PIs) and metrics are essential management tools. They provide synthetic objective measures to monitor the progress of a process, set objectives, assess deviations, enabling effective decision making. They can also be used for communication purposes, facilitating the sharing of objectives and results, or improving the awareness on certain phenomena, thus motivating more responsible and sustainable behaviors. Given their strategic role, it is of tantamount importance, as well as challenging, to guarantee that the intended meaning of an indicator is fully shared among stakeholders, and that its implementation is aligned with the definition provided by decision makers, as this is a pre-condition for data quality and trustworthiness of the information system. This tutorial aims to provide an introduction to recent semantic approaches for modeling indicators and metrics, focusing on applications in distributed and collaborative information systems, where semantic specifications promise to have the greatest impact. The tutorial is tailored to researchers and PhD students. Professionals like managers, data scientists, Chief Data Officers, Chief Information Officers can benefit from a systematization of issues related to PIs semantics and of advanced approaches for PIs management.

2 Organization

The tutorial first provides the notion of PI and introduces motivating scenarios where heterogeneities in the definition of PIs can determine interoperability and quality issues: PIs integration and exchange in distributed and collaborative organizations, alignment of managerial and IT views and data quality, analysis and exploration of PIs. Then, it surveys the state of the art in PIs modeling, focusing on (i) models for sharing and querying statistical and linked data [7, 11], (ii) models to represent indicators and their dependencies [2, 8], and (iii) models for the representation of PIs' calculation formulas [6, 9]. The third part of the tutorial is devoted to show how the presented models support the development of applications dealing with the above mentioned issues [1, 3–5, 10].

© Springer Nature Switzerland AG 2019
P. Giorgini and B. Weber (Eds.): CAiSE 2019, LNCS 11483, pp. 696–697, 2019.
https://doi.org/10.1007/978-3-030-21290-2

References

1. Atzori, M., Mazzeo, G.M., Zaniolo, C.: QA3: a natural language approach to question answering over RDF data cubes. Semant. Web J. (2018, accepted)
2. del Rìo-Ortega, A., Resinas, M., Cabanillas, C., Ruiz-Cortes, A.: On the definition and design-time analysis of process performance indicators. Inf. Syst. **38**, 470–490 (2013)
3. Diamantini, C., Potena, D., Storti, E.: Multidimensional query reformulation with measure decomposition. Inf. Syst. **78**, 23–39 (2018)
4. Diamantini, C., Potena, D., Storti, E.: Analytics for citizens: a linked open data model for statistical data exploration. Concurrency Comput. Pract. Exper. **2017**, e4107 (2017)
5. Diamantini, C., Potena, D., Storti, E.: Extended drill-down operator: digging into the structure of performance indicators. Concurrency Comput. Pract. Exper. **28**(15), 3948–3968 (2016)
6. Diamantini, C., Potena, D., Storti, E.: SemPI: a semantic framework for the collaborative construction and maintenance of a shared dictionary of performance indicators. Future Gener. Comput. Syst. **54**, 352–365 (2016)
7. International Organization for Standardization: ISO 17369:2013 Statistical Data and Metadata Exchange (SDMX), https://statswiki.unece.org/display/ClickSDMX
8. Horkoff, J., et al.: Strategic business modeling: representation and reasoning. Software & System Modeling, vol. 13, pp. 1015–1041 (2012)
9. Matè, A., Trujillo, J., Mylopoulos, J.: Specification and derivation of key performance indicators for business analytics: a semantic approach. Data Knowl. Eng. **108**, 30–49 (2017)
10. van der Aa, H., Leopold, H., del-Rìo-Ortega, A., Resinas, M., Reijers, H.A.: Transforming unstructured natural language descriptions into measurable process performance indicators using Hidden Markov Models. Inf. Syst. 71, 27–39 (2017)
11. W3C: The RDF Data Cube Vocabulary. In: W3C Recommendation, 16 January 2014 https://www.w3.org/TR/vocab-data-cube

Ontological Patterns and Anti-patterns for the Modeling of Complex Enterprise Relations

Nicola Guarino[1(✉)], Giancarlo Guizzardi[2], and Daniele Porello[1(✉)]

[1] ISTC-CNR Laboratory for Applied Ontology, Trento, Italy
{nicola.guarino,daniele.porello}@cnr.it
[2] Free University of Bozen-Bolzano, Bolzano, Italy
giancarlo.guizzardi@unibz.it

Enterprise modeling requires of course to pay attention to different kinds of business relationships. In many cases, we really need to talk about such relationships, for instance, when the contractual conditions that regulate them evolve in time, or when such conditions are violated. In terms of conceptual modeling, this means that relationships need to be *reified*, they need to be put in the domain of discourse.

In this tutorial, we shall first introduce the ontological basis of relationships reification, according to which relationships are construed as *truthmakers* of relational statements. We shall then illustrate different kinds of ontological patterns and anti-patterns based on the different nature of such truthmakers, by discussing concrete case studies related to enterprise modeling.

The material presented in the tutorial is based on a novel theory of relationships and reification that was first published in (Guarino and Guizzardi (2015, 2016)) and later used to evolve the Ontology-Driven Conceptual Modeling language OntoUML (Guizzardi et al. (2018)).

The theory has since then been successfully applied to model economic transactions (Guarino et al. (2018a)), legal relations (Griffo et al. (2018)), service contracts (Griffo et al. (2017), complex service life-cycles (Nardi et al. (2015)), preference relations in economics (Porello and Guizzardi (2018)), and strategic enterprise relationships (Sales et al. (2018)).

The approach to complex relation modeling by employing Ontological Design Patterns has been discussed in (Guarino et al. (2018b)); The approach for Anti-Pattern detection and systematic model rectification employed here has been discussed in (Guizzardi (2014)).

References

Griffo, C., Almeida, J.P.A., Guizzardi, G.: Conceptual modeling of legal relations. In: Trujillo, J.C., Davis, K.C., Du, X., Li, Z., Ling, T.W., Li, G., Lee, M.L. (eds.) ER 2018. LNCS, vol. 11157, pp. 169–183. Springer, Cham (2018). https://doi.org/10. 1007/978-3-030-00847-5_14

Griffo, C., Almeida, J.P.A., Guizzardi, G.: From an ontology of service contracts to contract modeling in enterprise architecture. In: 21st IEEE International Enterprise Distributed Object Computing Conference, EDOC 2017, Quebec City, QC, Canada, 10–13 October 2017, pp. 40–19 (2017)

© Springer Nature Switzerland AG 2019
P. Giorgini and B. Weber (Eds.): CAiSE 2019, LNCS 11483, pp. 698–699, 2019.
https://doi.org/10.1007/978-3-030-21290-2

Guarino, N., Guizzardi, G.: We need to discuss the relationship: revisiting relationships as modeling constructs. In: Zdravkovic, J., Kirikova, M., Johannesson, P. (eds.) CAiSE 2015. LNCS, vol. 9097, pp. 279–294. Springer, Cham (2015)

Guarino, N., Guizzardi, G.: Relationships and events: towards a general theory of reification and truthmaking. In: Adorni, G., Cagnoni, S., Gori, M., Maratea, M. (eds.) AI*IA 2016. LNCS (LNAI), vol. 10037, pp. 237–249. Springer, Cham (2016). https://doi.org/10.1007/978-3-319-49130-1_18

Guarino, N., Guizzardi, G., Sales, T.P.: On the ontological nature of REA core relations. In: Proceedings of the 12th International Workshop on Value Modeling and Business Ontologies, VMBO 2018, Amsterdam, The Netherlands, 26–27 February 2018, pp. 89–98 (2018a)

Guarino, N., Sales, T.P., Guizzardi, G.: Reification and truthmaking patterns. In: Trujillo, J.C., Davis, K.C., Du, X., Li, Z., Ling, T.W., Li, G., Lee, M.L. (eds.) ER 2018. LNCS, vol. 11157, pp. 151–165. Springer, Cham (2018b). https://doi.org/10.1007/978-3-030-00847-5_13

Guizzardi, G.: Ontological patterns, anti-patterns and pattern languages for next-generation conceptual modeling. In: Yu, E., Dobbie, G., Jarke, M., Purao, S. (eds.) ER 2014. LNCS, vol. 8824, pp. 13–27. Springer, Cham (2014). https://doi.org/10.1007/978-3-319-12206-9_2

Guizzardi, G., Fonseca, C.M., Benevides, A.B., Almeida, J.P.A., Porello, D., Sales, T.P.: Endurant types in ontology-driven conceptual modeling: towards OntoUML 2.0. In: Trujillo, J.C., Davis, K.C., Du, X., Li, Z., Ling, T.W., Li, G., Lee, M.L. (eds.) ER 2018. LNCS, vol. 11157, pp. 136–150. Springer, Cham (2018). https://doi.org/10.1007/978-3-030-00847-5_12

Nardi, J.C., et al.: A commitment-based reference ontology for services. Inf. Syst. **54**, 263–288 (2015)

Porello, D., Guizzardi, G.: Towards an ontological modelling of preference relations. In: Ghidini, C., Magnini, B., Passerini, A., Traverso, P. (eds.) AI*IA 2018. LNCS (LNAI), vol. 11298, pp. 152–165. Springer, Cham (2018). https://doi.org/10.1007/978-3-030-03840-3_12

Sales, T.P., Porello, D., Guarino, N., Guizzardi, G., Mylopoulos, J.: Ontological foundations of competition. In: Proceedings of the 10th International Conference on Formal Ontology in Information Systems, FOIS 2018, Cape Town, South Africa, 19–21 September 2018, pp. 96–109 (2018)

Conformance Checking: Relating Processes and Models

Josep Carmona[1]([✉]), Boudewijn van Dongen[2], and Matthias Weidlich[3]

[1] Universitat Politècnica de Catalunya, Barcelona, Spain
jcarmona@cs.upc.edu
[2] Eindhoven University of Technology, Eindhoven, Netherlands
B.F.v.Dongen@tue.nl
[3] Humboldt-Universität zu Berlin, Berlin, Germany
matthias.weidlich@hu-berlin.de

Extended Abstract

Process mining bridges the gap between process modelling on the one hand and data science on the other [2]. In many practical process mining applications, relating recorded event data and a process model is an important starting point for further discussion and analysis. Conformance checking provides the methods to analyze the relation between modeled and recorded behavior [1].

In the course of the last decade, many approaches to conformance checking have been developed in academia. With the respective methods becoming more mature, the field of conformance checking is subject to consolidation. That includes convergence on essential properties of conformance checking (e.g., in terms of axioms on how to quantify aspects of the relation between event data and process models), significant improvements of conformance checking efficiency that enables analysis of large, real-world processes, and, most prominently, an increasing take-up in industry (e.g., by companies such as SAP and Celonis).

While a large number of scientific results on conformance checking have been published in recent years, there is a lack of a concise introduction to the essential concepts underlying it. With this tutorial, we intend to contribute to making these results more broadly accessible, for practitioners and researchers with, so far, little exposure to approaches for data-driven analysis of information systems in general, and process mining in particular. Our goal is to introduce the essential ideas of how to relate modelled and recorded behavior on an intuitive level, and outline the space of applications that may benefit from conformance checking.

References

1. Carmona, J., van Dongen, B., Solti, A., Weidlich, M.: Conformance Checking. Springer, Cham (2018). https://doi.org/10.1007/978-3-319-99414-7_1
2. Aalst, Wil: Process Mining - Data Science in Action, 2nd edn. Springer, Heidelberg (2016). https://doi.org/10.1007/978-3-662-49851-4_1

© Springer Nature Switzerland AG 2019
P. Giorgini and B. Weber (Eds.): CAiSE 2019, LNCS 11483, p. 700, 2019.
https://doi.org/10.1007/978-3-030-21290-2

Author Index